كم صالئت ميوه در اقصبة صالحية
اسم لسم بلد انجه در ملا مواسط

ديوار بده مرسول مصر ديم ودحما داعر ماسده داعلم حوا
ملحه التي تمات حصار ديوار نكجوب ما ملا سد ادمير ولها مصا
ومرصه لي بوبده مصر مقدرغه اصره سود لها عمدا لندر مراعوس
ولها سد نماربده بريير لوتيا انجنده مرا صا صواما ر اما
دومر مده اولا علمه بدا محدده در عدد جوا مهما سلاطي
حملا جاعد نعر مده مالا اسلو حصاري السلطان بازيد طينت نحية
محمد انتدى تكيه ح جامعد انت يكو تبود دن ا بح يبو قبوح
حصايو محمد انك حامر كندمو ماروحصاره ه ما ما جاوس حامر آنت موما ره
در دفاتر مدارس مقر مسل حمله اوح عدد مدرسه لو
حمله عدد دارالنعلم المحدحوار سراندحملا معى مس
ما حر وحصار در خانقاه درويشا بجذو حمله الموعد
نم لها عرسده مره ما اسم محمد امدى بلد سم ما مه مرو س
سره ا نسا نه عصمد مورد بجاو ومعر ما مه صاحم خرقه يوسر
كو حو كح عمد امد عنكيه سم در عدد مساجدها يحلا ص

AN OTTOMAN TRAVELLER

AN OTTOMAN TRAVELLER

SELECTIONS FROM THE
Book of Travels of Evliya Çelebi

TRANSLATION AND COMMENTARY BY
Robert Dankoff and Sooyong Kim

ELAND

First published by Eland Publishing Limited
61 Exmouth Market, London EC1R 4QL in 2010

Translation and Commentary © Robert Dankoff & Sooyong Kim
except where credited in the text, acknowledgements and bibliography

ISBN 978 1 906011 44 4

All rights reserved. This publication may not be reproduced,
stored in a retrieval system or transmitted in any form or by any
means, electronic, mechanical, photocopying, recording or
otherwise, without permission in writing from the publishers

Cover Image: 'Iskandar lies dying' from the *Tarjumah-i Shâhnâmah*
© Spencer Collection, The New York Public Library,
Astor, Lenox and Tilden Foundations

Typeset in London by Antony Gray
Printed in the United Kingdom
by MPG Biddles

CONTENTS

	Introduction	7
	Literary allusions	23
	Glossary	27

VOLUME 1
Istanbul

1	Introduction: The dream	3
2	The Süleymaniye Mosque	8
3	The antiquity of smoking	17
4	Galata	17
5	Kağıthane	21
6	Guilds' parade	24
7	Lağari Hasan Çelebi	31

VOLUME 2
Anatolia and beyond

1	Setting out	35
2	Hot Springs of Bursa	38
3	Return to Istanbul	42
4	Hamsi in Trabzon	44
5	Black Sea adventure	47
6	Tabriz	55
7	Cat-brokers of Ardabil	68
8	Oil wells of Baku	68
9	Cathedral of Echmiadzin	69
10	Ankara	70

VOLUME THREE
In the Retinue of Melek Ahmed Pasha

1	Nasreddin Hoca in Akşehir	91
2	Safed	92
3	Sheikh Bekkar the Naked on the road outside Damascus	94
4	The girl who gave birth to an elephant	97
5	Armenian	99
6	The cats of Divriği	100
7	Witchcraft in a Bulgarian village	101
8	Sofia	102

VOLUME FOUR
Safavid Borderlands

1	Diyarbekir	113
2	Bitlis	116
3	The ruined city of Ahlat	134
4	On 'extinguishing the candle'	136

VOLUME FIVE
East Anatolia and the Balkans

1	Highwaymen in the Bolu Pass; return to Van	141
2	Escape from Bitlis	142
3	Diplomacy in Split (Spalato)	163
4	The bandit Yano	169

VOLUME SIX
Hungary and the German Campaign

1	An incident on the battlefield	173
2	Shkodër (Scutari)	174
3	The Samakov iron works	180
4	An adventure near Komorn; Tatar raid into Western Europe	181
5	Dubrovnik (Ragusa)	204
6	The great bridge at Mostar	213

Contents

VII

VOLUME SEVEN
Habsburg Borderlands, Crimea and beyond

1	Raiding expeditions in 'Germany'; a fabulous tree in Krokondar	219
2	The battle on the Raab River (Battle of Saint Gotthard, 1664)	222
3	Comparison of Austrians and Hungarians	230
4	A pleasure resort near Vienna; the free conduct of women	231
5	Vienna	232
6	Crimea	249
7	A meal of strange honey in Circassia	253
8	Kalmyks and cannibalism	254

VOLUME EIGHT
Greece and the Conquest of Crete

1	Return to Crimea	259
2	Report to the Sultan in Edirne	274
3	The Gypsies of Gümülcine (Komotini)	276
4	Athens	278
5	Balibadra: A great cypress tree and the five ethnic groups of the Morea	293
6	Siege of Candia: Ministrations to the wounded and Saint Green-Arm	295
7	A captive woman in Kolorya	297
8	Fair at Doyran	298

VOLUME NINE
Pilgrimage

1	Setting out on the Hajj	303
2	Brigands at the Alman Pass; Ephesus	306
3	Safed and the land of Canaan	311
4	Jerusalem	315
5	Sheikh Bekkar the Naked in Damascus	338
6	The Hajj caravan; Muzayrib, the Hajj bazaar	340
7	Medina	345

8	The People of Mecca	359
9	Uyun al-qasab	362
10	St Catherine's Monastery on Mt Sinai	365

VOLUME TEN
Egypt and Sudan

1	Adam's prayer for Egypt in 'Hebrew'	371
2	Relation among Nile overflow, plenty and poverty, crowdedness of Cairo, people and donkeys	372
3	Snake medicine and snake charming	373
4	Rain, snow and hail in Egypt in 1083 (1672)	387
5	Crocodiles	388
6	The Cairo underworld and unusual trades	393
7	Trades and products lacking in Egypt	399
8	Chicken incubation; Sabil Allam stones	400
9	Exploring a pyramid	403
10	Weddings, circumcision, etc.	406
11	Mevlud of Seyyid Ahmad al-Badawi in Tanta	414
12	Mountain of the Birds	436
13	Map of the Nile	439
14	Meeting with Kör Husayn Qan	439
15	Meeting with Qan Girgis; encounter with two Bektashi dervishes	442
16	Elephants and monkeys	448
17	Envoi	450

APPENDIX

Outline of Journeys and Events in the Ten Volumes of the *Book of Travels*	453
Bibliography	472
Acknowledgements	477
Index	479

ILLUSTRATIONS

Illustrations in the text

Süleymaniye Mosque by Melchior Lorck (Royal Library, Copenhagen)	1
Entertainers at the circumcision of the sultan's sons (Topkapı Palace Museum)	33
A wandering dervish (National Library of Sweden)	89
Diyarbekir by Matrakçı Nasuh (Istanbul University Rare Works Library)	111
Map of Split (Spalato) (Newberry Library, Chicago, 171.5 M858 12(a)1)	139
Bridge at Mostar (Courtesy of Special Collections, Fine Arts Library, Harvard College Library)	171
A Tartar Khan (National Library of Sweden)	217
The Parthenon, Athens by Christian Hansen (akg-images)	257
The Great Mosque, Medina (The Stapleton Collection/Bridgeman Art Library)	301
An Ethiopian Woman (The David Museum, Copenhagen)	369

Colour illustrations between pages 256 and 257

Map of Athens by Piri Reis
(The Nasser D. Khalili Collection of Islamic Art, MSS 718)

Rålamb Costume Book illustrations
(National Library of Sweden)

Map of Athens by Piri Reis
(Topkapı Palace Museum)

Map of Diyarbekir by Matrakçı Nasuh
(Dost Yayinlari/Giraudon/Bridgeman Art Library)

Maps of Tabriz and Galata by Matrakçı Nasuh
(Istanbul University Rare Works Library)

The Ottoman State on the move
(© British Library Board, Sloane 3584)

Mevlevi dervishes perform the Sema'

Entertainers at the circumcision of the sultan's sons
(Topkapı Palace Museum)

Astronomers at work in Istanbul
(Corbis)

Headwaters of the Nile, from a map attributed to Evliya Çelebi
(The Vatican Library)

Endpapers

From the *Seyahatname* by Evliya Çelebi
(Topkapı Palace Museum, Ms. Bagdat 308, fol 338b)

INTRODUCTION

The *Book of Travels* (*Seyahatname*) of Evliya Çelebi occupies a unique place in the literature of travel. It is probably the longest and most ambitious travel account by any writer in any language, and a key text for all aspects of the Ottoman Empire at the time of its greatest extension in the seventeenth century. It is also the product of an unusual personality – a cultured Ottoman gentleman, pious yet unconventional, observant and inquisitive, curious about everything, obsessive about travelling, determined to leave a complete record of his travels.

Who was Evliya Çelebi?[1] Born in Istanbul in 1611, during the reign of Sultan Ahmed, he was the scion of an established Turkish family with ties to the court. His father was chief goldsmith to the sultan. As a young boy he had a medrese education. In 1623, the year in which Sultan Murad IV assumed the throne, he was apprenticed to the sultan's imam, Evliya Mehmed Efendi, who tutored him in Koran recitation. 'I became his pupil,' he writes, 'and he made me his spiritual son.' Perhaps he owed his name to his teacher and spiritual father.[2] He goes on:

1 Practically everything that we know about Evliya must be derived from the *Book of Travels*, since no other Ottoman source has yet turned up that mentions him. Only a list of the retinue in Kara Mehmed Pasha's 1665 embassy, discovered in the Vienna court archive, includes an 'Evlia Efendi', which must be Evliya Çelebi (published in Teply 1975; also in Kreutel 1957 2nd ed. 1987, 17). Recently Pinelopi Stathi turned up the draft of a Greek patriarchal letter, of uncertain date, recommending Evliya as 'a man of honour, and peace. He has the desire and the inclination to be a traveller of the world, and describe places, cities and nations of men, having no harm in his heart to make injustice or hurt anyone' (Stathi 2005/2006, 267; and see MacKay 2007). This is similar to the 'patents' or safe-conducts that Evliya mentions several times (e.g., see Volume 7, selection 6; Volume 9, selection 10). Also, five actual graffiti have been preserved. Four of these have been known for a long time; see Prokosch 1988–89 for photographs, hand-drawn copies, transcriptions and translations. A fifth has been reported by Mehmet Tütüncü. See Dankoff 2004, 149–50 for comparison with the thirty or so graffiti that Evliya records in the *Book of Travels*. In addition, a map of the Nile in the Vatican library can be attributed to Evliya; it was made known in Rossi 1949; an edition is being prepared by Nuran Tezcan and Robert Dankoff.

2 Evliya, which designates the 'friends' (Arabic: *awliya*) of God who, according to

> From Evliya Efendi I mastered the science of reciting the Koran from memory, and I could recite the entire Koran in eight hours, without addition or subtraction, and without error whether open or hidden ... And every Friday eve (Thursday night) I was appointed to complete a Koran-recital. God be praised, from childhood until the present, whether at home or during my travels, I have not abandoned this practice.[3]

Soon he was performing Koran recitations in public, including in Aya Sofya – the great Byzantine church of Hagia Sofia that served, since the Ottoman conquest in 1453, as the chief imperial mosque. It was on one such occasion, in 1636, that he attracted the attention of Sultan Murad IV himself, who drew him into the palace. The sultan was so taken with the young man's skills – which included singing and witty conversation as well as Koran recitation – that he made him a royal entertainer and boon companion.

Evliya writes:

> God be praised that my noble father served as chief goldsmith to all the Ottoman sultans from Süleyman to Ibrahim, and that I was honoured with the companionship of such a noble sovereign and jihad warrior as Murad Khan Gazi. Just before the Baghdad campaign I received his blessings and graduated from the harem into the cavalry corps with a daily allowance of forty *akçe*.[4]

Sultan Murad IV earned the title Gazi – warrior for the faith – with his two successful campaigns against the Shi'i (and therefore heretical) Safavids of Persia, recovering for the Ottoman Empire Revan (Erevan in Armenia) in 1635 and Baghdad in 1638.[5]

Despite Evliya's claim to have graduated into the cavalry corps, he did not graduate to officer status (which would have earned him the titles

---

Koran 10:62, 'have nothing to fear or to regret.' *Evliya* is also the term for saintly individuals whose tombs are the objects of pilgrimage and visitation (*ziyaret*). The usual translation in this anthology is 'saints'.

3 Vol. 6, fol. 47a–b; Dankoff 2004, 31.
4 Vol. 1, fol. 73a.
5 The Revan and Baghdad Pavilions, added to the Topkapı Palace, may be considered Murad IV's counterpart to the great imperial mosques of earlier *gazi* sultans – Fatih (Mehmed II), Süleyman, and Sultan Ahmed. These pavilions were later used as libraries, the Baghdad pavilion eventually housing the autograph ms. of the *Book of Travels*, which accounts for the designations in the bibliography. (Only Volume 6 got separated from Volume 5 and ended up in the Revan Pavilion instead.)

Agha or Pasha). All his life he avoided official appointment, whether military or bureaucratic, which would have limited his travel options. Instead, he took advantage of inherited wealth and family and court connections in order to pursue his avocation. Free of marriage ties, renowned for his wit, his learning, and his fine voice, Evliya had no trouble attaching himself to the retinue of various pashas sent to all parts of the Empire as provincial governors, or outside the Empire as emissaries. He served them as secretary; as prayer-leader (imam) and caller-to-prayer (muezzin); as messenger and courier; and as boon companion, confidant, and raconteur. The religious offices, including Koran recitation, qualified him for the title Efendi, by which he is sometimes designated. But Çelebi – a title roughly equivalent to Gentleman or Esquire – better suited his status as courtier, musician, and littérateur.

With all his *savoir-vivre* and cultural refinements, Evliya nevertheless likes to portray himself as a dervish or Sufi type – a man without worldly ties, not dependent on the employment or favours of others; thus one who does not have to flatter and deceive. This personality trait, if we can take it as such, coexists with what seems to be its opposite, for we often find him flattering and seeking gain, and taking account of his personal goods. At one point an interlocutor characterises him in this fashion:

> Evliya Çelebi is a wandering dervish and a world traveller. He cries the chant of every cart he mounts, and sings the praises of every man who feeds him. Wherever he rests his head, he eats and drinks and is merry.[6]

Even the inclination to travel is itself associated in his mind with worldly attachments as contrasting with the inclination to perform pious deeds, such as sojourning at the Prophet's mosque in Medina.[7]

Wanderlust was his dominant passion – the urge, as he puts it, to be a 'world traveller' (*seyyah-ı alem*). Growing up in Istanbul, he explored all aspects of the metropolis and at the same time eagerly imbibed accounts of the far-flung conquests of Sultan Süleyman (reg. 1520–1566) and Sultan Selim II (reg. 1566–1574), as related by his father and other veterans.[8] Once he ventured outside the capital, it was his father who told him to

---

6   Vol. 5, fol. 9b = Volume 5, selection 2 in the present anthology.
7   Vol. 9, fol. 282a = Volume 9, selection 7.
8   Vol. 10, fol. 42a; Dankoff 2004, 160.

The Ottoman Empire in 1600
(also including dependent states)

Introduction   xv

keep a journal, and even suggested the title *Seyahatname* or *Book of Travels*.[9] The initiatory dream – a highly stylised narrative, in which the Prophet Muhammad blesses his intention to travel[10] – sets this urge within familiar Islamic parameters: pilgrimage to the holy cities (Hajj); visitation of the tombs of saintly individuals (*ziyaret*); fighting for the faith (*gaza*).

It was the Ottoman elite – including the sultan, court officials and artisans like his father, military leaders and statesmen like his uncle Melek Ahmed Pasha, and other administrators, religious personnel (ulema) and literati, both in Istanbul and the provinces – who provided him encouragement, employment, and patronage. Whenever Evliya returned from one of his journeys, he found in one of these elite circles a forum for recounting his adventures. Thus in May, 1656, returning to Melek Pasha's entourage in Van after eight months travel in Kurdistan, Mesopotamia and Azerbaijan:

> I was not absent from our lord Melek Pasha's company day and night for a single moment. He inquired about my travels over eight months, the great fortresses and ancient cities that I had seen, the wonders and the marvels, and the condition of every region, whether thriving or ruined, and how justice was administered. I played the part of royal companion, and we had wonderful conversations . . .[11]

On his way back to Istanbul from travels in Özü (Ochakov) and the western Black Sea region in October 1659, he stopped in Edirne, which at that time was serving as the capital:

> I resided in the houses of all the statesmen and nobles, and attended the salons during that winter season with all my patrons and lords. I regaled them with descriptions of the towns and villages I had passed through and the fortresses I had toured, and we conversed heartily, day and night.[12]

In 1665, while Kara Mehmed Pasha waited impatiently on the outskirts of Vienna for the Habsburg emperor's invitation to court, Evliya went off touring the city and in the evening reported back what he had witnessed. He wheedled a passport out of the young emperor himself (Leopold I)

---

9   Vol. 2, fol. 241b = Volume 2, selection 1.
10 Vol. 1, fol. 6b–8a = Volume 1, selection 1.
11 Vol. 5, fol. 5a; Dankoff 2004, 185–6.
12 Vol. 5, fol. 100a.

Introduction XVII

after impressing him with his knowledge of the Christian holy places in Jerusalem. And following his second (largely fictional) trip to Western Europe he again regaled listeners when he set foot on Ottoman territory.[13]

Two years later Evliya's audience was the Sultan himself. Sultan Mehmed IV made his court in Edirne in order to indulge his passion for the hunt and also to avoid the plague raging in Istanbul. In May of 1667, when Evliya returned from the Crimea and the Caucasus, he first stopped at Edirne to report to the Sultan's deputy and promised to bring him the falcons he had captured in Circassia in order to present them to the Sultan. He then went home to Istanbul where, he reports, six of his slaves died of the plague in a single week. Setting out toward Crete in late December, he again stopped at Edirne, delivered the falcons, and this time had a direct interview with the Sultan.[14]

At the end of his road in 1672 Evliya found a patron in the governor of Egypt, Kethüda Ibrahim Pasha, who even provided him an apartment in the Cairo citadel where he resided, so he tells us, for seven years. Aside from Ibrahim Pasha, whom he explicitly names as his patron, Evliya provides long lists of religious personnel in Cairo during that period and of '*beys* and notables who are my benefactors and to whom I owe a debt of obligation.' They are, almost exclusively, members of the Turkish ruling elite. The first to be named in the second list is Özbek Bey, Emir of the Hajj for Egypt in the 1670s, with whom Evliya had struck up a friendship during the pilgrimage journey. Pierre MacKay may be right in speculating that the autograph manuscript of the *Book of Travels*, of which volumes 1–8 have come down to us, was in Özbek Bey's private collection from the time of Evliya's death around 1684 until it was brought to Istanbul in 1742.[15] In any event, it is clear that Evliya had no lack of patrons and supporters during the time that he was completing the final redaction of his work.

* * *

The *Book of Travels* encompasses much of what was considered in Evliya's day the Ottoman realm, which comprised a multitude of peoples – Christians, Jews, and Muslims; Armenians, Greeks, Serbs, Hungarians, Arabs, Kurds, and Turks – and whose sway extended over the traditional

---

13 Vol. 7, fol. 62b–63a, 73a, 77a6.
14 Vol. 8, fol. 203a (= Volume 8, selection 2), 204b.
15 Vol. 10, fol. 76b, 79b, 247a; MacKay 1975, 279.

seven climes, from the first – Dongala at the equator – to the seventh – the Volga River. Evliya ventured north to Azov in the Crimea, south to Ibrim in Lower Nubia; he visited Baghdad on the eastern frontier, Stolnibelgrad on the western frontier. But his ambition as a traveller was not limited to the Ottoman realm. North of Azov, he spent some time in the land of the Kalmyks; southward from Ibrim, he travelled to the Funj kingdom in the Sudan. He went on two official missions to Persia, in the wake of the Ottoman-Safavid truce of 1639; and he joined an Ottoman embassy to the Habsburg court in Vienna. His travels beyond the borderlands of the Empire paralleled Ottoman efforts to secure their strategic and territorial interests. Evliya also participated in a number of military campaigns, most notably the battle on the Raab River (Battle of Saint Gotthard) in 1664 and the Candia campaign that resulted in the final Ottoman conquest of Crete in 1669.

What kind of traveller was he? For Evliya, travel was not a diversion but an obsession. He had to see everything, and he had to record everything he saw. He was nothing if not systematic. The town descriptions – the most characteristic literary unit of the *Book of Travels* – generally follow the same pattern, with subheadings introduced in elaborate Persianate phraseology. Sometimes the headings are all we have, followed by a blank space where he provides no information. It looks as though he had a checklist drawn up and for each town he simply went through and filled out the list. Sometimes he is at pains to explain why he cut his description short. For example, he apologises for not counting the shops in Sidirkapsi, in northern Greece, saying that he was too depressed because of the loss of his runaway slaveboy.[16]

For one whose primary identity was 'traveller' Evliya had a strange distaste for sea travel. He soured early in his travel career when he suffered shipwreck during a storm on the Black Sea – an episode he describes with great pathos.[17] Returning home after a long recuperation, he vowed never again to venture by boat onto the Black Sea – a vow he seems to have kept, despite subsequent journeys around its littoral.[18] Mentioning a trip on the Caspian in 1666, he says that he has always had an aversion to sea travel, and that this was the main reason he did not go either to the

---

16 Vol. 8, fol. 212a.
17 Vol. 2, fol. 264b–268b = Volume 2, selection 5.
18 Vol. 2, fol. 268a. At Vol. 1, fol. 138b he states that he made the circuit three times.

Introduction

Maghreb or to India.[19] Of course, he did go to Crete and other islands off the Turkish coast, including Cos and Rhodes. But when he boarded a frigate heading to Cyprus in 1671, it was attacked by enemy galleons and had to return to port; Evliya disembarked, consoling himself that he had seen enough of Cyprus when he went there in 1650 – a journey mentioned nowhere else![20]

Evliya rarely travelled alone. Even when not leading an official delegation, or attached to an Ottoman governor or commander, he was generally accompanied by friends, a suite of servants and hangers-on, often a bodyguard when the roads were unsafe; not to speak of horses, for which he had a special fondness, and even at times dogs. For example, setting off in 1671 from Istanbul – for the last time, as it turned out – intending to go on pilgrimage, he had in his train three travel-companions, eight slaveboys, and fifteen Arab horses.[21] More than once, his itinerary was interrupted by the need to pursue a runaway slave.[22]

Travelling in the Sudan in 1672, Evliya encountered two Bektashi dervishes, one riding a rhinoceros and one an oryx. They joined his party and accompanied him all the way to Suakin on the Red Sea coast. When the rhinoceros died and the oryx ran away, Evliya provided camels as substitute mounts.[23] Some of this, if not all, is surely fictional. But he did like having travel companions. At one point, in Dagestan in 1666, he even lists the names of five of them – all dervishes of one stripe or another![24]

Evliya frequently expresses the notion that a traveller must conform to the ways of the country he is in. Thus, in the Sudan in 1672, he complains of his host's stinginess but remarks: 'I was in a foreign land, so I bowed to necessity.' He was unaffected by the heat in the Sudan, and says that he conformed his dress to the climate.[25] The cold was more difficult for travelling, which is perhaps why he eventually settled in Egypt. Azov is a

---

19 Vol. 7, fol. 166b. In the Sudan in 1673, Evliya says that he contemplated travelling overland to the Maghreb but was dissuaded from doing so by a dream, and so returned to Egypt instead (Vol. 10, fol. 431a).
20 Vol. 9, fol. 149a.
21 Vol. 9, fol. 3b.
22 MacKay 2009 has analysed some of these episodes and concluded that they are largely fictional.
23 Vol. 10, fol. 411a (= Volume 10, selection 15), Q339b.
24 Vol. 7, fol. 165b.
25 Vol. 10, fol. 403b, 416b.

proverbial hell because of the cold, he tells us, just as Damascus is a proverbial paradise because of the pleasant climate. In January 1667 while he was in Azov he slipped on the marble floor of a bath that was icy; and after returning to Istanbul he suffered pains and discharges in his eyes for two months, symptoms (of glaucoma?) that he attributed to the cold weather he had just endured.[26] He occasionally complains of fever and other ailments, but in general had a strong constitution.

What were the circumstances under which he undertook his journeys? The Ottoman Empire fell heir to a system of road networks and sea-lanes going back at least to Roman times. These networks were maintained for official uses: military – the transport of armies, garrison troops, and supplies; bureaucratic – raising taxes that were forwarded to the capital, issuing orders from the capital to the provinces, and circulating state agents and their retinues;[27] and religious – the annual Hajj pilgrimage and dispersal of state monies to the holy cities of Mecca and Medina. Just as important were the private uses of these networks: commercial – the transport of merchant caravans[28] and the attendance at periodic markets and fairs; religious – the visitation of shrines, the search for religious knowledge or for spiritual guidance, and the attendance at annual festivals and birthday celebrations of the great Sufi leaders; and touristic – seeking out natural and man-made wonders, enjoying pleasure parks, summer pastures, and hunting grounds, glorying in the achievements of present and bygone civilisations.

Evliya participated in all of these activities. What made him distinctive as a traveller was the systematic nature in which he conducted his journeys and recorded them.

We must imagine a typical travel party of ten or twenty individuals, consisting of the traveller (merchant, scholar, government agent, or tourist) and his associates, his servants or slaves, and their mounts – generally horses, but also donkeys, mules or camels as pack animals. In many cases this travel party was accompanied by an armed guard. In any case, it had to be strong enough to counter bandits and wealthy enough to purchase

---

26 Vol. 7, fol. 184b, 185b, 203b.
27 These included pashas assigned to govern according to *kanun* or sultanic law, and *kadis* assigned to govern according to Sharia or sacred law.
28 The merchants found refuge within city walls in inns known as *hans*, in the countryside in fortified inns known as caravanserais.

Introduction

supplies along the way. For Evliya the scholar and writer, it had to accommodate his books and his writing equipment.

It is clear that Evliya kept systematic notes en route, and that during the periods he was home – first in Istanbul, then in Cairo – he organised the notes into a coherent narrative, the *Book of Travels*. What were his aims in writing this huge book, and how did he compose it? An analysis of the ten volumes[29] shows that throughout the work there is a clash between two organising principles: on the one hand, spatial or geographical; on the other hand, temporal or chronological.

Evliya's first aim was to provide a complete description of the Ottoman Empire and its hinterlands. In pursuing this aim, the spatial or topographical survey is the favourite mode. These town descriptions generally follow the same pattern, beginning with the history and administrative organisation of the town, its names in various languages and their etymologies, and its geographic position; continuing with a description of the town's topography, with particular attention to fortifications; including descriptions of houses, mosques, medreses, primary schools, *hans*, baths, and fountains; town quarters and religious affiliations; climate; the appearance, dress, manners and customs of the populace; proper names and speech habits; the ulema, poets, physicians, and other notables; markets, shops, products, and comestibles; and parks, gardens, and picnic spots; and concluding with graves and shrines, along with biographies or hagiographies of the dead.[30] His second aim was to provide a complete record of his travels. In pursuing this aim, the first-person account of his itineraries and adventures comes to the fore.

The first mode is imperial in scope, having sources in the 'Roads and Kingdoms' (Arabic: *masalik wa mamalik*) tradition of Muslim geographers.[31] Evliya's human geography embraces history, customs, folklore, and much else; but all tends to fit into pre-established formulas and grids. The second mode is personal or autobiographical, with sources in the *rihla* tradition of Muslim travellers, the best known of whom is Ibn Battuta (fourteenth

---

29 See Dankoff 2004, 10–20. Note that in Dankoff 2004 and elsewhere, the term 'Book' is used where here we have used 'Volume' in accordance with Evliya's own usage.

30 The structuring of travel accounts as a succession of descriptions of towns or of peoples, lands, and their products is also found in contemporary European works. See Rubiés 2000, 25–28.

31 See *EI2* 'DJughrāfiyā (S. Maqbul Ahmad).

century), whose life and travels overlapped with those of Marco Polo.[32] Evliya's junkets and adventures follow recognisable narrative patterns and tend to be quirky and anecdotal, sometimes sliding into satire or fantasy. At certain points Evliya adopts a different kind of chronological ordering, viz. according to historical sequence, based on the *ta'rikh* tradition of the Muslim annalists.

Evliya belonged to a group of educated men at the time who had a keen interest in geography. The scholar Katib Çelebi, at his death in 1657, left unfinished the first major Ottoman work on world geography. His 'Cosmorama' (*Cihannüma*) incorporated the writings of Arab geographers, the itineraries of Ottoman military campaigns, and European cartographic works such as the *Atlas Minor* of Gerhard Mercator.[33] Evliya was familiar with some of those sources and consulted them before composing his own account. Yet what makes the *Book of Travels* distinct from the 'Cosmorama,' or other comparable works, is the mixture of the factual and the personal. Indeed, as Cemal Kafadar has observed, the *Book of Travels* is the most monumental example of first person narratives in Ottoman literature.[34] The generic novelty of the *Book of Travels* perhaps explains its relative neglect among Ottoman literati until the middle of the nineteenth century. Nevertheless, parts of the *Book of Travels* parallel another kind of travel writing that now appears – the ambassadorial report (*sefaretname*). One of the earliest was written by Kara Mehmed Pasha about the embassy to Vienna in 1665.[35]

The *Book of Travels*, with its first-person narrative and focus on human geography, is also reminiscent of another tradition of travel writing altogether – the Chinese 'lyric travel account' (*yu-chi*). In these accounts, the travel itineraries were primarily domestic and, compared with early modern European travel writing, there is little evidence of 'the idea of self-fashioning, both of the individual traveller and of the collectivity of home society.'[36] This is also the case with the *Book of Travels*. And when Evliya

---

32 See *EI2* 'Rihla' (I. R. Netton); also Beckingham 1993, 86–94. For an assessment and summary of Ibn Battuta's travels, see Dunn 1989.
33 On Katib Çelebi, see Gottfried Hagen in Dankoff 2006, 227–33.
34 Kafadar 1989, 126.
35 For an assessment of Evliya's place within the broad category of Ottoman travel writing, see Vatin 1995.
36 Alam and Subrahmanyam 2007, 15. On the Chinese 'lyric travel account' see Strassberg 1994.

did venture into the realm of the 'other' we do not get the impression that any of the encounters was transformative. Evliya usually felt out of his element beyond the Ottoman borders, and seemed most at home among the Tatars, who were partially Ottomanised.

* * *

The trajectory of Evliya's travels – of his life – follows a path between the two great metropolises of the Empire: Istanbul, his birthplace and home town; and Cairo, where he lived his last ten years and where he drew up the final redaction of his magnum opus. Thus, Volumes 1 and 10 are devoted to these two cities. Evliya's description of Istanbul is without question the best guidebook to that city ever written. If Evliya had left us nothing but chapter 270 of Volume 1 – the panorama of the Istanbul craftsmen and merchants parading before the sultan – he would still enjoy a reputation as one of the greatest Ottoman writers. His description of Cairo in Volume 10 is equally impressive, the most elaborate and complete survey of that city written between the two *Khitats*, that of al-Maqrizi in the fifteenth century and that of Ali Mubarak in the nineteenth.

These two volumes, while serving as the frame for the larger work, appear to be modelled on each other in various respects. For example, the description of the shops and guilds in Cairo (Volume 10, chapter 49) is a reduced and more straightforward version of the corresponding sections in Istanbul (Volume 1, chapter 270). And the survey of quarters and villages up and down the Golden Horn and the Bosphorus (Volume 1, chapters 235–66) has its analogue in Evliya's trips up and down the Nile (Volume 10, chapters 65–74), although in the latter case these are tied in with the chronologies and itineraries of the work as a whole.

Only Volumes 1 and 10 have the chapter organisation. What about Volumes 2–9? While these do not have the same tight structure as the frame volumes, there is clear evidence that Evliya intended to provide a kind of shape to each volume. The dividing points are not haphazard, although all ten volumes are roughly the same size. Volume 2 begins with a reprisal of the dream, described much more elaborately at the beginning of Volume 1. This is a clear indication that Evliya conceived of the *Book of Travels* as a single text, since his journeys, and his account of them, all have a common motivation and share common goals. These goals include the traditional triad of *seyahat* ('travel', i.e., tourism, satisfying curiosity), *ticaret* ('commerce', i.e., making one's fortune), and *ziyaret* ('pilgrimage', i.e., fulfilling religious obligation).[37] But they also include such things as serving the Ottoman state; eulogising patrons and associates; and providing his contemporaries – and later generations – with instruction and amusement. It is suggestive that Evliya's first foray outside of Istanbul is the old Ottoman capital of Bursa; and that his last journey before settling in Cairo is the pilgrimage to Mecca, of which his account provides a *vade mecum*. When he sets out on the Hajj at the beginning of Volume 9, again from Istanbul, he has another (much shorter) dream in which his long-dead father and his old teacher Evliya Efendi both appear and urge him to go.[38] Compositionally, this dream parallels the reprisal of the initiatory dream at the beginning of Volume 2.

Although his itineraries over forty years repeat and crisscross, his accounts of them tend to be coherent and interrelated. Broadly speak Volume 2 can be characterised by the rubric 'Anatolia', Volume 4 by 'Safavid Borderlands', Volume 6 by 'Hungary', Volume 7 by 'Habsburg Borderlands', Volume 8 by 'Greece', and Volume 9 by 'Pilgrimage'.

Evliya's account naturally begins with the capital, also his birthplace, Istanbul, to which he devotes an entire volume. The historical and geographical surveys of the metropolis proceed systematically, although with frequent digressions and anecdotal asides. Volume 2 opens with Evliya's early journeys outside Istanbul, first to the old Ottoman capital of Bursa, then along the Black Sea coast as far as the Caucasus region, the homeland of his mother's kin, and around to the Crimea. He participates in raids against the infidel. He suffers shipwreck. Returning to Erzurum in the train of the newly appointed governor of that province, his kinsman Defterdarzade Mehmed Pasha, he accompanies an envoy to Tabriz in the country of the heretical Kızılbaş (i.e., the Safavids of Persia), his first venture outside the Ottoman realm. Later Mehmed Pasha is caught up in one of the frequent Anatolian disturbances of that era, a revolt by a disaffected provincial governor or 'Celali'. Learning of his father's death, Evliya returns to the capital in time to witness the deposition of the extravagant Sultan Ibrahim and the accession of the seven-year-old Sultan Mehmed IV (1648).

---

37 Cf. Vol. 2, fol. 369b, Vol. 7, fol. 72b, 131b, Vol. 9, fol. 3a = Volume 9, selection 1, Vol. 10, fol. Q350b. *Seyahat* (Arabic: *siyaha*) was also used for Sufis travelling abroad to seek spiritual guidance.
38 Vol. 9, fol. 2a = Volume 9, selection 1.

Introduction

In Volume 3 Evliya accompanies the newly appointed governor of Syria, Murtaza Pasha, to Damascus. Luckily he is back in the capital when his kinsman Melek Ahmed Pasha is appointed grand vizier (1650). From that time on he is almost constantly in Melek's service, following him to Özü, Silistre, and Sofia, and back to Istanbul where the pasha serves as deputy grand vizier until the arrival of Ipşir Pasha from Aleppo. Ipşir 'exiles' Melek to Van. After reaching Van, in Volume 4, Evliya once again goes on an embassy to Persia, and takes the opportunity to travel to Baghdad and make an extensive tour of Mesopotamia and Kurdistan, returning to Van only at the beginning of Volume 5. The remainder of Volume 5 covers the latter part of Melek's career, as governor of Özü and Bosnia, interrupted by the blow caused by the death of his beloved wife, Kaya Sultan. At the beginning of Volume 6 Melek is recalled from the Transylvania campaign to marry another sultana, Fatma Sultan, the daughter of his original patron, Sultan Ahmed I. The unhappy match is short-lived, ended by Melek's death in 1662.[39] Though left patronless, Evliya rejoices in the lack of family attachments and goes off to join the German campaign. The remainder of Volume 6 includes a detailed description of Hungary.

Volume 7 includes eyewitness accounts of the Battle of St Gotthard (1664) and the Ottoman embassy to Vienna under Kara Mehmed Pasha (1665), followed by travels in the Crimea, Circassia, and Kalmykia. Volume 8 is largely devoted to Greece, including an eyewitness account of the Candia campaign and the final Ottoman conquest of Crete (1669). Pilgrimage to the holy cities of Jerusalem, Mecca, and Medina is the subject of Volume 9. In 1672 Evliya finally reaches Egypt, his goal and haven after forty years of travel; and his leisurely description of Cairo in Volume 10 (plus journeys up and down the Nile) recalls his description of Istanbul. In the second half of Volume 10 he engages in expeditions and safaris in the Sudan and Ethiopia, finally returning to Cairo to write up his memoirs. The last date mentioned corresponds to 1683. Evliya probably died in that year or shortly thereafter.

* * *

---

39 All of Evliya's accounts of Melek's career are translated in Dankoff 1991.

His autograph manuscript – of which eight of the ten volumes have come down to us – apparently languished unread until 1742 when it was brought to Istanbul and copied.[40] Modern scholarship begins with Joseph von Hammer [-Purgstall] who hit upon a manuscript of the first four volumes as early as 1804. Hammer thought that these comprised the entire *Book of Travels*. He began to publish excerpts and translations (in German) in 1814. These efforts culminated in an English translation of Volumes 1 and 2.[41] Hammer's translation – though hastily done, abbreviated, and faulty in detail – captured the spirit of the original, and has served to make Evliya known to the English-speaking world.[42]

Meanwhile, an imprint of the complete Turkish text appeared between 1896 and 1938.[43] The first six volumes suffered from bowdlerisations, rewritings, errors, omissions, and censorings. Volumes 7–10 were much better, though still falling short of a critical edition. It was not until the 1970s that Richard Kreutel and Pierre MacKay showed the way.[44] A new edition, based on the autograph manuscript and a critical evaluation of other manuscripts, appeared between 1999 and 2007.[45] There is also a 'corpus of partial editions' with English or German translations.[46]

Aside from several translations into modern Turkish, substantial portions of the *Book of Travels* have been rendered into Arabic, Armenian, Greek, Hungarian, Romanian, Russian and Serbian. These portions were chosen based on national and geographical criteria – thus the sections on Greece were translated into Greek, the sections covered by the Soviet Union into Russian, etc. Especially noteworthy is Richard Kreutel's German translation of the Vienna section from Volume 7.[47] An attempt to break the mold is Faruk Bilici's French translation of three battle accounts.[48] Most

---

40 The person who had it brought and copied was the intriguing figure of Hacı Beşir Agha, the chief black eunuch of the Ottoman palace. See MacKay 1975; Hathaway 2006.
41 Hammer 1834–1850.
42 See Lybyer 1917; Pallis 1941, 1964.
43 *Evliya Çelebi Seyahatnamesi*, ed. Ahmed Cevdet etc. See Bibliography.
44 Kreutel 1972; MacKay 1975.
45 *Evliya Çelebi Seyahatnamesi*, ed. Yücel Dal et. al. See Bibliography.
46 Published by Brill: Bruinessen and Boeschoten 1988; Dankoff 1990; Buday 1996; Tezcan 1999; Dankoff and Elsie 2000.
47 Kreutel 1957.
48 Bilici 2000.

Introduction XXVII

recently, Hasan Javadi and Willem Floor have published their translation of Evliya's travels in Azerbaijan and the Caucasus region.[49]

The choice of texts for the present anthology was governed by several criteria. We wished to have samples from all ten volumes, and to have examples of the various descriptive and narrative types – the city monograph or town description; the itinerary; descriptions of mosques, churches, and other monuments; language specimens; descriptions of natural phenomena such as oil wells (Volume 2, selection 8) and manufacturing processes such as iron works (Volume 6, selection 3); descriptions of processions, festivals, and entertainments; narratives of battle and the hunt; dreams; pilgrimage accounts; and personal adventures, such as narrow escapes and encounters with bandits.

While most of the translations are new, we have made use of some published elsewhere. For Volumes 1 and 2 we have occasionally borrowed Hammer's phraseology. The Diyarbekir and Bitlis selections in Volumes 4 and 5 and the Albania selections in Volumes 6 and 8 are based on materials in the 'corpus of partial editions' mentioned above. Some shorter selections are borrowed from *An Ottoman Mentality* and other books and articles by Robert Dankoff. For the Vienna section in Volume 7 we profited from Kreutel's German translation and also made use of Livingston's version of the surgical operations.[50] For Dubrovnik (Volume 6, selection 5) we consulted the translations of Turková and Rocchi;[51] for Cairo and the Funj kingdom (Volume 10), those of Prokosch;[52] for the pyramids, that of Haarmann.[53] Some parts of the Athens section in Volume 8 employ earlier translations by MacKay.[54] And for the sections on Safed and Jerusalem in Volumes 3 and 9 we made use of Stephan's versions from the 1930s.[55] In all cases, we made revisions and corrections based on the original Ottoman Turkish text, and other changes for the sake of readability and stylistic uniformity.

Evliya Çelebi is not an easy author to translate. He wields a vocabulary greater than any other Turkish writer.[56] His own style tends to prolixity

---

49 Javadi and Floor 2010.
50 Livingston 1970.
51 Turková 1965; Rocchi 2008.
52 Prokosch 1994, 2000.
53 Haarmann 1976.
54 MacKay 1969.
55 Stephan 1935–1942.
56 See Dankoff 1991, 2008.

and exuberance and abounds in word play. He swings between the factual and the fanciful. He is sometimes exhaustively detailed to the point of tedium, sometimes vivacious and sparkling with wit. We have tried to convey his meaning accurately and, occasionally, to suggest his stylistic virtuosity. Where uncertainties remain, we have signalled this by a question mark (?).

The selections from each of the ten volumes are preceded by brief introductions. An appendix provides an outline of the entire work. It lists all the chapter headings for Volumes 1 and 10, and gives a rough outline of the untranslated portions for Volumes 2–9. It shows where all the translated selections fit and indicates the folios of the original manuscripts that have been translated.

Koranic citations are given in the Dawood translation,[57] sometimes adjusted to fit the context. These and other quotes in Arabic and Persian are given in *italics*. **Bold** in the main text corresponds to overlining or orthographical prominence in the manuscript, mainly used for headings. Rounded brackets { } enclose Evliya's own marginal notes, added when he was revising the text. Blanks left in the original text the size of a single word are indicated by (—). The large number of such blanks is characteristic of Evliya's descriptive style, which strives for exactness. Rhetorically, the blank means, 'To be filled in when more information is available'. Lines left blank are also indicated. Otherwise parentheses enclose explanatory notes supplied by the translators.

Evliya invariably refers to Istanbul as *Islambol*, meaning 'Islam-plenty'. In the translation, the city's name is rendered as Istanbul. Frequently he calls it *Kostantiniyye*, rendered here as Constantinople. The term *Rum* at this period usually referred to Asia Minor or the core Ottoman lands extending into Thrace; we have usually rendered it as Turkey or left it as Rum. A common designation for Christian Europe is *Kafiristan* meaning 'Land of the Infidels' (the coinage Infidelia suggests itself as an equivalent); we have consistently rendered it as Christendom. On the other hand, we have let *Frengistan* – meaning land of the Franks, i.e., Western Europe – remain in the translation. When he refers to himself, Evliya generally uses the locution *bu hakir* which we translate as 'this humble one' or, more often, simply 'I' or 'me'.

As a general rule, we have rendered Turkish personal names and place

---

57 *The Koran*, 5th rev. ed. (New York, 1990).

Introduction XXIX

names in modern Turkish orthography, Arabic and Persian ones in a transcription compatible with that of the *Encyclopedia of Islam*. Thus Turks will have names such as Mehmed, Ömer, Osman, Hüseyn as opposed to Muhammad, Umar, Uthman, Husayn. Note that in the Turkish orthography, *c* is pronounced as English *j*, *ç* as *ch*, *ş* as *sh*, *j* as *s* in *measure*. This orthography is also used for the specimens of various languages.

LITERARY ALLUSIONS

A notable feature of Evliya's literary style is the plethora of references to Islamic and Persian lore. He could assume that his audience – the Ottoman elite – would instantly recognise allusions to Koran and Hadith, and to such Persian classics as Firdawsi's *Book of Kings* (*Shahnama*, completed in 1010) and Sa'di's *Rose Garden* (*Gulistan*, completed in 1258).

Especially the legendary Persian kings and heroes served as templates; the mere mention of their names was enough to lend a rich associative gloss to whatever is under discussion. Thus Jamshid, an early king and culture hero, stands in for majesty and inventiveness; Kay Kavus for fine cuisine; Farhad for mining and engineering. Chosroes (Khusraw) is famous for his monumental vault, which still stood near Baghdad; while his beloved Shirin is associated with fine royal structures. The tyrant Zahhak stands in for a grim executioner, hence 'sword of Zahhak'.

A mountain suggests Mt Qaf which, in the traditional geography, surrounds the inhabited world; or else Bisutun, a lofty range in Iran. A strong fortress or dam elicits a comparison to the Wall of Iskandar, referring to the rampart against Gog and Magog constructed by Alexander the Great, who was identified with Dhu'l-qarnayn – 'The Two-Horned' – mentioned in the Koran (18:83). Or a mighty fortress is likened to that of Qahqaha (near Alamut in Iran); while a glorious palace is likened to Khawarnaq (near Najaf in Iraq). A fountain may evoke that of Salsabil, mentioned in the Koran (76:18), and a river that of Kawthar (108:1); while a beautiful garden invariably recalls that of *the many-columned city of Iram* (89:7). In Muslim lore, this last was built by Shaddad ibn Ad, who for Evliya serves as another example both of a great builder and a tyrant.

Mani – the founder of the Manichaean religion, but remembered for the artistry with which he adorned his book of revelation, the *Arzhang* – is often conjured up in connection with painting or any fine handiwork. (Evliya apparently thought that Arzhang was the name of another painter.) The other figure invariably mentioned in this connection is Bihzad, the famous master of the Persian miniature, who lived in Herat in the fifteenth century. Evliya also mentions more recent Persian masters such as Shah

Quli, Vali Jan and Agha Riza. When it comes to calligraphy, first place goes to the Persian Yaqut Musta'simi (d. 1298); then the Turks take the palm with Karahisari (d. 1556) and Sheikh Hamdullah (d. 1519); and also the master of paper cutouts, Fahri Çelebi of Bursa (d. 1611?).[1] Musical performances, on the other hand, invariably recall those of Sultan-Husayn Bayqara, who presided over the Timurid court of Herat in the late 15th century.

There are frequent allusions to pre-Islamic sacred history, from Adam to Jesus. A seductress is dubbed Zulaykha, referring to the figure known as Potiphar's wife in the Old Testament who tried to seduce Joseph. (In the Koran she is simply called 'His master's wife' – 12:23.) The Biblical Korah (Qarun in the Koran, 28:76) is proverbial for great wealth. Also in the Koran he is joined with Haman and Pharoah as figures of tyranny (29:39, 40:24), and Evliya follows suit, sometimes adding the Umayyad caliphs Marwan and Yazid to the list. Loqman, on the other hand, is proverbial for wisdom (31:12).

Hızır (Arabic: al-Khidr) is associated with the Water of Life that bestows immortality; and he comes to the rescue of those in distress, especially seamen. These traits are based on interpretations of the Koranic figure identified simply as 'one of Our servants' (18:65) who guided both Moses and Dhu'l-qarnayn/Iskandar. David – both a king and a prophet – is patron saint of ironsmiths stemming from his association with 'the armourer's craft' in the Koran (21:80). Someone sleeps like the Seven Sleepers of Ephesus, referred to in the Koran as Sleepers of the Cave (18:9).

Other allusions are to figures or events in Islamic history. Any cave – or something that just resembles a cave – calls up the Cave of Orphans, which probably refers to the cave near Mecca where the Prophet Muhammad and his companion Abu Bakr took refuge from their enemies. Salman – known as the Pure (*Pak*) or the Persian (*al-Farisi*) – was a Companion of the Prophet who became the patron saint of barbers and was thought to have a role in the initiation of various craft guilds. Bilal the Ethiopian was the Prophet's muezzin, and so the patron saint of Evliya himself in that role. Hassan ibn Thabit, known as the Prophet's poet, serves as a figure for poetic skill. Sa'd ibn Abi Waqqas, a leading Companion of the Prophet and commander of the Arab armies during the conquest of Iraq, was the patron saint of archers; Amr Ayyar al-Zamiri, the Prophet's messenger, of runners

---

[1] On Fahri and Ottoman paper cuts, see Atasoy 2002, 73-79.

Literary Allusions xxxiii

and tumblers. A certain Mahmud Piryar Veli was the patron saint of wrestlers, Kassab Cömerd that of butchers.

Ma'di-karib, associated with the semi-legendary exploits of the Prophet's uncle Hamza, was proverbial for his large appetite; while Ma'noghlu, a Druze rebel in Mt Lebanon whom the Ottomans executed in 1635, was proverbial for his imprisonment. Abu Muslim, leader of the Abbasid cause in the eighth century, was known as a halberdier and so his name gets associated with hatchets. The ascetic and saintly Rabi'a al-Adawiya (d. 801) was a model of chastity. The philosopher Ibn Sina (Avicenna) (d. 1037) had a reputation as a great physician, but also as a great magician. And an elephant can be qualified as Mahmudi, named for Mahmud of Ghazna (reg. 998–1030) who famously used elephants in his military exploits.

Sunnis as well as Shi'is recalled the trials of Husayn and his followers, who were martyred at Karbala in Iraq in the year 680; and so the Plain of Karbala is a figure for all who suffer thirst or are wounded in battle. The villain of the Karbala drama was the Umayyad caliph Yazid, whose name is enshrined in the pejorative term Yazidi for a certain heretical group.

GLOSSARY

Measures by weight

dram	[*dirhem*] approx. 3.2 g.
miskal	approx. 4.8 g.
okka	[*vukiye*] approx. 1.3 kg.
batman	approx. 23 kg.
quintal	[*kantar*] approx. 80 *okkas* or 100 kg.

Measures by volume

bushel	[*kile*] a dry measure used in Egypt
ardeb	approx. 5 bushels

Measures by length

cubit	[*arşın, zira*] approx. 28 inches
span	[*karşı*] approx. 6 inches
parasang	[*farsah*] approx. 3 miles

Currencies and measures of account

akçe	asper, a small silver coin, the basic unit of the older Ottoman monetary system
para	small coin worth one-fortieth of a *guruş*
guruş	piaster, Groschen: a foreign (Venetian or Spanish) silver coin worth about 80 *akçe*
dinar	a Venetian silver coin
ducat, goldpiece	[*altun*] a Venetian gold coin
Egyptian purse	[*Mısır kisesi*] a unit of expense, equivalent to 833 *guruş*
Egyptian treasure	[*Mısır hazinesi*] a unit of expense, equivalent to 1200 Egyptian purses
Groschen	see *guruş*
kızılga	a Tatar word for goldpiece
purse	[*kise*] a unit of expense, equivalent to 500 *guruş* (but see Egyptian purse); sometimes applied to other coins
scudo	[*uşkuta*] a Venetian silver coin
Thaler	a German silver coin worth less than a Groschen

tuman	a Persian unit of account, originally 10,000
yük	'load' = 100,000 *akçe*; sometimes applied to other coins

Administrative terminology

agha	title of officials, especially military officers; member of a pasha's retinue
azeb	an auxiliary infantry troop
Ban	title used in the Balkans for a prince or a governor
bey	a military title (= *emir*); governor of a *sancak*
beylerbey	governor of an Ottoman province (*eyalet, vilayet*)
celali	name given to fugitive soldiers and to provincial rebels engaged in armed insurrection against the state
cizye	tax paid by non-Muslims
çelebi	title given to Ottoman gentlemen
divan	the imperial council
efendi	title given to members of the religious or bureaucratic organisations
emir	commander; in Ottoman context a synonym of *bey*
gaza	warfare on behalf of Islam (= jihad), a term used for Ottoman military campaigns
gazi	one who engages in *gaza*, a term used for an Ottoman soldier
gönüllü	an irregular militia unit (others mentioned in the text are *deli* and *levend*)
has	an imperial grant to a governor, a *timar* providing an annual income of over 100,000 *akçe*
harac	tax or tribute; poll-tax on non-Muslims (= *cizye*)
kanun	statute, custom; Ottoman dynastic law (as opposed to Sharia)
janissary	[*yeniçeri*] main Ottoman infantry troop
kadi	qadi, judge in a Sharia court and administrative governor of a *kadi*-district (*kaza*)
kashif	in Egypt: district governor
kethüda	steward; deputy
khan	title of Ottoman sultans, Crimean *khans*, Kurdish chieftains, and Safavid provincial governors
molla	title for the chief *kadi* of a province
muezzin	caller to prayer
mufti	jurisconsult; one who issues a *fatwa*; the chief *mufti* is the *şeyhülislam*

Glossary

müteferrika	the elite mounted personal escort of the sultan
nakibüleşraf	officer in charge of tracing genealogies and maintaining the registry of *seyyids*
padishah	a title of the Ottoman sultan and other rulers
pasha	title reserved for high officers of the Ottoman state (*beylerbeys* and viziers)
sancak	administrative division of an Ottoman province; the officer in charge is *sancak-bey*
Sarıca	one of the irregular provincial levies, especially infantry
Segban	one of the irregular provincial levies, especially cavalry
seyyid	title for descendants of the Prophet, who were accorded a number of privileges including exemption from payment of taxes (see *nakibüleşraf*)
sheikh	title of the head of a religious order; Arab tribal chief
sherif	title for descendants of the Prophet, in particular hereditary governors of the Hijaz
şeyhülislam	title for the chief *mufti* of Istanbul and other major cities, head of the religious establishment
sipahi	timariot cavalryman (see *timar*); member of one of the six standing cavalry regiments at the Porte
surre	the sultan's annual gifts to the Holy Cities
timar	a grant of land in return for military or administrative service (see *zeamet, has*)
ulema	religious personnel, including *kadis, muftis, imams, sheikhs* of religious orders, etc.
voyvoda	voyvode, a military agent appointed by a governor to oversee tax collection in a *kadi-district*
zeamet	a *timar* providing an annual income of over 20,000 *akçe*

Religious terminology

besmele	the formula 'In the name of God the Compassionate the Merciful', recited when undertaking an activity
cami	congregational Friday mosque
Fatiha	the first *sura* of the Koran, often recited as a prayer
fatwa	a ruling or legal interpretation issued by a *mufti*
hacı	title of one who has performed the Hajj pilgrimage
Hadith	a traditional saying attributed to the Prophet
hafız	one who has memorised the Koran
hoca	title of a religious teacher

imam	prayer-leader; one of the twelve successors to the Prophet recognised by the Shi'is, and also honoured by the Sunnis; one of the four founders of the Sunni legal schools
Kızılbaş	pejorative name for Shi'is or Safavids
medrese	school to train *ulema*, especially jurists and theologians
mevlud	birthday celebration of the Prophet or the founder of a religious order; poem celebrating the birthday of the Prophet
Mu'avvizeteyn	the last two *suras* of the Koran, often recited as a spell to ward off evil
palheng	a carved stone the size of a hand with twelve flutings, worn at the waist by Bektashis.
qibla	the direction of prayer
Sharia	the Islamic sacred law, administered by a *kadi*
Sura	a chapter of the Koran
Sunna	a practice of the Prophet
temcid	a chant sung from the minarets at night about an hour after the last service of worship during the months of Rajab, Shaban, and Ramazan
tevhid	proclaiming God's unity; term used by Evliya for *zikr* and *sema'*, ecstatic mystical practices, often in conjunction with *tezkir* meaning *zikr*
waqf	endowment of property for the building and maintenance of a religious or charitable institutions
zikr	[Arabic: *dhikr*] lit. 'remembrance of God', a term applying to various Sufi rituals

Other

bedestan	covered market
boza	a beverage made of fermented millet
han	an inn or caravanserai
jereed	[*cirid*] a short javelin thrown on horseback as a military exercise

VOLUME ONE

Istanbul

EVLIYA BEGINS THE *Book of Travels* with a volume devoted to Istanbul, the capital of the Ottoman Empire and his birthplace. The volume opens with an account of the dream he has on his twentieth birthday, 19 August 1630, in which the Prophet Muhammad blesses his desire to travel. It proceeds with a historical and geographical survey of Istanbul, including its suburbs along the Golden Horn and the Bosphorus.

The opening volume of the *Book of Travels* is like a guidebook to Istanbul as well as a tribute, offering a vast panorama of life in the city, with descriptions of buildings, monuments and gardens, dress and cuisine, types of occupations and social groups. It also provides a template for Evliya's narrative and descriptive styles, which aim both to instruct and amuse. And as the centre of his world, Istanbul would become the touchstone and measure of everything he witnessed during his travels.

We have included here Evliya's description of one of the great imperial mosques of the city; also the churches and taverns of Galata; and the pleasure park of Kağıthane.

The systematic nature of Evliya's account is reflected in the chapter divisions – a feature found only in this and in the final volume. By far the longest is chapter 270, comprising the 47 guilds of Istanbul craftsmen and merchants parading before the sultan. The excerpts included here (furriers, circumcision barbers, tightrope walkers) give the flavour of these sections that are such rich sources for Ottoman life.

1. Introduction: The dream

In the Name of God the Compassionate the Merciful, and to Him we turn for help.

Praise be to God who has ennobled those honoured with worship and travel, and has vouchsafed for me the path to the holy places and shrines. May blessings be upon him, who laid the foundations of the fortresses of Sharia (the sacred law of Islam), and established them on the basis of prophethood and tariqa (the mystical path of Sufism), and upon his good and pure family. And may abundant blessings and the most excellent salutations be upon him, the protector endowed with exceptional character, the most noble and perfect of creation, the model for prayer who said, 'Pray as you saw me,' the infallible guide, Muhammad, who spoke Arabic best. In his honour, God, the Lord of the Realms and Creator of the Heavens, made the earth a pleasant home for the sons of Adam and made them the most noble of all the creatures:

> *Blessed be God, who ordered all affairs by His will,*
> *Without oppression, and without injustice!*

May blessings be upon the shadow of God on earth and good order of terrestrial things, sultan and son of the sultan, Sultan Gazi Murad Khan IV, son of Sultan Ahmed Khan, son of Sultan Mehmed Khan (III), son of Sultan Murad Khan III, son of Sultan Selim Khan II, son of Sultan Süleyman Khan, son of Selim Khan I, son of Bayezid Khan II, son of Sultan Mehmed II the Conqueror. *May God's mercy be upon them all.*

May God's mercy be especially upon Sultan Murad (IV), the *gazi* khan, *may his earth be sweet*, the Padishah majestic as Jamshid, the conqueror of Baghdad, with whose service I was honoured when I began these jottings. It was in the year 1041 (1631), in the time of his reign, that while making tours and pleasure outings to the villages and towns and thousands of parks and Iram-like rose gardens around the pleasant land (*belde-i tayyibe*, cf. Koran 34:15), i.e. Constantinople, the desire to make extensive travels came to mind.

I beseeched the Creator at every moment to grant me health of body, complete journey, and faith to the last breath, asking myself, 'How can I get free of the pressures of father and mother, teacher and brother, and become a world traveller?' I was always on good terms with heart-wounded dervishes and glad to converse with them. And when I heard a description of the seven climes and the four corners of the earth, I longed to travel with all my heart and soul. So I became utterly wretched, a vagabond crying out, 'Might I roam the world? Might it be vouchsafed to me to reach the Holy Land, Cairo and Damascus, Mecca and Medina, and to rub my face at the Sacred Garden, the tomb of the Prophet, glory of the universe?'

By God's wisdom – **Reason for travelling and roaming the land** – this humble one and poor supplicant full of fault – world traveller and boon companion of mankind, Evliya the unhypocritical, son of Dervish Mehmed Zıllı – always desired God's guidance in dreams while praising Him abundantly, and sought His succour for a sick heart while reciting Koranic chapters and verses. So I lay down on the pillow of lamentation, in the corner of my hovel, in my birthplace Istanbul, to a sleep of wish fulfilment. It was the night of Ashura in the month of Muharram, the year 1040 (10 August 1630), in a state twixt sleep and wake, that I had a dream.

This humble one saw myself in the Ahi Çelebi mosque, near the Yemiş landing – a mosque built with money lawfully acquired, an ancient mosque where prayers are accepted by God. There were soldiers bearing arms. The door was opened and the light-filled mosque was crowded with a luminous congregation, who were busy performing the dawn prayer. It seems that I stood motionless at the foot of the pulpit and gazed in astonishment at this congregation with their beaming faces.

'Good sir,' said I, turning to the person beside me, 'please tell me who you are, and what your noble name is?'

'I am one of the Ten Promised Paradise, the patron saint of archers, Sa'd ibn Abi Waqqas,' he replied. I kissed his hand and said, 'And who, good sir, are the lovely congregation immersed in light on this right side?'

'They are the spirits of the prophets. In the row behind them are the spirits of the saints and the pure ones. And these are the spirits of the Companions of the Prophet, the Emigrants (from Mecca), the Helpers (in Medina), the People of the Bench (*Arbab-ı Suffa* – a group of pietists during the lifetime of the Prophet), the martyrs of Karbala, and the Friends. Those to the right of the prayer niche are Abu Bakr and Umar; those to the left, Uthman and Ali. The man in front of the prayer-niche wearing a cap is Uways al-Qarani, the Prophet's brother in this world and the next. The dark-skinned man at the left wall of the mosque is Bilal the Ethiopian, your patron saint and the caller to prayer of the Prophet. The short-statured

Introduction: The dream 5

man who groups the congregation into rows is Amr Ayyar al-Zamiri. These soldiers marching with the standard, whose garments are dyed red with blood, are Hamza and all the spirits of the martyrs.'

Thus he pointed out to me the entire congregation, one by one. As I gazed at each in turn, I held my hand to my breast, nodding in acquaintance, and I found my soul refreshed.

'Good sir,' I asked, 'what is the reason of this congregation's gathering in this mosque?'

'The fleet-footed Tatar soldiery, among the Muslim forces in the vicinity of Azov, have come here to Istanbul which is under the protection of the Prophet. Later we will go to help the Crimean Khan. Now the Prophet is coming to perform the morning prayer. With him are Hasan and Husayn and the rest of the Twelve Imams, and the rest of the Ten who were Promised Paradise. He will signal you to begin the call to prayer. So cry out loud, *God is great*. After the salutations, recite the Throne Verse (2:255). Bilal will repeat, *Glory be to God,* and you, *Praise be to God*. Bilal will repeat, *God is great,* and you, *Amen, Amen*. The entire congregation will join in to profess His unity. Then after you say, *And blessings upon all the prophets and messengers, and praise be to God, Lord of the Universe,* rise immediately and kiss the Prophet's hand while he is sitting in the prayer niche. Say, *Intercession, O Messenger of God,* and make an appeal.'

Sa'd ibn Abi Waqqas gave all these instructions while sitting at my side. What should I see next?

A clear light broke through the door of the mosque. While the inside had already been filled with light, it was now *light upon light* (24:35). All the noble Companions and the spirits of the prophets and the saints rose to their feet and stood ready. The Prophet appeared felicitously at the foot of his green standard, with face veiled, staff in hand and sword girded at his waist. Hasan stood on his right and Husayn on his left. He placed his right foot inside the light-filled mosque, uttering, *In the name of God*. Then he removed the veil from his face and said, *Peace be with you, my community*. The entire congregation replied, *And with you be peace, messenger of God, lord of the religious communities.*

The Prophet at once advanced towards the prayer-niche and performed the two prostrations of the dawn prayer. This humble one was overcome with fright and my body trembled, yet I was able to observe all of his features. They were just as described in the *Hilye* of Hakani (on the Prophet's physiognomy, completed 1599). His veil was of crimson

Kashmir cloth. His turban was a white Arab-style turban with twelve bands. His mantle was of camel hair, yellowish in colour. On his neck was a yellow woolen shawl. On his feet were yellow boots. And a toothpick had been stuck in his turban.

After the salutation, the Prophet looked upon this humble one, struck his right hand on his knee, and commanded me to begin the call. I started immediately, according to Sa'd ibn Abi Waqqas's instructions, by intoning in the *segah* musical mode, *May God bless our lord Muhammad and his family and grant them peace,* and completed the call with *God is great.* Then the Prophet, in the same mode and with a mournful voice, recited the Fatiha and followed it with the decade of verses beginning: *We gave Solomon to David, and he was a good and faithful servant* (38:30). The entire congregation listened, the Prophet leading them in prayer. After the salutation, this humble one recited the Throne Verse. Bilal repeated, *Glory be to God,* and I, *Praise be to God.* Bilal repeated, *God is great,* and I did the call to prayer in sequence with Bilal. Following the benediction there was a royal *tevhid* that made me drunk with divine love, as though I had just awakened from sleep.

To sum up the dream: I completed my duties according to Sa'd ibn Abi Waqqas's instructions. The Prophet recited *Ya Sin* (Sura 36) in the *uzzal* musical mode with a doleful voice, *al-Nasr* (Sura 110) three times, and the *Mu'avvizeteyn*. Bilal recited a Fatiha. As the Prophet rose to his feet in the prayer niche, Sa'd ibn Abi Waqqas at once lay hold of my hand and brought me before him, saying, 'Your loving and faithful servant, Evliya, begs your intercession.'

He told me to kiss his blessed hand. As I shamelessly put my lips on that blessed hand, out of awe and dread, instead of saying '*Intercession (sefa'at), O messenger of God!*' I said, '*Travel (seyahat), O messenger of God!*' The Prophet smiled and replied, '*My intercession and my travel and my pilgrimage, may God give you health and well-being.*' He recited a Fatiha, and all the noble Companions recited it after him.

I kissed the hands of everyone present in the assembly and received each one's blessing. Some of their hands smelled of musk, some of ambergris, some of hyacinths, some of roses, some of sweet basil, some of wild basil, some of violets, some of carnations. But the scent of the Prophet was of a blooming saffron rose. And when I kissed his right hand, it felt as if it had no bones and was soft as cotton. The hands of the other prophets were scented with quinces. The hand of Abu Bakr had a scent of melons, Umar's of ambergris, Uthman's of violets, and Ali's of jasmine; the hand

Introduction: The dream 7

of Hasan smelled of carnations and that of Husayn of white roses. *May God be pleased with them all.*

When I had duly kissed the hands of the entire congregation, the Prophet again recited a Fatiha and his Companions repeated it in a loud voice. *Peace be with you, O brethren!* the Prophet pronounced from the prayer-niche and made his way out of the mosque. The Companions gave this humble one various benedictions and they too left the mosque. Only Sa'd ibn Abi Waqqas removed his bow-and-arrow case from his waist and girded it on mine, uttering *God is great.*

'Go forth,' he said. 'Perform the *gaza* with bow and arrow. Be in God's protection and safety. And receive these good tidings: Of all the spirits you met in this assembly and whose hands you kissed, you are vouchsafed to visit their tombs. You will be a world traveller and unique among men. The well-protected kingdoms through which you pass, the fortresses and towns, the strange and wonderful monuments, and each land's praiseworthy qualities and products, its food and drink, its latitude and longitude – record all of these and compose a marvellous work. Make use of my weapon and become my son in this world and the next. Do not abandon the path of truth. Be free of envy and hatred. Pay the due of bread and salt. Be a faithful friend but no friend to the wicked. Learn goodness from the good.'

Having finished his counsel, he kissed my brow and departed from the mosque.

Waking from the sleep of comfort, I was in a quandary, uncertain whether it was a dream or reality or a true vision. As I pondered, my mind was at ease and my heart filled with joy. At dawn I performed my ablution and the morning-prayer, then crossed over from Istanbul to Kasımpaşa and consulted the interpreter of dreams, Ibrahim Efendi, who gave these good tidings, 'You will be a globe trotter and world traveller. Your journey will be sealed with a good ending. You will be admitted into paradise by the intercession of the Prophet.' And he recited a Fatiha.

Next, I went to Abdullah Dede, the sheikh of the Mevlevi convent in Kasımpaşa. I kissed his hand and again related my vision. He told me, 'Since you have kissed the hands of the twelve Imams, you will be a champion in this world. Since you have kissed the hands of the Ten Promised Paradise, you will enter paradise. Since you have kissed the hands of the first four caliphs, you will have the honour of conversing with all the padishahs in the world and will be their boon companion. Since you have beheld the beauty of the Prophet, kissed his hand, and received his blessing, you will attain happiness in both worlds. Following the counsel of Sa'd ibn Abi Waqqas, do your utmost to chronicle our dear Istanbul; then you will surely obtain the lot that is decreed for you, in accordance with the dictum, *What is destined will happen.*'

He gave me seven rare and valuable books of chronicles and said, 'Go forth, may your affair come out right. A Fatiha!' Having received his benediction, this poor humble one took the treasure of books to a corner of my hovel. And now, having studied some of those histories, I begin the account of my birthplace, the envy of kings and harbour of vessels, mighty fortress of the province of Macedon – Istanbul.

2. The Süleymaniye Mosque

Description of the Mosque of Sultan Süleyman

May God's mercy and forgiveness be upon him

It was begun in the year 951 (1543) and finished in the year 963 (1557), and is an exemplary mosque beyond description. The learned men who compose histories, and thus strike the die on marble, have confessed the inability and failure of the best chroniclers to celebrate this unequaled mosque. Now, this humble Evliya ventures to write down its praises as much as I am able.

First, this mosque divides in half the ground of the old palace that the Conqueror had earlier built. On top of the high hill, Süleyman Khan built a unique mosque overlooking the sea. How many thousands of master architects, builders, labourers, stonecutters and marble cutters from all the Ottoman dominions had he gathered! And for three whole years 3000 galley slaves, foot-bound in chains, would lay the foundation deep into the ground, so deep that the world-bearing bull at the bottom of the earth could hear the sound of their pickaxes. They dug until they had reached the deepest part, and in three years, by erecting a platform, the foundation was built up to the surface.

In the following year construction was halted while workmen cut stones for the buildings above the foundation. A year later, the prayer-niche was installed to the same measurement as that of the mosque of Sultan Bayezid II the Saint. In three years they completed the walls as far as the vaults of the dome on all four sides. After that, they constructed the lofty dome on top of the solid square pier base.

Features of the Süleymaniye mosque. The bowl of the indigo-coloured dome of this great mosque, up to its lofty summit, is more spherical than that of Aya Sofya, and is seven royal cubits in height.

Apart from the square piers supporting this incomparable dome, there are four porphyry columns on the right and left sides of the mosque, each one worth ten Egyptian treasures. These columns were from the city of (—) in Egypt,[1] transported along the Nile to Alexandria. From there Karınca Kapudan ('Admiral Ant') loaded them onto rafts and, with favourable wind, brought them to Unkapanı in Istanbul and then to Vefa Square. When he delivered the four columns to Süleyman Khan at the mosque, he recited the verse:

> The ants presented Solomon
> A locust's leg;
> Whatever of ours suits you
> Accept, I humbly beg.

Süleyman Khan was pleased, and, as a reward for his service, Karınca Kapudan was duly granted the governorship of Yılanlı (Spurie) and Rhodes islands. These four columns of red porphyry are each fifty cubits high. God knows, there is nothing like them in the four corners of the world.

A semi-dome above the prayer-niche and another one above the qibla gate opposite it are fixed to the great dome. But there are no semi-domes resting on the aforementioned piers. In order not to overload them, the chief architect Sinan put windows of cut glass and crystal, (—) in number.

The multicoloured stained windows above the prayer-niche and the pulpit are the work of Sarhoş ('Drunkard') Ibrahim. Mere men are too impotent to praise them. At noon, when these windows let in the rays of the world-illuming sun, the mosque interior shines with light, dazzling the eyes of the congregation. Each pane contains a myriad of varicoloured glass bits, in designs of flowers and of the beautiful names of God in calligraphy. They are celebrated by travellers on land and sea as a sight not matched in the heavens.

The prayer-niche and pulpit and the muezzins' gallery are made of pure white marble. But the master stonecutter set the muezzins' gallery above (—) columnettes so that it is like the galleries of paradise. The lofty pulpit is made of raw marble and has a crown-like canopy, matched only by the

---

1 In Vol. 10, fol. 383a Evliya identifies the source of these columns as Luxor.

pulpit in the Sinop mosque. And the prayer-niche could be that of Solomon himself. Above the niche, gold on azure by the hand of Karahisari, is inscribed the verse, *Whenever Zacharias visited her in the Niche* (3:37).

To the right and left of the prayer-niche there are columns with spiral braids that are white magic. Also there are candlesticks tall as a man, gilded with pure brass and gold, which hold candles of camphor wax, each one twenty quintals in weight. The candles are reached by wooden staircases of fifteen steps and are lit every night to illuminate the mosque interior.

In the left corner of this mosque, there is a lofty gallery raised on (—) columns, with a separate prayer-niche, for the sovereign's private use. Apart from this gallery, there are four others, one in each corner of the four piers, for the Koran reciters. On either side of the mosque there are (—) side benches of stone. Inside the mosque and flanking the side galleries there are congregational galleries resting on columnettes of various sorts. Outside the mosque and overlooking the sea there are again galleries on slender columns, similar to those indoors, and on the right side, the market. When the congregation gets crowded, people perform their devotions on these galleries.

Within the mosque, around the dome, there are two more rows of galleries supported by columns, which on holy nights are lighted with oil lamps. There are 22,000 lamps in total and thousands of chandeliers. And there are (—) windows all around the mosque, through each of which blows a gentle breeze that refreshes the congregation as though they had entered paradise. By God's command, this mosque has a pleasant fragrance that perfumes the brain; but it has no resemblance to the scent of earthly flowers.

On the side of the qibla gate and next to the two piers in the back of the mosque there is a fountain. The entire congregation drinks from the clear water, satisfying their thirst. And beneath some of the arches on the upper storey there are storage rooms where the notables of the province and thousands of travellers keep their money, the amount of which the Creator only knows.

Praise of the calligraphy of Karahisari. There has never been to this day, nor will there ever be, any calligraphy like that of Ahmed Karahisari both inside and outside this mosque. The Creator granted him success in this field. First, in the centre of the big dome, is inscribed the verse: *God is the light of the heavens and earth. His light may be compared to a niche that enshrines* *a lamp, the lamp within a crystal of star-like brilliance* (24:35). He has truly displayed his skill in rendering this Light Verse.

In the semi-dome above the prayer-niche is written: (—). In the semi-dome above the qibla gate is inscribed: *I will turn my face to Him who has created the heavens and earth, and will live a righteous life. I am no idolater* (6:79). On one of the four piers is inscribed *Allah*, on another one *Muhammad*, on another *Abu Bakr*, and on the last *Umar, Uthman, Ali, Hasan,* and *Husayn*. And above the window to the right of the pulpit is the verse: *Temples are built for God's worship; invoke in them no other god besides Him* (72:18).

Apart from these, over the upper storey windows, are written the beautiful names of God. These are in the *şikafi* style, while the large inscriptions in the dome are in the *güzafi* style where every *alif* and *lam* and *kaf* is ten cubits tall – they were written in proportion to the height of the dome, so that they can be read plainly from below.

This mosque has five doors. On the right side is the imam's door; on the left, below the sultan's gallery, is the viziers' door; and there are two side doors. Written over the left side door is: *Peace be to you for all that you have steadfastly endured. Blessed is the recompense of paradise* (13:24). Written over the right side door is: (—) (—) (—) (—). And the inscription above the qibla gate is:

[2 lines empty]

In this inscription is added: *Ahmed Karahisari wrote this in the year* (—).

Description of the white courtyard. A flight of (—) stone steps leads up to the above mentioned portals of felicity of the noble mosque and to the three lofty gates of the delightful courtyard. This courtyard is a white plateau paved with white marble, every slab the size of a carpet, smoothed and polished and even, forming a crystalline valley. It is square in shape and, along with its side galleries measures (—) feet. But the mosque interior is larger than the courtyard, the distance from the qibla door to the prayer-niche being (—) feet and the width (—) feet. Above the side galleries, forty feet wide, that go all around this courtyard, over the varicoloured piers, there are (—) precious columns. And rising above these column are varicoloured stone arches, giving the impression of a rainbow. Still further above and all around are (—) domes.

Overlooking this courtyard on all four sides are (—) windows, each with iron gratings and bars thick as one's arm. The master ironsmith wrought these windows with the skill of David, wielding his file so that even now no trace of dust affects their polished surface which gleams like Nakhchivan steel. And over these windows are (—) panes of glass.

In the middle of this white courtyard is a square basin that has to be seen, a work of white magic. But it is not for ablutions – all four sides have marble latticework, and the congregation drinks its Water of Life. It is roofed by a squat dome covered with flat leaden tiles. The strange thing is that because jets spring up from the basin, it is called a fountain, but the water actually flows down from the dome like the Salsabil fountain in paradise. It is a marvellous spectacle that amazes anyone who inspects it.

Over the windows along the qibla gallery of this courtyard, the verse (—) (—) (—) is inscribed on azure porcelain tiles. The verse (—) (—) (—) is written over the gate on the left side, the verse (—) (—) (—) over the gate on the right side, and the verse (—) (—) (—) over the qibla gate.

This qibla gate is the tallest of all the gates and unequaled on earth in its fine white marble filagree decoration. The master stonecutter has joined the blocks together such that no man can differentiate between them. Above the lintel and within the marble recesses resembling a prayer-niche, there are nodding tulips and an array of other carvings, and marble chandeliers suspended by chains, wrought with the skill of Jamshid. On either side of this gate, in cells four stories high that reach up to the dome, dwell the timekeeper, the caller of the hours of prayer, the gatekeepers and caretakers.

Just inside this gate, the floor is paved with a large round block of red porphyry that is an unparalleled piece of polished stone. It is the size of a Muhammadan dinner-spread, and one side is slightly cracked.

Then, to the right, is a square slab of porphyry on which a cross was engraved, traces of which are still visible. The infidels offered a million of money for it, but it was not for sale. Finally, during a water festival, a *şahi* cannon was deliberately fired over the mast of the infidel galleons moored at Galata. The ball broke the threshold of the left gate of the courtyard of the Süleymaniye mosque, rolled onto the slab with the cross and came to a stop. But since it was set in the ground, it was not damaged. The import of this is that the cursed Franks were so hostile, and the master gunner so skillful, that they could take aim from Galata and strike the threshold of the Süleymaniye. Traces of the strike are still visible, and people come to view it.

On the pedestals of the columns along the four sides of this courtyard, there are brass plates on which are incised all the great events, such as fires and earthquakes, enthronements and public uprisings, and the like. The

The Süleymaniye Mosque 13

engraver of the chronograms is provided for by the endowment. They are marvellous pedestals with dated inscriptions.

Description of the minarets. This mosque has four minarets, each one used for the Muhammadan call. Since Sultan Süleyman Khan was the tenth Padishah of the Ottoman dynasty, ten galleries were built on the four minarets. The two adjoining the mosque have three galleries each, and the climb to these incomparable minarets is (—) hundred steps. The two minarets in the rear corners of the courtyard are lower and have two well-proportioned galleries each.

The minaret on the left with the three galleries is called the Jewel Minaret. The reason is that, in order for the foundation to settle, Süleyman Khan had the building of this mosque stop for a year and built other pious works. Shah Tahmasp, the king of Persia, when he heard of the halt to construction, dispatched a great embassy with 1000 purses of money and a box of all kinds of valuable jewels. In his letter he wrote, 'I heard that you did not have the funds to complete the mosque and so you put a halt. Due to your friendship, I have sent to you this amount of money from the treasury and these jewels. Sell them and spend the money, and take pains to finish the mosque. Let us have a share in your pious works.'

The emissary arrived with such taunting letters before Süleyman Khan, who was surrounded by a sea of labourers and masons employed about the mosque. Süleyman was incensed by the letter. In the presence of the emissary he distributed the 1000 purses of money to the Jews in Istanbul, and not a grain was left. He addressed the emissary, saying:

The heretic on judgement day
Will be an ass beneath the Jew.

To your masters the Jews then, who will mount you when the time comes, let your money be allotted, so that when they do mount you on judgement day, they may spare you the spur and whip. Otherwise, what do folk like you who reject ritual prayer have to do with pious works like founding a mosque?'

Then he gave the architect Sinan the box of jewels while the emissary was still present and said to him: 'The so-called precious stones he sent are worthless beside the stones of my mosque. So put them with the rest and use them in the construction.' When the emissary had understood the situation, he was dumbstruck. Several facetious letters were written in reply to the emissary's letter, and he set out toward Revan (Erevan, part of the Safavid kingdom at that time).

Meanwhile, the chief architect used the jewels to decorate the grooves of that minaret with artistry of all sorts, also for the marble roses decorating the inscriptions. This is why it is called the 'Jewel Minaret'. Some of the stones shine when the sun's rays strike, but others have faded and lost their lustre from exposure to the heat, snow, and rain. However, in the centre of the arch above the qibla gate, there is a Nishapur turquoise as large as a round bowl that dazzles the beholder.

On both sides of this mosque, there are forty taps for renewing ablutions.

Description of the bower of the light-filled tomb. Within a bow-shot's distance from the prayer-niche wall, in the midst of a rose garden, is the tomb of Süleyman Khan, *may his earth be sweet*. He lies under a lofty dome that has no match beneath this celestial dome. For the master builder has put a larger dome on top of a smaller dome. Such a well-wrought dome, with such a strange and wonderful design, and such artful and intricate carvings of marble, is not to be seen in any other country.

Description of the outer courtyard. On three sides of this mosque there is also a single-layered outer courtyard. Two sides are an arena long enough for a horse to gallop in. It is a vast courtyard adorned with lofty plane trees, weeping willows, cypresses, lindens, and ashes. And on its three walls are (—) windows in total.

The courtyard has ten gates: two on the qibla side, the Mera Gate and the Old Palace Gate; on the south side, the Mekteb Gate, Market Gate, Sağmedrese Gate, and Chief Physician's Gate; on the west, the Imaret (Soup Kitchen) Gate, Tevhane (Guesthouse) Gate, and the Agha's Gate, reached by (—) steps. On the north is the Dome Gate of 1001 Nails, reached by twenty stone steps – it is called so because that was the number of nails used to construct the dome. And on the east side is the Hammam Gate, with (—) steps leading down to the public bath. On this side, the courtyard is not enclosed by a wall but by a low parapet so that one can view Istanbul. The entire congregation stops here to enjoy a panoramic view of the imperial palace, Üsküdar, Boğazhisar (Rumeli Kavağı), Beşiktaş, Tophane, Galata, Kasımpaşa, and Okmeydanı. And there are fine views of the Golden Horn and the Bosphorus, with thousands of ferries and caiques plying the waters and other boats unfurling their sails.

The circumference of the Süleymaniye mosque, around the four sides of this courtyard, is (—) thousand paces.

There is also a small courtyard between the Süleymaniye and the walls of the old palace. It is known as the Pehlivan Demir square, after the chief of the wrestlers. All the champions from the Lodge of Wrestlers grapple with one another at that pleasant place after the mid-afternoon prayer. The proper Turkish term is *güreş*.

To the right and left of this mosque, there are the four great medreses for the chief muftis of the four schools of law, filled completely with men of the most profound learning.

There is also a Hadith school, a Koran recitation school, a medical college, a primary school, a hospital, a soup kitchen and dining hall, a guesthouse, a caravanserai for travellers, and a palace for the Janissary Agha; markets for goldsmiths, button makers and boot makers; a resplendent public bath; quarters for theological students; and 1000 houses for servants. 1001 domes can be counted in the vicinity of this mosque.

Seen from Galata, the Süleymaniye complex seems like a vast city covered with dark blue lead. There is a total of 3000 servants attached to it. They are maintained by secure endowments from Süleyman Khan, including the revenues of several islands in the Aegean – such as Sönbeki (Symi), İstanköy (Cos), Sakız (Chios) and Rhodes – that are governed by the endowment's administrator and his 500 agents.

Because Süleyman Khan is the conqueror of the seven climes, his name is mentioned not only here but in (—) Friday sermons. And in all the lands of Islam, there is no building stronger and more solid than the Süleymaniye. All architectural experts agree on this, and also that nowhere on earth has such an enamel dome been seen.

Within and outside this mosque the foundation is firm, the buildings elegant, and every piece of ornamentation the work of wondrous magic of extreme perfection. When the construction ended, the Grand Architect Sinan said, 'My Padishah, I have built for you a mosque so solid that on Judgement Day, when the mountains of the world are carded like cotton, the dome of this mosque will roll like a polo ball before the carder's bow string of Hallaj Mansur.'[2]

---

2 The mountains 'carded like cotton' are reminiscent of the Koranic image of the mountains on the Day of Judgement being 'like tufts of carded wool' (101:5); while the mention of carding evokes the ninth-century Sufi martyr al-Hallaj whose name means 'The Carder'.

Indeed, built on a lofty hill, the foundations are firmly supported by walls below, beginning from the upper wall of Tahtakale, to the wall of the palace of Siyavuş Pasha, to that of the Janissary Agha, to the cistern wall of Küçükbazar, and to the walls of the Agha's school, the guest house, the soup kitchen, the lead magazine, and the hospital.

Once, this humble one observed ten Frankish infidels with expert knowledge of geometry and architecture who were touring this light-filled mosque. The gatekeepers had let them in, and the caretakers had given them special shoes so they could walk around and see it. Wherever they looked, they put finger to mouth and bit it in astonishment. But when they saw the doors inlaid with Indian mother-of-pearl, they shook their head and bit two fingers each. And when they saw the enamel dome, they threw off their Frankish hats and cried out in awe, 'Maria, Maria!'

Then they saw the four vaults at the skirt of the dome, resembling the Vault of Chosroes. They are like the rainbow, in accordance with the verse:

> Like the milky way, with head raised high
> He threw the lasso to the vault of the sky.

– each one as it were a vault created by the hand of God. {In fact, these vaults can be dated from *kudret kemeri* ('Vault of Power'), the year 944 (1537).}[3]

They gazed at these arches and at the rest of the mosque's interior for an entire hour, with finger in mouth, then went outside into the courtyard. When they saw the four minarets, the four pedestals, the six lofty gates, the delightful courtyard and surrounding arches and domes, the columns and row on row of well-proportioned cupolas topped by gilded Muhammadan finials, their eyes were dazzled from the splendour. Once again they threw off their hats and walked all around this noble mosque bareheaded. Now in their awe they bit all ten fingers, that being their way of expressing extreme astonishment.

This humble one requested their interpreter to ask them how they liked this building. One of them turned out to be capable of speech. He said, 'All things, whether created beings or man-made structures, are beautiful either on the inside or on the outside. Rarely are the two beauties found together. But both the interior and the exterior of this mosque were constructed

---

3   An example of a chronogram, in which the numerical value of the letters add up to the date.

The Süleymaniye Mosque

with such grace and refinement. In all of Frengistan we have not seen an edifice built to such perfection as this.'

'How does this mosque compare with Aya Sofya?' I asked.

'To be sure,' they answered, 'that is a larger building, constructed with brick, and an ancient work, solid and well-built for its time. But this is a finer construction in terms of grace, elegance, and beauty. It also required greater expenditure than Aya Sofya.'

In fact, they say that every ten *miskals* of stone used in this mosque cost one gold piece.

Expenditures for the Süleymaniye Mosque. When the mosque was completed, all its expenses – according to the accounts of the superintendent of construction, overseer, and treasurer – amounted to 890,383 *yük* of florins.

3. The antiquity of smoking

A curiosity. This ancient mausoleum (tomb of Sultan Mustafa), was built by King (—) at the time of the construction of Aya Sofya, (—) years before the Prophet. So it is a thousand and (—) years old. While (recently) the master builder and miners, with chisels like that of Farhad, were carving a hole in the south wall to put in a window, an iron tobacco pipe appeared between two bricks. All of them saw it, and they could still detect the scent of tobacco smoke. This is evident proof that smoking tobacco is an ancient practice.

4. Galata

Chapter 246: Account of the ancient edifice and great fortress of the city of Galata, its founding, its features, the buildings within it, and all its qualities

First, King (—) built the fortress of Constantinople after the time of Alexander the Great. The area of Galata was a meadow of pleasant air and a rich pasture where shepherds tended their sheep and cows, always milking them and bringing the milk to the king. Since delicious milk came from this fertile pasture, it was named Galata – *galata* being the Greek word for milk. Later, in order to quarter the shepherds, a fortress-like shelter was built near the present-day Kurşumlu Mahzen ('Lead-Covered

Magazine'). And so Galata became more and more built up, until the reign of (—).

{It is north of Istanbul, and a mile-wide strait separates them. It is eighteen miles long, reaching Kağıthane at its western extremity. One crosses from Stanbul to Galata by caique, ferry, or barge. In the era of the infidels there was a bridge of chains.}

[...]

Circumference of the walled town of Galata. Its circuit is 10,060 paces. In the year (—) (1634), when Sultan Murad IV went on his expedition to Revan, his lieutenant Bayram Pasha repaired and whitewashed the walls of Galata and measured them with an architect's cubit. The circuit, together with all the towers and ramparts, was calculated to be 18,000 cubits. There are 205 towers and 13,000 crenellations. The height of the walls is forty royal cubits. Some of the towers are eighty royal cubits in height.

But Galata Tower, built by Mehmed the Conqueror, is 118 cubits high, and its sky-scraping summit is covered with lead. From nowhere can one see the entire circuit of the walls of Istanbul, and its triangular shape, except from Galata Tower. In clear weather, the Mountain of Monks (*Cebel-i Ruhban*, today Uludağ) which looms over Bursa is visible, and even the buildings of Bursa can be seen through a spyglass. {This tower, cylindrical in shape, is visible from three parasangs' distance.} The tower interior was a dungeon in ten layers; it is now a storage for Ottoman naval equipment. It has a single iron gate that opens to the south and is reached by a stone staircase of (—) steps. This humble one used to fly paper from there (i.e., from the top of the tower). One time I strung a rope to get a tightrope walker's view of Istanbul.

On the land side of Galata Tower is a deep moat, extending from Meyyit Gate to Tophane Gate. I have seen thousands of fortresses but never a moat like this; only that of Akkerman, where the Dniester flows into the Black Sea, might match it. There are always sailors in this trench twisting ship cables, marlines, and life ropes. It is broad and deep, and all along its edge are graveyards and cemeteries. {But there is no moat on the sea side, which is entirely covered with markets.}

[...]

This city has eighteen Muslim quarters, seventy quarters of Greek infidels, three of cranky Franks, one of Jews, and two of Armenians. No infidels reside in the first castle, and none at all in the second castle as far as the Arab mosque – the inhabitants of the quarter possess a noble rescript

Galata 19

from Mehmed the Conqueror according to which no infidel is allowed in, and if they see an armed Christian they give no quarter and kill him immediately. The majority of these inhabitants are grief-stricken Mudejars who came from Spain, driven out by the infidels, in the time of Sultan Ahmed. If *they* see an armed infidel in Galata, they kill him right away.

Aside from these two castles, the two walled areas of Galata as far as Tophane are filled with Franks of the Seven Kings (i.e., from the Habsburg Empire) and other Christians. According to the land survey of Murad (IV) Khan, there are 200,000 infidels and 64,000 Muslims. May God preserve it.

There are seventy churches. First, the Church of the Organ belonging to France. It is on a dyke; the gate is reached by a staircase of seven steps.

Near it is the Venetian church. It had burnt down, and lay in ruins for twenty years until it was restored at the time of the Candia truce (1669) by permission of Köprülüzade Ahmed Pasha. It has a sky-scraping square bell tower.

Inside and outside these churches, there are strange and wonderful images and icons that seem to be alive.

[2 lines empty]

The Greeks have (—) churches.

[1 line empty]

They have one hospital according to their false claim.

[1 line empty]

The Armenians have three churches.

[1 line empty]

And the Jews have two synagogues. But the Jews are always in fear of these infidels (i.e., Christians).

As for the infidel quarters, they are patrolled day and night, because they have girded their loins for rebellion more than once, and many of them were put to the sword.

[...]

The manners and customs of the inhabitants of Galata. The people of Galata are in (—) categories: the first are sailors, the second merchants, the third craftsmen of various sorts, and the fourth joiners and caulkers. Most of them wear clothing of Cezayir (the Aegean archipelago) {because they are mainly marines. There are fabulously rich captains, among them Elvan Kapudan.}

The Greeks are tavern keepers. The Armenians are sellers of pressed meat (*pastırma*) and wealthy merchants. The Jews are intermediaries in the marketplace. The Jewish boys are male prostitutes – there is no more despised group of catamites than they.

The praiseworthy food and drink of the city of Galata. First is the fine white Mudejar *francala* bread. The thousands of coloured candies, flavoured with musk and ambergris and worthy of a padishah, in the glass jars at the confectioners' market are found nowhere else, unless it be paradise-scented Damascus. The Mudejars also sell spiced sweetmeats topped with decorative leaves and spiced ring-bread (*simit*).

Among the artisans are sellers of compasses and watches, cut-crystal lenses and hourglasses, and infidel apothecaries.

As for drinks, in the taverns – named Taş Nerdüben ('Stone Steps'), Kefeli, Manyalı, Mihalaki, Kaşkaval, Sünbüllü, Kostanti, and Saranda – are sold various notorious forbidden ruby-dripping wines, including *misket* (from Bulgaria) and wines from Ancona, Syracuse, Mudanya, Erdemit, and Bozcaada (Tenedos). When I pass through that wicked locale and see hundreds of downtrodden tavern-slaves lying in the highway, bareheaded and barefooted, and inquire about their wretched state, some put forth this verse:

> I am so drunk I do not know
>   What is worldly or divine.
> Who am I? Who is the cupbearer?
>   What is the crimson wine?

Or:

> I have quaffed his ruby wine:
>   Drunk I am, drunk I am!
> Captivated by his locks,
>   Mad I am, mad I am!

Or:

> My foot takes no step but to the tavern,
> My hand holds nothing but the cup of wine.
> Stop the rant, preacher! My ear hears nothing
> But the bottle's glugging and the drunken cry.

Galata 21

Some denizens of the tavern recite this couplet:

> Ascetic, to the tavern
> Politely go.
> What this convent is
> Do you think you know?

This humble one swears by God the Knower of Secrets that I have never partaken of a single drop of these intoxicants. Being of a sociable and impertinent nature, I have mingled among all the craftsmen and learned their secrets. But I only drank sherbet of Athenian honey, known as Mudejar sherbet. Galata has such types of craftsmen. But these bankrupted drunkards and addicts are put in the dungeon just inside the Yağkapanı Gate to reform their manners.

This city, because of the delightful climate, is famous for its darling boys and girls. Its blessings are abundant for rich and poor alike. All the people are impertinent lovers, of dervish temperament. They are famous for their salons in wintertime. When the grand ship captains return from their voyages, they take all their friends in their faluccas and frigates to the vineyards in Boğazhisarı and have intimate gatherings.

The harbour of Galata, being an extremely fine one, is protected from the eight winds, and in winter time 1000 ships lay anchor here without fear. The suburb to the north of the walled town of Galata is considered to belong to Tophane, because it has a separate governor. There is no record of (Muslim) pilgrimage sites in Galata.

5. Kağıthane

The pleasure-park and resort lodge of world-adorning Kağıthane.
It is a promenade famous among travellers in Arabia and Persia, India and Yemen and Ethiopia. The Turkish poets have penned the praises of its air and water. It is a delightful river that flows through the valleys of Levendçiftlik near the Bosphorus. Fullers wash their turbans and shirts and trousers without the need for soap – after two rinses the garments come out fresh as a white rose. Some Indian merchants bring their stuffs to Kağıthane and dip them in the water just once, which is sufficient to clean them.

On both sides of the river are grassy meadows with clover, alfalfa, couch grass, *levşe* (?), buttercups, and tulips; and shady bowers adorned with thousands of plane trees and poplars and weeping willows. In the river one gets sweet flag, the like of which is not found at Azov or in the lake of Kanizsa and whose root is extremely beneficial.

On holidays, thousands of old and young lovers come to this place to flirt with one another and go out in caiques and ferries. Some come with their boy sweethearts to take a plunge in the river and swim and embrace without fear. It is a river of love. But the tree roots along the banks sometimes catch the feet of swimmers like fishing nets and drag them down to a watery death, crying, 'Oh, a sea sprite has got me!' So one must be cautious, even though there are no sea sprites. Withal, thousands of sweethearts wrap their rosy pink bodies, like peeled almonds, with indigo-coloured silk aprons, then dive into the river like fish and flatter their lovers. There is much commotion, with musical entertainments in every corner worthy of Husayn Bayqara. In charge of this place of enjoyment is a regiment of janissary conscripts and their colonel, who also oversee the gunpowder mill.

Praise of the gunpowder mill. Bayezid the Saint built it at the border of this Spring of Life in the year (—). Later, Süleyman Khan made it into a stone building roofed with lead. But the dome is not made of stone. The staff, from the munitions corps, includes the chief gunpowder maker, his warden and guards, and 200 soldiers.

In this factory are 100 bronze mortars, each weighing ten quintals; and various wheelwork mechanisms that have to be seen and cannot be explained in words. There are also water wheels on the river. When the barrages are opened, the water wheels turn, as do the wheelworks inside them. Then iron pestles, each weighing 40 to 50 *okkas*, pound and grind the gunpowder in the mortars, while the workers stir it with wooden sticks. *Heaven help us*, if an iron pestle strikes a mortar and a spark lights the gunpowder, all the workers get blown in the air like the birds of Ababil (105:3). It is a dangerous place, and not a pretty sight. And the thundering noise from the wheels turning and the pestles pounding makes a man tremble to the marrow of his bones. It is a noteworthy sight for reckless tourists. Those who are sensible will view it from a distance and then will repair to the lodge of Kağıthane for carousing.

For this lodge has thousands of benches and galleries for lovers to sit in, a seventy-hearth kitchen and pantry worthy of Kay Kavus, twenty shops, a bread oven, a coffee house, a mosque, and a well of sweet water. There are 200 cells for the janissary conscripts, and storerooms full of dishes, pans, ladles, kettles, and copper utensils. Lovers who wish may put up here as guests for fifteen nights and enjoy themselves.

Once every forty years,[4] in this meadow of Kağıthane, the guild of goldsmiths assembles and holds parties for twenty days and nights according to the *kanun* of Süleyman Khan the Goldsmith. Guildsmen from all the Ottoman dominions flock to this festival, 300 purses are spent on it, and 12,000 journeymen graduate to become master goldsmiths. And it is a *kanun* of Süleyman Khan that the Ottoman Padishah in person attend this great gathering, pitch his Solomonic tent-pavilion, and give the chief goldsmith a gift of twelve purses. For when Süleyman was a prince in the city of Trabzon, he apprenticed under the Greek master Kostanta and himself became a goldsmith. Later, when he became sultan, he founded the goldsmiths' workshop near the Water-carriers' fountain.

First, twelve goldsmith apprentices kiss the hand of the glorious Padishah, then that of the *şeyhülislam* and the other great viziers, then the hands of the chief goldsmith, their sheikh, and their warden, and lastly the other masters, as established by Süleyman Khan. Then the chief goldsmith presents gifts to the Padishah – such as a chest, an inkstand, a bridle, a sword, or a scimitar – all encrusted with jewels.

In short, in the valley of Kağıthane, five to six thousand tents and pavilions are pitched. It is a sea of men for twenty days, and powerful torches turn the nights into bright days, as on the night of the Feast of the Sacrifice.

Once every twenty years the saddle makers' guild also has an outing here, and that is also a noteworthy event. And every year, from the first day to the last day of the month of Sha'ban, the people of Istanbul pitch tents in this plain of Kağıthane in anticipation of the fast of Ramadan. For a whole month they make amusements, under the name of *şeb-bük*.[5] Such a place of joy is Kağıthane.

The town of Kağıthane is situated 1000 paces north of this promenade. It has 200 houses of Muslims with Iram-like gardens. There is the mosque of (—) Hatun who was (—)'s wetnurse (*daya*), with the following chronogram over the qibla door:

[1 line empty]

---

4 Elsewhere (Vol. 1, fol. 186a) Evliya reports that this festival is held once every twenty years, and that he attended it three times.
5 A rare word apparently signifying hand-clapping or the like; see Dankoff 2008, 215.

There are also a fine bath and twenty shops. In Byzantine times there was a paper mill (*kağızhane*) here, a large structure with masonry domes. And there were water wheels turned by the river that passed beneath the Daya Hatun mosque. The paper mill is now in ruins, but it could easily be restored and turned into a gunpowder mill.

In this place and as far as the wooden bridge there are lofty plane trees on both sides of the river, reaching up to the sky, on whose branches nest myriads of herons. Their plumes, that are left behind on their perches, are collected by the keeper of Emirguneoğlu's garden (today's Emirgan).

Convent of the fire-worshipping Hindus. It is on the western side of this town, a small convent with a grassy meadow and a few weeping willows. If a Hindu dies in Istanbul and its environs, the body is brought here and cremated. This humble one witnessed it three times.

Convent of the Indian Kalender dervishes. It is at the head of the Kağıthane bridge. They are all Muslims. Sultan Ibrahim Khan, like Ibrahim ibn Adham (a famous Sufi, d. 777), used to set aside his crown and share food with the dervishes at this Indian convent.

6. Guilds' parade

Chapter 8: Guild of Mediterranean captains

[...]

Following the procession of the Mediterranean Sea captains, the butchers were supposed to pass, according to imperial decree. But all the great Egyptian grain merchants, including dealers in rice, hemp, Egyptian reed mats, coffee and sugar gathered together and began quarrelling with the butchers. Finally they went before the sultan and said, 'My Padishah, our galleons are charged with transporting rice, lentils, coffee, and hemp. They cannot do without us, nor we without them. Why should these bloody and tricky butchers come between us? Plagues have arisen from cities where they shed their blood, and for fear of this their stalls and shambles in other countries are outside of the city walls. They are a bloody and filthy band of ill-omen. We, on the other hand, always make Istanbul plentiful and cheap with grains of all sorts.'

Now the butchers' eyes went bloodshot.

'My Padishah,' they said, 'Our patron saint is Kassab Cömerd and our occupation is with sheep, an animal that the Creator has made the object of mercy, and whose flesh He has made lawful food for the strengthening of His servants' bodies. Bread and meat are mentioned as the foremost of God's gifts to mankind: with a small portion of meat, a poor man can subsist for five or six days. We make our living with such a lawful trade, and are known for our generosity (*cömerdlik*). It is we who make Istanbul plentiful and cheap. As for these merchants and dealers and profiteers: concerning them the Koran says, *God has made selling lawful and profiteering unlawful* (2:275). They are such a despised group that after bringing their goods from Egypt they store it in magazines in order to create a shortage, thus causing public harm through their hoarding.

'The Ottoman state has no need of their rice in the first place, because there is excellent rice already available from Filibe and Beypazarı and (—). Nor do the people Turkey have a need for Egyptian hemp which they praise so highly, since there are various kinds of hemp available from Manastır, Florunya, Serfice, Tırhala, and Drama in Rumelia, and from numerous places in Anatolia, not to speak of the linen and cotton shirts from Trabzon which are sold for a straw – one can get a *beddavi* shirt for 20 dirhems – so why do we need your hemp, which anyway has been the cause of so many huge fires in Istanbul? As for the lentils you speak of, this is a product found all over Rumelia and Anatolia.

'Egyptian sugar? But in the Koran the rivers of paradise are praised as being made of *pure honey* (47:15). Now we have honey from Turkey, Athens, Wallachia, Moldavia, each with seventy distinct qualities. Furthermore, if my Padishah wished, thousands of quintals of sugar could be produced in Alanya, Antalya, Silifke, Tarsus, Adana, Payas, Antakya, Aleppo, Damascus, Sidon, Beirut, Tripoli and other such provinces – enough to make it plentiful and cheap throughout the world – so why do we need your sugar?

'As for coffee: it is an innovation; it prevents sleep; it dulls the generative powers; and coffee houses are dens of sedition. When roasted, it is burnt; and in the legal compilations know as *Bazzaziya* and *Tatarkhaniya*[6] we have the dictum that *Whatever is carbonised is absolutely forbidden* – this holds even for burnt bread. Spiced sherbet, pure milk, tea, fennel, salep, and almond-cream – all these are more wholesome than coffee.

6 *Bazzaziya*: a compendium of fatwas by Hafiz al-Din al-Bazzazi al-Kardari, d. 1414. *Tatarkhaniya*: a compendium of Hanafi law by Alim ibn Ala'al-din al-Hanafi, d. *c.*1351.

'You speak of henna. True, it is a Sunna of the Prophet, used by women and to dye the white beards of old men. But if you pound laudanum root in a mortar, mix it with water, and rub it in your hair or beard, it makes an excellent red dye, and furthermore rids hair and beard of lice and dust; so we have no need of your henna either.'

To these objections of the butchers, the Egyptian replied, 'Our rice is fine and white and cooks nicely, especially that grown in the regions of Manzala, Damietta, Faraskur and Birimbal, which has a wonderfully fragrant scent when cooked with butter. Before the Prophet there was no rose-water, rice, bananas, or jujubes; so the creation of rice is one of the miracles of the Prophet. As for our lentils, they are mentioned in the Koran – *and lentils* (2:61) – and grow in the soil of paradise and in the water of Egypt, and are tastier and cook better than the lentils of Turkey. No henna in any other land compares with our henna, and there is no argument that its use is a prophetic Sunna. It is true that Turkey has no need of sugar and hemp, and that sugar from Frengistan is also very fine. But tell us this, O band of butchers: What benefit and return do you offer to the public treasury?'

The butchers had nothing to say to this, and the Egyptian merchants continued, 'My Padishah, the goods arriving in our galleons provide the public treasury an annual revenue of 11,000 purses from customs dues. As a matter of justice, we ought to have precedence in the Muhammadan procession and the butchers ought to come after us.'

The *şeyhülislam* Yahya Efendi and Mu'id Ahmed Efendi cited the Hadith, *The best of men is he who is useful to mankind*, and the sultan gave the Egyptian merchants a noble rescript authorising them to go first, and the butchers to go second.

Chapter 28: Guild of furriers

They are 1,000 men, with 500 shops, and their patron saint also is the prophet Idris, since they work with needles. But it was Hushang Shah who first hunted animals and wore their skins.[7] He roamed the mountains in the guise of those animals in order to hunt them. Other people wore them in imitation of him, and took pleasure in wearing them. The patron saint of

---

7 Elsewhere (Vol. 3, fol. 47a; Vol. 9, fol. 70a) Evliya attributes the tanning of animal skins and the wearing of furs to the innovation of Jamshid rather than Hushang. In the *Shahnama* Jamshid, son of Hushang, is a culture hero, founder of the civilized arts; and in the *Book of Travels* he is the patron saint of many things (see Dankoff 2004, 92).

Guilds' parade

furriers at the time of the Prophet was Amr ibn Amiri. His light-filled tomb is in (—) (—) (—) and he is the fourteenth patron saint to be girded by Salman Pak.

A marvellous battle broke out between the furriers and the tanners. Finally the sultan and the nobles and grandees decided that wearing furs was a necessity and the order was given for them to go in advance accompanied by a special military band.

So they file past with their shops on drawn carts and carried on shoulders, adorned with the furs of sable, ermine, marten, red squirrel and Russian silver fox, the head and leg furs of sable, the neck furs of duck, swan and goldfinch, the neck and belly furs of fox, and the furs of astrakhan lambskin, all worth hundreds of thousand of *guruş*.

Next, the Greek furriers in the Mahmudpaşa market form a separate grand procession, wearing hundreds of furs which they put on backward.[8] On their heads are outlandish bearskin caps. Their trousers are also animal skins. Some are covered head to foot with skins of leopard, tiger, lion and wolf. Others have sable kalpak crowns on their heads and pikes and javelins in their hands, and pass with their horses, also smothered in animal skins.

Another group wrap themselves in animal skins, pretending to be wild men, each one dragged along by five or six men with chains. These wild men of strange aspect – *Heaven help us!* – make mock attacks on the spectators, frightening them out of their wits. Others dress up as demons or fairies and stand on their heads, then leap to their feet and attack the crowd. Some are strangely attired as jinn, confounding the minds of any who see them. Still others put on lion or leopard or tiger skins and go on all fours, giving the onlookers threatening glances, and are hardly restrained from attacking them by their keepers who drag them along by chains and strike them with rattan staffs.

---

8   This means wearing them fur-side out, as we do today – as opposed to wearing them with the furry side next to the skin, which Evliya takes to be the norm, and which was apparently the common practice among the Russians and the Tatars (the source of furs for the Ottomans), for the practical reason that they provide greater warmth that way. Elsewhere (Vol. 10, fol. 173a) Evliya asserts that Hushang Shah, the patron saint of furriers, started out wearing furs backward or fur-side out (*ters geymek*) – apparently because he could hunt other animals more effectively dressed in animal-like fashion; but his more sophisticated imitators began to wear them fur-side in; although fur-side out is still the fashion in the Caucasus and parts of southern Russia and Tatary.

Next some men in skins of bear, boar, wolf, stag and roe deer enter the arena unchained and swaying back and forth. Behind them come a band of hunters with their motley hounds and brandishing pikes and maces. They attack the first group as though they were hunting boars and bears and wolves, and so pass before the sultan.

Guild of sable kalpak makers. Eighty shops and 105 individuals. Their patron saint is unknown. This headgear is the crown of the Chingissids. They deck their shops with sable kalpaks and entertain the crowds by stuffing kalpaks with cotton and manipulating the resulting puppets with strings.

Guild of sable merchants. 1,000 individuals, all of them Rumelian Greeks – from the cities of Serfice, Florunya, Liçista and Gölikesri – with no religion and no patron saint. They are wealthy merchants who every year import sables and squirrels and other furs from Muscovy. They put their sables on backward and pass in parade with their litters and horses adorned head to foot with sables and with leech teeth, also known as fish teeth.[9]

Guild of falconers {and other hunters}. 200 individuals. They are the furriers' hunters and possess sultanic rescripts exempting them from taxes. None of the other hunters – whether the chief falconers, or the keepers of hounds of the palace gardeners or of the janissaries, or the janissaries of the Istıranca hunters' corps – can interfere with these furriers' hunters. They shoot swans, goldfinches, mallard drakes and speckled ducks in the Great and Little Çekmece inlets and in the Terkoz lakes, and give their throat-fur to the chief furrier and their wings to the chief arrowsmith. They too pass in procession with their game.

Guild of leopard keepers. One agha – his shop is in the Lions' Den (*Arslanhane*) – and fifty-five individuals. Because the chief furrier possesses leopard skins and lynx skins, these leopard keepers parade with all the

---

9   Perhaps walrus ivory. There is a confusion of *sülük* 'leech' and *süñük* 'bone'; see Dankoff 2008, 213, citing Vol. 7, fol. 169b on 'the bone known as fish tooth', one of the imports from Muscovy.

10 At this point in the description appears the phrase *seraser çullar ile* which might mean 'with embroidered hair cloth bags' (used to restrain the animals?) or else 'dressed in hair cloth from head to foot' (but unclear whether this would refer to the animals or their keepers).

sultan's leopards, dragging them along by gold and silver chains[10] and keeping them in check with rattan staffs, crying 'My leopard did not take it, my leopard did not see it!'

Guild of lion keepers. Their patron saint was Ali, the Lion of God, at whose feet all the wild beasts used to grovel. The chief lion keeper, in charge of lions and tigers, was originally supposed to march with the mastiff sheepdog keepers under the authority of the chief butcher; but the chief furrier persuaded the sultan to have them under his authority instead, since he had control over the skinning and tanning of lion and tiger skins. So the fifty lion-keepers too go in the procession with the furriers, dragging their chained lions and tigers – and panthers, bears, wolves and hyenas – like so many vicious dragons.

Following them come the Greek and Muslim darling boys (i.e., apprentices) of all the furriers, with their Tatar kalpaks and armed to the teeth.

The chief falconer of the furriers, the chief leopard keeper, the deputy of the chief lion keeper, and the chief furrier go together in front, stirrup to stirrup and bridle to bridle, dressed in the finery of their respective guilds. Following after are their darling boys and their eightfold band, all passing in ceremony.

This guild of furriers is very necessary to the Ottomans, whether at home or on campaign.

Chapter 34: Guild of barbers

[...]

Guild of circumcision barbers. They are 400 men, with 300 shops, and their patron saint is Abu'l-Hawakin Muhammad ibn Talha ibn Abdullah. Salman Pak girded him and he circumcised all those who were honoured with the glory of Islam. But the Prophet, by God's command, when he was born from his mother Amina, was already circumcised, and his eyes were tinged with kohl.

The wife of Abu'l-Hawakin Muhammad was Rabi'a, daughter of Abdullah ibn Mas'ud. She circumcised her chaste-starred daughter by cutting off the excess flesh called the 'little red tongue' in the middle of her vagina. This was first done by (—) (Sarah), Abraham's wife, who out of anger at Hagar had circumcised her by cutting off that very flesh. Since that time, the practice of circumcising girls has become peculiar to Arabia.

Even in Egypt there are a people known as Hadari who make great merriment on the night of the circumcision of girls. The advantage of this for women, reportedly, is that it eases childbirth.

Here the circumcisers adorn their shops drawn on carts with various circumcision razors and, as they pass by in procession with drums and tambourines, pretend to circumcise some boys.

Chapter 41: Guild of acrobats
First are the master acrobats, i.e., tightrope walkers, who perform world-admiring feats. In Istanbul today there are thirteen masters, each one capable of climbing to the sky on rope ladders and conversing with Jesus and the cherubim. First is Mehmed Çelebi of Üsküdar, then Hacı Nasir of the Maghreb, Hacı Ali of Alexandria, Şaşı Hüsam of Harput, Kubadi of Bursa, Kara Şücah of Arapgir, Kemberoğlu, and Kız Pehlivan. They exhibit their skill in the Padishah's presence, wearing Kubadi slippers, some with balancing beam, some without, some with a tray in each hand and a donkey on their backs, or with a naked sword in each hand – in short, demonstrating their skill with one of the 260 props used by acrobats. They are Arab and Persian, Indian and Yemeni masters, who have set foot in the heavenly sphere at the summit of Galata Tower.

Chief of the guild, appointed by a noble rescript, is Mehmed Çelebi of Üsküdar, who performed in the Hippodrome on the occasion of the imperial circumcision. According to his register, there is a total of 200 tightrope walkers wandering about this island world, with 2,000 men in their train.

Their patron saint is Dawud Habli, son of Imru'l-Qays. Dawud scaled the fortress of Khaybar by tightrope and upon its conquest was girded as patron of the tightrope walkers by Salman the Persian. His tomb is in Hamadan. His father Imru'l-Qays was unique of his age, one of the most eloquent of the Arab poets, from the tribe of Quraysh. He recited these couplets –

> *In summer man desires winter;*
> *When winter comes, he desires summer.*
> *He is never satisfied with one thing.*
> *Let him perish! How ungrateful he is!*

– before the revelation of the Koran. Later, the Koranic verse: *Let man perish! How ungrateful he is!* (80:17) was revealed. Imru'l-Qays eventually went to King Heraclius and was buried in Caesarea.

7. Lağari Hasan Çelebi

On the sixth night after the chaste-starred daughter of Murad (IV) Khan, named Kaya Sultan, was born, in celebration of her hair being shorn, this Lağari Hasan created a rocket with seven prongs, to be fired by 50 *okkas* of gunpowder paste. Overlooking the sea at Sarayburnu, in the Padishah's presence, Lağari mounted the (main) rocket and his assistants ignited it. As he was soaring to the summit of heaven, he cried out, 'Goodbye, my Padishah. I am going to converse with Jesus.'

Offering praises to God, he ignited the rocket prongs around him, illuminating the sea below. But as he mounted to the roof of the sky, the gunpowder for the main rocket ran out and he plummeted back to earth. He had attached eagle wings to his arms in order to break the fall. Now he plunged into the sea before the palace of Sinan Pasha and swam ashore. Emerging naked, he kissed the ground before the Padishah and joked, 'Jesus greets you, my Padishah.'

He was rewarded with a purse of gold and an appointment in the cavalry corps with a salary of 70 *akçe* per diem. He went on to serve Selamet Giray Khan in the Crimea, and died there. He was my close friend. *May God's mercy be upon him.*

VOLUME TWO

Anatolia and beyond

EVLIYA RELATES that he always wished to travel and make the Hajj pilgrimage but found it difficult to escape family obligation; and he recalls his dream of the Prophet. Finally, on the eve of his thirtieth birthday in 1640, he departs Istanbul without informing his family and ventures to the old Ottoman capital of Bursa, famous for its hot springs (cf. those of Sofia, Volume 3, selection 8).

In August 1640, Ketenci Ömer Pasha, a protegé of his father, is appointed governor of Trabzon, and Evliya seizes the chance to set out in his retinue. One of the features of Trabzon is the fish known as *hamsi* (anchovy), of which he gives an amusing account. In October 1642, after many adventures, including shipwreck during a storm on the Black Sea, he returns to Istanbul. (While he claims to have witnessed the Canea campaign in 1645 – the opening salvo in the twenty-five year long Ottoman conquest of Crete – the account lacks veracity).

It is not until August 1646 that Evliya again hits the road, this time in the retinue of Defterdarzade Mehmed Pasha, a kinsman who is appointed governor of Erzurum. Once in Erzurum, Evliya accompanies an envoy to Tabriz, which marks his first excursion outside Ottoman territory. While shocked at some of the Shia religious practices and the harsh punishments meted out to criminals, he also finds things to approve of in this provincial capital of Safavid Persia. Stopping in Ardabil, he finds Divriği cats being auctioned (cf. Volume 3, selection 6). His roundabout journey in the Caucasus takes him to Baku, where he observes oil wells, and to the Armenian religious centre of Echmiadzin, as well as parts of Georgia, before returning to Erzurum.

Later Mehmed Pasha forms an alliance with Varvar Ali Pasha, the dismissed governor of Sivas who had turned rebel ('Celali'). Eventually the rebel forces are defeated outside of Ankara, but both Mehmed Pasha and Evliya are spared. Meanwhile, Evliya learns about the manufacture of mohair, visits the shrines of saints and has an encounter with a festival of tightrope walkers – all narrated with his typical flair. Getting news of his father's death, he returns to Istanbul in July 1648 and witnesses the events surrounding the deposal of the mad Sultan Ibrahim and the accession of the child Sultan Mehmed IV.

1. Setting out

Praise to the Creator of specks and scents, Fashioner of the pied universe, Who brought into existence this lowly slave from the realm of non-being and commanded me to obedience and service. With the Koranic injunction *I created mankind and the jinn that they might worship Me* (51:56), He enjoined upon His slaves the five daily prayers and the other obligations of Islam: fasting, alms, and pilgrimage.

This humble slave too wished to perform the Hajj pilgrimage and avidly desired to set out on the journey. How, I asked myself, can I get free of the pressure of parents and siblings and become a world traveller?

Then, on the first day of Muharram in the year 1040 (10 August 1630), as I aimlessly wandered the streets of Istanbul, I wrote down in Volume 1 the complete description of this matchless city, recording, as far as possible, its important buildings and noteworthy matters; all of its guilds, with their patron saints and rules and statutes, in forty-seven chapters; and the parade of the army as Gazi Sultan Murad (IV) set forth on his campaign to conquer Baghdad.

So my desire to travel and sightsee, and to visit the tombs of the saints, was satisfied within Istanbul. Still, day and night I longed to gird my loins and set out for the Holy Land, towards Baghdad and Mecca and Medina and Cairo and Damascus.

One blessed night – as I recorded at the beginning of Volume 1 – while asleep in my hovel, I dreamed that I saw the holy Prophet in person. I kissed his hand and, instead of begging him for intercession, by a slip of the tongue begged for travel instead. He raised his blessed veil, revealing his beauteous countenance, smiled, and said: '*My intercession and my travel and my pilgrimage, may God give you health and well-being.*' He recited a Fatiha, and the entire congregation of the Prophet's companions recited it after him. Then I kissed their hands and woke up – as I recorded above in detail.

When God desires something He prepares the intermediate causes. The following morning, by God's wisdom, I happened to visit my old friend Okçuzade Ahmed Çelebi in the Gedikpaşa quarter. What should I see? They were making preparations for a journey to the city of Bursa. That faithful friend and dispeller of grief said, 'Come join me, my brother Evliya. *First the companion, then the road.* Be my companion for five or ten days. We'll tour

Bursa with its magnificent countryside. Thus we'll gladden our saddened spirits and scour the rust of grief from the mirror of our hearts. We'll see thousands of noteworthy monuments and visit the tombs of hundreds of saints and Ottoman sultans. In particular, we'll enlighten our hearts by rubbing our faces at the threshold of his holiness Emir Sultan. And we'll have loads of fine conversation.'

At this I was lit with an inner fire, overcome with the desire to take up my loyal friend's proposal and go to Bursa. As though overtaken by a divine inspiration I uttered a *besmele* and cried out to all the friends and lovers who were present, 'May the journey be blessed, and God vouchsafe us a safe and prosperous return!'

I uttered a benediction and recited a Fatiha. Then immediately, without informing parents or siblings, I joined the party of twenty friends. We came to Eminönü and boarded a caique for Mudanya.

Account of my first journey, to Bursa, setting out in the year 1050 from my birthplace Constantinople; comprising the stages, villages and towns and noteworthy monuments, countryside and ancient cities; recording what I observed with careful attention; travelling about on the face of the earth according to the definitive Koranic texts *Roam the earth* (27:69, 29:20, 30:42) and *Travel through them by day and night in safety* (34:18); day and night viewing the sights of the seven climes in the four quarters of the world; also the hardships encountered in mountain and plain, on land and sea; and how my precious life was spent according to the dictum, *Travel is a fragment of hell, though it be but a single parasang*.

Setting off from Eminönü with a *besmele* amidst the surging waves, we struggled across the whirlpool of the Golden Horn in front of the Kurşumlu Mahzen, as it is called, located at the Galata promontory. The sea was rough at first, and we recited the Koranic verse, *It is He who guides them by land and sea* (10:22). It quieted down as we sailed in front of the town of Fındıklı, where we took on some passengers, expert seamen and wayfarers according to the saying, *First the companion, then the road.*

It was the first Friday of the month of Muharram in the year 1050 (27 April 1640). At mid-morning the burning sun stood in the sky at a height of two javelins. 'Praise God, the winds are favourable,' said the mariners, as they weighed anchor and raised the yard. All the sailors, after hauling up the anchor, presented themselves and hoisted sail with prayer and praise, crying 'May God ease the journey!' and reciting a Fatiha. With wind astern we quickly crossed the whirlpool current at Sarayburnu (the Topkapı Palace promontory) and headed in the direction of Muradiye in Bursa province. All on board were having lively discussions, and some singers in our party were intoning the hymn:

> O God our Guide
> Stand by our side
> And hold our hand
> As we cross sea and land.

It turned out that among our party were some musicians – playing the pandore, zither, reed flute and fiddle – from the retinue of Sefer Agha, Sultan Ibrahim's chief snow procurer; also a guitar player and two singers from the retinue of Kara Recep Agha, the grand vizier Kara Mustafa Pasha's courier. 'Come,' they said, 'we'll play you a concert in the *segah* musical mode which will scatter your cares in this whirlpool of grief.' This lowly one kept the beat as we modulated through the *segah* and *maye* and *gerdaniye* musical modes, settling at the last of these. After two overtures we performed a *sema'i* concert consisting of three quatrains composed by Dervish Ömer. It was delightful, a concert worthy of Husayn Bayqara, such as was never performed on the sea since the sea of mercy was created. Some of the mariners – Kışlakcı Dayı, Çördüm Dayı and Cıvık Veli – came with their own guitars and also played some rapturous pieces, which made the other guitar owners' mouths water.

Proceeding in this delightful manner we stopped at Heybeli Island. It is eighteen miles from Istanbul and nine miles in circumference. It has a flourishing monastery where once a year thousands of Christians foregather, having come over from Istanbul in their caiques. They visit the grave of the monk Angilia who is buried here – the one who through his austerities took flight from Aya Sofya during Byzantine times. The people of the island are wealthy Greek ship-captains. The island has a delicious stream of water and some orchards; its administrators include a chief gardener and a janissary constable.

Departing from Heybeli we sped across the sea like lightning – it was as though flames were emerging from the prow – until five hours later, by the grace of God, we reached the shore and dropped anchor.

> *On the boundless sea*
> *Are benefits galore*
> *But for security*
> *It's best to stay ashore.*[11]

11 A well-known verse from the *Gulistan* of Sa'di.

2. Hot Springs of Bursa

There are a total of (—) ancient hot baths. The one with the best atmosphere and the cleanest attendants and furnishings is the Çelebi Sultan Mehmed (I) bath, beyond description. Then there are the İnebeği market bath, an endowment of Bayezid the Thunderbolt; the Tahtakale bath; the Kayağan market bath; the Gardener's (Bostancı) bath; the Castle (Kal'a) bath; the Knifemaker's (Bıçakcı) bath; the Muradiye bath; (Bayezid I) the Thunderbolt bath; etc. [...] These are all double baths (i.e., with separate compartments for men and women), open to all and sundry.

In addition there are 3,000 private baths in people's houses – there are so many because water is very abundant in this city. Some people have turned their private baths into public establishments for profit, giving access from outside their house through a new door that they open up for this purpose.

Description of the natural hot springs

In Anatolia hot springs are called *ılıca*, in Arabia (—), in Persia *germab*, in Turkey *kaynarca*, in Bursa *kaplıca*, in Mongolia *kerense*, in Rumelia *bana*. They are found in many countries. According to the natural philosophers, wherever, by God's decree, a water source comes in contact with a sulphur mine, that water boils up as though placed over a fire. It would – *Heaven help us!* – cook a man to death, except that cold water mixes in and moderates the hot spring. Furthermore, more benefits accrue the more one washes in it or drinks it. The ancient physicians record seventy beneficial properties. They warn, however, that drinking too much causes teeth to drop out; and that is correct, since those who take pills with sulphur or with mercury lose their teeth.

Bursa has hundreds of these hot springs. In Byzantine times the infidels were unaware of their beneficial properties and so did not build any baths here.

The Eski Kaplıca ('Old Bath') was built by Gazi Hudavendigar (Sultan Murad I, reg. 1362–89). In the middle of a domed space is a large pool, ten-by-ten in dimension according to Imam Zufar.[12] On all sides are Hanafi basins, and there are two cubicles. It is life-restorative to anyone who enters

---

12 The Shafi'is require a pool ten cubits by ten cubits for the canonical ablution. This contrasts with the 'Hanafi basin' typical of Turkish baths, a small basin with a spigot. Imam Zufar (d. 775) was an early disciple of Abu Hanifa.

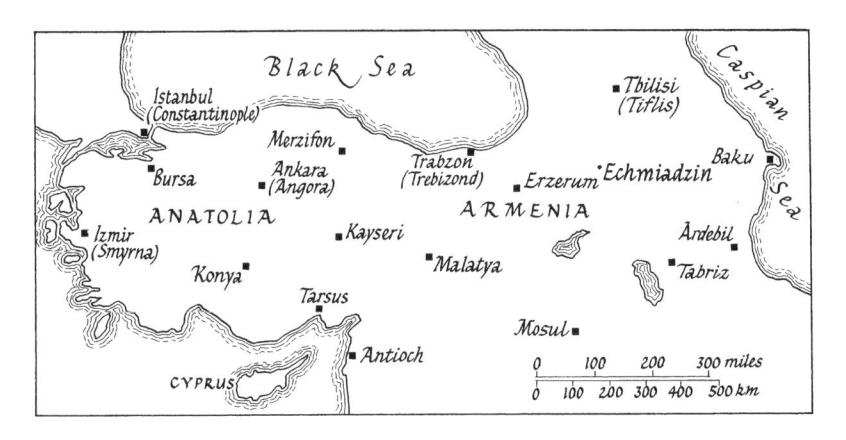

the pool; it makes one's skin as soft as one's earlobes and so smooth that one's hand slides over it like soap. The water is extremely hot by nature, but is moderated by mixing it with cold.

This is a most beneficial hot spring. Drinking the water wards off palpitations, dysentery and heart murmurs. Entering the water, however, is curative only if you know the proper procedure; otherwise it can give you pleurisy and in a single day can land you in the hospital or the graveyard. The procedure is as follows:

> Go to the edge of the pool. Perform a canonical ablution. Wash your head well first with the hot water, then pour it over your body so that you become gradually accustomed to it. Now you may put your feet in the pool, immerse your entire body, and enjoy it. But you must not stay immersed for very long, and when you go out to the changing room you must not remain naked; because the body, enervated by the hot pool, is subject to a variety of illnesses when out in the cold. So you must cover yourself quickly, rest a while, let the wholesome sweat be absorbed by the bath-cloth and wiped off by towels, then put on your clothes.

If you follow this procedure you will find it life-restoring; otherwise you will renounce your own life and give heartache to others. So be very cautious in this hot spring, for however beneficial it is, it is five times more harmful.

This Hudavendigar is the most beneficial of the Bursa baths; and the outer changing room, since it is built in the old style, is not too cold.

The Bath of Çekirge Sultan is also under the protective gaze of a great saint. The building is small. The water is effective against mange and leprosy. Someone who has suffered from leprosy for forty years may be cured of that affliction by entering the water and also drinking it for forty days. His facial hair will be restored, his voice will be as loud as the prophet David's, even his sexual prowess will return so that he can have progeny. It is known that lepers lose their brows and lashes, and their voices, and their sexual prowess. And, God save us, it is said to be a contagious disease from which one should flee as from a lion. That is the reason why in towns throughout Turkey the lepers dwell in a separate quarter, outside the city.

The Sulphur Bath is also a small building, but the water is very hot and extremely sulphurous. It is also very beneficial, especially for those who have scabies or the red itch, like the people of Banaz and Honaz. There are special bath attendants who are very knowledgeable about this disease. They rub down the scabby patient with clean bath-gloves. He then enters the cubicle and stays in the sulfurous water for half an hour, if he can bear it that long. When he comes out he puts on an old shirt which he wears for one day and night until he begins to witness the wonderful effect, fashioned by God: his scabs peel off in black scales like the skin of an onion, leaving the body shiny and smooth as pearl or silver. So beneficial is the Sulfur Bath – the more so if one drinks the water.

In short, this town of Eski Kaplıca has about 300 houses, each with orchard and garden, and each with its peculiar hot spring. Some are for men, some for women, some for children, some for youths, some for old men or old women. Each one has its special characteristic which is known to the populace of Bursa, who flock here with their families to stay for five or ten days in the homes of their acquaintances, making the rounds of the hot baths and engaging in conversation. The experts know that there are so many baths and that God has endowed each one with a special property.

Near the city, situated in a rocky gorge, is **the Yeni Kaplıca** ('New Bath'). It too, like the Old Bath, is a large building completely covered with lead shingles. Originally it was small, but Sultan Süleyman visited it several times and found it curative for his gout. So he ordered his grand vizier, Sarı Rüstem Pasha, to build a large bath-house here, and Rüstem Pasha completed this New Bath in the year (—). Travellers from Samarkand and Balkh and Bukhara and Laristan and Multan agree that they have never seen such a grand and well-constructed bathhouse.

The changing room, in a spacious field, is a large domed structure, like the dome of heaven, a huge space that can accommodate 1000 men. On the wall, in large *ta'lik* script, is appropriately written this verse:

> Don't put on airs with your fancy clothes.
> This is the world, this is the changing room
> Where everyone leaves behind his corporeal garment.

In the middle of the changing room is a pool of raw marble, and within that a jetting fountain of pure water. There are over 100 bath-attendants with their clogs, handsome and clean young men who dance attendance on their love-struck patrons.

The bathhouse itself has a pool surmounted by a large light-filled dome that some geometricians claim to be 100 cubits in circumference; an azure-coloured dome with 600 windows of glass and crystal, and overlaid with indigo-coloured leaden shingles.

The pool is ten-by-ten (cubits) in dimension, like a large island or a lake. Six marble steps lead down to it on all sides, and hot water flows into it from four directions out of the mouths of dragons and lions fashioned from raw marble.

The room known as the tepidarium (*sovukluk*) has a fountain with water jetting up to the dome.

The great pool is surrounded by eight vaults surmounted by a lofty dome. Beneath each vault is a Hanafi basin where those who have bathed gather to take their ablutions and to ogle the bathers swimming in the pool.

This resplendent bath is completely paved with varicoloured marble, like a goldsmith's enamel-work.

There are two cubicles, the one on the right containing a small pool with very hot water. But there is cold water nearby, and the two are mixed to provide lukewarm water.

While this bath is not famous for its curative properties, yet it is a delightful bath of splendid construction.

In all these baths lovers dally freely with their darling boys, embracing them and going off to a corner. It is considered youthful exuberance and not improper behaviour.

During the long winter nights all the lovers flock to these baths, which they illuminate with candles. They go in the pools with their sweethearts and perform leapfrogs and somersaults. They dive below the surface and emerge to salute a pretty boy.[13] They climb on one another's shoulders, join hands, and while the ones below turn in a circle, the 'gentlemen' above them do all sorts of acrobatics. They leap into the water, or inflate their bath-cloths like bubbles and use them to float, or make fountains with their hands or jets with their mouths and teeth, or lie motionless on the water for an entire hour. Or all the lovers join hands and turn in a circle, raising a hue and cry like the mariners' cry *Ya mola!* when they are casting off, and causing the water to swirl in waves like a whirlpool in the Arabian sea, so no one can stand but gets swept up in the flood; then they all stop at once, but the water is still swirling around them.

This kind of marvellous acrobatics is a speciality of the Bursans. People make fun of the Bursa youths who frequent these baths, saying, 'Don't pull, you'll start leaking.' This is an inside joke; for some reason the Bursans don't like it – *The meaning is in the belly of the poet.*

Then there is **the Kaynarca Bath**, which also has curative properties. There are others as well; but being a stranger here – *The stranger is like a blind man* – and this being my first journey, I don't know all their names, nor have I entered each one.

3. Return to Istanbul

We returned to Istanbul on the 25th of Safar in the year 1050 (16 June 1640). When I arrived at my sorrowful home, I kissed the hands of my father and mother and stood before them with hands respectfully crossed.

'Welcome, traveller to Bursa, welcome,' said my father. But I had thought that no one knew I was gone.

'Sir,' said I, 'how did you know that I was in Bursa?'

'On the blessed night of Ashura, the tenth of Muharram in the year 1050 (2 May 1640), the day that you disappeared, I recited several traditional prayers, and I recited *We have given you* (Sura 108, *al-Kawthar*) 1000 times. That night I dreamt that you were visiting the tomb of his holiness Emir Sultan in Bursa, seeking help from his spirituality, requesting travel, and weeping.

'Also that night several great saints sought my permission for you to set

---

13 Male preoccupation with beardless boys – ranging from Platonic affection to pederasty – was a feature of Ottoman culture. In Evliya's usage, the *dilber* (translated in these pages as 'pretty boy', 'darling boy' or 'sweetheart') was the object of erotic attention, while the *mahbub* (translated as 'lovely boy') was more the object of aesthetic appreciation.

out on your travels. By their grace I granted you permission that night, and recited a Fatiha. Come, my son, henceforth you are marked out for travel; may God bless you. But I have some advice to give you.'

He took my hand and I sat on my knees before him. With his right hand he grasped my left ear, and began to give his counsel, 'Son,' he said, 'man is a miserable creature. Never eat without uttering a *besmele*. If you have a secret to keep, don't tell it to your wife. Never eat while in a state of ritual impurity. Don't sew over a tear in your garment. Don't lend your good name to a bad end. And don't take a bad man as your wayfellow, or you will suffer his harm.

'Walk ahead, my dear, don't stay behind. Don't break ranks. Don't tread on a field. Don't pounce on your friend's share. Don't reach for something where you haven't put it. When two people are talking, don't listen. Pay the due of bread and salt. Don't look on a stranger with contempt. Don't go somewhere without an invitation. If you go, go to honourable people in a safe place.

'Keep your confidences. Guard the words you hear in every gathering. Don't spread evil reports from house to house. Don't indulge in slander and backbiting. Be good-natured. Stay on good terms with everyone, and don't be contentious or insolent. Don't go in front of your superiors. Respect your elders. Always be clean and renounce forbidden things. Perform the five daily prayers, attend to your moral state, and busy yourself with religious knowledge. [...]

'As for this world, my son, I advise you always to be jovial and light-hearted. When you attend on viziers and deputies and other great notables, never beg for worldly goods, lest they hate you and find you burdensome. Be content with what you possess, but also don't lavish your possessions on others. *Contentment is an inexhaustible treasure,* as the saying goes; it is useful in both sickness and health. Guard your worldly possessions for the sake of your own food and dress, and don't become dependant on others. [...]

'Wherever your travels take you, bind the sash of zeal to your belt in two places. And always be on your guard, for water sleeps, but servants and strangers and enemies do not sleep.

'Occupy yourself with visiting the graves of the great saints. Record all the shrines that you visit; also the stages of your journeys, the lowland plains and the lofty mountains, the rocks and the trees. Write down descriptions of the towns and cities, their climates and their noteworthy monuments, who built their fortifications and who conquered them, and what their dimensions are. Compose a scroll recording all these things, and call it *Book of Travels*.

'May your final end be good. May you be safe from the evil of foes. May God, mighty and glorious, be your helper and aide. May you be secure in this world, vouchsafed with faith at your last breath, and gathered in the afterlife at the foot of the standard of God's messenger. Keep this counsel of mine like an earring in your ear.'

With that he gave me a resounding slap on the back of my neck, twisted my ear, and said, 'Go forth, may your final end be good. A Fatiha!'

I was still reeling from the force of his slap. When I opened my eyes, our house seemed to be full of light. I once again kissed my father's hand and stood silent. Then what should I see? My father presented me with a sack containing twelve excellent books of religious guidance, including *Kitab-ı Kafiya* and *Kitab-ı Shafiya* and *Monla Jami* and *Quduri* and *Multaqa* and *Kitab-ı Quhistani* and *Hidaya* and *Ganjina-i Raz*.[14] He also gave me 200 musk-scented *şerifi* gold pieces for road expenses.

'Go forth,' he said, 'you are permitted to go in whatever direction you will; but when you are in a strange country, stand on your own two feet, be well-provided for yourself and be a friend in distress for others.'

He kissed my forehead and took me to Abdülahad Efendi in the Wednesday Bazaar, whose benediction I received; then to Sheikh Mısri Ömer Efendi and Sheikh Gafuri Efendi and Sheikh Ehl-i Cennet Efendi and Sheikh Bektashi Hasan Efendi – in short, to twelve great sheikhs, each of whose hand I kissed and each of whom imparted their spiritual support, saying, 'Go forth, may God bless your journey!'

By the grace of God, the eye of the soul of this humble one was opened, a kind of ecstasy overcame me, and I rejoiced, returning to our humble abode. That week, the first of Rabi' al-awwal in the year 1050 (21 June 1640), I took passage to Izmit on the boat of our kinsman Captain Kuloğlu Mehmed. I kissed my father's hand and set out with a *besmele*.

4. Hamsi in Trabzon

The favourite fish – the one they sacrifice themselves for a thousand times over and have bloody battles over when it is bought and sold – is the *hapsi*

---

14 Referring to standard books on grammar, jurisprudence and mysticism.

(or *hamsi* that is anchovy), dear to their hearts. It is called *hamsi* because it appears on the day of *hamsin* (Pentecost).

The reason is that during the time of Alexander the Great, a master of magic arrived and, in order to provide the monks and patriarchs with sustenance, he erected a column in the sea outside the Moloz Gate and placed on it a bronze fish, fashioned like a hamsi. On the day of Pentecost this talisman emitted a sound that made all the hamsi in the Black Sea swarm into Trabzon harbour and hurl themselves on shore.

At the birth of the Prophet Muhammad thousands of such talismans were destroyed and Nimrod's fire-temple was extinguished. This hamsi talisman also fell into the sea, but because it is connected with the sea it has retained its efficacy to this day.

Every year, on the day of Pentecost, the hapsi fish run to shore, or else fishermen go out to catch them in caiques known as *meneksile* which they fill up and return. Fishmongers at the wharf cry their wares in this patter (mixture of Greek, Turkish, and nonsense):

> *Ey muhterun ey muhterun*
> *Esi çağ ata zun*
> *Den hurdesin samur bada taraşa*
> *Ey lağ ata karun*
> *Ehgi kolup ipsarya*
> *Ele pamun ey umet-i Mahmet ele pamun*

They also have special trumpets made of elder-tree wood. They only have to blow on these trumpets once and, by God's dispensation, if people praying in the mosque hear it they immediately leave their prayer and come running for the hamsi. 'Prayer is forever,' they say, 'but hapsi is not forever.' Even the imams and muezzins break the ritual worship. 'By your father's life,' they cry, 'give me a handkerchief of hapsi for my little *akçe*,' and they fill those delicately embroidered handkerchiefs with fish. People joke that they are sorry to see the brine dripping from the wrapping, and say: 'Hey, you're letting the fish juice drip out, why don't you toss in a little pilav!'

Once a certain Çiço Husayn was having sex with his wife when he heard the trumpet announcing the catch. He immediately pulled his 'fish' out of his wife, tied up his drawers and ran to the wharf to buy his *hapsi paluğı*.[15] This is a well-known story, but I never witnessed it.

---

15 Trabzon dialect; standard Turkish is *hamsi balığı*.

Another time when the *meneksile* trumpet sounded, five naked men ran out of the public bath panting and sweating, jumped into a fishing-boat and filled their bath-cloths with hamsi, leaving their private parts exposed. The fisherman demanded payment, but since the men were naked and had no money on them they offered a pledge.

'The fish-tax agent doesn't accept pledges, only cash,' said the fisherman.

'Look here,' one of them replied, 'let these men bear witness, I offer you my religion!'

'I too am fed up with my religion and its daily prayers,' said the fisherman. 'Take it, you can have mine as well!'

The town wits of Trabzon relate this sort of hapsi anecdotes, which have become proverbial among them. The Trabzon sophisticates also taunt the Çiços or simple townsfolk with verses such as:

> Trabzon is our home,
>   Our hand can't keep a penny.
> Because of hamsi fish
>   We have no cares, not any.

To such a degree is this fish beloved of them.

With regard to its properties, it is first of all an elegant fish, about a span in length, rather purplish and shiny and plump. Its benefit is such that if a man eats it for seven days he will go to his wife and have his own 'fish' eaten seven times every night. It is very invigorating, easy to digest, has no fishy smell at all, and does not produce heat when you eat it. It is a cure for typhoid fever. If someone has snakes and scorpions in his house, he burns hapsi fish heads and fumigates the house with them, and the smell of it kills off all the vermin. This fish has hundreds of benefits and curative properties.

The Trabzonites have forty different ways of cooking hamsi, each with its own peculiar flavour, including various kinds of soup, stew with onions, kebab, stuffed pastry, and baklava.

They make a kind of stoneware pan called *pileki*. First they clean the fish and line them up on reeds in rows of ten each. They chop up parsley, celery, onion and leeks and mix with cinnamon and black pepper. They line the *pileki* pan with a layer of celery and parsley, then a layer of hapsi. Then they pour over it some Trabzon olive oil that is like the Water of Life and cook it over a hot fire for one hour. It is like congealed light, and one who eats it is light full of light. This dish benefits the eyesight and the digestion.

This fish is indeed a *table from heaven* (cf. 5:112), fit to be a favourite; glory be to the eternal Creator!

5. Black Sea adventure

Description of the walled town of Balıklava. While participating in so many campaigns, I had no free time to note the climate and monuments of the Crimea, including this walled town of Balıklava; so I dare not give a description of it.

In the month of (—) in the year (—), along with 350 other passengers, I boarded a *şayka*[16] belonging to a certain Captain Ucalı Sefer. Sleeping on board that night I had some frightful dreams, and in the morning went ashore to give alms to the poor in order to ward off calamity. I reboarded and we weighed anchor. A small boat guided us out of the harbour. Because we gave no heed to whether the hour was auspicious – in accordance with the Koranic verses *On a day of unremitting woe* (54:19) and *Over a few ill-omened days* (41:16) – and made no prayers for saintly intercession, we hoisted sail with a north wind and, putting our trust in God, sailed for one day and one night with a favourable wind at our stern until we reached approximately the middle of the Black Sea. [...]

The Anapa mountains to the north and the Suluyar mountains near Balıklava behind us were not visible, nor was there any sign of the Sinop and Amasra mountains in front of us. For another day and another night we were tossed about in a whirlpool of grief, the wind now before us, now behind us, not knowing in which direction we should go. In that inauspicious open sea, where *neither road nor guide was evident* and the sun rose in the sea and set in the sea, we sailed aimlessly, tossed about by the waves.

By God's decree, black clouds appeared in the eastern sky. A whirlwind arose, squalls with thunder and lightning, and huge waves. All the mariners turned pale and began to rub their hands. They looked at the compass in the stern and at their mariners' compasses, then looked at one another and began to think how to save their skins. One of them, an old salt named Dede Dayı, spoke up, 'Avast, my hearties! What are you afeared of? God is generous. Look, a storm is brewing. Lower the topmast with the sail.'

They all jumped to and lowered the sheets and brought down the mainsail mast. But the tossing of the sea did not calm down, it only grew

---

16 A kind of boat used on the Black Sea, especially associated with Cossack raiders.

stronger. With the passengers assisting, the crew began to heave cargo overboard – sacks of wool, reed mats, barrels of pickled fish, ship's timbers. The 200 captives who were aboard, young and old, were put in the hold, with the cover tightly shut. God be praised, the ship lightened a bit. Still the waves reached to the sky, the hurly-burly increased and the wind grew stronger, as in the verse:

> If the boat of my heart, when we are apart,
>   Is tossed in a whirlpool of grief,
> What can I do? The winds of time
>   Offer us no relief.

By God's dispensation, the tossing of the waves began on the fourth of Safar in the year 105- (if 1051: 5 May 1641) and for three days and three nights we suffered thunder and lightning, whirlwind and tempest, rain and snow, blizzard and cyclone. The sailors could no longer stand up; each one cowered in a corner. As for the passengers, God bless them, some threw up, others threw their hands up seeking God's forgiveness, some made sacrifices, others made vows to give alms.

'Fellow worshippers,' I cried, 'let us join together in continuous recital of the Sura of Deliverance /al-Ikhlas (112) which God may be pleased to grant us.'

All those present immediately began to repeat the *al-Ikhlas* from the depth of their hearts. At that moment, by God's decree, the darkness lifted, the sky became clear, the thunder and lightning ceased.

The tossing of the sea, however, did not abate. The huge wave known in those coasts as the Seventh Wave (*yedişerleme*) gave no quarter. Now it rose to the zenith, the ship's mast touching the clouds; now it sank to the bottom of the sea, as though to the depths of hell, and the Black Sea loomed up all around us like Mt Bisutun.

Eventually we opened the cover of the hold and heaved all the heavy merchandise overboard, but still we found no relief. The next thing we saw was that the rudder bolt broke in the ship's stern and the rudder flew overboard. All the mariners struck their knees with their hands and huddling together began to make amends with one another as though on their death beds.

At this point those sailors who were spirited and courageous grabbed axes and cut the sheets, then all together began chopping at the mast. At once the mast snapped and fell into the sea, crushing eleven men to death.

We tossed the corpses overboard. Weeping and wailing arose as everyone despaired of life and thought about how to save his skin.

Now another squall struck and tore the ship in two. The passengers and prisoners in the hold all rushed out in a panic. Some made amends, asking one another to forgive their debts. Some of the crew began to strip their clothes off. Everyone tried to find a plank, a gourd or cask or barrel, anything to hold onto.

As for this lowly one, I too was overcome. I continuously recited *Ya Sin* (Sura 36), giving no thought to my slaves and goods and provisions, but entrusting my affairs to the Lord of glory from the depth of my heart, and occupying myself with reciting the Witness formula and the Koranic verses *To God I commend myself* (40:44) and *He that fears God, God will give him a means of salvation and will provide for him whence he does not reckon* (65:2–3).

I noticed that some infidels had brought down the launch by its rope and scrambled into it. On the other side of the ship the other mariners hurled themselves into the sea holding planks, or the like. I and my seven companions drew our swords and leapt into the launch, just as the infidels already there were cutting the rope. Two of them drew their swords against us. Şerif Ramazan Çelebi from Ayntab was struck in the chest above the nipple. The seven of us attacked the eight of them and killed four, while the other four, fearing for their lives, hurled themselves into the sea. So the launch was left to us seven companions. We threw overboard any heavy baggage, and the boat tossed in the waves, lightened of its load.

Meanwhile the ship had been split asunder from stem to stern. The 300 passengers and merchants and the roughly 400 slaves and seamen leapt into the water with a cry of 'Allah!' Some drowned, others kept afloat on planks or other props, struggling with no cash to make a purchase in the bazaar of life. Some, swimming for their lives, swarmed our lifeboat. Among these was the story-reciter Emir Çelebi. I grabbed him by the arm and hauled him into the boat. As others too tried to climb in we realised that our launch was bound to capsize with so many people. So the seven of us again drew our swords and fended them off.

As we got our distance from the shattered ship it disappeared from sight, and eventually there was no one else visible. We tried to recover our wits, as the boat oscillated between the tip of heaven and the depth of the sea. We used our turbans to bail out the boat. We were exhausted from this activity and from the rough weather.

What should we see? There was the *kadi* of Menkup, Ali Efendi, diving through the waves like a heron, making his way toward us. With God's help we got Ali Efendi aboard. So now we were ten people in the lifeboat. We kept on bailing water and reciting *Ya Sin*, but all of us despaired of our lives.

We spent one day and one night in this manner, tossing on the sea and shaking like leaves in autumn, hungry and miserable and weeping and naked. The *kadi* Ali Efendi and the story-reciter Emir Çelebi succumbed to pleurisy and died. Saying it was God's decree we threw their corpses overboard and the eight of us were left in the boat as before. A large pinewood plank, twenty cubits long and one cubit wide, kept harrying us, now battering the boat, now drifting apart. Saying 'What can we do? It is God's to command,' we kept bailing and were dizzy from the cold and exhaustion.

At noon on the third day, by God's decree – and according to the verse,

> Through cautionary measures
>   You can't thwart destiny;
> Though you be a thousand times cautious,
>   Still what will be will be.

– a huge wave came and turned the boat upside-down. This humble one too was plunged headlong into the sea. Fearing for my life I struggled in the water, thrashing with my hands and arms – because I did have some skill in swimming. I emitted a heart-burning sigh to the Lord of truth. From the depth of my heart I held to the noble Koran as my intercessor, and inwardly sought succour from the spiritual qualities of the great saints whose graves I had visited.

The Lord of Glory fashioned a fire in my heart. The mirror of my heart was polished. From the depth of my heart I concentrated on the declaration of God's unity, and took great consolation. I recalled the mystics in the countries where I had travelled. I was free of fear and my wits were restored.

Apparently that mighty and eternal One, the Sustainer who is forever, desired to rescue this sinful slave. As I was swimming fearlessly and furiously, like a diver, suddenly that long and broad plank – the one I mentioned above that kept battering our boat – heaved into view. I quickened my stroke, thinking that I should try to grab onto that plank rather than drown in this black and merciless sea. Saying 'Come what may' and performing death-defying feats in this life-and-death bazaar, I slithered onto the plank like a snake and grasped it tight. It was like encountering his holiness Hızır, the saviour of seamen.

I had no idea what became of my companions in the boat. But as I was bobbing up and down in the waves, shivering with cold and fear, I heard a cry behind me. Looking back, and afraid for my life, I saw there were several other people clinging like bats to the selfsame plank that I was riding. There were two Georgian slaveboys, two Circassian girls, and one Russian slave.

'Oh dear,' thought I, 'these people will be a heavy weight on my plank and will cause me to drown. Oh what is my sad fate? What can I do, I wonder, to lighten the load and have this plank all to myself?'

By God's wisdom, a water barrel was floating by like a gourd. The Russian boy heaved himself off our plank and onto the barrel, but was unable to get his arms around it and – as though one should say, 'Haul up the guest!' – the poor lad drowned. That left the other four captives to contend with. Murmuring 'God is generous,' I did nothing.

We were in the middle of the sea with no coast in sight. But, praise God, the weather calmed a bit. The sun shone and warmed us up. The tossing of the sea died down. An east wind sprang up and drove us forward. God be praised, on the third day some lofty mountains came into view, and at noon the waves drove us ashore. I fell onto the sand utterly exhausted, recalling the verse:

> *On the boundless sea*
>   *Are benefits galore*
> *But for security*
>   *It's best to stay ashore.*

Gathering my strength, I gave a hundred thousand praises to the Lord Creator. Consider that Lord of generosity, Who bestowed on me eighteen slaves in Mingrelia and Abkhazia and Crimea, then took them away. When I despaired of life in the merciless sea he again gave me four captives, lovely boys and girls, each of them one in a thousand.

As we were sheltering on the shore at the foot of the cliffs, some Muslims came and seeing us in this state removed their overgarments and draped them over this humble one and my slaves. I questioned them as they conducted us to the top of the cliffs. It turned out that these tall cliffs and orchards were part of the Keligra Sultan mountains which came down to the Black Sea in the province of Silistria (Kaliakra in Bulgaria).

The upshot of this adventure is that from the time the ship capsized we wandered in our lifeboat, hungry and miserable, for three days and three nights; and when the lifeboat capsized we clung to the plank for a fourth day and night until, on the fifth day at noon we came ashore and found salvation, like Noah the Saved, at the foot of the cliffs of Keligra Sultan. We were cheered up by the dervishes at the shrine of Keligra Sultan, where they assigned a room to me along with my slaves whom God had bestown on me.

I was in a delirium for the first ten nights in this convent. Various illnesses had taken root in our veins from the exposure and the terrible suffering we had undergone in the storm. I spent an entire winter here, crestfallen and weeping on my pillow, and completed ten entire Koran-recitations of gratitude. In this place I calculated that I had completed a total of 1,060 Koran-recitations since my childhood.

So I spent eight months recovering my health in this shrine of Keligra Sultan, having delightful conversations with the Bektashi dervishes, sometimes serving them as imam or muezzin. During this time not one of my slaves said that they belonged to anyone else, but all acted as though I were their legitimate owner.

[...]

(Legends of Keligra Sultan, i.e. Sarı Saltık)

This shrine of Keligra Sultan, where we were hosted after being delivered from the sea, is a lofty promontory that projects into the Black Sea like an elephant's trunk. Ships from Istanbul going toward Kara Hırmen and Köstence and Kili take a bead on these Keligra cliffs, which rise up toward the sky and are visible from 150 miles away. Directly across the sea in an eastward direction in Anatolia is the Sinop Promontory, the distance between that and the Keligra cliffs being (—) miles. In very clear weather the mountains of Sinop are visible from Keligra, and the mountains of Keligra are visible from Sinop. At the very tip of the Keligra Promontory is a cave where Keligra Saltık Sultan is buried – that is where the dragon was stopped.[17]

The shrine itself is a large convent, founded by Dobruca Ali Muhtar. The saint's wooden sword and sling, tambourine and drum, standards and banners are kept within. There are a variety of rooms, and a summer plaza

---

17 Referring to legends about the Turkish warrior-saint Sarı Saltuk. See *EI2* Sarı Saltūk Dede' (G. Leiser).

and winter plaza furnished all around with immaculate sheepskins. On each sheepskin sits a spiritual master, excelling in knowledge and virtue. All are strict Sunnis, believers and monotheists, who perform the five daily prayers in their mosque. There are over 100 mystical lovers. Indeed, during my eight-month stay they studied Koran-recital with me according to the reading of Hafs.[18]

The windows of this convent, and of the light-filled tomb, all face the sea. The kitchen of Kay Kavus is marvellous to behold. It has a suspended dome-shaped chimney. Cauldrons are over the fire continuously day and night, and food is dispensed freely to all comers and goers. The dervishes own no buildings or estates; their income is wholly derived from begging. The cooks have assistants, barefoot and bare-headed devotees, lively and stalwart fellows who burn with divine love and mystical devotion. Such a great convent it is.

To the left and right of the convent, at the top of the cliffs, are hundreds of well-mouths. The rock cliffs rise perpendicularly, like Mt Bisutun, but the bases are hollowed out, forming natural harbours. Ships with top-gallant masts a hundred cubits tall enter below the overarching cliffs and drop anchor. The ship captains buy wheat and barley from the peasants which they transport by cart and pour into the well-mouths at the top of the cliffs. The grain falls down the shafts into the holds of the ships waiting below until they are full. These shafts were excavated in ancient times by the infidels, digging like Farhad, in such a way that ships can dock next to them. It is a marvellous sight, peculiar to this region. For it is impossible to bring wheat and barley and other goods down to the ships in sacks; that would require men on foot to scramble like goats up and down the mountain paths, which are three or four hours away from the cliffs and harbours.

In the entire perimeter of the Black Sea, this is the only place with such lofty cliffs. The southwesterly gale and the south and east storm winds batter these rocks with a thunderous roar that can be heard in Aflatar and Alhanlar near Silistra, a full day's journey away (about twenty miles). So lofty are these mountains, reaching up to the Milky Way. The cliffs house nests of peregrine and other falcons, also musky eagles the size of sheep. Some men in the convent make sacrifices and feed them to the eagles. If

---

18 Hafs, d. 796, propagated one of the standard 'readings' of the Koran. See *EI2* 'Kirā'a' (R. Paret).

the eagles eat the sacrifice, the men's wishes are granted, if not, not. At least that is what people say.

With regard to this Keligra Sultan, there are hundreds of legends, but I have given an abbreviated account.

Near the convent is the castle of Keligra Sultan which was built by King Yanvan, brother of Yanko ibn Madyan and author of the history of the Greeks.[19] It was conquered from the Byzantines in the year (—) by Musa Çelebi, son of Sultan Bayezid the Thunderbolt. Administratively it belongs to the *kadi*-district of Balçık in the province of Özü. It is a small square castle 1,000 paces in circumference, located on the seashore; a towering fortress, as though built by Shaddad. There is a single gate, facing west. Inside there are no houses, no mosque or *han* or shops, no warden or garrison or arsenal. On the eastern side are rock crevices a hundred fathoms deep. The lower part of this castle is also hollow, since it is situated on top of the Keligra Sultan cliffs.

In the year (—), when Nasıf Paşazade Hüseyn Pasha was governor of Özü province, the ill-omened Ukrainians who are the Cossacks of Özü raided these coasts several times and enslaved the populace. Hüseyn Pasha repaired this Keligra castle with his own money and put in a warden and garrison, so when the cussed Cossacks raided, the people took refuge in the castle and were safe from harm. It is a very strong castle. Afterwards grand vizier Mustafa Pasha removed the garrison back to Özü, in spite of Hüseyn Pasha, and the castle was left vacant.

God be praised, after suffering the vicissitudes of the sea I was rescued before the bird of my soul flew from the cage of my body and spent eight months in this convent of Keligra Sultan having delightful conversations with all the dervishes and seeing all sorts of sights.

In the spring, the month of (—) in the year 1050 (if error for 1052: 1642), I bade farewell to all my friends and acquaintances, made a farewell visit to the tomb of Keligra Sultan, seeking succour from his noble spirit, and boarded a caique with my four slaveboys. We hopped from harbour to harbour along the Black Sea coast, drawing the caique ashore by cables in stormy weather to be safe from the tossing of the sea. We docked at Kavarna, Balçık, Varna, Ahyolı, Suzebolu, Müsevre, Burkas, Çingene, etc. ... Terkoz ... Karataşlar. ...

---

19 This probably refers to the tenth-century Arabic work *Kitab al-Unwan* by Aghapios; see Dankoff 2004, 27.

Black Sea Adventure 55

With a *besmele* we entered the Bosphorus in the month of (—) in the year (—) and dropped anchor at Kavak where I disembarked, made a prostration of thanksgiving and a sacrifice of gratitude for God's mercy, and distributed the meat to the poor. God be praised, although we suffered the tortures of purgatory in this journey, still we accomplished many travels and jihads and managed to tour the entire perimeter of the Black Sea.

(Description of the Black Sea)
This lowly sinner travelled the perimeter of the Black Sea and returned to Istanbul through the Bosphorus on the first day of Shaʿban, 105- (if 1052: 25 October 1642). I immediately proceeded to his holiness Abu Ayyub Ansari,[20] rubbed my face at his felicitous threshold, started a complete Koran recital on behalf of his noble spirit and made a sacrifice in the path of God. I then came home to my father and mother who pressed me to their bosoms.

At this time I made a solemn vow never again to set out by ship on the Black Sea. May God Most High keep all the community of Muhammad from harm; amen, O Helper!

Then, in Ramadan of (10)5– (if 1052: November–December 1642) I became imam to the customs inspector Ali Agha. Our nights were like the Night of Power, our days like the Day of Festival.[21] We had intimate conversations with all the sweethearts, and accumulated substantial gifts and emoluments. Thus did the Lord Creator compensate us for our property that was lost in the Black Sea, and for our nineteen slaves who were drowned.

6. Tabriz

I received gifts from the governor of this city (Marand) and set out together with the ambassador of the governor of Tabriz, travelling south in the midst of countryside for thirteen hours. Both sides of the highway were

---

20 i.e., the shrine of Eyüp outside the city wall of Istanbul, named after the Companion of the Prophet whose grave there was discovered during the siege of the city in 1453.
21 The Night of Power (27 Ramadan) is celebrated as the night on which the Koran was revealed. The festival days are the two *eids* or Bayrams, the Festival of Sacrifice at the end of the Hajj pilgrimage season, and the Breakfast Festival at the end of Ramadan.

lined with weeping willows and verdant and lofty plane trees, leaving no opening for the sun to strike. So we proceeded in complete shade as under an arbour, occasionally stopping to rest and drink from the purling streams, until we arrived at **Kahriz**.

This is a village of 1,000 houses belonging, they said, to the Tabriz governor's secretary. It has six mosques, three public baths and two *hans*. A flourishing village with orchards and gardens beyond number – may God the Avenger destroy it! Because all the inhabitants are Shi'is and caliph-cursers. This was the first time in Persia that I heard them – God forbid! – cursing the Caliph Umar. I nearly went out of my mind. But I was weak and tired, not yet in a position to do anything about it. Otherwise I could easily have killed that accursed curser; because when Ottoman envoys come to Persia they have the liberty of killing up to four Kızılbaş cursers for the sake of the Four Companions of the Prophet, no questions asked. For now I bore it patiently.

Seven hours south of Kahriz we came to the village of **Sahlan**, a royal *has* belonging to the governor of Tabriz. Situated in a level plain, it has 1,000 houses, orchards and gardens, seven mosques, a *han* and a public bath, and some small royal shops. It is a fine village, with weeping willows and plane trees lining the main road, and pleasure-pavilions in the orchards and gardens. The people, however, are again those damned Rafidis (i.e., Shi'is), although they pretend to be Shafi'is (i.e., Sunnis). But the climate and the lovely boys and girls are highly reputed.

As we set out from Sahlan we could make out the domed tomb of Sham-ı Ghazan Muhammad Shah looming up on our right side, six hours away.[22] I recited a Fatiha for his spirit. We stopped to rest in a meadow and sent a man ahead to Tabriz. Three hours later we put on our armour and mounted, with my horse and that of the Tabriz envoy head to head. In front of the envoy marched his soldiers, with their magnificent garments, and in front of me forty horsemen composing my train, while a large contingent approached us from the other direction.

This, it turned out, was the deputy of the governor of Tabriz who had come out to meet us. We proceeded together, stirrup to stirrup, in grand procession, entering the city of **Tabriz** nine hours after leaving Sehlan. It

---

22 This refers to the mausoleum, now in ruins, of the Ilkhanid ruler Mahmud Ghazan (reg. 1295–1304) which he had built for himself in the village of Sham, west of Tabriz.

was the (—) of the month of (—). Thousands of people turned out in the marketplace to see the sight, and I did my own sightseeing of them. It took two hours to go from the edge of the city to the governor's palace. The noble khan or governor, Kelp Ali Khan, came out to greet us.[23]

We took our places in the audience hall, sitting knee to knee. Three times they sounded the imperial kettledrums and the horns of Afrasiyab[24] and the trumpets and shawms of Jamshid. With great pomp and ceremony they presented us with fine silken stuffs, as row on row of pageboys stood in attendance with hands folded, fully armed, with plumes in their Safavid turbans.

After the drumroll I stood up and removed from my breast the jewel-studded and love-styled letter of our lord and vizier, the governor of Erzurum, Defterdarzade Mehmed Pasha. I kissed it and gave it to the Khan, hand to hand. He too rose to his feet, took it in his hand, kissed it and put it on his head. The master of ceremonies indicated that I should resume my place, but as the Khan remained standing so did I, following Muhammadan protocol. The Khan gave the letter to his secretary who kissed it reverentially and read it out loud. At mention of the Prophet and the Four Companions all present in the council rose to their feet and magnified the name of the Prophet, but at the names of the Four Companions some of them immediately sat down.

After the letter was read, and its contents understood, the Khan said, 'God willing, with the help of the Lord and Nourisher of mankind, within this month I will send out a caravan of 1,000 camels. Upon my head and eye!'

'Welcome,' he continued, addressing me. 'A hundred welcomes. Your step is auspicious, delight of my life and light of my eyes!' He went on in this vein with polite talk and light-hearted conversation as we sat knee to knee. With hand on breast he arranged a huge feast, followed by incense

---

23 In the Persian context, Khan and Sultan are titles for provincial governors appointed by the Shah. Javadi and Floor 2010, 21 point out that the governor of Tabriz at that time was Pir Budaq Khan Pornak Turkman. Kelp Ali is apparently based on *kalb-i Ali* 'Dog of Ali', a self-deprecating nickname.
24 One of nine kinds of trumpet that Evliya mentions in Vol. 1, fol. 208a, where he says that it was invented in Iran by Afrasiyab (the arch-enemy of the Iranians in the *Shahnama*).
25 The term is *hârâ*, Evliya's spelling of *khârâ*. Javadi and Floor 2010, 21 interpret it in this passage as glasswork, elsewhere as porcelain (2) or fabrics (83).

and rose-water.

From the Pasha's gifts I picked out a set of pearl prayer-beads, a gold-embroidered silken quiver, and some Genoese and Venetian moiré stuffs.[25]

'The noble pasha your brother greets you,' I said, 'and sends these tokens of his love to your majesty so that you will not go empty-handed.' He was very pleased with the prayer-beads and the quiver of arrows.

'And he sends two thoroughbred horses, swift as the wind, for your felicitous attention.' With this I stood up, came to the edge of the audience hall and made a signal.

First they brought forward the horse with jewelled saddle and jewel-encrusted bridle. Praise God, when that piebald and rose-bodied Arabian cantered into the plaza, whinnying and prancing, all the Persian courtiers put finger to mouth in astonishment. With a *besmele* I handed over the reins to the Khan saying '*May it be a blessing!*' He jumped with joy, mounted the Arab steed without a stirrup, cantered about the plaza a few times like a knight in the field of eloquence, and dismounted.

Then they brought the caparisoned horse. The Khan was immensely pleased at that one too, and gave it over to his (—).

Following this the Khan gave orders to his sons and servants, who brought rice-water sherbet and, once again, rose-water and incense. He then entrusted us to the care of his hospitality officer and chief of the guards and prefect and mayor who conducted us in procession to the mayor's world-adorning garden where we were housed. At our heels came *tumans* of *bisti* coins as bath-money, one Karaçubuk ('Black Rod') thoroughbred with saddle and bridle, one piebald sorrel ambler, and seven camel-loads of food and drink and fruit. Our house overflowed with these gifts.

Cryers circulated throughout the city with the announcement, 'As long as the Ottoman Sunni envoys are here, it is the royal proclamation of the governor that you will not engage in ritual cursing. If you do, the Sunnis may shed your blood without recrimination. Be advised!'

God be praised, cursing of the Four Companions of the Prophet ceased. To be sure, they do not curse Abu Bakr and Uthman; their main concern is Umar, upon whom – God help us! – they continually vent their spleen.

That same day the Khan sent us ten pages, prancing like peacocks and smothered in chintz and silk brocades. Our host Hoca Sirac brought them to us and they kissed my hand. Apparently it is the *kanun* of Persia for the governors to send each of the Ottoman envoys ten boys who are ordered to obey their every command. The ones who showed up were named Jivanaramish, Sadiq Jan, Ramish, Mirza Khan, Yazdan Ali, Kakunj, Qurban Bay, Suhrab, Mazid Khan, and Yar Quli. They were choice and splendid youths, congealed light, like so many denizens of paradise.

Finally we began to tour the city.

[...]

One of the sights is the polo grounds. In the middle of an open field are two lofty columns of juniper wood nailed together, at the apex of which a silver bowl has been affixed. On Fridays the servants of the Shah and of the Khan mount their wind-swift steeds and do sports, one of which is to shoot arrows at this bowl, as the love-struck spectators look on. On the Khwarazm-shah's New Year's Day in particular they stage a battle between horses that have been reared in darkened quarters for forty or fifty days. It is a great spectacle. They also have combats between camels, buffaloes, rams, donkeys, and dogs, as well as cockfights. These New Year's entertainments are peculiar to Persia.

Another marvellous and noteworthy spectacle is the Ashura ceremony held every year on the tenth day of Muharram. All the notables and citizens, young and old, come out to these polo grounds where they pitch their tents and stay for three days and three nights. They boil innumerable cauldrons of Ashura pudding, in remembrance of the martyrs in the plain of Karbala, and distribute it among rich and poor alike, devoting the religious merit accrued thereby to those martyrs' spirits.

And water carriers dispense cold water and sweet sherbets, poured from their waterskins into bowls of glass or crystal, even agate or turquoise. The thirsty spectators drink these beverages in remembrance of the martyrs who suffered thirst in the plain of Yazid on the day of Ashura, intoning the verse:

> For the love of Husayn of Karbala, to health!

Or they cite the Koranic verses *Their Lord will give them pure nectar to drink* (76:21), and *as lawfully yours* (4:4). Several of the great notables, setting aside their dignity on this day, hang a waterskin on their neck and dispense water for the sake of the spirit of Husayn.

The great event of the day is when the Khan pitches his parti-coloured pavilion in this open field and all the Tabriz notables gather round knee to knee to hear the recital of 'The Martyrdom of Husayn' which is comparable to the recital of 'The Birthday of the Prophet' in Turkey. All the lovers of the Prophet's family listen with dejection and humility, moaning and sighing. Finally, at the words, 'The accursed Shibr, the oppressor, martyred his holiness Imam Husayn, the oppressed, in this fashion,' a curtain opens behind the reciter and a severed head and trunk of a body, with blood flowing, are thrown in front of the Khan's pavilion. Then they bring mannequins of the Imam's innocent children, who died of thirst. The audience wail and lament and are caught up in a woeful ecstasy.

At this juncture some hundreds of professional barbers circulate among the lovers with razors in their hands. Those wishing to demonstrate their love for Husayn on that day have the barbers slash their arms and breasts, shedding so much blood that the verdant green ground turns tulip red. Some of the lovers brand their heads with the Mark of Submission, or brand their arms with the marks of Hasan and Husayn and Aqil, or have tattoos pricked on their arms, shedding their blood for the love of Husayn.

Eventually they remove the dummy bodies, complete 'The Martyrdom of Husayn' amidst weeping and litanies, eat up the Ashura puddings, and enjoy spiritual intercourse for three days and three nights. What a grand spectacle!

Due to the delightful climate, the orchards and rose-gardens here are beyond number. The entire city is like the garden of *the many-columned city of Iram* (89:7) and the parks and picnic places are like the gardens of Meram (in Konya), Aspuzu (in Malatya) and Sudak (in Crimea). The Persian-style pavilions of Shirin and courtyards of Vamık and Azra (lovers celebrated in poetry) are bywords of beauty. One of them is the pavilion in the mayor's garden where we were housed; it has the following chronogram in the calligraphy of Qutb al-Din Muhammad Yazdi:

> O place of Shirin, lofty arch.
>
> Year 982 (1574–5)

There are many other such noteworthy monuments, but there is no profit in enumerating those that are obscure or not worth dwelling upon, and the prolongation of discourse gives rise to tedium, so this much will suffice.

God be praised, we spent two full months enjoying the pleasures of Tabriz and contemplating the youths of Azerbaijan. We also went off on a junket with the noble Khan and a retinue of 1,000 soldiers to visit the surrounding towns and villages. We went as a hunting party, with hawking drums beating, and accompanied by hawks and hounds. We toured villages in the flourishing districts of Mihranrud . . . Saravrud . . . Didahar . . . Urdniq . . . Rudkat . . . Khanumrud . . . and Badustan. . . .

Tabriz

If I were to record the hunts and other delights of these villages, to the extent of my experience, over the twenty days of our expedition, God knows, it would require an entire volume. Because in the entire kingdom of Persia there is no city and no countryside as fine as Tabriz, the ravisher of hearts, and Isfahan, known as half the world. It is a large and ancient city with delightful climate, lovely boys and girls, lofty buildings and numerous foundations and institutions. May God vouchsafe that it once again belong to the Ottomans[27] – although that would bring about its ruin; may God Most High cause it to flourish forever!

Returning to the city I once again was honoured with the company of the Khan and had intimate converse with him on a daily basis.

One day, in the course of one of these conversations, the Khan offered me some wine.

'I swear by God,' said I, 'and by the pure spirit of Ali, that from the time I was born to this day I have never tasted any forbidden food or intoxicating beverage or aphrodisiac substance or mind-altering drug. From the time of my great ancestor, Turk of the Turks, Hoca Ahmed Yesevi ibn Muhammed Mehdi,[28] none of my forbears has drunk wine or taken narcotics or stimulants. Please excuse me in this privy council of yours.'

'My brother, light of my eye and delight of my heart!' he said. 'I beg you. My own Mirza Shah is standing before you and offering a cup of pure wine. If you do not quaff a cup of ruby wine for his sake, from whose hand will you take a goblet? Who are you afraid of? Is it your shah, the Caesar in Constantinople? He is a five months journey away. Is it your khan in Erzurum? That is a forty-stage journey from Tabriz. So who is it that you fear? I who am Kelp Ali Khan – khan of khans of the Shah of Persia and Turan – I do not forbid it. I do not follow the edict of my beautiful Shah who said that he would tear out the gall of any of his governors who were caught drinking wine. No, I break his edict and, covertly, have drinking parties with wine and music and entertainment. So who are you afraid of? You must drink!'

'My handsome Khan,' I replied. 'If your beautiful shah has forbidden you to drink wine, the Shah of Shahs, the Padishah Whose edict one does not question, has forbidden me a single drop, in the definitive text: *Wine*

---

27 The Ottomans occupied Tabriz from 1585 to 1603.
28 Turkish Sufi sheikh of Central Asia, d. 1166, to whom Evliya traced his ancestry. See *EI2* 'Ahmad Yasawī' (F. İz).

and games of chance, idols and divining arrows, are abominations devised by Satan (5:90). It is God the Avenger that I am afraid of, He who brought all things into existence out of non-being. I will not break His command and will not drink wine.'

'By God, you are a fine believer and fanatic.'

'By God, my Khan, I am not a fanatic, only a pure adherent of the school of Nu'man ibn Thabit (i.e., a Hanafi). Otherwise I am a world traveller and boon-companion to mankind, a lover of the family of the Prophet, and a man of God.'

This put all the courtiers and boon-companions in a stupor and a quandary. The insistent khan stood up with all his darling boys and came over to me, saying, 'Come, light of my eye. I beg you, my Evliya Agha, take one of these slaveboys of mine. Which one do you fancy? Yazdan Shir? Mirza Shah? Firuz? Parviz? Ali Yar? Zulyazan? Shahlavand? Sayf Quli? Khal Khan? I'll give him to you. If you love 'Red' Murtaza Ali and the Twelve Imams, come, my believer, quaff a cup of wine from the hand of one of these boys, that heads may grow warm and breasts grow soft, that we may get a bit of pleasure and a moment of gratification in this banquet-hall of evanescence.'

All his slaveboys – radiant as congealed light – embraced me and started kissing me. And I kissed them back. Still I sought the assistance of the Munificent, the Absolute.

'My Khan,' I said, 'is this what you call an intimate gathering, when now Hoca Naghdi has knocked off a cup of wine, and is drunk, and belches and farts in your presence? Is this what passes in Persia as having a party and living it up?'

At this the Khan began kicking Hoca Naghdi and knocking him on the head, getting him on his feet. But Hoca Naghdi was so drunk that he seemed to be intoning the verse:

> I am so drunk I do not know
> What is worldly or divine.
> Who am I? Who is the cupbearer?
> What is the crimson wine?

I saw that the Khan was still going to insist that I drink. Realising that the council chamber is a place of security, I said, 'My Khan, you drink wine and get heated and intoxicated. But divine intoxication is what we need. Have them bring me a tambourine and I'll show you what divine intoxication is.'

'Yar Ali!' he cried, 'For the love of Ali, bring my brother a tambourine.' Yar Ali brought me one with Indian inlay-work on the hoop and a pinewood cymbal. Taking it from his hand, I began to improvise in the Turkish manner, in the *segah* mode, singing:

> My love for you betokens
>   Eternal life.
> Each love-struck one on your behalf
>   Gives up his life.

I sang three quatrains and one *sema'i*, and finished the session with a two-couplet piece. All those present put finger to mouth in astonishment. The khan rewarded me in the Persian manner, draping a sable fur-piece over my shoulders with his own hand.

'A thousand bravoes!' he cried. 'A million blessings on you, O impudent one of the land of Caesar!' He showered me with presents, including a Georgian slaveboy; ten *tumans* of *abbasi* coins; and a 'Black Rod' horse, swift as the wind. Now he was safe from me, and he stopped offering me wine.

We spent an entire month in this fashion, engaged in intimate converse with the Khan, or else seeing the sights of heart-ravishing Tabriz. So our nights were like the Night of Power, and our days like the holiday of the Festival of Sacrifice.

But let me express my boundless admiration for the justice of his administration, the safety and security of the city, his fostering care for his subjects, the law and order, the cleanliness of the marketplaces, the schedule of fixed prices of Sheikh Safi,[29] and the prevailing orderliness. To be sure, the people are all pleasure-seekers and party-goers. But one never sees anyone intoxicated on the public thoroughfare. Everyone is extremely well-behaved, befitting these eloquent verses:

> *Devoted to their pleasure, the people of Tabriz*
>   *Are like a mirror, free of the rust of cruelty.*
> *And if you say they are not faithful to their friends,*
>   *The mirror can reflect but what it apprehends.*

To sum up the praiseworthy customs of Tabriz:
1) They sweep the public thoroughfares day and night with brooms, then sprinkle them with sparkling water – something they can do because of the

---

29 Referring to the eponymous founder of the Safavids, Safi al-Din Ardabili, d. 1334.

many streams flowing through the city – leaving not a speck of dust. So even in July the marketplaces are clean and cool. One who goes there is refreshed, and one who looks at the faces of the youthful shopkeepers is astonished.

2) They never marry off girls of the noble family of Muhammad to slaves or converts, but rather they observe the principle of social equality in marriage. When I questioned them about this they replied, 'You marry non-Muslim women, arguing that the man plants the seed, and he is Muslim. This is a reasonable legal doctrine. But you do not marry off girls observing the principle of social equality. If you marry a girl to a man who has converted to Islam, it is possible that he will apostatise. Since the man plants the seed, what about the children? Perhaps that convert will abandon them and run off to the infidels. Then we could not consider the children to be descendants of the Prophet through their mother, since according to your doctrine the man plants the seed. Based on this you marry non-Muslim women; but in that case what happens to the children of an apostate and a woman descended from the Prophet?'

'The Lord Creator,' I said, 'causes all children – no matter what religious community they are born in, whether Jewish or Christian – to be born Muslim; then they are led astray by the teaching of their parents.' And I cited the Hadith, *The messenger of God, May God bless him and give him peace, said: There is no one born except in the natural state of Islam; then his parents make him a Jew or a Christian or a Magian.*

'*The messenger of God speaks truth,*' I said. When they heard this noble Hadith they fell silent.

3) It is the *kanun* of Sheikh Safi that all commerce in the royal bazaars be conducted with *bisti* and *abbasi* coins and with gold. Coins of other kingdoms are not allowed, only Safavid coins have currency. They are minted in seven places, marked as 'struck' in Ardabil, Hamadan, Baghdad, Isfahan, Tiflis, Nihavand, or Tabriz. The inscription on one side is: *There is no god but God; Muhammad is the messenger of God; Ali is the friend of God.* On the reverse is the name of the regnant shah, as *Unworthy slave, dog of Ali, Shah Abbas.* Only the *kazbeki* – this is the name given to the copper coin – is marked 'Struck in Tiflis' or 'Struck in Tabriz' and on the other side is the year of mintage. These are the only coins in circulation.

All their measures of length have *There is no god but God* written on one end. The same for measures of volume, as well as finely sewn fabrics. The drams and scales are also marked with the Name of Glory (i.e., Allah).

Woe to him who commits a fraud while using weights and measures with *There is no god but God* – he will be punished by inserting a stylus in his eye and putting a burning plate on his head.

All the royal markets and the small shops have scales suspended by brass or iron chains. They are permanently suspended, never touched by human hands. When a customer wants something – food or drink or fruits and vegetables – he selects what he prefers and places it in the pan of the scales, then gives the shopkeeper the price corresponding to the weight; because his *akçe* is pure (i.e., the coin is unadulterated) and he has purchased what he himself selects.

Furthermore, all foodstuffs in the marketplace – whether bread, meat, vegetables, barley, wheat, flour, chickens, pigeons, walnuts, hazelnuts, or any prepared foods sold in the cook-shops – are sold by weight according to the schedule of fixed prices of Sheikh Safi. Wheat, rice and other grains are always sold by weight, not by volume. Woe to that man who commits a fraud while using dram weights with *There is no god* – he will have his gall bladder drawn out from under his armpit; that is the Persian *kanun*.

Cloth goods and fabrics are sold by the royal cubit. Animals and slaves also are sold at prices determined by the law of Safi and transactions are supervised by professional assayers. The royal *kanuns* prevail.

4) The cookshop keepers in all the royal markets cannot open their shops until they have washed the china dishes hanging on the wall and the copper utensils and the cups and the porcelain and celadon bowls that they use to serve the food. They open their shops at dawn, uttering a prayer, and serve out – after weighing them on scales – portions of pilavs, whether with boiled wheat, roasted meat, omelette, boiled rice, saffron or rice-water. These are the favourite dishes.

The waiters are clean and lovely youths. They serve the food on pewter dishes with inscriptions in *ta'lik* lettering such as *They give sustenance* (76:8) or aphorisms such as *There is no nobility loftier than Islam* or *The nobility of a place depends upon the one who occupies it* or *The nobility of a house depends upon its inhabitants and the nobility of its inhabitants depends upon their generosity*. After dining, notables of the town are given napkins and clean bowls and ewers to wash their hands; but servant types and hangers-on wipe their right hand under their left armpit and their left hand under their right armpit or under the right skirt of their robe and take off like dogs in a field. That is the way things are.

As for the condemnable customs of the Persians:
1) It is the ancient *kanun* of Azerbaijan that only certain groups cook food in their houses. These include the twelve military regiments – for love of the Twelve Imams – consisting of several thousand men; also twelve groups each of the ulema and of the other notables. The rest are not permitted to light fires in their chambers, except in order to make coffee or tea or fennel or salep or mahaleb, and in order to heat water to wash their clothes. So all the retinue types and soldiers and bachelors get their food in the marketplace. This is why they are 'bad-living' (*bed-ma'aş*) Kızılbaş, since their living (*ma'işet*) is in this respect really bad, although it is cheap. You can get anything to eat that you want, and for bachelors and people on payrolls this is convenient.

Indeed, if a soldier takes his meals in the bazaar for three months, when the royal clothing allotment comes up, the cook goes to the *divan* and says, 'I am Kurban Kuli's cook,' and takes away Kurban Kuli's clothing. But he cannot take any item more or less than allotted; if he does, he will have his tongue pulled out through the back of his neck. After this the cook feasts the owner of the clothing gratis for twelve days. That is the *kanun*.

When the Shah or his general goes on campaign, the largest contingent of felt tents in the army bazaar belongs to the cookshops, since all the soldiers have need of them.

2) Law and order are maintained as follows. They do not put criminals to death by hanging, or the like. Rather, the prefect (*darugha*) and the market inspector take them to the execution grounds and there – God forgive us! – the professional executioners administer 360 tortures over three days and three nights.

First they give the offender 300 lashes with a whip or *şubend* (?) or elephant-penis. Then they strike his knees with drumstick breakers. They drive pieces of straw under his fingernails. They brand him all over with branding irons. They force him to swallow a greasy rag, then pull it out by a thread, which pulls out his stomach and guts as well, and the man is certain to confess his crime. They make him swallow a greased sponge. They bind anklebones of gazelles to his temples. They nail horseshoes and horseshoe nails to his temples. They bore holes in the elbows with a musketeer's auger; or they bore through the knee so it comes out beneath the sole of the foot, then pour molten lead into the hole so that the lead runs out with the marrow. They tie together his thumbs and big toes and hang him by a noose on a gibbet, then burn sulphur and donkey's urine until the fumes make the poor man scream. They pry out his shoulder blades and his ribs and collar bone, then crucify him with straps drawn through his back and wind-tapers attached to his shoulders. They crush his testicles with a noose. They shove gorse up his nostrils. They put a burning plate on his head and insert a stylus in his eye. Or they may pull out his penis through his anus, or his anus through his navel so that – *God forgive us!* – he excretes through his navel. They draw out the man's gall bladder from under his armpit. If he is a thief they hamstring him. If he has given false witness they mark him with a brand and dock his nose and ears. If he is a persistent thief they cut off both hands and both feet. They have seven ways of hanging a man on the hook, and seven types of impalement.

These are the tortures they inflict for three days and nights in order to set an example for others and to reform mankind (or, as exemplary punishment and corrective punishment).

One day, as the Khan was having these tortures administered in his presence, and was taking pride in them despite our discomfort, I asked, 'My Khan, what is the purpose of torturing people to this degree?'

'My brother,' he said, 'these are criminals whose guilt has been established by probationary witnesses and who deserve to die. Instead of putting them to death all at once, we subject them to these torments in order that they may serve as warnings to the heedless. They are rebels against God, like Pharaoh who said *I am your supreme Lord* (79:24). That is why we torture them.'

'But these are not canonical punishments according to the Sharia,' I objected. 'Nor are they effective. Punishments laid down by the religious law are bitter; such as those in the definitive Koranic texts, *As for the man or woman who is guilty of theft, cut off their hands* (5:38), and *We decreed for them a life for a life* (5:45). If you followed these commandments your subjects would have greater fear of committing those crimes.'

'Truly, you give good counsel,' he replied, acknowledging that I had the better argument.

But they practice these kinds of extreme tortures in order to maintain strict law and order, and because their subjects are riotous and heretical. Also, such arbitrary punishments are traditional.

7. Cat-brokers of Ardabil

By God's wisdom, because cats in Ardabil have short lives, there are very many mice, more than in other regions. The mice chew up the people's clothing – their woolen cloaks, for example. So this city has a royal auction for *hirre*, i.e. *gürbe*, i.e. *kutta* – i.e. cats. There are professional cat-brokers, much in demand, who sell cats in cages. The Divriği cat is a particular favourite, fetching a price of up to 100 *guruş*; still, it does not live long here. When the brokers cry their wares, this is the patter they sing, in a loud voice, in the *beyati* mode:

> You who seek a feline,
> A cat to hunt your mice:
> To rats it makes a beeline,
> But otherwise it's nice;
> An enemy to rodents,
> And yet it's not a thief;
> A pet to share your grief.

8. Oil wells of Baku

The water here smells of petroleum because near the city in seven places are petroleum wells, each of a different colour – yellow, red, or black. In the districts of Müskir, Sindan and Zeyneb (?) the people do not use candles of beeswax or of ghee, but only lamps burning black petroleum.

[...]

We got an armed retinue of 100 soldiers from the governor of Baku and from Taqi Ali Khan, the governor of Revan, and departed Baku heading south. There are salt marshes along the (Caspian) coast and also, in seven places, wells of petroleum of various colours. We stopped to inspect them – a natural wonder! There are some along the coast and some in the district of Müskir.

By God's decree, the petroleum bubbles up out of the ground. But, in the manner of hot springs, pools of water are formed with the petroleum congealed on the surface like cream. There is a special agent who gets revenues for the Shah from these wells amounting to 7000 *tumans* of *akçe* per year. The agent's men wade into the pools, collect the petroleum with ladles, and fill goatskins with it, which the oil merchants take to various regions.

There are seven or eight colours of petroleum. The yellow kind is highly regarded. The black kind is a monopoly of the Shah. He transports it to his forts and castles along his borders with the Uzbeks and with the Mughals of India and with the Ottomans in Iraq, Kurdistan, Georgia and Dagestan. When one of these castles is under siege, they use it to light torches around the castle at night. And they soak quilts and old clothing in it which they set ablaze and toss at the army of Islam (i.e., the Ottomans). It serves other important functions as well in their castles and cities. In fact all the torches used in the presence of the Shah and in the royal courts are made from this Baku petroleum. It is a great natural wonder!

The wells are guarded day and night, since any fire sets them ablaze, and then they are not extinguished until the end of time. So mountains of pure soil have been piled up at the rim of each well. If a spark falls on one of the wells, all the subjects rush to the scene and scatter the soil, stopping the fire in this way, by God's command. There is no other remedy. I have heard that there are also oil wells in other places, amidst rocks or in caves; but the only ones I have seen are these in Baku.

9. Cathedral of Echmiadzin

Üç Kilise ('Three Churches') is said to have been built by the Byzantine emperor. It is a wondrous and lofty church, actually three great monasteries, occupied respectively by Armenian girls, by Greeks, and by Armenian men. Of the famous ancient churches in Persia, one is this Üç Kilise; another is Yedi Kenise ('Seven Churches') on the road to Nakhchivan.

This too is a mighty church full of wonders and marvels. One noteworthy item is the holy oil or chrism that is manufactured here. The priests and patriarchs gather the grasses and herbs that grow in abundance here and boil them in a huge cauldron that is placed on top of a cloth spread out like a silk carpet. The herbs cook for three hours, but the fire, which is directly beneath the carpet, has no effect on it. Eventually the oil rises to the top of the cauldron. They fill jars and bottles with it and send these as a blessing to Frengistan and throughout Christendom. In return they receive votive offerings from those places. They claim that this oil has medicinal effect against various illnesses, and that it cures wounds when rubbed on them.

Another marvel: in the courtyard of this church, in plain view, there is a thick iron bar suspended underneath a vault. It is permanently suspended, although not attached to anything in any of the six directions. This is indeed a mysterious phenomenon, amounting to white magic. According to the false claim of all the infidels, it is suspended due to the miraculous grace of Simon the Pure (St Peter), one of the disciples of Jesus. Foolish Muslims also are amazed when they see it, and believe in it; because this little iron column trembles when struck by wind. To prevent people from touching it, some devils have set up a railing all around it made of hard acacia wood.

The true explanation is that the ancient sages who constructed the church placed one large magnet at the apex of that vault and another in the ground directly beneath it. The iron bar has been positioned in such a fashion that it remains suspended between the two magnets. So it is not a miracle of Simon or a talisman of Samson. Still, all who see it put finger to mouth in astonishment. This humble one, full of fault, with my faulty intellect, explained it in this fashion; God willing there is no error in my explanation.

This church has roughly 500 priests and monks. Every night five or six hundred people arrive here from Persia and the same number from Turkey. Even before they dismount and remove their horse cloths and sacks, the monks offer their hospitality, bringing date-milk and sugar cane of Hama and Damascus – whatever food they have – and serving them day and night. It is a wonderful convent of his holiness the Messiah.

10. Ankara

Description of the land of Selasil ('Chains'), the invincible fortress of Ankara, the prosperous walled city of Engürü

First our billeting officer, entering the city with our horse-tail standards, proceeded to the Sharia court where the notables of the province told him, 'Your pasha holed up in Erzurum intending to become a Celali. The suspicion he aroused then has now proved true. He has raised an army of 10,000 men and has leagued himself in rebellion with Varvar Ali Pasha. We cannot allow you to occupy a walled city belonging to the Padishah.'

Nevertheless, since many of these notables were protegées of our lord the Pasha, they said that we could remain for three days as their guests. The agreement was sealed with the recitation of a Fatiha. Diplomas were issued by the court assigning 2,000 lodgings, and the Pasha was quartered in the house of Çavuşzade.

The following day we entered the castle of Ankara in grand procession, the likes of which the people of Ankara had never seen. The entire populace turned out to greet us. Twenty welcome cannons were fired from the castle walls. When the Pasha was settled in his quarters, all the great notables and small tradesmen came to offer him gifts.

This humble one was a guest in the house of Kederzade, a noble *seyyid* and a molla with salary of 500 *akçe* per diem. I went straight to the light-filled tomb of Hacı Bayram Veli, where I rubbed my face on his threshold and began a complete Koran-recital for the sake of his noble spirit. As I had vowed when I got my windfall in the village of Balıkhisar, I paid my votive of 100 *guruş*, distributing it among the dervishes at the convent of Bayram Veli, and receiving their benedictions in exchange. Then I began to tour the city.

It was founded by the Roman Caesar and passed down from kingdom to kingdom until in the year (—) it was conquered for Islam by Hezardinar, vizier of Ya'kub Shah of the Germiyan dynasty of Kütahya. Later it was conquered by the Ottoman sultan (—) in the year (—).

It is a gleaming castle and world-famous. When viewed from the village of Erkeksu, which is a day's journey north, it rises in layers one above the other, like a pearl of great price or like a white swan. Among Ottoman castles it is comparable in this respect to Buda, rampart of Islam, which when viewed from Vac castle a day's journey north and across the Danube has a grandeur beyond all other Hungarian frontier fortresses, resembling as it does a barge with masts raised and decked out from stem to stern. Another is the castle of Van, rampart of the faith, in Azerbaijan, in description of which the tongue falls short – God willing, it will be recorded in its place. And another is this exemplary castle of Ankara, envy of kings, whose might and prosperity are noted in all tongues and in the chronicles of kings and emperors.

The Persian chronicles, to begin with, report that in Persia this city is called *Anguriya* because of the abundance of grapes (Persian *angur*). In the time of the Caesars this city provided 40,000 workers every day for seven years and their daily ration was forty walnuts and one loaf of bread; and based on this *ankariye* or forced labour the city was called *Ankariye*. According to oral tradition, both Kayseriye (Kayseri, Caesaria) and Engürü (Ankara) were constructed according to this accounting of forty walnuts and one loaf of bread. The Arab chronicles call it *Mutabbak* or 'Layered' since it is built layer on layer and the layers intertwine. The chronicle of

Tuhfe calls it *Selasil* or 'Chains' because in the year of the birth of the Prophet the emperor Heraclius laid siege to this castle and surrounded it with seven layers of chains. Its name in Mongolian is *Anagra*; in German, since it is an Ottoman possession, *Anguriyaopol* and *Kostantinopol*; in Tatar *Kirmen-i Angar* (fortress of Angar); in Turkish *Engürü* and *Ankırı* and *İnkırı* and *Aydınkırı* and *Unkuru* and *Anguru*. Many terms are applied to it, but in the Ottoman imperial registers its name is *Ankara*.

The walled town or castle is like a white rose, with layered walls hard to conquer, surrounded by a moat. Poets have praised it in their city eulogies (*şehrengiz*), and chroniclers have said about it:

> *All the world's castles have we seen,*
> *But never have we seen one like this.*

It is the seat of an independent *sancak-bey* in the province of Anatolia. Several times it has been awarded as *arpalık* or stipend to viziers of three horse-tail standards. According to *kanun* the imperial *has* provides an annual income of 263,400 *akçe*; the *sancak* has 14 *zeamets* and 257 *timars*. Administrative officers include a cavalry marshal, troop commander and captain. During campaign the timariots with their armed retainers along with those pertaining to the governor's prebend amount to 3,000 armed soldiers. It is the *kanun* of the Ottoman dynasty that if a timariot fails to be present under the banner of a *sancak-bey*, his prebend is transferred to someone else.

A total of (—) constabularies pertain to the imperial *has* of the provincial governor. These include that of the city itself and those of the valleys of Murtat, Yaban, Çubuk, Çorba, etc. They provide the governor with a legitimate tax revenue of 40,000 *guruş* per annum to support his campaign expenses.

The Sharia administration is headed by a molla with salary of 500 *akçe* per diem. The total number of sub-districts is (—) flourishing villages. The *kadi*-districts are the following:

[1.5 lines empty]

They provide the Molla with twenty purses per annum. There are also a *şeyhülislam*; a *nakibüleşraf* named Kederzade with salary of 500 *akçe* per diem; *kadi* notables in charge of 600 high offices; and countless descendants of the Prophet.

Military officers include an army deputy and a magnificent janissary sergeant in place of a janissary commander, since the populace consists of either *kadis* (!) or soldiers.

Municipal officers include a city clerk, a market inspector, and a customs agent. The stamp officer of Ankara is a separate agency farmed at the rate of 40 *yük* of *akçe* per annum.

There are also a castle warden and deputy, officers of the *azeb* corps, chiefs of the armourers and the gunners, and a garrison of (—) fully-armed soldiers.

The castle itself, situated at the top of a high mountain, is a mighty fortress like that of Qahqaha, a splendid fortification built of four layers of white stone walls, each layer higher than the next. The layers are separated from each other by 300 paces. The height of the walls is 60 cubits, the width of each wall is 10 royal cubits. The base of the foundations reportedly consists of hollow vaults around the entire perimeter, but I didn't see it. The reason is to prevent an enemy from undermining the walls during a siege.

This citadel is situated sidelong to the south and oblong from east to west. There are four layers of iron gates, one leading to the next, on the western side; no other castle has such strong iron gates. Between the gates are iron cages suspended by iron chains. The bars forming these cages are the thickness of an arm. When a siege occurs they are lowered in front of the gates within the castle to block the way.

The red-coloured stones of the upper and lower thresholds are also not seen in other castles. Above the arch of the upper threshold of the outermost gate, that opens to the west overlooking the horse market grounds, are hung maces belonging to the heroes of old, also fish skeletons and other marvellous things. Garrison troops guard this gate day and night from within and from without. If the warden ever leaves the castle he is either put to death or dismissed from office. This is because so many enemies have attacked it and a thousand lives have been lost for every stone.

Indeed, when Abaza Pasha turned Celali in Erzurum in the year (—) he laid siege to this castle with 100,000 troops and took possession of the lower town. As Abaza Pasha was sitting in his palace while the siege of the citadel was going on, an expert gunner shot a cannon ball directly at him and wounded him in the rear end, so he returned to Erzurum disappointed. Since that time it has been forbidden for the castle warden to go outside beyond the front gate, and the garrison keeps watch day and night, with their night cry of 'God is good, He is good!'

To be sure, there is no moat around the upper citadel; but it's perimeter consists of sheer cliffs and conquering it from any direction is impossible. Nor is it easy to mine the walls, since they are layered and have 366 towers that overlook and protect each other – in such wonderful fashion were they planned and laid out – and the four layers of walls have a total of 1,800 crenelations. The citadel is 4,000 paces in circumference.

There is a hill to the east – it is called Hıdırlık and has a shrine – that is slightly higher than the castle. But no possible harm can come to the citadel from there, since the distance between them is a long cannon's range, and the area between consists of a deep crevice, betokening the chasm of hell, from the bottom of which it is extremely difficult to climb up to the castle.

There are a total of eighty-one cannons, large and small, in the citadel, but no large balaramada guns, though many culverins and *şahi* and *zarbzen* guns. And there is a sufficient quantity of munitions and weapons.

Within the castle are 600 pretty houses, with no orchards or gardens. The ancient mosque of (—) is located there, converted from a church ages ago. All the houses and public buildings are covered with pure clay. In short, this citadel is noteworthy from the point of view of its construction and of its architecture.

As to the lower town, in the year (—), from fear of the Celalis, Cenabi Ahmed Pasha,[30] with the help of the people of the province, built a strong single-layered wall around it. It has four gates. It is 6,000 paces in circumference on three sides; the fourth side is the upper citadel, which the lower castle surrounds. On the eastern side one can go down the cliffs from the upper castle to the Hıdırlık valley. There are water conduits in the cliffs, and in the citadel there are cisterns and wheat storehouses; but in this lower castle, because of the abundance of streams, there are no cisterns but 170 fountains and 3,000 wells.

The gates in the perimeter of the castle are, first, on the (—-) side
[2 lines empty]
This large suburb has (—) quarters, first
[2.5 lines empty]
There are a total of seventy-six prayer-niches of which (—) are Friday mosques. First is the Cenabi Ahmed Pasha mosque, and the Hacı Bayram Veli mosque; these two were constructed by Sultan Süleyman's architect Sinan.
[1.5 lines empty]
Few of the mosques are covered with lead tiles; rather they are all covered with pure clay. The remainder are small neighbourhood mosques.

---

30 *Beylerbey* of Anatolia and governor of Ankara, d. 1561.

There are eighteen dervish convents with prayer-niches. The most flourishing is that of Hacı Bayram Veli with over 300 mystics who have wasted their bodies with divine love. Their sheikh, Koca Abdurrahman Efendi, is considered to possess the miraculous graces of a saint, and one whose prayers are accepted by God.

The Bayramis are an independent branch of the Hamidi Sufi order, Hacı Bayram Veli having received the equipment of poverty from Sheikh Hamid whose disciple he was. The spiritual lineage is traced back to Hoca Abd al-Qadir al-Jilani (founder of the Qadiri Sufi order) and through him back to the Prophet. But in Turkey the Bayramis have been reviled, and some of their sheikhs killed, on the grounds that they are Hamzawis going back to Sheikh Hamza and Sheikh Idris. They have no badges on their cloaks and turbans. And while they have committed no act contrary to the Sharia, they are accused and held in suspicion, a band of liver-roasted (i.e., suffering) dervishes.

Then in Ankara is the convent of his majesty Mawlana Jalaladdin Rumi, *may his secret be sanctified*, a Mevlevi lodge constructed by Cenabi Ahmed Pasha, an orchard of Iram with rose-gardens on three sides.

[1.5 lines empty]

There are (—) medreses, including those of Mustafa Pasha, Cenabi Ahmed Pasha, Taşköprüzade, Seyfeddin, Husrev Kethüda, etc. The ones I have named are the most famous, each with numerous cells and domed classrooms, and each providing its students with room and board and candles.

There are three schools of Prophetic Hadith.

There are a 180 elementary schools.

There are (—) public baths, including those of Tahtakale, Sunkuroğlu, Cenabi Ahmed Pasha, etc.

[1 line empty]

These are delightful baths with invigorating atmosphere. There are also 200 private baths, according to the boast of the notables of the province.

There are seventy great and lofty palaces with their orchards and gardens – delightful mansions with layer on layer of walls, all of which are brick, however, not stone. Also none of the public buildings in this city has a tiled roof but rather all are covered with pure clay. And all the houses are made of brick, since the Ankara brick is famous and hard as granite. Note the popular expression, 'lined in a mold like Ankara bricks' – when anything is lined up in order it is likened to Ankara bricks. It is a great city, with

6,066 flourishing houses made of brick. And among the palaces are those of Kederzade, Çavuşzade, Ahmed Pasha, etc. There are many others, but these are the ones I am familiar with.

There are (—) *hans* of the merchants, including
[1 line empty]
The rest are small guest-houses.

There are 200 fountains of *pure nectar* (76:21), the famous ones being those of Hacı Şa'ravi and Hacı Nasuh.

There are 2,000 shops and an ornate bedestan with four chained gates. Most of the markets are situated at a high elevation. Long Market and Army Market and, in the lower castle, Tahtakale Market are very crowded and prosperous. The coffee shops and barber shops are also famously crowded. All the sultanic markets and all the major roads in the quarters are paved end to end with pure white stones.

Notables and *seyyids* and viziers, ulema and sheikhs and poets, are beyond number and beyond compare. True, this is Anatolia and the province consists mainly of Turkish peasants; still, one finds writers and authors, Koran interpreters and experts in Hadith, and Koran reciters who chant it with proper enunciation. And there are over 2,000 mature and clever boys and girls who have memorised the Koran. Thousands of people have also memorised the *Muhammediye* of Yazıcızade Mehmed Efendi (completed in 1443) and the *Tarikat-i Muhammediye* (of Birgili Mehmed Efendi, completed in 1572).

Indeed there are many pious men who follow the Muhammadan path (*tarik-i Muhammedi*). One of these is Abdurrahman Efendi – the one who is considered to possess the miraculous graces of a saint. His transfigured face is characterised as 'four-stroke' meaning that it is free of moustache, beard, eyebrows and eyelashes. He is a descendant of the sainted Hacı Bayram Veli whose face also came to be characterised in that manner, as the following legend goes to show.

One day a deceitful woman invited him to her house in order to recite the Koran for the spirit of her late father. Bayram Veli, who was at the beginning of his ministry, agreed. After reciting a portion of ten Koranic verses, that notorious Zulaykha approached Hacı Bayram and said, 'My dear, what fine eyebrows you have, and what a fine shapely beard, and what eyelashes, and what doe-like eyes daubed by the hand of Power.'

'Lady,' said Hacı Bayram Veli, put off guard by these advances, 'wait just a minute, I need to go to the bathroom.' He took a ewer, secreted himself in a corner, and prayed, 'My lord, you know my condition. Don't blacken my face (i.e., shame me) in your glorious presence. Let me be the most loathsome creature in the world, but free me from these brows and lashes and moustache and beard.'

That instant, by God's command, no trace of hair remained on his radiant face, which now shone like a polished gourd. Thanking God profusely he returned to the woman and greeted her. She, however, now finding him repulsive, cried, 'Girls, strike this pimp who has no place in the harem!'

They drove him out of the house. Thus did our saint escape that predicament. He remained shaved in this fashion for the rest of his life. That is why many of the gentlemen who descend from his daughter have pretty faces and wispy beards.

[2 lines empty]

While in this city I associated with many another saint and lover (of God); may God be pleased with them all.

Generally the great merchants here wear sable cloaks; the middle class wear broadcloth *serhaddi* and *kontuş* cloaks of various colours; the tradesmen wear white cotton twill and mohair; and the ulema woolen cloaks of various colours, since Ankara is a major source of wool. The women also wear varicoloured woolen cloaks and go about very modestly.

Since it is in the fifth true clime and seventeenth conventional clime[31] the latitude is (—) and longitude is (—). The climate is very mild, the people's complexion ruddy, the lovely boys and girls praised around the world.

Of foodstuffs and other products, first of all Ankara trotters are equal to those of Kütahya. Ankara pressed meat cured with seeds of fenugreek is very tasty, as is the meat of Angora goats that feed on holm oak leaves in the mountains.

The Angora goat is a snow-white he-goat found nowhere else. The goat hair is the source of wool thread used for multi-coloured woolen garments worn by emperors. If the hair is shorn the thread is rough, but if it is plucked out it is as soft as Job's silk. When the poor goats' hair is plucked out their bleats reach high heaven. But sensitive individuals have found a solution to this lamentation. They mix lime and ashes in water and wash the goats with this limed sherbet just before plucking them. Then the hairs come out

---

31 True clime (*ıklim-i hakiki*) refers to the seven traditional zones of latitude extending north from the equator. Conventional clime (*ıklim-i örfi*) refers to the twenty-eight regions or countries of the later Muslim geographers.

painlessly, leaving the goats naked and bleating. The thread made from this goat hair is woven into woolen cloth and mohair. All the populace, including the women, are involved in this enterprise.

How waved wool (or mohair) is manufactured. They put a large cauldron, half-filled with water and the desired dye, over a fire. They pile the woolen cloth layer by layer over wooden trestles and place these inside the cauldron, which they then cover and daub with fermented dough. They then stoke the fire so the water in the cauldron turns to steam which strikes the cloth with varicoloured streaks. It is the work of God (i.e., a natural process), producing an effect that even the pen of Mani or Bihzad would be incapable of.

This mohair is also a speciality of Ankara, impossible to find elsewhere. Some bastard Franks brought some of these Angora goats to Frengistan and tried to spin their wool and weave the resulting thread. By God's command the goats died within a year, and they were unable to give a wave to the wool they wove. Finally they brought some of the woollen thread that had been spun in Ankara, but still could not make mohair out of it. So now they only make the thin black waveless homespun woolen cloth that their monks wear.

The Ankaraites attribute the special qualities of Angora wool to the miraculous grace of Hacı Bayram Veli and to their salubrious climate. Indeed, the woolens produced here do not have their equal elsewhere, and the mohair is particularly famous, as is Ankara brick, etc. Most of the populace are merchants on land and sea, trading in mohair wherever it is esteemed – Izmir, Frengistan, Arabia, Egypt, and the seven climes.

There are many Armenians and Jews; of the city quarters, ten are Armenian and two are counted as Jewish congregations; but there are few Greeks or Gypsies. Orchards are few but gardens are many. But the villages in the countryside are flourishing; the populace of the city wealthy and happy; the buildings excellent; the people handsome and hospitable; the crops plentiful; charitable institutions abundant; blessings overflowing; streams and rivers ever flowing. An altogether prosperous city and incomparable castle – may God maintain it in the hands of the Ottomans until the end of time!

The righteous dream of lowly Evliya. On the same day that I entered the walled city of Ankara I visited the shrine of Hacı Bayram Veli and began a complete Koran recital, then came to my quarters. Following the evening prayer and the recital of my litanies I uttered the prayer for a dream-omen and went to sleep. In my dream I saw a man of middle height with a blond beard and wearing a honey-coloured woolen cloak. On his head was a Muhammadan turban with twelve folds wrapped around a *veledi* cap. He approached me and said, 'Look here, my son. Is it right that you should go to visit my pupil Kösec ('Wispy-beard') Bayram Veli and step over me? Is it right that you should begin a Koran recital for him and pass me by without even a Fatiha?'

'Noble sir, who are you? I don't think I know you. And where do you reside?'

'In your youth, when you cried the prayer for wrestlers in the Lodge of the Wrestlers and in the presence of Sultan Murad, didn't you used to say, 'In Ankara lies Er / In Rum Sarı Saltuk'? Well, I am Er Sultan in Ankara. I lie inside a dismal tomb in the Woodcutters' Market near the lower citadel. Visit me there. Cheer me with a Fatiha, and you will be cheered and get your wish in this world and the next. Tomorrow after the morning-prayer I will send you a man who will look just like me. Put your hand in his, tour the city with him and come to visit me. *Peace be upon you.*'

With that he disappeared. I awoke, performed my ablutions and stood waiting for the time of the dawn prayer. After the prayer one of the Pasha's servants arrived and invited me to breakfast. 'No my son, today I am fasting,' I said, and got rid of him.

Suddenly, the person whom I had seen that night in my dream appeared. He greeted me and said: 'Evliya Çelebi, is that you? In our dream Er Dede Sultan sent me to you. Come, let us go visit him.' But his speech seemed to emerge from under the ground. To be sure, his face was radiant and his words were sweet and touching. I donned my cloak and stepped outside with a *besmele*.

As we proceeded on foot, he named and described the great saints buried in eleven places within the city, making me stop at each one and pay a pilgrimage-visit. 'This is my pupil,' he would say; or else, 'This is the successor to the saintly Hamid Efendi.' He held my hand fast and we made a complete tour of the pilgrimage sites; God willing, they will be recorded below. But, though he held my hand fast, his own hand had absolutely no bones: whichever way I bent it, it gave way like dough. Occasionally he would remove his hand from mine, point out a pilgrimage-site, and again clasp my hand.

We went on, discussing matters related to the afterlife, until we arrived at the place known as the Woodcutters' Market. At the western side of the square there was a small tomb, hardly visible. 'There is the tomb of Er Sultan,' he said, pointing with his right hand. I looked in that direction, and when I looked back, he had disappeared. 'Oh dear,' I said, 'I shouldn't have let go of his hand. Now what will become of me?' I wandered about in a daze, in the dim light of dawn. The place where that person disappeared was a main road, but now it too had disappeared both in front of me and behind. 'He must have gone inside that little door covered with felt,' I said. I opened the door and went in.

Would you believe it? The place turned out to be a tavern! And there were a bunch of the Pasha's servants and muleteers and donkey-boys, some playing the guitar and the lute and raising a hullabaloo. 'Evliya Çelebi!' cried one of them, 'Come and have some *boza*.' When I realised that I had been seen entering a tavern, I wanted to sink into the ground from shame. I ran outside, went over to the tomb of Er Sultan, opened the door and entered.

'Peace upon you, O saintly sheikh,' I said, weeping the while, and rubbing this rebellious face of mine in the dust of the threshold. 'You appeared in my dream and told me that you would send me a guide on the path, and you kept your word. But you took him from my hand before I could be guided aright. I have come to visit you and to rub my face at your gate. For the sake of God's beloved (i.e., the Prophet Muhammad) do not leave me forlorn in this world and the next. I swear by God that I will perform a complete Koran-recital for the sake of your noble spirit,' and I began the recital then and there. Meanwhile I crawled beneath the green woolen coverlet that lay over the noble cenotaph, crying, 'Protection, O Er Sultan, protection!'

I fell asleep almost immediately – I was sweating so much that the sweat poured from my clothes – and again I saw the figure of Er Sultan, dressed as in my previous dream. He greeted me and I returned the greeting. 'My lord,' said I, 'I lost the man you sent to conduct me here, so I have come to your gate without intermediary. Do not turn me back empty-handed.'

'You will not be left forlorn,' he replied, 'for you are one who preserves the Koran in his memory, and one who loves God's friends and rubs his face at the thresholds of the great saints. Out of my love for you I appeared in your dream and said that I would send someone to conduct you here, and I told you to hold his hand; and the next morning I arrived and clasped your hand in mine. I am your perfect guide who will lead you to the path of Truth.

'Do not distress yourself. Your final path in the end, safe and sound, is the Straight Path. But keep to the straight and narrow while you are roaming about with these ruffians. Take pity on the poor and the weak. Try to extricate yourself from these ruffians. Tell your pasha that while he is shutting himself up as a Celali in this dear little Ankara of mine he should not harm the people who are in my precinct.

'As for you: God grant completion of your journey, faith at your final breath, intercession of the Prophet as your share (in the next world), and bodily health as you roam about (this) world. Eat little, speak little, and sleep little. Do much for the sake of knowledge – in the end one must perform good deeds in order to find the path of truth; as the Koran states: *The good word is heard by Him and the good deed exalted* (35:10). Keep to this counsel of mine, and carry out your obligations to your parents. Do not forget me in your prayers, and hold in reverence the holy sheikhs and patron saints. Go, may God bring you right, may your end be good.'

'A Fatiha on this intention,' said I, and recited a Fatiha. As I was kissing his hand a clamour rose outside the door of the light-filled tomb, and someone shouted: 'Doesn't this tomb have a keeper?' At this I awoke and crawled out from under Er Sultan's woolen cenotaph-cover, in a daze and drenched in sweat. It seems that quite a few pilgrims had come to visit the noble grave. 'Are you the tomb's keeper?' they said. 'Yes,' I replied, 'I have become a servant at this shrine.' They performed their visitation, and I, uttering the Fatiha of farewell, shut the door of felicity behind me and returned weeping to my quarters.

I immediately reported my dream to the Pasha. 'I beg God's forgiveness,' he cried. '*Turn to God in true repentance* (66:8). Tell the regiment commanders and the Segban and Sarıca soldiery to deliver up the munitions and muskets and other arms. Henceforth it is forbidden to shut ourselves up as Celalis in this walled city of Ankara.' He gathered the arms from all the military regiments, and the town fell quiet.

It turned out that the Pasha had also seen Er Sultan in his dream which, as he narrated it to me, fit mine exactly. So it seems that the Pasha actually had conceived the idea of shutting himself up in Ankara as a Celali.

After this I took it upon myself to visit the tombs of Er Sultan and of Hacı Bayram Veli Sultan every day, and I also finished the complete Koran-recitals that I had started.

Account of the shrines of the great saints resting in Ankara. First the magnificent Pole and esteemed Column, ascetic of the age and worshipper unique, speaker of truths and counsellor of virtues, chief of men and point of perfection, absolute sheikh and verified Pole, mine of divine wisdom and dweller in the godly hut, his holiness Sheikh Hacı Bayram Veli, *may God sanctify us with his precious secret*.

Born in the village of Sol on the bank of the Çu River (— illegible), he received the equipment of poverty from his holiness Sheikh Hamid and under that sheikh's spiritual guidance was the Pole of Poles for some years and exhibited thousands of miraculous graces. In the course of travel he came to Edirne in the year (—), during the reign of Sultan Bayezid the Thunderbolt (1389–1402), and mounted the pulpit of the Old Friday Mosque (Eski Cami), built by that sultan as a blessing, to preach; that very pulpit is still standing in that ancient light-filled mosque. It often happened that other sheikhs mounted that pulpit and, finding themselves tongue-tied, were unable to preach; for a sheikh qualified to sit lightly on that prayer-rug had not appeared, let alone one who could preach fearlessly. Bayram Veli was such a great saint. He died during the reign of the Thunderbolt and was buried in the splendid light-filled dome of the convent in the castle of Ankara, as mentioned above – *may God have mercy upon him*.

Then the tomb of the one whose prayer is answered, source of saintly lights, revealer of the mysteries of truth [...] his holiness Sheikh Er Sultan. His noble name was Mahmud. He was a disciple of Sheikh Hamid in the Qadiri Sufi order. Thousands of his miraculous graces became evident. Praise God, this humble one was vouchsafed the visitation of his tomb, and also the vision of him in my dream. Thus I got a share of his mystical guidance although he was already in the other world – *may God have mercy upon him*. He rests in a small domed chamber in the Woodcutters' Market inside Ankara and is visited by elite and commoners alike – may his secret be sanctified.

Then the tomb of his holiness Hızır, on a lofty mountain overlooking Ankara castle to the east (i.e., Hıdırlık, see above). People go there for a picnic and to take in the view of the entire Ankara plain spread out before them like varicoloured paper.

The tomb of Sheikh Hüsameddin, disciple of Ahmed Sarbani. While imprisoned in Ankara castle he said 'Bury me tomorrow' and on the next day, although no man or jinn had access to his prison cell, he was found wrapped in a yellow shroud of date-palm fibre, his body washed and perfumed. All were amazed at this. He is buried in the enclosed graveyard of his convent.

The tomb of Katib Salahaddin. As an astronomer he was a second Pythagoras. He is the author of such works as *Melheme* (on eschatology) and *Ta'birname* (on dream interpretation).

Aside from these shrines there are several thousand tombs of authors and scholars and saints, both inside and outside Ankara. But because I only stayed there a few days these few were all that I recorded – *may God have mercy upon them all.*

As we were about to depart from Ankara, and the horse-tail standards were going with the billeting officer, I wished to lighten my load. So I sold one of the mule-trains I had got from Hacı Baba to the Pasha for a purse of *guruş*, which I gave away as alms to the poor, receiving a goodly reward in exchange, in accordance with the Koranic verse: *He that does a good deed shall be repaid tenfold* (6:160). As for the rest of my heavy baggage, and all the windfall treasures that the above-mentioned Hacı Baba gave me in the robbers' den, I deposited them for safekeeping with my host and benefactor Kederzade Efendi. Thus I was left with seven armed slaves and one lightly-furnished packhorse, ready to depart the following morning.

But the next day, at the time of the morning prayer, a tremendous hubbub broke out and a hue and cry that shook earth and sky. As we wondered what was going on we heard the cries of so many thousands of soldiers. Some said, 'We are pleased with the Pasha, he is innocent!' Others said, 'It is the Sultan's to command! The Pasha is a Celali in alliance with Varvar and his followers are bandits!'

It turned out that one of the imperial chief porters, Mustafa Agha, had arrived with forty men bringing a noble rescript demanding that the Pasha be put to death. They shut the castle gates and had criers go about announcing a call to arms.

By God's wisdom, that night the Pasha had had a fearful dream, so he had put on a disguise, mounted an Arab steed, slipped out the castle gate and gone to the shrine of Hüseyn Gazi, the father of Seydi Battal Gazi. This was his usual practice in such circumstances. When the chief porter and his men raided the Pasha's palace, they could not find him. They scoured the city inside and out but found no trace of him.

When the Pasha got wind of all this he decided not to go back into Ankara but proceeded to the place called Erkeksu north of the city. He sent a peasant with a message to his deputy Ali Agha requesting him to send his troops.

Meanwhile, when the Pasha was not found, the castle gates were opened and criers announced that, by imperial decree, any of the Pasha's men who were found henceforth would be killed and their wealth confiscated. All the Pasha's banished men were conducted out of Ankara and warned not to enter any city with a minaret if they valued their lives.

As for this humble one, I bid farewell to our host, made farewell visits to the tombs of Hacı Bayram Veli and Er Dede Sultan, and proceeded seven hours north of Ankara to the stage of **Erkeksu**. It is a flourishing Muslim village at the foot of a cliff in the district of Ankara, with 200 houses, a Friday mosque, an imposing *han*, but no orchards and gardens.

From there, after another (—) hours, we came to the great town of **Istanoz**, on the border of the Murtat valley district. It is administered by a constable of the governor of Ankara and a *kadi* with salary of 150 *akçe* per diem. It is situated at the edge of a narrow ravine between two high cliffs. There are 1,000 houses, without orchards and gardens, a Friday mosque, a public bath, and a small marketplace. The river (—) flows through it.

Formerly there were large gates at both ends of this town, but they were destroyed when Celali Karayazıcı pillaged it during the reign of Sultan Mehmed III. If they were repaired it would be impossible to conquer this town from any direction. Because on both sides rise sheer cliffs, red and yellow, where hawks and falcons and eagles have their eyries, so lofty that a person would not dare look down. These are imposing and frightful rocks such as those of Van, Şebin(karahisar) and Mardin castles. Some are hollow at the base like Mt Bisutun, some swoop down from above like dragons, or have wondrous shapes like lions or elephants.

Most of the populace are Armenians. There are reported to be 1,000 looms for the processing of mohair. Being inside a valley, the weather gets very hot; nevertheless the mohair produced here is of a fine quality. Also the Armenian girls are famous. There are caverns in the cliffs where you could comfortably fit a thousand horses tied together. And there is a small ruined castle dating from antiquity atop one of the sheer cliffs.

By God's wisdom, on the day we entered this town it was swarming with people. It turned out that a tightrope walker convention was going on.

Spectacle of master acrobats, the tightrope walkers. Once every forty years all the tightrope walkers gather here to vie and contest their skills.

There are two places in Anatolia where these tightrope walker conventions take place, one being this valley of Istanoz and the other the town of Gediz. We too, now idle and unemployed, had nothing better to do than attend as spectators. What should we see?

The ropes – whipcords, of Frankish manufacture – were strung across the ravine from one cliff to the other and secured at either end by sheepskins, lest they be frayed by the rocks. Also armed guards were stationed to ensure that no rival cut the rope while a master was performing. Thousands of people gathered in the ravine below and on the cliffs above to observe the spectacle. In the previous week benches and bleachers had been set up on both sides of the river, and tourists had pitched their tents in the fields nearby. The governor of Ankara province had sent his military band and it was banging away on both sides and crying blessings upon the Prophet. Now the master tightrope walkers issued challenges to each other.

First up was chief of the guild, Sipah Mehmed Çelebi from Üsküdar.[32] With a *besmele* he seized the balancing beam in his huge hands and proceeded boldly out on the rope, crying *Allah Allah!* The sound of his voice mingled with the banging of the drums and resounded among the cliffs like thunder. His rope, known as a testing rope, was extremely thin, but he flashed out on it like lightning. When he reached the middle he suddenly turned and scampered back, like a rabbit turning before a hound. The spectators, amazed at this feat of white magic – for it is beyond human capacity to turn on a rope while running at full speed – all cried out: 'God help you, O Pehlivan!' Sipah Mehmed performed this manoeuvre three times, shouted a benediction to the crowd, then rushed down to his tent, leaving his servant-boys to go out among the crowd and gather coins.

Next came Civelik Ali, a veteran tightrope walker from Isparta. He bowed to the chief of the guild, uttered a benediction, and climbed up to the rope. His speciality was to grasp the balancing beam at the end by one hand – the standard practice being to grasp it in the middle by both hands – and, letting it hang down, cross to the other side like a bolt of lightning. Performers and spectators alike marvelled at this feat. He then switched hands and returned, walking backwards. As he accomplished this superhuman feat the audience cried 'God make it easy!' Once back at the

---

32   He was the guild chief according to Evliya's account in Vol. 1, fol. 204a = Volume 1, selection 4.

starting-point, Civelik Ali slithered down the pole upside-down and kissed the ground in front of the chief of the guild who said 'God bless you, Pehlivan!' and pressed him to his chest.

Third was Pehlivan Şücah from Harput, who didn't bother with a balance beam at all, but instead he held in each hand a jar full of water. At the end of his performance he flung himself from the pole onto the ground, while the spectators held their breath. By God's command, he neither harmed himself nor broke the two jars. This feat won him the admiration of the crowd and the congratulation of the guild chief whose hand he kissed.

Fourth was Hasan Zavil from Tokat, a seventy-year-old master who had performed before the Mughal emperor in India. He too kissed the guild chief's hand. He wore a pair of new Kubadi slippers and had a celadon bowl full of water perched on his gilded turban. He too scorned the use of the balance beam, but instead held tight to the sleeves of his stiff cloak of red broadcloth known as *muvahhidi*. Thus he crossed over and back, and the crowd went wild.

Fifth up was Pehlivan Sührab from Gerger (a town on the Euphrates between Malatya and Siverek). On his feet he had a pair of tall clogs of the sort that women wear to the baths, and on his shoulders he bore a live calf; but he did make use of the balance beam in going back and forth on that thin tightrope in those clogs – an acrobatic feat.

Sixth was Pehlivan Nasır from the Maghreb. He too used the balance beam, but crossed the ravine blindfolded and carrying on his back one of his servant-boys who beat the drum all the while.

Seventh was Pehlivan Selim from Arapgir, wearing only leather tights and carrying a flintlock musket in each hand which he shot off as he crossed, then reloaded and shot again as he crossed back.

Eighth was Pehlivan Nasreddin from Djerba in Tunisia. His speciality was to cross on the tightrope, not only without using a balance beam, but also without even using his feet. He accomplished this feetless feat by attaching rings to his sidelocks and hanging the rings from the rope, and thus, suspended by his hair, he gradually slid along the tightrope by propelling himself with a kind of ball the size of a watermelon that he turned with a string like a top. No one could even have imagined such a feat.

Ninth was Kızkapan Süleyman from Galata, an apprentice of the chief of the guild, who also appeared in leather breeches. His trick was to go inside a little box, which he first held out to the audience to demonstrate that it was nothing more than a plain square wooden box lined with paper, and to speed back and forth across the tightrope while inside the box, which was suspended to it by an iron ring. He returned in the same way, then emerged from the box and bowed before his master. This feat too was beyond the comprehension of a rational observer.

There were many more than these. In fact, the convention went on for three days and nights, and a total of seventy-six tightrope walkers displayed their various skills. If I recorded all of these I would become a professional eulogist for tightrope walkers; so what I have recorded is sufficient. They also graduated 300 apprentice tightrope walkers, all of whom performed their stunts. In the course of three days the townsmen, especially the Armenians, produced 600 woollens and the same number of mohairs, and received as reward a purse of *guruş* from our lord the Pasha.

(Eventually Evliya falls into the hands of İpşir Pasha who has been pursuing the rebels. He fearfully asks to be dismissed, insisting that he is with Mehmed Pasha only 'for travel's sake'. He recovers his property in Ankara.)

VOLUME THREE

In the Retinue of Melek Ahmed Pasha

EVLIYA DEPARTS for Damascus with its governor Silihdar Murtaza Pasha in September 1648. On the way he stops briefly at Akşehir, home of Nasreddin Hoca, the legendary subject of so much Turkish humour. His peregrinations in the Holy Land include a stay in Safed (cf. Volume 9, selection 3) where he encounters a community of Sephardic Jews. He considers Ladino (or Judaeo-Spanish, which he had also heard in Istanbul and was later to hear in Salonica) to be the Jewish language par excellence. While in Damascus he has encounters with the colourful Sheikh Bekkar the Naked (cf. Volume 9, selection 5).

A year later Murtaza Pasha is appointed governor of Sivas, and Evliya accompanies him there. At the end of his long description of the city, we find the satirical story of the girl who gave birth to an elephant, and his description of the Armenian language. Stopping at Divriği, he sees the cats that he had found auctioned in Ardabil (Volume 2, selection 7). With the Pasha's dismissal from office, Evliya returns to Istanbul in July 1650.

He now attaches himself to another kinsman, Melek Ahmed Pasha. For the next twelve years Evliya is in Melek Pasha's service, and his travel itinerary follows the various posts to which the Pasha is assigned as governor (*beylerbey*). In this volume we hear about Evliya's travels with Melek Pasha in Thrace and the Balkans. He reports on witchcraft in a Bulgarian village; on hot springs (cf. those of Bursa, Volume 2, selection 2) and prostitution in Sofia; and, in the countryside, on a fountain that tests for homosexual proclivities.

Evliya returns to Istanbul in 1653.

1. Nasreddin Hoca in Akşehir[33]

Description of the saints' tombs of Akşehir
First, in the cemetery outside the city to the south is buried the scholar of worldly and religious matters, Simurgh of Mt Qaf of certainty, the sheikh Hoca Nasreddin. He was born here in Akşehir during the reign of Gazi Hudavendigar (Sultan Murad I, reg. 1362–89) and grew up during the reign of Bayezid (I) the Thunderbolt (reg. 1389–1402). He was a great saint, with many virtues and a ready wit, and displayed miraculous graces.

He consorted with Timur[34] who enjoyed his company and, for his sake, exempted this city of Akşehir from pillage. The counsels and pleasantries of Nasreddin Hoca are on everybody's lips and have become proverbial. For example:

One day Timur went with the Hoca to the public bath. As they were bathing themselves, each wrapped in a bath-cloth, Timur said, 'Hoca, if it were necessary for a world-conquering emperor like my humble self to be sold, how much would you buy me for?'

'40 *akçe*,' he replied.

'Hey Hoca,' he said, 'my bath-cloth is worth 40 *akçe*.'

'Yes, and I would buy the bath-cloth for 40 *akçe*. Otherwise you're a lame and wounded fellow from the band of Mongols, you're not worth a Hille penny!'

Timur enjoyed this display of wit and showered him with gifts.

There are many such jokes and pleasantries. After the death of the Thunderbolt he lived until the reign of Çelebi Sultan Mehmed (I, reg. 1413–21). He is buried in a domed shrine outside this city of Akşehir, and a railing surrounds the tomb.

Adventure of this humble one. When the trumpet signal for departure was sounded at midnight and the heavy baggage had left, I too sent off my

---

33 n.b. Evliya was probably never in Akşehir since, aside from some administrative details derived from a written source, and the passage above, the only information about it he mentions is that it is famous for its apples.
34 Tamerlane or Timur the Lame, who defeated the Ottomans at the Battle of Ankara in 1402

servants and left the city at midnight with one slaveboy. I recalled the belief that if one visits the tomb of Hoca Nasreddin and remembers some of his pleasantries, one is bound to laugh. Wondering if this was true, I veered left off the main road with my horse and went straight toward his noble tomb.

'Peace upon you, O people of the graves!' said I. Thereupon a voice came from within Nasreddin's shrine, 'And upon you peace, O princely soul!'

My horse started with a grunt, rose up on its hind legs and tore through the cemetery. I had a hard time reining him in. One of his legs tripped on a grave, and I nearly suffered the torment of the grave.

'Agha!' cried the voice from the Hoca's tomb. 'Give alms and go laughing, but be sure to come back.' It turned out to be the tomb's keeper.

'Hey, fellow, I greeted the people of the graves (*ehl-i kubur*), you are people of the backsides (*ehl-i dübur*), so why did you return the greeting?' I gave him a few *akçe*.

'Go, may God be your helper.' He sent me off with this benediction, and I indeed went laughing at these events.

2. Safed

Description of Kafr Nahon, i.e. the notable city of Safed, country of the Jews, province of Canaan, town of the Yids[35]

After the Deluge its founder was Shem, son of Noah – peace be on him. Until the time of Jacob this city prospered so much that even cities like Askalon, Hasan (Bilbays), Palestine, Tiberias, Jerusalem and Zagzaga were not so prosperous as this city of Safed. That is because all the Children of Israel originated from Safed and had their ancient Temple here. This city has become their Ka'ba – *saving the comparison!* – and remains so even to this day.

When Sultan Selim (I) took this city from the Sultan al-Ghawri of the Egyptian Circassian (Mamluk) dynasty in the year 922 (1516) it had, according to the register of Tavaşi Sinan Pasha, a *harac* tax on 600,000 Jews. Today between seventy and eighty thousand Jews still live here, their houses layer on layer. According to their vain belief, a Jew cannot be considered anything but a Karaite Yid if he does not visit this city once in

---

35 n.b. Cuhud and its derivative Çufut are derogatory variants of Yahud meaning 'Jews'.

his life; or, if being unable to do so, he does not rub his face with its dust; or if he does not drink from its water; or does not fumigate himself with the (smoke of the) autumnal leaves of its trees.

I have recorded elsewhere the founder of this city and its being the capital of the Jews together with its public edifices and buildings, pious foundations, and chronograms. In volume (—) (9) of our *Book of Travels* dealing with the Hajj, I have written a detailed account of all the shrines of the sons and daughters of Jacob and the sons of Ishmael; Jacob's House of Sorrows; and the houses of Ephraim son of Joseph, Isaac, Ishmael and Job, together with a thousand other notes.

For this year's journey I will record here the language of the Jews according to the language of the Torah, since those who are world-travellers and boon-companions of mankind must have a smattering of every language.

Description of the Language of the Jews. The Yid Jews are an ancient and accursed people. Of the 124,000 prophets, 4,000 did not die in their beds but were martyred by this tribe of Jews. The fact that they martyred such prophets as John, Zachariah, George, etc. is recorded in thousands of commentaries and histories.

Two books were revealed to one religious community. One is the Book of Psalms which God revealed to the prophet David; as attested by the Koranic verse: *To David We gave the Psalms* (17:55). David was initially a preacher and counsellor who recited the Psalms in a loud Davidic voice. He made his living by fashioning iron into armour. Then God commanded David to wage war on King Goliath. King Saul believed in David. There was a great battle in the plain of Marj Dabiq near Aleppo where David crushed Goliath's head with a sling shot and killed him instantly. God gave David Goliath's kingdom, and thus he became both prophet and emperor, as attested by the verse in the Sura of al-Baqara: *David slew Goliath, and God bestowed on him sovereignty* (2:251).

The Book of Psalms, revealed to David, does not contain promise and threat, narrative, command and prohibition, permitted and forbidden; rather it consists entirely of prayers. All that the rabbis recite from their leather straps in the synagogues of the tribe of Judah are psalms, and what they swear by is the book of Psalms. As for the Torah, revealed to Moses, it is entirely promise and threat, command and prohibition, narrative, permitted and forbidden, paradise and hell and purgatory, resurrection and judgement. Everything in the Torah has to do with judgement, as in the Koranic verse: *Nor anything green or sear, but is recorded in a glorious Book* (6:59).

Aside from the Jews, among the Christians as well – the infidels of Sweden, Holland, Dunkerque, Denmark, Germany, etc. – they all read the Torah and the Psalms and they speak Jewish (*Yahudice*). But the Jews are a bunch of erring infidels whose sect is contrary to that of the Christians.

The Jewish language is this: *un* 1 *dos* 2 *tire* 3 *kotra* 4 *çinko* 5 *si* 6 *sete* 7 *ota* 8 *nova* 9 *deç* 10 *kim anda* What are you saying? *venki* Come! *un dos* Where were you? *inkaza* I was at home *miyalom* My dear *ki kaziyan* What were you doing? *avra porta* Open the door *serele porta* Shut the door *miyaloma sinyor vamoz sadaka* My dear sir, go to alms *miyaloma ono pa çuz dami* My dear, give me a vagina *miyaloma bono andam* My dear, look at me nicely *miyaloma andami sinyor si* My dear, look, my dear sir.

Jewish names: *Abraham* Abraham *Mordahay Nisim Mayliho* Ishmael *Yaho* Jacob *Duşenho Isra'il Musiko* Moses (*Musa çelebi*) *Kazeliko Harun Zehirya*

[2 lines empty]

Names of Jewish women:

[2 lines empty]

pastaliko pastry *kaşar* pure *turfa* impure *sinago* synagogue

[5 lines empty]

The tribe of Jews has countless words and expressions other than these, but this much will suffice. Also there are many things to describe about the city of Safed, but they are all recorded above (i.e., below in Volume 9).

3. Sheikh Bekkar the Naked on the road outside Damascus

Description of the Stages and Castles and Cities on our Journey from Damascus to Turkey in the year 1059 (1649)

On the first day of the month of Dhu'l-qa'da in that year (6 November 1649) Emir Pasha, removed from office in Egypt, arrived in Damascus and set up camp in the Blue Square (*Gökmeydanı*). On the same day our lord Murtaza Pasha departed from Damascus. We went north, skirting the Damascus orchards, to the stages of Harasta ... Kusayra ... Katife ... Karalar castle ... **Caravanserai of the Two Gates** (*İkikapulu hanı*).

This is a great *han* with two gates, like a castle, in one of the Damascus districts. Its governor and benefactor is (—) Pasha, as I recorded above. Departing from this place we were proceeding north through the desert with all the troops.

Saintly deeds of Sheikh Bekkar the Naked. A certain Sheikh Bekkar showed up from the east, with bare head and bare feet and bare chest, both hands on his shoulders, and his penis and testicles swaying back and forth.

'*I came Baghdad!*' he cried to the soldiers (in ungrammatical Arabic) as he passed us by. The chief muleteer Halil Agha, who was a very upright person, said, '*O Sheikh Bekkar, where is your gift from Baghdad?*'

Sheikh Bekkar had both hands on his shoulders. With a *besmele* he pulled out a bunch of dates with his right hand. They were *hastavi* dates that seemed freshly picked from Rum-nahiye in Baghdad, a bunch weighing 40 Ottoman *batmans*.

'*This grew Baghdad,*' he said and gave the dates to the chief muleteer. Then he approached Murtaza Pasha and said with a smile, '*O Murtaza, go Turkey then went Istanbul and went Erzurum, went etc., went to Baghdad and went to the land of the Kurds, died from the love of God, martyred in the castle of Dühük.*'

No one had any idea what these mysterious words meant. Sheikh Bekkar turned toward Damascus and in a moment vanished like a shadow. The chief muleteer gave the Pasha the bunch of dates he had received from Sheikh Bekkar.

'Praise God!' said the Pasha, 'they are *hastavi* dates of Baghdad, freshly picked.' He gave them to this humble one in a copper bucket. I ate three of them as a blessing and kept the rest. I plan to give one to anyone suffering from epilepsy or paralysis.

God knows, this saintly deed of Sheikh Bekkar happened exactly as I have recounted it. To be sure, dates do grow in Damascus, but not productively, and *hastavi* dates of Baghdad grow nowhere else but there. Sheikh Bekkar one day previously was walking about and exchanging banter with us among the tents in Karalar castle, and the next day brought a bunch of *hastavi* dates to this place near İkikapulu. The strange thing is that none of the date palms – whether in Qurna, Jawazir, Samawat, Arja, Hilla, Baghdad or Damascus – was in flower. The miracles of the saints are true.

He was a great and naked saint, one suspected of miraculous graces – may his spiritual support be ever present. God be praised, I associated with such a great saint and received his benediction. Also this humble one had a tambourine in my house (i.e., while residing in Damascus?). Whenever he came to my house he would find the tambourine, put it in my hand and say *'Play the tambourine,'* and as I played he would dance ecstatically.

He was originally from Baghdad where he was the muezzin at the (—) Friday mosque. One night while reciting *temcid* and seeing that the gate of God's mercy was open, he flung himself from the minaret, disappeared from Baghdad, and appeared naked in Damascus.

He used to go about the marketplace naked. He would enter the women's bath-houses, only a bath-towel around his loins, and rub the women down with soap and a bath-cloth. 'The baby in your womb,' he would say, 'will be my daughter in this world and the next, or will be my son,' and by God's command the baby would be born precisely as he indicated.

One time he did this to the wife of a certain janissary colonel. After rubbing her down he placed his hand on her womb and said: 'The baby boy in your womb will be my spiritual son and will go about like me.' When the woman delivered, it was a boy like a gold piece, congealed light. Sheikh Bekkar showed up at the door and said 'Give me my boy.' Taking the baby in his arms he recited the call-to-prayer in its ear and puffed on its head, then returned it to its mother and left. By God's wisdom, the newborn began to squirm and babble and refused any swaddling or any garment. Before he was three years old this son of the colonel began to go about naked alongside Sheikh Bekkar. Indeed, all his movements and gestures and attitudes are exactly those of Sheikh Bekkar. Only Sheikh Bekkar is not very talkative, but this spiritual son of his talks non-stop. He chats with anyone who catches his eye, and if there are no people he talks with animals and even with stones and trees. He is such a pure innocent child – may his spiritual support be ever present.

4. The girl who gave birth to an elephant

In the year 1059 (1649), while Silihdar Murtaza Pasha was governor of Sivas in the province of Rum, a delegation appeared before the Pasha from a village near Turhal. They had a box in which was the corpse of a white baby elephant. 'My lord,' they said, 'this little elephant was born in our village of a girl who is a virgin maiden. Now our magistrate has imprisoned the girl along with her father and mother and other relatives. The baby elephant was born alive, but the prefect had the midwife smother it. We beg my lord to dispatch one of your agents, a fair-minded officer, to have the girl and her mother freed from prison and brought here so that you may determine the truth.' The provincial councillors of Rum were amazed at the sight of this baby elephant.

'Evliya Çelebi,' said Murtaza Pasha, 'this is a job for you. Let's bring all of them before the provincial council. Let's see how a virgin maid can give birth to an elephant. This is a divine mystery. Go quickly, punish those who have committed this deed, and bring them before the council.'

I was nonplussed. 'You tell me to punish those who have committed this deed. But the one who has committed this deed is the Free-choosing Actor, the Lord of the Worlds. He has done this in order to manifest His creative wisdom. Whom should I punish? My lord, I beg you not to reveal this mystery. The whole world will start to say that women in the Ottoman Empire give birth to elephants. Just ignore this case.'

Some of the Pasha's companions spoke up: 'My lord, there is an issue here of income and expenditure. The matter requires a strong and brave individual, one who fears neither God nor man, who will investigate why they had the elephant killed and will haul the murderers and all the villagers in chains before the council. If they had not killed the elephant, you might have sent it to Sultan Mehmed, who recently assumed the throne, and it would have been a gift the likes of which no previous sultan has received since the world has stood.'

They pointed to the elephant corpse in the box, marvelling at its ears and lips, its trunk and eyes, its tail and legs. 'God be praised, my lord,' they said. 'You should exact 10,000 *guruş* from the person who smothered this innocent baby elephant, and 40,000 or 50,000 from the girl who bore it and from her parents.' At their insistence a decree was drawn up and the head of the military band was ordered to go and summon all the villagers and the girl who had given birth to the elephant along with all of her relatives.

Three days later seventy individuals were brought before the provincial council in chains. The first to be questioned was the girl who had given birth to the elephant.

This was her story: 'My lord. Three years ago a delegation from the sultan of India, bearing two elephants as a gift for Sultan Ibrahim, stopped in our plain of Turhal. All the townsfolk and the people from the surrounding villages went to see them. I was with a group of five or ten girls. We arrived at a pleasant spot and mounted some carts to get a better view. As they passed they cried, 'You are too close, get down from the carts.' Some of the women near me were whispering to each other, 'Allah! what a big animal this is.' I went forward, saying, 'Mommy, where is the elephant?' I saw a black house on five pillars. One of the pillars was swaying back and forth. I kept going forward, saying, 'Mommy, where is the little elephant?' Then I heard everyone shouting, 'Hey, girl, stop!' The next thing I saw was that big black house walking toward me. Something snatched me up in the air. I was in a dark warm place. I floundered about, crying for help, and my hands and feet kept sticking into warm flesh. Suddenly, after about an hour, something took hold of me and left me outside in the sunlight. I lay senseless for three hours, then they took me home. My belly began to swell. It got bigger day by day. Three years later I gave birth to this baby elephant. It was alive for one month. Then the midwife, urged on by the prefect, killed my elephant son. I demand justice.'

When she made this plea all the people of Turhal and Eynebazar and Kazova testified that it was so. Murtaza Pasha clapped the seventy individuals in chains and, keeping them confined for twenty days, got 20,000 *guruş* out of them. He also preserved the baby elephant in salt, planning to send it to the Felicitous Threshold (i.e. Istanbul).

These events occurred as I witnessed them, by divine mystery. *God is capable of everything* (2:20). The Free-choosing Actor wrought His eternal will in such a way that the elephant swallowed that virgin. She became pregnant by remaining in its belly for three hours, and a baby elephant was born. *God does what He wills by His power and judges what He wishes by His might.* This is clear proof of the wisdom of the Koranic verse: *For His are the creation and the command; blessed be God, Lord of the Worlds* (7:54).

5. Armenian

Language of the Armenians, called Soul of Yarmeni, an Ancient Community

This land of Sivas is an ancient city that has been in the hands of the Armenians ever since the time of its builder, Amalek. They trace their descent back to Esau, son of the prophet Isaac. They were a people of giants (or tyrants). According to their own claim, it was Amalek who created the Armenian language, which is spoken in its most elegant and refined form in the city of Sivas.

They belong to the Jacobite religious community. Since they believe in the Messiah, they are all Christians and followers of the Gospel. Furthermore, they are divided into seven sects and speak seven dialects. But being Christians, they all act according to the Gospel and recite the Gospel.

The Armenians of the Arab lands are called Jacobites, all of whom – in Damascus, Aleppo and Iraq – speak the Jacobite dialect and their false and unorthodox rituals are of a different sort; the Jacobite dialect is recorded in its place. The dialect of the Mighdisi people is a different dialect, of which some words and phrases are close to Persian; it is the most elegant of their dialects. The dialect of (—) is close to the language of the Kurds. The dialect of (—) is close to Arabic. The dialect of (—) is close to Georgian; these are Anushirvanis. The dialect of (—) does not resemble any other language; they are the Gypsies of the Armenians.

But they all follow the Gospel and belong to the Christian religious community. Only their false doctrines are not like those of the Greeks. The Armenians eat oily foods on the eve of the Christian Festival of the Egg (Easter), while the Greeks eat oily foods on the following morning, according to their false fast.

The world traveller and boon-companion of mankind greatly requires to know some of this Armenian language. Therefore this small amount has been recorded here so that he will know enough to get sustenance in the stages of his journey and in the villages and towns, and so that he will be on good terms with everyone he meets.

First are the numbers for counting in Armenian, which differ in the seven dialects: *meg* 1 *erguk* 2 *erek* 3 *çors* 4 *hink* 5 *veç* 6 *yot* 7 *ut* 8 *ını* 9 *das* 10 *meg das* 11 *erguk das* 12; *asvas* God *haç* bread *çur* water *mis* meat *gavoh* grapes *çamic* raisins *eku* Come! *kına* Go! *nıste* Sit! *el* Get up! *kını* Sleep! *hıncor* apple *zu kına per kari* Hey, go bring barley *çıka* There isn't any *kına pındırdı* Go look for some *yur kıdınam* Where shall I find some? *lına kıdını zu gınikıd kunem* Go get some or I'll fuck your wife *zu kına* Hey, come *kurtank bostanı kini hmenk* Come let's go to the garden and drink wine *ah imhokiz dıga* O my dear boy *ahbar eku inç kuzes imhokiz* Brother, come, what do you want my dear? *bahadır hist kezi kısirem* My hero, I love you very much *yes iz kezi kısirem* I love you too *eku ertank mer dunı* Come let's go to our house together *bak mı dur inc bake ah dıga* Give me a kiss O my dear boy *vagı kıkum tun kini* ... I'll come tomorrow, you get wine right now *ez nıstenk hımenk* Let's sit and drink *bahadur inc kıgına ez kişer kıgına eku kınik* My hero, whatever happens will happen tonight, come let's go to bed.

6. The cats of Divriği

Among the Turks and Arabs and Persians there is no cat more coy and cuddly or more trained to the hunt than this Divriği cat. True, the cats of Al Wahat (the oases in the Western Desert) in Egypt and those of Trabzon and Sinop are also famous. But this Divriği cat is fat and sturdy, with a shiny coat like sable fur, and comes in a thousand colours.

Indeed these cats are brought as gifts from Turkey to Persia, in particular to the city of Ardabil where they are sold at auction by cat-brokers who put them in cages on their heads and parade them around the royal market and the bedestan crying 'One *tuman*, two *tuman*s of *akçe*!' The Divriği cat goes for a great price, especially if it is spayed. Because cats in Ardabil have short lives, and so the mice of that city are notorious. The Persians, to be sure, have round trim beards, but their moustaches are all mouse-eaten, and that is why Divriği cats are so expensive.

Cry of the Ardabil cat-brokers:

> You who seek a feline,
> A cat to hunt your mice:
> To rats it makes a beeline,
> But otherwise it's nice;
> An enemy to rodents,
> And yet it's not a thief;
> A pet to share your grief.

This is their patter, sung in the *beyati* mode, as they peddle the Divriği cats in cages perched on their heads. Because in Ardabil the mice chew up the people's clothing – their woolen cloaks, for example – and so this city has an auction for *hirre*, i.e. *gürbe*, i.e. *kuta*, i.e. *sennure*, i.e. *merrabe*, i.e. *maçı* and *pistan* and *mistan* – i.e. cats.

That is how famous Divriği cats are. But some of the *kadis* of Divriği have gone bankrupt because of these cats and so bear a grudge against them. Every year forty or fifty cats are secretly killed and their skins tanned and made into furs to be worn in the winter. They are very like the squirrel furs of Muscovy, and the cats with red coats are no different from the *cıkava* furs of Azov.

7. Witchcraft in a Bulgarian village

Adventure of Evliya the humble. In that mountainous Balkan region my servants and I were guests in the house of a certain infidel, and I was comfortably settled in a corner near the fire. Suddenly an old woman entered. She was very ugly, with her hair going in all directions, and was in a rage. She sat herself next to the fire and let out a stream of expletives in her peculiar dialect. From what I could understand, the servants outside had somewhat mistreated her. When I went out to scold them, they denied it. Then seven young children came in, male and female, and gathered about her, jabbering away in Bulgarian. They did not leave any place for me near the fire, so I observed the strange scene from a little distance (before falling asleep).

Around midnight I was awakened by some footsteps. What should I see? The old woman came inside, took a handful of ashes from the fireplace, and rubbed them onto her vagina. Then she recited a spell over the ashes left in her hand and scattered them over the seven little boys and girls who were lying naked next to the fireplace. At once all seven turned into plump chickens and started to go 'cheep cheep'. She scattered the rest of the ashes over her own head and in an instant was transformed into a big broody hen going 'gurk gurk'. She marched out the door with the seven chicks right behind.

'Hey, boy!' I shouted out, in a fright. My slaveboys awoke and came over, only to see that my nose was bleeding profusely. 'What's going on?' I cried. 'Go outside and see what that racket is.' They rushed outside and saw that witch-hen and her brood of chickens marching about among our horses, which had got loose and were tearing at each other. This seemed unusual, since horses normally like chickens, and they also like pigs, and they are never affected by scrofula or red mite (when those animals are present), and that is why you never see farriers' shops without chickens, or horse-driven mills without pigs, or wealthy people's houses without Jews. But this time the horses were just tearing at each other, so some peasant infidels from the village had to come and tie them down. The bewitched hen and chickens went off. One of my slaveboys, who followed them, reported what happened next, 'One infidel took out his penis and showered the chickens with a rain of piss. At once all eight of them turned back into their human form. The one who had urinated over them gave the old hag and the children a good beating and took them away. We followed them into a house, which turned out to be their church. He gave the woman over to a priest, and the priest anathematised her.'

My slaveboys swore that this account was true; and Antabi Müezzin Mehmed Efendi's servants and my chief canteen-man's servants also bore witness that they had seen human beings turn into chickens.

Whether out of fright, or because my blood was so excited, my nosebleed kept up all that night and only stopped toward dawn. In the morning I questioned my muezzin's servants and also Mataracı Mehmed Agha's servants. They swore that when the infidel pissed over the chickens they turned human, and they offered to bring the very man who did it. When the infidel was brought and I questioned him, he laughed and said: 'My lord, that woman is a different breed. She used to turn into a witch once a year on a winter's night, but this year she turned into a hen. She doesn't harm anyone.' He went away.

Such was the adventure that this humble one, full of fault, experienced in the above-mentioned village of Çalık-kavak. It really unnerved me.

8. Sofia

Description of the pure hot springs in the city of Sofia. In this country hot springs are called *bana*, in Persia *germab*, in Arabia *humma*, in Türkistan (i.e. Turkey) *ılıca*, in Yörükistan (i.e., among the Yörüks or Balkan nomads) *kaplıca*, among the Tatar *ılışı*, in Kürdistan *çermik*, in Serbian *köstence*, among the Türkman *ılığın*.

Here in Sofia there are five such hot springs. The first is the women's bath – beneficial to women but not to men. If a man enters this bath he loses his hair and beard and is turned into a shiny-pated boy or a *cevellaki* dervish (i.e., one who shaves off all facial hair). But if a woman enters she loses all her body hair, including pubic hair, and the flesh around her vagina becomes as soft and smooth as her earlobes.

The second is reserved for Jewish and Christian women.

The third is reserved for Greeks, Latins, Bulgars and Armenians; other Christians are not permitted.

The fourth is only for Rabbinic Jews; all other religious communities are loath to enter it.

Each of these four baths has its own beneficial properties. But they are not imposing stone buildings. Also, the overflow from their pools forms streams that flow through the tanners' quarters and are used for tanning.

The fifth one, the great hot spring, is in the middle of the city. It has a large domed dressing room – spacious enough for 1,000 men – and, in the middle, a pool and jetting fountain. Then one enters another domed space, so large you can hardly recognise someone on the other side. It has six vaults around the periphery, each with a Hanafi basin and water flowing from a spout in a stream as thick as your arm.

And there are two private chambers. One – called the White Chamber because it is paved with shining white marble – has a basin with the picture of a frog, as if to say, 'You are human beings, don't stay in the water too much like a frog.' The other is called the Black Chamber, and indeed it is dark.

There is also a basin on the left side of the great pool called the Stopping Basin (*Diner Kurna*). If you stick your finger in a hole that is in the opposite wall, or just blow on the hole, the water stops flowing from the spout. Remove your finger, or stop blowing, and the water starts to flow again. It is a strange spectacle.

In the middle of this domed space is a large pool, ten-by-ten (cubits) in dimension and as deep as a man's height, full to the brim with hot water. Six marble steps lead down to it on all sides, and fresh water flows into it from marble heads of dragons and lions. But the water is very hot. Lovers dally freely with their sweethearts in this pool. The bathers swim about like herons, leap and tumble, join hands and dance like dervishes or turn and croak like a flock of cranes. Or they huddle in a circle with some standing on others' shoulders and turn in a circle with a great hue and cry.

I call this pool Lovers' Lair because everyone here embraces his darling boy uninhibitedly and they can go off in a corner to dally undisturbed. It is such a spacious pool. Also there are numerous small basins in the changing-room where individuals may wash their garments. Others, meanwhile, are getting rubdowns with bath-gloves and soap. This gets them very clean, though some who don't know the rules of ritual purity soil themselves (by ejaculating). It is altogether a marvellous scene, verging on mayhem.

In this bath there is no distinction between rich and poor. As long as you have a bath-cloth you can get out without giving the bath-keeper a single *akçe*. If you want him to guard your clothes, it costs a penny. This is worth it, since there is a mixed multitude of unsavoury individuals who come and go. If you don't have a bath-cloth you can rent one from the bath-keeper and also get rubbed down with bath-gloves and soap for two *akçe*.

During the long winter nights seventy or eighty of the town notables rent this *bana* for a private party. The space is illuminated with hundreds of lamps and candles. They party until dawn while the city sleeps, having intimate conversations, enjoying delicious foods and musk-flavoured fruit drinks and the scents of rose-water and aloes-wood and ambergris.

The more sophisticated residents of Sofia make it a practice to fill clean jars with water from this bath and drink it when it cools, as it betokens the Water of Life. Generally the water of hot baths smells of sulfur and arsenic and tarnishes silver. This water, on the contrary, has no smell at all, nor does it tarnish metal but rather gives a shine to both silver and gold.

Bathing in this water is beneficial for leprosy, syphilis, scabies, jaundice, palpitations and baldness. Drinking it is good for diarrhoea, pleurisy and haemorrhoids. Entering it several times is a cure for fever. But there are certain rules. Sofia gets very cold in winter, so you must not stay too long in the hot bath, nor stay too long in the changing-room when you get out, for that could prove fatal. The first rule is to put on a shirt and trousers as soon as you exit the bath.

One delightful custom in Sofia is that when anyone dies, male or female, the water-carriers of his or her neighbourhood attach honey-barrels called *çılır* to poles and fill them up with hot water from the *bana* which is used to wash the body, and then it is buried, all at the expense of a pious foundation. On this occasion the soap combined with the hot water from the natural spring causes so much foam that it is like the water of Lake Van.

Another, less savoury, innovation has to do with the womenfolk of Sofia. They are covered and modest ladies who never go out into the marketplace unless there is a dire necessity. There are, however, several thousand loose women who do go out every night to 'wash themselves' or 'do their laundry'. They put their clothes in a bundle, get permission from

Sofia 105

their so-called husbands, take lanterns and go to the *bana* or to some other house and 'wash their soiled clothes'. It is a disgraceful practice, peculiar to this city. Our lord Melek Ahmed Pasha wanted to put an end to the practice but the notables of the province would not let him. So every night women of this sort gad about in groups until morning.

Another class of females are the very pretty Bulgar Voynuk girls employed here as household servants. Every house of the notables has five or ten, or at least one or two of these girls, who are called *orfana*. Elsewhere this term refers to prostitutes, but in Sofia it just means servant girl. You see these girls, with their faces uncovered, in the houses and in the markets, performing services very capably.

In short, these are the customs of old in this city. But going to the *bana* at night is most improper.

It was the martyr at Kosovo, Gazi Hudavendigar, who founded these hot springs. Due to his benevolence everyone here goes to the *bana* for free, which accounts for there being only two public baths in Sofia. The notables of the province do assert, however, that there are seventy private baths in the palatial residences of the city.

[...]

Description of the picnic grounds and great summer pasture of Mt Vitosh. The brethren of purity should know that of all the summer pastures and lofty mountains in the Anatolian region, the greatest is Mt Alburz around the countries of Dagestan and Persia and Georgia and Circassia and towering over the Caspian Sea. Next is the great summer pasture of Bingöl overlooking the Erzurum region, as we recounted above in Volume 2[36] when discussing the summer pastures of Anatolia that number (—) in toto.

But now in Rumelia we observed this lofty mountain pasture of Vitosh, one day's journey from Sofia, where I came to spend the month of July with seventy companions. Having climbed to the most flourishing site we set up our tents and busied ourselves with picnics, parties and pleasure excursions.

---

36 The reference to 'Volume 2' (*cild-i sanimiz*) must be to an earlier redaction of the *Book of Travels*. As we have the text now, the listing of Anatolian summer pastures is found in Vol. 3, fol. 89a, that of Rumelian summer pastures in Vol. 3, fol. 18b. Cf. Dankoff 2004, 55.

The peak of this mountain is the summer-pasture for Salonica, Kavala, Serrez, Zihne – in short, all the cities of Rumelia. Flocks of sheep numbering in the hundreds of thousands spend seven months of the year here. From these sheep we got over 100 lambs to make into kebabs.

And every day we feasted on trout that we caught in the lakes and cooked in butter. There are fish here weighing six or seven *okkas* the likes of which are not found in the summer pastures of Bin Göl, Göksün or Ramazanoğlu. There are ruby-coloured gold-sprinkled musk-scented trout, as well as carp and fish known as *şibe* and *dilçe* that are found here and nowhere else.

Another speciality of the region are the sour cherries growing on a kind of squat shrub. There are also strawberries and, in the lower valleys, chestnuts, wild pears, sour plums, medlars and rowanberries. Day and night we drank sour-cherry juice cooled with pieces of ice like crystal.

According to the local authorities there are on this mountain 3,000 sheepfolds called *eğrek* or *saya*. The shepherds – Serbian and Bulgarian and Voynuk infidels – live in long huts that resemble caravel galleons and their daughters are Bulgarian mountain beauties. There are lovely boys as well, but the plump and ruddy girls of the Yörüks and Çıtaks and the other country bumpkins win the beauty-prize of the Franks.

We stayed for five days in the Yörük tents savouring their milk and cream and yoghurt, curds and whey and buttermilk and beestings and cheeses, and their butter-baked breads and pastries, and other such light-fare specialities of these summer pastures, and fattening ourselves on roasted lamb.

In sum, we spent a total of forty days among the Yörüks and Çıtaks, going from tent to tent and savouring the regional delights. Eventually we got a Yörük guide to take us back to Sofia. He told us about a fountain nearby, springing from the rocks, called the Fountain of Luck (*Tali' Çeşmesi*). 'Go try your luck there,' he said, and took us through that valley. As we were making our way on that difficult road, Refi'izade Şefi'i Çelebi, who was from Sofia, spoke up, 'Do you know what the Fountain of Luck is that this old Yörük is taking us to?'

'No,' we replied, 'we've never heard of it.'

Description of the Fountain of Luck, the Spring of Plato the Divine
'Listen, O brethren of loyalty,' said Şefi'i Çelebi. 'It is a fountain of pure water that refuses to flow for any man who has ever committed murder, or any man who was sodomised in his youth. But any man who is clean-skirted can drink freely from that Water of Life. If you can't get water from

it you will be shamed and blamed among your peers. Is it a good idea to go to such a fountain?'

Some of our companions started teasing him, 'Şefi'i Çelebi has been a homeless vagrant for the past forty days. He's anxious to get home and make up the Friday night prayers he missed and dally with the beauties of Sofia.'

'Let the mare that mothered you feel shame,' said Şefi'i Çelebi, stung by their taunts. 'Whoever doesn't go is an old woman. Onward, father Yörük, show us the way!'

So we proceeded toward the Fountain of Luck. But most of our companions began to complain that the road was hard or the road was long. Finally, having arrived at that Water of Life, we dismounted in a shady grove and set up camp.

Adventure of the brethren of purity. Before us was a sheer cliff rising to the sky and a pure stream flowing out of the rocks. The group urged one another on, and withdrew to this corner and that to consult, but no one would dare approach to drink. Finally Şefi'i Çelebi said: 'God be praised, I know that I have been innocent and pure in all respects, from the time I was a child until now.' So he came forward, uttering a *besmele*, fearlessly drew some pure water from the spring, and drank it.

Next to dare was Müezzinzade Ali Çelebi. Taking up his wooden begging-bowl, he reached out for the water, but suddenly the spring stopped flowing. Everyone made fun of him, crying, 'You're a catamite.' The poor fellow turned pale and couldn't say a word.

Now the party started quarrelling, some claiming that they had drunk but the others could not, some saying 'Let's drink,' others saying 'Let's go.' Eventually they all swore not to reveal what happened, and began to draw water one by one.

When Şefi'i Çelebi's brother approached, as soon as he stretched out his hand the water stopped flowing, and again the others started to make fun.

Then there was Hımhım Mehmed Çelebi, who was Şeyhzade Çelebi's boy: the spring stopped while he was still ten paces from it. They all burst out laughing: 'This one must have been sodomised quite a lot!'

Resmi Çelebi uttered a *besmele* and drank without hesitation.

When Muhzırzade approached, the water stopped but then began flowing again and he drank – a sequence that the others in the party did not know how to interpret.

Now one of my slaveboys came forward and fearlessly took a drink. Immediately all the party fixed their attention on me and insisted that I too should drink.

'O friends and lovers,' said I, 'you know that I am a world-traveller, free and easy and friends with all. Please don't force me to do this.' The more I objected, the more they laughed and kept pressing me, 'You have seen how it stands with us, now let's see about you!'

Of course, I was aware of my own situation; still, I couldn't shake off a nagging fear. Seeking spiritual succour from my great ancestor, Turk of the Turks, the saintly Hoca Ahmed Yesevi, I took up the begging-bowl with a *besmele*, drew some pure water from the spring, and drank it. My friends all rejoiced.

Now Sarrac Mehmed Çelebi drew water and drank, thanking God.

Then it was the turn of the old Yörük who had brought us to the spring. He expressed misgivings, saying, 'Children, my luck is bad, the water might stop' – and indeed, he was unable to draw from the spring.

'Hey old man,' they joked, 'you're a catamite too!'

The upshot was that seventy individuals tried to drink from the spring at this bare rock, and only five were able to do so. It is a strange and wondrous spring, under a talismanic spell. No one could fathom the mystery of this fountain.

The next day we entered Sofia, having been absent forty-one days.

[...]

A marvellous and noteworthy spectacle. Upon the lead-tiled roof of the ancient Friday mosque named the Çelebi Mosque, which is in front of the Pasha's palace in the city of Sofia, a pair of storks made their nest and deposited their eggs.

One day a notorious rogue named Debbağoğlu ('son of the tanner') climbed up to the roof of this mosque, removed the stork eggs, and put crow eggs in their place. Eventually these hatched and two crow chicks emerged, according to the verse:

> If you put crow eggs beneath a blessed peacock
> What hatches are crows, despite a thousand schemes.

When the father stork returned from his foraging, what should he see but two black crow chicks squirming in the nest. He gave the mother stork a sound drubbing with his beak, then flew up and began to cry and wail as he soared about over the entire city of Sofia. Thousands of storks assembled and flew straight to Çelebi Mosque, landing on the domes and covering the roof so that you could not see a single lead tile.

All these birds came forward one by one to peer into the nest and take a look at the grafted crow chicks. They raised such a hue and cry on the mosque dome that it frightened the wits of the passers-by. None of the birds ate or drank that day; they just kept up their crowing and cawing. So there was no peace of mind in Sofia on that day. All the people stopped what they were doing to watch the storks.

Finally the crowd of storks killed the crow chicks. Then they rushed upon the mother stork, accusing her of adultery, and cut her to pieces with their beaks. After some further stork talk they gave the father stork another mother stork as his mate, and all flew back to their own nests.

The townsfolk marvelled at this incident, and our lord Melek Ahmed Pasha too was quite astounded. 'Have that scoundrel who exchanged the eggs brought here immediately,' he said, 'we'll punish him.' But then he decided to bide his time saying, 'Be patient, God almighty will punish that rogue as he deserves.'

A few days later – by God's wisdom – that notorious outlaw who had exchanged the stork eggs – he was a Segban servant named Uşkurta Debbağoğlu – was tipsy and went to visit his lady friend. Just as he was shuttling on her loom like a master weaver, the lady's husband suddenly entered and saw that the workshop was in full swing. This householder bared his sword in a fit of zealous rage, rushed upon his wife and on Uşkurta Debbağoğlu, and led them outside wounded and manacled, crying, 'See, O people of Muhammad!'

When they reached Bana-başı, the gathering place of Sofia's mystics and lovers, some Zadra janissaries were squabbling over a woman, and it turned out that this woman was the original whore of that very Debbağoğlu who had exchanged the stork eggs. So now Debbağoğlu freed himself from his captor and began trying to rescue his whore. In the midst of the struggle the janissaries bared their swords and cut up both Debbağoğlu and his whore, and left them in Bana-başı.

A band of youthful tanners from the town brought Debbağoğlu's corpse to the Pasha's palace, crying, 'The janissaries killed our Çelebi, here is his corpse!' Since the Pasha was rather displeased at this plea for justice, the tanner youths put Debbağoğlu's corpse under the eaves of the mosque in front of the Pasha's palace.

So you see the divine plan! Because this Debbağoğlu took the stork eggs and put crow eggs in their place, when the crows hatched, all the birds cut the female stork to pieces and dropped them from the eaves of the mosque. A few days later – according to the verse,

> Avenger is one name of the Eternal One

– God had him cut to pieces, as well as his whore in place of the female stork, and had them leave Debbağoğlu's corpse in the very place where the storks had left the stork. For God is just.

When the Pasha heard of this he said, 'I ought to have punished him, but I cast him to God, and a few days later God punished him. He got what he deserved. Have that damned fellow's corpse removed from the courtyard of the mosque, shrouded in a mat, and buried.' So the tanner brigands took away the hide of the tanner's son and brought it to Banabaşı to be tanned. It was quite a spectacle. Many moral lessons can be drawn from this event.

After the Debbağoğlu affair our lord the Pasha banished all the prostitutes of Sofia from the town. A few of them, by leave of the Sharia and for the reform of the world, were strung up like chandeliers to adorn the town at the street corners in the silk market. The notables of the province were grateful that their town was now tranquil and free of prostitutes. But the rogues and the brigands, for the sake of their carnal pleasures, bruited it about that the town's resources had grown scarce, and there would now be famine and dearth, even plague.

And indeed – by God's wisdom – the plague did begin to spread in the city from day to day. By the end of a month, 500 people, men and women, were dying from it daily. It reached the point that thousands of people fled from Sofia to other regions. Seventy-seven of our fortunate lord's renowned aghas, among his highest officers, died. The Pasha too had to take to his bed from illness. His head swelled up like an Adana squash, his tongue was scorched and turned black, his ears oozed with pus. More than once he was on the verge of death.

(Melek Pasha recovers from his illness, but is dismissed from office.)

VOLUME FOUR

Safavid Borderlands

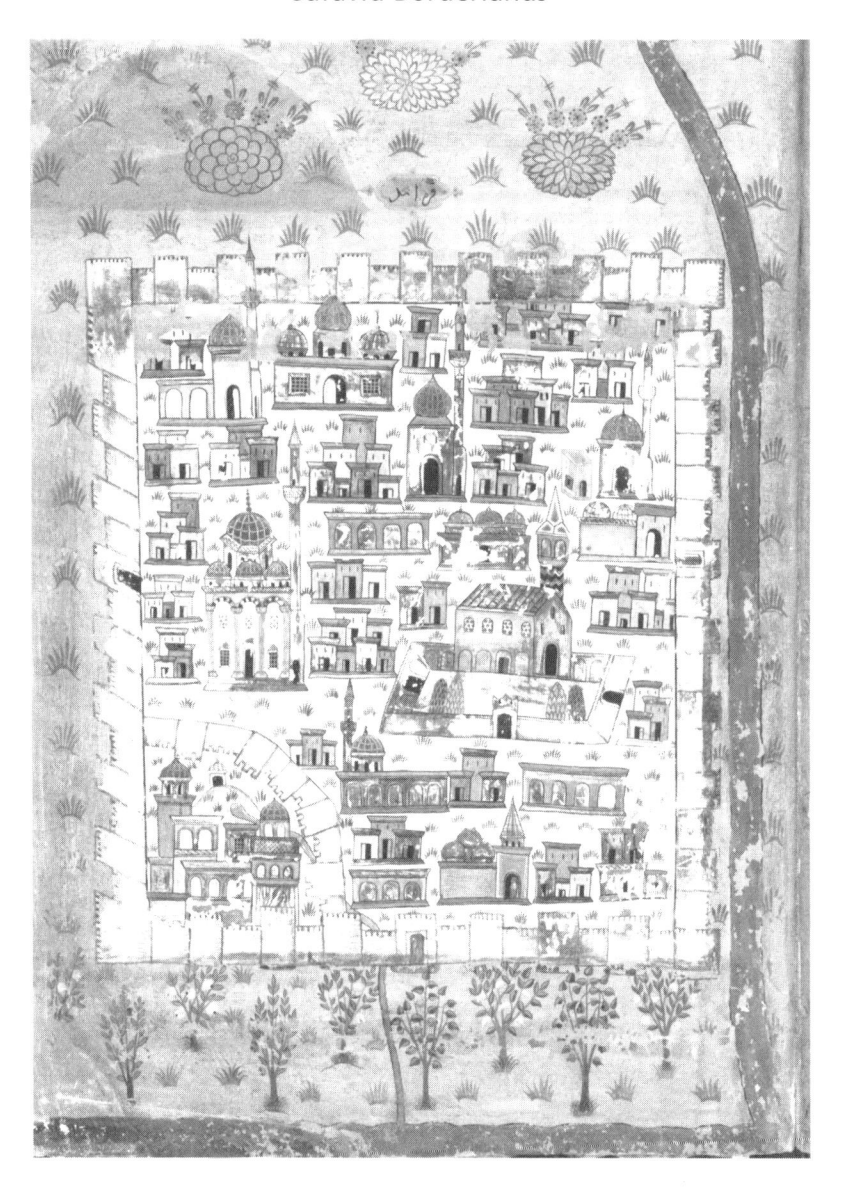

IN MARCH 1655, Evliya sets out to join Melek Ahmed Pasha at his new post in Van. On the way he stops in Diyarbekir and then Bitlis, where he and Melek Pasha are entertained by the flamboyant, quasi independent Kurdish ruler, Abdal Khan. (With regard to the acrobatic performances, cf. Volume 10, selection 11 for similar entertainments in Egypt.) Evliya's travels in the region include a visit to the ancient city of Ahlat.

Once in Van, Melek Pasha finds an excuse to mount an expedition against Abdal Khan and to reassert Ottoman authority in Bitlis. Evliya is once again sent on an embassy to Tabriz. While in Urmia he deals with the slanderous rumours about 'extinguishing the candle'. After some jaunts in Azerbaijan and Western Persia, he takes the opportunity to travel to Baghdad and makes an extensive tour of Iraq and Kurdistan.

1. Diyarbekir

On the royal covered bazaar. Altogether 2,008 shops constitute the well-built area of the bazaar, the Market of Beauty. Firstly, there is the bazaar of Hasan Pasha, then the army bazaar, the druggists' bazaar – the brains of those who pass through it are scented with perfumes – and the goldsmiths' bazaar. All these bazaars are constructed with vaults of fitted stone, huge as the Vault of Chosroes.

Further, there is the market of the blacksmiths, the bazaar of the locksmiths, the bazaar of jewellers and goldsmiths, the bazaar of the boot makers, the saddlers' bazaar, the bazaar of the silk manufacturers and the bazaar of the traders in cloth. In short, there are shops of 366 different trades and crafts. But the market hall in the army bazaar is a well-kept, beautifully ornamented solid building of fitted stone, with iron gates on both ends. It is crowded with the richest merchants, and one finds here valuable goods of the highest quality and the most expensive sorts of jewellery from all countries.

Swords, scimitars, maces, axes, arrows, daggers, spear-blades and arrowheads such as those forged hereabouts are made nowhere else, except perhaps by the weapon-smiths of Isfahan.

The Armenian blacksmiths, while beating their hammers and pumping their bellows, sing songs with their fine voices – *kâr* and *nakş*, *zecel* and *tasnifat* – thus earning their profit (*kâr*) while singing songs (*kâr*). And their servants strike their hammers in twenty-four different rhythmic patterns – beating a *tırtaka tırtak tırtırtak* in the double two-one (*çifte dü-yek*) meter – and pump their bellows in the *sofiyane* meter.

When the cotton carders beat the cotton, the strings of their carding bows produce sounds in various musical modes, some in *segah*, others in *dügah* or *yekgah*. The meter is 'bow's hoop' (*yay çemberi*) or else 'heavy' (*sakil*) which is: *tırtaka tırtakataka tırtaka tırtırtak tırtak tak tırtaka tırtırtak tırtak tırtırtak*.

The kettle makers, working in a group of twelve, hammer the red copper on their anvils in the *sofiyane* metre of *tañ taña tañ taña*. Even musical experts are struck with amazement when they hear the *hüseyni* melody produced by their hammers and observe their metrical motion.

Such is the degree to which the artisans here are perfect masters in every respect. Unrivalled masters as well are the jewellers and goldsmiths making silver vessels and golden headgear and bejewelled vessels of pure gold. And the embroiderers are as accomplished in the art of multi-coloured designs as the painters Mani, Bihzad and Arzhang.

[...]

Description of the excursion spots of Diyarbekir the unparalleled. We have described all such far-famed parks that we have seen, as the Meram garden of Konya in the country of Rum-ı Yunan, the Istanaz garden in Antalya, the Fayyum garden in Egypt, the Manjik garden in Damascus, the Darende garden in Darende, the Aspuzu garden in Malatya. But Diyarbekir's basil garden and regularly laid out vegetable plots on the bank of the Tigris have no equal in Turkey or Arabia or Persia.

In spring, when the flood period of the Tigris has passed and its limpid waters begin to flow again in a stable current, all Diyarbekir's inhabitants, rich and poor alike, move with their entire families to the bank of the Tigris. They set up camp with their tents and pavilions along this wide water, on plots they have inherited from their fathers and ancestors, and cultivate their gardens with melons, watermelons, various vegetables and flowers.

They cultivate here a special type of basil that everyone plants along the borders of his plot. In a month's time it becomes thick as a forest and tall as a spear, impenetrable to the glance. All their humble houses along the bank of the Tigris have their doors and walls and roofs made out of basil. The basil stems remain rooted in the earth and the leaves remain green and continue to grow finding moisture in the soil. It is impossible to see from one house to the next through these walls of basil. The huts are so overgrown that the brains of the men and women living in them are perfumed night and day with the fragrance of basil and the other flowers in these gardens, such as roses, Judas trees and hyacinth. The women's quarters of each garden pavilion are also such pleasure-huts of basil. And each hut has a pool and fountain drawing water from the Tigris which is diverted into numerous tributaries and canals that flow among the gardens.

Here on the bank of the Tigris there is a merry tumult day and night, with music and song, for a full seven months. Everyone parties in his hut with his lovers and friends, enjoying the delights of Husayn Bayqara. The artisans, however, are not idle during this garden season. Thousands go to the city (in the morning) and pursue their occupations, and return to their gardens in the late afternoon where food and drink are stored and they can indulge in pleasure and enjoyment.

The melons that grow in these gardens have no match, except perhaps the melons of Bohtan in the province of Van. The Diyarbekir melons are huge, very juicy and sweet, and with a delicious aroma as of musk and ambergris. If you eat one of them the fragrance of melon will not leave your brain for an entire week. There is even a tradition among the ulema of Kurdistan and the scholars of Soranistan that Abu Bakr the Faithful exuded a fragrance like that of melon; and the ulema of Diyarbekir claim that this can only be their Tigris melon. The aroma is such that the brain of one who eats it or just smells it is imbued with ambergris.

Some of these melons attain a weight of 40 or 50 *okkas*. They all have a green colour. People take them as presents to various countries, as far as they remain fresh. Some people use them to prepare *zerde* (a yellow-rice dish), flavoured with cinnamon and cloves, according to the recipe of the Caliph Mu'awiya. Not even Athens honey could make a *zerde* so fragrant as this dish is with Diyarbekir melons.

The watermelons, however, do not deserve much praise. The basil on the other hand grows into such huge trees that in seven or eight months they can be used as tent-poles or stakes, and when one burns them in a fire they smell like Chinese hyacinth.

In short, the people of Diyarbekir are the envy of the world for the delights they enjoy for seven or eight months of the year along the bank of the Tigris; when their nights are like the Night of Power, and their days like the holiday of the Festival of Sacrifice; holding concerts worthy of Husayn Bayqara; and thinking to snatch a bit of pleasure from this transitory world.

Every night the bank of the Tigris is illuminated with oil lamps, lanterns, wind tapers and torches. They place boards on the water with oil lamps and wax candles arranged in a thousand artful ways so the lights float from one end to the other and dark night is turned into brilliant day. In each hut are singers and musicians, clowns and minstrels and story-reciters, players of various instruments.[37] They perform until the break of dawn like the musicians at Bayqara's court. Then the muezzins with their sorrowful

---

37 Mentioned in the text are: lute, four- and six-string guitar, *berbut* (a kind of lute), *kanun* (zither), *çeng* (harp), *rebab* (three-stringed violin), *musikar* (panpipe), *tambur* (pandore lute), *santur* (zither), *nefir* (trumpet), *balaban* (shawm), *ney* (reed flute), and *dehenk* (?).

voices chant the glories of God, and the mystics and lovers recite their litanies. Since the people of Diyarbekir all belong to the Hacegan (Naqshbandi) and Gülsheni orders, they do not miss the ecstatic joy and delight of the ritual chantings.

In sum, as such busy intercourse and buzzing conversation go on in this garden of Iram, the people continually pray for the welfare of the imperial state. May God elevate their station.

2. Bitlis

The meeting of Melek Ahmed Pasha and the noble Khan for the purpose of the bounteous feast. At this juncture, in those rough steep regions, the Khan of Bitlis, Abdal Khan, appeared with his soldiery. Dismounting, he rushed over and was about to kiss the Pasha's stirrup when the Pasha too dismounted from his zephyr-swift steed, and the two of them embraced and kissed. After much conversation, the Khan said: 'Please mount and go a little ahead where you will have a breakfast.' The Pasha mounted and proceeded with great ceremony, playing his eightfold band, until we came upon a meadow in a valley, a veritable tulip garden of brightly coloured tents: *derim obas* in Persian, Turkman, and Kurdish style; Persian *ten-getirs*; and Ottoman baldachins. The Pasha came to that delightful spot and alighted at the Khan's pavilion.

At once an enormous spread was served, with golden and silver dishes and porcelain and onyx and celadon bowls. Such a bounteous and delicious banquet no latter-day sultan has given since the time of Jamshid and Iskandar and Kay Kavus. As God is my witness, there was enough to feed the 3,000 soldiers of our lord Melek Ahmed Pasha, and the 3,000 retainers of the Khan, as well as the town notables who had come out to meet us, and the swarms of Kurdish vermin in the surrounding districts. Aside from this, thousands of vessels of food of every sort were spilled out on the grass. When it was time to leave, the noble Khan bowed before the Pasha, as did his twelve sons and the seventy-seven tribal chieftains who were submissive to him.

'My lord,' said the Khan, 'please regard with favour and accept the seven pavilions where you have alighted; also the fifty silver dishes and hundred porcelain and celadon bowls, and all the carpets and vessels, plus four each of Circassian, Abkhazian, and Georgian slaveboys.' And he kissed his hand. The Pasha removed a sharp-pointed dagger from his own belt, one of

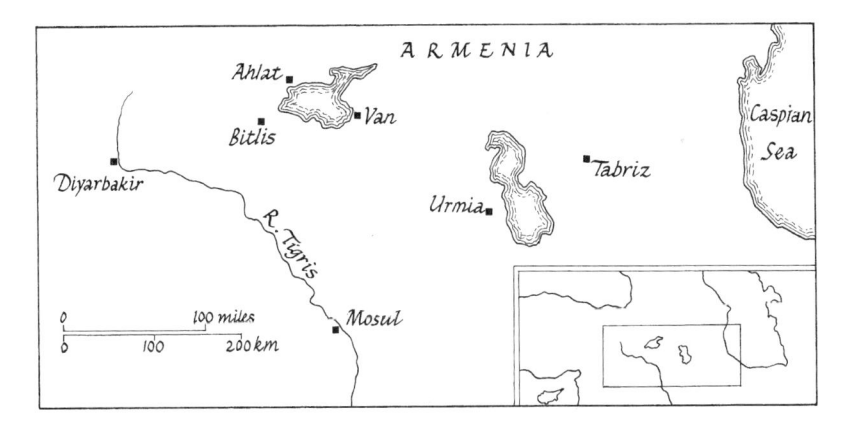

Sultan Murad's daggers, and with his own hands fastened it to the Khan's waist. He also gave a sable cloak to the Khan, three fur pieces to his children, and 170 gold-embroidered robes of honour with sashes to the Khan's attendants. Then mounting his fleet courser and playing his band, he proceeded over hill and dale toward the town of Bitlis.

Meanwhile all the Khan's attendants had gathered about someone and were proceeding amidst a great deal of laughter and joking. I went ahead, wondering what all the commotion and jesting were about.

A strange scene. There was a Kurd, of strange and wondrous aspect, hideously ugly, with a turban so tall it could serve as a sparrow's nest; a flaming beard— yellow, red, blue, green and white – reaching down to his belt; and mounted on an emaciated horse. In his hand he held a huge snake, and he was beating the poor *King and Beggar*[38] beast with it as with a whip. The horse put one foot forward, but seemed to have the other foot in the grave. Spittle ran down its mouth like a fountain, the eyes were completely lustreless, the legs were like sprigs of mint, the bones stuck out so they could be counted one by one. It tottered left and right like a drunken man. On each haunch hung two sacks of barley, but the poor beast had one foot in the grave. This merry fellow, meanwhile, kept striking the meagre animal's belly with his stirrup, or whipping it with the snake, hopping off

---

38 i.e. very emaciated. The reference is to an incident in the poem *Şah u Geda* by Yahya Bey (d. 1582): 'Geda next obtains a wretched old horse, and on it rides to Shah's house to visit him. On his arrival there the horse drops dead, and Geda bewails its death in a poem wherein he incidentally laments his own unrequited affection.' (Dankoff 1990, quoting Köhler).

and remounting, and doing all sorts of acrobatic tricks, so that the people roared with laughter.

One of the Khan's servants, named Kurban Ali, gave him a gold piece. 'Molla Mehmed, my dear fellow,' he said, 'let us see you put this stallion through its paces.'

'Hey my mystical friend,' said I, 'if you keep putting it through its paces, it will take its final pace to the Hereafter!' Suddenly he scrambled up the craggy rocks and flew past the Khan and the Pasha like lightning on that emaciated horse. All the Pasha's men were dumbstruck with amazement, but the Khan's soldiers merely laughed. Then, coming at full speed from the opposite direction, and spurring his horse from rock to rock, he passed through like thunder and re-entered the Khan's soldiery.

I rushed over to the fellow and looked at the horse's face and eyes to see if it was panting. Its eyes were still lustreless, but it was not panting, nor even standing still, but prancing about and chomping at the bit. Examining this emaciated beast more closely, I found no sign of its being either a stallion or a mare, or a gelding – just nothing! While I was praising God and marvelling at this mystery, the rider smiled and addressed me thus, 'Mister, why are you looking so much? Do you want to buy it? This is my horse, which has come down to me from my forefathers. Even if your Pasha wanted it, I would not give it to him. The whole world could not come up with its price.' He grew quite heated.

'Evliya Çelebi,' said the chief taster, Mustafa, 'what do you think of this emaciated horse? It was a log in a pile at the stokehold of the Khan's bath. The Khan refused to give this Molla a horse to ride in the parade, and warned him, saying, 'You will make a mockery of my procession in view of Melek Ahmed Pasha's procession, so do not join the parade!' The Molla got offended. He went straight to the stokehold and put a spell on that log, which turned into an emaciated horse, and he mounted it and performed the tricks you saw. But now the Khan is quite irritated. He is worried that your Pasha will get wind of the fact that this horse was produced through sorcery, and will think that the Khan has people who practice sorcery and alchemy and magic.'

I was at a loss. 'My dear chief taster,' I said, 'for the love of the Prophet, what do you say about this?'

'By the pure and noble spirit of Evhadehullah,'[39] he swore, 'it is this

---

39 The Abbasid ancestor of the Rozhiki Kurds, according to the Bitlis lore recorded by Evliya in this section.

way: that Molla is one of the holy Friends, a jokester and a trickster. He can mount a pole or a trough, a jar or a sheepskin, or else a log such as this, utter a spell, and ride on it wherever he wishes. And if he mounts a cat or a sheep or a dog or other animal, he can make it dance and can play jereed on it as though it were Ali's mount Duldul or a rose-bodied Arabian steed.'

'I don't believe it, I must get to the bottom of this mystery,' said I, and requested the taster to help me.

'Come with me,' he said. We followed Molla Mehmed at a distance and came to the Khan's Garden. The Molla entered the garden through the back gate and, supposing that no one else was around, went straight into the stokehold. I got off my horse and watched him with my three servants. He dismounted, put the snake that he was holding inside his trousers, and squatted down. Then he took a waistband from his trousers, fastened it round the emaciated horse's neck, and let out a tremendous shout. It turned somewhat dark, and my eyes dimmed. When I could see again, there was a log with branches and stems right in the middle of the stokehold.

'So,' said the chief taster, addressing the Molla, 'You have re-attached the courser to the stokehold.'

'That lousy so-called khan would not give me a horse,' he replied, 'and so I did this. By God, I should have mounted the court sweeper Bağdu Kafir, but the Ottoman procession came and I thought they would make fun of me, so I mounted this log.' He did not deny a thing.

'Who are these?' he asked, meaning myself. The chief taster had just made acquaintance. 'He is a *hafız* and the Pasha's boon companion,' he said. The Molla was very pleased, and we became friends. God willing, I will relate below many more of his marvellous skills.

Meanwhile our lord Melek Ahmed Pasha entered the town of Bitlis with a great procession and was greeted on every side by the populace coming out to meet him. He showered on them a huge amount of gold pieces and shiny silver coins. With such pomp and ceremony he came to the noble Khan's Garden, where he was put up as guest, and he ordered a ten-day halt.

[…]

We spent the ten-day halt in his palace with our lord the Pasha. Each day from dawn to dusk there was a constant stream of musicians and buffoons and acrobats, displaying their wares and receiving gifts from the Khan and the Pasha. Because of the Khan's reputation as patron of the arts and sciences, skilled men would come to him from every country, and if they were well-rounded and cultivated individuals, the Khan would give them gardened palaces and slavegirls and *timars* and dye works in order that he might keep them tied down in the valley of Bitlis and so acquire some of their skills. Thus the Khan became a second Jamshid, spending all his free time learning new skills. And thus the city of Bitlis was filled with skilled masters.

As for the master players on the shawm and the trumpet and the kettle drum and the cymbals in the Khan's band, their like is not to be found in the imperial workshop itself, let alone in that of a vizier. For he himself performs concerts and is knowledgeable in the various musical sciences. And he has masters in his band who perform *küll-i külliyat*, zencir in the twenty-four rhythmic cycles, *şükufezar*, and *peşrevs* in the saba mode and the zarb-i fetih rhythmic cycle. Each one is like Jamshid who invented the shawm. When they perform in the evening, or in the pre-dawn when no one is stirring, they delight the listener.

The Khan's pleasure garden. On the harem side of this garden palace there is a garden as long and broad as the range of a bow-shot. If the seas were ink and the trees were pens, and all the scribes gathered, they could not record a drop in the ocean or a mote in the sunlight of due description and praise of this garden. Suffice it to say that all the fruit-bearing trees are planted in rows, each one swaying with the zephyr breeze like beauties with girded loins. Aside from the fig, the sycamore, the banana, and the cypress, all varieties are present. In some nooks and crannies there are even lemon and orange saplings which are protected with felt coverings during the winter. There are also charming and lavish pleasure-domes, like so many castles of Khawarnaq, each one different in style from the others, and each the work of a master of a different land.

The pools and jets and fountains here are not to be found in Turkey. Each pool is surrounded by a mosaic floor of varicoloured marble, like Indian-style mother-of-pearl and marquetry inlay. Streams of water as thick as a man's neck flow into the pools from the mouths of various demons, lions, and dragons; then pour down into the reticulated garden beds. There is also water springing up from jets. In certain cases, forty or fifty streams jet out of a single hole and mingle together like a beauty's tresses. The marvellous thing is that they all issue from one mouth. Some of the pleasure-domes have suspended glass and crystal bowls, which give a melancholy sound when the water jets strike them, while the larger ones channel the water so that it cascades like rain. Some of the jets have a wheel suspended above, which turns when the jet stream strikes. Others have a hollow ball the size of a watermelon, which turns and bobs in the air. In short, the master craftsmen of every land have created such wonders that the tongue cannot express.

There are beds with thousands of flowers of various sorts, including rose, hyacinth, sweet basil, violet, judas tree, jonquil, *nebati* (?), camel's nose (*deve boynı*, a type of iris), camphor tree, peony, Roman musk (*müşk-i rumi*, a wildflower in the hyacinth family), carnation, syringa, lily, iris, narcissus, cyclamen, jasmine, tulip, and hollyhock. Each bed is laid out differently, and they intoxicate with the scent of jonquils and other blossoms. As for the varieties of fruit trees, there are saplings from as far away as Isfahan, Tabriz, and Nakhchivan. Even though this garden was constructed only recently, when Sultan Murad IV saw it during the Revan campaign, he was astounded.

The Khan's artificial lake. Behind the aforementioned garden on the northern side there was a flowing spring called Ayn-i Taklaban. The Khan dammed up the lower part of the stream and made a sea-like lagoon. The dam is like the Wall of Iskandar or the Wall of Magog, and myriad fishes swim in the lake. The Khan had caiques constructed and decked out, and he himself used to row alone, or else he would take his household out for excursions, thereby dissipating his longing for the sea.

One day, by God's wisdom, the women were not sitting properly in the caique and it capsized, leaving several slavegirls drowned. After that he gave up the sport, only occasionally going fishing. The lake is very deep. Once, when the flood waters were severe, one side of the dam broke and the rushing waters destroyed quite a few houses in the Taklaban quarter. When the Kurds cursed the Khan, wishing that he too would be ruined, he reconstructed all of their houses.

The garden bath. A delightful bath goes off the treasury room of the above-mentioned Khan's palace, and gives onto a dressing-room. It has gardens on three sides, and the dressing-room has windows overlooking the gardens, all with bronze and iron grating like Fahri cutouts, also shutters of Arab-style carved (wood), which the khans of Persia sent from Tabriz as gifts. The shutter carvings are filled in with raw black ambergris, and as the zephyr breeze strikes them from without, the men within enjoy the fragrance.

All four walls of this dressing-room are covered with varicoloured porcelain tiles. And going all around the lofty dome and over the upper sills of the windows, in calligraphy written enchantingly on the tiles by the hand of Muhammad Riza of Tabriz, is Fuzuli's 'Bath Kaside'.[40] The couplets inscribed there are as follows:

[3 lines empty]

In the very centre of this dressing-room are fountains full of water shooting toward the dome from 300 places. Its floor is paved with Egyptian-style varicoloured marble. The jet in the centre of the pool strikes the glass bowl at the peak of the dome and then rains down. All the servants here are lovely Circassian, Abkhazian and Georgian pages, each outfitted with a jewelled belt worth 1,000 *guruş*, adorned with daggers and knives, and walking about on clogs with inlaid mother-of-pearl, like so many peacocks of paradise. They give the bathers silk waist-wrappers and clogs like their own, and serve them respectfully.

When one enters the bath from the dressing-room, one finds oneself in a large domed room called the tepidarium (*sovukluk*), but the water of the pools and fountains in the middle of this room is all hot, and the walls are all covered with varicoloured tiles. The floor here too is paved with marble mosaic 'China-rose' while the sturdy enamel dome is brightened by porcelain tiles and ornamented with numerous chandeliers.

The next room is the caldarium (*hammam-ı germa*). It is as though one entered a pool of light, for there is no sign of a wall rising on all sides to the lofty dome. Rather, this great round dome is perched on tall columns, and between the columns are windows of clear and polished rock crystal and cut glass. When the sun strikes the windows, the inside of the bath become *light upon light* (24:35). In the garden of Iram outside these windows a thousand nightingales wail and cry, as the bathers within listen and watch them feed their chicks, and observe the flowering trees and the singing birds' nests and the tall and brightly coloured flowers arrayed on the ground.

In the middle of this bath is a large pool with jets spouting up on all sides, the jet in the centre reaching as high as the bowl in the dome and then pouring down into the hot water. Ruby-coloured petals of rose and carnation are floating in the pool and stick to the bathers' skin, imparting their perfume. Each cubicle has a two-jar sarcophagus bath. This room also is paved with marble that dazzles the eye, since it is inlaid with precious stones, like the eye of a bird: jade, onyx, amber, fish-eye,

---

40 The reference is to a celebrated ghazal (not a *kaside*) by the sixteen-century Turkish poet Fuzuli.

Yemenite agate, and garnets. And attached to the columns that are between the windows are washbasins of onyx, porphyry, *yerekan* stone, *ferah* stone, and Chinese porcelain, carved to such perfection that the marble cutters of today could not even strike a chisel at it. The craftsmen made the water flow out of the marble columns into the basins in a marvellous manner. All the spouts are gold and silver, the bowls as well, and the jet pipes are pure silver. The atmosphere is so delightful that one seems to be enjoying eternal life. As the fountain streams strike the various chandeliers and wheels and suspended crystal bowls, they turn in the air, which is also a rare sight. On the lower level of this dome are fine calligraphic inscriptions with verses relating to the bath. Lovely slaveboys, with silken indigo waistbands wrapped round their naked bodies, service the bathers with fütuni bath gloves and scented soaps. When they loosen their tresses, the distraught lover goes out of his mind. Some of them light censers and incense-burners with aloes and ambergris, so the bath is filled with fragrance.

In sum, the tongue falls short in describing this bath, or the grand palace, or the garden of Iram. For in the expenditure of filigree-work in these buildings, and in grace and elegance and cleanliness, it is a peerless bath of unique design whose like I have not seen in forty-one years of travel.

The master builder in each of his works brought forth such marvels of art that no former architect under the sun achieved such a construction. Only God knows what it cost to make such a wondrous mansion. Even Sultan Murad (IV), during the Revan campaign, when he entered this bath and found the cold water flowing with rose-water, and the hot with steam; and in one cubicle five lovely male attendants with black tresses, and in another five fairy-graced and angel-faced virgin maiden attendants; – even he exclaimed with delight: 'If only this bath were in my palace!' It is truly a wonderful and charming bath. When our lord Melek Ahmed Pasha entered it, he remarked: 'No bath like this has ever been seen on earth.'

The Khan's feast for Melek Ahmed Pasha. When the Pasha emerged from this bath, a sumptuous feast was spread out in his honour, in the arena, according to the Khan's regulation. 200 silver platters, full of culinary delights, ornamented the arena, their delicate odours perfuming the brains of those attending. There were numerous kinds of pilavs – *kükü* (omelette), saffron, *çilav* (plain boiled rice), twelve roasted meats, mulberry, *şille* (?), pomegranate, aloes, ambergris, rice-water, meatball, pistachio, crushed almond, raisin; and soups – *mastaba* (yoghurt), *kıjı* (cress or mustard), and vermicelli. But the pilavs of partridge and pomegranate and various juicy and well-cooked kebabs were incredible.

Aside from these 200 silver platters, 200 of the Khan's pretty pageboys with such names as Siyavuş, Kazım Sührab and Husrev Bakır, with their turbans at a rakish tilt, decked in gold and jewels and wearing waist-cloths with embroidered silver fringes, stood in rows before the Pasha like so many cypresses, respectfully offering china and porcelain dishes, crystal ewers carved in relief, and celadon bowls. The tongue falls short in praising the table-napkins, the jewel-handled spoons, the sherbet bowls, and the other utensils on display at this feast. In sum, the Khan and the Pasha sat kneeling at the spread, with the Khan's sons Ziyaeddin, Bedreddin, Nureddehir and Şerefeddin on either side of the Pasha; they recited the *besmele* and then, the Pasha's aghas on one side and the Khan's on the other, laid into the 400 platters and bowls, each with the appetite of Maʿdikarib or Muʿawiya ibn Sakayat. This hungry tribe began to eat as though they were just released from Maʿnoghlu's prison, or as though they were infected with canine hunger.

After dinner, hands were washed with musk-scented soap with ewers and bowls of bejewelled gold. Then a long gilt-thread napkin was laid down. The company was provided with spoons of phoenix, tortoiseshell, mother-of-pearl, walnut, emerald, garnet, agate, and *yemeni*, each worth a fortune. Fifty lovely pageboys, each robed in a splendid garment, held out fifty splendid bowls with fifty kinds of juices and sherbets, prepared with Hamah and Damascus sugar, indescribably delicious. These too were consumed by the Pasha and the Khan and all the aghas and note worthies. Ewers and bowls were again brought in for ablutions, this time made of porcelain set with gold and jewels. And spiced Yemenite coffee, salep, mahaleb, tea, fennel, hot rice-water, sweet sherbet, hot flour-water, and milk were served in jewelled cups.

Each day regularly after that, for breakfast we were regaled with hundreds of sweetbreads and jams and jellies and other confections – rhubarb, lemon, pear, wild carrot, nutmeg, cassia, and club-foot; for lunch, a sumptuous spread of the type described above; and another Muhammadan feast at supper time. For ten days and nights the noble Khan entertained Melek Ahmed Pasha in this manner, providing for all 3,060 men in his camp, from the aghas' Segbans and Sarıcas down to the lowliest torchbearers and grooms. He did not let them want a hair cloth or a nose-bag for their horses. Even their coffee was provided by the Khan.

After dinner the Khan addressed the Pasha thus, 'My lord, we have in our service several master entertainers. If you wish, come to the lower pavilion overlooking the arena and you will observe the finest masters of sorcery and traversing of space and target-shooting and acrobatics that you have ever seen.'

'Well,' said the Pasha, 'let us see.' So they seated themselves in the pavilion overlooking the arena, and people gathered in rows on all four sides, awaiting the spectacle.

Marvels of magic and acrobatic skills. First, from Persia, a renowned acrobat named Pehlivan-zen-güzer came into the arena dressed in black deerskin. He kissed the ground before the Pasha; uttered benedictions upon the Prophet, the four companions, the twelve imams, the house of Osman, Melek Pasha, and the Khan and all his children; rubbed his face with his hand saying, 'Give leave, O enlightened vizier!' and recited the following verse:

> *Though all faults are in this slave,*
> *Every fault the sultan favours is a virtue.*

He kissed the ground once again, then began to strut and prance in the arena, faster than any noble steed, with the vigour of Amr Ayyar in his bearing, and the grace of Abu'l-Ma'ali in his speech. After that, he leapt before the Pasha crying *Yallah*, turned a somersault three times in the air and landed on his feet. Crying *Ya Hayy* he turned a quadruple somersault, spinning like a ball so that none of his limbs was visible; and as soon as he landed he made a short backward triple somersault – an amazing feat! He finished by holding head and hands and feet together and rolling in the arena like a top, with his limbs invisible.

Fourth number. Six men stood in the arena holding stretched open a sixteen-cubit-long muslin turban cloth. That swift acrobat raced like lightning and leapt across the sixteen-cubit-long band from one end to the other without stirring it the slightest. Truly a magical feat of running!

The next number: At two places in the arena he put three wine bottles one on top of the other. Leaping from the opposite side with the cry *Yallah!* he made a fearless somersault and landed squarely on top of them without losing balance or breaking the delicate bottles. Then he jumped to the ground and put three more bottles on each of the piles, making twelve in all. These were fragile glass decanters of Genoese manufacture, empty, and piled six atop one another the height of a man, such that the slightest breeze would make them sway.

'A difficult feat,' he said. 'May God assist. Now hand to tambourine!' With that, he went back forty or fifty paces. He pawed the ground and neighed like a horse. Crying 'O Lord without equal!' he leapt forward like a flash of lightning, or like an arrow released from a taut bow; and shouting *Ya Hayy!* when he reached the foot of the bottles, he sprang up like a fly and landed squarely with one foot atop each of the piles of six bottles. As Heaven is my witness, though he was stockily built, neither he nor the bottles budged in the slightest, nor was any broken. Standing on the bottles, he uttered benedictions on the Pasha, then jumped down, kissed the ground, and stood to one side.

A strange and wondrous spectacle, the science of magic. Molla Mehmed, the same who rode the emaciated horse during the grand entrance into Bitlis, now entered the arena in his dirty ragged turban and patched woolen cloak. After a perfunctory bow before the Pasha, he said pointedly, in his Kurdish dialect, 'Why summon me to this arena of execution? You don't invite me to the arena of feasting, because of my ragged clothes. And now you want me to show my skill.' He went on in that vein, then cried: '*Arise to prayer!* May the Khan's hearth burn forever, may Melek Ahmed Khan stand upright, may the spirits of Pythagoras and Avicenna and his brother Abu'l-Harith be joyful!'

He threw a sack into the arena. Pehlivan-zen-güzer's assistants struck the drum and the tambourine. Molla Mehmed raised his hands and cried: 'Brothers and dear ones, know and be aware! If you are firm-hearted men of God, then watch me with steadfast foot, otherwise put one foot forward and proceed to the exit.' Suddenly he was naked as the day he was born, and prancing impudently about the arena. Approaching his sack, he cried: 'My dear Khan, and my dear Melek Ahmed, perhaps it is impolite to walk before you naked like this. But you think I have private parts!? No, friends, I have no penis. Just take a look!' – and then he turned about so that everyone in the audience could see. There was nothing – not penis nor testicles nor buttocks – only two flaps of skin in front and back like boards. He was neither male nor female, nor was he a eunuch. There was no sign of a posterior either. He had become a manikin.

After prancing about, he took a waist-cloth out of the sack and girded it round his waist. This was a cloth of marvellous weave, like the reed mat of Yemenite manufacture known as Aden cloth. Fixing this waist-cloth to his belt – a great spectacle – he began to hop up and down the arena like a large fluttering bird about to take off. And indeed, his feet lifted off the ground, and he began to fly in the air. As he soared about, he cried all the while to the spectators, 'O wise ones! O foolish ones! O so-and-so son of so-and-so!' – greeting by name people in the Pasha's retinue whom he had never seen before.

The astonished audience was delighting at this spectacle, when Molla Mehmed, who was circling in the air at a height of four or five men's statures and occasionally dropping down to touch the spectators' heads with his feet, suddenly removed the waist-cloth, put it over his shoulder, and revealed a huge penis like that of Og son of Anaq.[41] Holding this in his hand, while he sailed through the air, he started pissing, and sprayed the spectators who filled this palace arena. They all became soaking wet – only their armpits stayed dry. Some ran out the door; others exclaimed: 'We just looked at the Molla naked and saw that he had no penis. Now, what is this enormous tool, and where did this damned rain of piss come from?' But those Kurds who understood what was going on just drank up this 'urine' and pronounced it 'water of life'.

Molla Mehmed hovered above the Khan and the Pasha, pissing and spraying. The Khan and his sons ran inside. The Pasha too, crying, '*No power and no strength (except in God)!*' took refuge within the courtyard, as the Molla poured a shower of pee into the gilt-furnished pavilion where he had just been sitting. The Khan was laughing his head off. 'Someone shoot that devil!' he exclaimed. After a while, the Molla landed, put the waist-cloth back on, and kissed the ground.

There was no more sign of a penis, nor of the rain of piss, nor of soaking-wet people. All the spectators were back in the arena with their clothes as dry as before. The Pasha put his finger to his mouth in astonishment, saying '*Praise be to God!*' Now the Khan took the sable fur from his own back and presented it to Molla Mehmed. 'O Molla,' he said, 'if you love me, perform another wonderful and perilous deed.' 'Just as you wish,' replied the Molla.

Another marvel. 'My Khan,' said Molla Mehmed, 'have all the doors of the arena shut, also the doors to the stairs going up, so that you and the viewers below will concentrate on the show.' The Khan gave the signal, and all the doors were shut, so that it was like a castle wall on all four sides.

---

41 A giant who lived during the time of Moses.

Molla Mehmed took out some rags and tatters and bits of cotton from his sack and, with his servants, stuffed all the vents and holes in the doors.

Returning to the arena, he removed a cup from his sack, drank some water, and hid the cup back in the sack. Once again he took his penis in his hands and started to piss in the direction of the spectators. Even one who suffered incontinence of urine could not pee that much. As the Molla's urine invaded the palace arena and began to form a lake there, as though the Great Zab and the Batman and the Charqa and Diyala Rivers were flowing into it, the thousands of frightened spectators raised a hue and cry. They kept up their moaning and wailing, but there was no place to escape. Then the Molla mounted his sack and began to float in this lake, while the people saw that they were about to drown. With one voice they cried: 'Mercy, Melek Ahmed Pasha, mercy! Have them open the doors and let us escape this inundation.'

'What's going on here?' said the Pasha. 'Will you let so many people drown in your own house?'

The Khan kissed the Pasha's hand. 'My lord,' he said, 'it is a display of skill. There is no danger to life here. Be patient a while.'

When the crowd saw that no help was forthcoming from the Khan or the Pasha, those who could swim stripped naked, and several thousand men began to swim in this palace arena as though swimming in the sea. Others sought solace by embracing one another. Some scrambled together on the steps leading up, or began to climb the walls, or get on top of one another. Some uttered the witness-formula as they were drowning, or just gurgled in the water. In short, it was a scene from the Last Hour, there was so much shouting and commotion. As for me, I watched the entire spectacle from the Pasha's pavilion. When Molla Mehmed had pissed out what he had originally drunk from the cup, the water on the ground only came up to a man's heel; still, the onlookers below nearly drowned. Now the Molla took a crystal bowl out of his sack and struck it with a stone. It resounded like the bell of a clock. At once, not a single drop of water remained in the arena, nor any sign of a penis or a rump belonging to Molla Mehmed. Only several thousand men, stark naked, were clinging like bats to the palace windows, or scrambling up the walls. Looking at them, the Pasha and the Khan and the other notables laughed themselves silly. The poor fellows sunk into the ground from embarrassment, or went about in the crowd crying, 'My clothes! My knife and dagger!' If a man travelled for a thousand years he would not see such a sorry and funny spectacle.

Now Molla Mehmed again kissed the ground before the Pasha and the Khan.

'For the Pasha's sake,' said the Khan, 'show us another small part of your skill. We would not ask you to do something beyond your capacity.' The Pasha tried to intervene, 'Hey Khan! Get rid of this damned magician. He has frightened all my followers out of their wits.'

'There is no danger here, my lord.'

Seeing that the Khan was enjoying the entertainment, the Pasha turned a blind eye and said, 'Well, as long as he shows his skill in a reasonable manner.'

Another and final marvel. Molla Mehmed approached his sack and took out a multi-coloured embroidered waistband, which he concealed beneath his waist-cloth. After sitting upon it a moment, he removed the band from beneath the cloth, uttered a charm, and put it back in the sack. Suddenly the sack started to convulse and emit thunder and lightning. From its mouth emerged the head of a huge serpent, which slithered out and lay coiled up on the hot sand, facing the sun. But as it heaved, its body kept swelling, its eyes flamed like a torch, its teeth jutted like elephant tusks, and it became covered with hair like a deer. That dragon kept up like this for half an hour, until it was as large as an elephant. Then it writhed and stretched its long body in the heat, twisted and turned a while, and came up to Molla Mehmed. 'I think I'll ride this dragon,' said the Molla; but the serpent struck him with its long tail, and he fell on his head and lay sprawling on the ground.

At this juncture the spectators began to get alarmed, saying, 'If this dragon treats the Molla in this fashion, what will it do to us?' And they tried to find a way out. Willy-nilly they broke down the garden gate of the palace and started to run away. Suddenly Molla Mehmed stood up from the ground, took a wand of red spiraea from his sack, struck the dragon, and mounted it. The dragon raised its head and tail into the air, let out a roar, spewed flames from its mouth, and stirred up a huge cloud of dust with its tail. Again it began to writhe and twist, and the crowd broke into a great hubbub, some fainting on the spot, others getting trampled underfoot. The poor chief bread-maker was so frightened he had an epileptic seizure.

'Damn you, Molla Mehmed,' cried the Pasha upon seeing this melancholy sight. 'I won't forget this!' The Molla realised that the Pasha was upset. He made one turn with the dragon, came beneath the Pasha's pavilion, and cried, 'I commend you to God, my Pasha. *Ya Hu!* My blessings!' With that, mounted on the dragon, he flew out the garden gate toward the mountains, and disappeared from view. Meanwhile the crowd gathered again in the arena, and everyone chattered in amazement.

The ocean of grace of the science of magic. Now Molla Mehmed's sack was left in the arena. 'Bring me that sack,' said the Khan, 'let's take a look at Molla Mehmed's meagre equipment.'

'Hey Khan,' cried the Pasha, 'get rid of that devil's things!'

'For goodness' sake, Pasha,' said the Khan, let's just take a look,' and he opened the mouth of the bag.

There were multi-coloured threads of sheep's and camel's wool; hempen cords; various medicaments in boxes; thorns of gorse; camphor, gum benzoin, and myrrh; aloes and ambergris; pitch and tar; balsam and oleander; and all sorts of camphor candles; also old rags and pieces of striped Yazdi cloth, Kashani velvet, and Damascene *kutni*[42] not worth a penny; various ointments in small canisters; taffies and confections; seeds of melon, watermelon, cucumber, squash, and a thousand and one kinds of seeds of this sort; also tin bottles of ink, arac, vinegar, wine, naphtha, and sandarac; sheep and goat heads and trotters, salted and unshorn; a lion's head; numerous dead snakes, skinks, lizards, scorpions and centipedes; the hooves and teeth of a donkey, a horse, a mule, a camel and a pig; several canisters with live leeches, centipedes, dung beetles, earthworms, and large ants; and boxes with live snakes, scorpions, snails, and bugs of various sorts from Lake Van; even a dried human head; also lion, tiger and leopard heads; and all sorts of animal skins, including sable, marten, ermine, and lynx. The entire contents were not worth a dime, but all existing things were in this magic ocean of a sack. The medicinal herbs and the aromatic woods in this bag could not be found in any apothecary's or charcoal-seller's shop.

'My dear Khan,' said the Pasha, 'what did this devil do with all these worthless things? He has wine and raki and vinegar.' 'I swear by God, my lord,' replied the Khan, 'he has been with us for three years, and he has not once taken wine or tobacco or coffee.

'He prays at night and fasts by day, and subsists on the fast of David. He has never eaten food of a slaughtered animal, and has never missed one of

---

42 Defined by Redhouse as a kind of striped goods, with a face of silk and a body of cotton.

the five daily prayers. He learned this science of magic in the Maghreb, in the city of Marrakesh, and has demonstrated before my lord a small portion of his skill, at my behest. All the rest is merely a hypnotic trance, of no harm to anyone.'

'What about these animal skins, and these live animals in boxes?'

'A good question,' said the Khan. 'All the magical feats that he performs have their basis in the things of nature created by the hand of God, or the items which you see here. He expends his skill upon them as required. For example, he rubbed the oil from one canister on his body, uttered a charm, and appeared to be lacking a penis. He rubbed on oil of hoarfrost and dew, and appeared to fly in the air. He poured water over the people from a flask, and the crowd said, 'He is pissing on us.' He poured charmed water on the ground, and the people stripped off their clothes, thinking they were drowning. He took one of these snakes from the bag, uttered a charm, and it appeared in the shape of a dragon. Then, fearing my lord's wrath, he flew off with the dragon, leaving his sack behind him as you see. Whatever animal skins he has in this sack, he can make appear to be alive – which of course only God could do actually – so he keeps one piece of each kind in his sack like his own head and soul.'

In this manner the Khan tried to justify his patronage of Molla Mehmed. But the Pasha said, 'Take away that sorcerer's sack.'

'I did enjoy that flying acrobat,' continued the Pasha. So Pehlivan-zen-güzer, whose name means 'free and pure and beyond women,' began to strike his drum and tambourine in the arena.

Another marvellous feat. The roofs of the houses on the eastern side of the Khan's Garden palace, which was described above, are higher than the palace wall, and below them are bare cliffs, the height of two Süleymaniye minarets, such that a man dare not gaze down. A day or two previously, some hundred or so miners with their Farhadi picks had demolished the rocks in that perilous gorge, opening up a vast arena into which they poured sand. This was at the order of Pehlivan-zen-güzer, who knew that he would be displaying his skill, and who also had placed on top of the Khan's palace a sack full of earth and horse-dung. Now Pehlivan said, 'O my lord, Melek Pasha, brave vizier! If you wish to observe another feat performed by this lowly slave, please proceed to the balconies overlooking the cliffs, and you'll see a marvel.'

The Pasha and the rest of the spectators moved to that side. While his assistants beat their drum and tambourine, Pehlivan, atop the roof, uttered a benediction, and cried, 'O lovers! This is not a mere display of skill. It is a life-risking feat. I commend you to God. May you also commend me, and do not forget to pray for me. Whoever here is a Muhammadan, let him shower invocations on Muhammad's roselike beauty. God bring it right!'

The thousands present echoed the cry: 'God bring it right!' With that, cruel Pehlivan took the sack of dung and earth mentioned above, held it tight under his buttocks, and hurled himself eagle-like from the palace roof, shouting *Yallah!* as he plunged the two-minaret distance. When he was just a man's height above the ground, he did a somersault flip over the sack that was under his buttocks, and by God's grace landed safely on his feet. He uttered another benediction. There was a horse ready there. In a wink he mounted, spurred the horse, and kissed the ground before the Pasha, who presented him with a purse of *guruş*. The Pasha then returned to the pavilion at the palace arena to watch the next spectacle.

Another marvellous acrobatic feat. Once again Pehlivan's servants beat the drum and tambourine, while he performed turns and somersaults in the arena. He then took a hammer and two large nails out of his sack.

'O my Khan,' he said. 'With your permission I will scale this lofty wall the height of eighty cubits.'

'Permission granted,' said the Khan. 'May God make it easy for you.'

He approached the foot of the wall, uttered a benediction, then drove one of the nails in the wall as far up as his hands could reach, stuck his hammer in his belt, and with a flip and a cry of *Yallah!* mounted the nail and did some tricks. Then standing on this nail and clinging to the wall, he removed the hammer and the other nail from his belt, drove it between two rocks as high as possible, again stuck the hammer in his belt, and sprang spider-wise atop the second nail, where he again performed some tricks. The strange thing was that the nails were only a span and a half in length, and when they entered the wall three fingers thick, there was hardly room left, or any instrument left, with which to perform these feats.

Suddenly he slid upside-down like a snake and, holding the lower nail fast in his hands, caught hold of the upper nail claw-like with soles and toes curled around it, thus freeing his hands for some upside-down prestidigitations. Removing the hammer from his belt while suspended by his feet, he struck the lower nail until it came out, then slithered back to the upper nail, stood on it upright, and again drove in the first nail as far up as his hand could reach. He repeated this procedure several times, each time performing a hundred different gymnastics.

When the nails were up nine men high, he pulled out his tobacco pouch from his belt, placed it on the nail, and stood on his head waving his feet in the air. It was wonderful to see a human body go through such contortions atop a nail in the wall.

He continued to remove the lower nail while hanging from his feet and driving it in overhead, forty-seven times, without repeating any of the tricks he performed on one nail on another, until he rose forty-seven men's heights to the top, where he uttered a benediction upon his masters and patron saints. He then drove both nails in together, threw down the hammer, and said: 'O people of Muhammad! My tools were a hammer and two nails. Now the hammer is gone, and the nails cannot be removed. How shall I get down from this roof? My soul is in God's hands: I will hurl myself down! God is my witness: I do not hold you responsible if I am killed. But do not forget to pray for me.'

He pulled out a pair of gloves from his bosom and put them on his hands saying *Bismillah, Yallah!* Then he hurled himself from the roof to the arena floor. The thoughtful spectators cried, 'God preserve us, we are guilty of bloodshed!' It turned out that the gloves he had put on were actually whipcords made of raw silk, with one end attached to the two nails that he had driven into the roof. Just as he was about to land on the ground, he took fast hold of the glove- cords in his hands, his body swung over to the wall, and he remained suspended by the cords. From there he flipped down to the ground and kissed the perfumed dust before the Pasha, who showered him with two handfuls of gold.

A most strange and phenomenal spectacle. While the Pasha and all the soldiery were watching these marvellous events, sitting next to the Pasha was a certain worthy and learned gentleman whose name I cannot recall – it was either Ismail or Molla Ali – a kinsman of the governor of Hakkari. This contentious individual, as though struck by a point of Kurdish honour, addressed the Pasha and the Khan thus, 'This thief and knave of an acrobat and nail-climber goes right up to the roof of your harem. If he wished, could he not enter your harem one night and commit fornication? You don't think of that. Instead, you put a sable robe on his shoulders and shower his head with perfumed gold. Now I'll demonstrate the skills I learned from my ancestors. Let's see what you'll give me!' With that he leapt down from the pavilion, tore off his sable fur, and started to strut around the arena crying, *Ya Hayy, Ya Qayyum!*

'That Pehlivan scales walls using nails,' he went on. 'Let's see how I'll do it.' At once he struck the face of the wall opposite once with his hand – and it stuck to the wall. Then he struck the other hand a bit higher – and it stuck too. In this manner, crying *Ya Hayy, Ya Qayyum!* all the while, he walked up, sticking to the face of the wall like a bat. With his *kohik şanpur* (?) turban on his head, and shoes with pointed tails on his feet, he circled several times round the face of the wall on all four sides of the palace arena – these walls are eighty or ninety cubits in height – shouting *Ya Hayy, Ya Qayyum!, Ya Wahid, Ya Majid, Ya Ahad, Ya Fard, Ya Samad!* (calling on various names of God). Finally he descended into the pavilion from the wall just above, settled himself back into place next to the Pasha, and demanded from him a large reward.

'My Bey,' said the Pasha, 'you are of the House of Abbas. I know without having to ask. In fact you displayed a similar skill when you came to me in Diyarbekir from Hakkari in '53 (1053/1643–4). God be praised that we meet once again in the town of Bitlis, here in the palace of our brother the Khan.'

'Yes,' answered the Bey, 'and since we have not seen each other for so long, neither have I seen your favour.' So the Pasha gave him a purse, and the Khan gave him a purse of *guruş*, and they each gave him a robe of honour and an Arab horse with all the trimmings, and sent him on his way to Hakkari with letters for Khan Yezdenşir.

In sum, if I were to record all the strange and wondrous things that were our daily fare in Bitlis during our ten-day halt, it would be a scroll of delights.

3. The ruined city of Ahlat

According to the Persian chroniclers this is one of the cities of Armenia in the eighteenth of the conventional climes. The ruined city contains hundreds of domed buildings and splendid ancient mosques that seem to have just been released from the hands of their architects. All the cupolas are constructed of stone; some, pertaining to once-flourishing mosques, are covered with limewash. But they are now deprived of congregations and have become the nests of pigeons and crows and owls.

There is one flourishing mosque that has remained, however: that of Emir Kay. Its walls all around are intact, completely up to the roof, and smooth as Chinese paper. The owner of this mosque, Emir Kay, was an author of the ancient city, and for this reason the walls all around are covered with an inscription that shows how flourishing the ancient city was. It lists all the great buildings – Friday mosques, neighbourhood mosques, medreses, *hans*, baths, and royal markets. It is written very clearly, as though engraved on a seal, in Musta'sımi script. This humble one read it and recorded as much as I could, though but a drop in the ocean and a speck in the sun. I was so assiduous in reading it that I had to use my spyglass in order to make out the part next to the roof. The language that was used in Old Ahlat is an unusual dialect of Turkish close to Chagatay and Mongolian and contains many interesting expressions, such as, *İşven, gitmişven* I have departed; *gurumıza varmışmız* We have gone to our graves; *bizim Kay gibidir, boğaz eyitdi; dükeli geleserlerdir* All of them will come; *meni suncamışdır, şad bay kişidir, ayıtdım şol kişi menfadınadır; savular sayladım* – i.e., I was left weeping; *barumız uruş kişisimiz* – i.e., we are all men of war.

The inscription records that when this city was thriving it had 35,000 prayer-niches, 2,000 medreses, 1,000 baths, 2,000 *hans*, 1,000 Hadith schools, 6,000 primary schools, 800 dervish convents, 18,000 fountains, 8,000 water dispensaries, 10,000 Muslim quarters – there was no mention of infidels or Christians, 200,000 Muslim houses, 70,000 palaces of the notables, 3,000 caravanserais, 2,000 bachelor quarters, 600,000 shops, 150 covered markets with lofty cupolas – some of these are still intact albeit swarming with snakes and vermin, and 700 soup kitchens.

This city stretched a three-day's walk along the shore of Lake Van when it was thriving. It had 40,000 excursions, 900,000 orchards and gardens, 70,000 lofty shrines, 600,000 ulema notables, 400,000 physicians, 100,000 surgeons, 150,000 sheikhs, thousands of saints suspected of miraculous graces, also 40,000 muftis belonging to the four legal schools, 70,000 descendants of the Prophet, 600,000 armed soldiers, 40,000 watchmen, 2,000 Sharia courts, 700 administrative officers, and 3,000 public scales officials.

On the slopes of the summer pastures are 3,000 caves, still visible, in many of which lived travellers on the spiritual path, withdrawn from society, who subsisted on bran for seventy or eighty years.

The summer pasture of this city is Mt Subhan, which ranks just after the summer pasture of Bingöl. It had 3,000 milk cisterns. They milked their sheep and goats, water buffalo, cows and horses, and there were separate cisterns for storing the milk of each kind of animal. There were also 7,000 milk fountains down in the town. The owners of the milk would send men with word to the city where people would draw the milk down to the fountains and pay a tithe to the emperor of Mahan. This imperial tithe was absolute and the people never objected to it; it is for this reason that the chroniclers call Ahlat the Land of Bumpkins.

There were so many saints here that whatever they prayed for was granted.

Even now the conduits are visible that brought milk from the summer pasture to the fountains. In fact, there is a marketplace consisting of 3,000 shops near the Ali Kay mosque with stone placards above each section saying 'Bazaar of the Saddlers', 'Bazaar of the Weavers', 'Bazaar of the Silk-makers'. There are even placards saying 'Sheep's-milk Fountain', 'Goat's-milk Fountain', 'Mare's-milk Fountain' – the word for mare in this case being *baytal*. Hence one may conclude that the populace were Tatars, since they drank mare's-milk, and since the inscriptions are all written in the Tatar Chagatay dialect.

When this city was thriving, no animal other than horses could enter it. Animals were slaughtered outside the city limits and brought to the 7,000 butcher shops in town. And cattle of all sorts were milked in the summer pasture; the milk was then brought down in conduits and sold at the milk fountains. The pastures and mountains and orchards are on the northern side of the ruined city, whereas on the southern side is Lake Van.

One of the mosques has its endowment charter written on the mosque's wall. It states that the endowment consists of 1,500 shops, 1,000 fields, 100 mills, and 500,000 gold pieces. At the end it says: 'If anyone destroys these endowments, may the curse of Haman and Korah and Marwan and Pharaoh and Yazid be upon his descendants and himself.' And underneath is the Koranic verse: *None should visit the mosques of God except (those who believe in God and the Last Day …)* (9:18) [...]

4. On 'extinguishing the candle'

Shrine of Salih Efendi. He was the chief deputy of Sheikh Safi, the forefather of all the Persian shahs who are buried in the pure ground of Ardabil and belonged to the Vahidi Sufi order. Following the miracles that occurred when Sheikh Safi extinguished the candle, this Salih Efendi prohibited the practice – may his grave be sanctified.

Notice concerning 'extinguishing the candle'. Sheikh Safi achieved the rank of Pole of Poles in the city of Ardabil in the year (—). One day, due to divine inspiration, he went into an ecstasy and summoned the thousandfold congregation to the Muhammadan *tevhid*. He also summoned their womenfolk to attend. So all the women came, with their veils and head-covers, and thousands of them were in a corner occupied with *tevhid*. After night fell, Sheikh Safi produced a lighted candle and said, 'Come, my daughters, you too enter the *tevhid*, just like my sons.'

Just as all the men and women together were performing *tevhid* and *tezkir*, the saintly Sheikh Safi extinguished the candle and all the men and women mingled together and performed the royal *tevhid* for seven full hours. Finally Sheikh Safi uttered the words, *'and blessings upon all the prophets and the apostles.'* He passed his hands over his face, then commanded, 'Let everyone, dark as it is, embrace the ones next to him and go home.'

It turned out that all the men, by virtue of the saintly grace of Sheikh Safi, in that massive confusion had embraced their own wives and daughters and went home. It is truly a miracle that in that dark of night and in that mingling and whirling crowd of people, everyone should have found his very own wife.

During Sheikh Safi's lifetime the candle was extinguished several times, and each time all the men found their own wives and daughters. But after his death, when certain of his deputies extinguished the candle, they missed finding their own womenfolk and the Persians began to be villified as 'candle extinguishers'. So this saintly Sheikh Salih, buried in Urmia, prohibited men and women from performing *tevhid* together and prohibited extinguishing the candle.

People say that in Persia there are still those who do it. But as God is my witness, I travelled to Persia from Erzurum in the year 1056 (1646); in 1055 (1645) I went from Baghdad to Hamadan and Darguzin; later, in 1077 (1666–7) I went from the Crimea to Daghestan and from there through the Iron Gate of Persia (i.e. Darband) to Shamaki in Shirvan and Baku in Gilan; and in the present instance (1065/1655) I visited, aside from Urmia, also Khoy, Marand, Tasuj, Qumla and Tabriz; and I never saw anything resembling 'extinguishing the candle.' But the people of this world are slanderers and libelers and cavilers.

It is also reported about the province of Sivas, in the *sancaks* of Keskin and Bozok, and in Sunkur and Imad, that they extinguish the candle and that everyone embraces another man's wife and lies with her in a corner – God forbid! This humble slave has traversed those regions often since the conquest of Baghdad (in 1648); and during our lord's governorship of Sivas (i.e. Murtaza Pasha, in 1650) I carried out several offices in Keskin and in Bozok; and I never observed anything like that.

Again, these officious people claim that there are Shah-lovers and candle-extinguishers and men and women who wear the Shah's diadem in Rumelia, in the province of Silistria, in the districts of Deli Orman and Kara Su, and in the Dobrudja. As God is my witness, I have sojourned in those countries perhaps fifty times, and have carried out offices there, and I never observed any such illegitimate activities – although, to be sure, there are those who fail to pray, or who run after singing girls.

There is however, in Damascus a quarter called Sazenekler whose populace do pay allegiance to Persia. And also there are people belonging to the Nukhudi sect throughout the Druze and Teymani mountains of Syria, who are seventy times worse than the Kızılbaş. I have recorded them in detail in Volume (—) (3) in the account of my travels in Damascus and Syrian Tripoli.[43]

---

43 The reference is to the discussion of the sects in Jabal Naqura in Vol. 3, fol. 40a–b.

VOLUME FIVE

East Anatolia and the Balkans

IN MAY 1656, Evliya returns to Van. On a lightning trip to Istanbul, where Melek Pasha sends him as courier, he has an encounter with highwaymen in a treacherous mountain pass near Bolu (cf. Volume 9, selection 2). Then he is sent to Bitlis to collect arrears, and has to flee when the angered Abdal Khan returns from exile at the news of Melek Pasha's removal from office. The highly dramatised account of his escape reads like an adventure novel.

In May 1657, Evliya accompanies Melek Pasha on the Polish campaign and later that year assists in repelling a Cossack siege of Azov. In March 1659, he enters the service of vizier Köprülü Mehmed Pasha and joins the campaign against Celali rebels in western Anatolia; then the Moldavia, Wallachia and Transylvania campaigns, before reuniting with Melek Pasha in Sarajevo in the summer of 1660.

Melek Pasha sends Evliya on a mission to Split, giving him the opportunity to observe the Venetians (cf. Volume 6, selection 5) and practice his Italian. In January 1661, he joins Melek Pasha at his new posting in Sofia. Sent into the countryside to collect arrears, Evliya has another confrontation with a bandit.

1. Highwaymen in the Bolu Pass; return to Van

Account of our journey from Istanbul to Van
Departing from Üsküdar with a *besmele* – stage of Gegbizye (Gebze) – stage of Iznimgit (Izmit) – stage of the city of Bolu – stage of the town of Çerkeş.

Setting out at sunset we ran into seven highwaymen. After some words they bared their swords and told us to strip. My three servants and I dismounted and we showed them the orders and letters in our saddlebags.

'What should we do with these?' cried one of them. 'Do you have gold and jewels?'

'No, I swear by God, only these, and in this saddlebag our shirts and underwear.'

'God bless you, we are mountain men, we have need of shirts,' he said, and took the bag with the shirts.

I leapt to one side, thinking that I would be able to grab my sword, but all seven rushed upon me with their muskets in hand.

'*Gazis!*' I cried. 'Attacking a courier who has ridden until he and his horse are both exhausted is like striking a pregnant woman. Don't you know that there are no strangers among people of faith? What you are doing, even Köroğlu did not do in these mountains. If you are men of God, let us go free.'

I kept talking and pleading in this fashion, until one of them untied his sword from his waist and said: 'Young man, this is a very fine sword. Keep it in memory of me. And you give me the silver-decked sword at your waist: I too will wear it as a keepsake from you.'

'Of course,' said I, and gave him my sword in return. Then we all kissed and became brothers. God be praised, they did not touch anything else.

Stage of Tosya. That night we passed Osmancık and the towns of Gümüş and Kerkez. Stage of Amasya – pass of Çengalli, very dangerous, which we crossed at night – stage of the castle of Niksar – stage of Koyluhisar – headlong down the crevice, stage of the village of Keremli. We passed the city of Erzincan, took fresh horses and went via the Erzurum plain. Stage of the walled city of Erzurum – eastward, stage of Malazcird – stage of Erciş. There we took fresh horses, passed Amik castle.

Stage of the castle of Van, frontier of Azerbaijan
At the break of dawn they opened the postern gate. God be praised, on the thirteenth day (after leaving Istanbul) I saw the blessed face of our lord Melek Ahmed Pasha. He read the orders and noble rescript and the letters, expressed his delight that Siyavuş Pasha was now the grand vizier, and bestowed on this humble one a purse of guruş and one set of clothing with a sable's head fur-piece.

'Evliya,' he said, 'my condolences, your slaveboy named Kazım has died. Here are two Georgian slaveboys in compensation.' Very pleased, I went to my dwelling and rested for a week.

One day the Pasha said: 'My Evliya, you brought me good news in your capacity as courier. Now I have another task for you: to bring the letters of investment to my son the Khan of Bitlis and to the emir of Ziriki. Leave in the morning, without delay, for the time is already late. Join forces with the canteen officer in Bitlis, get the remaining seventy purses from my son the Khan, and bring them here as soon as possible. For you know what is written in the noble command and friendly letter that you have conveyed.'

2. Escape from Bitlis

We were again greeted by the Khan and outfitted with a sumptuous room. Night and day we caroused with the Khan and his twelve brothers – God be praised, the nights were like the Night of Power and the days were like the Day of the Festival of Sacrifice. Following the Pasha's instructions, I joined forces with the canteen officer and with great effort we managed to collect fifty purses from the noble Khan, which we sent off to Van with 300 musketeers along with our own goods, so we were left in Bitlis free of care. Now the new Khan owed only twenty purses, and the canteen officer kept pressing him for them. This humble one, meanwhile, got along splendidly with all the princes and the tribal emirs and the Bitlis grandees, receiving gifts and favours from each one, so that in a short time I amassed four wardrobes of clothing and other rare and precious items, plus seven purebred horses. Each day we celebrated as though it were the Khwarazm-shah's New Year.

By God's will, in the year (—) (1066), on the first day of Jumadi al-awwal (26 February 1656) we got news that our lord Melek Ahmed Pasha had been removed from office, and that the governorship of Van had been given to Pehleli Ahmed Pasha. But, since it was the dead of winter, the Pasha

Escape from Bitlis

remained in Van, as the new governor's agent took charge. Along with this news came a letter from our Yusuf Kethüda regarding the collection of the remaining twenty purses. 'Do not come back without them,' he wrote.

The following day, what should we see but Abdal Khan, who had fled during the battle with our lord Melek Ahmed Pasha on Monday 24 Ramadan 1065 (28 July 1655), entering the town of Bitlis. There was great commotion among the populace. Everyone thought, 'Now that Melek Ahmed Pasha's removal from office has been confirmed, Abdal Khan, having fled to the mountains of Mudiki, has returned to Bitlis. What will he inflict on our town now!' Out of fright, they all rushed with their gifts to greet the old Khan.

I too went to see Abdal Khan, bringing as gift a finely calligraphed Koran. He rose to greet me, took me by his side, and showered me with favours and flatteries.

'My little Evliya, so you are here?' he said.

'Yes, my Khan. For twenty years now I have been eating the bread and licking the bowls of your noble house. For the sake of the pure soul of your noble ancestor Sultan Evhadehullah, set me up in this town as your protegé, and accept me in your service. I will no longer go to Melek Pasha's gate.' He removed the cover from a small cabinet by his side.

'Here is the deed to a dye works which will provide you a daily income of four *guruş*. I will also give you an estate in Muş. And I'll give you some slavegirls, and set you up as a married man.' Aside from this he gave me a *Shahnama* (of Firdawsi), a *Gulistan* (of Sa'di), a hundred Spanish *guruş*, and a suit of clothes.

What should we see next but his son Ziyaeddin, whom Melek Ahmed Pasha had set up as his protegé, coming and falling at his father's feet. He laid before him the imperial warrant of khanship and the noble orders that Melek Pasha had brought from the capital, also the letter of investment and the robe of honour that I had just conveyed from the Pasha. Rubbing his face in the dust at his father's foot, he said, 'My father, my lord and Padishah: I swear by God that during the war with Melek Pasha they demanded me as khan, in consultation with all the people of the country, in order to prevent anyone from the outside interfering in our rule. I have served for a year as your deputy. Now that Melek Pasha too is removed from office, may God bless you once again with crown and fortune!'

'Now my son,' replied the Khan in a prudent fashion, 'I have entered my eightieth year. Many a time have I strung my bow and shot my arrow, and hung my bow in the firmament. I have won fame and fortune from heaven, and have borne the hot and the cold of this celestial sphere. God forbid that I should henceforth accept the khanship. Here are you, my twelve beloved sons and lights of my eyes. Join your hearts, and rule Bitlis with wisdom and singleness of purpose, so that you not be a laughing-stock to the people. Just provide for my needs, and let me withdraw with your mother and my household to a quiet corner, where I will pray for your welfare. Take away these warrants, may God bless you!' But all the time he spoke he was choked with rancour and his words were full of contempt.

In short, there was a great deal of discussion. After we had dined and washed our hands, the Khan said, 'My Evliya is one of us, not just now but previously as well. Prepare a chamber for him near mine so that we may converse together.' I again kissed the Khan's hand, then returned to my room and lay down for a nap.

In a dream I saw my late father. 'Son,' he said, 'you will manage to leave this town and flee via Ahlat castle. Don't worry, just continue to recite the Koran.' I woke up, renewed my ablution, and at once began a complete recitation of the Koran, which I completed two days later.

Adventure of Evliya the sincere, in the city of Bitlis. One morning this humble sinner emerged from my chamber at the Khan's Garden, withdrew to a quiet corner in the treasury room of the *divan* hall, and, while everyone else was still asleep, occupied myself peacefully reciting my litanies. Suddenly from the harem the old Khan (sent me) a silver tray with ten porcelain plates containing pears, lemons, myrobalans, olives, sour cheese, filtered honey, all kinds of conserves, fine white folded bread like rose pinks, also a jug of ambergris-flavoured soup and a jug of rice-water sherbet. As I sat in a corner eating alone, a certain Tavaşi Amber Agha emerged from the harem door, a eunuch with scowling face but Jesus-like disposition. He handed me a bag of clothing.

'My lady Hanım Sultan greets you,' he began, 'and says that you should put on these clothes and leave immediately. Go to your Pasha, and when you are again in the company of Kaya Sultan, do not forget my lady in your prayers. But you must leave immediately.' Thus did I 'get news from Loqman' from this Loqman-like eunuch. I was non-plussed, and began to think all sorts of dark thoughts, when the negro said, 'Guard the bag and the clothes carefully, and don't tell a soul.' Then he slipped away.

I was quite bewildered, wondering what the purport of this unexpected visit might be. As I resumed eating my breakfast, the harem door again opened, and the two elder sons of Abdal Khan appeared, the eldest Bedir Bey and the next eldest Nureddehir Bey. They were still in their bedclothes and had nightcaps on their heads.

'Good morning, Evliya Çelebi, how are you faring? I see you are again eating from father's silver tray. The Khan our father has honoured you with a breakfast. If you don't mind some partners, we can eat together.' They sat down next to me, and I recited the verse:

> All is yours, my heart and soul;
>   Just take the trouble to advance one foot.
> All that I own is a thank offering
>   I place in your path – don't you know?

As a joke I added: 'This food is mine, but you may eat it as though it belonged to your father the Khan. It is yours to have and enjoy, it is your Seyf Kuli Agha pilav (?).'

As we were eating, Nureddehir spoke up, 'God be praised, one silver tray and these porcelain plates were left unplundered in our father's war with Melek Ahmed Pasha.' He smiled as he spoke, and I knew he was testing me, but I did not answer a word, just kept on chewing and munching. Now it was Bedir Bey's turn.

'Evliya Çelebi,' he said, 'so now your Pasha too has been removed from office. What did he hope to gain by putting this town to the sword like that, ruining our province and our city, massacring so many thousands of men, and committing such outrages on that blessed Ramadan day that ten Egyptian treasures were plundered from our town. Do you think Melek Pasha and his followers and the Van garrison brigands will get away with this? Do you think they will be able to keep all that plundered wealth?'

'To tell you the truth, my princes,' said I, 'there are many kinds of dervishes in this world. I am the kind who goes out among people, rides horses, and keeps servants. Still, I am unconcerned with the affairs of the world. A war happened, a province was plundered and ruined. I know nothing of that. I only know that I am your well-wisher, and that for twenty years now I have been a wandering dervish longing for your house, to which I have finally come. God be praised, this very day your father the noble Khan has given me the deed to a dye works, and has set me up as his protegé. Now treat me in whatever manner suits your noble dignity. I am a wayfarer at this threshold, arrived here out of my love, and have the impertinence to seek your favour.'

I said all kinds of humiliating things, as I continued to eat my breakfast, but it was like swallowing poison. Then Bedir Bey, God bless him, said, 'It's true. Evliya Çelebi is a wandering dervish and a world traveller. He cries the chant of every cart he mounts and sings the praises of every man who feeds him. Wherever he rests his head, he eats and drinks and is merry.'

While we were still talking and the breakfast dishes were still before us, the door of the *divan* hall opened, it being dawn, and in walked Halhali Haydar Kethüda, whom Melek Ahmed Pasha had made Ziyaeddin Khan's steward. He was a decrepit grey-beard, 110-years old, and had an earring swaying from his ear. As he entered he greeted us warmly, 'Greetings to you, my princes, and good morning to you, my Evliya.' The princes did not return the greeting, but I said, 'And good morning to you, O knight Haydar, seeing far, and heart-weary as you are.'

'I am rather far-sighted,' he said. 'But why did my princes not return this old man's greetings and salutations?' And he began bustling about the audience hall.

Upshot of the adventure. As poor Haydar Kethüda was bustling about the audience hall, he came up to the *biheri* or fireplace which was next to the princes, cleared his throat with an 'Ah-tu' and spat out a wad the size of a mullet-oyster, which spattered over the princes and myself. He made some disdainful remarks and kept mumbling, 'The princes didn't return

Escape from Bitlis

my greeting,' then went 'Ah-tu' and spat again, raining saliva over the stone tiles and over Bedir Bey.

At this Bedir and Nureddehir leapt to their feet, crying 'Kill that old fart!' At once the door of the closet next to me opened, and out came Güzel Dereli Musli Agha with drawn sword. He leapt right over my head and brought his sword down upon Haydar Kethüda. Poor Haydar, wounded, drew a dagger from his belt and began to struggle with Musli Agha. As they were wrestling like Mahmud Piryar Veli's dancing-boys, Abdurrahman Bölükbaşı and Kanah-dereli Deli Mahmud also dashed out of the closet and came up with their swords flashing. Old Haydar Khan, fearing for his life, kept hitting at them with his dagger, as they kept striking him. The poor old man ran about the *divan* hall shouting for help. Finally he rushed upon the princes, brandishing his dagger. The pages surrounded him, and as they were cutting him up with dagger and sword, Nureddehir said, 'He is you Pasha's protegé, Evliya. If you love the Khan, why don't you strike him with your dagger?' I darted from my place, and tore off the turban from his head, the ring from his ear, the Haydari *palheng*-stone from his waist, and his dagger sheath and knife. But his sable fur was already cut to pieces.

It seems the poor fellow still had some life in him. He latched onto my foot, heaved a sigh, stood up, then fell again. While the pages were slicing at him, all of a sudden his own servants, who had been standing outside the door holding his slippers and boots, rushed in with drawn swords and began some swordplay with the pages, so that several people aside from Haydar Kethüda lost their lives, and the carpets turned into a lake of blood. God knows, those Kurdish braves who rushed in from outside hacked away with their swords like Kassab Cömerd with his butcher knife. But what could five or six men accomplish against seventy or eighty warlike pages? The princes and I huddled in a corner and were bathed with blood. Finally, citing the adage, 'the minority must bow to the majority,' I started to help the princes take the corpses by the legs and drag them away. As we were lugging the guts, huffing and puffing, a watch fell out of Haydar Agha's pocket. I picked it up, and also removed his rings just outside the door. We dragged the corpses away and threw all four down over the balustrade and into the palace arena.

By now I was nearly out of my mind. During breakfast Nureddehir had said, 'Do you think Melek Ahmed Pasha and his followers will get away with this?' And before that, Hanım Sultan had sent me a bag of clothes from the harem and said, 'You should go to your Pasha immediately.' When this latest event also took place, I kept reciting the Witness formula (expecting imminent death); otherwise I was speechless.

After this my heart was on fire. I could not sleep at night. I was constantly making plans to escape, though I revealed this to no one. Beginning that very day, though it was the dead of winter, I mounted with my slaveboys and we exercised the horses, forcing paths through the snow. But whenever I was in the company of the Khan and the princes, I would recount our heroic deeds, saying, 'We struck Haydar Agha thus, he struck us thus,' and they would say, 'Wasn't it that Haydar who brought Melek Ahmed Pasha to this town with eighty thousand soldiers? He got what he deserved!'

The next day, however, 10,000 select musketeers, all troops from Haydar Agha's clan, had mustered within Bitlis town and on the hills overlooking the Khan's Garden, demanding blood for blood, and clamouring that the case be settled according to the Sharia. The ulema and the sheikhs intervened, saying, 'This Haydar Kethüda is the one who brought Melek Ahmed Pasha to this town; that is why he was made steward. He got what he deserved.' In this way peace was restored between the clansmen and the Khan. So poor Haydar Kethüda, and three of his servants, and five of the Khan's retinue all shed their blood for nought. The clansmen consoled themselves with the thought that at least their chief, the knight Haydar, did not die alone. And so they returned home.

Until now Abdal Khan had not emerged from his harem. That very day, after the suit of Haydar Kethüda's clan had been disposed of, he came out to the *divan* hall and sat down in a corner, intending to be unobtrusive and merely listen. He did occasionally say a few words relating to affairs of state, and some wits observed that 'the Khan has some mischief up his sleeve.' Later the Khan said, 'My Evliya, what do you think about this matter of Haydar Kethüda?'

'Ants take wing when they are about to perish,' I replied. 'He was contemptuous of everyone, and not subtly, but in view of all the courtiers. In fact, on the auspicious day he was killed, he came over to where I was sitting with my princes and, as though spitting into the fireplace, he let out such a gob of slime that my princes' suits were spoiled and my own face was covered with a rainstorm of spit.' Along with such disparaging remarks I also cracked some jokes, which made the Khan laugh and cheered him up quite a bit. While he was still in this merry mood, I kissed the Khan's noble hand and said, 'My lord and patron, most noble Khan! It is now forty-one years that I have been a world traveller and boon-companion to mankind. I am tired of roaming the seven climes.

> Know you, my soul, what in this world
> > Ought not to cease?
> I've been everywhere, and there is nought
> > Better than – Bitlis!

The climate is mild – especially that my Khan is the reigning spirit in this country. True, you have given me a dye works, and have thus raised me from the dust. But give me a house and a slavegirl too!' I sealed this request with a kiss on the knee, and he turned to Çakir Agha, who served as his vizier.

'Çakir,' he said, 'go bring my jewel-encrusted casket that I keep with me in the harem.' When he brought it, the Khan said, 'You see, my Evliya, your pasha came with 8,000 soldiers and ruined this house of ours. They pillaged ten Egyptian treasures' worth of my wealth, reducing me to penury. Of all my properties and goods, only this little case escaped unharmed, since it was whisked away by my wife Hanım Sultan, Zal Pasha's daughter. I also managed to convey seven mule-trains of goods and treasures to the Mudiki mountains before your pasha could get to them – they are there still in the Mudiki country. Now, just take a look inside this casket.'

He removed the cover and I peered in. Glory to God! It was filled with rubies, emeralds, pearls, chrysolites, garnets, turquoises, cats-eyes, fish-eyes, and tomcats-eyes. The middle compartment alone was overflowing with brilliant diamonds, each one 20 or 30, even 40 carats. The outside of the casket was Frankish enamel work, painted in gold as though by Mani, and studded with pure gems. Indeed, the rulers of the world could not afford to purchase such a thing, they could only seize it by force. Even I, who have seen something of the world, was dazzled at the sight of this case, and bit my finger in astonishment.

'What is it, my Evliya?' said the Khan when he saw me in this state.

'By God, my Khan, I have roamed the world for forty-one years and visited eleven kingdoms; I have been boon-companion to nine padishahs and have sat with them knee to knee; but I have never seen anything like this highly-wrought jewel-encrusted casket.' The Khan was immensely pleased.

'Now my Evliya,' he said, 'since you love us, and since you have left

Melek and wish to remain here, henceforth you are my son, and I appoint you as tutor to my sons. From now on you may rest easy. Forget about the anarchy and rebellions of Kurdistan. You stay with me and enjoy your leisure in whatever orchard or garden you wish. I swear by the spirit of my ancestors of the House of Abbas, and by the soul of Sultan Evhadehullah, and I swear by God: I will drown you in wealth, to spite Melek Pasha; I'll give you one of my daughters in legitimate marriage; and I'll give you several slavegirls and a fine pleasure-garden. Now, accept these deeds. They are for a garden plot in the Avih valley, including a multitude of courtyards laid out like Persian avenues, a variety of chambers, and a bath with pool and fountain.' He took the title deeds out of the jewellery case and handed them to me, and I rubbed my face upon his felicitous foot.

When I came out, I displayed these gifts to all the courtiers and pretended to be deliriously happy at this good fortune. But the truth was that all joy had vanished from my heart ever since Haydar Agha was cut up at my side. I could only think about mounting my horse, girding my sword, and running away. My joy had turned to sorrow, my wine to poison; as in the verse:

> Not everyone knows what pain I suffer;
> Only I know, and the only God knows.

I remained in Bitlis two more months in this state, unable to go anywhere, since we were completely snowbound.

One day, letters arrived from Melek Ahmed Pasha for Ziyaeddin Khan and for myself, instructing me and the canteen officer to collect without fail the twenty purses still outstanding. Old Abdal Khan got wind of this, and said, 'He stole ten Egyptian treasures of wealth from this town, and claims that twenty purses are left. God willing, now that he is removed from office in Van, and he cannot return via Erzurum in this dead of winter, he will decide to take the milder route via Diyarbekir, so he will have to pass through the valley of Bitlis. God willing, I will turn old Melek into a monkey bombarded by cannon shot all the way to Donkey Valley. I'll make him bray like a donkey and make his followers groan, I'll strip him naked and cook him raw, I'll pour a chamber-pot over Melek's head as I did to Boynueğri Mehmed Pasha, I'll smear his cheeks and his eyes with filth, and taking a few of my favourite pages I'll capture all his drums and standards!'

Escape from Bitlis

He took a solemn oath to this effect, and all present in the council applauded, crying: 'What you say is quite just, my Khan.'

Then he addressed me: 'What do you think, my Evliya?'

'My Khan,' I replied, 'still, you are a noble padishah, with heart as bounteous as the sea. Still, you will act with forgiveness. You will ignore what the Pasha has done, and if he comes here out of office, you will receive him just as when he came before. You will repay kindness for the evil he has done, saying, "He is an imperial son-in-law and a noble vizier, I will do what befits my dignity and preserves my reputation." Then all the people of Kurdistan, and all the people in the lands of the House of Osman, will applaud and sing your praises, while they curse Melek with a million curses reserved for the likes of Haman and Pharaoh and Korah and Yazid. Melek will suffer malediction, while you, my Khan will enjoy benediction. You know the saying:

> Cast goodness upon the waters:
> God knows, what matters if the fish do not?'

'Bravo, Evliya,' said the Khan, 'you are truly a man of chivalry, who knows the due of bread and salt. I was fired up with righteous indignation, and said that I would do this and that. But if Melek does come to this humble valley, I'll embarrass him with gifts and favours, I'll give him enough stores to last until he reaches Diyarbekir, I'll give him my own sons as an entourage, including my son Ziyaeddin whom he made khan, and they'll accompany him as far as Diyarbekir by my order.'

He spoke many such vaunting words. But every day in Bitlis town some innocents would be the objects of slanderous accusations: 'You are the ones who instigated Melek Ahmed Pasha and brought him to this region;' or, 'You are Haydar Kethüda's puppet.' And every day they would toss innocent Muslims from the tower of Bitlis castle, or else they would gang up on them and hack them down with swords, or they would throw them with hands tied to their necks off the Garden cliffs, or from Mt Deh-divan, or the Avih cliffs, and the poor victims would lunge down like the birds of Ababil (105:3) and be dashed in a hundred pieces on the rocks below. Only God succoured one man: as soon as they tossed him down from the castle, the fellow's shirt opened like a sail and caught on a rock, where he was left hanging. By my request they attached lassoes to the fellow, drew him up, and let him go free.

Noteworthy adventures. There was a certain Molla Mehmed the Sorcerer, a veritable Avicenna in the science of magic. He was described above, when Melek Ahmed Pasha first arrived in Bitlis and this Molla mounted a bath log and rode it as a *King and Beggar* horse.

One day the Molla and I were in the Avih valley in the town of Bitlis, watching the young lads of the town skiing over the snow and the ice on their *tahuk* or skis. All the lovely Rozhiki boys were hugging and romping, skiing down to the bottom of the valley, then climbing back up the slope to show off their skill again. And quite a few of us old lechers were having fun watching their antics.

'Tell me, Evliya Çelebi,' said my companion Molla Mehmed, 'which of those boys would you like to see ski down the hill, and then keep on skiing up this side so we can get a closer look?'

I pointed out two lads wearing pied headbands and holding their skis in their hands. 'Those are the ones I would like to see.'

'And I,' said the Molla, 'have fallen in love with those two boys over there, with pied bands on their heads, Küfre jackets on their backs, and their skis underneath them. Now I'm going to make all four of those lovely lads ski uphill on this side and come right toward us.' He turned to face the other way, covered his head with the skirts of his coat, and recited some mumbo-jumbo. All at once the four pretty boys whom we had pointed out skied like lightning down to the bottom of the valley, then kept right on skiing up the hill on our side, shooting up like a fountain, until they came to a halt in front of us. It seems they knew Molla Mehmed, and they kissed his hand. Then they again took off down the slope toward the watermills below the Khan's Garden, and from there continued skiing uphill until they reached their starting point.

All of us lovers were astounded at this feat – it made me feel quite giddy. But now all the boys began skiing in a row, one behind the other like a flock of cranes. When they reached the bottom, suddenly all of them reversed direction and returned to the top, like a lightning bolt, skiing backwards! All the onlookers were lost in amazement. In short, that day Molla Mehmed demonstrated his prowess to me and to the people of Bitlis with these and other such tricks.

However, by God's wisdom, despite his being such a skillful magician, as the saying goes, 'When destiny strikes, the eyes go blind.' Verse:

> Through cautionary measures
> You can't thwart destiny;
> Alhough you be cautious a thousand times,
> Still what will be will be.

Also: *There is no turning away His decree, and no preventing His judgement.* In other words, there is no remedy for fate.

As we were viewing these marvellous spectacles, I happened to look behind and saw a white hand beckoning me from one of the windows of the Khan's Garden. I ignored it and again became absorbed in watching the boys ski. A little later I glanced behind again, and once again a hand appeared at one of the Khan's Garden windows and motioned rapidly several times. As I was pondering what this signal might mean, who should appear but Altı Kulaç – he was a tall Sarıca, all the taller because of his conical cap, which was a good fathom long, so they used to call him Altı Kulaç or 'Six Fathoms'. He always went in front of the Khan and carried a huge battleaxe in his hand. Now this Altı Kulaç appeared at our sides like Destiny's cloud.

'Evliya Çelebi,' he said, 'the noble Khan beckoned you several times from the Garden window grill with his own blessed hand, but you paid no attention and failed to come to the Garden. Get up now, he wants to see you, alone.'

'Well then, let's go,' said I, as I started to get up from the snow. Molla Mehmed started to get up as well. Suddenly Altı Kulaç brought down his axe on the Molla's head, giving him such a blow that his brain spurted out. My face and shoulders were spattered with it, even before I had completely got to my feet; and I leapt up from the spot in sheer terror, outleaping even Amr Ayyar. Altı Kulaç removed the Molla's clothes and tossed his corpse down the cliff onto the snow below.

'God's mercy!' I thought as I began to mount the slope. 'One day in these valleys they will kill me too for some reason, just like this.' Then I saw that the Khan had sent along his own horse for me. Praising God, I jumped up on the horse without even using the stirrups, and galloped before the Khan, cracking all sorts of jokes, and using dialect to make fun of 'Molla Mehmed's funeral obsequities' and 'meritorious intention against the valiant magician.' All covered with blood and gore as I was, I greeted the Khan, saying, 'May your Holy War prosper!'

'My Evliya,' said the Khan, 'what happened to your face?'

'The magician's brain spattered on it,' I said.

'Well, Evliya, I did wave to you several times from the window, but you failed to come.'

'My Khan, how was I to know what a naked waving hand meant? There was no body, only a waving hand. I remarked at it, and I was also freezing out there; but Molla Mehmed – may God not rest his soul – kept saying, 'Please sit a while longer and I'll show you another trick, so when you go back to Turkey you will sing my praises, and they'll summon me to Turkey by royal decree to see for themselves what skills I possess'; and so he kept me sitting there in the cold.

'But, my Khan,' I continued, 'what was that poor magician's crime, that you had him killed in this manner?'

'My Evliya,' replied the Khan, 'that damned infidel ate my bread for so long now, and drank cup after cup of rice-water sherbet from my own hand. But he paid no regard to the due of bread and salt. He conspired with Haydar Kethüda, saying: 'You, Haydar Agha, make common cause with Melek Ahmed Pasha, and have him come to this town with the Van soldiery. I will plant a charm among the Khan's troops assuring that they will be routed, and also plant a talisman among Melek Pasha's troops assuring that they will be victorious and will kill the Khan. Then one of his sons will become khan; you, O knight Haydar, will become steward in perpetuity; and I will become *kadi* of Bitlis.' That is exactly what he did when I was battling with Melek. So on that day my soldiers were routed like ants and snakes, and I had to flee to the mountains of Mudiki. God be praised, I have returned to my throne safe and sound, and now I have had that devil killed by Altı Kulaç's axe.'

'My Khan,' said I, 'may the spirit of Abu Muslim, the halberdier of Merv in Khorasan, rejoice, that Altı Kulaç with his axe has beheaded such a Yazidi. He got what he deserved! If that devil's crime was as you say, my Khan, give me leave to go and piss on his corpse. And let me join the Kurdish rabble in stoning the devil – I'll bury him with stones of damnation.'

At this, the Khan gave the order, and everyone in the town, great and small alike, even the servants and the Christian boys, came with one or two stones to 'stone the devil', leaving the magician's filthy corpse buried beneath a hillock of several thousand stones.

But he was – may God rest his soul – a true master in the science of sorcery, more skilled than anyone I have seen in the seven climes. True, in 1058 (1648), the year Sultan Mehmed IV assumed the throne, when I accompanied the governor of Damascus, Kara Murtaza Pasha, on his expedition against the Druzes, there was in Acre a certain tightrope walker who was a veritable Mirzad in the science of magic. But this Molla Mehmed was a Koran commentator and a purveyor of Hadith, as well as having written books on magical science. Many of his skills were noted above, when he displayed them to Melek Ahmed Pasha and his retinue in the Khan's palace. *God have mercy on his soul.*

This humble sinner and the Pasha's poor canteen officer were full of anguish at these latest events. But what could we do? Verse:

> Now and then I moan and sigh:
> It's not in my hands.
> A captive of grief, I cry:
> It's not in my hands.

All we could do was continually recite: *We belong to God, and to Him we shall return* (2:156). The rigours of winter grew daily worse and the roads were blocked. The Pasha on his side, though dismissed from office, had not set foot out of Van. But I could not discuss going to the Pasha while I was with the Khan and his cronies. I did, however, mount horses every day, and make paths through snow and storms toward Rahva or toward Kefender. I would stop in at the farms belonging to the Khan or to the others, have a meal, and return to the city. If the Khan questioned me about it, I would say: 'I went to your farm, my Khan,' or, 'I went to Arab Khalil Agha's farm, and I ate *kükü* (omelette) pilav with rice-water.' I never lied, but told him exactly where I had gone; and when they questioned their farm men, my reports were confirmed.

In this fashion I spent another month, in constant agitation, but I kept my feelings hidden. Day and night I busied myself praying and reciting the Koran, reading books of Hadith and the Koran-commentary of Daylami,[44] and discussing matters of the Sharia as far as I was able with the Kurdish ulema. At the same time, I did not want them to think I had become some kind of humourless fanatic. So when I was in the Khan's presence, or in the company of his sons Bedir and Nureddehir, or with the other tribal chiefs, I would play the clown, joking and jesting, and also would sing different kinds of songs, including *kâr, nakş, savt, zikir, zecel, amel, tasnifat* and mournful *kavi*. And so they accepted me as one of their retinue.

By this time the new khan – i.e. Melek Ahmed Pasha's protegé, Ziyaeddin

---

44 Muhammad ibn Abd al-Malik al-Tusi al-Daylami, twelfth century.

Khan – would not let me out of his sight for a moment: he even made me sleep in his own room. For my part, I had despaired of them all and I took refuge in God alone. Terror had settled in my heart. I maintained vigilance night and day. Downstairs, in the stable, the horses were kept saddled at night, bedded down on some dried horse dung a cubit thick, while my servants slept with their clothes on and with all their weapons ready at hand. If I said 'boo' the horses were already saddled, all they had to do was remove their fetters and mount.

A notable adventure and a sorrowful calamity. In this town of Bitlis, and this mine of Iblis; our nights were spent like the Night of Power, our days like New Year's Day; but our food was our own hearts' blood, our comrades and companions were the invisible Saints. Finally, one evening, the youthful Ziyaeddin Khan proposed to the company, 'Tonight, while everyone is asleep, let's all go to the bath house, where we'll apply henna and depilatory, get rubdowns with *fütuni* bath gloves, and have a party.'

On every side they applauded the idea. At sunset, we had our usual sumptuous banquet, and after the evening prayer we were informed that the bathhouse of the noble Khan – described above – had been adorned and prepared. Six of us – Ziyaeddin Khan, his eldest brother Bedir Bey, his next elder brother Nureddehir Bey, myself, the chief taster Mustafa Çelebi who was kinsman to the Sheikh of Urmia in Diyarbekir, and the story-reciter Molla Dilaver-i Isfahani – we six rascals entered that bath, which was the envy of kings. And a right royal time we had, somersaulting into the pools, swimming about left and right, joking and pranking. After nearly drowning in these sports, some superb slaveboys rubbed us down with bath gloves and soap. We lit pastilles of raw ambergris in censers, and savoured the fragrance. We quaffed all sorts of musk-flavoured beverages. Cleansed and pure, we retired to the dressing-room for some fresh air. Then we returned to the bath, where we were enjoying the white magic spectacle of the fountains and jets.

'Brother,' said Nureddehir Bey to Ziyaeddin Khan, 'outside with my clothing is a canister with some aphrodisiac taffy. A person who eats just one ounce of it can engage in sexual intercourse seven times. If we each eat a little, we can also dispel the heat of our bodily humour; and if the spirit moves us, we can even get off on one another.'

'If I eat some,' said I jokingly, 'I'm sure I could get off on my own brother – even on Molla Dilaver here!'

'Tell Seyf Ali to bring that canister from the dressing room,' ordered the Khan. Seyf Ali came into the bath fully clothed and handed over the canister to the rascal, Nureddehir Bey, who said, 'You're very stupid, treasure-boy Seyf Ali. How can we eat this taffy without a spatula? Give me that dagger stuck in your belt.' Nureddehir grabbed the dagger from Seyf Ali's belt. Then, with the canister in one hand and the pointed dagger in the other, he began to strut about the bath like a raging lion. I nearly fainted with fright, for I knew how many people Nureddehir had stabbed that day some time back when they cut up Haydar Kethüda, and I knew how many times he had stabbed Haydar Kethüda. Seeing him now, brandishing a dagger, I recalled that scene and was scared out of my wits. For all of us in the bath were naked – and there was Nureddehir with a naked dagger in his hand.

'If you say this taffy is bad, let me eat some first,' cried Nureddehir. Using the dagger, he removed a big chunk from the canister and ate it. Then he gave some to me. 'O God, I take refuge in You alone,' said I to myself, and, unclean as it was, I ate it. He took another chunk on the tip of the dagger, eyeing his brother the Khan. Suddenly he bounded over to the Khan, roaring like a lion, and offered the taffy in a menacing fashion, as though he were striking the Khan's naked breast with the dagger.

'Ah, brother,' said the Khan, 'with what kindly attitude and friendly disposition you give me this taffy.' He tried to take the dagger together with the taffy from his brother's hand, so he could feed himself.

'Brother,' said Nureddehir, 'won't you imbibe the Water of Life from the hand of Hızır?' The Khan snatched the taffy from the tip of the dagger, tossed it in his mouth, and immediately plunged into the pool. I knew he would not swallow it, but spit it out into the pool instead. After frolicking a bit in the water, he came out and got dressed. Nureddehir gave some taffy to Molla Dilavere and Mustafa Çelebi as well, then they went out to the dressing room. The rest of us finished our ablutions and followed suit.

Retiring to Ziyaeddin Khan's quarters, we lit incense of rose-water, aloes and ambergris, and enjoyed music and conversation until midnight. We also played gencefe which is known in the land of the infidels as 'cards'. It consists of seventy or eighty rectangular painted cards – these particular ones were painted with lacquer and came from Persia – and the players form two teams. I was on the Khan's team and had such good luck that I won seventy *abbasis*.

We finally tired of card-playing as well. Towels were brought, we washed our hands, then snacked on candies and sweetmeats, devouring so much that you would say, 'These men are wholly made of sugar.' Next came the fruit, fit for a padishah: plums, apricots, pomegranates, peaches, *meleçe* and *abbasi* and *ordubari* pears, and seven varieties of grapes. We washed this down with musk-scented juices made of sour cherry, Mardin plum, red Bukhara prune, and Shahraban pomegranate. After towels were brought and we washed our hands a final time, they ordered the bedclothes to be laid out. The Khan's brothers Bedreddin and Nureddin-i-bi-din (i.e., Bedir and Nureddehir) left for their rooms along with the chief taster Miskin (i.e., Mustafa Çelebi) saying, 'Good night, my Khan.'

Excusing myself to urinate, I too went out and made my way from room to room to the *divan* hall, where I unexpectedly ran into Kara Mehmed Kethüda – he was made steward to the new khan after Haydar Agha was killed. This Kara Mehmed was on night-patrol duty in the divan hall, with a guard of 500 musketeers who were conversing pleasantly and playing various instruments.[45]

I passed through them, greeting this one and that one, and proceeded downstairs to the stable where, as was my custom, I inspected my horses and gave instructions to my slaveboys.

When I returned to the Khan's room I saw that he was lying in his bedclothes on a couch next to the fireplace. Molla Dilaver had fallen off while reciting a story, and was now sleeping the sleep of the Seven Sleepers and snoring in the *rehavi* musical mode. His bed was situated at the foot of the closet, while mine had been laid out near the door, as usual. As I lay my head on the pillow with a sigh, I prayed from the bottom of my heart to God the Dispeller of cares. The Khan's coffee-server, a fine lad named Rustam, who was lying next to the fireplace at the foot of the Khan's couch, was also dozing like Rustam's father Zal.[46] All of them snoring away like pigs made me quite depressed. As I was consulting our inborn companions – bile and melancholia and satanic whisperings – the Khan interrupted my dark thoughts: 'Evliya, why did you go out?'

'My Padishah,' I replied, 'urination – *kertem pereset*.' He giggled and said, 'Evliya, what language is this *kertem pereset*?'

'My Khan,' I said, 'it is called 'male Persian' and was handed down from

---

45 Mentioned in the text are: *çögür* (a kind of guitar), *tanbura* (pandore lute), *karadüzen* (a kind of guitar), *ıklığ* (a kind of violin) and *revza* (a kind of lute).
46 In the *Shahnama* the white-haired Zal is the father of the hero Rustam. In Evliya's usage, he is the figure of a decrepit old man.

Escape from Bitlis

my forefather Alkıravün Çelebisi.' Laughing out loud, he came out from under the covers and sat up on the couch.

'I can't sleep, my dear Evliya. My heart is on fire. Come lie down over here, let's chat like working-men. I can confide in you. Also, you have been my tutor for some time now. What do you think about the situation here in Kurdistan?'

'It can't be helped, my Khan,' I replied. 'God knows, the rising star of this town of Bitlis is fixed in the constellation of Scorpio, the mansion of Mars, fiery. Therefore Mars the executioner always has his sword drawn and ready to strike in this town. It can't be helped, my Khan. That is the way of this old, perishing, workhouse of a world.'

Well, we talked for two entire hours – how can I record every word? Finally he said, 'My Evliya, I swear by God, if it weren't the dead of winter, I would cross Mt Kuskunkıran in one night, and would rub my face at the horse's hoof of my father Melek Ahmed Pasha in Van. For me it would be a relief even to wash dishes in his service.'

'God forbid, my Khan,' I said; 'if you submit to the Ottomans, they will treat you well for a few months, but after that they won't look in your face. Now, tell me why you are so sad?'

'Don't you see how they cut up the man my father Melek made my steward? And how many of my men they have thrown from the castle cliff? And didn't you see just now how threatening Nureddehir was, when he gave me the taffy on the dagger?' He heaved a sigh.

'My Khan,' I said, 'the taffy must have affected your brother, and that is why he was so excited when he offered some to you.'

'You don't understand, Evliya. Let's leave it at that.' He lay down and pulled the quilt over his head.

I too returned to my bed, saying, 'O perverse and perishable world! That is how sultans' deputies act – and the sultans themselves. What comfort or joy is there in that? As the verse has it, *Truly, the greatest sultanate is to be free of marriage bonds.*' I crawled under the covers fully clothed, as usual, having just loosened my waist-cloth but now removed my trousers. But Satan's whisperings again prevented me from sleeping. God knows, it was two hours past midnight.

Upshot of the calamitous adventure. I was lying in bed, and my eyes were on the door. Suddenly, who should appear there but Nureddehir Bey, with a waistband round his middle and his sleeves rolled up. Softly he crept in, stretched and yawned, cracked his knuckles and snapped his lower vertebra, then fingered his dagger and straightened his belt. As I lay there watching, he first came over to me, saying, 'Evliya the dervish. What are you doing in this land?'

My heart was in my throat. Taking refuge in God, I gave a snort as if in my sleep, and began to snore like a pig, just as the others were. I was really trumpeting in a comical fashion. Seeing me thus, Nureddehir said, 'This dervish's beauty-sleep is also like the sleep of swine,' and he passed me by.

Moving on to the story-reciter Molla Dilaver at the foot of the closet, he said, 'You pimp from Isfahan, get to work, or go to your house down in the city and sleep there!'

He passed him also and went over to the coffee-server Rustam, lying next to the Khan, and looked him over too. Then his eye fell on his dear brother the Khan, who was lying on the couch and slumbering peacefully, 'bedded on roses and covered with hyacinths.' He glanced about furtively, then returned to gaze at the Khan. I was peering out from under my coverlet like a dog from under the skirting-board of a privy, wondering if they had some private matter to discuss.

Suddenly he drew the dagger from his belt, flung off the Khan's gold-embroidered quilt, and gave him a kick, shouting, 'Get up, you catamite!'

Groggy with sleep, the Khan opened his eyes and saw that it was his own dear brother. As he cried out, Nureddehir plunged the sharp dagger in his breast, then again at the midriff, twisting it into his belly. Grasping in terror and futility for his own dagger, the Khan fell to the floor, where his brother stabbed him once again.

Now the coffee-server Rustam got to his feet, crying, 'O my Bey, what have you done to my Khan? You have doomed my Khan and his house, O Nureddehir the damned!' They began to struggle, but Nureddehir stuck the dagger into his midriff with such a terrific blow that Rustam's blood came gushing out and his guts trailed down to his feet.

Nothing daunted, I myself was about to leap into the fray, but I must have fainted, for I did not have the strength to move from my place. Meanwhile the poor Khan was struggling for his life, wrestling with Nureddehir as Rustam tried to hold him from the other side. But the Khan, with his delicate frame, was no match for the powerful and merciless Nureddehir, who got the upper hand, and left him as full of holes as a powder-maker's sieve. In the end, that highway robber Death, who cuts all threads of Hope, befell his victim; the Khan quaffed the poison cup from the pointed dagger at the hand of Nureddin-i-bi-din (Nureddin the Irreligious), and was transported from this abode of vanity to the palace of joy and eternity; may God have mercy on his soul.

With the Khan lying lifeless on one side and Rustam on the other, Nureddehir tore through the treasury-room door and recklessly began to open the cupboards and chests. God be praised, I came to my senses and, shooting from under the bedclothes like a basilisk, darted through seven doors out to the *divan* hall, where I emerged holding my trousers band as though I were going out to urinate. The sentries were all half asleep.

'Evliya Çelebi,' said one, 'is it near morning?'

'Is Nureddehir conferring in there with the Khan?' asked another.

'The conference is over,' I replied, 'I am going to pee.' I flew down the twenty steps from the *divan* hall to the stable.

'Up my lads! Hurry! Mount, you bastards!' I cut the horses' fetters with my dagger, bridled my own horse right away, and girt on my sword. My slaveboy named Hüseyn was up and ready, God bless him; but the others were still rubbing their eyes and tying on their waistbands, and I saw they would be of no use. Kazım, however, was also ready, since he too slept in his clothes. He grabbed his sword, which he kept next to his bed, clapped it to his waist, took his musket in his hand, and released his horse's fetters. I grabbed two muskets in addition to my sword, and also attached a battleaxe to my belt. We tightened the horses' girths and the three of us mounted – myself and my two slaveboys – leaving behind my other four slaveboys, six horses, and a great deal of money and clothing.

From the Khan's Garden we flung headlong down the slope, swooping hawklike over ice and snow, clattering over the ice to the bottom of Değirmenler valley. There I shouted to Menteş Bölükbaşı, 'Hey brother! Mount! They've gone too far!' The fellow apparently was not used to getting up before dawn. 'They've killed the Khan,' I cried, 'what are you waiting for?' He came to his senses, flew down to his stable, mounted his horse bareback using a spurred bit, took his sword and musket from his servant and threw his fur coat over his shoulders.

With extreme caution and much difficulty, we passed through the Husrev Pasha market in the dark. What a huge town this city of Bitlis was! It took us some time to get up through the town. When we reached the point known as Butcher's Fountain we heard wails and cries from the direction of the Khan's Garden, also musket shots. Finally we came out to the Rahva plain. The snow was as high as a minaret. Fortunately, I had mounted every day and had opened paths, trampling down the snow drifts with five or six of my servants as a daily exercise. So the four of us pushed through; now at a jog-trot, now at a gallop, now at a run; often sinking in the snow, and looking back in the dark.

An hour before dawn we reached Tatvan Han on the shore of Lake Van. An agha of Pehleli Ahmed Pasha had recently been posted there as commander. We asked him for news of Melek Ahmed Pasha.

'You can reach him tomorrow near Adilcevaz castle.'

'Please, my Agha,' said I, 'we have urgent business with Melek Ahmed Pasha. We have to go on the double!' He gave us a ten-man escort and we set off immediately along the shore of Lake Van, keeping to the sandy beach where there was no snow. Postponing the dawn prayer to a more opportune time, we galloped for an hour, when, glancing back, we could just make out forty or fifty horsemen advancing over the white snow like eagles seeking their prey. We wondered whether they were fugitives like ourselves, or else a party sent to pursue us, and we climbed a snow-covered dune to take a look.

Dawn was just breaking. Behind this group of fifty or so horsemen another group appeared of roughly 100 mounted troops. As we watched, they caught up with the first group and the two forces engaged in battle. Finally the second troop cut down all the earlier group of fifty, stripped them of their clothes, and rounded up their horses. 'Power to our cruppers and blessings on our whips!' we cried as we decided to flee.

'My brother,' I said to my old friend Menteş Bölükbaşı, 'they have seen our hoofprints, they will pursue us too. God help us! If only we can reach Ahlat castle.'

We started off again, but the ten-man escort we got from the commander of Tatvan stayed behind at the shore of Lake Van. As we fled for our lives and cried blessings to our whips, we glanced behind. Those assassins caught up with our ten escorts. They gave no quarter, but cut them all down before our eyes, and began to gather their mounts and trappings. The four of us cried to God for help and pushed our horses to the limit.

Suddenly my poor Hüseyn's horse swerved and began to shy. 'God help you, my lad, press on!' I cried. 'If the horse shies, dismount, throw off your weapons, and run along the shore. God willing, you'll reach such a haven as Ahlat castle.' No matter how much he whipped it, the horse kept shying, so he dismounted and began to run. My poor Hüseyn! Those Rozhiki devils caught up with him, bared their swords, and mercilessly cut off the lad's head. Terrified, the three of us who remained let the reins loose and galloped as hard as we could, fleeing along the shore of Lake Van. God be praised, our horses were in top condition, and went like lightning; for we had withheld their straw to make them lean, and we had mounted every day in Bitlis and trained them hard by pushing through the snow.

By now the world-illuminating sun had risen out of a breach in the firmament and stood a spear's height, casting its rays over the snow. It revealed Papşen Han to our left and Ahlat Castle ahead. Those damned Kurds were still pouring after us, although quite some distance behind, as we trotted like Tatars and flung ourselves exhausted into Ahlat castle, reciting the verse: *And he who enters it is secure* (3:97). I immediately dismounted and shut the castle gate behind us.

3. Diplomacy in Split (Spalato)

Description of the walled city of Split

When the castle came into view, we sent ahead Baba Ahmedzade Baba Ismail Agha. Suddenly a party of infidels appeared to greet us – 1000 musketeers on foot and 400 horsemen. They brought us in procession to the guesthouse called Nazarete (lazaretto) in the lower suburb. It was grandly furnished. As soon as we settled in, they fired 1000 cannons to demonstrate their majesty. And they sent a young and princely officer, with a retinue of 200 infidel musketeers, to serve us. He brought forty or fifty porcelain dishes piled with various breakfast items. We ate them, but they were mostly sugary confections.

The next day another officer came and, in accordance with their ancient pomp and ceremony, invited me to the quarters of the general. Together with my armed retinue, all of us mounted our Arab steeds and proceeded at a slow pace as far as the skirt of the castle, where their captain of the guards told our servants to leave their weapons before entering. This struck me as an outrageous demand.

'According to our *kanun* it is disgraceful to break our formation and enter unarmed,' I said. 'If you do not allow us to enter the castle in our formation we will go back.'

After a good deal of disputation they eventually let us go in with our weapons. When we arrived at the council hall, the general rose and we took our places, I on one chair and the general on another. I kissed the letter, placed it on my head, and gave it to the general, hand to hand. He had it read by an interpreter and its contents explained.

'God forbid,' he said, 'that we should do anything on this frontier contrary to the treaty, or that we should repair and garrison castles that you have destroyed. Only we do fear the Ottomans, and so we do keep in good repair those castles that are ours of old. They should just leave us alone. But look how many of your troops have been sacking our territory for the past five months. Moreover it is recorded in our registers that you have taken 3,000 of our men captive over the past six months.'

'Well,' I replied, 'you are on bad terms with the frontier population. For their part, they cannot sit quiet but mount raids and take captives and booty.'

'God grant that this endless conflict on Crete will be resolved, either in your favour or in ours,' he said. 'As long as there is no peace there, neither you nor we will live in peace here.'

After much discussion I presented him the prayer-rug and a pile of *köse* (?) turban-cloth that the Pasha had sent, saying, 'Your intimate friend, the courageous Pasha, requests that you give us the Ottoman prisoners languishing in your dungeon: our chamberlain, two of our janissaries, and six of our Bosnian *gazis*.'

He immediately had all ten youths brought and delivered them to me. The fact is that the Pasha had no inkling of all this. I had learned about these prisoners from some merchants in Split and requested them extempore. God be praised, the general did not hesitate, and he gave me an Ottoman horse as well.

'Please do not be offended,' he said, 'that we lodged you in the lazaretto and not in the castle. It is our *kanun* that all guests and all merchants be lodged in that quarter for forty days before mingling with our people. We have them stay there for forty days to determine whether anyone has the plague. But we brought you to our presence after one day.'

They then served a grand feast, laid out on tall benches called *tirpeza* (i.e., table). There were various roasted meats; also vinegar stews cooked with parsley, mint and celery root; and sweetmeats. After dining we washed our hands according to Ottoman ceremonial and drank a goblet of musk-flavoured sherbets. Then we proceeded in formation back to our lodgings outside the wall and began a leisurely tour of the castle and the suburb.

This castle, according to their own report, was conquered by Farhad Pasha and Husrev Pasha during the reign of Sultan Süleyman, but was occupied by the warlike Franks in the same year and is now in the hands of the Venetians. It is a solidly built pentagonal fortress, with a thick three-layered wall, on the shore of the Venetian Gulf (i.e. Adriatic Sea). Because it is quite ancient it is repaired every year and the stones whitewashed so that it resembles a swan.

All the munitions are in a state of readiness. There is a series of great redoubts, sticking out like hedgehog quills toward land and sea, that protect the harbour and the Klisz strait. Each of these has forty or fifty balaramada guns, and each of these guns shoots cannon balls weighing 40 or 50 *okkas*.

The harbour is spacious enough to accommodate 200 bargias, galleons, carracks and galleys.

Indeed, there were two Venetian barges in this harbour that I would need a separate book to describe properly. Suffice it to say that each of them was like a mountain, with ten balaramada guns at the prow and ten at the stern. The three masts – at the prow, in the middle, and at the stern – were topped with pennants and flags depicting the cross and Saint Mark. fifty oars on the right side and fifty on the left were pulled by Muslim captives. There were 100 wind-sails, each with four infidels lying ready. And each oar had eight Muslims ready to pull. 300 armed infidel warriors stood ready at the prow and at the stern – Croatians, Slovenians, Carinthians, Montenegrans, Clementi Albanians and Uskoks (Christian Bosnians). These barges are like floating castles, conveying merchants and goods from this port of Split to Venice. The Venetian infidels possess six such barges, such as no king has ever had.

Around this harbour are *kavata* towers, meaning guard towers.

On the sea side the castle wall is a single layer, since there is no fear of attack from the sea; and two gates lead out to the harbour. But on the land side the wall is fortified in three layers. The moat, carved out of the rock, is very deep; and armed infidels stand ever ready between the layers of the threefold iron gates on the land side, stopping anyone from crossing the moat bridge.

The citadel is situated atop a hill and is quite small, but the main parts of the castle are filled layer on layer with houses. The lower castle has three large monasteries and several ancient churches with their idolatrous Christian ceremonial. There are 300 shops. I was told that there were baths as well, but I did not see them. The grandest of the houses is the general's palace. The merchants have magazines along the harbour filled with sheep's-wool and broadcloth, satins and brocades, silken and leathern stuffs. The trade in these commodities is very brisk, since this port is an entrepôt for goods going to Bosnia and thence to Turkey. The commerce is carried out in finely constructed stone buildings near the magazines.

Beyond the walls on all three sides, and stretching as far as the mountains of Clissa (Klisz) and the orchards of Salona, are 77,000 orchards – that is the number they cite – mainly olive groves laid out like Persian avenues, also figs, pomegranates, pears, lemons, oranges and citrons.

As this city is on the gulf coast the climate is mild. It is famous for the lovely lads and maids who sit in the shops selling their secret wares. We viewed them in the bazaar, and indeed the doe-eyed girls with their bright faces and sweet speech drive their lovers mad, as in the verse:

> This is a spectacle at which
> The spectator loses his wits.

Reportedly there are also prostitutes in the taverns. As for the men, they are very slim and elegant, with black vests and conical black hats.

We toured this city for three days. As we were resting on the fourth, the general showed up at our quarters with twenty trays of sugary confections. I rose to greet him, then we sat knee to knee in our secluded corner and ate the food. I presented the general with one gold-embroidered turban and two multicoloured Kaya Sultan handkerchiefs. He was extremely pleased with these gifts and put one of the handkerchiefs on his hat.

For his part, he presented me with ten black Sarajevo fur pieces – these are astrakhan lambskins black as beaver skins; ten suits of varicoloured broadcloth; ten rolls of varicoloured Frankish satins; 300 Venetian scudos – these are silver coins weighing ten drams apiece; one watch; one spyglass; one book with illustrations of the world called *Mappa Mundi*; and 100 musk-scented ducats. When he left he gave each of my forty-seven servants five ducats and one piece each of broadcloth and fine stuff. He had former obligations toward Baba Ahmedzade İsma'il Bey, and also feared him since they lived in close proximity; so he gave him one purse of *guruş* (i.e. scudos) and one suit of broadcloth, and also sent his father Baba Ahmed 100 gold pieces and one suit of broadcloth.

We bid farewell to the general and he went to his palace while we continued pursuing our own pleasures.

I record here some phrases of their Frankish tongue that I got from their interpreters who spoke excellent Turkish.

Language of the warlike Franks. Their language is called Italian (*Talyan*). Now the kings of Spain, France, Genoa, the grand-duchy of Livorno, Portugal, Dunkerque, Denmark, Holland, and England – all of their peoples

Diplomacy in Split (Spalato) 167

are Franks, but some are Catholic (*Papişta*), some Protestant (*Luteryan*), and some of the Italian sect, but they are all Christians; although the Swedes, the Czechs, the Karelians and the people of Sol (?) are Magians. And the Germans, Hungarians, Poles, Wallachians and Moldavians all have different languages. But the above-mentioned Franks all speak Italian; although each one has its own special dialect and terminology, and they communicate with one another only with interpreters. The most eloquent is the language of the Frankish Venetians. To be sure, there is an old saying that *Arabic is eloquence, Persian is elegance, Turkish is an offence, and all other languages are filth*. But the Venetian tongue is the sweetest of them all. To begin with the numerals:

uno 1 *duy* 2 *tire* 3 *kotrá* 4 *çinko* 5 *sey* 6 *sete* 7 *ot* 8 *neve* 9 *deçe* 10.

marya the name of Mother Maria *sanmarka* name of saints *pan* bread *akwa* water *bono çorno* Good morning *bono zeribonani* Good morning indeed *vino* wine *porko* pig *mele* honey *venko* Come! *pos* Sit! *Persiade duka* Where have you been? *mela* apple *esta dona bella* Is your daughter pretty? *bardaş* boy *be ko fotut fotut ladona* – begging your pardon – Let me fuck your wife *kosa voli* What do you want? *dolim po di pan* I want a piece of bried *tirom pürolates* I'll split your head *kane* dog *un çekinno tedonero* I'll give you a gold piece *senta baş bardaş* Don't move, boy! *mancá merda* Eat shit! *manca du merdo* You eat the shit!

In fact *manca* means 'shit' in the language of the Franks. What does it mean that they say their food is shit? To one who is a Muslim it should be called food, and then it should be eaten.[47]

Praise of the musk-scented Venetian gold pieces (i.e. ducats). According to their own correct report, it is truly alchemy, since no wicked king has ever possessed such gold. That is why in Turkey gilded silver vessels are white (?); but this Venetian gold is very red in colour and gives gilded copper and silver a reddish sheen. Indeed, on the gold pieces that in olden times they struck as votive offerings for Mawlana there is a staff with a forked banner at the top that is blood-red in colour, though of gold. If a strong youth rubs it in his hand it rolls and crumbles like dough. If one (of those old gold pieces) were found it would serve to gild 50 (today). In the period of Sultan Ahmed (reg. 1603–17) I saw many of them in my father's possession. But these days we never see them – even viziers don't have them. We get by with pennies and coppers weighing ten a dram. God grant

---

47 The translation of this passage is quite conjectural.

us blessings! What has happened to our zeal for Islam? We have to get our currency into good order!

I asked a number of their knowledgeable monks and patriarchs: 'Why, when his holiness Mawlana Jalaladdin Rumi was alive, did you sent 10,000 of those gold pieces every year as votive offerings?' Here is what they told me, 'Our doge (*pirinc-pirim*) was a knowledgeable person. When he heard about the saintly revelations and miracles of Shams (Tabrizi) and Mawlana, he wondered what sort of man he was and sent an envoy with gifts. When our envoy arrived in Konya and visited Mawlana, they received the gifts and then entertained the envoy according to their ceremonial with ecstatic dance and music and singing.

'The musicians then came before Mawlana and held out a tambourine for a reward. Mawlana, as our envoy watched, stretched out his right hand with the sleeve of his green cloak toward the west and said '*Bismillahi – In the name of God!*' At once a handful of Venetian ducats poured down into the tambourine. The ducats, which were red-hot as embers, burned the skin of the tambourine and fell onto the ground. When our envoy saw this he was struck with amazement and carefully recorded the exact time of the incident. The musicians took the gold and left.

'Our envoy took leave of Mawlana and returned to Venice. As soon as he arrived he was informed that a white hand in a green cloak had appeared at the wall of the well-fortified mint and, through a hole in the wall that also suddenly appeared, took a handful of ducats that were being forged in the fire; and that this had occurred at the exact moment which he had recorded in Konya.'

Now the envoy told the doge all he had witnessed in Konya; and the prisoners working in the mint also testified that 10,000 ducats had been taken by a white hand at the very time the envoy had recorded it in Konya. The doge, after consultation, decided to send 10,000 ducats with depiction of the banner every year to Mawlana in Konya. The Mevlevis, for their part, accepted the gift on the grounds, citing the line of verse, *Property of infidels is permitted for believers* and distributed it as alms to the poor.

Description of the Venetian gold piece (ducat). On the Venetian ducat, the tall figure to the right (sic; error for left) of the staff is Mawlana whom they began to depict on their ducats after the occurrence of the saintly miracle (recorded above). The figure opposite, to the right of the staff, with the squat headgear like that of Hacivad,[48] is their doge (*pirinc-pirim*) –

Diplomacy in Split (Spalato)

i.e. their king and chief of forty *beys*. Only the doge's headgear is a cap not a crown.

Jesus (on the reverse) has sheep's-wool stockings on his feet that somehow made their way from Edessa to Venice. One of the forty infidel *beys* becomes doge and on their false festival days dons the headgear and keeps it on his head thereafter. The staff on the ducat signifies that 'The staff of Moses and the stockings of Jesus are with us.' The inscriptions along the edge of this side of the coin (the obverse) are the names of Mawlana and the doge.

But on the reverse, the single tall figure inside the dotted oval is Jesus. He is surrounded by twelve dots with clawed edges representing the twelve constellations of the zodiac; or they are twelve stars standing for Jesus's twelve disciples; because the science of astrology is more advanced in Venice than in other infidel lands. The inscriptions around the figure of Jesus are blessings and greetings upon Jesus, in Latin, as follows:

[2 lines empty]

After confirming the information about this ducat and other matters, and touring the city to our satisfaction, we got letters and gifts for the Pasha from the general – including muskets, twenty rolls of brocaded silk and seven rolls of varicoloured broadcloth – plus one horse and one suit of broadcloth for each of the men released from captivity. The general accompanied us for one hour, then we bade farewell on the highway and he returned to Split.

4. The bandit Yano

There was an infidel named Yano in the Sheshan hills who was pillaging the city of Manastır. It was impossible to collect the money due from the villages in those hills. So I left all my attendants behind and rode up Mt Sheshan with a single slaveboy. **Adventure of this humble one.** After three hours an infidel with a mace appeared.

'Hey Turk,' he said. 'What are you doing in this mountain?'

'I have come to my friend Yano Bey. I must see him.'

The infidel went off, then came back and said, 'Come with me.' We dismounted and proceeded through thick forest. Five or six hundred infidels lined our path, each with a pike and a mace in his hands and two or three

---

48 A figure in the Karagöz shadow-puppet theatre.

muskets in his belt. On both sides men were roasting kebabs of lamb and pork, perhaps 300 animals. Several hundred tailors were cutting out clothing for the infidels from the cloth they had taken on their raids from the city of Manastır and the fair at Maskoluri. I viewed all this activity as I advanced.

'Hello, my good man, welcome!' cried a warriorlike infidel, as he rose to his feet. He had a feather in his cap, a dark brown vest, and was clean-shaven.

'Thanks,' I replied. 'I've come to see your smiling face.'

'How did you come up this mountain so fearlessly?'

'He who comes on foot is not put to death – that is so in the religion of Muhammad and in the religion of Jesus – but I *have* come to die. The villages in this mountain still owe three *yük* of *akçe* for the grain requisition. The *kadi* has given a court order. What if Melek Ahmed Pasha says 'Where is my money?' and we say 'I haven't got it!' and he says 'Where is the *kadi*'s appeal?' and the *kadi* hasn't given an appeal? Then Melek Ahmed Pasha will put me in prison and bleed me for the money owed in this mountain. So fearing for my life I put my head behind my saddle and came to you. Do as you like – here is my head and my soul!'

'You are not to blame,' Yano replied. 'It is all the fault of your infidel *kadi*. He gave the order, and the harassers of the province along with the *kadi*s are oppressing the peasants. But God willing, we will kill that *kadi* and make an example of him. Look here, young man, do you know who I am?'

'No,' I said.

'Don't you recognise me? I am Yano, the one with the sherbet shop near the Mahmud Pasha bath in Istanbul. One time you withheld my tax receipt from the customs agent, Ali Agha.'

'Now I know who you are,' I said, and since it was in a good cause, I added, 'my dear friend!' We kissed each other, exchanged pleasantries, ate a lamb kebab. Then he loaded three *yük* of *akçe* on a packhorse, and also gave us ten rolls of Prankona cotton, fifty pieces of satin, ten pieces of Frankish printed cloth, and ten packhorse loads of tobacco; also 100 Venetian ducats for myself, and an outfit of fine broadcloth for each of my forty attendants down below. He even accompanied me down to the valley and made sure I had rejoined my attendants before going back up, and he left all the packhorses behind.

My attendants were stunned. I gave them the broadcloth, which made them quite happy. God be praised, thanks to this adventure I got 300 *yük* of *akçe* instead of 100. So in this fashion I collected the due of the *kadi*-district of Cum'abazarı.

VOLUME SIX

Hungary and the German Campaign

During the Transylvania campaign, Evliya's adventures include a comical if embarrassing incident on the battlefield. In February 1662, Melek Ahmed Pasha is recalled to Istanbul to become the deputy grand vizier, and Evliya is sent to Albania to collect the Pasha's debts. His description of Shkodër includes information on the Albanian language. On his way back to Sofia, he stops to observe the Samakov iron works. He finally returns to Istanbul in April of that year.

In the following year, Melek Pasha dies. Left patronless, Evliya joins the German campaign in March 1663 and travels extensively in Hungary. Following the successful siege of Uyvar, he claims to have ridden off with 40,000 Tatar horsemen on a raid into Western Europe as far as Amsterdam.

His account of this apocryphal raid (it all takes place between Oct. 12 and Oct. 22 of 1663!) allows him to imagine what Western Europe is like, and what a large and ruthless Tatar force might accomplish if it made a concerted effort in that direction. His tongue-in-cheek attitude makes it difficult to judge the degree to which he is critiquing Tatar predatory habits and satirising the tall tales of travel writers.

Returning to Hungary and reality, he participates in several other military campaigns and a mission to Dubrovnik, with more reflections on the Venetians (cf. Volume 5, selection 3). His travels in the region include a stop at Mostar where he views the famous bridge.

1. An incident on the battlefield

A strange and comical adventure, a wondrous and foolish *gaza*. This adventure happened to your humble servant. If it is bad manners to relate it, I hope to be covered with the skirt of forgiveness.

After the battle, feeling the call of nature I retired to a lonely spot, loosened my drawers and was busy relieving myself when, from a thicket just above my head, I heard a rustle and a snap. Before I could determine what this noise meant, an infidel soldier, fearing for his life, suddenly hurled himself from a low rock just above my head and landed on top of me, so that I plopped right into my own filth. I had been holding on to the rein of my horse, but the horse started and stood off at a distance. For a moment I lost my wits: there I was, topsy-turvy with that infidel, my belt and drawers swimming at my feet and my clothes all covered in shit – I almost became the shitty martyr.

Thank God, I recovered my wits and wrestled with that infidel like Mahmud Piryar Veli until I was on top. Baring my dagger, I stabbed him several times in the neck and breast, then cut off his head. By this time I was soaked in blood as well as in shit, and I had to laugh, seeing that I had become the shitty *gazi*. I used the dagger to wipe the shit off my clothes, then began to draw my drawers together when suddenly a brave youth came panting to the rock above my head and said, 'My friend, I was chasing that infidel whom you just killed through the mountains. Fearing for his life he hurled himself on top of you and you cut off his head. Now that head belongs to me!'

I was still tying up my drawers. 'Well,' I replied, 'take this head,' and I showed him my little brother who was born together with me (i.e. my penis).

'What an ill-mannered man you are,' said the elegant fellow and, despairing of the head, he went on his way.

As I was pulling off the infidel's filth-spattered dolman with its silver buttons, and his drawers, I discovered 105 Hungarian gold pieces and one ring and 40 Thalers in his waistband. Putting these items in my saddlebag I mounted my horse – his name was Hamis – and deposited the head before Ismail Pasha.

'May the enemies' misfortunate heads always roll like this one,' I said, kissed his hand, and stood at attention. Those next to me moved off because of the smell.

'My Evliya,' said Ismail Pasha, 'you smell strangely of shit.'

'Don't ask, my lord, what calamities have befallen me!' And I recounted my adventures blow by blow. All the officers at that victory celebration laughed uproariously. Ismail Pasha too was tremendously pleased. He awarded me fifty gold pieces and a silver turban-crest, and I cheered up considerably.

2. Shkodër (Scutari)

From here (Lezha) we set off westwards, crossing the Drin River, and journeyed to **the walled city of Shkodër**. It was founded by Iskandar Dhu'l-qarnayn and thus was called Iskenderiye (Alexandria). It was subsequently taken over and enlarged by Spain, then passed from the king of Puglia into the hands of the doges of Venice. When Mehmed the Conqueror received the dreadful news that the Venetians had begun to loot and plunder the lands around Skopje, Prishtina and Vushtrria, he resolved at once to pacify the region and, arriving with a huge expeditionary force, he conquered the fortress from the Venetians in the year 883 (1478) after a siege of forty days and nights. He then made it the capital of a separate *sancak* in the province Rumeli, bestowing it as a hereditary land grant (*ocaklık*) upon Yusuf Bey, the first *sancak-bey* of Shkodër. And so its rulers are still known as Yusuf Bey Oğulları.

The present governor, Mehmed Pasha, came out to meet us and accompanied us into the fortress where we were quartered in the house of the castle warden, (—) Agha. When Mehmed Pasha had read the affectionate letters I gave him from Melek Pasha he expressed delight. 'God willing,' he cried, 'I shall meet my obligations and repay my debt within ten days and you may continue your journey.' He gave me a purse of *guruş* for bath-expenses and a set of clothing, and gave my thirty companions and servants ten *guruş* each. We frequently resorted to the Yusufbeyzade palace in a village called Bushat, where we were well received and had an excellent time. But we always returned to Shkodër because the Venetian infidels were up in arms.

There are three Iskenderuns or Alexandrias in the Ottoman Empire. One is this Albanian Iskenderiye (Shkodër). The second, called Iskenderun, is on the shore of the Mediterranean one caravan stage from Aleppo and

Shkodër (Scutari) 175

serves as the port for that city. The third is Alexandria in Egypt, which in Greek is called Alexandria Pyrgos or Alexander's Castle.

According to the *kanun* of Süleyman Khan, the Bey possesses an imperial *has* worth 459,200 *akçe*, plus 19 *zeamets* and 205 *timars*, and for every 3000 *akçe* he must provide one armed retainer. These, together with the troops of the cavalry marshal, troop commander and constable, and the Pasha himself, provide a force of 4000 select armoured soldiers. In time of war, this force is put under the command of the vizier or else the *sancak-beys* of Rumeli. And indeed, all of these brave *gazis* were with us during the Transylvania campaigns.

The *sancak* also provides forty purses for the Pasha who, with the help of 1000 warriors under his command, guards and defends the *sancak*. Among the Sharia authorities in Shkodër are the *şeyhülislam*, the *nakibüleşraf* along with various notables and descendants of the Prophet, the *kadi* with a salary level of 150 *akçe*, the steward of the *sipahis*, the commander of the janissaries, the castle warden along with the garrison soldiers, the market inspector, the *voyvoda*, the toll collector, the chief engineer, the mayor, and the poll-tax official.

Plan of the fortress of Shkodër. It is situated upon a lofty and very steep cliff overlooking a great lake called Boyana. It is square-shaped, somewhat slanted. The fortress is constructed of chiseled stonework and is fully functional, with no obstructing higher ground in the vicinity. Though small, it is strong and impregnable. It has no moat on the lake side or on any other side, but does have many towers and crenellated battlements. There are two gates, one facing east, the other overlooking Küçük Ova. Inside this second gateway is the shrine of Muyo Baba Sultan. Within the fortress there are few houses and only one congregational mosque, i.e., the radiant mosque of Sultan Mehmed, covered in tiles and constructed in the old style. There are seven or eight cisterns which fill up with rain water. Descending from the fortress to Lake Boyana are water channels known only to those in the fortress. They cannot be seen by the enemy outside. It is through these channels that they fetch water during sieges. There are no shops inside the fortress, only 100 houses for the garrison soldiers and storage bins for wheat. There are also ammunition depots and fine imperial cannons. It might be possible for an enemy to bombard the fortress from Mount Tarabosh, which looms above on the other side of Lake Boyana, but they would need cannons forty spans in length. Smaller guns pose no threat, because the lake is in between. At the foot of the fortress, near the cliffs down at the lake, there are fishing weirs built on pinewood pilings. These weirs are administered on commission from the fortress garrison.

The open town (*varoş*) of the fortress of Shkodër. The town outside the walls consists of 1800 one- and two-story stonework houses with slate and tiled roofs and surrounded by vineyards and gardens. The inhabitants are all Muslim. There are fifteen quarters, of which the best known are: Bayezid Khan quarter, Ali Bey quarter, Hüseyn Bey quarter, Iskele-başı (Docks) quarter, Mufti quarter, Kara Hasan quarter, and the Mahkeme (Courthouse) quarter at the end of the bazaar.

Mosques of the monotheists. There are eleven prayer-niches. First is the mosque of Sultan Bayezid II the Saint at the end of the bazaar. In front of it is a well with delicious water and an iron chain. It is definitely the finest of the mosques, an exquisite building with a tiled roof, and has a large congregation. Then comes the mosque of Hüseyn Bey in the Ali Bey quarter; the Mufti mosque at the Docks; and the mosque of Kara Hasan. These are all well-known and radiant mosques with tiled roofs. Aside from these, there are seventy other prayer-houses.

There are seven medreses, each congregational mosque having its own, but there are no special schools of Koran recitation or Hadith. There are (—) primary schools, six dervish convents, and (—) *hans* of which the Ulama Pasha Han is the strongest in construction and the most imposing, with all kinds of precious furnishings. There is a single very spacious and attractive bathhouse that gets its water from Lake Boyana by means of a water wheel. There are 500 shops in the covered market, all the skills and handicrafts being represented. The fish-market at the lakeside is well maintained and furnished.

Clothing of the manly men. They all wear broadcloth garments and tight-buttoned trousers with *teybend* silk waistband and Kubadi shoes. On their heads they wear Albanian kalpaks made of sable. Learned scholars and rakish youths alike carry *kortela* knives in their belts, and the youths are never to be seen without their swords and shields.

Clothing of the demure women. They all wear full-length broadcloth coats and a strange conical headpiece, like the caps worn by the imperial guards, and they wrap themselves in white muslin wraps. On their feet they wear soft yellow indoor boots and shoes. They go about very well mannered.

Men's names.

Women's names.

Praise of the lovely boys and girls. They have silver limbs and rosy cheeks.

Praise of the salubrious climate. Because of the fine climate, all the people reach the age of seventy or eighty without diminution of their faculties.

Praise of the sparkling Water of Life. On one side is the Drin River, like the Water of Kawthar, and on the other side is Lake Boyana, whose water is like *pure wine* (76:21).

Climes and latitudes of towns and countries.

The rising star of auspicious prosperity.

Churches of monks.

Cereals and plants.

Manufactured goods.

Meats and foodstuffs.

Fruits.

Beverages.

Natural wonders. The hand of the Almighty Creator fashioned seven grassy islands of various sizes in the middle of the lake, no bigger than one or two or three or five threshing-floors. During some years a violent storm arises and these little islands become dislodged and move to another part of the lake. Sometimes the islands even meet in the middle of the lake and join together. They each have a variety of shrubs and grassy plots. The townsfolk like to sail out to these little islands in their caiques for picnics.

Sometimes a strong wind arises and one or two of the islands get dislodged and float from one end of the lake to the other, taking the people with them as though borne on the throne of King Solomon's audience-hall. The people delight in sailing about on the islands, and they boast of their exploits in years gone by. No one ever suffers any harm, for that is the nature of these islands – *God is capable of everything* (2:20). It takes an extremely strong wind to dislodge the islands, or so it is reported. There were quite a few storms during the time that I was in Shkodër, but I never saw those islands moving, though I did see them *not* moving. In my curiosity I questioned the old people about the past, and they related the following, 'In the year when Sultan Osman II advanced against Chotin (i.e., 1621) there was a severe winter storm which caused even the Bosphorus in Istanbul to freeze over. Here in Shkodër the storm blew down houses and uprooted large trees, whirling them in the air like falconers' lures. That year, these little islands in Lake Boyana floated about for forty or fifty days, from north to south and from east to west.' This is what the old-timers told me.

Praise of the Lake of Albanian Iskenderiye (Lake Shkodër). The body of pure water at the foot of the fortress is known as Lake Boyana. It stretches lengthwise from east to west and is 11 miles in circumference. Mt Tarabosh, which looms up on the other side of the lake, is a cannon's range distance. It was from there that Mehmed the Conqueror bombarded the fortress. The other banks stretch lengthwise, forming a kind of freshwater strait, with Mt Tarabosh at the mouth of it, where the water runs out of the lake. There is a delightful promenade at that end of the lake. From there a tributary flows westward for four hours until, after passing through vineyards and orchards, it empties into the sea. At the foot of the cliffs on which the fortress is built are ten weirs for catching fish. These are state-owned; the income deriving from the fish caught in the weirs and in the lake is confiscated by the agent on behalf of the garrison of Shkodër fortress and goes to pay the salaries of the preachers and imams of the imperial (i.e., congregational) mosques in the city.

Many kinds of fish are caught in this lake, and in immense quantities. Plaice, carp, sea bass and mullet swim up the tributary from the sea into the lake. Eels are found in quantity and quality that outmatch those in the lakes of Kastoria, Ohrid, and Beşik. They are fat and have a musky scent that is peculiar to the eels of Lake Shkodër and not to be found elsewhere. Also, they are a marvellously beneficial fish. Anyone suffering from fevers and ailments can be cured by cooking and eating these eels, or merely by carrying eel-heads on their persons. Because of the presence of this type of musk-eel, the people of Shkodër suffer from no ills of any kind.

The pure water of this lake, when drunk regularly, brings about a loosening

Shkodër (Scutari) 179

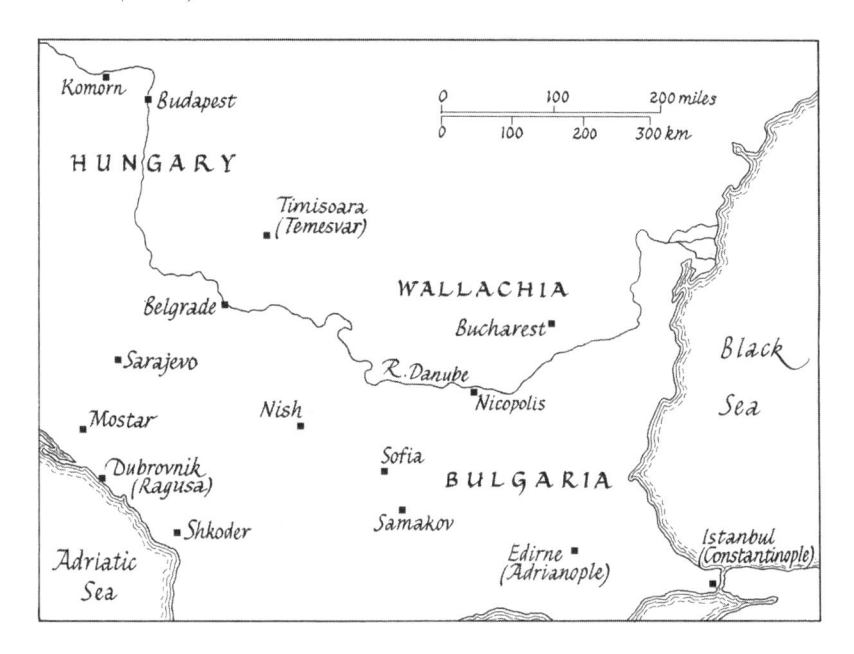

of the bowels and a cure for problems of the spleen and gallbladder, and for phlegm, headaches, constipation, swellings, and similar illnesses.

Professions. There are fishermen, soldiers, merchants who trade on land and sea, handicraftsmen, scholars and ulema, and vintners for the 23,000 vineyards. This place is the home of brave and diligent Albanian *gazis*, who, like Farhad, earn their living by hard toil. There are no other nationalities in this city.

They all speak Albanian, which is like no other tongue. In origin, the Albanians were one of the Arab tribes of Quraysh in Mecca. That is why there are some Arabic words still in use among them. When these Albanian tribesmen emerged from the mountains of Shkodër and Vlora, they mingled with the Italian Franks, and so, during the Caliphate of Umar, produced a language between Arabic and Frankish. We will give an account of the reason for this and of the origin of the Albanians in another place.

For now – **Language of the Albanians** – it is called the language of *Arnavud* or, in Persian, *Ar-na-bud* ('May there be no shame'), and certain chroniclers write it this way. It is a delightful language that they speak humbly and gently when addressing one another with respect. The infidels among them pass as Christians, although this, too, is at the insistence of the Spaniards and the Venetians. Otherwise, they are a company of scriptureless infidels and fornicators who, like the Zoroastrians, know nothing of the Book or of Judgement Day. Their language is as follows:

First, *pörtuni zoti* For God's sake!

When buying and selling they count coins thus: *ñe* 1 *dü* 2 *tiri* 3 *kotrá* 4 *pensı* 5 *gaşt* 6 *iştat* 7 *teti* 8 *nandı* 9 *dhit* 10.

falemi müre Greetings, men *aye şendoş enbahi* Hey, are you well? *mir niştıra nişe* Good morning *miliserde* (Welcome) *palá mizuni* (Thank you).

buk bread *uy* water *miş* meat *dele* sheep *pulı* hen.

bayá müre Come, man *aha buk* Will you eat bread? *ku kıye* Where have you been? *miyalt* honey *akı te ki* Is there barley? *nuku kám* There isn't *ruş* grapes *akı mebe teşin kurd* Bring barley or I'll split your head open *pörtuni zoti nuku kám akı* For God's sake, there is no barley.

támu mother *motrá* sister *şoke* wife.

The following are foolish expressions, but the traveller needs to know them since he might be the object of cursing or a beating: *hak mut* Eat shit! *tıkifşatı támu* I'll fuck your mother *tıkifşatı şoke* I'll fuck your wife *tı pirişte bıhund* I'll fart in your nose *tıkifşatı büthı* I'll fuck your ass *iç kıvırdım* catamite, pimp.

In short, when dervishes are travelling, they should know such expressions as well, so that they can avoid trouble by not going to places where they will be abused.

Conclusion of the eulogy of Shkodër. In the open town there are two bridges over the Drin River, the Hüseyn Bey Bridge and the Ali Politina Bridge.

[4.5 lines empty]

Places of pilgrimage. Inside the fortress is the shrine of Muyo Baba, may his mystery be sanctified.

3. The Samakov iron works

Among the noteworthy products (of Samakov) are highly-wrought iron lanterns with cages; tinned iron trays with hinges for serving food – fine objects that can even be taken on campaign; all kinds of locks; horse-baggage clamps; iron wolf- and lion-traps; coffee mills in small iron boxes – they can also be used in a pinch to grind flour; and nails of various types –

fireng, lofça, zağra, ortasayış, yüleme, miyane, tahta – that are exported from Samakov to all countries of the world.

There are a total of 110 iron works in the city of Samakov and in the surrounding districts. In this region *samakov* has become a generic term for 'iron works'.

The huge fires in the forges are fanned by bellows operated by water mills; even ten men would be unable to operate one of them. The iron anvils are as big as the belly of an elephant. The red-hot iron emerges from the fire, glowing like Yemeni carnelian, and master ironsmiths place it on an anvil. The hammers used to beat it are operated by water wheels, each hammer being the size of a water-buffalo head, causing the ground to quake. Two smiths work at one anvil. They keep the iron, which may weigh one or two quintals, moving back and forth beneath the blows of the hammers until it stretches out into a rod. They stop the hammers by stopping the water wheel.

This operation goes on day and night. It is a kind of ironmongery that even David, son of Solomon, patron saint of ironsmiths, never accomplished. Few travellers have ever seen this and, as the verse has it, *How can hearing measure up to seeing?* It is hard to imagine unless you have seen it with your own eyes. The same is true for forging cannons in the Istanbul gun foundry; casting cannon-balls in Danzig; forging the iron Tatar kettles in the village of Çüyençi in the Crimea; and forging iron here in Samakov – it is a craft of white demons rather than of human beings. Anyone who sees it is dumbstruck.

Every year 8,000 carts of iron go from this Samakov to the entrepôts of Salonica and Varna, from where it is shipped to all parts of the Ottoman Empire, and the ironsmiths in every city use it to fashion things as they wish.

4. An adventure near Komorn; Tatar raid into Western Europe

Beginning of the adventure of the world-traveller Evliya the unhypocritical

By God's wisdom, while Uyvar castle was being renovated and repaired, this humble one ran short of fodder for my horses. On an inauspicious day, Gürci Mehmed Pasha and his troops from Aleppo province constituted the vanguard of an Ottoman force going to forage below the walls of Komorn castle. 10,000 men set out from below the walls of Uyvar castle in the direction of Komorn, striking up their military bands. This humble one also, with four of my slaveboys on mounts and two packhorses, joined Gürci Pasha. 20,000 more soldiers joined this advance party from the Wallachian and Moldavian and Tatar troops camped along the way, plus 5,000 mounted servants.

Seeing this rabble army I heartened my slaveboys with such pleasantries as 'Opportunity is plunder' and *First the companion, then the road*. We accompanied all these vermin out of Uyvar and along the Litre River in a southern direction.

After proceeding for four hours, we came to a verdant grove. Gürci Mehmed Pasha suddenly dismounted and gave his banners and military band to his deputy, (—) Agha.

'You go ahead,' he said, and stayed in that park.

We continued toward Komorn through the grassy plain, a body of soldiers without a head. In three hours Komorn castle appeared, like a white swan; it is situated on a populated island in the middle of the Danube.

Now Gürci Pasha's deputy, having ridden up a hill, also dismounted without striking up his military band. The pasha's men tumbled down all about and, neglecting to set guards, fell asleep and began to snore. The rabble army dispersed in all directions like ants and snakes, ostensibly to forage, but actually to pillage the surrounding villages. Had our commander's deputy remained an hour behind and protected us, he would have guarded the Ottoman troops.

This humble one too, at this juncture, entered a prosperous village with a few companions and – on the consideration that *Property of infidels is permitted for believers* – we filled our sacks with oats and wheat and barley, loaded our packhorses with another forty bundles of wheat, grabbed a few geese and chickens and were on our way when my slaveboy named Seyfi spoke up, 'Agha, over there is a lot of sifted flour, and some white honey in barrels. Let's take some of that too, bring it to the camp and eat it there.'

He darted through a hedge into a house and began gathering up the honey and butter. Just then gunpowder sparks appeared above Komorn castle.

'Hurry up, my boy,' I cried. 'They've made a gunpowder signal from the castle. It isn't a good sign.'

Suddenly a cry of *Allah Allah!* rose up from the direction of the Pasha's deputy and from amidst the troops who had gone foraging. Our party let out a cry of woe. There was a clash of swords and a thundering of muskets among the Ottoman soldiery. Everyone was trying to save his skin.

An adventure near Komorn; Tatar raid into Western Europe 183

This humble one was left in the middle between Komorn castle and the place where our commander's deputy was doing battle. It seems I had gone quite a ways ahead. It was a perilous situation.

'My boy,' I cried, 'I've given up the honey and oil. We're going to give up our lives. Come out of there!'

Now seven banners with crosses and 1,000 infidels appeared from behind the village we were plundering. I cut the ropes of the packhorses with my sword and, leaving the goods behind, joined the animals to my spare horse and was ready to go with my two slaveboys. The infidels were approaching the village, and we were cut off before and behind.

'Hey Seyfi, my boy! Come out of the house. We're being attacked by some infidels.'

Seyfi emerged. He had become quite the hero: the two pockets of his shalwars (baggy trousers) were filled with all sorts of items that he had tracked down. As he was scrambling through the hedge the poor lad's shalwar got caught on a stake. By the time he freed himself and got to his horse, the infidels had surrounded us. Some of them entered the village.

At this point my two mounted slaveboys fled toward our troops, leaving me there alone. I tried to help Seyfi mount, but ten of the infidels saw us and came galloping toward us, shooting bullets and shouting, in Hungarian, '*Ey beştelelen kurafıya!*'

Taking refuge in God, I too shot at them with my hand-musket. One of the infidels fell headlong from his horse. I was just reaching for my quiver when the infidels stopped to look after their dead comrade. I headed toward Seyfi, but noticed that his horse had a bullet wound and was rearing up. The infidels drove the boy ahead of them in my direction.

But now ten brave youths from our soldiery came to my aid. As they were doing battle with the infidels, I brought my packhorse to Seyfi and told him to mount that. The poor lad had go free of the infidels, but was exhausted from running. He grabbed the pommel of the packsaddle and tried to mount, but by bad luck, the packsaddle slipped beneath the horse's belly and the boy tumbled onto the ground.

Ten or fifteen infidels rushed upon him. Twenty others penned me in on one side and were shooting at me from all directions. God be praised, none of the bullets hit their mark, but my horse had been struck and wounded at the first onslaught and now began to rear up.

I was at my wit's end. The world darkened and narrowed about my head. By now I realised that the situation was hopeless. The ten youths who had come to my aid had increased to twenty, but all twenty were laid low by the sword. I looked around me and could see neither earth nor sky.

Fearing for my life, I again grabbed my quiver, notched an arrow, crouched on my horse's neck and galloped forward. As I approached my slaveboy and was about to pass him, the poor lad cried, 'Agha, don't leave me among the infidels!' He heaved such a burning sigh that my heart was cut in two. But what could I do? The infidels had both of us surrounded and were trying to capture me as well.

Noticing a space where there were no infidels I raced like thunder in that direction and made my way toward the Ottoman soldiery, crying, 'Giddup, my horse Hamis!' But what a horse! One of Solomon's *prancing steeds* (38:31), noble as an Arab thoroughbred, dearer to me than my own brother.

I was out of sight of the infidels. But now I noticed blood gushing from the bullet wound at my horse's withers down to his shoulder blade. I snatched my handkerchief from my bosom, tore it in two and stuffed the pieces into his wound. Thank God, the blood stopped flowing.

But now a party of fifty infidels appeared on my right side. Driving me forward they came within musket range. A divine inspiration came over me. Gathering my strength, I turned to God with utmost sincerity and began to pray, 'O Lord, You who are worshipped by all creatures, You are my refuge. On this field of battle and amidst a thousand hardships, convey this lowly slave from the abyss of destruction to the frontier of salvation.'

Meantime I pressed my poor wounded horse to the utmost. God be praised, I came to the field where the Ottoman troops were fighting and soon was in the midst of the fray. The infidels were getting reinforcements on all sides, while our troops were being decimated.

Just then, by God's wisdom, a troop of Tatars arrived and showered the infidels with a volley of arrows. On our side the Ottomans who were routed wheeled about to attack. In an instant 3,000 infidel souls were consigned to the fires of hell.

In this fashion a heated battle was kept up for one sidereal hour. Thousands of infidel corpses adorned the Uyvar plain like the tree of Waqwaq.[49] Praise God the Absolute, in this illustrious *gaza* thousands of

49 'A legendary element which Islamic geography shares with the Thousand and One Nights are the Waqwaq Islands, located somewhere in the southeast of the world ... on those islands a tree produces fruit in the shape of human (female) bodies. The only sound they give is the waq waq which has given them the name. It is said that sailors who land there sometimes pluck them, and even have intercourse with

gazis hung their soul-melting swords on the roof of the celestial Throne.

What should we see next? Seventy banners with crosses appeared in the woods and groves from the direction of Komorn castle. Infidel soldiers, drawn up for battle like a herd of swine, came regiment upon regiment, hauling their cannons and sounding their trumpets in the *rehavi* musical mode.

The infidel Wallachian and Moldavian regiments of our own victory-tokened soldiery, who were assigned to one wing as guard troops and were standing by quietly, took flight as soon as they saw the enemy's banners with crosses. The tricky infidels, finding an opening, attacked the Tatars, shouting *Yajuj Yajuj* (Jesus! Jesus!) and shooting a volley of cannons and muskets. The Tatars for their part, unhappy with cannonballs and bullets, took flight toward Esztergom.

Now the infidels became even more daring, regiment upon regiment attacking our muleteers and equerries coming to forage. A huge battle ensued that lasted an entire hour, during which several hundred of our brave *gazis* quaffed the sherbet of martyrdom from the goblet of this world and their spirits wafted to the gardens of paradise.

Next the infidels galloped toward Gürci Mehmed Pasha's deputy, hurling cannon- and musket-shot. All the Pasha's Segban troops – according to the grammatical rule to *flee the succession of plurals* – abandoned their drums and fifes and banners and fled toward Uyvar.

As for this humble one, I was left behind with a band of poor men who had lost their horses. Taking stock of the situation and overcome with dread, I wondered whether I too would have to drink from the cup of martyrdom in this field of battle; or would I be able to get in safety to Uyvar? Gathering my wits – for I was intoxicated enough without quaffing the cup of martyrdom – I made common cause to flee with those routed soldiers and distraught and grief-ridden individuals. Some had tumbled from their horses and lay sprawling on the ground. It was like the day when the dead will be gathered from their graves.

---

them, although, once severed from the tree they decay within a couple of days. This colourful legend was seriously discussed by a man as rationalistic and critical as the seventeenth century polymath Katib Celebi. Its popularity is attested by the fact that the janissary uprising of 1656, during which the corpses of dignitaries killed by the insurgents were hanged from a plane tree in Istanbul's central square, the Hippodrome, was remembered as the Waqwaq incident.' (Gottfried Hagen in Dankoff 2006, 222–3)

While contemplating this sad scene, a band of Hungarian cavaliers, some on horse, some on foot, emerged from the forest like pigs from a grove and attacked us with great vigour. Our distraught soldiers were like birds fallen in a trap. For my part, I bowed to destiny, saying 'It is God's to command.' We all fled in different directions.

To my left was a marshy reed bed along a tributary of the Vak River. I galloped over to it and plunged in. I was quite dizzy, and up to my ears in water. My horse beneath me whinnied and started swimming. The infidels behind me showered me with bullets like the rain of damnation. Glory to God the Preserver (*Hafiz*) who preserved this preserver (*hafiz*) of the Koran and did not allow me to suffer any harm.

Eventually my horse's hooves touched the ground. At that moment my eyes filled with bloody tears, for I realised that I had emerged on the opposite bank of the Vak River, which was infidel territory. Considering this, I prayed as follows, 'O Lord, strength and power and victory are Yours. Do not let this Koran of Yours, which I bear (in my memory), fall to the infidels as their share. For the sake of Your ancient Speech (i.e. the Koran), do not let me fall captive to the infidels. Deliver me from this whirlpool before the bird of my soul flies from the cage of my body, and let me reach my place of birth safe and sound.'

With such sincere prayers, and seeking intercession from the 124,000 prophets and succour from the spiritual graces of the 77,000 great saints, I wandered aimlessly in a grassy plain. There was no sign of man or jinn. But now and then I could still hear the report of muskets from the battlefield across the river.

As I wondered which way to go, I heard the shot of ten balaramada guns to the north and I took heart, realising that Uyvar lay in that direction. So I proceeded fearlessly toward the sound of those guns. Meanwhile, though my life was in danger, my mind could not let go of fancies and worries regarding my worldly possessions – my heavy baggage on one side; my miserable captive slaves on another; and my four Arab thoroughbreds on another.

Meanwhile my soul's companion, my zephyr-swift steed Hamis, was going slower and slower, exhausted from his wound. My own heart seemed to be wounded because of his wound. I went on aimless and downcast, recalling the verses:

> No sign of the door through which you came,
> No sign of the ford you will have to cross.

And:

> Where is the place of safety, where, oh where?

For there was no place to turn. On one side was the vast Vak River; on the other side the white castle of the infidels, Komorn. No friend, no grief-dispelling companion, and no road leading anywhere.

I continued on in this state of confusion, murmuring my litanies. Suddenly, on my right side, by God's wisdom, a white ram appeared in an oak grove. My horse underneath me began to paw the ground and prance about like a piebald or sorrel, rose-bodied Arabian steed. I took comfort at this and looked at the ram. It was fat and plump, with a curly white fleece, lovely black eyes and black horns, a fat tail like a Karaman sheep – congealed light. It did not shy away from me, but rather approached and seemed to rub against my horse, keeping pace with it. Sometimes it bleated with a sad voice – in my whole life I have never heard a sheep bleat in this fashion.

Watching this spectacle I forgot all the pains we had suffered. It was as though I had found eternal life. My horse underneath me likewise kept up its strutting and prancing. Sometimes the ram ran in front of the horse, looked back to us with a kindly expression and bleated. I wondered at this mystery and concluded that it was the Men of the Unseen World who had taken this shape and were guiding us. We both – my horse and I – found great comfort in this, and I decided to follow the ram wherever it led.

We went and went until we came to the shore of the great Vak River. On the other side I could see rose gardens and date groves and vegetable gardens. The ram plunged into the water and headed across, now swimming, now walking with its feet touching the river bed. It stepped onto an island, turned toward me and began to bleat louder and oftener. It went into and out of the water, bleating the while, as if to say: 'You too come this way, cross to where there is safety.'

Now I was unable to restrain my horse underneath me. With a leap my horse Hamis plunged into the water, which soon came up to the saddle. But after going twenty paces it only came up to the stirrups. We reached the island. Both the ram and my horse underneath me frisked and frolicked. I could hardly keep from falling off the saddle. *'This is my Lord's favour'* (27:40), I cried, weeping with joy.

Once again the ram plunged into the river and crossed to the other side. This time its feet never touched the ground, but it swam all the way in a zigzag course. With my sword I cut an oak branch and trimmed it like a spear. Holding it in my hand, and uttering a *besmele*, I spurred my horse into the river. It was rather deep, but using the branch to sound the depth, with God's help I crossed safely. Once again ram and horse pranced and danced like Venus.

Then the white ram began to run in the direction of Uyvar. It bleated back to us and we joined it. It kept on bleating toward Uyvar, then plunged into the river and disappeared. A little later I saw it on the other side.

God be praised, I crossed that raging Vak River in safety with the help of God and, no doubt, the men of the unseen world. I realised that the prophet Hızır had taken that shape and guided us. By the grace of God, and with the blessings of the prophets and the saints whose shrines I had visited in the seven climes over forty years of travel, I had escaped from this whirlpool.

With countless praises to God for this salvation, I proceeded in the direction of Uyvar. It seems that some of our men who had been routed in the battle had strayed into these forests.

'Comrade,' they said when they saw me, 'are there any infidels ahead of you or behind you?'

'No, there's nothing,' I replied.

Now all the wounded men who were hiding in the forest came out into the open. Most were horseless and helpless. They tried to approach me, but I kept them at bay. How often it has happened that someone who appeared to be ill or wounded would knock a man from his horse, mount it himself and flee! As the proverb has it: 'The horse belongs to him who mounts it, the sword to him who girds it on.' So I put off the wounded men, consoling them with words of encouragement, or exchanging banter with them about our escapades.

As I went ahead, looking back and forth, a party of our Tatar friends came riding up, 2,000 swashbuckling Tatars with their spare mounts. True, they are ruthless soldiers; but – God forgive them! – at my bidding they let those wounded Ottoman soldiers mount and ride alongside them on their spares. So now over 600 wounded and exhausted men rode along with us in comfort.

We went on for another two hours. Here and there we saw our martyred troops, their heads cut off and the nubs of their penises slashed. More wounded troops came and were mounted on the Tatars' spare horses.

We met another party of 10,000 men going to reinforce our troops who

An adventure near Komorn; Tatar raid into Western Europe 189

had recently been routed. They inquired about the battle and we told them in detail what had taken place. May God be pleased with them and with their commander Sührab Mehmed Pasha. Even in the midst of battle they gathered the corpses of all the martyrs on this plain, performed the prayer for the dead, and buried them in two large ditches that they dug out.

God be praised, we entered the grand vizier's camp safe and sound. I directed a thousand prayers of thanksgiving to God. When our benefactors in the Ottoman camp heard about our sad plight, they showered this humble one with presents, including five thoroughbred horses and three Hungarian captives. Three days later, by God's wisdom, two of my slave-boys who had fled during the earlier battle were delivered to us, along with their horses and equipment, by the routed deputy of Gürci Mehmed Pasha. God be praised, I felt that I had acquired my possessions anew.

Stages of the journey from Uyvar castle with 40,000 enemy-shattering, wind-scattering Tatars to Germany and the Atlantic coast and Holland and Sweden

First, my lord Ahmed Giray Sultan, son of Mehmed Giray Khan, at the order of the grand vizier, made his coastal officer (—) Agha commander over 40,000 Tatars who stood ready with their 200,000 mounts and spares. This humble one, being restless, got leave from Ibrahim Kethüda and Defterdar Ahmed Pasha to join them. Having lightened my load in true Tatar fashion, with only my three slaveboys and six horses, I set forth with a *besmele* and the intention of performing *gaza*.

From Uyvar, heading west, we passed Nitre castle, then crossed the Vak River dismounted. That day after a forced march we stopped at the source of the Vak. This river rises in the White Summer Pastures (*Ak yaylalar*) in the vicinity of the Castles of the Mines (*Ma'den kal'alari*), passes before Uyvar, and joins the Danube in front of Komorn castle.

In the morning we crossed the Summer Pastures of the Mines (*Ma'den yaylalari*) and pressed on at a rapid pace for a full day and night. We found no thriving villages, only country that had been burned and devastated by Kurd Pasha and Hacıkey Pashazade. We made a halt that night in a grassy meadow and, having buckled and bitted and bridled our horses and girded our bow-and-arrow cases, we remounted our geldings at the break of dawn and galloped northward.

On the second night we arrived in **Tot**, a very flourishing country, incomparable in Christendom for productive land and cheap prices.

Indeed, the astronomers have likened this prosperous territory to a peacock's tail, so rich and beautiful is its soil.

It is bounded by Middle Hungary (*Orta Macar*) in the south; Poland in the east – the Tot language is like Polish; the Czech lands in the north; and Germany in the west. But the Tot people are under an independent Ban who has 200,000 soldiers. But since they are subject to Middle Hungary they are Christian and, like the Hungarians, of the Lutheran sect – cross-worshippers, not idol-worshippers (i.e., Protestants, not Catholics).

So many thousands of Tatars entered this flourishing country, laid waste their villages and towns and thriving cities, burned their houses and took 18,000 infidels captive. They sent all the captives along with the booty back to the Ottoman camp. So the Tatars were left unencumbered and could conduct raids for another day and night.

Next we came to the country of **Holland**. North of this, on the Baltic coast, is the port of Danzig which is governed by the king of Poland – I had already gone once to Danzig in the year (—) during the time of Islam Giray Khan. Bordering the capital city of Holland on the west is the Czech kingdom; toward the southwest is the kingdom of Sweden; in the south, where the German River (i.e. Rhine?) flows into the Atlantic,[50] is Amsterdam, seat of the king of the Flemings. This too was a great and flourishing city, whose infidels were happy, villages fine, and soil productive.

At dawn our Tatars set fire to this city of Holland and took all the naked infidels captive. The booty was too great to carry, so millions worth of goods and furnishings went up in flames. Countless infidels fled to the fortresses, which in this country are quite strong and defensible, since the Tatars have no means to lay siege. Still, 10,000 infidels fell captive in this raid. God be praised, my share of the booty was one girl, one boy and seven horses.

This country is in the seventh clime. We headed north and, doing no harm to Poland with which the Tatars have a treaty, pressed on over the plains for three days and nights to the country of **Korol**. Its ruler is Varşalka Ban, a notorious and ruthless infidel. I had already come here once in the year (—) during the time of Bahadır Giray Khan – at that time this King Varşalka was just a lad, and his father Yoranda was king.

---

50 *Bahr-i muhit*, lit. 'The Surrounding Sea', i.e. the sea surrounding the inhabited world according to the old geographers.

An adventure near Komorn; Tatar raid into Western Europe

This flourishing country is bordered on the north by the Baltic coast; Poland is in the east; the Czech country in the west. Korol has always been subject to Poland; but this year it was at odds with Poland and, on the principle that *The odds can never be even* (lit., *Opposites never join*), the Polish king laid it waste and took booty without limit and captives without number.

This country is as rich as the meat of a walnut. The Ottomans have never set foot on its territory, but the Tatars have trampled it numerous times. The people here also know Polish and Russian.

So 40,000 Tatars, give or take a few, went burning and pillaging with impunity throughout Korol country – north, south, east, and west – taking captive whomever they did not put to the sword. After three days they reached the Baltic coast where they again laid waste to several cities and took countless Korolian youths captive.

That day we headed west and came below the walled city of **Şivekoron**, a castle like the Wall of Iskandar, its towers reaching to the sky. In the harbour were seven India ships and several Dutch and English and Portugese vessels. Forty or fifty balaramada guns were shot from the battlements at our soldiers, and the suburb below the walled town was also highly fortified, so we were unable to pillage here at all.

Turning to our right, which is east, we continued with guides all night by moonlight until, at the time of the morning prayer, we came to **Heyvaroş**. It is in a great plain, a large city without surrounding walls but nevertheless a strong fort surrounded by a deep moat. It has 20,000 houses like the garden of Iram.

As soon as the Tatars arrived they positioned themselves upwind. 40,000 Tatars fitted their bowstrings with two *tabur* arrows each, and to each arrow tied a match stick. Then they rained these fiery arrows into the city like rain from hell. The wooden houses began to crackle and burn in the flames fanned by the wind. As the infidels were scurrying amidst this woeful conflagration, the Tatars seized the opportunity, found a path through the palisades, poured into the city, took 20,000 captives and much booty, and put all the strapping Cossack warriors to the sword.

We stayed in this city of Heyvar for two days and two nights, camping in our Tatar tents without fear of reprisal. God be praised, here too I got three Korolian boys bright as coral, one exceptional virgin maid, and several vessels of silver and gold. The Tatars also ransacked the basements and found myriads of precious items. If I were to enumerate all of the booty taken in these cities, and if I were to record all of these sojourns in detail, God knows it would require a separate volume.

From there we headed west, galloping for three days and three nights, taking captive anyone we ran into on the way, but passing by villages and towns without burning them. On the fourth day we arrived in the country of the **Christian Czechs** with flourishing estates. It is bordered by Poland and Korol country to the east, Holland to the south, Germany to the southwest, Sweden to the west, and the Atlantic Ocean (or Baltic Sea) to the north. The cosmographers place this country too in the middle of the seventh clime. Being a coastal region, the climate is mild, growing sugar cane, lemons and citrons, pomegranates, olives, figs and cotton.

It is an independent kingdom. The ruler was formerly one of the Seven Kings (or Seven Princes, i.e. Kurfürsten or Electors) of the German emperor, but since the time of Sultan Süleyman has been subject to the king of Sweden. The people here too are Christian, but Protestant (*Luturyan*) rather than Catholic (*Papişte*) – i.e. cross-worshippers rather than idol-worshippers. Their king is a splendid youth named Joachim, his mother being the daughter of the Swedish king. He mints his own coins, a round gold piece and also a pure silver *guruş* piece called Thaler.

Paying no heed to the seventy-six castles with their suburbs in this country as well, we pressed on toward the north in a forced march and, praise God, reached the Magellan Sea which is a tributary of the Atlantic. The infidels along the way who saw us did not flee but smiled, and we took them all captive. Apparently the people of this region during their long lives had never seen Tatars, though they had heard of them, and had not seen enemy soldiers before at any time in their history.

In this region we got splendid stuffs and rare textiles and countless lovely boys and girls. Praise be to God, this humble one too got as my share three slaveboys and three virgin maids, six wind-swift steeds, several gold-embroidered women's dresses and vests and silver crosses.

From there, again using our captives as guides, we undertook great raiding expeditions to the west for two days, stopping at night. Weary of this, on the third day we came to the beadless and meadless country of **Sweden**. This too is a huge fertile territory and an independent kingdom, with seventeen subordinate Bans and seventeen Herzogs, and, as subjects, 800,000 nomadic Tatars. But the latter are Zoroastrian infidels. Several hundred of them fell captive to our Tatars; but they spoke Italian and did not know the Tatar language.

As for the Swedes, they too are Christians of the Lutheran sect. The king is independent and mints his own coins. Ever since the time of Sultan Süleyman they have been bitter enemies of the Germans and have taken seventy-six German castles. They are brave warriors, but no horsemen. All these infidels wear black vests and black Eflatuniye hats, just like the Franks.

Having set foot in this country of Iram we conducted a raiding expedition to the west for one whole day until we arrived at the great city and inauspicious castle of **Kallevine**. It is an entrepôt on the shore of the River Vistula (? – *Vo*) and very crowded. It is located at the bottom of the earth (i.e. the northernmost part), the extreme of the seventh clime. The longest summer day, as well as the longest winter night, is 18½ hours and one degree and two minutes. The latitude is (—).

The Vo River has its source in the mountains of Danzig and waters the regions of Sweden and the Seven Kings before it empties in the Atlantic – or so they say, for I have not seen the mouth of the river. But as it flows at the foot of this city it is bigger than the Danube and somewhat smaller than the Volga and the Ural. I judge the Danube to be smaller because in this river of Vo were India ships and galleons of Dunkerque and Denmark.

South of this great city lies an endless plain with village upon village, very thriving and prosperous, where there are everywhere estates with two mansions each and orchards and gardens.

We were unable to tour this city as we wished, since we were too busy raiding and plundering. But it is a merciless castle which shot perhaps 1,000 cannons at the Tatar soldiery. God be praised, no one was hurt.

Remarkable creatures and plants in this region

One is the India hen that comes from India. Also the Egyptian hen. And there is another hen that comes from the New World, with a flat head and flat nose and eyes at the top of its head, a marvellous and ridiculous creature. Its feathers are curled like the fleece of a sheep. Its wings are like those of a chicken, but it has long legs for wading in the water. Sometimes it dives into the water and re-emerges; but since its feet have claws like a hen, it cannot swim.

There are also abundant ducks and geese. All these birds lay two eggs each day. The egg laid in the morning is white, hard and big; the egg laid in the evening is small and soft and, when cooked and eaten, smells like musk.

While this city is at the extreme of the seventh clime, nevertheless, due to its mild coastal climate, it abounds in lemons, oranges, olives, pomegranates and figs. There are no date palms or sycamores or banana trees; but cypresses and pine trees are everywhere.

By God's command the flowers in this region are very different from those in Turkey, and have different smells.

This city has myriads of marvels and wonders and noteworthy spectacles; but since I was with the restless Tatars, and had no safe-conduct, I was only able to find out this much about the country.

After that we set fire to the surrounding villages and took captive the infidels fleeing to the mountains, amounting to 7,000 choice Frankish lads and lasses. But I got none of this booty, and consoled myself with the verse:

> However much you strive to gain your desire,
> No more will come to you than your fated share.

Heading south from this city of Kallevine we passed by 800 villages, burning none of them. We just galloped for three days with our captives and booty in tow until we reached the country of the city of **Holland**. It is governed by (—) (—). This too is a huge fertile territory. Our Kallevine captives told us that this country has a total of 700 castles. The city of Holland was so crowded that we decided not to harm it. We did spend one day and one night on a raiding expedition of the surrounding villages. Since no stranger or enemy had ever set foot in this region before, all the infidels stayed in their houses. Their villages are called Pranda (?).

We took so many splendid captives from this country and so much loot that only God could reckon it. My share consisted of seven girls and three boys. Their males are ugly, but their females have doe eyes, radiant faces and sweet speech. Most of the populace are Czechs, with here and there some Poles, and the peasants are all people of Tot. They are sometimes subject to the Czechs and sometimes to the Swedes. In short, when the Czech king conquers them they are Czechs, when the Swedish king conquers them they are Swedes.

Our return journey in safety from the above-mentioned country of Holland

First we all assembled for *keñeş* which is to say, consultation, in the language of the Tatars. Of the seventy or eighty thousand captives, we released ten who promised to take us in safety via a different road and through a country even more abounding in booty. We handed them over to the foraging officers to serve as guides, and set out in a southwesterly direction from this country of Holland. Travelling for three days, we took 6,000 more captives en route, burning no villages and destroying no houses.

We came to the great city of **Kariş** in the country of the Frankish Flemings. It is located in a vast plain on the shore of the German Sea and is adorned with orchards and gardens. Our eyes were dazzled by the gilded crosses in the churches. This large town is at the extreme of the sixth clime. It is governed by the Flemish king, an independent ruler who mints his own pennies and Groschen and round and fragrant florins. He has 3,000 galleons and bargias and carracks, as well as merchant vessels that operate in India and China and the New World.

The Flemings also pass as Christians, but are actually fire-worshipping Zoroastrians like the English infidels, although their scripture is the Gospel. Their Lenten fast for the Red Egg (Easter) festival is like that of the Germans, viz. they eat no oily foods but only fish eggs. Unlike the Germans, the Flemings and the Swedes eat hens' eggs and sheeps' liver. So their sect is contrary; and while their scripture is the Gospel, it has been translated into Flemish.

The Flemish language is as follows:

[2.5 lines empty]

They have all sorts of expressions, but what we have recorded is what we heard from our captives.

We remained for one day in the plain and the infidels did not stir. The city is without surrounding walls, a great unwalled habitat spread out over a vast fertile plain. But it is surrounded by a deep moat and has a fort with a single-layered hedge wall.

It happened that five or ten of Mehmed Agha's men – he is one of our Tatars – captured six infidels and brought them to the camp. One of the prisoners was put to death and the others served as informants. They said, 'There is a ruined area of the wall on the sea side. If you enter the city from there you will conquer it.'

All the Tatars immediately mounted, tied a burning match stick to each of their arrows, and attacked the fort with a rain of arrows, setting it aflame. The infidels inside the fort started to flee to the mountains southwest of the city, but the Tatars caught up with them and, with a shower of arrows, killed several thousand and took up to 10,000 captive. Others of the *gazis* entered the city from the places indicated by our infidel guide and pillaged to their hearts' content.

However, the number of captives we took from this city was small in relation to its size. The reason is that the inhabitants heard that we had gone as far as the Atlantic coast burning so many cities and villages, and so they fled, some by boat, some by horse to the mountains. But although we got few captives, we got much booty. Our Tatars were aware that there were many (potential) captives in the mountain forts and redoubts; but since the mountains were steep and thickly wooded, the Tatars did not enter them for fear of being shot at and because they would have to dismount. So they settled with few captives.

We remained for one day in the plain outside this city, grazing our horses and picking up booty with impunity. The flourishing villages at the foot of the snowy summer pastures to the east of this city provided booty consisting of 10,000 Flemish horses, which suited our Tatars very well, for we had many captives and the captives had no mounts.

Natural wonders of the country of the Flemings
The fields of these villages on the skirt of the snowy summer pastures become cracked from the heat of summer. The bees make hives in the cracks and these produce a fragrant honey like musk and ambergris, which the infidels consume. But many of the hives are deep in the cracks and inaccessible except to foxes, jackals and bears. Of the honey combs that remain in the ground, the honey gets washed away by the winter rains, leaving the beeswax behind. The following spring, by God's wisdom, the wax begins to seep out of the ground like sprouting grass. If the honeycombs left in the ground were yellow, the wax comes out yellow as saffron; if red, red; if white, white; if green, then green as grass. Thus, by God's command, waxes of various colours grow out of the ground and perfume the air. When the beeswax reaches its full height of three spans it begins to melt in the heat of the sun. The infidels of that region know its season. They go out to the mountains and orchards and fields with their wives and children to gather the wax. From it they make candles of various colours. They also make dolls out of their white camphor which they sell, and all sorts of idols which they worship.

Again, in the mountains of this city of Kariş in the land of the Flemish Franks, there is a yellow tree like boxwood, tall and decanter-shaped like the cypress in Turkey. People put the leaves, that have a musky scent, in their cupboards, which leaves their homes and their clothing smelling like musk and ambergris. The leaves never fall from the tree, it being an evergreen. At the right season the people gather the leaves and extract a juice from them, like rose-water, which they export throughout Christendom.

The branches and leaves of this tree resemble those of the cypress, except that they are yellow as amber and shiny as gold. The tree bears a fruit, with a pod like a bean, but inedible. From it they extract an oil that they rub on the skin as a curative for scabies and leprosy; it even cures syphilis when applied to the affected limb. The fruit smells like the laurel in Turkey. When they have extracted the oil, they use the pod for incense in their houses and churches. The wood of this tree is used to make cupboards, chairs and tables.

By God's wisdom, what they call 'French itch' (i.e. syphilis) is endemic in this land of the Flemings. To be sure, all Franks have the itch. But God has created this *filva* (or *nilva*?) tree as a cure for these ills of theirs. They rub the oil from its fruit on their skin, and anoint their faces and eyes with the juice from its leaves. This humble one too, counting it as a blessing, took some leaves and put them in my clothing.

Departing this city with so much booty and countless captives we pressed on toward the southwest for two days at a forced march, taking captives but burning none of the thousands of villages along the way, until we arrived at **Amsterdam**, capital of the king of the Flemings. It is a huge walled city, more populous and prosperous than any in the Christian country of the Seven Kings.

We set up camp in a plain to the east of this city, beyond gun-range, and observed it from a distance. We could make out the towers of the 170 great churches rising to the sky, topped by golden crosses the size of a man that flashed in the sun, the roofs covered with fine indigo-coloured lead. Such a built-up city reminded me of Danzig. We could also make out the king's palace, very beautiful, dazzling our eyes with its rooftops and cupolas and balconies.

Unfortunately we could not enter the city and tour it properly, nor could we get closer to it than we were, since it was so bustling with people and bristling with 200,000 fire-spouting infidel Fleming musketeers. Also, the surrounding walls, with its towers and redoubts, is like the Wall of Iskandar or, to vary the image, like Mt Alburz. Not only could we not approach this paradise-like city, we could not even get beyond the (surrounding) orchards and gardens and approach the moat.

So we kept our distance, only raiding areas within one day's distance and taking innumerable captives. Those who escaped our swords crowded onto caiques, in fear of the army of Islam (i.e. the Tatars), and remained offshore in the German sea. Most of the boats capsized. One notable captain could not reach his ship and was taken captive with his 300 men. We stayed in camp away from the walled city, setting up watch-posts on all four sides.

Natural wonders
An unusual kind of cabbage grows in some of the garden plots in the countryside surrounding this city. Its leaves are in layers, like a cabbage, and very green, but tart like sorrel. At the very centre of these leaves, where the heart of the cabbage would be, is a white gourd, about the size of a man's head. This gourd has no seeds but is filled to the brim with millet, like the inside of a fig, and with yellow honey that also tastes like a fig, but sweeter.

I was brought some of these cabbages when they were ripe. The gourds split open like figs and the honey and millet spilled out. In some cases they split in two and, when the honey and millet flowed out, the skin was left behind.

The Frankish physicians ascribe seventy beneficial properties to this fruit. First the outer green leaves, when roasted and eaten, make the complexion ruddy, remove wind from the belly, and sharpen the eyesight. The inner gourd is wholesome and fattening. When it is very ripe, the honey is made into a sherbet that rejuvenates the liver. If the sherbet stands still for three days, it turns into mead, intoxicating without causing hangover, and bracing to the body's faculties.

This plant is only found in the country of the Flemings. But in origin it is a New World vegetable. Just 200 miles to the west of this country in the Atlantic is England, an island 8,000 miles in circumference; further west, beyond the Atlantic, is the Magellan Sea; and 4,000 miles beyond that is the New World, discovered in the year of the chronogram *Fütihata* ('Both are conquered'). The New World ports in this Old World are Western France (*Dış Fransa*), Sweden, Dunkirk, Denmark, Lonçat (Rotterdam?), and Amsterdam of the Flemings. The above-mentioned cabbage was brought to these ports from the New World and now grows in the Flemish country. Its name is *hunza*.

I brought a sample of this cabbage to the camp, and even brought it as far as Uyvar where I cooked it with rice and saffron. All who ate it were amazed and said it tasted heavenly.

On the third day we departed this plain of Amsterdam and again headed southwest. After burning villages and gathering captives and booty for two days we arrived on the third day in the country of **Prandaporosk** (Brandenburg?). This is a vast city with orchards and gardens, spread over a territory like snowy mountains, and governed by the German Kaiser or emperor. Huge numbers of infidels drew up their wagons in a defensive circle and prepared for battle, so we camped a good distance away. We made sure our captives were tightly bound, placed watch-posts all around, tethered the horses with ropes and let them roll in the dust, then saddled them and prepared for battle ourselves.

This city of Prandaporosk is situated at the foot of a great snow-covered summer-pasture and thickly-wooded mountain range. Its infidels had all gone up into the steep mountains a few days before our arrival, while its soldiers had emerged from the walled city and prepared for battle in their Wagenburgs. For this reason we were unable to get any loot here, not even a needle.

The surrounding villages are as flourishing as the garden of Iram. Since it is summer-pasture country, the grapes in its orchards are sweet, and the wine is drunk neat, but the infidels are all drunken on their feet. Orchards and gardens and fields are very fertile and productive. Rivers flow freely and blessings abound.

We could make out a very strong fortress in the middle of the city.

The people of this region are sophisticated and refined. I deduced this from the fact that the bedding and pillows of the peasants in the villages that we plundered were all stuffed with feathers, while the bedsteads were made of balsa wood and holly oak.

As for the climate, the winter is very severe; it rains for six months straight, and the whole country turns into a muddy swamp.

The fortresses here are for the most part like that of Kanizsa, wooden palisades in the midst of reed beds and swamps. Still, each one is a Wall of Iskandar. The infidels of this region make their fortresses very strong out of fear of the Swedish king.

And most of the cannons are wooden as well, made of ash or elm or *sarma* (?) and shaped like barrels with iron hoops in five or ten places. It takes ten men to lift one cannon. They put ten wooden cannons on a cart, take them where they want them, then affix the iron hoops and begin shooting. They can only be fired fifteen or twenty times, however; sometimes they burst after being fired three or four times.

After getting a bit of booty from the countryside we departed this city of Prandaporosk and again headed southwest, arriving in one day at the border of **Germany**. The country is mainly forest, and subject to the German Kaiser. Being in possession of Alexander's crown, which is called Corona, he takes precedence over the Seven Kings and holds sway over 760 castles.

The people are Christians and their scripture is the Gospel, but they have translated that into German; they also recite the Psalms. Their sect is Catholic (*Papişte*), meaning that of the pope. They all wear black vests and Eflatuniye hats. The hats, however, are not black as with the other Franks, but yellow, blue, green or red, with crane and ostrich feathers stuck in.

After setting foot on this pure and fragrant territory we spent one complete day at a forced march raiding German villages and towns until we came to the great city of Isinriye, capital of the German Kaiser. It is one of the most prosperous and beautiful cities that we observed during this happy campaign, with layer upon layer of buildings. When viewed from one stage distant, the golden crosses atop the indigo-coloured cupolas and on the bell-towers of all the churches glitter in the sunlight. As the city is situated at the skirt of a lofty mountain, we could also make out the streams flowing through it like Salsabil in paradise.

In the endless plain that is eastward of the city, the sweet fragrance of the plants and flowers in the orchards and gardens perfumed the brains of our Tatars. There are parks and picnic spots in all the grassy meadows surrounding the city, with tall shady trees and pavilions and pleasure-domes and benches, and wondrous sights, gardens of rose and hyacinth and sweet basil like the garden of Iram. But they were empty of people, since all the infidels had fled within the city walls out of fear of our Tatar soldiery.

While we were considering with the Tatars whether to set fire to the surrounding villages and towns, a contingent of 300 infidels appeared from the direction of the city of Isinriye with a white flag. Three of the infidels rode up crying 'Mercy, O Chingissid soldiers, mercy!' They brought a letter, written in Turkish, the gist of which was as follows, 'Welcome to you. Thus far you have not burned our villages and our thriving orchards and pavilions. May Jesus and Mary be pleased with you. In exchange for this kindness we have sent you and your soldiers two carts with 20,000 Groschen and fifty carts of grain. Please accept these and depart without destroying our prosperous and beautiful city that is the envy of kings.'

When the letter was read the gifts of money and grain were accepted and distributed among the *gazis*. My share consisted of 100 Thalers.

We learned that the governor of the city was a certain Joachim, a kinsman of the German Kaiser, who by this stratagem got the Tatars to leave and saved the city. Our commander, the coastal officer (—) Agha, took the gifts as hush-money and said: 'Henceforth it makes no sense to destroy the country of Germany.'

So we proceeded along the Danube, keeping the walled towns of German Hungary (*Alaman Ungurus*) on our right side and refraining from pillaging them, since they belonged to the German Kaiser and we had accepted the gifts of his magistrate Joachim. These included the castles of Serinbe, Tancavar, Anpirvar, şinvardo, Prague – one of the Kaiser's capital cities; (—) (—) (—); Vienna – another of his capitals; Peşpehel Porok, Frau, Ovar, Kastel, Senmartin, Porok, Pojon, Yanık; Tata, Papa, Pirespirim – these last three are in the mountains; and Komorn.

Stages of our journey from the lands of Germany to the country of Middle Hungary

Departing from below İsinriye we trotted eastward for three entire days, covering in that time a distance of seventy-six hours, until we set foot on the border of Middle Hungary at the castle of **Holçar**. It is situated in the midst of a vast plain, so we were able to take it by surprise attack and set fire to its large suburb. The booty we got there was beyond reckoning, including 2,000 choice captives, 150 cartloads of goods, various silver and gold vessels, precious stuffs and rare commodities.

Also, since this is the cavalry country of the Hungarian infidels, we took 7,000 horses of the Hungarian cavaliers. God be praised, this lowly one got as my share seven horses, six infidels, one slaveboy and two virgin maids.

So the large suburb was burnt; but the walled city was intact, and there was nowhere for the Tatars to find refuge. Now the damned infidels inside the castle fired several hundred of their cannons from a single wick and, in a trice, 200 of our Tatar *gazis* were martyred and 600 wounded. During the entire time of this happy campaign, and throughout the four kingdoms that we covered, no one's nose had been bloodied, and only twenty of our brave soldiers had been killed; but now so many doughty champions quaffed the cup of martyrdom below this castle of Holçar. Thank God we did not leave any of the noble bodies of these *gazis* in the field, but loaded them all on horseback and buried them in the mountains, setting fires over the burial ground in order that their graves not be known. *May God have mercy upon them.*

While our *gazis* were plundering and destroying the villages in this plain of Holçar castle, a very large troop of infidels appeared on our western side. This rather disconcerted us, and as we prepared for battle we decided that if the troop proved large and hostile we would first of all massacre our captives. But then it appeared from their flags and banners that they were Polish soldiers. I took a look through my spyglass and confirmed that the troop belonged to the king of Cracow who was subject to the king of Poland.

They sent a contingent to our side under a white flag, and we did the same to theirs. It seems that the Polish king had a customs agent living in Holçar castle. The Polish soldiers paid no attention to us but went straight into the castle and, almost immediately, sent fifty cartloads of grain to our soldiers. They were able to do this because at that time the Poles and the Tatars were allies. The coastal officer distributed the grain among the Tatars.

Then the Polish captain, with 300 infidels, brought fifty purses of Groschen in two *hinto* coaches and ransomed the 2,000 captives whom the Tatars had taken in the Holçar suburb. At first I was reluctant to part with my seven infidel captives, but eventually gave them up for two purses of Groschen. When it turned out that one of them was a town official, I regretted having given him up so cheaply, but it was too late to do anything about it.

The Poles took the 2,000 captives and went with them into Holçar castle. So many cannons were fired in celebration that earth and sky shook. We learned later that this castle or Middle Hungary was right on the border with Poland.

From there we headed southwest

[11 lines empty]

In seven places in four lofty mountains there are **silver mines** (with veins) as thick as an arm. But they are all underground, and since there is no one there, the workshops stand idle. Although this territory belongs to Middle Hungary, the German Kaiser has seized these mines and derives income from them to the tune of 10,000 purses. It is a wonderful sight.

From there we went seven hours, by-passing several prosperous Hungarian villages that had been burnt, and came to **Derinma'den** ('Deep Mine'). The Uyvar *gazis* had pillaged the extramural settlement and villages here as well, but had not set fire to them. So we raided the suburb at the break of dawn, lit all four sides with Tatar fire, and disturbed the sleep of all the infidels. We took 1,500 captives, shackling their legs and shattering their hearts, and lopped off the hapless cabbage-head of their trollopy metropolitan, commending his wicked soul to the fires of hell.

[3.5 lines empty]

We passed the walled town of Litre and, with a forced march for one day, passed the profitless places that had been burnt. In (—) days, on the (—) day of the month of (—), returned to **Uyvar**. We paraded before the grand vizier's tent-pavilion below the walled town, displaying all our captives numbering (—), 2,060 carts loaded with precious stuffs and goods, and horses taken from 26,000 infidels.

The grand vizier presented robes of honour to the coastal officer and to 105 Tatars and the foraging officers; but not even a snakeskin to this humble one. I frowned and pouted and looked down in the dumps. As I was leaving, the grand vizier said, 'Hey, isn't that Evliya?'

'Yes my lord, it is he,' came the reply.

'Did he go on this campaign too? He has turned into a Tatar! Well, he is the Mother of Narratives. Let's inquire wisdom of Loqman. Call him here!'

He clothed me in a gold-embroidered robe of honour, gave me 50 gold pieces, and stuck a crest in my turban. I in turn kissed his noble hand and showered him with benedictions, for he had honoured me among my peers.

'Go for now,' he said, 'you are tired. Come back this evening and give us an account of these glorious *gazas*.'

'Certainly, my lord,' said I, and went off to my tent.

As we were leaving, the presents from the coastal officer to the grand vizier arrived and were handed over to the treasurer, including 300 excellent slaveboys and girls and 300 *hinto* coaches with crystal-glass windowpanes loaded with precious items.

God be praised, this lowly and weakly one went on this *gaza* and returned without uttering a sigh, and without my servants grumbling even once. Thanks be to God, I came unscathed to my tent and was reunited with the rest of my servants, bringing with me a total of (—) lovely slaveboys and (—) girls like unpierced pearls and unopened buds, and (—) splendid cavalier's horses, and one *hinto* coach and plenty of stuffs. Praise be the Lord Creator who recompensed me a thousand times in this *gaza* for my horses and my captive Seyfi, taken from me earlier in the battle below Komorn castle, and for all the pains and hardships I suffered on that day. *This is of my Lord's favour* (27:40).

The next morning I presented one lovely slaveboy to my lord, the grand vizier's deputy, and one lovely slavegirl to my lord Defterdar Ahmed Pasha. In order to lighten my load, I kept only three of the captives and sold the rest along with the horses and the items of booty, and rested content.

5. Dubrovnik (Ragusa)

Stage of the Han of the Nazarete of Bandışka

Here in Christendom, Nazarete (lazaretto) is the term for the *han* or guesthouse where merchants and diplomats – whether from India or Yemen or Samarkand, Arabia or Persia, or from the Ottoman sultan or the vizier of Bosnia or the Pasha of Herzegovina – are lodged. Generally they must stay for forty days, in special circumstances for ten or seven or, at the very least, three days, to make sure they are not plague-ridden before they enter the city, and to ascertain other intelligence.

In this lazaretto, a military officer with fifty of his infidel subalterns stand guard over the resident guests. If a merchant has something he wants to bring to the city, but his forty days in the lazaretto are not yet up, they rub some vinegar on one end or one edge of the merchandise and give it to one of the infidels waiting their turn, who takes it to the city and sells it. They vainly suppose that plague will not enter the city with that item as long as it is rubbed with vinegar.

This Han of the Nazarete is located some distance away from the walled town of Dubrovnik, on the western side. It is a square building, very like a *han*, with numerous and well-outfitted rooms, one after the other, and kitchens and stables and rooms for the infidel soldiery. Those standing guard over the guests shut the gates every night and open them again in the morning.

Outside the lazaretto are some houses belonging to Gypsies and to other poor Lasman infidels, also graveyards with an effigy of Jesus. They say that Simon the Pure (St Peter), who was Jesus's successor and one of his disciples, is buried here. The lazaretto itself is a large square *han* built on a rocky site along the seashore.

The infidels, after treating this humble one with due care, on the third day invited us to enter the city in our formation.

Description of the capital of the Latins, the castle of Dubrovnik of the Satans

There are two Venediks on the face of the earth. One is called *Bundukani Venedik* – this is Venice the rebellious that has been at war with the Ottomans for the past twenty-five years. The other is this one, called *Dobra-Venedik* (i.e. Dubrovnik), a separate ancient community. To be sure, they are Christians, but they have translated the Gospel into Latin and recite it thus. They go so far as to claim, preposterously, that the Gospel was revealed by God to the prophet Jesus in their own Latin language, and they take pride in this.

Indeed, Latin is the most correct and eloquent of the various languages of Christendom; and, like Persian, it is an ancient and elegant tongue. And the Latin chronicles are the most reliable and authoritative. In fact, when a chronicler writes a history, it is first examined by an ecclesiastical board to make sure that it contains no errors or exaggerations. Only after it has been approved by the board, and the Twelve Bans have given their imprimatur, can it be printed.

The infidels here are very critical and deductive scholars: astrologers, diviners, surgeons, phlebotomists and historians. In fact, by their mastery of astrology they know about the Prophet Muhammad's being the possessor of this world. They know that the Ottomans have emerged and their state will last forever, that they will not leave a single infidel on the face of this earth, that they will reign until the coming of the Mahdi and the second coming of Jesus. In their books of prognostication they find the destiny of every ruler.

In the year (—), when Osman Gazi was besieging Bursa, these Dubrovnik infidels realised that the future world conquerors had emerged. So they sent their ambassadors to Osman Gazi in Bursa with (—) gold pieces and plenty of silk brocades and other precious stuffs. Finding that Osman Gazi had died and that his son Orhan Gazi had conquered Bursa, the Dubrovnikers gave all the presents to Orhan Gazi and made a peace treaty with him, agreeing to send the specified sum of treasure every year with their ambassadors. The treaty contained 150 articles, in return for which they received 150 imperial decrees.

For this reason the infidels of Dubrovnik have accepted peace with the Ottomans to this very day. They are a bunch of foresightful and farsighted infidels who never do anything contrary to the treaty and whose envoys never fail to arrive (in Istanbul) at the beginning of every year, before any others.

But despite the fact that they have renewed their treaty with the Ottomans every year since Orhan Gazi, still they are like the great plague under the wing of the Ottoman state, damnable swine who maintain the pretence of truth but whose satanic machinations infect all the infidels. To be specific: it is these Dubrovnik infidels who have led astray those of the great *Bundukani Venedik* – the Venetians, who are now our enemy – and secretly supply them with grain. They are the wealthiest of all the infidel kings, but make a show of poverty and humility in order to protect their state, and craftily maintain peaceful relations with all other rulers.

To make a long story short, these infidels treated this humble one also with courtesy and kindness and brought us in our formation to their capital and castle named (—) (—). Both the Pasha of Bosnia and the Pasha of Herzegovina have highly-placed customs officials residing in this castle, and I and my retinue were lodged in a palace near them. A military officer was assigned to keep an eye on us. We were given ample supplies of food and drink, but had to stay where we were: our infidel guards did not permit us to wander about. After the time of the evening prayer they shut the gates upon the customs officials and upon us, and opened them in the morning. Peculiar guards these, God damn them!

Shape and dimensions of the castle of Dubrovnik
It is a mighty fortress and thriving walled city of dressed stone built on a rocky site along the seashore. Its name in Latin is (—) (—). Its founder was (—) (—) Ban of the Latin people, who founded it before Jesus according to the Latin chronicles. They also write that since its founding it has never been taken by the hand of an enemy, nor have its walls ever been breached.

It is fortified on all sides, like the Wall of Iskandar. On the land side, which is the eastern and northern side, is a lofty tower like the Rampart of Gog. The entire gulf is visible from this tower, as though spread out beneath its feet, and big balaramada guns protect both the land walls and the harbour. There are forty-seven such mighty towers outfitted with balaramada guns.

This castle is two miles in circumference, although I was unable to pace it out. The fortification on the land side consists of two layers of walls and one layer of moat carved out of the cliff. The surrounding walls are very fine and firm. On the land side, however, there are five hills that loom above it; at these five points there are two walls, each twenty cubits thick, and a three-layered redoubt, also the moat doubles back on itself. The sea wall, on the other hand, is a single layer.

There are a total of (—) gates. It is a mighty city[51] situated at the mouth

---

51 The term used here is *rabat* which usually refers to the extramural settlement.

of a small gulf inside the great Venetian Gulf (Adriatic Sea). It has a total of 700 cannons, small and large. But again, because of the tremendous hazard posed by the places looming above it, it has established peace treaties with the Seven Kings (i.e., Habsburgs) and with the Ottomans and pays them tribute and duties. But again, they are devilish infidels who have tricked the emperors with whom they are at peace to provide them twenty times the amount they pay them in tribute.

Within the walls the streets are so narrow and the houses so built up that there is not a single empty or idle space. Only there is a public square for executions and another for the marketplace, and also twenty-two courtyards of churches and monasteries.

The most imposing of these is the church of (—) (—) belonging to the king of Herzegovina. It is like a citadel to this castle, its cupolas covered with lead from end to end. May God vouchsafe that it one day become a prayer-hall of the Muslims. Aside from this there are also churches of the Venetian doges and of the bishops and the Bans and Herzogs. A Byzantine king once fled here from Macedonia – i.e. Istanbul – and had a church built which is also noteworthy and lead-covered.

The houses here are layer upon layer, like those of Galata in Istanbul, built of brick masonry and covered with tiles of slate or tin. And there are myriads of bells, large and small, hanging on every house and every church. They ring these bells on the eve of Sundays; on the festivals of St George (*Sarı Saltık*) and St Nicholas; Hızır Ilyas and Kasım (the spring and autumn equinoxes); the Virgin Mary and Kara Koncoloz; or on the Festival of the Christians (i.e., Christmas?) or a town council (*turvin*) or any one of their inauspicious holidays, and from the sound you would think the Antichrist had appeared.

This city has numerous Armenians, Greeks, Jews, Persians and Franks; but no Hungarians, Germans, Russians, Czechs, Poles, Swedes, Muscovites, Wallachians or Moldavians. Being a place of security and a safe haven of Christendom, it is a very prosperous entrepôt.

A remarkable spectacle, the strange and wondrous ceremony of the infidels

One night while sleeping peacefully in this city I was awakened by a great crashing noise and a hue and cry. At my wit's end, I wondered whether the infidels intended to massacre us. We saw that all the Dubrovnikers were passing in procession in front of the house where we resided. They came group after group, young and old, male and female, officials and armed soldiers, all carrying two lit candles that illuminated the surroundings. We watched through the chinks in the windows which, as was their nightly custom, they had closed upon us.

Everyone was shouting, 'Catch him! He went this way! He went that way!' The soldiers and executioners went in and out of some houses of the Greeks and Armenians and Persians. They leapt up and down, and threw stones at the windows – even the windows of our lodging. 'He's in this room! He's in that room!' they cried, searching frantically for something. We, of course, having no idea what it was all about, merely marvelled at the spectacle.

After a while all the infidels started celebrating and prancing and dancing, crying *Pişkindos pişkindos!* They set off a myriad of muskets and rockets and cannons, with the cry *Yajuj Yajuj!* We were stunned and thought they had burned down the city.

Now all the hell-bound infidels drew up in regiments, passing row on row and wave on wave, crying *Pişkindon!* and sounding their organs and trumpets and Lutheran horns and clappers and pipes and drums, and boys with fine sad voices intoning songs in the *rehavi* mode.

Then came the monks and patriarchs and priests and cardinals, swinging their censers and perfuming the air with aloes and ambergris and storax and angelica. There followed troop on troop with tabors and drums and bells reverberating through the walled town. Then came twelve thousand women seated on jewelled palanquins; these were the wives of the officials, who conducted them through the streets. Others passed carrying ships' masts, like cypresses, adorned with a myriad of little camphor candles that illuminated the city and turned dark night into bright day.

After this procession of women came the twelve Venetian officials, mounted on horses richly adorned with gold-embroidered trappings, themselves fully armed and magnificently attired, accompanied by their armed retainers and, on foot next to them, a gaggle of priests intoning the Gospel in the *rehavi* musical mode.

When they had passed, another large contingent appeared bearing a litter shrouded in fine gauze that was embroidered with gold and pearls and other gems. Inside were statues of Jesus and Mary – save the comparison! – smothered in jewels and silk brocades. The jewels alone were worth five Egyptian treasures.

Jesus – save the comparison! – was clothed like a priest, with a black vestment and a black mitre (?) on his head. His light-filled face set off the blackness of his locks, and he was seated on a throne.

Mary too was seated on a throne. On her head was a *Mayfirav* (i.e., empress or queen) crown, covered with various kinds of jewels that had been sent as votive offerings by the wives of all the kings. Around her neck were hundreds of pearl prayer-beads. Her nails were diamonds of 40 or 50 carats, and her eyes were carbuncles.

These were magical images, not at all like paintings on paper, but with clockwork movements and gestures just like human bodies, so that the viewer would think them to be alive. They are white magic statues, the utmost degree of artifice of the infidels; though lifeless and speechless mannikins, recalling the verse:

> You can depict the fuzz on his cheek
> And the beauty-mark on his arm;
> But, O Bihzad, how can you draw
> His coquetries and charm?

On either side of these statues people carried a myriad of candles and lamps, lighting up the night as though it were New Year's Day. When the monks bearing these two statues on their litters had passed, and then the patriarchs with their gilded and jewelled and enamelled crosses, behind them came a band playing kettledrums and fifes and drums and organs and trumpets, who conducted the King of Herzegovina to his monastery.

These joyful celebrations kept up the entire night, illuminated by candles and lamps. I have hardly begun to describe them all. The next morning, when I questioned the military officer who was serving us as to the origin of this strange spectacle, this is what he told me, 'Well, my lord, when our Lord Jesus was alive he summoned the Jews to the religion of Jesus. So one night the Jews kidnapped him and his mother Mary and imprisoned him. They intended to kill him, but since Jesus was the Spirit of God (cf. 4:171) the Jews were unable to kill him and just kept him imprisoned. Now our Latins of Simon the Pure (St Peter) got wind of this, armed themselves, and began to search for Jesus in the Jews' houses in Nablus with a great hue and cry, just like last evening. They found Jesus and Mary in a Jew's house and massacred all the Jews. Then they rejoiced, shouting *Pışkındos pışkındos!*, attired Jesus and Mary in garments and sashes, and brought them to a church. From that time until this, our

Latin people have made statues of Jesus and have celebrated his rescue from prison on one blessed night of the year. This ceremony is peculiar to the Latins and not found elsewhere in Christendom. It was our Latin people who rescued Jesus from the Jews, and for that reason we are a harmless nation of Christians esteemed throughout the Christian community.'

This is what that infidel of a chief soldier related to us. So that night we were all amazed at this tremendous spectacle. But that night we had many frightful dreams.

Meeting with the Ban on the following day
The next morning a magnificent captain came with several soldiers and conducted this humble one and the treasurer of the Agha of the Nova janissaries in procession to the Doge's Ban (*pirinc-pirim ban* – i.e., the Venetian governor of Dubrovnik). As we proceeded through the city, all the infidels came out to greet us, and as we could hardly move because of the crowds, we were able to take note of the marketplace.

Most of the shopkeepers are broadcloth and satin dealers, jewellers, paper makers, wood turners, knife makers, bead makers, bottle makers, candle-snuffer makers, ironmongers, butchers, barbers, tailors, and all the other merchants and craftsmen. The shops are laid out in good order, and very fine and busy. But there is no covered market, and the number of mercantile establishments is small in proportion to the size of the city. Quite a few of the craftsmen work at home; buying and selling in the marketplace being handled by women – both matrons and lovely maiden girls – who display their wears openly. In Christendom this is not considered shameful behaviour.

So we made our way through the city, viewing the markets and also the noteworthy houses of the infidels, until we arrived at the *korta* or palace of the Ban. If I were to describe this happy palace as it deserves, it would constitute prolixity and a hindrance to our travels. It is well-constructed, indeed, but somewhat narrow in proportion to the city. It is a mighty stone palace in five layers, with no point at which the walls could be breached. It has over 300 rooms, with vaulted halls, pantries and kitchens.

The walls of the audience hall are covered with paintings of bygone magistrates. In addition, there are depictions of future Ottoman sultans and of their own future Bans, with their precise features and dress, marvellously done according to the science of astrology.

During the reign of Sultan Murad IV (1623–40) Abaza Pasha[52] – who as a Celali had shut himself up in Erzurum, then gave up his rebellion and came with Husrev Pasha to the Porte, where the pen of forgiveness was drawn over the register of his crimes and he was made governor of the Bosnian frontier – heard about the paintings in this audience-hall of the Dubrovnik palace, and wondered why these infidels had depicted the Ottomans below their own Bans. So he came in a forced march from Sarajevo to this castle of (Dobra)-Venedik and asked permission to enter, intending to destroy the palace. Some of the infidels were willing to let him enter, but one pestiferous priest said, 'Once he has entered the castle, who can tell him to leave? He entered Erzurum once and shut himself in. Eight viziers over eight years could not get him out. Finally he left of his own accord and came to Sultan Murad, and his crime was forgiven. So if he enters here now, who can get him out? Let's give him a little and beg him a lot.'

The Venetians gave Abaza Pasha 100,000 ducats, which was enough to persuade him to give up entering the castle. But he stopped to visit the shrine of Simon the Pure (St Peter), who is buried next to the above-mentioned Nazarete (lazaretto), and saw him lying in the tomb with a black *manlifke* headdress.[53]

'Look here, infidels,' said Abaza Pasha. 'Wasn't Simon the Pure the successor of Jesus?'

'Yes my lord, that is so,' they replied.

'O damned ones! Since he was a Muslim, why have you put such a hat on his head?'

With that he removed the hat from St Peter's head and replaced it with the *selimi* turban that was on his own head. The infidels were aghast. They gave him another 100,000 ducats. He removed the *mücevveze* turban[54] and said,

---

52 The following story is apparently based on an incident reported by Naima (III, 201; ed. İpşirli II, 776–7) that Abaza, then (1633) governor of Bosnia, wanted to visit Zadra. The Venetian authorities held a council and were about to grant permission when they were dissuaded by the argument that once Abaza was inside, they could not made him leave, nor could they kill him, from fear of breaking their treaty with the Ottomans. Refused, Abaza laid siege to the city, but the Zadraites sent an urgent message to the bailo in Istanbul who managed to get Abaza removed from office, so he had to lift the siege.
53 Probably the *kallimavchion* or cylindrical hat of the Greek orthodox priests.
54 Both large ceremonial turban types; for comparison, see Zygulski 1992, 105 (fig. 21), 111.

'Look here, infidels, I want you to erase the images of your kings from above the pictures of the Ottomans in your palace. Otherwise, when I come again, if I find them still there I will level your castle to the ground and put all of you to the sword.'

With this he left. From that time on they have repainted the depictions in this palace so artfully that not everyone is aware of them; but someone knowledgable in the science of painting who examines them carefully can appreciate their painterly qualities.

I entered the palace and toured it to my heart's content, then came out through the Ban's harem and sat on a chair. Now the twelve magistrates emerged through a door of this audience-hall. When they saw this humble one they stopped, took their Eflatuniye hats in their hands, and greeted me. I was obliged to get up, though I did so unwillingly, and stood in a respectful attitude, while they took their seats.

These magistrates have no claim of precedence among themselves; they simply sit in a circle, and thus no one of them is in a more prominent position. The government circulates among them, each ruling for one month of the year. But when they consult, they are always in agreement. If one of them dies, there is a pool of forty others, one of whom comes and enters the circle of twelve. If one of these forty dies, there is an outer group of 300, one of whom is prepared to enter among the forty. But none may enter the circle of twelve and sit on the throne until he is forty years old and in his prime. Such is their ancestral custom.

In short, when the twelve magistrates were seated on their thrones, I handed over the Sultanic orders and the letters of the grand vizier and of his deputy Ibrahim Agha. The magistrates all stood up and took off their hats again while inquiring after the health of this humble one and the health of the grand vizier and of the deputy. When the imperial orders were read out and their contents made known, they said, 'It is the Sultan's to command. Our treasure and our envoys are ready. According to the imperial command, we will give the salaries of 3,000 musketeer guards to Sührab Mehmed Pasha and Praçalı Mustafa Pasha.'

They cried benedictions upon the Sultan and grand vizier, and then continued, 'However, the Nova galleys are always attacking our villages, taking our Christians captive and driving off our sheep and goats and cattle. If they do not give back our sheep, we will have our envoys, who are about to leave, register an official complaint and inform the Sultan about our plight.'

Now this humble one had in my hand orders from Sührab Mehmed Pasha empowering me to obtain the Dubrovnikers' sheep from the Novaites. When I showed these decrees to the magistrates, they were very pleased and showed me even greater courtesy and increased my rations. They also showed great favour to the treasurer of the Agha of the Nova janissaries.

I stayed there a few days. Some of the magistrates feasted me and some came to greet me as 'the grand vizier's agha.' I gave them embroidered handkerchiefs of the Kaya Sultan variety; they each gave me a *honta* (Italian *conto*?), meaning a sum of 20,000 dinars, also stuffs and muskets and falcons. The *dinar* is a silver coin, very fine and white and pure, but very thin. On one side is the figure of their chief Ban, on the other the figure of Jesus and the date since his birth. It is round like a penny; four make one drachm. It is the standard currency here; they have no other silver coins (*guruş*) or gold pieces; but their treasuries are very full.

6. The great bridge at Mostar

The Grand Architect Sinan son of Abdülmennan Agha built this noteworthy bridge in the year (—) at the command of Sultan Süleyman. It rises into the sky like a rainbow, spanning the water from one cliff to the other, a single arch like the Vault of Chosroes in Baghdad. The Neretva River flows beneath it in the middle of the city of Mostar. Each end of the bridge is a fortified castle, so it is impossible to pass from one side of the city to the other without crossing this bridge.

The loyal brethren who hear my tale should know that this lowly slave, Evliya the unhypocritical, has been travelling non-stop for the past twenty-seven years. I have sojourned in sixteen kingdoms and have examined hundreds of thousands of buildings and monuments. Among these are the Çoban (Shepherd) bridge over the Araz River near Hasan-kal'a in the province of Erzurum; the Altunhalkalı (Golden Hoop) bridge, also over the Araz River, between Erzurum and Malazgird; the Batman bridge between Hazzo and Mifarkin; The Hasankeyf castle bridge; the Antioch bridge over the Asi River; the Cihan bridge in Misis; the Adana bridge; the Tarsus bridge; Eğriköprü (Crooked Bridge) in Sivas; the Çaşnigir (Taster) bridge over the Kızılırmak; the Osmancık bridge over the Kızılırmak; the Geyve bridge, built by Sultan Bayezid, over the Sakarya River; and hundreds of other noteworthy bridges in Anatolia.

As for Rumelia, the bridges that must be seen are those of Sultans

Suleyman and Selim II at the Çekmeces (two Marmara inlets near Istanbul); the Burgaz bridge; Sultan Murad's bridge over the Ergene River; the Mihal bridge in Edirne; the Yeniköprü (New Bridge) and Sarrachane (Tannery) bridge, again in Edirne; the Koca Mustafa Pasha bridge near Edirne; and the great twelve-arch bridge of Vishigrad over the Drina River, built by Sokollu Mehmed Pasha.

But of all these bridges, the most noteworthy and the one most worth seeing is this peerless bridge of Mostar. For this humble one has journeyed in the lands of the Arabs and Persians and Turks and Franks, and as far as Balkh and Bukhara (!), but in all the inhabited quarter of the world I have never seen a lofty bridge like this. To be sure, the Batman and Hasankeyf bridges in Kurdistan, which I mentioned above, are extremely well-constructed bridges; but (they don't match up to this one).

It is a single lofty arch, like the Vault of Khawarnaq, stretching from one cliff to the other, so high that a person crossing dares not look down. The total length of the bridge, from gate to gate of the fortified castles at either end, is 100 broad paces. The width is 15 feet.

Another noteworthy feature, and a mark of tremendous skill, is the channel consisting of bronze pipes that runs over this bridge from the Tabahane (Tannery) suburb on the western side to the marketplace on the eastern side. It was installed by Sultan Murad IV's day-book clerk, Ibrahim Efendi. The channel carries water from the Radobola River for the baths, mosques, *hans*, imarets, medreses, fountains – in sum, for forty-five places in the city. The poets of Mostar have commemorated this good work with the following chronogram: (—) (—) (—) (—) (—) (—) (—) (—) (—)

This is a unique feature, unseen and unheard of elsewhere by travellers on land and sea, that water should flow both below a bridge and above it as well. A surpassing marvel!

The building of the bridge by Sultan Süleyman is commemorated in the chronogram *kudret kemeri* ('Vault of Power'), the year 974 (1566–7). Another chronogram is this:

> This bridge has been built exactly like a rainbow.
> Is there anything like it in the world, my God?
> Drawing the lesson, a wise man stated its date:
> The bridge that others cross, we too will cross, my shah.
>
> Year 973 (1565–6)

There are many chronograms for this matchless bridge, but these are the ones I can recall.

Truly, the master builder of old expended all of his skill in bridging the gap from one cliff to the other with a single arch. When viewed from a distance (i.e. with its reflection in the water) the bridge appears rounded, just like an archer's thumbstall.

Nowhere else in the world is there such a bridge. No ancient architect has constructed anything like it for elegance and refinement. Actually, if you consider it, this spot calls for exactly such a one-arch bridge. On either side of the river are lofty cliffs, and the wide Neretva River flows below to a depth of a minaret. Accordingly, the Grand Architect Sinan made such a single grand vault, the likes of which no traveller has ever seen.

Despite the great height of this bridge, when some viziers and deputies and great notables and exalted magistrates come to sightsee and while they are residing in one of the above-mentioned two castles, some brave boys stand ready at the edge of the bridge and, in the presence of the viziers, cry *Ya Allah* and leap into the river, flying like birds. Each boy displays a different skill, whether somersaulting or plunging upside-down or sitting cross-legged; or they go in twos or threes, embracing each other and leaping into the water. God keeps them unharmed and they immediately clamber onto the shore and up the cliffs to the head of the bridge where they get rewards from the viziers and notables.

Other men do not dare look down, let alone jump off; if they did, their galls would burst; because the height of this bridge from the surface of the water is 80 fathoms, and the depth of the Neretva River is another 80 fathoms. Also there are rocks in the river the size of bath-house cupolas, and the river itself flows very wildly, with many eddies and whirlpools, flashing like lightning and roaring like thunder. It takes tremendous courage to plunge into water like that.

But the boys have trained. First they jump off low rocks, then higher and higher. Another form of training is that the boys who are apprenticed to tradesmen in the city, when they bring lunch from their masters' houses to their shops and have trays of food and loaves of bread in their hands and on their heads, do not go in the middle of the bridge with these heavy loads but rather hop up and down on the thin railings that run along the bridge on either side. Prudent men do not even dare approach the edge of this bridge when they are crossing it, but immature boys hop on the railings! It is quite a spectacle.

VOLUME SEVEN

Habsburg Borderlands, Crimea and beyond

EVLIYA ENTERS 'GERMANY' (i.e., Austria) and leaves a German graffito on a huge tree. He participates in raiding expeditions in the Habsburg borderlands of Hungary. In the summer of 1664, he is an eyewitness to the Ottoman defeat at the Battle of St Gotthard ('Battle on the Raab'). His experience in the field allows him to make generalisations about various European groups.

In the spring of the following year, he arrives in Vienna as part of the Ottoman embassy under Kara Mehmed Pasha to King Leopold I. The occasion for the embassy is the signing of the Peace of Vasvár between the Ottomans and the Habsburgs. Evliya's account of Vienna is by far his most extensive of a European city. He is especially struck by the clockwork mechanisms in the city's public squares and markets; the surgical techniques and medical practices in the hospitals and asylums; and the paintings and books, organ music and singing in the cathedral. His description of German language includes a prayer to the Virgin Mary.

The remainder of this volume covers Evliya's travels in Rumania, Crimea, southern Russia and the Caucasus. He spends the winter of 1665 in Bagche-Saray, capital of the Crimean khanate, and participates in Tatar raiding expeditions under the auspices of Mehmed Giray Khan. In the following year he ventures to Circassia and the land of the Kalmyks. The outlandish customs and food-ways he observes in these places occasion some amusing stories, which have to be taken with a large grain of salt. He returns to Azov in January 1667.

1. Raiding expeditions in 'Germany'; a fabulous tree in Krokondar

Account of our heading toward the merciless country of the Germans
One of the captive guides said, in private, 'Would you like to do some more pillaging and get some more plunder without any trouble?'

'Yes, we would,' we answered, and he led us westward for six hours on a broad highway. The other infidels did not approve of us going on this road.

'Why do you not want us to go this way?' we inquired.

'Not a Tatar or a Turk or any enemy has ever set foot in this country,' they replied. 'It is completely heedless, and there is much spoil to be had. But when you have got your fill of spoil, it will tie down your feet. Your Turkish army is far from you. They call these lands the German country. Kasım Voyvoda and 40,000 of his men were martyred here. You too will have difficulty getting out alive with so much booty. Also, all the German infidels have heard of you. Eventually, on your way back, they will attack you from behind.'

This reply and other like arguments seemed plausible, and some of us found it convincing. Others, however, said, 'What will be will be. What they say is nonsense. We want some spoil now!'

The minority followed the majority, and that day we set out from Prondok and headed westward. We proceeded at a forced march along the skirt of the German mountains (i.e., the Alps?).

Description of the Fortress of Raytinad. It is a big city, under the authority of the mother of the German Kaiser. We left behind in the mountains all of our captives and abundant spoil with 2,000 *gazi* warriors and stormed into the city via a sparsely wooded grove on the north side of the fortress. In the twinkling of an eye, we overcame the garrison infidels with our swords. We found so much money and goods in their market and churches and ill-omened houses, and captured so many boys bright as the sun and girls lovely as the moon, each one a rose that had not yet bloomed and to whose skirt no thorn had yet attached.

The armies of Islam got so rich from the booty that they repeatedly let go what they had plundered and grabbed more costly items. In sum, the spoil got here amounted to 300 cartloads of assorted rare and precious things, a wealth of goods and wares beyond description. And all the Muslim *gazis* got their share.

In the centre of this city of Raytinad there is a huge ancient monastery, a Shaddad-like edifice more imposing and stronger than a fortress. It has a lofty dome resembling that of Aya Sofya in Istanbul, and 300 smaller domes, all covered with indigo-coloured lead. Surrounding it are four bell towers that reach up to the sky. The big dome in the middle is topped by a cross as tall as five men, the 300 others by silver crosses as tall as three men. All the crosses are gilded with pure gold. This huge monastery is prominent in Christendom and throughout the world because of these crosses.

The army of Islam laid siege to this convent, saying, 'There is much money in this church!' But the infidel convent turned out to have much artillery and in an instant seven of our *gazis* were martyred. We split open their dead bodies' bellies, stuffed them with salt, and loaded them onto carts.

As we retreated from below this fortress with our spoil, we turned north and proceeded through thick forest, on German territory. Happening upon the trail of a large army, we questioned our captives about it.

'This is the road to France,' they said. 'God knows, the French king must have sent reinforcements from Dunkerque and Denmark and elsewhere in Western Europe to our king. They have crossed the German mountains and gone to the fortress of Yanık (Yenikale/Zerinvar).'

We examined the tracks closely. They were the footmarks of a sea-like army that had just gone by.

From there we travelled westward for one day.

Description of the prosperous city and fortress of Krokondar. It is first and last a great city untouched by an enemy's hand. It is German country under the authority of the German kaiser. Since it is surrounded by marshland, it was not possible to raid and plunder the place. We therefore halted in the open plain.

In the centre of this city also there is a huge fortress-like monastery like the Wall of Iskandar. Wayward King Ferdinand, who did battle with Süleyman Khan in Buda, is the founder of this unpraiseworthy building. It is a solidly constructed and prosperous convent, like a white pearl.

Passing this city we proceeded north through mountainous country, gazing at the lofty trees, God's creation. By God's Wisdom, there was one mammoth tree situated in a broad plain. No tree in the turning world gives such shade and bears such leaves and fruit. It has 300 branches, each as thick as an elephant's trunk, with thin tart-tasting leaves like the parsley in Turkish salad. Although, by the Creator's wisdom, everything sour is constipative, these sour leaves are as laxative as senna.

Its fruit is curious. All the fruit grows on the tiny tips of the branches, and the green-shelled fruit lines the tree's 300 thick branches like acorns. When ripe, by command of the Living and Omnipotent One, they taste like *hastavi* dates from Baghdad and smell like musk and raw ambergris. And they are very invigorating (i.e., aphrodisiac). But there are no seeds.

This tree is unique; there is none like it on the face of the earth. 10,000 sheep can lie under the protective shade of each branch. There are chapels and little platforms with stone benches in seven places underneath its shade, and more than 300 taverns and brothels.

This tree rises up to the zenith of heaven. Its trunk is so thick that, as many of the *gazi* youths who were sitting in its shade gathered round me, seventy-seven of us, circling it hand in hand, could hardly embrace it. God's creation is especially remarkable in this respect: a mighty river leaps into the air like a jet from seventy or eighty forked branches on this great tree's lofty summit, and pours down into a large pool built of white German marble some distance away. As the water gushes forth, it makes a terrifying noise. The trunk out of which it spouts is as tall as a minaret, and the water jets up to the height of another minaret before it pours down into the pool. It is truly a grand spectacle.

In the environs of this large pool is an assortment of galleries fashioned in the Frankish style, ornamental fountains, water jets, and gilded pavilions with gushing springs. There are also kitchens and grottoes, orchards and gardens, every one constructed by a bygone king who made the endowment saying, 'Let it be a picnic spot and pleasure park.' It is a noteworthy attraction.

This humble one pleaded with the *gazis* and did not let them damage a single building. Now I got the iron chisel and hammer from my saddlebag and, mounting my horse, carved the following inscription on the huge tree's bosom, in German language and imitating the German script:

Maria	meaning, For Mother Mary
Kot kapurhand	For God Almighty
Makar fand	Evliya prays.

But the truth is that I carved this inscription in order to leave my mark in Germany.

When this humble one asked several of the captive priests for information – root and branch – about this tree, they related, 'Our prophet Jesus was a world-traveller. He came here and planted this huge tree, a miracle to behold, as a sign pointing to the Danube in the German mountains. Thus the Danube River leapt into the air from inside this tree and poured down to the ground. Later our kings constructed this pool, the pavilions and the forts, as pious works.'

Indeed, in the seven climes and the lands of the ten kings, this humble slave has not seen such a magnificent tree and such an ancient and exemplary bearer of fruit to be endowed with spirit. *God is capable of everything* (2:20, etc.).

2. The battle on the Raab River (Battle of Saint Gotthard, 1664)

Summary of the *gaza* on the Raab River and the bad planning that led to the defeat of the armies of Islam at the river's edge

All the veterans of the imperial council convened at the edge of the Raab. The decision was made to build bridges over the river, then to proceed past Nemet Uyvar against the fortress of Vienna in order to lay siege. A Fatiha was recited (to seal the decision). No one was able to speak up and say, 'Since the beginning of winter, the army of Islam has conducted three campaigns. They drove out the infidels from the fortress of Kanizsa. They conquered Yenikale in twenty-eight days, and conquered seventy-seven other fortresses. So there is no strength left in the army of Islam. Now it is the depth of winter, and men, horses and donkeys are starving. How can we march to Vienna or Prague or Yanık in this winter rain?'

Because Gürci Mehmed Pasha and Ismail Pasha did not allow anyone to speak up, the officials continued their illusory deliberations, saying, 'Today is Friday, so there is no battle. But tomorrow is Saturday and according to the Hadith, *God has blessed Saturday and Thursday*, let us cross the river tomorrow and devastate the land of the infidels. But since today is Friday, let bridges be constructed over the river at several points, and escarpments on both banks, and wide roads and huge ramparts and trenches at the bridgeheads.'

Yet there was no inclination in the army of Islam to cross the river and do battle.

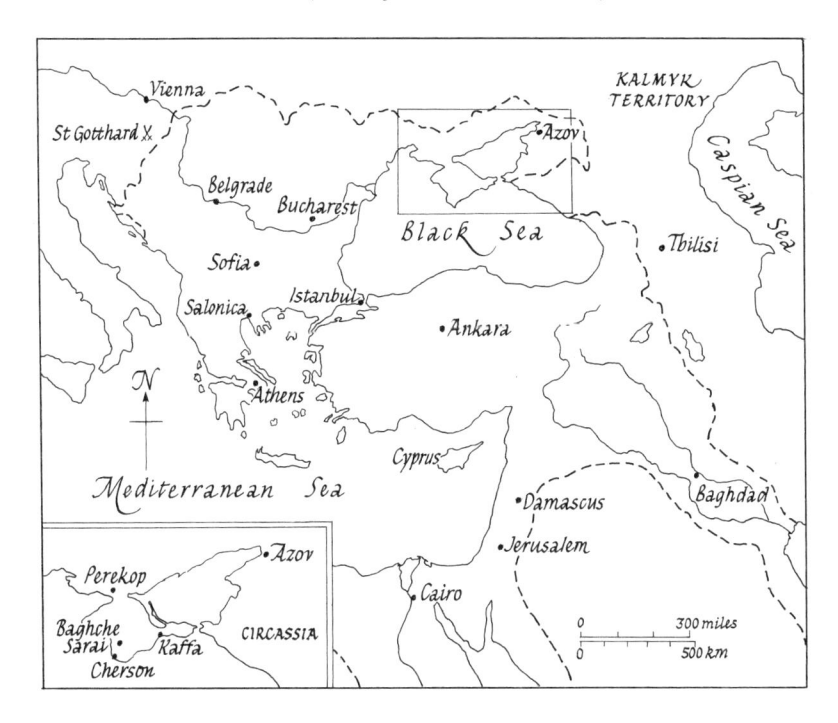

The battle on the Raab River (Battle of Saint Gotthard, 1664)

This humble one soon realised the misery of the situation and the bad planning. Therefore I, with my sixteen horses and eleven servants, all starving because of reduced rations, one night secretly crossed over to the Tatar army, pretending that we were merely changing our campsite. I made camp in a place next to Ahmed Giray Sultan. The horses were happy moving from pasture to pasture, and this humble one forgot the cruelty and suffering. But not for a moment was I, along with one or two of my servants, ever separated from the presence of Ibrahim Kethüda and the grand vizier (Köprülü Fazıl Ahmed Pasha).

Because the battle was planned for Saturday, on Friday the sergeants-at-arms gave firm warning and instructions, saying: 'Tomorrow morning we will cross the river and there will be a great battle. Today let everyone go foraging and make provisions.' So all the servants and thousands of brave youths went out to the fields for grain and fodder, and the army camp was deserted like a mill whose stream has been cut off.

On this Friday the grand vizier gave the imperial decree to Defterdar Ahmed Pasha, and five or ten thousand soldiers assembled before the courageous vizier's tent. Right away logs were nailed together and a compact wooden bridge was constructed for the army of Islam to cross on foot. The gun carriages were tied with ropes, and ten companies of janissaries (commanded by) the keeper of the Sultan's mastiffs, Abdi Agha, slowly made their way across the bridge. On the first day of the month, all the janissary *gazis* entered the trenches at the bridgehead on the bank of the Raab and erected ramparts before the trenches. Once they were settled in, several thousand horsemen crossed the river in the water.

This humble one too, thinking that I ought to cross and get some easy spoil while there were no infidels about, joined 5,000 soldiers and went westward for an hour at a forced march, arriving below Nemet Uyvar at mid-morning.

[...]

Account of the cause for the Ottoman army's defeat on the bank of the Raab River

Because on this Friday the armies of Islam had some slight victories, raiding parties left to plunder the countryside. The emirs and the officials of the imperial council, however, had all become bigheaded and did not keep a watchful eye on the infidels. While the soldiers in the army were scattered about seeking spoil, news came that the spoil-seekers had in fact fled, and that the hell-bent infidels had set out from their staging-points west of the battlefield —the cities of Beşluka, Gratz and Brandeburg – and were on their way towards the fortress of Nemet Uyvar.

Since our arrival in German country, we had completely ravaged the land of the infidels. The infidels were left homeless and, saying 'How can we take vengeance on the Turks?' were stampeding like a herd of swine and, with their black hats and black heads, were sharpening their fangs like boars. Smothered in iron and armed to the teeth, and hauling their artillery guns, they came to the battlefield where we had previously fought and massacred them. Wherever they set their unclean feet they saw that the entire field was covered by infidel corpses. They sulked amidst the corpses for a good while and roamed about, then mounted their horses and slowly marched towards the janissaries' trenches on the bank of the Raab. With them were their Generals and Grafs, Bans and Herzogs, cardinals and monks, advancing like black swine, inexorable.

On the left, all dressed in red as though soaked in blood, the French army appeared in red garments and green velvet, with white standards, and passed to one side marching rank on rank.

The battle on the Raab River (Battle of Saint Gotthard, 1664) 225

After them, the troops of the Zirinoğlu, Beganoğlu and Nedajoğlu, Kepanoğlu, İslovin, and Mekemorya passed, covered wholly in buckskin and wearing green broadcloth kalpaks. Each soldier had two horses and five or six flintlock muskets.

In sum, the troops of the Seven Herzogs passed by displaying their formations and consolidated on the right bank of the Raab.

After them, 40,000 or 50,000 German infantry passed in their battalions, with balaramada guns, commanded by the viziers named Zoza and Montecuccoli.

After them, the army of the Czech king filed past.

After them, the troops of the Girl King (Turk Louis) marched by, and the thousands of mastiffs they brought in carts that they would unleash onto the battlefields. They went and stood ready on the west flank.

After them, the army of the king of Dunkerque marched.

And after them, the troops of Denmark marched.

In a word, the Seven Herzogs, Seven Bans, Seven Kings, and two viziers came together, and all the infidels stood in their ranks.

Then all the monks, patriarchs, clerics, and priests lit ablaze the sticks of aloes wood and balsam in the braziers they held in their hands and intoned in the *rehavi* musical mode verses from the Psalter in the language of the Psalms: *Fin sonderbares cuder gebbet alerheyligesten den kapuçinar Marya Kot*. These verses thousands of the monks recited in a loud voice. And from hundreds of places, also in the *rehavi* mode, they sounded organs and trumpets and Lutheran horns. Some priests went around and distributed cups of wine to the infidels, but as though mounted on ants (i.e., at a snail's pace), until they halted on the battlefield.

On this side was our bloodthirsty army of Islam. But they had got their spoil in the earlier skirmish. They were tired and weak. For twenty days they had suffered from nonstop rain. Men and horses were sapped of their strength, hungry and starving. Most of the soldiery were out foraging in the fields or pillaging a day's journey distant. What good were they against the infidel army on the opposite side, wearing their black hats and covering the ground like a black cloud?

At this juncture the grand vizier took offence at the Tatar prince and did not invite the Tatar army to join the battle.

Now all our viziers and *beylerbeys* and the chiefs of the janissary corps drove the army of Islam against the infidels. The Muslim *gazis* cried, 'In the name of God, we intend the *gaza*!' Beginning with Ismail Pasha, the *gazis* from Sirem, Semendire, Kanizsa, Buda, Egri, and Esztergom joined us, and all prostrated before the Prophet's standard, then advanced saying, 'Don't forget us in your prayers. Continue to recite *Victory/al-Fath* (Sura 48).' And we recited verses from the Koran with musical intonation.

Once all of our seventeen *beylerbeys*, seventy *sancak-beys* and twelve viziers stood in their columns, first the infidels began to march out, then the army of Islam. Ismail Pasha with the army of Buda and the other frontier troops formed the vanguard and moved out. In the right column was the Aleppan vizier Gürci Mehmed Pasha and Salih Pasha; in the middle column, the army of the grand vizier, the army of Bosnia, and the regiment commander Ismail in the van. In the centre were 12,000 of the grand vizier's picked soldiers, Segbans and Sarıcas of Croatian, Albanian, and Bosnian youths, and other champions. There were 20,000 other musketeers and janissaries. But the grand vizier did not cross the Raab, staying across the river with the rear troops.

The janissary infantry emerged from the trenches they had dug that morning at the river's edge. As they advanced towards the infidels, the cavalry squadrons, in accordance with *kanun*, kept pace with them like two wings, wave on wave, and came to a halt. The four lesser divisions also stood in their ranks.

But there were several instances of poor planning. One was that they failed to bring forty or fifty light cannons that the army of Islam had across the bridge. Another was that they had the janissaries leave their trenches and sent the infantry to battle the infidels in the open plain.

At once, Ismail Pasha, the regiment commander Ismail, the Sultan's sword-bearer Zülfikar Agha, and the keeper of the Sultan's mastiffs, Abdi Agha, stuck their egret plumes in their turbans and put on their helmets. Smothered in blue armour, they urged on the cavalry to battle.

The agha of the janissaries Salih Pasha and the regiment commanders (—) Agha, (—) Agha, (—) Agha – in short, all the janissaries of the Sublime Porte – had emerged from their trenches at the river's edge by the vizier's command and moved a bow-shot's distance forward. In the twinkling of an eye, they had dug some new compact trenches and entered them. Now they were ready for battle, as was the entire army.

First the infidels charged the army of Islam, beating on large and small kettledrums, blowing trumpets, ringing bells, and crying *Yajuj Yajuj!* The Muslim *gazis*, with all their heart and soul, cried back *Allah Allah!* and rushed upon the infidels as hungry wolves upon sheep and sheep upon salt. First on

The battle on the Raab River (Battle of Saint Gotthard, 1664) 227

the field of bravery, on leaping horses, were the regiment commander of the Bosnians, Ismail, and the Sirem and Semendire *beys*. Besides them, other *beys* and *beylerbeys* and *gazis* entered the field of battle. They were so heroic in combat that they decimated the infidels like pigs in the first encounter.

The first of the base infidels to be broken was the German column, who fled to the mountains and vineyards. There were even infidels who took off to the fortress of Nemet Uyvar, which was in sight. The Muslim *gazis* saw straight away that the infidels were fleeing in this fashion and informed one another, proclaiming that the infidels had been routed. But as they pursued the routed troops, the French infidels, all wearing red, emerged onto the battlefield from the forest on the left side. From the right side came the soldiers of the Girl King. The Czech musketeers – fresh infidels armed to the teeth – also entered the battlefield in droves, bound to one another by chains, and attacked our army of Islam from behind.

Now the two armies engaged and there was intense fighting for six entire hours. On every side fresh and unscathed reinforcements for the infidels kept arriving. Drunken and berserk, they paid no heed to musket and cannon. In their zeal for their false religion they rained cannon and musket fire from seven columns, and nearly half of the grand vizier's Segban and Sarıca troops were martyred at the first encounter. The other Muslim *gazis*, caught in Nimrod's flames from the barrage of musket and cannon fire, gave way slightly. But the tricky infidels never stopped their onslaught. They continued to come, crying out, *Piyan piyan!*

Now the Muslim soldiers who had pursued and driven away the routed German infidels returned to the battlefield safe and sound. Realising that the base infidels had taken the field of battle and gained the upper hand, they immediately put their captives and the priests to the sword. The *gazis*, with all their heart and soul, shouted *Allah Allah!* and entered the fray, striking the infidels with swords. 10,000 of these able-bodied youths did not come out alive but quenched their thirst with the sherbet of martyrdom – for they were like a drop in the sea of infidel soldiers. Intoxicated with *elest*,[55] they remained in that valley.

As for this humble one, assisted by God's wisdom, I took not a single step from the shelter of the Prophet's noble standard but continued reciting the Koran with my fellow reciters. At a certain point, an infidel was coming toward me chasing one of my slaveboys. The blood of this

---

55 The primordial pact between God and mankind, based on Koran 7:172.

humble one, full of fault, stirred with zeal. I spurred my horse and went over to the battlefield, thinking that I should be a friend and protector to my slaveboy. It seems the infidel had another musket which he aimed in my direction. I ducked and the bullet struck my horse in the neck. The horse reeled beneath me and reared up, and I saw blood gushing from the wound.

When my slaveboy saw that the infidel had shot his musket, he himself released a splendid arrow of Sa'd ibn Abi Waqqas. The infidel toppled from his horse, and the boy cut off his head and took it while the horse ran away toward the infidels.

Meanwhile, at a loss because my horse was wounded, I returned to the Prophet's standard and turned my mind to God. Still I was distraught and said to Musahib Hacızade, the chief of our Koran-recital troupe, 'Master, let me go back across the river. Look, my horse has been shot. One of my slaveboys can stay here in my place. Let me cross the river and get another horse. I'll be back soon, God willing.'

'That's right,' Hacızade replied. 'Go to the grand vizier with this wounded horse; he'll give you another one. And take with you the boy who cut off the head; get a reward for him as well. Also, we're very hungry; have them send us what food is available in food tins.'[56]

This humble one realised that the field belonged to the infidels. For the army of Islam was in disarray and slow in battle, while the infidels were quick and fighting courageously.

I took my horse by the leading-rein, walking at a slow gait, and came with my slaveboy to the bank of the Raab. As we were about to cross, the scouts of the imperial council and the army drovers on the opposite bank cried out, 'Shoot that pimp! Kill that pimp! Keep clear, pimp!'

I am an unmarried man, but I have often been cursed out with the term 'pimp.' I pointed to the blood flowing from the bullet-wound on my horse's neck and shouted, 'Men! my horse was wounded and has no strength left. I'm going to get another horse, then I'll cross back.'

'Well, who's that boy next to you?'

'He's my slaveboy. He has cut off a head. He's going to get a reward from the grand vizier.'

In short, a man needs a faithful friend and a loving companion in this

---

56 The *sefertası* was a tin-lined metal box for food used by travellers or soldiers on campaign. Several of them could be stacked together.

The battle on the Raab River (Battle of Saint Gotthard, 1664)

world. Quite a few of the men recognised me and said, 'Leave that man alone. We know him. Let him cross and exchange horses.'

'Evliya Efendi,' said Ali Çavuş, who was Eğirkapulu Oruç Çavuş's protégé, 'come, cross over here. It's deep but not hazardous. Just hold tight to the horse's mane.'

He pointed the way. I struck the horse and we plunged in together. I did go under once – it was deep next to the shore – but I held tight to the horse's mane.

'Boy, don't get separated from me!' I yelled and, swimming Tatar-style on my horse, with a thousand hardships we managed to cross the river to safety. I again took my horse by the rein and came before the grand vizier.

'Welcome, Evliya,' he cried. 'What news of the army?'

I answered thus (in rhymed prose):

> 'Here in your presence it is evident:
> A battle intense and without end.
> If some of the soldiers of Karaman
> Came to our aid, the army of Islam
> Would find renewed life.'

I continued: 'Hacızade, your slave, rubs his face in the dust at your feet and sends greetings. While we were reciting the *Victory* Sura (48) under the protection of the Prophet's standard, my horse was struck with a bullet.' And I showed him my horse.

'Quickly, give Evliya a doughty horse,' he said.

My slaveboy rolled the head before the vizier, and I continued, 'In partnership with this boy of mine we cut off this infidel's head before the Prophet's standard.'

He gave the boy fifty gold pieces and this humble one eighty gold pieces, plus a purebred Arabian horse. I kissed his hand, then went to Hacızade's tent and informed them that their master requested them to send over some breakfast in food tins. Then I went to my tent and dressed the horse's wound with egg, salt, and alum. I mounted another horse and rode to a high spur on the bank of the Raab. Gazing across the river, I saw – great God! – that the infidels were victorious and our army verging on defeat. There was still fervent fighting going on. But our army at times could not endure the infidels' attacks and often gave way or again drove the infidels.

[...]

(With the battle's conclusion) I had no doubt at all that this day of rout at the Raab was like Judgement Day. And my complete faith in the Lord of the Worlds increased further. All the viziers had conferred together and thought they had made good plans. But *Man proposes and God disposes.* The strange thing was that due to one ill-planned order the janissaries left the trenches and this became the reason for the infidels' taking the field, although at first the field belonged to the army of Islam. This verse in the Sura of al-Sharh is definitive proof: *With every hardship there is ease. With every hardship there is ease* (94:5-6). I witnessed this noble verse first-hand in this battle, since victory and defeat are in God's hands; but in one moment the Lord Creator showed forth myriads of His creations.

3. Comparison of Austrians and Hungarians

The Hungarians are Protestants while the Austrians are Catholics. Therefore these two infidel groups are opposites to one another, despite their both being Christians. And, as the saying goes, *Opposites do not join.* Even though the Austrians are in control, from fear of the Hungarians they never venture into the region of Esztergom and Stolnibelgrad, whether armed or unarmed, except in large force. They communicate at the point of a spear, and never cross one another. To be sure, *Unbelievers are a single community.* Nevertheless, the Austrian state is solid, while the Hungarian state is quite puny ever since the time of Sultan Süleyman when the Corona (the crown of St Stephen) and Esztergom and 300 other walled towns were lost to the Ottomans. After that happened, the Austrians prevailed over the Hungarians and made them into their subjects.

Still, compared to the Hungarians the Austrians are like the Jews: they have no stomach for a fight and are not swordsmen and horsemen. Their infantry musketeers, to be sure, are real fire-shooters; but they have only a single rapier at their waist, and when they shoot they brace their muskets on a forked gun-rest – they can't shoot from the shoulder as Ottoman soldiers do. Also, they shut their eyes and shoot at random. They wear large hats and long pointed shoes with high heels, and they never remove their gloves, summer or winter.

The Hungarians, on the other hand, though they have lost their power, still have fine tables, are hospitable to guests, and are capable cultivators of their fertile land. And they are true warriors. Like the Tatars, they ride wherever they go with a span of horses, with five or ten muskets, and with real swords at their waists. Indeed, they look just like our frontier soldiers, wearing the same dress as they, and riding the same thoroughbred horses. They are clean in their ways and in their eating, and honour their guests. They do not torture their prisoners as the Austrians do. They practice swordplay like the Ottomans. In short, though both of them are unbelievers without faith, the Hungarians are more honourable and cleaner infidels. They do not wash their faces every morning with their urine as the Austrians do, but wash their faces every morning with water as the Ottomans do.

4. A pleasure resort near Vienna; the free conduct of women

The river (—) flows through the centre of (Peşpehil/Schwechat). It is rather small, but a Water of Life nonetheless. It flows from Little Germany and sustains many villages, towns, and cities. It joins the Danube River at this city's lower end after irrigating its gardens and orchards. These lie on both sides of the city, from end to end – rose gardens and paradisical parks like the Aspuzu garden (in Malatya). There are also lofty palaces and pavilions adorned with pools, water jets and water wheels. And there are belvederes and villas in the Frankish style, each artistically fashioned by a master craftsman. In every one of the Khawarnaq-like palaces, built with much expenditure, there are magical works of paintings, finely variegated, by painters like Mani and Arzhang, whose skill in the art of the brush is amazing. All the infidel notables and sophisticates of the walled town of Vienna take their pleasure for weeks and months in this city and in its gardens and orchards. And their darling boys and lovely girls swim in the river that flows through the city. Warmed with wine and arak, they embrace one another and enjoy themselves in every nook and cranny.

Because the climate is delightful, the lovely boys and girls of this city are renowned. Indeed, the men and women do not flee from one another. The women sit together with us Ottomans, drinking and chatting, and their husbands do not say a word but rather step outside. And this is not considered shameful. The reason is that throughout Christendom women are in charge, and they have behaved in this disreputable fashion ever since the time of the Virgin Mary.

5. Vienna

On bazaars and bedestans

There are altogether 5,500 shops, neatly organised and uniformly built. So prosperous and well stocked are they that each shop is worth an Egyptian treasure.

Street by street, each trade occupies a different main street. The watchmakers, goldsmiths, book-printers, barbers and tailors have shops that are decked out like Chinese picture galleries. And the shops are unequaled in the operation of wonderful objects and strange instruments. Alarm clocks, clocks marking prayer times, or the month and day, or the signs of the zodiac, clocks on a monthly or daily calendar, chiming wall clocks – all are functioning. And they make clocks in the form of various creatures, with moving eyes, hands, and feet, so the viewer thinks those animals are alive; whereas the master clock-makers made them move with wheel mechanisms.

Whatever mills there are in the city, not a single one is turned by a horse or an ox or a man. The mills – and the kebab skewers, the buckets of water drawn from the wells, even the carriages travelling in the countryside – are all set in motion with devious and devilish clockwork mechanisms, not with a horse or an ox. They are marvellous contrivances.

Furthermore, a carriage travelling in the open country can carry a load of a hundred quintals. The wheel mechanisms move what ten water buffaloes cannot. But this is so only on flat ground; going uphill is not so easy, and going downhill the carriage has to drag a heavy ballast load in the rear in order to reduce the speed. Perched on top is an infidel with an iron-tipped forked stick which he uses to steer the carriage right and left. To increase the speed, he winds up the carriage wheels like a clock.

[…]

Noteworthy features of the walled town of Vienna

First, in the above mentioned Elephant Square, there is a bronze elephant beneath a lofty arch that is as tall as a minaret. It stands on its four legs, and its eyes, ears, and trunk are always moving. When it is noontime, the elephant roars once, flaps its ears, rolls its eyes and lifts its trunk in the air. It raises its trunk as high as the roofs of the houses across the street, then strikes it once against its chest, giving out a booming sound like that from a large earthenware jar. Its chest is actually the bell of a clock. When the elephant strikes its chest twelve times with its trunk, they know that it is noon. It is an elephant clock, dreadful and marvellous. This place is called Elephant Street.

Another spectacle. In yet another corner and beneath an arch, there is a white elephant. It is a lovely and skilfully made elephant figure that strikes the night-time hours. Its inside is of bronze, but its outside is of elephant hide. Its behaviour is like that of the black elephant; but it is white magic, a masterpiece of art, that astonishes the viewer.

Another noteworthy object. At a crossroads, in a rather broad square, there is a gilded copper peacock, set in a copper tray the size of a large dining-tray, perched atop a red porphyry column. When it is midday, the peacock shrieks once, flaps its wings, and goes around the edge of the copper tray. It does this twelve times, sounding the hour with a deafening noise of shrieking and wing flapping.

Another work of art. In another corner is a gilded bronze goat. This is a most marvellous statue, as though it were an actual billy goat.

Another noteworthy object that has to be seen. In the place called Execution Square, beneath arches on both sides of the road, there are two rams, made of bronze but covered with sheepskin. When it is noontime, these rams are set in motion. They paw the ground once, then butt their heads against one another, right in the middle of the road. They butt one another's heads so hard that the ground shakes from the blow. At noontime they butt their heads twelve times and the clock bells in their heads toll the hour.

When a man has been condemned to execution, they bring him before these rams, tie together his thumbs and big toes, and hang the criminal by hand and foot like a bag from the arch that is midway where the two rams butt one another. If the criminal has despaired of his life, he dies and his soul goes to hell. But if in fear of the butting of the rams' heads he confesses his guilt, either he is released, or else the two rams butt the fellow twelve times in the square of execution. Such a butting would crush a Mengerusi elephant, let alone a delicate fellow like him.

When Süleyman Khan set out to besiege Vienna, they put the aforementioned clocks and these noteworthy statues on ships and took them to Prague, then later brought them back. In the year '90 (i.e., 1090/ 1679) they will take them there once more, so it is said (referring to the prophecy of another Ottoman siege in that year). The streets are individually named after these noteworthy statues and are known by them.

The strangest spectacle. This humble one, full of fault, while sightseeing the city of Vienna, arrived at the market of the physicians. There are 100 shops. In front of a number of the shops, on chairs, sit Muslim captives wearing white turbans, Bosnian kalpaks, Tekke and Hamid caps, and Tatar kalpaks, even with the appearance and dress of Tatars. All have their hands and feet chained, and some of the captives from the community of Muhammad are dark Arabs, some youths, and others white-bearded old men. With sad expression and bent necks, they sit on their chairs busily pounding medicaments in huge bronze mortars – mace, cubeb, cinnamon, black pepper, cardamom, ginger, orris root, etc. Standing behind them are men with swords, as if to say, 'Pound quickly!' But the older men pound slowly and feebly, looking right and left, their strength all spent.

Feeling pity for these older captives, I took out my purse and was about to give them a few *akçe*. But Boşnak Ali Zaim of Esztergom proved one of *those who prevent good works* (cf. 50:25).

'Leave them alone for now,' he said. 'Give them alms when we come back through this quarter towards evening. Now the owners of these captives are standing next to them and will take from their hands whatever you give.'

This seemed reasonable and I put the purse back in my pocket. After touring the markets and quarters and the ancient monuments that we had not yet seen, we returned towards evening to those captives. While we observed, the shops began to close. Several infidels came and unfastened the belts from the waists of the Muslim captives, then removed the turbans and kalpaks and caps from their heads and took off all of their clothes. They inserted a watch key into each one's armpit and turned it. Immediately the hands and heads and eyes and eyebrows of all the Muslim captives stopped moving.

When they removed their headgear and clothing I noticed that they were bronze effigies of men, wound up like a clock and moving by means of clockwork mechanisms. I was lost in astonishment.

'Evliya Çelebi,' joked my companion Ali Agha, 'give these captives a few *akçe*, for God's sake!' It was truly a strange and wonderful spectacle.

[...]

Dispraise of the cathedral of priests and monks

There are altogether 366 churches of patriarchs and metropolitans, lairs of the stubborn and dirty priests. But sixty-six of them are great monasteries, each house of mis-worship the un-good work of a non-upright king, and 300 are small chapels inside and outside the city.

Of all, the monastery named (St) Stephan in the very centre of the city is such a grand and ancient structure that nothing like it has been or will be built in Turkey, Arabia and Persia, or in the seven climes of Christendom. Travellers coming by land and sea say that it has no equal in the inhabited quarter of the world, and it is true.

While this humble one was sojourning in the Polish country I saw the (—) Monastery in the port of Gdansk at the ocean's edge, and in Middle Hungary the (—) Monastery in the city of Kaschau – great cathedrals, finely constructed and richly adorned. But the Stephan Monastery in this city of Vienna is an ancient building and very prosperous. The amount of money in the treasuries found here, and the number of jewels and precious stones, God only knows.

Of all the churches that I have seen until now, this Stephan Cathedral is the biggest. The lofty domes,[57] partially of masonry, are set on sixteen huge piers. And some parts have painted ceilings, finely variegated, supported by long cypress beams over vaults of Khawarnaq. The paintings and gildings are strange and wondrous works of magic in the Frankish style. The ridged roof over these ceilings is covered with fine indigo-coloured lead. And some parts of it are covered with varicoloured glazed tiles.

If a man looks at this convent from a far distance, his eyes will dazzle from the sparkle of the window panes of cut glass and crystal and from the gleam of the gold crosses, tall as a man, in 300 places. This great cathedral glitters like the gold mine of Mt Akra in Kurdistan and dazzles the eyes like a mountain of light. It is such a brilliant temple of Messiah-worship (Christianity).

The sixteen huge piers inside this cathedral are made of porphyry and 'honeycombed' and 'jaundiced' marble, each one worth ten Egyptian

---

57 As Kreutel points out (1957, 237), the Stephansdom in Vienna has arches and vaults, not domes. Evliya applies to the gothic building the language he customarily uses for Greek-style churches. Köhbach (1979) has shown that Evliya's description of this and other European cathedrals follows a set of architectural clichés ('Beschreibungs-Topoi').

treasures. The tall columns were brought from the city of Sheba in the country of Yemen, which now lies in ruins and is the birthplace of Mother Balqis, the wife of Solomon. There is nothing like them in all the lands of the earth, syenite columns, God's handiwork which has to be seen.

The length of this convent, from the back gate to the prayer-niche of Jesus, is exactly 300 feet, and its width 180. Between the galleries and arches are slender columns of nephrite, onyx, obsidian and jasper.

The walls and the small and large domes are covered inside and outside with mosaics of varicoloured precious stones and carved alabaster. The scoops in the moldings of the domes, walls and arches are adorned with glass beads and precious stones of various colours, white, black, green, red, etc. The jewels give lustre and beauty to this church. And the wall on the south side is decorated with valuable gems such as ruby, olivine, Nishapur turquoise, Yemenite carnelian, garnet, cat's eye, fish's eye, yellow sapphire, blue sapphire, amber, mother-of-pearl, and Ethiopian pearl.

The walls of the cupboards have niches plastered with raw ambergris and housing copies of the Gospel, the Torah, the Psalms, and the Koran. Important books by various authors in every language of the world are found here. There are hundreds of thousands of bound books, with special priests appointed for their care. It is a great library that has to be seen. There is no such collection of books anywhere in the world, except in Cairo at the mosques of Sultan Barquq and Sultan Faraj, and in Istanbul at the mosque of Mehmed the Conqueror, the Süleymaniye, the mosque of Bayezid the Saint, and the New Mosque (mosque of Valide Sultan). God only knows the number of books in those mosques. But the number is greater in this Stephan monastery in Vienna, since there are numerous illustrated books in the infidel script of every language, including anatomical texts and cosmographies with the titles *Atlas, Minor, Geography*, and *Mappa Mundi*. Our libraries, on the other hand, have none of these illustrated books, since 'Pictures are unlawful.' That is why there are so many books in the Stephan Monastery. When this humble one had a tour of it, with the permission of the head priest, I was lost in astonishment, and the fragrance of musk and pure ambergris suffused my brain.

Now, my dear, the import of this long disquisition is the following: These infidels, in their own infidel manner, consider these books the word of God. They have seventy or eighty servants who sweep the library and dust off the books once a week. In our Alexandria, on the other hand, there is a great mosque known as the Perfumers' mosque supported by many pious foundations including hundreds of shops, *hans*, baths and storerooms; but the mosque itself lies in ruin, and its library that houses thousands of important volumes – including priceless Korans calligraphed by Yaqut Musta'sımi, Abdullah Kırımi, Şemsullah Gamravi and Sheikh Cuşi – is rotting because of the rain. Worshippers who come to this mosque once a week for Friday prayers can hear the moths and worms and mice gnawing at the Korans. No one from the community of Muhammad stands up and says, 'These Korans are being destroyed, let's do something about it.' That won't happen, because they do not love the word of God as much as the infidels do. I only wish that God make that mosque as prosperous as this church, and that its servants and governors regard that abandoned mosque with the eye of compassion.

Thousands of servants bustle about this cathedral of Vienna on a daily basis. And there are priests and bishops, popes and cardinals and monks from the eighteen kingdoms of Christendom. Each of the Christian sects has its own corner where the infidels practice austerities day and night. And ever since the infidels lost Stolnibelgrad (in 1543) they have buried their kings and cardinals and archbishops in front of the prayer-niche and in the crypt of this cathedral. Both sides are lined with tombs, while the centre, up to the prayer-niche, is a treasury erected on 200 columns.

The amount of gold stored here the Creator of the Two Worlds only knows. The Groschen (i.e., silver) treasury is beneath the outer courtyard. Furthermore, when the chaste-starred daughter of a former king died – her name was İzarila Son (Isabella Asszony [Hungarian for 'Lady']) – thousands of millions of money (or goods, *mal*) and hundreds of millions of gold were endowed to this convent, and the endowment is still in force. Millions of money (or goods) such as these are buried here. For that reason, when the Swedish king drinks a full bowl of wine he takes the following oath: 'May this crown and throne of Alexander, my grandfather's throne, be unlawful for me if I do not gain possession of the money in the Stephan Monastery in the walled town of Vienna in Germany, and may this Swedish state be unlawful for me and my children.' Such is the limitless amount of treasure to be found in this great church.

There are thousands of idols (i.e., statues) each worth an Egyptian treasure; myriads of highly wrought chandeliers, each the product of a master craftsman and a royal workshop; and so many thousands of gold and silver and jewelled oil lamps, candlesticks, lamp-stands, censers and chafing dishes, the viewer is stunned.

But the floor of this monastery is not covered with rugs; rather it is paved with the varicoloured mosaic stones and pieces of marble and alabaster, each resembling a bird's eye, as recorded above. All around are 300 chairs, skilfully made from whatever materials God created on the face of this earth, each one donated by an erring king or a miserable nobleman. The infidels sit on them and worship Jesus according to their false doctrines. No chair, indeed, resembles any other; and the *stolni* – i.e., chairs – are made of bird bones and human bones, fish teeth and elephant teeth, and every kind of wood.

Just inside the south gate, at the back of this church, there is an organ gallery resting on eight slender syenite columns. The master stonemasons of our day cannot wield pick and saw to produce such a highly wrought pavilion. Only Sultan Süleyman's gallery in the Kızılelma ('Golden Apple') mosque in Esztergom bears a resemblance; but this gallery of Vienna is taller. And there is nothing like the organ of David found here in the churches of any infidel country. It comprises 300 musical instruments, including drums and kettledrums and horns and pipes. The effect cannot be described by words, either spoken or written; one must hear it to understand it. It is an organ that has to be seen; as the verse has it, *How can hearing measure up to seeing?*

Indeed, all its musical instruments (i.e., the organ pipes) are arranged in rows over this gallery. To the right and left of these instruments are bellows made of water buffalo hide, with pine planks below and above. The priests pull up the top planks by pulleys and one bellow goes down while another goes up, so that the wind does not get cut off from the instruments and they continuously resound. Twenty priests are assigned to operate each of the bellows.

Ladders have been erected alongside these bellows. When the infidels wish to play this organ on one of their ill-fortuned days, there are seventy master magicians expert in the science of this organ – each one a paragon in the science of musical instruments according to *Kitab al-Adwar* (a famous thirteenth-century treatise on music), each one a master at the level of Pythagoras, Abdullah Faryabi, Ghulam Shadi, or Husayn Bayqara – who come and turn its wheels and tighten its screws, adjust its pipes and reeds, and begin to pull on the bellows. Meanwhile some German castrati climb up the ladders that are alongside the bellows and stand ready. When the top plank rises to its limit and starts to go down, the castrati get off the ladders and on to the planks and go down with them. As this is going on, a kind of cold wind blasts from the bellows that actually causes the pipes to vibrate and a different sound emerges from each one, astounding the listeners. When one of the bellows goes down, the castrati climb up ten (rungs of the) ladders and again get on the bellows. The other bellows are going up and down in the same fashion with the boys mounted on them.

The function of these boys is not merely to provide a weight to the bellows. The reason they have been castrated is to prevent their voices from cracking, so they can sing along with the sound of the organ and sadly intone verses from the Psalter in the *rehavi* musical mode.

It may be asked: 'While the Jews recite the Torah and the Psalms because they are Mosaic and Davidic, these Germans are Christians, so why do they recite verses from the Psalter?' The answer is provided by the Koranic verse, *And We gave the Psalms to David* (4:163), which proves that the prophet David recited verses from the Psalter. During his auspicious time, the German people had faith in David and acted according to the Davidic rite. Later they rejected the rite of David and adopted the rite of Jesus and so became Christians.

Now according to the Germans' false doctrine, while David recited psalms in a mournful voice, he also played the organ. God gave David a sweet voice, and whenever he recited the Psalter, the cherubim would listen to his voice and cry out, 'Glory be to the Creator!' The organ is David's miracle, through which thousands of unbelievers converted to the faith when he recited the Psalter.

{At the present time, among all religious communities, the prophet David is famous for the loud voice in which he recited the Psalms. Indeed, the most eloquent of the Koranic commentators have interpreted the verse, *He multiplies His creatures according to His will* (35:1), as referring to a mournful voice, on the grounds that a sweet voice is the sound of the world of spirits.}

So when the German priests and monks play the organ in the *rehavi* musical mode – and the castrati mounted on the two bellows in groups of ten recite the Psalter with their sweet voices and manifold tremulations in the *rehavi* mode – one's lungs fill with blood and one's eyes with tears.

Although the Germans recite the Psalter, they do so not in the (—) language as revealed by God to David, but translated into their infidel German language which I will record below.

Truly, this organ has an awesome, liver-piercing sound, like the voice of the Antichrist, that makes a man's hair stand on end. In short, an unlettered man who listened to this organ would say it is the miracle of the prophet David and of Jesus the Spirit of God.[58] But really it is neither a saint's miraculous grace nor the miracle of a prophet. It is only white magic, a concatenation of musical instruments that scatters the wits of the listener.

Furthermore, inside this church, the head priest has a pulpit which he mounts to harangue the congregation on their ill-omened un-holidays. The tongue falls short in describing this pulpit. And there is another enclosure, a jewelled gallery reserved for kings, the work of a German master who truly demonstrated his skill. The master architects of old expended their best efforts and the master builders executed their finest work on this gallery and on this highly wrought church. No ancient architect on the face of the earth produced such a masterpiece. Only the Eternal Master could inspire such a marvellous work.

Account of the spectacle of images in the church of Vienna
There are so many statues and icons in this church, images of the sons of Adam, and so many idols – I had not seen so many since the conquest of Uyvar when I toured the great cathedrals of Poland, Czechia, Sweden, Hungary, Dunkerque, and the port of Danzig. I was on good terms with several priests and, partly as polemic, partly in jest, I said, 'How many gods you have – God forbid! – that whenever you pass by one of them, you remove your hats and bow down and worship.'

'God forbid,' they replied, 'that we should consider them gods. The sole Creator of you and of us is God, the Holy Spirit. God forbid that we should bow down and worship these images, or that we should pray to them for sons and daughters, blessings and worldly fortune and long life. They are only images of our prophet Jesus and his disciples, of our saints who came afterward and our monarchs who were world conquerors and pious endowers of good works. Whenever we behold these images, we respectfully offer our benedictions. Most of all, we show reverence to the prophet Jesus, because he is the Spirit of God. In our religion, it is permitted to make images. When our priests harangue the people, just as your sheikhs do, they have difficulty conveying their message with fine words alone. So we convey the message through images of the prophets and saints and paradise, depictions of divine glory. And we show hell with

---

58 *Ruhullah* – an Islamic designation of Jesus, based on Koran 4:171 *a spirit from Him*.

demons, flaming fire and boiling water, depictions of divine wrath. When our priests give sermons, they point to these images saying, 'Fear God!' But we do not worship them in any way.'

But when one sees the depiction of paradise in this Stephan Church of Vienna, which is the ill-fortuned seat of the German king, one wishes to die and go to heaven, recalling the Koranic verse (89:30), *Join My servants and enter My Paradise*. They have depicted the Gardens – of Eden, of Paradise, of the Heights, of the Lote Tree, of the Refuge (cf. 9:72; 11:108; 7:46; 53:14–15) – in an open space, layer on layer, pavilions of Iram, with great rivers and the pools of Kawthar, orchards and gardens with houris and youths, brocades and satins, Buraqs and angels, the Throne and Tablet and Pen. Truly, when it comes to painting, the Franks prevail over the Indians and Persians.

Opposite this heaven, in a dark corner, on the surface of a wall 50 paces in length, they depicted hell. When this humble one saw it, I recited from the Fatiha, *Guide us to the straight path* (1:6). When I saw the balance and scales, I recited from the Sura of al-Rahman, *That you might not transgress the balance* (55:9). When I saw the lowest valley of hell, I recited the verse, *The hypocrites shall be cast into the lowest depths of the Fire* (4:145). And when I saw the Ghayya pit of hell (cf. 19:59), I recited the verse, *Woe to every back-biting slanderer* (104:1). The valley of woe, the hill of scorching heat (*saqar* – 54:48; 74:26), the valley of perdition, the valley of the dungeon (*sijjin* – 83:7–8), the ridge of the flaming fire (*sa'ir*), and the other levels of hell: all these did the master painters of the Frankish style illustrate with Mani-like precision. Those who see once the depictions of these tortures – men roasting in the fires of naphtha and tar; groaning at the hands of demons and the whips of tormentors; bitten by scorpions, snakes and centipedes, vipers as long as camels' necks – will repent their ways of Nimrod and Pharaoh, Korah and Shaddad. They will cleanse themselves of backbiting and slander, adultery and fornication and pederasty, usury and wine drinking. They will leave off eating and drinking and spend the remainder of their precious life in a hermit's cell, having washed their hands of the filth of this world, and will say, 'It is God's to command: if it is not to be heaven, at least let my place be purgatory and not hell.'

But the master painters, to demonstrate their skill, have depicted purgatory in this church such that those who see one part will be gladdened and those who see another part will be saddened. On one side is illustrated the place where the resurrected are to assemble, a jostling and woeful crowd, moaning and lamenting. Seeing these figures, one's body trembles like an autumn leaf.

In short, my account of these depictions of heaven and hell and the place between is but a drop in the sea or an atom in the sun. It is impossible to describe them; you simply have to see them for yourself.

[…]

On hospitals and asylums
There are seven hospitals in this city. The busiest and best adorned is the hospital of the Stephan Church, where the sleeping garments and the quilts and sheets are made of silk and satin and cloth-of-gold. The king himself comes to this hospital if he is sick, because the physicians here are like Plato and Hippocrates, Socrates and Ptolemy, Feylekos (Philip) and Feylesof.

The infidels (in Vienna) wear black vests and Eflatuniye hats. But these physicians wear only plain white garments and a kind of cap of Russian leather and buckskin with seven gores. Their hands never come out of their gloves, since their hands always have to be soft. And the moment they take their patients' pulse, they know the illness and treat it accordingly.

It happened that, in the battle on the Raab, a bullet struck the head of one of the king's kinsmen, next to his ear, and remained lodged inside his head. **Account of the perfect surgery of the masters.** This wounded infidel would neither die nor accept treatment. Finally the king said, 'There are so many excellent surgeons and phlebotomists who receive fixed salaries in the hospitals of my forefathers. Surely they can find a cure for this kinsman of mine. If not, I will cut off their provisions!'

This humble one heard that the chief surgeon of the Stephan Church was about to undertake the treatment, so I went to him. As we exchanged pleasantries, they brought in the wounded infidel and laid him down on a four-legged silken bed, as though he were blind. His head was like an Adana pumpkin, his eyes like Mardin plums, his nose like a Morean eggplant – everything was swollen.

The chief surgeon drove all the infidels out of the room, which was warm and had glass windowpanes. Only one of his servants and this humble one remained. The surgeon gave the wounded man a cup of saffron water to drink, which rendered him unconscious. He then lit a fire in a brazier and put it in a corner. While the servant held the wounded man's body to his breast, the surgeon tied a strap of leather, like a knee-garter, around the edge of his cap. He took up a sharp razor and, sitting himself in front of the patient, made an incision in his brow from ear to ear and flayed the skin slightly from the side of his right ear, revealing the pure white skull bone. He did all this without causing a single drop of blood to flow.

Then the surgeon lightly pierced the fellow's skull at the temple and inserted an iron clamp. As he turned the clamp's screw, the skull began to lift from where the skin was incised along his cap. This caused the fellow to move slightly.

As the surgeon continued to turn the screw, the fellow's bald skull, by God's command, was opened at the joints that held it together like teeth, revealing the brain. The inside of the skull, between the ears, was filled with humours resembling watery blood and mucus. There, lodged in the brain's membranes and glistening red with blood, was the bullet in its paper shell. It was apparently shot from a five-dram flintlock musket.

'Come, look,' said the master surgeon. 'See this man's sorry condition, all for a piece of bread!'

Taking my handkerchief from my bosom and holding it to my nose and mouth, I came forward and stared into the wounded fellow's skull. By heaven, the poor man's brain was all shrivelled, like a chick that had just emerged from its shell with its head, eyes, nose and wings shrunk and contracted. But the brain was covered with a thick envelope of skin, i.e., a white membrane.

The surgeon asked why I was covering my nose and mouth with a handkerchief.

'I might sneeze or cough, or just through my breathing a draft might enter the man's brain. I covered my nose and mouth to prevent that.'

'Bravo,' he said. 'A hundred blessings of God. If you were to study this science, you would become a master surgeon. And from the way you paid close attention when looking at the man's skull, I know that you have seen many things in the world.'

He deftly removed the bullet from the fellow's brain with a pair of forceps. Using something like a yellow sponge, he wiped away the dried blood and yellow humours where the bullet had been lodged all this time. He washed off the sponge with wine and again wiped clean the inside of the skull and around the brain. Then he quickly put the skull back into place and tightly wrapped flat leather straps around the crown of the head and beneath the jaw.

Now he brought a box into the room and set it down. **Spectacle of the**

surgeons' wisdom. The skin of the fellow's head had been incised from ear to ear, and now the two edges were brought together. Inside the box were giant ants known as 'horsemen' ants. The surgeon took one of these with his iron forceps and placed it head down where the skin of the fellow's head had been cut. When the hungry ant bit the two edges of the skin, the surgeon cut the ant off at the waist with scissors, leaving the head still biting the two edges of skin together. He placed another ant next to it in the same manner. In all, he made the heads of eighty ants bite the skin of the fellow's head from ear to ear, then smeared it all over with salve and bandaged it up.

Now he propped the fellow up in a corner on a down mattress, with pillows on both sides. He probed the wound with gauze, smeared it too with salve, and bandaged it.

Next, he fumigated the room with some foul-smelling incense; dabbed the man's nostrils with wine that was forty or fifty years old; and smeared his hands, arms, chest, and neck – indeed, every part of his body – with clay of Chinese ambergris. Finally, he once again fumigated the room, this time with bitumen.

Food was then brought in, and when we had been eating for a full hour, the fellow opened his eyes and wanted food. The physician gave him some almond paste and chicken broth, and perhaps five drams of wine, nothing else.

This humble one returned there every day for an entire week in order to observe. On the eighth day the fellow had recovered sufficiently to move about inside the hospital. On the fifteenth day, he presented himself before the king.

[...]

Another praiseworthy art of the master surgeons. One day, while I was sitting in a surgeon's shop, an infidel entered. He gave the surgeon a Hungarian gold piece and said, 'My tooth aches. Take it out.'

Upon seating him in a chair, the surgeon took up his stylus and struck the man's tooth. The fellow screamed.

'That's the tooth that aches!' he said.

So the master surgeon brought in a lit brazier and placed some yellow brass wires[59] in it. He also brought two bottles, one containing a blue liquid,

---

59 Evliya specifies the wires as *tanbura telleri*, lit. 'pandore strings'. The reference is

the other a red liquid. Taking up a pair of wooden tweezers, he opened the infidel's mouth, rubbed some of the blue liquid on the gum of the aching tooth, then laid hold of the tooth with the tweezers and pulled it out without difficulty and without any blood flowing. It was a magnificent tooth, a white, three-pronged molar.

He then took one of the red-hot wires from the brazier and applied it to the root of the tooth. It made a hissing sound from the marrow inside the tooth. He removed the tip of the wire from the rotten cavity and with it a tiny black-headed worm. He stuck another red-hot wire onto a second root of the tooth and a similar tiny worm emerged from the decayed part. Then, without touching the tooth with his hand, in the same fashion as he had extracted it he put it back into its socket. This time he rubbed on some of the red liquid and salt. He placed a small piece of wood over the infidel's pulled tooth and told him to bite on it. The infidel bit down and the pulled tooth was set in its socket.

'This tooth won't ache any more and it is stronger than before,' said the surgeon. All this time he never once touched the tooth with his hand.

As I observed this remarkable operation, a weight was lifted from my shoulders, because while playing javelin below Nemet Uyvar castle, Kıbleli Mustafa Pasha had struck my teeth with a javelin shot and three of them were dislodged. I showed them to the surgeon and he immediately rubbed some of the red liquid on the gums and had me bite down on a piece of wood, just as I described above. By morning my teeth had turned into Nakhchivan steel, strong enough to crack hazelnuts and walnuts. I was so delighted that I gave the surgeon a Kaya Sultan handkerchief. He was pleased and gave me half a dram of the red liquid in the little bottle.

'If you give me a hundred ducats,' he said, 'I will teach you how to brew liquids like aqua fortis. In whatever country you travel, you can extract a man's aching tooth with the blue liquid, then cauterise the marrow, reinsert the tooth and rub on the red liquid. So you won't be idle in this world but earn a living.'

'I'll give you fifty ducats.'

---

to the *tel tanburası* 'wire-strung pandore' which Meninski (3129) says is 'similar to our instrument' (*Cithara fere nostrae similis, sed plerumque trium sidium aenearum*); cf. Farmer 1936, 36. Evliya has quite a bit of information about this instrument (Vol. 1, fol. 207b).

'*No, no,*' he replied, 'I won't teach you for less than a hundred.'

I was too stingy to give that amount. But it is actually a wonderful skill, worth a thousand ducats to learn.

On another day, he took three Kreuzers (*kralıçka*) – i.e., three *akçe* – from an infidel and rubbed on the blue liquid. But he handed his tooth back to him, and the infidel left. Apparently the price of putting the tooth back in its place was one gold ducat.

[2 lines empty]

In short, no country boasts as many expert physicians and phlebotomists, of which there are hundreds, as this Vienna. If I were to record all of the displays of skill I observed here and note them one by one, my unprinted notebook would be like the *Canon* of Avicenna. Moreover, there is no strain or difficulty in their work; it is all done easily and relaxedly.

There are even barbers in many of the surgeons' shops. It is true that the German infidels wear their hear long and so have no need of haircuts. But they do shave a spot in the middle of their heads (referring to the monk's tonsure?) and they wash their hair with musk-scented soap. And numerous infidels reach the age of seventy or eighty and still shave their beards.

When they go to the barber, first they sit on a high chair and his servants wash their hair and beard. Then they sit on another chair that is set on a stylus and rotates like a top. The barber sits in his own chair and easily turns the customer's chair in whatever direction he wants as he shaves. The barber does not shave standing up as in Turkey. This is also something that has to be seen. The barbershops are pleasure resorts, adorned with fountains and other amenities.

And in no hospitals in any other country are there such endowments of buildings, food and drink and electuaries. First of all, any patient who recovers health at one of these hospitals brings the items he has vowed – plates and pots and trays and candlesticks of gold and silver and copper and tin. Every hospital has gold and silver vessels worth ten Egyptian treasures, and gold and silver skewers for roasting meat are leaning in every corner. Various dishes are cooked in gold and silver and copper pots and distributed to the patients according to their illness. Even delicacies such as bird's milk and date milk and sugar cane syrup from Hama are stored in their pantries. Then there are the master chefs – whenever a king gives a banquet to another king, or a vizier or an ambassador, these master cooks come from the hospitals and prepare all sorts of dishes.

Actually, none of the food throughout Christendom is worthy of note.

The infidels are abstemious at mealtime, eating fifty drams of food from the tip of an iron fork, and sipping fifty drams of wine. Dining is only found in the Ottoman Empire. Nor is there any cuisine to speak of in India and Persia – only their pilavs are worth mentioning.

Every hospital has a special kitchen where a head physician sits and prepares daily one quintal of sugary electuaries which they distribute to the sick and the poor. There are a myriad of canisters and jars for such pastes and beverages and sweets. Every hospital also has summer-rooms and winter-rooms with all sorts of basins and fountains. The winter-rooms have stoves as in a Turkish bath, the summer-rooms have fountains with jets. The windows of the rooms overlook gardens. Musicians come and perform concerts, playing various instruments, depending on each patient's temperament. Strange to say, by God's wisdom, there are not as many madmen in the German lands as there are in Turkey and Arabia. Still, there are many famous infidels in these asylums, and no one can find a cure for them.

[...]

Chapter: the ancient language of German

Some call it Nemçe, others Ungur, because it spans the provinces of Hungary (*Ungurus*), Germany (*Alaman*) and (—). It is an ancient Christian country that boasts its state goes back 2,600 years. Indeed, it is a powerful state that claims parity with the Ottomans and the kings of Muscovy. It is under the supervision of the Seven Kings. When one king dies, the others meet together with the emperor of this German Kaiser (!) and with his permission choose another king to take his place. First the king of Dunkerque, and the kings of Denmark, Holland, Czechia, Poland, (—) and (—) are all subject to the German Kaiser. In war time, each king comes to the Kaiser's aid with 100,000 troops.

Yet the king of Sweden – which is on the shore of the Baltic Sea opposite the New World – has been able to terrify and harass the German Kaiser despite his 700,000 troops; because the Swedish king possesses 1,200,000 troops of Tatar nomads, plus other infidels whose number God only knows. There has been continual warfare between Germany and Sweden for the past 127 years. Only recently, in fact, the Swedes took seven fortresses from the Germans, who report that each one was worth the seven climes.

'Indeed,' they say, 'we have concluded this peace with the Turks only because we have to deal with the Swedes. Otherwise, do you think we would make peace with the Turks after the Battle on the Raab (when we defeated them so soundly)?'

The Swedes pass as Christians and read the Gospel, but their language is different – I will record it in its place, God willing. They are, however, fire-worshippers (i.e., heretics) of the Protestant (*Luturyan*) sect, while the Germans are true Christians and followers of the Gospel of the Catholic (*Papişte*) sect – i.e., the sect of the pope. The German language, however, is not the Spanish language of the pope. It is a very heavy language, which also has many Persian expressions; because the Germans too came from Persia with the descendents of Manuchahr.

As I mentioned above, because David played the organ and recited the Psalter, the scriptures that were revealed to the prophet David have been translated into German, and they sing psalms with the organ accompaniment. Here is one such verse from the Psalter in German: *Fin sonderbares andaştiges gebet cuder alarheyligsten unt siligten yugunt firav Marya hilf avef den kapuçinar berkopa* {meaning, fortress} *soson*. It is a hymn to Jesus and to Mother Mary. Indeed, it is recited in a loud voice by the monks as they pass through the streets and go from church to church with their cross-adorned banners and flags and with their organs. But when they sing this hymn in marvellous fashion, in the *rehavi* musical mode, it stuns the listener.

Another verse from the Psalter, a prayer to Jesus, as translated into German: *Daler furtireflihste golorvirdiyaste alarheyligste ale çeyt unbeflekste yugunt firav Marya an matre unserris herres Yezu kırıstı in renigin der velt unt hersir in alarkıraaturen melke duniyemant verlest niyemant verehst avih niyemant ver cu dir mit raynin irt nirştend unt busfertigen Kot* {that is God} *Marya Firav* {Mother Mary}. When the monks and boys with their sweet and mournful voices sing these precious words of the Psalter to the accompaniment of the organ, one feels intoxicated with love. For one's heart expands when these verses are sung in the *sofiyane* meter according to the science of music.

As for the German language … First, when the Germans reckon in buying and selling they count as follows: *ans* 1 *isçpa* 2 *tiray* 3 *fir* 4 *finf* 5 *sekes* 6 *siben* 7 *ahet* 8 *nayin* 9 *çen* 10 *çiyançet* 20 *tiraysik* 30 *firçik* 40 *fufçik* 50 *siyihçik* 60.

burot bread *bosır* water *vayin* wine *lihit* candle *lihter* candlestick *meser* knife *feder* pen *fin tirdid* penbox and pen *tinte* ink *papir* paper *kot* God *marya* Mother Mary *kosıtin opol* sultan of Istanbul *çasar* king *inpirator* king of kings *lipolda inpirator engur* Hungarian king of the Germans *pampol* cotton *kam her* Come here *seçnide* Sit down *niksi* There isn't *uskut* It is good *na mayin hurbu* No my lord *may firav* my wife *yug firav* my daughter *furta* flee! *mayn foder* my father *mayn puluda* my brother *geher kılanı* Come little one *geher may herec* Come my dear *por pisli* Stay a while *kolt* common gold *dukat* gold piece *taler* royal piaster *qıraliçqa* two pennies *engörleş* penny.

6. Crimea

Perekop: The Khan writes a patent of safe-conduct for Evliya to travel in Crimea

The Nureddin Sultan (heir to the throne of the Crimean Khan), who defends this place, had hundreds of light cannons fired from the fortress, and there were great celebrations. Afterwards, a banquet was given for the army of Islam with kebabs made from 100 steers and twenty horses, and 100 casks of *boza* were drunk. Five *guruş* per captive were taken from the army of Islam as *savka* (tax on captives). According to the register, during this blessed year seven *gazas* were undertaken in a single campaign – something not recorded in any historical chronicle. And it was recorded that (—) thousand captives, 300,000 horses, and countless other booty were captured in these seven battles. God be praised, this most humble one got seventeen captives and forty horses.

Now the illustrious Khan remained behind to defend this fortress of Or (Perekop). He bestowed upon me five slaves, five ambling horses – one of them complete with harness and saddle, and one sable *çekman* (a Tatar caftan); and upon each of my servants one horse, ten gold pieces, and one suit of broadcloth. This humble one bowed before the Khan and said, 'My Padishah, I have come to the province of Crimea several times, and have participated in some felicitous campaigns, but I have not yet properly toured the province. I appeal to my Khan and offer my benediction.'

The illustrious Khan took up his jewel-scattering pen and said, 'O nobles and guardians of Crimea, statesmen and elders: to whichever trading port or city Evliya Efendi – my comrade and friend, my confidant and way-fellow, my ancient associate – goes with this royal decree, bestow favour and hospitality upon him for my sake; clothe him and gird him; give him an allowance of *kızılga* gold pieces; provide him with reliable escorts so that he may tour my province; show regard for himself and his companions and his horses, and give them provisions. And you Ahmed Agha, commander of the fortress of Gözlev (Eupatoria): when my brother Evliya

Çelebi arrives, house him in a palace; provide all of his food and drink; give him a daily allowance of one *kızılga* gold piece; when he departs, give him one sable caftan and 100 *kızılga* gold pieces; and in whatever direction he journeys, provide him with reliable escorts.'

Taking the papers, I bade farewell to the Khan.

[...]

The Karaites in Menkup

This mosque (of Sultan Bayezid the Saint) has one gate. There are no houses around it; it is an ancient place of prayer in a grassy plot. But a little below this mosque is a Muslim quarter with one neighbourhood mosque, 100 houses with tile roofs, a small bath, and two fountains. There are no other buildings.

Below this area are seven Jewish quarters from end to end. There are altogether 1,000 ill-omened Jewish houses, filthy and nasty, with tile roofs. There are eighty tanners' shops. All the Jews make buckskins and shoe leather – in the country of Crimea, the shoe leather of Menkup is famous. There are only two butchers' shops and one *boza* shop.

All the Jews are Karaite in rite, and the other Jews (*yahudiler*) do not like the Yids (*cuhudlar*) belonging to this rite. The Karaites do not distinguish kosher and unkosher foods. They eat whatever they are served, even if it is prepared with clarified butter, and any kind of meat, even with the tendon not removed. Indeed, they are the Kızılbaş of the Jews. On Judgement Day they will not mount the Kızılbaş but it will be the others, the Israelite Yids, who will mount the Kızılbaş. Or so people say, as in the verse:

> *The heretic on Judgement Day*
> *Will be an ass beneath the Jew.*

Although these Jews are Israelites and followers of Moses, and read the Torah and the Psalms, they do not know the Yid language (i.e., Ladino) at all. Instead, they all speak Tatar and they wear Tatar kalpaks of purple broadcloth, not hats. And due to Menkup's delightful climate, they have very many lovely boys – ruddy-faced Jewish lads with doe eyes and sweet speech. Indeed, men from all over Crimea who are fond of boys come here to engage in pederasty. One such dissolute boy-chaser intoned the following naughty verse:

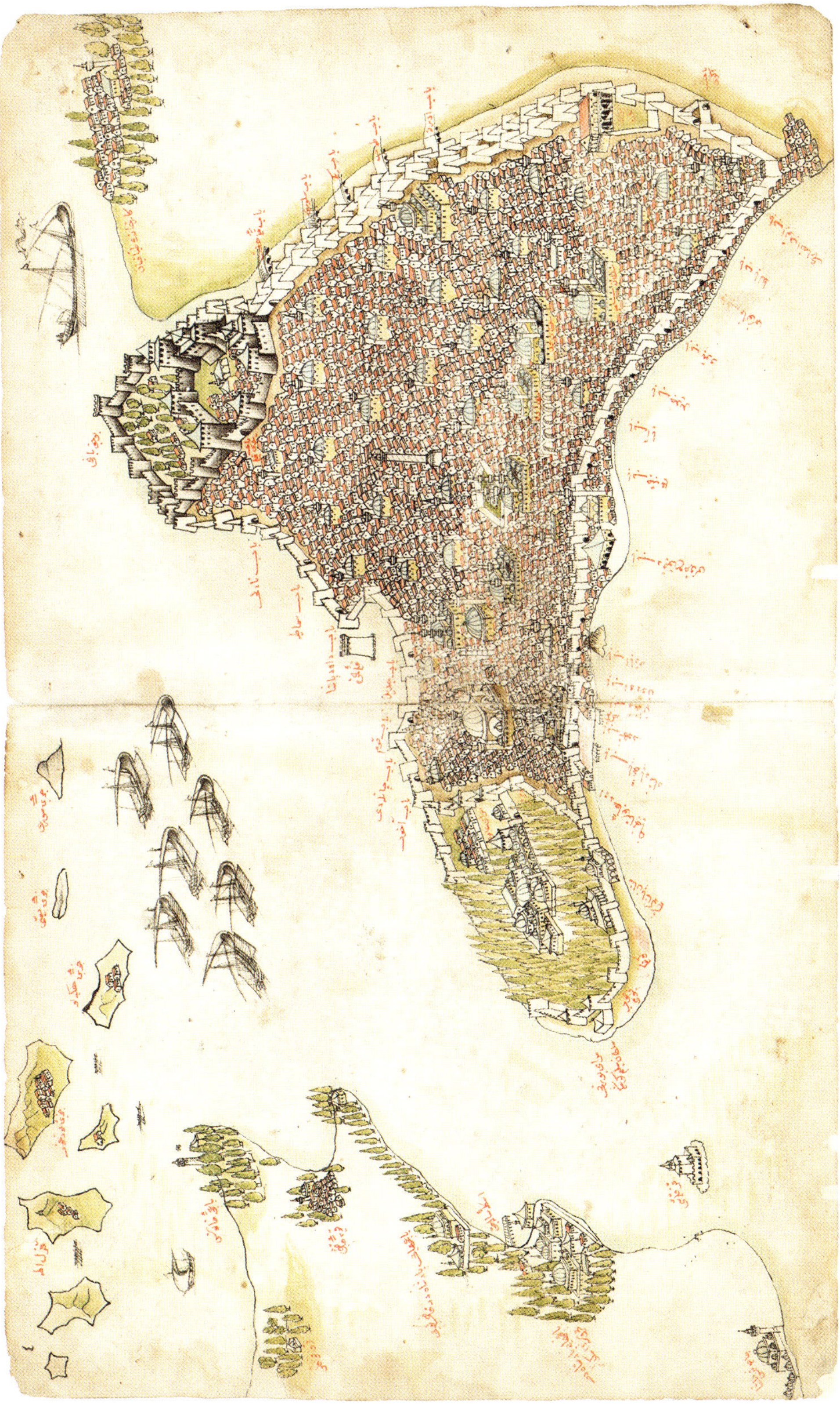

Preceding page: a topographic view of Istanbul from the *Kitab-ı Bahriye* by Piri Reis

This page:
Right, Sultan Mehmet IV (1648–87) was on the throne for most of the time Evliya Çelebi was travelling

Below, a Janissary guard and the Beylerbey of Rumeli, mounted

These illustrations were brought back from Istanbul by Claes Rålamb, who led a Swedish embassy to the Sublime Porte in 1657–8. Several costume books like this have survived from the period. Here we see *top*, an Imperial dog keeper and the Chief Falconer, and *below*, the Tartar Khan and a wandering dervish

Ottoman cartographers: *right*, the Bay of Athens, by Piri Reis, the 16th-century admiral, geographer and cartographer

below, Matrakçı Nasuh was a sixteenth-century Bosnian polymath recruited into the Ottoman navy and famous for his panoramic miniatures which mapped the cities of the Ottoman empire and beyond in beautiful, schematic detail. Here we see the city of Tabriz, visited by Evliya Çelebi in Volume Two

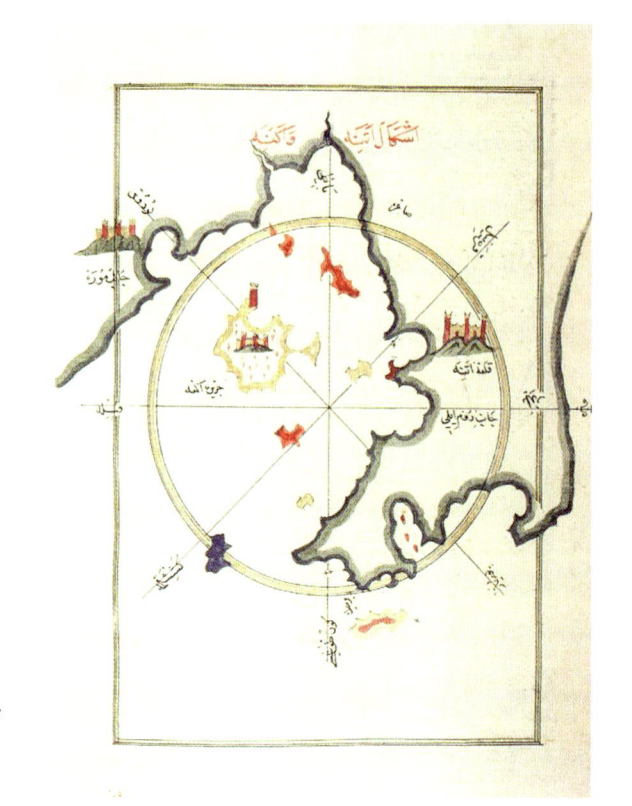

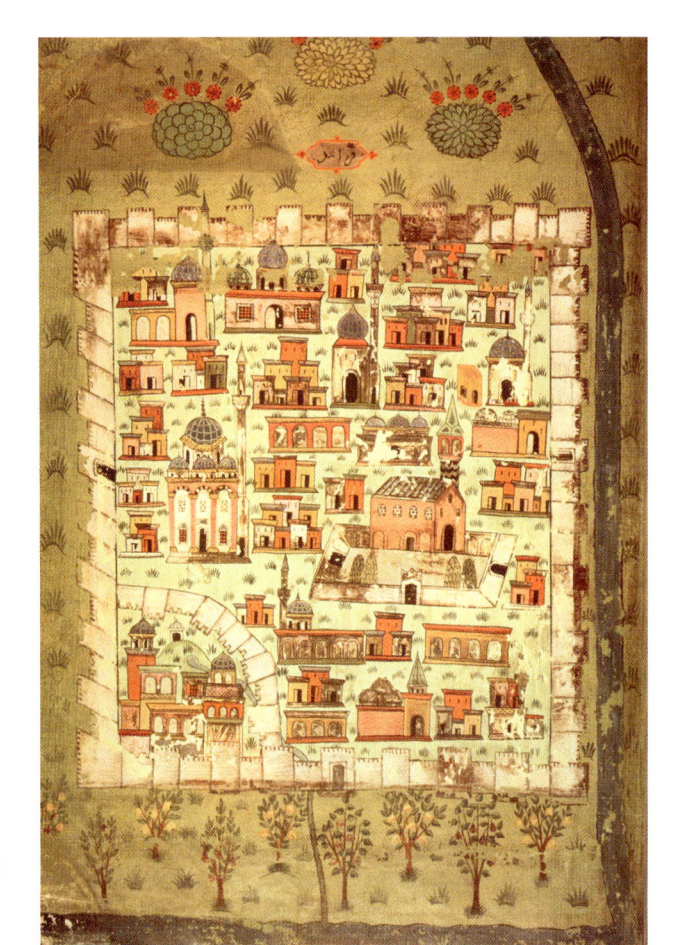

Right, Matrakçı Nasuh's Diyarbekir, which Evliya Çelebi visits in Volume Four

Below, Galata, the European settlement across the Golden Horn, described by Evliya Çelebi in Volume One on Istanbul

The Ottoman State on the move:
Kenan Pasha on his way to Drama in Macedonia, being waylaid by peasants asking for redress against the Albanians. Kenan Pasha's procession includes *azebs* wearing red caps and blue or red shirts and *sipahis*.

Civil society:
left, Mevlevi dervishes perform the Sema'

below, Astronomers at work around the great Taqi al-Din at the Istanbul observatory in the 16th century

below left, A tightrope walker, a man on stilts, dancers and musicians perform at a festival to celebrate the circumcision of the Sultan's sons in 1720

Part of a map of the Nile attributed to Evliya Çelebi, showing here the headwaters of the river. The map is in the Vatican Library.

> A Jewish lad did I pervert,
> To Love's religion did I convert.
> Satan cheered: 'Bravo! Well done!'

This verse is just a load of dirt.

[...]

Baghche-saray: Court protocol of the Crimean khans

First, whenever the illustrious Khan seats himself at the court, all the palace servants and ranking officials stand in their proper places according to protocol, with hands joined respectfully. On the right of the majestic Khan sits the Kalga Sultan (first heir to the throne). His territorial seat in this country of Crimea is the city of Akmescid (Simferopol). He governs 300 villages, as far as the fortress of Kiriş and the district of the villages of Güleç at the eastern end of Crimea.

On the left of the Khan sits the Nureddin Sultan (second heir to the throne). His jurisdiction extends from the Kaçı valley to the fortresses of Gözlev, Or (Perekop), Çikişke and Arbat. He adjudicates cases in 250 villages in this territory, under the authority of the Khan. The illustrious Khan, however, rules over all, including the Kalga Sultan and the Nureddin Sultan, and writes the royal decrees bearing the Khan's signature.

Again on the right side stand the Hanafi *şeyhülislam* and the muftis of the other three Sunni rites.[60] And on the left side sit the chief military judge Murtaza Ali Efendi and, below him, the molla of the city (chief *kadi* of Baghche-saray) and the twenty-four *kadis* of the Crimean peninsula. They adjudicate cases and decide lawsuits in their juridical districts. Should one of the *kadis – God save us!* – make a decision contrary to the Sharia or weak in assertion, the Tatar ulema give the misjudging offender no quarter but immediately put him to death by stoning.

The Khan's vizier Sefer Gazi Agha remains standing; sometimes he sits by the Kalga Sultan. The superintendent of the ushers goes around with a silver rod in his hand and draws forward those with complaints; there are no gatekeepers at this court. The provisions officers also attend standing up, as do the finance minister who stands beside the Kalga Sultan and the court secretary who stands beside the Nureddin Sultan. The other officials –

---

60 The Ottomans and the Turks generally, including the Crimean Tatars, favoured the Hanafi *madhhab* or school of law. In Sunni Islam, the other three rites or schools – Shafi'i, Maliki and Hanbali – have equal authority with the Hanafi.

tax agents, treasurers, revenue contractors and court secretaries – stand to one side next to the daybook keeper.

After the council meeting, a Muhammadan spread is laid out with all sorts of dainties. A dish of horse meat is *de rigeur*, because the Tatar people follow the Shafi'i rite and for them horse meat is strictly *halal* (permitted). The Khan, Kalga Sultan, Nureddin Sultan, the *şeyhülislam*, the chief military judge, and the molla of the city all sit down to eat together. The other *kadis* eat separately. The vizier and the *mirzas* (tribal chieftains) – including those of the Şirinli and Mansurlu tribes – sit in another place. The superintendent of the ushers and the head gatekeepers sit in yet another place. The notable palace servants dine with the finance minister. The tax agents, revenue contractors and provisions officers eat together in a different place. The Kazak sultans dine together with the princes. The court secretaries eat with the daybook keeper. In short, on the day of the high council, Muhammadan spreads are laid out in twenty-two places and all the members of the council enjoy the feast, after which they recite prayers and benedictions.

[...]

Anatolian refugees in Cherson

The Karasu River flows through this city, and its two sides are very prosperous and flourishing. The slopes on the south side mainly have houses of the Armenian subjects. The west side is a flat plain with orchards and gardens, and altogether there are 5,500 two-storeyed houses with tile roofs, occasionally thatched roofs. All around the city, lofty two-storeyed palaces have been built, so the city is thriving more and more. The majority of the populace have migrated here from the cities of Tokat, Sivas, and Amasya because of oppression in Anatolia. Having come to the Crimean peninsula, they now see justice. For that reason, the Crimean cities are becoming prosperous and beautiful.

This city is in the middle of Crimea, yet most of the houses only have a hedge around the courtyard. Since there is nothing to be afraid of, hundreds of houses have no stone walls but are only fenced in by hedges. And every house is sure to have a flowing stream.

[...]

Alchemy in Kaffa

In the forty-one years that I had been roaming the world until this time, I never saw a genuine practitioner of alchemy, although I saw thousands of impersonators. I rejected this science, considering that it was without foundation. But, God be praised, when I saw this Naib Ibrahim Efendi in this city of Kaffa, I witnessed the genuine article. He even gave me an ingot of gold, which I crumbled in my hand like wax. In fact, Ibrahim Efendi used to make tablets out of these gold pieces. He would swallow one in the morning and three in the evening, and eat nothing else that entire day.

Yet for someone to reach this level, this dervish status, he must be an upright mystic, one who busies himself with austerities and contemplation, preserves the mysteries, and withdraws from the world. In short, this work is the lot of him who belongs to the class of great saints.

7. A meal of strange honey in Circassia

A strange adventure
God is my witness that this took place. One day we were guests in a certain village and the Circassian who was our host wished to do a good deed. He went outside where he tarried a while. When he returned he brought a dinner-spread of elk skin, also a wooden trough – like a small vault or portico – full of honey and other troughs with cheese and *pasta* (millet gruel).

'Eat, O guests, may it be permitted, for health of my father soul,' he said (in ungrammatical Tatar).

We were starving, as though we had been released from Ma'noghlu's prison, and we laid into the honey so fast that our eyes could not keep up with our hands. But the honey was full of strange hairs that we kept pulling out of our mouths and placing on the spread.

'Eat,' said the Circassian. 'This my father honey.'

Our hunger having abated, we continued to eat the honey at a slower pace, separating out the hairs. Meanwhile, Ali Can Bey, a native of Taman in Crimea, came in.

'What are you eating, Evliya Efendi?'

'Join us,' I replied. 'It's a kind of hairy honey. I wonder if it was stored in a goatskin or a sheepskin.'

Ali Can, who knew Circassian, asked our host where the honey came from. The Circassian broke out weeping.

'I took from my father grave,' he said.

I understood the words, but didn't quite grasp the import. Ali Can explained, 'Last month his father died and he placed the corpse in a box on a branch of a big tree in the courtyard outside. Honeybees colonised the area around the groin and penis. Now, as a special favour, he has offered you honey with his father's pubic hairs. These are the hairs you have been separating while eating the honey. Rather than excrement of bee, eat excrement of old man!'

Ali Can said this and went out. I followed him, with my gorge rising and my liver fairly bursting.

'What kind of trick has this pimp of an infidel played on us?' I cried.

Then what should I see? Our Circassian host also came out, climbed up the tree where his father was and refastened the lid of the coffin-box, all the while weeping and eating the horrible honey. When he descended from the tree, he said, 'Hajji! When want honey, I bring you much father soul honey. Just say prayer.'

This was certainly a strange and disturbing event.

8. Kalmyks and cannibalism

A Strange Spectacle among the Kalmyks

Some of the Kalmyks live to be 200 or 300 years old. When a man's vigour is spent and he can no longer mount and dismount, his kinfolk tire of dragging him around. They cook him a fat sheep's tail and stuff it into his mouth, forcing him to consume it entire. In this fashion they put him to death, saying that he died a martyr. They also eat one another's flesh, but this is done according to lot, as follows.

They have a man known as Karpa, next in authority after their Tai-shi or king. This Karpa has a four-sided wooden lot that has been passed down from his ancestors over several thousands of years. Each side is painted a different colour. When one of their leading men dies, they cast the lot to determine his fate. If the red side comes up, they interpret the oracle to mean 'Burn him in fire,' and they burn his body. If the black side comes up it means 'Bury him in the black earth,' and they bury his body. If the blue side comes up it means 'Throw him into the water,' and they throw him in the Volga River or in whatever body of water they happen to have camped near. If the green side comes up they cook his body and eat it. They only act according to the instruction of the oracle lot.

One day it happened that one of the Moyinçak Shah's sons had died. They roasted his body, poured out the fat and blood, and were eating the flesh, accompanied by great merriment and festivity. When I passed by they invited me to the feast, saying: 'Come, you too can partake of our emperor's son.'

'Can one eat human flesh?' I asked.

'Indeed,' they replied. 'We eat his flesh so that his soul will enter one of us. Thus he does not die, but goes on together with us.'

'And who is your father?' I asked.

'He who made you and me and the Shining Mountain.' Such was their blasphemous reply, and some words that I dare not write down. They have no sense of being infidels or going astray, no notion of the Last Judgement, of the Scales, of Paradise and Hell and Purgatory, of the Four Books, the Prophet, obligation and Sunna. They are simply beasts in the shape of men, the Yellow Tribe.[61]

'Sirs,' I cried, 'can one really eat human flesh? Isn't it bitter?'

'It is bitter,' an old Kalmyk said. 'Don't eat it. But if you want to know what it tastes like, just kiss a woman and see how sweet it is. If you eat human flesh you will derive eternal life from its sweetness and will live long, like us.'

In that meal, the body of one man was enough to feed forty or fifty Kalmyks. As for the fat, they smeared it over their faces and eyes and bodies; and they buried the bones.

---

61 *Bani Asfar* – a tribe that plays a role in eschatological musings.

VOLUME EIGHT

Greece and the conquest of Crete

RETURNING FROM AZOV to Crimea, Evliya encounters a landscape rich in fauna – horses, wild boar, migratory and hunting birds (on bird migration, cf. Volume 10, selection 12) – and in human drama: Kalmyk Buddhist weather magicians vs. Tatar Muslim fanatics. After reporting to the Ottoman court in Edirne, he returns to Istanbul in May 1667. By the end of the year he decides to leave the plague-ridden capital and join the Crete campaign, the twenty-five-year-long Ottoman attempt to conquer the island from Venice. After stopping in Edirne again to present Sultan Mehmed IV with some hawks he had obtained in Circassia, he departs on a tour of Greece.

In Komotini, he encounters a community of Romani (or Gypsies) and describes their language. His account of Athens reveals his attitude toward the ancients and their monuments – the Parthenon, now serving as a mosque; the Tower of the Winds; the Lion of Piraeus; also his knowledge of Greek, with which he was familiar growing up in Istanbul. His wide travels in the Morea (Peleponnesus) allow him to generalise on the ethnic make-up of the region. Taking passage from Corinth, he arrives in Canea in time to participate in the siege of Candia and the final Ottoman conquest of Crete in September 1669.

The following year, Evliya participates in the capture of Maina in southern Morea. A feature of warfare at that time was the taking and ransoming of captives; but in Kolorya Evliya discovers that not all captives wish to be ransomed. Later he is sent on another mission to Albania, where he attends a wedding in Ergiri Kasri. Stopping for one of the great Balkan fairs at Doyran (near Strumitsa in Macedonia), he returns home in December 1670. (The festive atmosphere of these fairs has its counterpart in the *mevluds* of Egypt; cf. Volume 10, selection 11).

1. Return to Crimea

We departed Azov with a *besmele* heading south through the Kipchak Steppe. We proceeded cautiously, posting guards in front and behind and right and left, and drawing up our wagons in defensive mode like a moving castle, with three cannons in front and three behind, and 500 light-armed cavalry in the van. After two hours we stopped at the stage of the **Güğemli River** and drew up the wagons in a defensive circle in a field of reeds and rushes, in fear of the Kalmyk Tatars.

By God's wisdom, in this place, due to the extreme cold, the sun rose in four places. We could not discern which of the four was the world-illuminating sun that rises in the east according to divine custom (i.e., natural law). The Azov veterans who were with us said that it was forty or fifty years since they had last seen the sun rise like this in four places. The reason it occurs is that, due to the extreme cold, the sun over this Kipchak Steppe has no effect, and suns appear, when it is not dark, at the zenith over the other regions that are near the sea and so milder. But there has never been a sun over the country of Muscovy; only in the southern and southwestern directions, over Crimea and over Istanbul, the suns have stayed suspended in four places like fishing nets or sacks. Sometimes, by God's command, suns appear in six or seven places, according to eyewitness accounts of the Nogay veterans and the veterans of the Muslim Bashkirs.

So this night we lay exhausted in the place called Güğemli. Only God knows what torments of cold and storms we suffered. As we were about to depart in the morning, forty or fifty horsemen came with letters from the envoy in Azov and from the Azov aghas, to the following effect, 'My lord, take caution. 5,000 Kalmyks are preparing to raid your party.'

We received the news, but could do nothing except trust in God's providence and sit at the Güğemli River waiting for help to come from Azov.

To be sure, this river was frozen; but its source is a two-month's distance away, in the middle of the Kipchak Steppe, from where it flows until it reaches this point. Here, where it meets the Sea of Azov, it forms a wide channel and a gulf with reeds and rushes. Its source is a tributary of the Volga, near the shore of the Caspian Sea, from where it flows for two months through the Kipchak Steppe until it meets the Sea of Azov at this point. It was Tohtamış Giray Khan who first diverted the stream from the Volga and made it flow in this direction with the idea of cultivating the Kipchak Steppe. In the course of time it has silted up with mud and sand, and the water does not flow constantly.

As we were about to depart, a reinforcement of 1,000 fully-armed troops arrived from Azov castle. We all took heart at this, and with caution proceeded southwest through the Kipchak Steppe by stages to Akkumlar ... Akkuğular ... Çibir River ... Kaburkalı well ... valley of Yey ... Üzengilik River. ...

At this place our troops were set upon by eight wild boars that emerged from the reed bed. The boars, each the size of a Merzifon donkey, wounded some of the horses. The Muslim *gazis* rained arrows on them and they ran out onto the ice of the Sea of Azov, where they were slipping and stumbling because their claws would not catch hold on the ice. Now this humble one had two mastiffs with me, named Palu and Çakır; they took after the boars and, after a struggle, tore seven of them to pieces. The Muscovy infidels, whom the envoy had sent as reinforcement, ate the boars – for them it was like the festival of the Red Egg (Easter).

Again proceeding south we crossed the valley of Ahıryan ... Kuru Eşim River ... Çalpaş ... stage of Akbaş ... stage of **Cibilli**. ... At this point the fresh meats and boiled meats that we had brought with us from Azov were all frozen hard as a rock and we had nothing to eat. Providentially, our Muslim *gazis* saw two wild buffaloes, each the size of an elephant, in the Kipchak Steppe and some took off after them.

'Hold up,' cried the other *gazis*. 'These buffaloes never used to emerge from the reed beds and thickets in winter weather like this. They must have done so now because they were harried by the Kalmyk Tatars. Beware, don't chase them!'

Some of the men paid no heed to this warning but, fully armed as they were, kept riding after the buffaloes, only to find themselves about to enter amidst the Kalmyk tents. The Kalmyk Tatars, of whom there were many, turned them around and began to do battle. Our men numbered only seventy or eighty, but these were very fine and fully-armed warriors.

In short, as the Kalmyks kept up the pursuit amidst fierce fighting, they came upon us. By this time we had readied the cannons and mounted our horses. We let out the cry *Allah Allah!* and attacked the Kalmyks all together. They could not even lift their hands, but in a trice 1,060 Kalmyks fell prey to the sword, seventy were taken captive and put in chains, and so many horses and garments and weapons were shared out among the *gazis*.

'Do you have any men left in your camp?' we asked the Kalmyk captives.

'No, we are the only ones left. Those still in the camp are our wives and children.'

All the *gazis* armed themselves and, with leave from Ak Mehmed Pasha, in a trice attacked the Kalmyks' (illegible) and returned, unscathed and full of loot, with myriads of animals and women and boys.

When God desires something He prepares the intermediate causes. When God the Generous wishes to be generous to one of His slaves, He creates the intermediate causes. In this instance, God sent those wild buffaloes, which prompted our men to chase them, which led them to the Kalmyks, which brought the Kalmyks to attack us, which led the army of Islam to massacre them and then to get all their wealth as booty. So, with no one aware of what was happening, and with the pretext of two water buffaloes, God granted the Muslim *gazis* countless benefits in that dead of winter. As they say in Persian, *He gives the pretext for buying but does not say how much it costs.*

That night, in this place called Cibilli, we hunted down several wild buffaloes and turned them into fat buffalo kebabs. Until this time we did not dare to light fires in fear of the Kalmyks; but this night we made bonfires with reeds and rushes to cook the buffalo meat. We also, using our axes, cut to pieces the frozen mutton and bread that we had taken with us from Azov. Some of that meat we re-boiled in cauldrons, some we re-roasted in the fire, and the bread we re-baked by burying it in ashes.

So that night we celebrated. But in the morning we again posted sentries all around, following our usual practice, and drew up the wagons in a defensive circle with the Kalmyk captives on their mounts in the centre. As we proceeded southward at a trotting pace, it began to snow, and in the late afternoon we halted at the stage of **Kertmeli** castle. It was originally constructed by the Genoese and was reportedly a great city before being destroyed by Timur the Lame. Its large moats and some traces of its buildings are visible in a meadow at the edge of a brackish lake that is an inlet from the Sea of Azov.

Here we again saw two wild animals, this time horses, and gave chase. When we caught up, I shot one of them with seven arrows but still could not bring it down – the arrows seemed to sink in the horse's body as though shot into a skin of butter. The horses reared up and ran off into the plain.

I headed off the same horse that I had hit before and shot a Rumi arrow right into its eye. It planted its head on the ground and broke the arrow. As it was doing this I hamstrung its hind legs with my sword, which finally immobilised it.

My companions caught up with me and cut both horses to pieces without skinning them. We shared the pieces out among several hundred men and that night feasted on horse meat kebabs. This was in addition to the cooked meat and bread that we had brought out of Azov, that had frozen and that we re-cooked; because ever since leaving Azov, our provisions consisted of nothing but rabbits.

In the morning we proceeded at a trot across the snow, shivering from the cold, and came to **Lake Biy**. It took an entire hour to cross as we struggled and stumbled through the reeds and rushes, the water not completely turned to ice, neither solid nor liquid. The pieces of ice lacerated the forelegs and breasts of the horses and of the animals taken as booty from the Kalmyks. Once we got across, we were relieved; but many animals were left behind in the lake. I was told that two men got caught beneath their horses and drowned, but I did not see them. The lake was actually not deep, but torturous to cross because of the cold and blizzards and because it was full of swamps and marshes.

Emerging exhausted from this ordeal, we continued south for another six hours to the stage of **Gölkonur**. The Tatars give their lives for this place, which they call Altı Su Boyu (Six River Banks) because they are the banks of six streams that form inlets from the Sea of Azov. In the summer there is so much vegetation and pasture along these six streams that horses and camels get lost amidst the flowering grasses. That is why the Tatars give their lives for this delightful place. However, the Kalmyk Tatars have taken it over and use it for their habitations. They even stop here in the winter, since it is a busy passageway of travellers to Azov; but we did not run into any, thank God.

Here too the troops went out hunting. They caught two wild camels and two *asgul* or antelope. By God's wisdom, while hunting here with my servants and companions and mastiffs and hounds, we ran across a wild horse. It was large and fat, the size of a Mahmudi elephant. I and my companions shot this horse with seventeen arrows and seven or eight bullets, but it still kept fleeing. Gradually the wounds took their toll and the horse slowed down, so that one of my slaveboys shot it in the girth by the ruddy foreleg, with a match-lock bullet. It fell once or twice to its knees and rose again. Finally I hamstrung it and, together with my companions, slaughtered and cut if up and shared out the pieces.

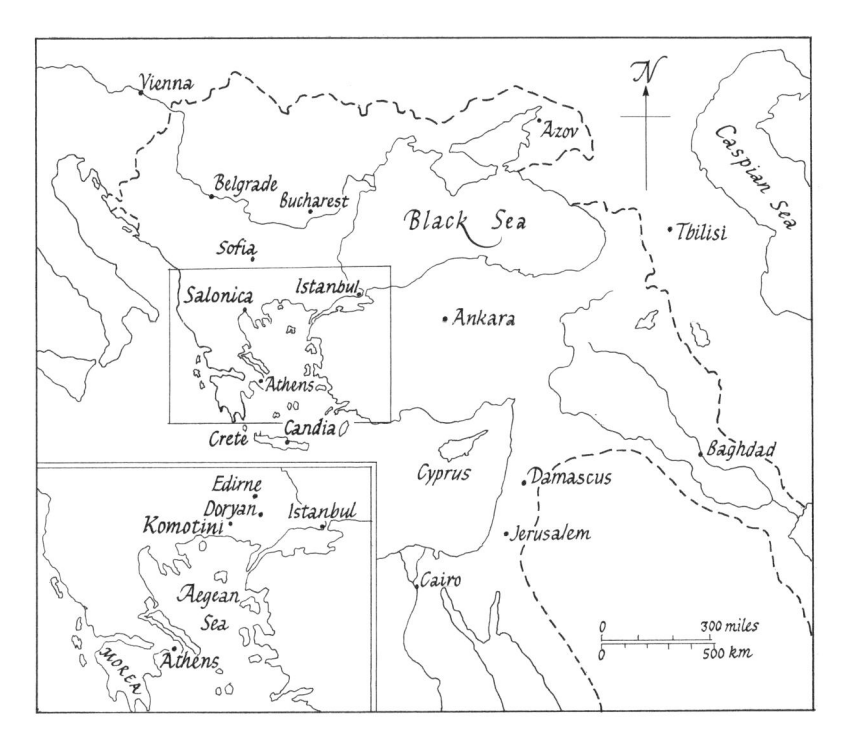

The reason I am relating this adventure is that, as God is my witness, I once had a dream during my childhood in which I was out hunting with hounds in a grassy plain, just like this Kipchak Steppe region, and I shot arrows at a wild horse and killed it. Now, forty-seven years later, my dream came true in this place, and I shot wild horses twice. It was quite a marvel!

When we came to this stage of Gölkonur we crossed the great inlets from the Sea of Azov in six places. They are wide bodies of water, some one hour across, some two hours; gulfs that penetrate a day's journey into the Kipchak Steppe. Between them are wells of fresh water.

Formerly, when we conquered Azov castle in the year 105(0) (1640), the various Nogay clans used to nomadise along these Six Rivers: Ulu Nogay, Kiçi Nogay, Urumbet Nogay, Şıdak Nogay, Yaman Sadak Nogay, Deveyeli, Nevruzeli, Çobaneli and Arslanbeyeli. They would reinforce the army of Islam (i.e., the Ottoman army) by bringing grain below Azov and by selling their musk-scented clarified butter for three *akçe* per *okka*. They then dug wells and drank the water during their migration. But now the entire region from the Kuban River to the Kipchak Steppe is impassable because of the harassment of the Kalmyks, and the Nogays have sought pasture elsewhere, for *God's earth is spacious* (4:97).

On the fauna of the Kipchak Steppe

The grassy meadows and beds of reeds and rushes of this Kipchak Steppe offer breeding grounds to geese, ducks, swans, bustards, shelducks, fieldfares, etc. The eggs of these birds rolled like pebbles beneath our horses' hooves. Foxes, jackals and other animals feed on these eggs.

Indeed, the cranes that winter in the countries of the Blacks – Isna and Aswan (in Egypt), Sudan and Funjistan (in Africa), and Irak of Baghdad – migrate in the spring to these beds of reeds and rushes to lay their eggs and breed their chicks. They cannot do this in Arabia where their eggs would be cooked from the heat. As soon as spring arrives they depart those coastal regions for this Lesser Kipchak Steppe (*Heyhat-ı Sağir*) and for the Greater Kipchak Steppe (*Heyhat-ı Kebir*) on the other side of the Volga.

Indeed, when this humble one was travelling along the Volga and as far as the Ural River, the crane and goose and duck chicks were skittering on the ground and getting crushed beneath our horses' hooves. We caught quite a few fat ones and cooked and ate them.

In this plain of the Volga there are more different kinds of falcons – called *karçığa, toykun, sunkur, albay, laçin, bödene, topalken, kırgı, küykenek* – than anywhere in the world. The ones called *toykun* and *sunkur*, each as large as a goose and having molted five or ten times, are known to have snatched up wild horses and wild camels and wild buffaloes and eaten them.

If you ask how that is possible, the answer is that the bird has trained itself and molted in such a fashion that its eyes become like red coral, and when it does not find enough ordinary prey to sustain itself it attacks a wild horse or camel. First it latches onto the horse's hide with its claws and tears at the horse's back with its beak while it settles on the horse's head and covers the horse's eyes with its wings to prevent it from running. Then it gouges out the horse's eyes and breaks its spirit. It eats it willy-nilly, horse or buffalo or whatever it is, tearing at its groin. When it is full it takes flight and goes back to eating its usual prey, which is the corpses of foxes and jackals and other animals.

But the *toykun* and *sunkur* do not attack wolves, foxes, jackals or lions, because those are themselves beasts of prey. As for lions: the fur of the

Kipchak Steppe lion is not sleek like that of the Baghdad lion, but hangs loose like the wool of an Angora goat; and the lion is a huge creature with a thunderous roar; so the *toykun* and *sunkur* cannot latch onto it with its claws.

The Bashkirs and Nogays train these Volga falcons – *toykun* and *sunkur* and other kinds that the Tatars call *laçin* – to attack people. When one of their enemies is riding alone in the plain, or any other place, they let loose two birds which harry the man from this side and from that and bring him down from his horse, no matter how stalwart and heroic the youth may be. Then they ride up and take their revenge on him.

God has endowed these birds with such splendour that they are dazzling to behold. Some have molted ten or fifteen times, so that they are milky white or milky blue or red like carnelian. Their wings are spotted with elongated black dots. Their eyes are like coral, or as though daubed with kohl. Their ears have more tassels than wool. Their beak is ruby-red like the beak of a phoenix. Their talons are as large as a lion's paws.

Not every young man can bear one of these falcons on his fist, since each one weighs ten or twelve or eight *okkas*. Some men let it perch on their horse's hide; or, if they bear it on their fist, they brace their arm on a forked stick wrapped in felt and stuck into the stirrup. Some young men bear it on their heads.

The birds are so well trained that while riding between stages they fly above your head and, when you shout to them, come and land on your arm. But if you dispatch them against a prey, the rustling of their wings makes the ground tremble and stuns the animal they latch onto. And these birds are not dispatched against geese or cranes or partridges, which would simply get crushed from the swoop of a *sunkur* or a *toykun*; rather they are usually dispatched against wild horses or wild camels or stags or buffaloes.

The animals in this Kipchak Steppe – wild rams, deer, fallow deer, antelope, roe deer, woolly Chinese gazelles, onagers or wild asses with black stripes on their backs, wolves, jackals, foxes, boars, bears, etc. – graze as *otav*, meaning herds of one or two thousand. And they live by eating each other, which is why the steppe is almost impassable because of the animal bones. The furs of red fox known as the Azov navel-bag come from here.

I could go on describing this Kipchak Steppe for a year and still not exhaust the subject, but this much will suffice.

We departed Gölkonur and again proceeded southward, galloping over the steppe, for eight hours until the stage of **Yamançc Karaağaç**.

From Azov to this point the journey across the Kipchak Steppe is fifty-four hours going at a brisk trot. Otherwise, going at a leisurely pace, it is twenty stages. The entire length of the Kipchak Steppe, from the Caspian shore in the east to Kılburun castle on the shore of the Özü River in the west, is ninety-seven stages.

God be praised, we came unharmed from Azov as far as Yamançe Karaağaç where we entered the forest, lit huge bonfires and cooked the meat of camels, stags and buffaloes. We feasted merrily, but still placed sentries on all four sides.

This is the only forest to speak of in the Kipchak Steppe; although there are many forests along the Volga and Ural and Kuban Rivers and the shores of the Caspian Sea. Leaving the forest of Yamançe Karaağaç we headed west, munching on wild pears and sloes and crab apples and acorns as we approached the river. Praise be to God, after galloping for (—) hours we reached **the great Kuban River** and took refuge in the forest along its shore.

The soldiers from Azov, who had come as reinforcement and escorted us to this point, now removed the heavy baggage from the carts and, leaving some carts with us, asked leave to return. Just then the governor of Azov, Monla Gani Pasha, crossed the Kuban River on the ice (coming from the Circassia side) to the Kipchak Steppe side with his 3,000 soldiers and camped in the forest where we were. Meeting with Ak Mehmed Pasha, he donned a vizierial sable fur and got letters from the Pasha for the Azov notables and for Süleyman Pasha. That very night, in the moonlight and the freezing cold, and taking along our military escort and the carts and fifty cannons, they turned and headed to Azov, putting their trust in God. They also took ten Kalmyk captives with their wives and children from Ak Mehmed Pasha to serve as hostages and to assure their safe return to Azov.

As for our party, several hundred clever individuals – indeed, the majority of our soldiers – as soon as the governor of Azov, Monla Gani Pasha, had crossed the Kuban River on the ice with his soldiery, decided to cross over on the ice into Circassia and set up their camps there. The rest of us remained in the great forest on the Kipchak Steppe side of the river, turning our kebabs and feasting merrily.

But many of those who had been exposed to the blizzards and extreme cold, and then sat down next to the fire, got frostbite in their hands or feet, or glaucoma in their eyes, and ended up lame or blind; some even died while sitting around the fire. Praise God, this humble one did not let my slaveboy companions too close to the fire, but even in the blizzard we sat on the snow under the trees, sipping hot toddies and supping on hot soups and munching on wild pears and apples and sloe plums.

That night we stationed sentries all around this copse, also 100 or 150 musketeers in the trenches on each side of the forest, in fear of Kalmyks and of Circassian robbers. We also took pains to transfer the heavy baggage over the ice to the other side of the Kuban River. Only light-armed horsemen remained on this side.

In the morning, by God's wisdom, the ice on the Kuban had broken up and the river was neither ice nor water (i.e., something in between). So we were left with the soldiery in the forest on the Kipchak Steppe side. Ice floes the size of a threshing-floor were flowing down the river, and it was impossible to cross to the Circassia side.

Finally a group of stalwart youths, fortified with arak and mead and *boza*, made rafts by tacking together rushes and reeds and thick dried branches. On these they loaded the wagons and the loads from several hundred pack-horses and conveyed them across the river. Everyone tried to put his horses on a raft, but most were brought across swimming. Once on the other side, the horses were stabled in the houses of the Circassians and Nogays. Some Circassian youths and Nevruz Mirza Nogays came across in their *çırnık* caiques to escort the rafts. They also brought across Ak Mehmed Pasha along with his aghas and his imam Ibrahim Efendi and Cafer Agha; they got to the other side in safety, thank God.

As for this humble one, I refused to be separated from my baggage. But I also did not expect the rafts to come back and get me. Making common cause with some tried and true *gazi* youths, we inflated goatskins and tied their mouths tight; tethered the horses to them by the tail; loaded onto them my sword and bow-and-arrow case and shoulder-muskets and other lightweight items. Then this lowly slave stripped naked in that wintry day of purgatory and – astride an inflated bladder between two horses, with my Tatar whip in hand and crying *Yov yov!* – I crossed the river together with my servants and horses. God be praised, I got wet only up to my knees. Quite a few youths crossed the Kuban River safely in this fashion.

It turned out that one of my horses – an *alaşa* or Tatar gelding – either would not enter the water because of the cold, or else had crossed back over, and was now stranded on the other side and stood there neighing – no one else was left. I summoned up courage and, taking refuge in God on that day of hazard, naked as I was, mounted my roan *alaşa* that had been given me by the military judge of Crimea, Murtaza Ali Efendi and, striking it with my whip, recrossed the great Kuban River between the ice floes and drove the other horse into the water.

One of my hounds, named Vaşak ('Lynx'), had also been left behind. I took it onto my saddle bow and plunged back into the river, then left it on a large ice floe. The dog made its way across, now skipping from floe to floe, now swimming in the water. I too reached the other side in safety.

As I was putting on my clothes and my fur-piece, we noticed a troop of 40 or 50,000 Kalmyks drawing up on the opposite shore. They were stymied when they saw that the river was no longer frozen solid and that all our troops had crossed to the other side. As they were standing there on the opposite shore like Azov foxes, the *gazis* of Mehmed Pasha's soldiery who still had functioning hands and feet began spraying them with bullets from their forty- or fifty-dram *dalyan* muskets, and the Nevruz castle garrison began shooting at them with their *şahi* cannons. In one volley several hundred Kalmyks fell to the ground of perdition on the snow in the forest, and seventy-five Kalmyk veterans tumbled down like sacks from their horses, while the remainder took flight.

When the Circassian and Nogay champions saw that the force of Kalmyk infidels had been broken in this fashion, 2,000 musketeers and 3,000 horsemen quickly crossed the river on rafts and pursued the fleeing Kalmyks. Soon they returned to the river bank with 2,000 heads and 300 live captives. There they stripped the corpses of the Kalmyks who had fallen from the volley of musket- and cannon-shot, taking their horses and equipment and even their filthy garments. Having recrossed the Kuban River on their rafts, duty done and booty won, and having rolled the 2,000 heads at Mehmed Pasha's feet, all the Circassians and Nogays were awarded a purse of *guruş*.

Now all the troops entered Nevruz castle, lest the Kuban freeze up again and the Kalmyks return. Those who found no room inside the castle fortified themselves in trenches outside the walls and appointed sentries all around, so they were also safe from Circassian robbers. That night everyone slept soundly.

[...]

We were proceeding in the dead of winter, wracked by blizzards and storms. Suddenly a *toykun* falcon that was perched on my arm died from the cold. It was a clever bird, molted seven times, with coral eyes – a bird fit for the Sultan. In fact I had brought it with me all the way from the

Volga and Ural Rivers, in the Muscovy country, thinking that I would give it to the Sultan as a present. *Judgement belongs to God.*

I had one other *toykun* and two *sunkurs*. Hoping to keep them alive, I took the jesses from the feet of the dead bird and the collar from its neck, tore out its (illegible) and pinions, and left its body there. They say that birds – like cats and dogs and other such creatures – do not have graves, meaning that one does not bury them. That is why I tossed this *toykun*'s body on the ground of perdition and went on my way. Because on a day like this, when we were being harried by Circassians and suffering the infernal torture of cold, if someone's packhorse were to collapse, his servants would not stop to pick up the load but would just continue on their way.

After suffering these torments for several days we arrived at the stage of the village of **Şağake**. It was described above in my earlier journey to Dagestan with Mehmed Giray Han. This time we camped here. Some of those who sat around the fire had their eyes dazzled and went blind. Some others – including Sarraczade Mehmed Çelebi and a few other of our lord Ak Mehmed Pasha's personal retinue, and the taster, and twenty of the *müteferrikas* – had frostbite on their hands or feet and had to have the limbs amputated with a saw and cauterised with boiling pitch. Those who survived this operation screamed to high heaven.

It is known to God, the Knowing and Wise, that none of this humble one's slaveboys or companions, as we passed from stage to stage of this journey, suffered a loss to any part of their bodies. But we generally dismounted and walked (to keep up the circulation); and when the horses got cold we remounted and rode them around for a bit until they reddened (i.e., warmed up). Each day we suffered a thousand such torments before coming to another stage. The old men in our company bore witness that they had not seen winter weather like this in forty years.

In short, we wanted to bury the seven men who died in this village; but though we struck the ground with thousands of picks, we could not break through a single inch. Eventually we had cauldrons of water boiled in the Circassian houses and poured on the ground, and in this way were able to dig up just enough to bury each man.

[...]

It is the *otar* – i.e., farm estate – of Ömer Agha, the kinsman of Sefer Gazi Agha who is the vizier of our lord Mehmed Giray Khan. We stopped here for seven full days and could not go out safely in any direction because both the Yeleşke and Adahon straits were in a semi-frozen state.

God be praised, on the eighth day we got news that the area in front of Kızıltaş castle was frozen over. We loaded our baggage onto carts and pack horses and made a forced march westward for two days until we arrived at the Kuban River. But it was not frozen over. Nor were there any boats. We were overcome with a grieving sensation difficult to describe. It turned out that those damned Circassians had got tired of feeding us for the last eight days and providing us with grain, so they made up the false report that the Kuban had frozen over.

Wondering how we were going to pitch our tents, since the tent-pegs would not go into the ground because of the ice, we had no recourse but to attach the tent ropes to the carts and to some trees. So we pitched the tents in this manner and thought they were stable. But then a very rough wind sprang up that tore apart all of the tents, whirling them into the air. The squall overturned many of the carts and hurled others, without their horses or oxen, far into the steppe so that we lost trace of their turning wheels.

Poor Ak Mehmed Pasha had crawled under a cart to hide, although he was a very dignified vizier. The wind turned the cart over and Mehmed Pasha barely escaped with his life. All hell seemed to have broken loose. Everyone was thinking how to save himself. Some of the experienced *gazis* said, 'Tatar *gazis*! We are the victims of magic!'

Mehmed Pasha, who kept his wits about him, told all of his staff to begin reciting the *Mu'avvizeteyn*. As they did this over and over, the strong wind died down, by God's command, and the weather cleared a little.

Still, on this side of the Kuban there was no village or any sign of civilisation. We were left in limbo, with no grain or even a mustard seed. Everyone began to tremble like autumn leaves. We were really in a quandary.

At this juncture an ancient Kalmyk Tatar with a scanty beard approached the Pasha and said: 'Pasha, swear that you won't harm me.'

The pasha put his hand on a Koran and swore: 'Neither I nor my servants will harm you.'

'My lord,' said the Kalmyk, 'it was I who just now raised this calamitous wind upon your heads and had it sweep away so many carts and so many tents. I did it to demonstrate a small part of the science that is in my possession. If you wish to cross this river, give me one horse and one bow-and-arrow case and one fur garment and 100 *guruş*. I will summon up calamity again and make the river freeze up. Then you will easily cross to the other side and to safety, and will be delivered from hunger on this side.'

Poor Mehmed Pasha, helpless, agreed and gave the Kalmyk even more than he had asked for. The Kalmyk took the items, tied them down a little ways off, then went into a wooded glade. He was still visible where he was standing in the woods. No one else knew what was transpiring, only this humble one and the Pasha and his secretary.

A marvel: the effects of magic of the Kalmyk Tatars
The sun by this time was shining brightly. I followed the Kalmyk and stayed hidden some distance away amidst some trees so I could observe. The first thing he did was to loose a shower of piss at the foot of a tall tree. Then he bared his buttocks – excuse the expression – and turned to face the open air. Standing up he took some excrement from his anus, put it in his mouth, then did three somersaults on the snow. Returning to the pile of his excrement he put both hands on the ground, raised his feet into the air and braced them against the aforementioned tree. He stirred up his excrement with his left hand and rubbed some on his forehead with his finger. For quite a while the Kalmyk remained upside-down perched over his shit.

What should I see next? The sky began to darken in the eastern and western and northern directions. The sun faded above us. The sky turned deep blue and then black. There was thunder and lightning. A horrible wind blew up. The bluish cloud seemed to break into pieces and descend to earth.

Now the Kalmyk brought his feet down from where they were braced against the tree. He turned around three or four times near his excrement. Occasionally he scooped up some of it in his hand and threw it into the air, at which lightning struck and all hell broke loose.

At this point our soldiers began to swarm around the shore of the Kuban. Everyone looked for some means to cross the river. The Kalmyk wiped off the excrement from his forehead with snow and started walking toward the soldiers. I ran behind him and, when I caught up, greeted him in the Kalmyk language, '*Mandu tav.*'

'*Tav mandu*,' he said, returning the greeting. He took a stone out of his mouth the size of a walnut, rubbed it on his eyes and put it back in his bosom. He wiped some more excrement off his forehead with snow. Twirling about, he approached the Pasha whom we found standing at the shore of the river.

'Don't cross yet,' said the Kalmyk. He himself crossed over the ice first with a hopping gait, then recrossed to our side. Now all the soldiers on foot began to cross back and forth. The ice was still paper thin but, as God is my witness, when the men crossed, the ice crackled beneath their feet and cracked into segments the size of a dinner-spread.

This place, opposite Kızıltaş castle, is the point where Circassian territory comes to an end. The garrison of Kızıltaş castle, on the other side of the Kuban, made their way on foot across the ice to pay their respects to Ak Mehmed Pasha. They bowed down to the ground and kissed his foot, then stood up.

'Hurry!' said the Pasha. 'This very hour, while the river is frozen, convey our baggage and carts and animals to the other side so they will be safe in Kızıltaş castle.'

The garrison soldiers responded to this insistent appeal by crossing back to fetch hundreds of sacks of sand from the castle. They poured the sand over the ice to make narrow roads for the horses, lest their hooves slip and pierce the ice. Then the first thing they did was to bring their sheep from the castle across the ice to Circassia.

As God and the Prophet are my witness, I swear that this is how it happened. In one month (!) the Kuban River, which is like a sea, was frozen solid to the depth of an arrow. But, by God's command, it was not ice like polished crystal such as one sees in Muscovy in the Volga and Ural Rivers. Rather, the thick ice was in some places sandy or muddy, though in some places it was clear.

The Kuban at this point is about as broad and deep as the Golden Horn from Unkapanı on the Istanbul side to the Meyyit landing in Kasımpaşa on the opposite shore. In some places the ice was so clear that one could see large fish swimming underneath.

At the lower part of this crossing one could hear the waves of the Black Sea crashing onto the shore. The waves came over the ice right up to the front of this Kızıltaş castle. Despite this, the people and children of Kızıltaş celebrated the arrival of the Pasha and pranced about on the ice without fear, skipping like gazelles.

First they sat the Pasha alone on a raft with two tall masts which they drew with cables. So the Pasha got safely across and sat down on a prayer rug waiting for the others.

First came his retinue, leaping across the ice single file like a flock of cranes. Whoever tried to cross slowly was drawn under the ice and drowned. God knows, if someone stamped on the ice, it made a hole, so thin was it in spots. If one went forward and stamped, the ice behind became flat but the ice in front formed a hole.

Return to Crimea 273

God be praised, all the horses got across, one by one. Then came the carts which were empty since men on foot had already carried across all the baggage. They removed the wheels, tied ropes to them and to the carts, and hauled them across while keeping their distance. The horses, similarly, were hauled one at a time by men on foot who pulled them by their halters, while keeping their distance, over the paths of sand that had been poured onto the ice. My slaveboys also crossed safely with their eighteen horses and horse carriages and proceeded to the quarters in Kızıltaş castle where they had been put up the previous year.

Meanwhile, however, the Pasha's secretary had remained behind with seven or eight narrow-minded individuals. 'We refuse to cross this ice that was produced through magic,' they said.

'They should cross over quickly,' said the Pasha, 'if they know what's good for them.'

But the secretary was very despondent and did not get out of the cart. The Dagestani fanatics who had stayed behind with him began to haul the cart while crossing on foot. At the same time, some were reciting the *Mu'avvizeteyn*, some calling on God with such beautiful names as *Ya Dafi'* (O Warder off of evil!), *Ya Hafız* (O Preserver!), *Ya Rafi'* (O Exalter!), *Ya Allah*.

Suddenly the secretary's cart broke through the ice and got stuck. Poor Ibrahim Çelebi – that was the secretary's name – fearing for his life, scrambled out of the cart and crawled some distance away from it over the ice. But the six fanatical Dagestani Muslims passed beneath the ice and were drowned. His other ten companions, calling on God and reciting the Koranic spell, kept falling through the ice as they stamped on it. Some drowned and some got back to the shore.

What apparently happened was this: as they called on God's names and recited the *Mu'avvizeteyn* with great fervour and sincerity, the magic that produced the ice was rendered null and void and the ice was broken through. Some were saved, some were drowned.

When the Kalmyk saw this melancholy state of affairs he approached the Pasha, removed his kalpak and threw it on the ground, crying, 'Woe upon my *yayşılık*!' – i.e., my magic.

'My lord,' he continued, 'warn those men not to recite anything in Arabic as they cross. And tell them to cross with a hopping gait. Soon it will be noon and my *yayşılık* will be neutralised. They should just keep crossing!'

By now all the soldiers had made their way across. But poor Ibrahim Çelebi, the Pasha's secretary, with his small retinue, was turned into a ship's monkey. He had managed to escape drowning. He approached the Pasha weeping, too exhausted to speak, a lifeless form. His servants brought him to his quarters and he took to his bed.

After the Pasha and all the soldiery had crossed to this side of the river they formed into regiments and paraded beneath Kızıltaş castle. The garrison responded with a welcome salute of ten cannon shots. This angered the Pasha's brother and the Bey's *hoca* and several other busybodies who berated the gunners and the castle warden, 'Hey you bastards! Why are you shooting cannons and spoiling our fun in this depth of winter?' They were shouting from a mile away. 'Stop shooting, you infidels!'

They came to the Pasha and requested him to cut off the heads of the castle warden and the gunners.

'Why should I kill them?' said the canny pasha.

'My lord, should cannons be shot in this depth of winter?'

'It is their *kanun* for castle wardens to have a gun salute whenever a vizier arrives.'

'Fuck their *kanuns*!' said the *hoca*. He went off to his quarters disgruntled.

The castle warden held a feast, after which, at noon, the muezzin began to deliver the call to prayer from the castle minaret. As soon as he cried *Allahu akbar! Allahu akbar!* by God's command, the river ice that had frozen because of that Kalmyk's magic started booming like cannons and cracking into pieces. Soon there was no trace of ice – it was as though the river had never frozen, as though it had all been a dream.

As God is my witness, this is how we crossed the ice in front of Kızıltaş castle. Afterward the Kalmyk took his presents and disappeared.

2. Report to the Sultan in Edirne

I went to the Sultan's deputy Kara Mustafa Pasha and presented him with the falcons he had requested when we last met. He in turn instructed the memorandum-keeper to take two of the most splendid birds to the felicitous Padishah. All the chief falconers and imperial hunters marvelled at their size and beauty, declaring that they had never seen anything like them. 'Tell whoever brought these to bring more,' cried the Padishah. When the Sultan's deputy informed me of this imperious command, I swore up and down that there were no more, but I could not get out of it so easily. Finally I showed him the wings and tails of the birds that had died in Circassia. He brought them with me to court and I respectfully presented them to the Padishah, explaining that they had frozen to death in Circassia and that I had no others. I took an oath to that effect.

Vani Efendi – God bless him! – piped up and said, 'My lord, I have known this Evliya Çelebi since our days in Erzurum and his service with Melek Ahmed Pasha. He is true to his word, a world-traveller and boon-companion to mankind, and your loyal servitor. If he had other falcons he would not keep them back from my Padishah.'

'Yes, I know him too,' replied the Sultan. 'When I was a child he did us great service in the household of Kaya Sultan.'

I twice kissed the ground before him, showered him with benedictions in Tatar dialect, and regaled him with my adventures tracking down those birds in Muscovy, Dagestan, Circassia, the Kipchak Steppe, and the lands of the Kalmyks; and in the land of the Bashkirs where there is no bedtime prayer for seventy days and we did not perform the evening prayer.

As I was relating this, Vani Efendi piped up: 'Yes, in that country they do not perform the evening prayer, because the time of morning prayer comes after two hours of darkness.' He too asked me all sorts of questions, and I duly answered them.

The felicitous Padishah questioned me for seven full days about my travels over the past three years – in Poland, Czechia, Sweden, Germany, Holland, Hungary, and Croatia – and more particularly about Vienna and Yanık. On the eighth day he rewarded me handsomely for the falcons and I returned to the Sultan's deputy and recounted the entire episode.

The next day I bid farewell to all my patrons, saying that I was going to Crete, and got quite a few favours from them. I sought leave of the Kaymakam Pasha, who fixed allowances on me and wanted to attach me to the suite of his other aghas. I kissed his hand and said, 'For the sake of your noble head and the spirit of the late Köprülü Mehmed Pasha: this poor servant is *one who struggles on God's path* (or, performs jihad). I have been conducting the *gaza* ever since the *gaza* of Azov. For seven years now I have wielded the sword throughout Christendom, along with the wind-scattering, enemy-shattering Tatars, from Crimea to the lands of the Cossacks and Muscovy and Poland and Cracow and the Czechs. For God's sake, don't keep me from this *gaza* of Crete. The Grand Vizier is now reportedly in the city of İstife – let me catch up with him there!'

'Now Evliya Çelebi, don't forget to pray for us in that *gaza*,' he said and gave me 200 gold pieces and a suit of clothing, also thirty gold pieces and one suit each for my servants, plus six courier horses and seventy or eighty letters.

We bid farewell. I left quite a few of these gifts in Edirne and departed for the Candia *gaza* on the island of Crete on Monday, the 15th of Ramadan, in the year 1078 (28 February 1668).

3. The Gypsies of Gümülcine (Komotini)

Ever since the days of the Pharoahs, the original home of the Gypsies of Rumelia has been this town of Gümülcine (Komotini). In fact when the Gypsies take an oath among themselves they swear 'by Egypt and by our Gümülcine.' As for the Gypsies of Anatolia, their original home is the town of Balat in the *sancak* of Menteşe. Even now Balat is the name of the quarter where the Gypsies settled when Sultan Mehmed the Conqueror transferred them from Balat to Istanbul. To be sure, Sultan Mehmed also transferred to Istanbul some Gypsies from this Gümülcine. But the Anatolian and Rumelian Gypsies did not get along well. The Rumelian Gypsies celebrated Easter with the Christians, the Festival of Sacrifice with the Muslims, and Passover with the Jews. They did not accept any one religion, and therefore our imams refused to conduct funeral services for them but gave them a special cemetery outside Eğri Kapu.

It is because they are such renegades that they were ordered to pay an additional *harac*. That is why a double *harac* is exacted from the Gypsies. In fact, according to Sultan Mehmed's census stipulation, *harac* is even exacted from the dead souls of the Gypsies, until live ones are found to replace them.

Finally the Rumelian Gypsies returned to their old hometown of Gümülcine, while the Anatolian Gypsies from Balat remained in the Balat quarter of Istanbul as quasi Muslims and as musicians and dancers. So the Bey of the Gypsies (i.e., the official in charge of collecting the gypsy *harac*) sometimes resides here in Gümülcine. For there are numerous Gypsies in the vicinity of the town, whether singers and musicians, or counterfeiters and thieves. Every people has its Gypsies, as does every one of the Christian nations. But the Gypsies in the vicinity of Gümülcine are notorious brigands.

[...]

The peculiar language of the Gypsies of Rum.
The various peoples spread over the seven climes have their various languages. But each people also – by God's command – has its Gypsies,

who speak the language of the country where they are settled. However, the Gypsies of Balat in Anatolia have their own peculiar language. And also these Gypsies of Gümülcine have their own peculiar dialect. The Gypsies in this region and throughout the Ottoman domains originated in Egypt, when Moses battled with Pharoah on the shore of the Red Sea near the Sinai desert and 600,000 of Pharoah's soldiers – along with his magicians and diviners and the tools of their trade – drowned in the whirlpool at the place known as the Strait of Kolundur. Moses put a curse on the people of Pharoah who were not present at that battle. As a result of the curse they could not remain in Egypt but were scattered abroad, condemned to wander from clime to clime and from town to town, hungry and homeless, dwelling in the mountains and the valleys, and raiding and thieving.

[...]

In the time of Moses the people of Pharoah split into two groups. One group, consisting of several hundred thousand who escaped drowning in the Red Sea at the Strait of Kolundur, fled to Rum, as mentioned above. The other group, who were neither on the side of Pharoah nor on the side of Moses, are known as Copts. Moses was not angry at them, but rather he blessed them, and today they are the much-respected Coptic people of Egypt. [...]

But the 'Copts' – i.e., the Gypsies – in Rum, because of Moses's curse, live in contemptible and squalid circumstances, and even their dead must pay *harac*. It was concerning this group, while they were still soldiers in Pharoah's service, that God revealed the verse: *from every stubborn tyrant* (11:59). Truly they are tyrannical, good-for-nothing, thieving, irreligious people; they pretend to be Muslims but are not even infidels!

Their language: *yek* 1 *duy* 2 *tirin* 3 *iştar* 4 *panç* 5 *şov* 6 *eftay* 7 *ohto* 8 *anga* 9 *deş* 10.

firahun god. One of their gods – *God forbid!* – was Pharoah, whom one group called Firahun.

haman hun great prophet *zeyyan hun* great sultan *dulke hun* great sultan of women (?) *kuluşe hun* great saints *misa hun* prophet Moses *harun hun* prophet Aaron *mesab hun* father prophet.

manro bread *pangi* water *maş* meat *dudum* gourd *şah* cabbage *mancan canes* fine eggplant *keral* cheese *sika* fig.

so kerez so bi kengan What are you doing, what did you sell? *şu karamtu so kerez* Good, fine, and what are you doing? *akı kay kerez* Well, we are working *nuki keraz* What are you doing? *urda parda kerez* We are doing this and that. *caba biken* Go sell! *so bi kengan* What did you sell? *bul bikin gum* – begging your pardon – I sold ass. *kanaste diyan* To whom did you give ass? *yek kal balame diyum* I gave it to a certain infidel. *davo les kere daya pupe* Let me fuck this one's mother. *dameyte peya puye* And let me fuck your sister. *nana yila cavo kadéntu ma* Isn't it shameful that you are quarreling and swearing at each other? *sartana des tut* And why shouldn't I quarrel? *saro gis avla aku şéla* Every day he comes and swears at me *cay icav oles kav kakés* Go take him to the master. *icav gum mar ker gum oles* I took him and had him beaten. *mos ecav gan oles* Because you took him and had him beaten. *haba ma minca tar* Why don't you eat my cunt? *sos kete hal morom teminç* My dear, why should my husband eat your cunt? *tena hala mahal mebu ya tar* If he doesn't eat my cunt let him eat my ass.

They have thousands of other such naughty expressions. For they are always quarrelling among themselves, day and night, and cursing each other out with obscenities. They commit murder for the sake of a penny. Or else they insist on bringing their case to the Pasha or to the Sharia court, and when it is adjudicated it turns out to be over a penny or less. For that reason gypsy legal claims are not heard. The Copts in Egypt, on the other hand, never utter an impolite word. Even the Anatolian Gypsies of Balat are upright citizens compared to these Rumelian Gypsies; I have given an account of their language above in Volume (—).[62]

These Gypsies too have twelve dialects, one uglier than the next – may God save His servants from their wickedness. But the world traveller must have some inkling of their dialects as well, and so I have recorded it here despite the impropriety of some expressions. Don't blame me; for these Gypsies made my liver bloody and my eyes red with tears.

4. Athens

Description of the great ancient city, the abode of sages, the walled town of Athens

We say Atina, but the Greeks say Athina, since *t* and *th* are very close in pronunciation. It means (—). In Latin it is called (—), in French (—), in Italian (—), in (—) (—).

All the Christian and Coptic chroniclers agree that the founder of

---

62 This is not found in the *Book of Travels* as we now have it.

Athens was the prophet Solomon. He had the fairies bring Balqis, the daughter of the king of Sheba, to him one night in her dressing gown and he married her. Balqis wanted to see the world, so Solomon commanded the wind to transport them. Flying from Jerusalem they landed first on the summit of Mt Sfakia, on the island of Crete, where Balqis built a lofty pavilion. Their next stop was this city of Athens where, in the place called Temaşalık ('Promenade'), they built a palace like the garden of *the many-columned city of Iram* (89:7).

Solomon's son, King Rehoboam, further developed the city, and after him King Feylekos (Philip), in the fifth generation after Solomon. He also founded Salonica and Kavala, and subjugated the Greeks and Arabs and Persians. It was during his reign that Alexander the Great came into the world. Feylekos raised Alexander who became the world-adorning emperor Dhu'l-qarnayn. Alexander embellished this city of Athens even further.

7,000 Greek philosophers and physicians forgathered here, which is why the chroniclers of all nations refer to it as the abode of sages. They include Pythagoras the Monotheist, Hippocrates, Socrates, Feylekos (Philip), Feylesof ('Philosopher'), Aristotle, Galen, Plato the Divine, Ptolemy, etc.

In short, all the wise men liked the Athenian climate and took up residence. They collaborated trying to find a cure for death, and although unsuccessful, they did find cures for myriads of illnesses – largely through diet and exercise – and each of them lived three or four hundred years. Hippocrates the physician not only found no cure for death, he eventually succumbed to his own illness and died of dysentery. Plato the Divine died shortly thereafter, so the philosophers abandoned his religion and adopted that of the prophet (—) (—).

Plato the Divine, in his travels, came to Pécs on the frontier of Buda where he resided for forty years. Finally he too ... despite his perfect intellect, gave the collar of his life into the hands of death. He is buried in a garden outside the Szeged Gate of Pécs. His last words were: 'O Athens, my garden of paradise!'

And what a goodly and prosperous city it was – lofty in construction, mighty in population, full of marvels and wonders and fine arts and crafts. Visitors are amazed at its architectural monuments carved out of white marble. Their eyes are dazzled at its marvellous paintings and statues, in the Frankish manner. The figures in the paintings seem to be alive, and the statues smile or frown or look askance.

In sum, nowhere on the face of the earth in all the seven climes are there such noteworthy wonders and sight-worthy marvels as this city of mild climate and ancient entrepôt of Athens and its surroundings, including the valley of Temaşalık, the ports of Ejder (Dragon – i.e. Piraeus) and Derzi (Tailor), the church of Koçbaşı (Ram's-head), the town of Kifse, and Mermerlik (Marble-quarry).

The Greek people originated in the time of the prophet David and, multiplying in the country of Greece and acquiring property and territory, first built the great city of Macedonia which is Filibe; then the city of Pozanta (Byzantium) which was latter called Kostantiniye (Constantinople) and now is called Islambol ('Islam-plenty' – i.e., Istanbul). Then they built this city of Athens on the Rumelia side of the Sea of Rum (i.e., the Aegean) at the end of the Gulf (of Corinth) to the north and west.

Later Constantine, the ruler of Istanbul, expanded and embellished it. His army ruled over this city of Athens, which already had a 1,700 year history as a great entrepôt and a medrese (!) and abode of philosophers. It passed from king to king and emperor to emperor, eventually passing from the hands of Spain to the Venetian Franks and then, in the year (—), being conquered by the Ottomans in the person of Sultan Mehmed the Conqueror.

Now Athens is in the province of Rumeli, under the governance of the Admiral, in the *sancak* of (—), an endowment of Mecca and Medina under the supervision of the chief black eunuch, 'cut off from the pen and separate from the foot,' an imperial *has*. The Sharia administration is headed by a *kadi* with salary of 300 *akçe* per diem and with (—) villages under his jurisdiction. There are also a mufti; a marshal of the descendants of the Prophet; a colonel of the cavalry troops; and a commander of the janissaries. The governor's salary, paid by the chief black eunuch, is 50,000 *guruş*. Other officers are the castle warden with his 150-man garrison, market supervisor, toll-collector, tax-agent, municipal deputy, chief architect, and chief of police. The Greek Orthodox community have a patriarch, no other magistrate.

Fortifications. The walled city (Acropolis) is in the middle of a broad plain, on a sheer red rock, unthreatened by higher ground. It is a very ancient construction in an oval shape elongated from east to west. No other place on earth has such a mighty fortress, because the rock towers up 100 cubits from the ground. The stones of the fortification are dressed white marble, polished and shining, each one the size of an elephant or a bathhouse dome. The master builders of old expended great effort to fit these stones together without using lime or mortar. No foe could gain victory over this castle, since it is impossible to dig siege trenches or to undermine the wall from any direction, and there is no higher ground looming above it.

The stone construction above the native rock is 50 cubits in height. The castle's circumference measured on the outer wall is 3,000 paces. There is no moat, as every side is a sheer rock chasm like the Ghayya pit of hell. There are three iron gates that give on to one another, the layers separated by fifty paces, only facing westward.

Within the wall are 300 castle-like houses, built of stone and completely covered with roof tiles. While they have no gardens, they do have windows and balconies with fine views of the vineyards and fields and gardens in the plain. In the time of the infidels, water flowed into the castle through subterranean channels, but no longer. Now all the houses have cisterns that catch rain water from the roofs. So there is ice-cold water even in July, but the amount depends on the rain. Many people get their drinking water from wells in the suburb below, hauled up by donkeys.

Mosques. There is one Friday mosque in the walled city (the Parthenon). It is a remarkable light-filled mosque, situated in the middle of this castle, and very famous among world-travellers. It is 250 feet long and 80 feet wide, and contains sixty tall and well-proportioned columns of white marble, laid out in two rows one above the other.

On every side of the mosque, above the columns, another gallery has been built, so all around there are two layers of well-constructed mosques. But four of the columns, between the prayer-niche and the pulpit, are lofty piers of red porphyry, marvels of God's creation, so shiny that they reflect one's face, each one worth the revenue of an entire clime.

Above these columns, where the qibla is located, is a lofty gold-embellished enamelled dome of aloes wood, like a paper cutout of Fahri, amazing to behold. Plato the Divine used to hang a lamp made of carbuncle in this dome constructed of aloes wood. On the eastern wall of the mosque he put paper-thin slabs of *harekan* marble, otherwise known as fire-stones. As the sun rose, those stones turned red-hot from the heat of the sun, igniting naphtha-soaked wicks that lit the carbuncle lamps and illuminated the interior of the mosque. The infidels revered this mechanism as a talisman, calling it Lamp of Divine Light.

In the year (—), during the reign of the Umayyads, Sultan Mansur came from the Maghreb with 1,000 ships and conquered the islands of Crete and Sicily, and also conquered this walled town of Athens. He took away the above-mentioned carbuncle lamps and the chains of jewels and thousands of precious idols and candlesticks and jewel-encrusted crosses. But they did not know that the enamelled dome was made of aloes wood and so did not take that. Even now no one knows about it. But it is a noteworthy enamelled dome, truly a wonder.

Now as well, next to our (!) pulpit are four emerald-like porphyry columns, in which one observes strange multicoloured shapes and wondrous flowers. Aside from the eight porphyry columns – the aforementioned four red ones and these four green ones – all of the sixty white-marble columns, rising one or two storeys high inside the mosque, are fluted and grooved.

Just to the left of the four green porphyry columns are six slender columnettes of white marble upon which the master carver has made a white-marble throne for Plato the Divine that dazzles the eye and amazes the mind of anyone trained in the science of architecture. Above the six columnettes are six highly-wrought little arches, all rising to a point where there is a small dome. Plato the Divine used to sit on that dome and harangue the people. It is surrounded by an intricate network of carved marble ornament. In the very centre of that small dome, where the little arches come together, a head of cheese has been carved out of white marble resembling a belly[63] – a magical work of art. And the central part of this throne is surrounded by a carved grating of cypress wood.

63 This is the reading the text requires (*Ol kubbeciğin ta ortasında göbek gibi bir beyaz mermerden bir kelle peynir tasvir olunmuşdur*). Thanks to Pierre MacKay who provides the following explanation:

> This is a description of the pulpit, or ambo, off to one side of the main aisle. The builders may have copied an *omphalos*, one of the commonest ornaments of classical Greek architecture – the most famous one is at Delphi – and one that properly belongs in the middle of something. I imagine Evliya asking, 'What is that called?' and on being told that it was an *omphalos*, looking at it in some bewilderment. The shape of an omphalos is the pointy half of a hard-boiled egg or an old-fashioned sugar-loaf. It is often decorated with vines, etc. I would guess that it didn't look like any navel in Evliya's experience, so he felt he had to describe it to his readers, and resorted to a cake of cheese, called 'a head of cheese' in Turkish (*Rd1*, 1564).

> See also Diana Gilliland Wright (2010), 'Evliya visits the Acropolis' http://surprisedbytime.blogspot.com/2010/01/evliya-visits-acropolis.html.

This mosque is completely paved with slabs of white marble, each one five cubits square and so wavy (i.e., polished?) that one's face is reflected in it.

The gate of this mosque, in three layers, is on the qibla side. As one enters, between the outer and middle gate on the left-hand side is a goblet carved from striated white marble, large enough for a man to fit inside. In olden days the building contractor used to offer wine in that goblet to the workers in the mosque, and they would drink it in one gulp. Nowadays it would require two waterskins borne by water carriers and their horses to fill that goblet. What tall and sturdy men those men of old must have been to drink that amount of wine without pausing for a breath. Now another stone-carver has hollowed it out further and attached a spigot, so it serves for ablutions.

The hall ceiling of the middle gate is delicately carved work, like a cutout of Fahri Çelebi of Bursa, with pure gilding. The door leaves are 20 cubits high and made of cypress wood. Formerly, in the time of the infidels, these gates were covered with gold and encrusted with jewels; the settings for the jewels are still quite visible.

Passing the inner gate, you are inside the mosque. The enclosure where the organ and bells would be played has arches with, in the middle, a hanging arch called an orphan arch, and over another arch is a hanging column. This is really worth seeing, but when you see it you still cannot comprehend it but must marvel with finger to mouth. The proper response is silence before something miraculous. Above this arch and column is a carbuncle shining so brightly that by its light the priests were able to read the Gospel and other scriptures on a dark night.

But this ancient temple, the upper part of the mosque, has no stone-built dome. According to Muhammad ibn Ishaq (biographer of the Prophet, d. 768), the Prophet Muhammad was born 600 years after Jesus. On the night of his birth, the Vault of Chosroes in Iraq collapsed, the fire temple of Nimrod was extinguished, and the domes of Ayasofya in Pozanta (Hagia Sofia in Byzantium, i.e., Istanbul), of Ayasofya in Salonica, and of this Athens cathedral were all destroyed. The Athens dome was subsequently rebuilt several times but never stayed firmly in place. So the king of Istanbul (i.e., the Byzantine emperor) had great arches constructed where the dome used to be, then had planks of cypress laid down over the arches and, above these, cypress columns topped by a cypress wood ceiling. All the wood was embellished with gold and coloured paintings of a quality surpassing that of

Mani and Bihzad, and the fragrance of cypress perfumed the brains of the large congregation.

These painted cypress planks are roofed over by lime and gypsum and a layer of white marble, rather than a lead-covered dome. Every marble slab is the size of a knotted rug or kilim. The marble is finer and shinier than lead, and sparkles in the sun like cut glass. The master stone-carver has sliced this marble roofing as thin as ceiling boards, so it does not weigh heavily on the building's foundation.

When rain falls on these marble roof-tiles it runs off, by cunningly incised channels, into a cistern that is built on six tall columns resting on a large stone terrace reached by six stone steps from the prayer-niche hall on the qibla side of the mosque. All the rain that flows from the marble slabs on top of the mosque gathers in this cistern beneath the prayer-niche. So there is plenty of fresh cold water for the thirsty congregants.

On top of this qibla hall where the cistern is located there is a stone structure with a half dome – not a dome constructed with wooden beams as the interior of the mosque. This half dome is also roofed over with white marble slabs the size of kilims. The inside of this enamelled dome is glassy (?) stone covered with gilding and embellished with blue and red paint.

I examined this qibla dome very closely both inside and outside. It is overlaid with varicoloured marble and precious stones. And the arches and walls have variegated beads and small precious stones – white, black, red and other colours – dazzling to behold, recalling the mosaics of the Dome of the Rock in Jerusalem.

As for the lofty red and green columns, their like is found nowhere on earth except in the Ayasofya and Süleymaniye mosques in Istanbul.

The tongue falls short in describing the prayer-niche and pulpit.

The shiny marble slabs on the walls of this mosque are each the size of an elephant. The strange thing is that even a master architect cannot detect the places where these slabs are joined – it is as though the entire wall, 40 cubits high, were a single slab. And the wall is so shiny that the slightest speck of dust is visible. In particular, the faces and kneelings and prostrations of the worshippers – *God save them!* – are all reflected in the surrounding walls as though in a mirror.

Another admirable feature about these walls is that no mortar or lime or gypsum was used in their construction. The entire mosque was built using lead and iron clamps, nothing else.

As for the sixty remarkable lofty fluted columns of the outer courtyard, they are each twenty-five cubits tall. Unlike the columns inside the mosque, however, they are not carved out of single blocks of marble. Still, no matter how closely you examine them, you cannot see where the pieces are joined and you would say they are each made of a single block. The reason is the grooves and flutings which the master stone-carver made in highly-wrought ancient style. These sixty columns are laid out like cypresses around the courtyard in measured rows according to the science of geometry.

Above the columns, which are sheltered by eaves, and above the walls are a remarkable and varied assembly of voluminous statues, made of white marble. If I were to describe these one by one, it would require an entire volume and would hinder the course of our travels. The human mind cannot indeed comprehend these images – they are white magic, beyond human capacity. One with the intellect of Aristotle would be dumbfounded at the sight of these statues and proclaim them a miracle, because to a discerning eye they seem to be alive.

In sum, whatever living creatures the Lord Creator has created, from Adam to the Resurrection, are depicted in these marble statues around the courtyard of the mosque. Fearful and ugly demons, jinns, Satan the Whisperer, the Sneak, the Farter; fairies, angels, dragons, earth-beasts (cf. 27:82); the angels that bear up the throne of God and the ox that bears up the earth; sea-beasts, elephants, rhinoceri, giraffes, horned vipers, snakes, centipedes, scorpions, tortoises, crocodiles, sea-sprites; thousands of mice, cats, lions, leopards, tigers, cheetahs, lynxes; ghouls, cherubs, Gabriel, Israfil, Azrael, Michael; the Throne, the Bridge, the Scales; and all creatures that will arise in the plain of resurrection and be assigned their places – those in the fires of hell depicted grieving and mourning and tormented by serpents and demons; and those in the gardens of paradise depicted in marble enjoying the pleasures of the houris and *gilman* (male denizens of paradise). In short, one who sees the depiction of paradise on these walls of the mosque's courtyard will be delighted, while one who sees the frightful and monstrous likenesses of the people in hell will be petrified and aghast.

If you do not travel to Athens yourself and see it with your own eyes, you can have no idea what it was like in ancient times. Description cannot do it justice and, as the verse has it, *How can hearing measure up to seeing?* It has been this humble one's pleasure to roam the seven climes of the inhabited world ever since the year 1050 (1640–1). But I have nowhere seen such marvels as in this city of Athens – as well as Rome (!) in the land of the Franks and Esztergom in Hungary and Vienna and Amsterdam in Holland. But the artistry displayed in this Athens mosque and in the courtyard is more wondrous and marvellous than in those countries. Anyone who has not seen this city should simply not call himself a world-traveller.

But when that terrible Sultan of the West, King Mansur, conquered this province, he gouged out the jewel-eyes of all the statues and 'blinded' them. He plundered all of the precious bejewelled lamps and candlesticks and carbuncles and crucifixes. He removed the rubies from the domes in the outer courtyard and set fire to the courtyard – some places are still shrivelled from the depredation of that fire. Still, there is not such a resplendent mosque anywhere else on earth; because no matter how many times you enter it, you will always discover some new example of artistry and workmanship. The verse:

> *We have seen all the mosques of the world,*
> *But we have never seen the likes of this!*

must be about this light-filled mosque, for there is nothing like this place of worship in all the inhabited part of the earth – may it remain firm on its foundations until the end of time. *Amen, O Helper of men!*

On a building of wonders. Below this mosque, just inside the castle gate, are the classrooms of the physicians and philosophers. The windows, set in the walls, are of fine white marble. After the conquest, the Ottomans stored their gunpowder in this school and made it an armoury. One day, by God's wisdom, it was struck by lightning and some parts of it were destroyed. It is now used as a caravanserai. This large building is also a marvellous sight, beyond description.

Nearby, between the two fortress gates, is the gun foundry, where there are a few large cannons. There is also a small prayer-hall used by the armed garrison troops who patrol the castle gate.

A hundred paces below this gate is the dervish convent of Hüseyn Efendi. It is a great shrine of the Halveti Sufi order. Above the door is the chronogram:

> Mahdemi uttered its date as follows:
> May that hero be acceptable to God.
>
> Year 1023 (1614)

The suburb of Athens. A lovely unwalled town, like the Garden of Meram (in Konya), situated to the north and north-east of the walled city. There are three Muslim quarters, the houses all clumped together in one place.

There are three Friday mosques – four prayer-niches altogether if you count the mosque in the citadel, described above. One is the (—) Bey mosque, built of stone with a dome, solid and thriving. The others are the Hacı Ali mosque and the Old Mosque. All three are built of stone and have domes with tiled roofs – none of the buildings in this city have lead roofs.

There are seven neighbourhood mosques; one medrese; three primary schools; two dervish convents; three baths – Bey Hammam, Hacı Ali Hammam, Abid Efendi Hammam – all with pleasant atmosphere; and two merchant *hans*. And there are a total of 105 shops. While there is no bedestan, still every kind of precious stuff and valuable merchandise can be found.

There are 7,000 tile-roofed houses, of both Muslims and Christians. They are sturdy houses, like castles with battlements and loopholes, and built completely of stone – there are no wooden houses or houses with earthen roofs or mud-brick walls, but only splendid houses with stone walls set with mortar and lime. Each house has a cistern into which rain water is channelled from the roof. In short, they are very solid and spacious houses, most having gardens and entertaining guests.

The streets are pure sandy ground. There are no pavements, since there is never mud in this city.

The number of infidels registered to pay the *harac* tax is 4,000, although the true number is over 10,000. It is very much like the city of Malta. Muslims here are a despised group, with no standing or dignity, because the Christians are great merchants who have business partners in Western Europe (*Dip Frengistan*).

Dress of the infidels of Athens. The older men and the magistrates wear Eflatuniye hats of black silk velvet and garments of black mohair. The Greek youths wear red fezzes, varicoloured broadcloth vests, magnificent silk waistbands of various colours and silk belts, and, on their feet, black boots or black or red slippers.

The women wear varicoloured dresses and tarbooshes on their heads and go about with their faces uncovered. But no one in this city has ever seen a woman, whether Muslim or Christian, go out into the marketplace during the day. At night it is another story. As soon as it is dark, thousands of women grab their lanterns and go to other houses, or to the baths, where they party until morning – as in the verse:

That is to say, I search for you from house to house.

There is one class of women that wear something quite strange on their heads: a flat headgear that is pied like a peacock's tail. It is a marvellous get-up. But the Christian peasants wear the kamelaukion (*manlifke*) – like the Frankish conical felt cap – and varicoloured woolen or felt cloaks.

Dispraise of the churches. There are a total of 300 houses of idol-worship, and 3,000 priests and monks.

Water fountains. In the time of the infidels there were fountains in 108 places and every house had flowing water. Now the roads are in ruins and one can make out where the fountains used to be.

Wells. In the houses are 4,000 wells.

The pleasure-dome of Balqis. The eastern side of this city of Athens is known as the Throne of Balqis (the Queen of Sheba). It was made by demons at the command of the prophet Solomon. I would require an entire quire to describe this as it deserves, with its variegated columns and vaults of Chosroes and lofty domes. These days it serves as the public prayer-grounds of Athens. All the Muslims of the city resort to it, fully armed, for the prayer for rain and for the two festivals; because there are hardly any Muslims left – the city has been left to the infidels. It is a sight worth seeing, an open-air prayer-ground palace with soaring columns in praise of which the tongue falls short.

There is another large palace in the city, in the place known as the Scala Gate – an ancient and splendid palace, beyond description, a sightseeing must.

Then, in the place known as (—), a magical site known as Uzun Kenise ('Long Church'), impossible to describe.

A wondrous building (Tower of the Winds). Near the Old Mosque there is a gathering-place of learned men known as Plato's Pavilion. It consists of a remarkable sort of stone tent with eight sides facing the eight winds, each side formed from a single slab. On each of the sides of this pavilion a human figure is depicted, carved from a single slab of white marble. Each figure holds in his hands the characteristic implements of

Athens

one of the winds. Four of the winds are depicted as male and four as female. The four males are shown with the moon-like features of a youth bright as the sun's rays, and the four females are portrayed as lovely women. The winds depicted as men are Northwest, North, Northeast and East, and the women are Southwest, West, South and Southeast. In truth it was the magic art that made these images so that each one stands facing one of the winds.

The dome of the pavilion is formed of white marble inside, and the twelve segments of the dome are laid out according to the twelve constellations of the zodiac. In one segment is depicted the constellation of Ares, the mansion of Mars, retrograde, fiery. In another is Taurus, the mansion of Venus, earthy. In another is Gemini, the mansion of Mercury, airy. In another is Cancer, the mansion of the Moon, watery. In another is Leo, the mansion of the Sun, fiery. In another is Virgo, the mansion of Mercury, earthy. In another is Libra, the mansion of Venus, airy. In another is Scorpio, the mansion of Mars, watery. In another is Sagittarius, the mansion of Jupiter, fiery. In another is Capricorn, the mansion of Saturn, earthy. In another is Aquarius, the mansion of Saturn, airy. In the twelfth segment is Pisces, the mansion of Jupiter, watery. Thus the seven planets relating to these constellations and the influences of the other stars are depicted. It is a unitary, instructional pavilion of well-wrought marble in twelve segments, at the level of manifest magic.

Inside this pavilion-shaped dome there is a tomb in which all the Christian infidels believe that Philip the Greek is buried, and on their infamous feast days they visit it. At the head and foot of this grave a chronogram has been written in the Greek language.

Atop this marble pavilion-dome is a thin stylus. They say that in the days of the learned ancients a world-mirror, like the mirror of Alexander (on the Pharos), was set on this stylus. Whenever an enemy started out against this city from any direction, the army and its commander were revealed in this world-mirror. Its perch remains, but the mirror is no longer there.

In those days also, each of the learned men in the city devised for it a different sort of wonderful talisman and marvellous charm. And so this city never had plagues, snakes, centipedes, scorpions, storks, crows, fleas, lice, bedbugs, mosquitoes or houseflies. The year has 366 days, and there were two talismans set on the seashore for each day, one toward the land and one toward the sea. These were operative until the day when the

Prophet emerged from his mother's womb. On the night of the birth of the Beloved of God, all the talismans and charms were turned upside-down and their effect was nullified. Even now I have seen many places where the talismans used to be, and even now the city of Athens has no mosquitoes, centipedes, storks or crows – if they do come they do not settle down, and if they stay for long they die.

If an ill man goes inside this pavilion-dome, he immediately feels nauseated and vomits up black and yellow bile and phlegm and other humours. That is because in one of the segments of the dome there is a piece of Yemeni alum, and in another there is a blue vitriol eye-stone (or copper sulphate). Anyone with fever who goes inside is affected by their fumes; once he has vomited he is cured of his fever. This is a well-tested remedy.

One of the learned men, an accomplished master, contrived a time-piece, based on astronomical calculation and the astrolabe, corresponding to the eight winds on the outside of this pavilion-dome. It consists of a quadrant, together with slanting lines of celestial declination, carved into the marble. Never in this devious firmament has such a finely-wrought time-piece been made, whether by one of the Ptolemies, or by al-Hakim Bi-Amrillah (Fatimid caliph, reg. 996–1021), or by Ali Kuşçu in the days of Mehmed the Conqueror.

In sum, it is a marvellous lofty dome.

At the bottom of the cliff that looms over (!) this Athens castle are caves with all sorts of domes and palaces and hermit's cells. All the ancient sages – Aristotle, Hippocrates, Socrates, Pythagoras the Monotheist, Galen, Feylekos, Feylesof, Ptolemy, Mihan (?), Michael, and Plato – had cells in these caves. If you go inside them your brain will be perfumed by the fragrance of nutmeg, cubeb, cinnamon, long pepper, ginger, aloes, pellitory and cardamon. Since some of these cavemen practised alchemy, you can also smell sulphur and mercury and arsenic.

In those days, the philosophers who came to this city took up residence in these caves where they taught classes and held learned discussions. They knew all the occult sciences and perfected all branches of knowledge. That is why some chroniclers of old call Athens the City of Illuminationists (i.e., Pythagoreans), the City of Walkers (i.e., Peripatetics) and the City of (—). There were philosophers then who day and night were in wordless communication with the philosophers of Baghdad (i.e., Babylon). It is quite a mystery how scholars in Baghdad and Athens could commune with each other, the two cities being a five-month's journey apart; indeed, it is a miracle on the level of Jesus's life-giving breath.

Athens at that time was so populous and prosperous that the entire way between it and the port of Ejder, which is two hours south of the city, was lined with layer on layer of palaces and gardens and shops and tourist attractions. Hundreds of these are still visible. Two hours in another direction is Mt Deli ('Crazy'). And to the north is the town of Kifse, which now is separated from Athens by thousands of vineyards. In short, it would take a man three days to go around this city by foot; and a letter could be passed from hand to hand and be delivered in Eğriboz or İstife or Corinth. These days the area between the city and Port Ejder is filled with vineyards and flower gardens and vegetable gardens; but there are myriads of ruined buildings with their domes and arches.

The wondrous building of Port Ejder (Piraeus). Two hours south of the city, at the end of a gulf of the Aegean Sea, is Port Ejder, known to sailors and merchants from sea to sea.

On the quay, at the foot of a great *han*, is the statue of a lion, the height of two men, made of white marble. It is sitting on its hind quarters and its mouth is open toward the sea, i.e. toward the south. The master stonecarver has crafted such a likeness that all the world's painters could not equal it. The lion's head is the size of a bathhouse dome. The two front paws are resting on the shore and the lion is squatting on its hind quarters and gazing out to sea as though watching the ships. It is because this huge lion resembles a fearsome dragon that this place is called Port Ejder ('Dragon'). This is another wondrous work of art.

This great gated harbour is circular, shaped like a bowl, and can hold 300 ships at anchor, safe from the five winds. When Canpoladzade Mustafa Pasha was admiral (1630–2), he anchored here with the imperial fleet and built a breakwater and a large tower at the mouth of the harbour. During that time he also went to observe this lion and decided to paint it in various colours. Traces of that paint are still visible on the lion's body. Then Sultan Murad IV summoned Canpoladzade Mustafa Pasha to the Porte and he left the breakwater tower incomplete. Were it to be completed, this Port Ejder would indeed become a dragon's lair and a safe harbour. The only drawback is that there is no fresh water anywhere along the harbour shore. But there are streams of fresh water in the nearby vineyards.

This humble one took a close look at the lion statue and concluded that in the time of the infidels it must have served as a fountain. It is sitting on its hind quarters and has its mouth open to the air, and the space in front of its front paws is a large pool. Hence it must have been used as a fountain. Water spurted from its mouth as thick as a man's torso and poured into the pool. The mariners got their fresh water from there. The source was a lofty mountain two hours east of Athens known as Mt Deli. The water was brought from there by pipes and made to flow out of this lion statue's mouth. There are still traces of that water course.[64]

[...]

Explanation of the Greek language. This verse, in the Gospel, was revealed concerning the coming of the Prophet Muhammad: *abitun* a boy *azeriyun* a son of Azar *porfonoton* will be the prophet *lev gıslin* he will not be a liar *nithu nitha* his birth *efzulad* will be in Mecca *ki kalevşir* he will have come with righteousness *to nomnin* his blessed name *mevamith u mith* will be Ahmad Muhammad *epsigodos* those who follow him *na kirdis* will possess this world *biystu bith* and will possess the other world.

Letters of the alphabet in the Gospel. *Alfa-u vdipşi gamaşi dheltafi e-i dhitata itathima thiteru yotepi kaba-u levdekşi mi-ni ubiru.*

Avta, mikraçko kalo the prophet Jesus; *mikraçko* little; when he grows up he becomes *kalo* good.

Another form of the alphabet. *Alfa vita gama zlta ezita ote yota kapa lavza mi ni iksi ro sima ta ipsi şi,* etc.

Samples of the language, beginning with the numerals. *ena* 1 *dhiyo* 2 *tiriya* 3 *tethera* 4 *pende* 5 *eksi* 6 *efta* 7 *ohto* 8 *enga* 9 *dheka* 10 *endeka* 11 *dodeka* 12 *dheka triya* 13 *dheka tethera* 14 *dheka pende* 15 *dheka eksi* 16 *dheka efta* 17 *dheka ohto* 18 *dheka enga* 19 *ikoş* 20 *tiryanda* 30 *saranda* 40 *peninda* 50 *eksinda* 60 *efdominda* 70 *ogdonda* 90 etc.

hiristos name of God *mikraçko kalo* little good Jesus.

Names of Jesus's apostles: Simyon, Pavlo, Petro, Anderya; Yovani – as the Gospel was revealed verse by verse this Yovani gathered them into a book; Manthego; Luka – he was an ecstatic, privy to divine mysteries; Marko – the Venetian Franks call him San Marko and the lion depicted on

---

64 This passage has been studied by Gunnar Jarring in an article published in Swedish and Turkish in 1978: 'Evliya Çelebi och marmorlejonet fran Pireus', *Fornvännen* 73, 1–4; 'Evliya Çelebi ve Pire'deki mermer arslan,' *Belleten* 42.168 (1978), 775–9.

their flags and banners is his image; Yakopi – he is Jacob; Thoma. Two are unknown. After the ascension of Jesus – *whom We raised to a high position* (19:57) – each of these disciples journeyed to a different region and made known the religion of Jesus. They made the Roman (or Byzantine) lands prosper and assembled in the ancient cities of Athens and Rome.

As for those who came after these disciples, the Greeks call them Aya Niko, Aya Yoro, Aya Kasim, Aya Vestos, Aya Hıdrellez, and Aya İsvet Nikola. *Aya* means saint and *kala yoroz* means great priest.

ipsomi bread *nero* water *tiri* cheese *kıryaş* meat *ankurya* cucumber *pe pon* melon *koromidya* onion *keri* candle *angeli* angel *İsvet Nikola* Sarı Saltık *nalderfim* sister *ipsarya* fish.

pu payistu Where were you? *esi sopa ela kaç kato* Hey you, be quiet, come, sit down *sika pano matyam* Get up my dear *doz mga fora nase dhoko ena folori* Give me once I'll give you a ducat *kali mera kiritsi* Good morning sir *kalisi mera mastori* Good morning to you master.

keratsa young lady *kiritsi* gentleman *pedaki* boy *magır, mahır* knife *kasro* castle *pirgaz* fortress *ela mesa* come in *ladhika* priest *mitropolid kadi patrigah* (ecclesiastical) magistrate at the rank of great king.

kafiro people of Azar the idol-worshiper who was Abraham's father. *hiristiyan* those who believe in Jesus.

In sum, this language of the Greeks is like an ocean, but we have only dared to record this much.

5. Balibadra: A great cypress tree and the five ethnic groups of the Morea

A huge cypress. In the seven climes and the inhabited quarter of the earth there is nothing like it, for God the Creator and Fashioner, the Eternal Gardener, has fixed His glance upon it. It is an emerald-like green cypress but, unlike other cypresses, it is not straight and tall; rather, it has four forks and 360 branches shooting left and right and upward. Forty or fifty strings of horses can be tied to it, and 40,000 or 50,000 thousand sheep can rest in its shade. Each of its branches would encompass fifty or sixty spans. I and my seven slaveboys holding hands could hardly embrace its main trunk – one of them had to remove his turban and holding the ends of the unravelled turban-cloth we were just able to encircle it.

At the very summit of this noteworthy cypress is an ancient cavity where honeybees have made their hive. Every year in the honey season the owner of this cypress climbs up and extracts 100 *okkas* of honey which he sends to various provinces as gifts for the great notables. As God is my witness, there is no honey on earth more fragrant than this. All the Frankish chroniclers agree that it is because of the world-famous honey (*bal*) derived from this 3,060-year-old cypress that this city has received the name Balibadra.

During the time of Azaryun, the father of Abraham, a group of infidels adopted this cypress as a god – God forbid! – and worshipped it. To this very day, whenever any member of the Christian religious community passes by this cypress, he removes his hat and bows his bare head to it several times. I have witnessed this myself, since I got hoisted up with slings to one of the branches of this cypress in order to leave behind a monument of myself in this pleasure-park as well. I took my penknife and carved out of the bark the following graffito in the Karahisari manner: For the spirit of the world-traveller Evliya, a Fatiha (*Seyyah-ı alem Evliya ruhiyçün el-fatiha*). This graffito was even finer than the one I carved out of the lofty plain tree on the island of Cos. God willing, it will last forever.

The climate in this city is rather unpleasant, since it is on the coast. Lemons, oranges and other fruit-bearing trees are not bad. Also, there are quite a few streams of fresh water here and there.

The people are *Rumyor*: they speak Greek (*Rumca*) and the populace are Greek (*Urum*) and Albanian infidels. To be precise, the Morea (i.e. Peloponnesus) is a peninsula 770 miles in circumference and contains five distinct ethnic groups:

First are the native Muslim believers and monotheists of the Morea. Their language is Greekish (*Urumşa*).

The populace of the Kalavrata, Vostiçse and Taraboliçse regions as far as Corinth are Albanians and they all speak Albanian.

In Benefşe (Monemvasia) and Anaboli and the Maina mountains live a distinct group known as Çakona (Tsakonians). Their language is neither Greek nor Italian but a strange dialect peculiar to themselves and requiring an interpreter to understand.

The Maina province is at the southern promontory of the Morea peninsula, opposite Crete. The language of the Maina infidels is also neither Greek nor Katofari (?), but a dialect with its own nasty expressions.

Finally there are the infidels of Mistra. They are Greeks whose speech is very elegant and eloquent.

Each of the five groups has its distinct terms and expressions which will be recorded in their proper place.

Here in Ballıbadra there are also many Jews, since all the customs officials and the brokers in the marketplace are Jews, as are the sentries on all the Frankish galleons in the harbour.

6. Siege of Candia: Ministrations to the wounded and Saint Green-Arm

This humble one, full of fault, acquired some courage from constantly witnessing these great battles. Day and night I girded my loins and recited the Muhammadan call-to-prayer, or I tended to the Muslim *gazis* who had entered the thick of battle with bloody hands and bloody sword, with burning heart and naked breast, and with the words of the holy Koran on their lips. God be praised, whenever God saved one of them from a mine or a stone or a bomb, or from the projectile of a cannon or a musket, I was ready with weapons or with ablutions. I buried several hundred martyrs, including some governors and commanders, and several hundred others who were wounded I brought to the surgeons to be tended. Indeed, I can say in all sincerity that this poor and humble one sometimes carried bread and soup to the wounded. For some, who were poor, I and my servants boiled and washed their clothes and re-dressed them, soothing their wounded hearts and pitying their tears. For others, whose beards and moustaches and ears were swarming with lice, I used my scissors to snip their hair, turning them into 'four-stroke' Kalenderi dervishes (i.e. who have shaved off all facial hair), and thus saved quite a few patients from lice. There were times when all hell broke loose, when father ignored son and son ignored father. Even then I would fill my little waterskin-of-the-poor with Water of Life and dole it out to the sick and wounded left behind in the old trenches without attendants and without the strength to move. So I gladdened the spirits of the martyrs in the Plain of Karbala and gladdened the grieving hearts of the wounded. May the Almighty not record this as hypocrisy, may it be found acceptable in the divine court.

Deeds of the saints, by God's wisdom. In the year 1079 on the Night of Berat,[65] in the middle of the night, as the night-watch of the grand vizier's regiment was stationed at the seashore, a fire appeared over the

---

65 The sacred night between the 14th and the 15th of the month Sha'ban, corresponding to 30 January 1668.

water about ten miles off the coast. All the Muslim *gazis* in the trenches saw it.

'Help!' they cried. 'The infidels have devised some trick to attack the trenches. *Gazis*, don't pay attention to that fire, just stand firm in your trenches and stay alert.'

But they did station all the berserkers and the irregulars at the seashore and directed them to monitor any fires of the infidels coming deceptively from the sea. So a few thousand *gazis* stood ready on the shore.

By God's wisdom, that fire was surging toward the shore on the waves. As it approached, myriads of muskets and cannons were directed against it and the sea was roiled with lead like bulgur boiling in a pot of water. The fire got brighter and brighter, with flames shooting toward the sky. The army camp in that dark night was lit up like day. The *gazis* kept pumping lead into the fire as the waves drove it ashore. Then what should they see?

Onto the shore emerged the corpse of a man, completely naked except that his genitals were concealed within a thick purse-like sack. Some of the braver soldiers, paying no heed to the flames that were emanating from his (right) hand, ripped open the sack-cloth and looked at his genitals. When they saw that he was circumcised according to the Prophetic Sunna, they knew that he was a Muslim martyr. The dead man raised his left hand and covered his genitals, at which some cried 'God be praised!' while others warned that it was a fire-trick of the infidels who had put a magical spell on a Muslim's dead body.

Amidst a jangle of rumours and contrary opinions they brought the blessed corpse onto the shore. Now they saw that his right arm was completely green, and from a hole in the hollow of the hand, green and blue and red flames were streaming forth. Light emanated from the skin, which was pure as crystal and unscathed by the countless bullets and cannonballs that had been shot at it. The fire emerging from the hollow of the hand turned out to be light as well, shining up to the sky. When the Muslim *gazis* observed this they realised that he was truly a noble martyr.

The grand vizier's deputy, Mahmud Agha, and the other commanders obtained fatwas from the grand mufti of the army. By vizierial command they informed this humble one, full of fault. I veiled his face, resplendent as the full moon, with my cloak and covered his pure body with an *ihram* (seamless white pilgrim's garb used as a shroud). In the morning, the multicoloured lights in his arm disappeared; only a faint light glowed like fire in the hollow of his palm.

After the dawn prayer I gathered round me a few hundred dervishes. As we recited our litanies we lifted the noble corpse from the shore on a kilim and conducted it to our graveyard called Kara Şehidlik ('Black Martyrs' Cemetery'). During our procession, shrouds sprinkled with Zamzam water came from thirteen places. This humble one washed the corpse. Along with several myriads of soldiers we performed the interment prayer and buried the corpse in that dervish cemetery. I dubbed him Yeşil Kollu Sultan ('Saint Green-Arm'), had a moat dug out and a stone structure built around his grave, and over the tombstone placed a wooden banner painted green, the symbol of martyrs. It has become a popular pilgrimage site – *may God have mercy on him.*

Subsequently, for love of God, I washed and buried my travel companion in seven kingdoms and three sultanates, Hindi Baba Mansur; also Karabaş Yunus Dede and another dervish sheikh named Tofu; quite a few dervishes; two of my slaveboys who were martyred during the siege; three pashas – Kara Mustafa Pasha, Katırcızade Mehmed Pasha and Vanlı Mehmed Pasha; several *sancak-beys*; and other notables and commoners. For the spirits of all the martyrs of the Plain of Karbala, and the martyrs of the Battle of Siffin, and the martyrs of the *gaza* of Candia – may God be pleased with them – a Fatiha!

And there were many other tasks and efforts that I accomplished – may the Almighty not record this as hypocrisy. I shot more than 3,000 arrows. I shot two and a half years' worth of bullets. I carried hundreds of loads of earth. I recited the Koran night and day over two and a half years, completing one Koran recital every Friday eve (Thursday night). And wherever I found a stray cannonball I carried it to the foot of the cannons. May God Most High find these tasks acceptable in His court.

7. A captive woman in Kolorya

As we were going about on horseback, I saw a pretty young woman sitting under an olive tree. Her head was covered with a green cloth, and in her arms was a baby, also wrapped in a green cloth. When we approached, she stood up, put the baby down on the ground, and with a Greek accent cried: 'O my dear Evliya Çelebi!' She caught hold of my horse's stirrup and wept bitterly.

I was moved with pity, but also taken aback. 'Woman,' I said, 'how in this land of infidels did you know I was Evliya Çelebi?'

'Don't you recognise me?' she said. 'I am Saime, daughter of the captain of Bardunya, Emir Hasan Agha. Don't you remember how much time you spent eating my father's bread and salt when you and your retinue stayed in our house? It is seven years now that I have been a captive.' She kept weeping, as she took up her baby again into her arms.

'Girl,' I cried, 'hurry, mount one of my slaveboy's horses, and let's be off. I'll return you this very day to your father and mother.'

'O no, my dear little Çelebi,' replied the hussy. 'This little baby in my arms belongs to my Captain Lemberaki. I also go to church with my husband. I don't want to have anything to do with the Emir.' She moved off quite a bit, then smiled and said: 'Go in health.'

It occurred to me that I ought to kill this cursed woman before I left. 'Come girl,' I said, 'let me take you to your father, my friend Hasan Agha.' As I rode up to her she ran off to her house, went inside, and locked the door behind her.

This province of Maina has thousands of such Muslim captives. God be praised, this humble servant has rescued 170 Muslims from captivity in the course of my travels. I know, of course, that many thousands have been sent off to the lands of the infidels, and that hundreds are wasting away in dungeons in villages like this. But it is impossible to help them – may God in His omnipotence rescue them from captivity!

8. Fair at Doyran

In the *sancak* of (—) at the border of the *kadi*-district of Usturumça (Strumitsa) there is a delightful wooded meadow and a broad plain. The fairgrounds are laid out like a chessboard, with several one- and two-storey stone buildings, like a large *han* with *porta* gates on four sides resembling a fortress. Lining the thoroughfares are over 1,000 shops roofed with tiles that comprise the fair. It was constructed by (—) and endowed by (—).

Over the gates are government offices as big as palaces where the magistrates and *kadis* and commanders with their troops sit on the market days. And there are quarters for the Sultan's agents and treasuries for the imperial tithe which they collect from the market.

Once a year, during the cherry season, 100,000 people gather in this plain. They come from Turkey and Arabia and Persia, Hind and Sind, Samarkand and Balkh and Bukhara, Egypt and Syria and Iraq, and Western Europe – in short, from the seven climes. All the merchants of land and

Fair at Doyran

sea arrive here with their merchandise and set up their tents and pavilions and huts-of-sorrow and booths of reed and straw in the surrounding valleys. It is like an army-camp bazaar for the troops of Alexander the Great or Darius or Kay Khusraw. This valley becomes a sea of men. Myriads of bales of goods are brought out and bought and sold, including bird's-milk and man's-milk and lion's-milk – bird's-milk is eggs, man's-milk is mother's milk, and lion's-milk is wine – you can find all of these. Indeed, of eggs, I have seen ostrich eggs. I have even see men sell their own children!

On the days of the fair, thousands of shopkeepers – purveyors of food and drink, bakers and cooks and tanners – from all the nearby towns and villages set up their tent stalls. The jostling crowds are like a rabble army, and the market is brisk for forty days and forty nights. Even women openly sell their secret wears. Thousands of people become wealthy as Korah, while other thousands dissipate their wealth in revelry and end up poor as mice.

Also there is a separate market for sheep and goats, another for horses and mules, and one for oxen and water-buffaloes. Only there is no camel market since there are no camels in Rumelia. But there is a market in human beings where thousands of lovely boys and girls are bought and sold; and a separate slave market for black Arabs with 40,000 or 50,000 customers, since blacks are highly prized as servants in these regions.

In the main fairgrounds the various shopkeepers are installed, including the great merchants, worth hundreds of thousands of *guruş*, who set up shop in the tiled stone buildings mentioned above. They lay out their wares – precious stuffs such as silks and satins and velvets; or jewels such as rubies, emeralds, chrysollite, turquoise, agate, etc. – turning their counter-tops into decked-out brides or idol temples of China. For this *han* bazaar is as secure as a fortress and everyone openly displays his most expensive goods.

Meanwhile the business in the outer fairgrounds is equally brisk. The vast plain is filled with row on row of tents, pavilions, covered stalls, booths made from kilims or from pilgrim-garbs – it resembles a tulip garden – and goods are being exchanged in every corner.

Also there are cookshops of Kay Kavus; maybe 1,000 places where whole lambs and sheep are being turned on spits; and over 1,000 coffee houses and *boza* shops and wine taverns. Invariably some people get drunk and brawls break out. Then the officers stationed here the chief *kadi* of

Serres, the colonel of the janissary troop, the tax-agent's *voyvoda* and comptroller – step in and mete out fines and punishments, so the place is actually very safe.

And whatever entertainers there are on the face of the earth can be found here in the public squares and in the tents – jugglers, tightrope walkers, gamblers; players with bottles or bowls or glasses; mace-wielders, strong-men, rope-dancers, puppeteers, shadow puppet players, tumblers, sword-swallowers; trainers of dancing bears, monkeys, goats and donkeys; cudgel-wielders, lassoers, snake charmers, bird fanciers; tricksters with straps or paper or mirrors or jars or heads – in short, all the world's conjurers and alchemists and illegitimates come here in swarms and display their skills. Then there are the singers and dancers and instrumentalists; clowns and comics; reciters of ghazals and *kasides* (i.e., shorter lyrics and longer odes); wrestlers and archers; pretty boys and lovers and singing girls and women.

Whoever has not seen this spectacle – and whoever has not seen the celebrations at the breaching of the Nile in Cairo, and the *mevlud* celebrations of Seyyid Ahmad al-Badawi and of Sheikh Ibrahim Dassuqi, also in Egypt – should not say that he has seen very much. As for the Doyran fair, the nights are like the Night of Power and the days like the Khwarazm-shah's New Year's Day.

After all the bustle and commotion and buying and selling – some making a profit, others left bankrupt – everyone returns home and the fairgrounds turn into a water mill whose stream has run dry, so a passerby would wonder if there were ever people here at all. The wise will take a lesson from this and withdraw from the pomp and show of this perishable world. But it is a wonderful spectacle!

VOLUME NINE

Pilgrimage

Die grosse Mosque' zu Medina.
La grande Mosquée à Medina.

PILGRIMAGE TO THE HOLY CITIES of Jerusalem, Mecca and Medina had been in Evliya's mind since he began to think of travelling. Here he recounts the dream in which his long-dead father and his old teacher urge him to make the Hajj. He sets out in May 1671, taking a leisurely route along the Anatolian coast, with – after another encounter with brigands (cf. Volume 5, selection 1) – a stop at the ancient city of Ephesus, and many other places. His peregrinations in the Holy Land include a return to Safed (cf. Volume 3, selection 2).

He finally reaches Jerusalem in January of 1672. He has very detailed descriptions of the Muslim sites – Dome of the Rock, al-Aqsa mosque; nor does he neglect the Christian sites, such as the Church of the Holy Sepulchre. Reaching Damascus in February, where he again encounters Sheikh Bekkar the Naked (cf. Volume 3, selection 3), he now joins the Syrian pilgrimage caravan.

The pilgrimage month of that year, Dhu'l-hijja 1082 AH, corresponds to April 1672. Evliya's Hajj account combines personal narrative with prescriptive details for other pilgrims. A good portion of the Medina materials are included here; of the more extensive Meccan materials, only the section where he characterises the populace of the city.

Having performed the Hajj rites, Evliya departs Mecca with the Egyptian caravan. He regrets that he had to travel hurriedly in both directions – toward Mecca with the Syrian caravan and from Mecca with the Egyptian caravan – rather than leisurely vice versa. After stopping at St Catherine's monastery on Mt Sinai, he arrives in Cairo in June.

1. Setting out on the Hajj

Reason for the journey to Mecca and Mina
This humble one Evliya in my youth, when my physical faculties were in their prime, wherever the drawn bow of my eyes took aim, the arrow of my glance struck the mark. By God's command, in whatever direction I set out, winter or summer, I reached that country. But now I remained in Istanbul for six months and it was like a prison.

Finally, on the Night of Power (27 Ramadan) 1081 (7 February 1671), invoking the aid of all the prophets and saints and noble spirits, I set out to visit the shrine of Abu Ayyub Ansari. For the Prophet has said, *If you are bewildered in a matter, turn to the people of the graves for help.* God be praised, I performed the visit and recited a noble *Ya Sin* (Sura 36), donating the merit therefrom to their noble spirit and beseeching aid from their spirits.

Aid came from God. That night, as I lay moaning and groaning in my corner of travail, free of hypocrisy and crass desires, I saw in my dream my teacher Evliya Efendi – he was a bearer of the Koran, a great sheikh and master of Koranic recitation, and served as prayer-leader to Sultan Ahmed and Sultan Mustafa. With him was my father Dervish Mehmed Ağa Zılli – he was boon-companion to Sultan Süleyman and chief goldsmith of the Sublime Porte, and a noted dervish.

I kissed their noble hands and, after much discussion, Evliya Efendi recited the Koranic verses: *Travel through them by day and night in safety* (30:50); and *Behold then the tokens of God's mercy* (34:18). 'Act according to these nobles verses,' he said.

Now my father – *may his earth be sweet!* – recited the verse: *Roam the earth* (6:11). 'Son,' he said, 'my advice to you is: *Reflect on God's blessings, do not reflect on God's essence.*'

After imparting their counsel they uttered a benediction and intoned a Fatiha. My father rubbed his blessed hands over my body and puffed over all my limbs. Then he took me firmly by the ear and, as though I were a schoolboy, gave me a slap on the back of the neck that caused my skull to resound like Nakhchivan steel.

'Bind on the waistband of zeal in two places,' he said. 'Do not divulge secrets. Wherever you go, stay well.'

And my master Evliya Efendi chimed in: 'Go,' he said. 'Travel the world in bodily health. May your helper be the Possessor of the Kingdom.'

At this I awoke, and it seemed to me that I had a different body. All my limbs throbbed with strength and a light shone on the eye of my heart. When morning came I immediately began to make provisions for my journey.

By God's wisdom, that same day Saili Çelebi, one of the pupils of the late Azmizade Haleti Efendi, came to visit.

> It was the day of festival and that moon stopped at my house.

He greeted me and said: 'Happy days!'

We embraced and exchanged pleasantries. Then that faithful friend and homeless companion said, 'O my brother! Why are you so despondent and indecisive? Come, let us roam the world together, let us go to Arabia and India. Haply God will provide us a leader on the path and a guide on the way, who will dispel our grief and lead us to Truth.'

Here, thought I, was the perfect wayfellow. I cheered up considerably, saying, *First the companion, then the road.* We swore not to besmirch ourselves with any kind of forbidden substances, intoxicants or narcotics.

'Brother,' said I, 'I have experienced much of the turning of this lower world and have undergone its vicissitudes. I have drunk liver-blood from its poisoned chalice. My own liver has turned on the spit of the turning sphere and been roasted to kebab.' (Citing a verse to this effect) I related my own ill fortunes and recounted one by one the pains and tribulations that travel entails.

My faithful friend Saili Çelebi took heed of my counsels and understood the dictum, *Travel is a fragment of hell, though it be but a single parasang.* And so he prepared to set out for the Hijaz.

Reason for writing down this *Book of Travels*

Those who roam the seas and the lands should know that this meanest of God's creatures, Evliya the unhypocritical, son of Dervish Mehmed Zılli – who was chief goldsmith of the Sublime Porte and who, at the behest of Sultan Ahmed and in the service of the imperial *surre*, erected the Waterspout of Mercy (or Golden Waterspout) on the roof of the Ka'ba, and when he returned to Istanbul uttered a benediction and prayed that I be vouchsafed pilgrimage to Mecca; this humble one – having reached the age of fifty and not once since emerging from my mother's womb having besmirched myself with forbidden substances, intoxicants or narcotics – nursed only one wish since the time of my youth: to travel.

Finally I left my home town and the place of my birth, the pleasant land (*belde-i tayyibe*, cf. 34:15), i.e., Constantinople. Tying my saddlebags and braving the heat and the cold; choosing to further my education in a land of exile; desiring to roam the world and see foreign parts, in accordance with the Koranic dictum: *Travel through them by day and night* (34:18); I made it my ambition to examine first-hand the monuments of the seven climes that have excited the admiration of the men of knowledge and insight.

Even so, I consulted with my conscience and said: 'Why in the course of my journeyings should I waste the precious time of my life? In addition to travel (*seyahat*) let me also engage in pilgrimage (*ziyaret* – includes visiting the shrines of holy men as well as the Hajj pilgrimage) and trade (*ticaret*).'

Thus I began the travail of travel, zealous to record the ancient monuments of the Well-guarded Kingdoms (i.e., the Ottoman Empire) – with its *hans* and mosques and medreses and other buildings, including latitudes and longitudes and the lengths of days and of rivers – for *Lofty zeal is part of the Faith*. And I searched out the wonders and marvels of the world, mounting my wind-swift steed, traversing the spheres and wandering from constellation to constellation like the seven planets; cutting stages and rolling stations; giving voice to my jewel-tongued pen; now describing the lands, now visiting the shrines of the prophets, now reciting the Koran; recording the hour and degree and minute of the castles that I stopped in and the mountains that I crossed; and drawing charts and figures like those in *Mappa Mundi* and *Geography* and the books of *Atlas* and *Minor*.

In the years of my journeyings I saw thousands of strange places and experienced thousands of wondrous events. Because we humans are creatures of forgetfulness, lest their traces be effaced and their names be concealed, I began to make a record of noteworthy items – both man-made and God-made (i.e., naturally occurring) – and to write them down in order to provide memory-clues, using well-worn expressions and a middling style, in accordance with the dictum, *Talk to people according to the measure of their intellects*.

Finally all preparations were complete. This humble one set out one day with my eight slaveboys, my three faithful companions, and my fifteen Arab steeds. We were ready, now to journey on land and sea, now to sojourn in village and city. Holding the reins of our will toward the sea, we mounted a wind-swift boat, unfurled the sails, and galloped over the waves in the direction of Üsküdar which is in the territory of the Holy Land.

2. Brigands at the Alman Pass; Ephesus

With a *besmele* we entered the merciless mountain pass of Alman, all our companions armed to the teeth. After advancing for half an hour we suddenly saw a band of twenty horsemen galloping toward us. We prepared to engage them, but then saw they were wounded and bleeding, fleeing from something.

'Community of Muhammad!' they cried. 'Where are you going? In front of you are forty or fifty bandits. They attacked us and pillaged our goods. Now they are chasing us.' They passed us by.

We drew ourselves together. Our janissary companions dismounted and sauntered ahead fearlessly with their muskets. At once forty men, mounted on Arab thoroughbreds, appeared from the direction of Alman Pass, some with muskets, others with bows and spears, or brandishing swords. We showered them with a volley of lead, and they halted at a distance. One of them approached and said, '*Gazis*! Just now there were twenty or thirty fleeing horsemen. Have you seen them?'

'Yes,' we replied.

'Help us. They are bandits who attacked us. Praise God, we got the better of them. But our horses are exhausted. Theirs are as well; but yours are fresh. Help us chase after them!'

Now we were in a quandary. The first group said *these* were bandits. Was one group bandits and one group rebels? Overcoming our doubts we mingled with the newcomers and realised that they were merchants. A few, whose horses still had some vigour, started to join us.

Now, with our twenty janissary musketeers, we gave the bandits chase. God be praised, galloping with our fresh horses we caught up with them outside Alman Pass in a plain with scattered pear trees. Their horses were exhausted, so as soon as they saw us they dismounted and stood their ground. We swooped upon them and shot at them. One of my slaveboys was wounded, and one of my horses was killed. But I managed to kill four of the bandits and take six of them captive, and I gave their horses and trappings to my servants. The rest of the bandits took to the hills.

At this point, those of the forty merchants whose horses still had some vigour caught up with us. One of these, brandishing his sword, struck one of the bandits whom I had taken captive and lopped off his head.

'This infidel killed my brother,' he said. 'God be praised, I have taken my revenge.'

The rest of the merchants also reached us. 'Praise God,' they said, 'you have captured these devils.' And they kissed my hands and those of our companions. 'But what happened to the rest of them?'

'They have taken to the hills,' we said, and immediately we all – foot-soldiers and horsemen alike – headed for the hills in pursuit of the fleeing bandits, whom we overtook. Three youths from the band of merchants were martyred in the ensuing combat. Two of our youths were wounded slightly, as was one of my slaveboys who ran into a tree with his horse. We bound the dead on horses and tied up twelve of the bandits, taking their mounts and weapons.

Now we made common cause with the merchants. 'You are Hızır!' they said to us, and we said to them: 'No, you are Hızır Ilyas!' We set out once again into the Alman Pass and returned to where we and they had left the heavy baggage, only to discover that a three-hour battle had taken place here too. Another seven bandits had been killed, while nine of the merchants had been martyred and seven horses had fallen. This river-valley was full of corpses and weapons and flowing with blood; it had turned into a tulip-garden of a battlefield. They had had ten pack-horses, and all their bales of goods lay scattered over the ground.

'Where is the boy so-and-so?'

'He was martyred, there he is lying bathed in blood in the river.'

'And what happened to so-and-so and so-and-so?'

'The fleeing bandits drove them ahead of them.'

It turned out that they were a caravan of fifty wealthy merchants headed for Kuşadası. The forty thieves had spotted them and attacked them here in the Alman Pass. Providentially, we turned up to aid them, and the affair came off honourably.

What should we see next? The brave servants who had gone after the bandits in the mountains now came back with seven more of them in chains, plus their horses and trappings, and three heads. One of those brave youths had been martyred. Some were rejoicing, others grieving for their brother or their master. For eleven of them had quaffed the sherbet of martyrdom during the battle in this plain.

So some of the merchants were very distraught. We tried to comfort them, and suggested that we leave this merciless pass of Alman immediately. But first we buried the dead – sixteen martyrs, including four of the merchants – in rows on a grassy hill and recited a Fatiha for their spirits. It was a great battle and they were brave men. Then we brought forward the twenty-eight bandits whom we had captured and began to question them.

'We swear by God,' they said, 'that we could no longer bear the oppression in our villages and for that reason sought to make our fortune here in the Alman Pass. Now, because of this battle, we have come to this pass and our fortune has been made. It is God's to command. The brave ram is born to be sacrificed. Destiny cannot be altered. What will be will be.'

We all assembled and deliberated about what to do. Everyone had his own idea on how to turn a profit from the situation. This humble one spoke up as follows, 'If we take these bandits in chains to the magistrate, they will say, 'I had so many jewels tucked in my waistband and so many weapons and thoroughbreds;' or else, 'They tortured us and made us tell where our money was buried in the mountains and made us dig it up and then took it.' Do you want the merit attached to performing the greatest Hajj? Then perform the greatest *gaza*, in accordance with the verse: *Thus were the evildoers annihilated. Praise be to God, Lord of the Universe!* (6:45) Here, next to your martyred brothers, let us kill them all and share out their plundered goods among ourselves. Otherwise each one of them will somehow or other get free from the magistrate's hand and resume highway robbery, and on Judgement Day you will be responsible.'

They lent ear to my advice and together we swore on the holy Koran that the matter would remain hidden in this valley. So everyone took one bandit and invoked one martyred kinsman; or, in the case of our companions, we took eight to avenge the blood of the martyred merchants. We made them kneel down and, in a single moment, with our sharpened swords, made their heads roll on the ground like polo balls and erased their inauspicious beings from the page of time.

Alman Pass was now secure. We shared out the weapons among us. The merchants only took four of the horses; the rest were distributed among our companions and slaveboys and the merchants' servants.

Loading the packhorses, we again set out from that battlefield in a southern direction and proceeded through that merciless, stony, Alman Pass. But God knows, we were brought to such a pass in this pass that we nearly passed out. It is not a German (*Alman*) pass but an unmerciful (*Alaman-ı bi-aman*) pass, and so stony that neither horse nor mule nor man can find a place to step. There are seventy or eighty narrow passages where one man with a stone could keep a thousand men from passing.

Brigands at the Alman Pass; Ephesus

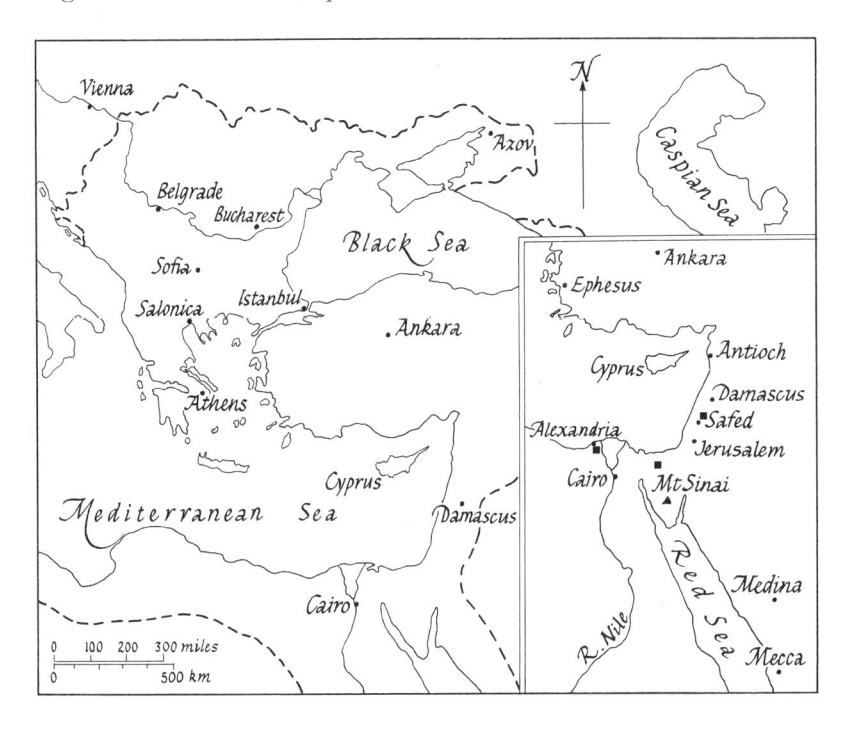

God be praised, we got through this pass safely in eight hours and reached a broad valley called Dalyan Ovası. Here we unloaded our packhorses and let our mounts graze. Whatever food and drink we had, we consumed. Then we continued on the road to Ayasuluk, passing the imperial fishing wiers at the place where the lake formed from the Alman Pass stream flows into the sea. We proceeded eastward in the Ayasuluk plain along the Menderes River, crossing the river by the seven-arched stone bridge, and went another hour southward through delightful sown fields until we reached:

Throne of Jamshid, the ancient Castle of Ayasuluk (Ephesus)
It was built at the time when Jamshid was a world-adorning emperor and he made it his capital. Later it was ruled by a Greek king named Aya Sulya, a descendant of Jamshid. Sultan Isa, the son of Aydın Bay, conquered it in the year (—) and it later was conquered by the Ottoman Sultan Bayezid the Thunderbolt at the hand of Timurtaş Pasha.

It is in the *sancak* of Sığla, governed by (—). It is a *kadi*-district at the salary level of 150 *akçe* per diem. It has a colonel of the local cavalry, a janissary commander, a castle warden and forty garrison soldiers. There are no town notables, but many indigents.

The fortification consists of a very strong, stone-built, oval-shaped fortress on a pointed blue rock-cliff, situated in a great plain with no higher ground looming above it. The circumference is 1,300 paces. There is no moat, since it is built on a sheer cliff and has forty strong towers. There is a two-layered iron gate looking down to the south. Inside the castle are twenty earth-covered houses and a small mosque. All the streets are paved since they are simply the sheer rock face.

Outside the castle, toward the south, is another castle with no buildings inside. It is a vast ruin, with noteworthy ruined structures. The gate, facing south, is a strange and marvellous, highly wrought ancient gate. Above the arches are a kind of fine depictions, like those of Bihzad, that dazzle the eye and puzzle the mind. Only in Athens does one find similar representations.

In the lower suburb outside this gate are noteworthy structures that cannot be expressed in words. It is clearly evident from the present remains of ancient buildings what a great entrepôt this city was in former times. It had 300 public baths, seven bedestans, 700 stone *hans*, 20,000 shops, 3,000 neighbourhood mosques, 800 Friday mosques, 200 medreses, 70 soup kitchens, 3,000 fountains, 1,500 primary schools; also several hundred thousand palaces and several hundred thousand private houses.

East of the city are lofty aqueducts, arches rising like rainbows into the sky. No sultan today would be capable of constructing a single such arch. They are amazing structures.

The ruined buildings are all made of white marble. Among the ruins are thousands of marble and porphyry columns, like those in Aya Sofya, lying on the ground helter-skelter. And there are thousands of arches like the Vault of Chosroes, and ruins of pools with fountain jets. Indeed, the noteworthy columns and precious rocks in the Süleymaniye and the New Mosque (*Yeni Cami*, i.e., the Valide Sultan mosque) in Istanbul have all come from here.

The reason why this city fell into ruins is that, according to the world-chroniclers, in the year (—) there was a great famine in Egypt. It reached the point that people were practising cannibalism. Finally the Egyptians sent a huge delegation by ship to the governor of Ayasuluk requesting money and grain, but they were spurned by the people of this city who did not give them even a mustard seed. So they cursed them, saying 'May your city go to ruin and may you yourselves be in need of bread and salt.'

Returning to Egypt empty-handed, they told their governor what had happened. He immediately gathered 200,000 men who removed their headgear and prayed for Ayasuluk to be ruined and for its people not to thrive. Even now, in the audience hall in Cairo, the Sura of al-An'am (6) is recited every morning as a prayer to bring about the ruin of seven cities. And one such city is this Ayasuluk, the reason for its destruction being the curse laid on it by such a great city (as Cairo).

In fact, the people of Ayasuluk are bankrupt and indigent, their granaries are empty, their salt stocks water-soaked and melted. Nevertheless, due to the spiritual influence of the great saints who rest in peace in this city, the lower suburb has about 100 earth-covered houses, twenty shops, one neighbourhood mosque, one small and oppressive bath, and one *han*. And there is one well of sweet water in the shade of a huge plane tree in the middle of the marketplace square – the water is like ice even in July. Here and there the houses have little gardens.

3. Safed and the land of Canaan

Description of the country of the Jews, the walled town of Safed

The first place on earth to be inhabited after the flood was the town of Cude (Judi) near Mosul. About it the Koranic verse was revealed: *The ark came to rest upon al-Judi* (11:44). Then Shem son of Noah built Damascus and this town of Safed. Until the time of Jacob it was so prosperous that hill and dale were full of people. It was the original homeland of the Children of Israel. Later on, when Nebuchadnezzar sought the blood of the prophet John, he massacred the Israelites and devastated Safed as well. In short, it was governed by seventy successive states until, in the year (—), Sultan Selim I took it from the despicable Circassians (i.e., Mamluks) without a blow. The troops who could not go on to Egypt he stationed there as garrison, before himself proceeding.

It is now a *sancak* in the province of Sidon. It is administered by farming the public revenues. The *sancak-bey*'s imperial *has* earns 373,800 *akçe* for him and 1,000 musketeers, leaving him a sum of 100 purses per annum. Previously it belonged to the province of Sham (Damascus) and when it was registered, had 106 *timars* and nine *zeamets*. The holders of these were not required to go on campaign but were put in charge of travellers and Muslim pilgrims, escorting them to the (Palestine) shrines, to Jerusalem and Damascus, and the seaport towns.

There are regiment commanders and commandants of janissaries in this city. It is a noble *kadi*-district at the salary level of 300 *akçe* per diem. The subdistrict (*nahiye*) consists of 400 rebellious villages, providing the *kadi* six purses per annum. The castle is in ruins. It has neither a warden nor garrison troops, nor a colonel of the local cavalry, nor a janissary colonel, nor notables. But there are many Jews. Each of the four Sunni rites has its *şeyhülislam*; and there is a chief of the descendants of the Prophet.

The citadel rises high into the sky. It is a lofty castle, which is within an hour's walk from the valleys and city below. At the very summit of the mountain is a round masonry building, an ancient, wonderful castle. At the time of the conquest, Melikü't-Tahir (al-Malik al-Zahir Baybars, in 1266) took it from the Franks only with great difficulty and had it dismantled at several places. Nowadays goats and sheep are kept there during winter. But no human beings nor any buildings are there, although the suburb below is inhabited. The houses are built one above the other, situated on places like the abyss of Ghayya in Hell. The city has seven quarters with 1,300 well-built houses covered with earth and lime.

There are (—) prayer-niches. The one with a sizeable congregation is the Sheikh Ni'ma mosque in the marketplace. A lofty dome of elegant design covers a square enclosure measuring 50 feet on each side. The interior is revetted with marble slabs to a height of a man. For two cubits above the marble the surface, made of tiles, is painted with flowers in a great variety of colours. Over the prayer-niche the following Koranic verse is written on glazed Kashan tiles: *None should visit the mosques of God except those who believe in God and the Last Day* (9:18). And over the windows flanking is the verse: *All that lives on earth is doomed to die* (55:26). Sheikh Ni'ma, the founder of the mosque, lies buried outside the qibla gate.

Nearby is the Overhanging Mosque (*Cami-i Mu'allak*). Its lower part is empty, being used as storehouses, which in fact gave rise to the name. It is reached by a flight of seven stone steps from either end. It is a large, ancient Friday mosque.

The Red Mosque is one storey but the largest of all. The governor of the city, Salih Bey, had it repaired and restored so that it is now a place like paradise. It measures 120 feet by 80 feet. Its interior is solid masonry, domed, with groined vaults. The chronogram on the pulpit reads:

> Salih renovated it in order to attain God's pleasure.
> O clever one, his Lord is the Generous, its date is: *leke'r-rıza*.
>
>   1082 (1671–2)

Over the prayer-niche the Throne Verse (2:255) is inscribed in large letters. Under the mosque and courtyard there is a cistern built with columns. In winter it is filled to the brim with water, which is drunk in July by all the populace to quench their thirst. It is collected rain-water, ice-cold, clear, and refreshing. The square courtyard is 100 feet on each side. Over the qibla gate there is a towering minaret roofed with lead. The roof of the mosque is plastered with lime.

The chronogram above the courtyard gate reads: *In the name of God the Merciful the Compassionate. Our lord and sultan, king of this world and the religion, sultan of Islam and the Muslims, slayer of infidels, heretics and rebels, Baybars al-Salihi, joint partner (?) of the Commander of the Faithful, ordered the building of this blessed Friday mosque in the year 674* (1275–6).

There are besides the Friday mosques of Eynesi; Eşertah (Eser Taha?) which is that of the Forty Martyrs; Sheikh Isa in the Suvabin quarter; one in the Kurdish quarter; and the Mismar ('Nail') mosque, called also the Mosque of the Medrese. Besides these there are neighbourhood mosques.

There are six medreses, including the Mismariye with its large building and sound endowments; one school of Koran recitation; seven primary schools; and seven dervish lodges.

There are six public baths, three of which operate both summer and winter. Near the Pasha's palace is the Amberiye bath, whose walls all around actually smell of ambergris. Its water and air and construction are very fine. The only bath I know that matches it is the Sultan Bath in Güzelhisar of Aydın. Then there is the New Bath, which is not so richly adorned. Another is the Apothecaries' bath. And one bath is now closed to the public.

There are three *hans*, including that of (—) Pasha below the citadel. It is a large *han* with an iron gate like that of a castle, and square in plan. The circumference measures 600 paces. It stands four storeys high. Previously 12,000 Jews lived in it, but at present they number only 2,000.

The city has three bedestans, two of which are unoccupied, their shops being locked up. They have now become guest houses for travellers. But the bedestan of Sinan Pasha near the Sheikh Ni'ma mosque is flourishing and in good repair. A flight of fifteen stone steps leads down to it. At both ends it is provided with iron doors. It consists of twenty shops, all built of stone. Besides these, there are another 120 shops in this city, where all precious goods are to be found.

All the houses are built of white ashlar. There is no wooden construction, except for the doors of the houses.

The most richly-adorned and solidly-built, airy and elevated, is the Pasha's palace, with seventy finely out-fitted chambers. It is reserved for the governor's residence. The upper audience hall has the following chronogram over the door:

> *My House, oppression never enter thee!*
> *Misfortune never do thy owner wrong!*
> *A charming house that shelters every guest,*
> *And grows more spacious as each guest appears.*

This is the imaret of Mehmed ibn Peri. In the year 980 (1572–3). *Honour be to our lord, the Sultan el-Melikü't-Tahir Ebu Sa'id.*

The orchards and gardens of Safed are mostly olive groves and mulberry plantations. Because it is situated on a high mountain its climate is healthy and agreeable. Its waters are exceedingly sweet. There are two springs of Melikü't-Tahir (al-Zahir Baybars) that flow from the hills about the city.

Yet, because of oppression, the inhabitants of the city are poor. Jews are more numerous than Muslims. The capitation tax from all the seven Jewish quarters is paid for 9,000. With previously 70,000 Jews living here, this was a magnificent city. Still the houses are well built and cover layer on layer of hill and dale. But there is no one living in them. They have all migrated to Salonica.

In former times Safed boasted 3,000 felt manufactories, of which forty have survived. The felt of Safed was known all over the inhabited world.

The reason for the large number of Jewish inhabitants is this, that it was the original homeland of the Children of Israel and – *saving the comparison!* – their Ka'ba and House of Sorrows. All the prophets and their descendants grew up here and here too they are buried. In the Jewish chronicles there are seven volumes treating of Safed.

Above the Jewish quarters are two Kurdish quarters. All their people wear striped cloaks. Lovely boys and girls are few. The women folk wear white head-covers.

Of the renowned kinds of food and drink, pure white bread, olives, and honey may especially be mentioned. Their handicraft and manufactures are kilims, felts, and prayer carpets. *May God increase you!*

[...]

Taking leave of the present governor, Salih Agha, and his nephew Mir Assaf, we descended from Safed a distance of one hour and a half with ten companions. On our left was **Mt Uqqab**. In olden times Nebuchadnezzar destroyed its castle. In the mountain there are over 500 caves, each one like the Cave of Orphans. The Children of Israel fled from the plague and hid themselves in these caves. Thereupon God sent them a barren wind so that all of them died in those caves. Their skeletons, heaped up, can still be seen there. At times people of the district keep their sheep and goats there during the winter.

Passing that place in a southerly direction, in one hour we reached a stream of fresh water known as the **Valley of Laymun**. It has its source at Mt Antar and here flows into Lake Minya. I passed this way when I was with Murtaza Pasha in the year 1058 (1648).

Going from there over hills and through dales and crossing barren mountains we arrived at **Ayn al-tin**, i.e. Stream of Figs. It has its source in the mountains of Acre and near this road flows into Lake Tiberias, i.e. Lake Minya. Its water is palatable and easily digested. The shores of this stream offer exceedingly dangerous ambush places and are the hunting-grounds of the brigands of the Turabi tribe.

Passing that in safety we came to **Ayn Wadi**, a small stream that comes from the mountains of the Turabi tribe and empties into Lake Minya. Though but a trickle, the water is sweet.

At this site was the great fortress of Tiberias, on the shore of Lake Minya, which Timur the unenlightened demolished on his way to Jerusalem. Reportedly it was a castle the size of Aleppo. Traces of its building are still evident. The lake is called after this fortress, properly Lake Tiberias, although popularly Lake Minya.

The province of Canaan (*Ken'an eli*) ends here.

4. Jerusalem

Description of the ancient fortress and former qibla, the Sacred House (Jerusalem)

It is called in Greek the province of Ilya (Aelia), in Syriac Makdine, in Hebrew Has (for *ha-'ir* 'the City'?), and in Arabic al-Bayt al-Muqaddas (The Holy House) or al-Quds (The Holy). It contains the shrines of 124,000 prophets. Before and after the Flood it was the qibla of mankind. When the Prophet, in response to a divine order, fled from Mecca to Medina, he was fifty-one years and nine months old. He lived for ten years in Medina. In the second year (of his stay there i.e. year 2 of the Hijra) the verse from Sura of al-Baqara *Turn your face towards the Holy Mosque* (2:144) was revealed from God through the mediation of Gabriel the Trustworthy. Thus the qibla was changed from Jerusalem to Mecca. The obligation of fasting was revealed at the same time. But the ancient qibla was Jerusalem, and it is said to be the qibla of the poor (or of the dervishes).

This noble Jerusalem has been the object of desire of the kings of all nations. Especially the Christians who, ever since Jesus was born in this city, have waged all their wars over Jerusalem. Yet other wars were also waged by Christians over Mecca – the stories of the People of the Elephant, Abraha, and the Tubbaʻ or kings of Yemen are well known.

The fortress of Jerusalem was originally built during the Caliphate of David, at the hands of Saul, because Goliath the king emerged from Aleppo and Azez and attacked Jerusalem several times. David built Jerusalem and together with King Saul fought a great battle in the place called Marj Dabiq near Aleppo. David killed Goliath with a slingshot, as attested in the verse: *David slew Goliath, and God bestowed on him sovereignty* (2:251). He became thereupon independent sultan and, duty done and booty won, returned to Jerusalem which he made even more prosperous with the booty from Goliath the king. In spite of his being a prophet and a sultan he occupied himself with smithery and produced mail coats. David is therefore the patron saint of the smiths.

Then in the year (—) Nebuchadnezzar emerged from the city of Nisibin in Kurdistan in order to avenge the blood of John the Baptist. Coming to Jerusalem he destroyed the fortifications and all its buildings, made mincemeat of its people, and killed thousands of Israelites. He did not stop wielding the sword until the blood stopped flowing from John's body. He also found Daniel in Safed, took him prisoner and brought him to Mosul.

After this Jerusalem once again flourished. During the reign of the Byzantine Emperor Heraclius, in the year 26 of the Hijra (647–8), it was besieged by Umar in person with 60,000 soldiers. It surrendered against safe conduct. Yet the inhabitants stipulated that the Church of the Holy Sepulchre, which is their main place of worship, should be left to them. Umar had a mosque built attached to the Church. He left 10,000 soldiers in the citadel and returned to Mecca, sending Amr ibn al-As to conquer Egypt.

Jerusalem

Then again, the infidels invaded Jerusalem in the year (—) (1099). Saladin, while vizier of the martyr Nur al-Din in Damascus, advanced toward Jerusalem with 100,000 soldiers and conquered it in a desperate fight (in 1187). He had the citadel dismantled, so that the infidels might not fortify it again, should they reconquer it.

In the year 922 (1516), when Jerusalem was in the hands of the Circassians (i.e., Mamluks), all the ulema and pious men went out to meet Sultan Selim I and handed him the keys to the Aqsa Mosque and the Dome of the Rock. Selim prostrated himself and exclaimed: 'Thanks be to God, I am now in possession of the first qibla.' He then made presents to all the notables and exempted them from onerous taxes. The Greek and Frankish monks showed him Umar's noble rescript. He passed it over his face and eyes and confirmed it with his own noble rescript, stipulating that the monks were exempted from the poll tax and that the Church of the Holy Sepulchre would be their place of worship as before.

He installed (—) Pasha as governor and Ahfeşzade as molla at the salary level of 500 *akçe* per diem. Jerusalem was registered as capital of a province which is still awarded as a stipend to its governor at the level of vizier, the imperial *has* earning him 257,485 *akçe* per annum. There are nine *zeamets* and 106 *timars*.

The pasha of Jerusalem has 500 soldiers at his command and is the commandant of the pilgrims' caravan of Damascus, charged with taking them to Mecca and bringing them back.

It is a prosperous province, providing its pasha an annuity of 40,000 *guruş*. But the timariots in his province are not ordered to serve in the field, but only to accompany with their banners the arriving pilgrims and conduct them to the places of pilgrimage. Altogether they number 600 men.

The Molla actually receives as much as the Pasha, because his district counts altogether 1,600 villages, to all of which his deputies are appointed, as his is a noble dignity of jurisdiction. It often happens that the priests and monks and patriarchs get material compensations and from these the Molla and the Pasha get 40,000 or 50,000 *guruş*. Especially on their infamous Festival of the Red Egg (Easter), the door of the Church of the Holy Sepulchre cannot be opened before the Pasha and the Molla arrive. From each of the five or ten thousand Christians (that come on that day) the priests take ten or fifteen *guruş* and give the Molla and the Pasha one tenth, which is a considerable sum.

According to Sultan Selim's register, the *sancaks* in the Pasha's province (of Palestine) are the following: Izzat al-Hashim (Gaza), Jabal Ajlun, Lajjun, Nablus, and Jerusalem which is the Pasha's seat. Besides there are five *sancaks* under the rule of the desert chieftains which they administer like their own possessions, yet at the same time they owe fealty to the Sultan. There are in this province some villages set aside as pious foundations, but most belong to the mounted feudal yeomen, the holders of *timar* and *zeamet*. There is also a cavalry marshal and a troop commander.

The timariots convey the Muslim pilgrims to Abraham God's Friend (*Ibrahim Khalil*, i.e. Hebron), to Bethlehem the birthplace of Jesus, and to Moses (i.e. the shrine of Nabi Musa), as the roads are insecure from the Arab brigands.

There is also a colonel of the mounted troops in Jerusalem, a commandant of the janissaries of the Porte, and a commandant of the janissaries of Damascus; muftis of the four Sunni legal rites; a supervisor of the descendants of the Prophet; and very many notables and nobles, ulema and pious men. There is also a castle warden and 100 garrison troops.

The Molla dispatches some of these troops to difficult districts and to the *kadi*-districts under his jurisdiction, which include Jerusalem, Hebron, Nablus, Ramla, Kerak, Lajjun, Jinnin. These have all been joined and form his jurisdiction. Additional *kadi*-districts may be joined to these according to the Molla's capability; or else he may only be appointed to Jerusalem. In short, it is a noble dignity of jurisdiction providing the Molla 40,000 *guruş* annually.

The Molla also has twenty officers appointed by imperial rescript for court service. First is the chief usher, appointed from the imperial stirrup, who is the porter with felt cap who seizes by imperial authority. Second is the water inspector appointed especially for Jerusalem to that office which is a coveted high post. Third is the chief architect. Fourth is the chief engineer. Fifth, the chief steward. Sixth, the chief cashier, who personally pays to the ulema the yearly gifts of the Sultan. Seventh is the treasurer. Eighth is the constable. Ninth is the market inspector. Tenth is the mayor. Eleventh is the supervisor of the bedestan. In short, the sheikhs of all the tradesmen are daily present at the Sharia court for duty.

Jerusalem has 700 *waqf*-endowments, each with its administrator who comes to the Molla with a gift and attends the court sessions.

It is a grand civil government and religious jurisdiction.

Description of the Fortress of Jerusalem

All chronicles call this country the land of Palestine. God has praised it explicitly in forty-two passages of the Koran. For that reason all the religious communities were anxious to get hold of Jerusalem, it was besieged hundreds of times and its citadel was destroyed. Finally, during the reign of Sultan Süleyman, Lala Mustafa Pasha with (jurisdiction over) twelve *sancaks* was charged with rebuilding the city walls. This was done in a manner that the tongue falls short in describing.

From the foundation of the castle that was destroyed in olden times, he built up the walls measuring forty or fifty Meccan cubits from the outside. He encompassed the Aqsa Mosque and the Dome of the Rock within the walls. It is a great square fortification like Qahqaha, every ashlar the size of a Mengerusi elephant.

The circumference of the castle and the amenities inside the wall may be described as follows:

First comes the Gate of the Maghrebis (Dung Gate), a small gate opening to the south. It has been given this name because the Maghrebis conquered the city through this gate. The chronogram above the lintel reads: *Order has been issued to construct this gate during the reign of the great sultan, Sultan Süleyman Khan, may God perpetuate his reign, in the holy month of Muharram of the year 947* (May 1540). This same chronogram is inscribed on all the gates and towers and on the corner bends in large letters.

Going along the city wall, which has here no moat, and leaving this Gate of the Maghrebis in a western direction, it is 500 stretched paces to the vault of the Water Tower. From there, again upwards to the westernmost point there are 1,000 paces until one reaches the Gate of David, which also looks south. It is new and twelve cubits high. From here to the corner of the Flat Tower (*Yassı Kulle*) is 200 paces in a western direction. This site is one corner of the fortress.

One goes from here in a northern direction. Following the edge of the moat to the east it is 600 stretched paces to the Gate of Khalil al-Rahman (Jaffa Gate). This gate opens to the west and is ten cubits high. It has a high double iron gate. It too has the chronogram above the lintel. Passing from here along the moatless skirt of the citadel in a western direction, it is 400 paces to the Crooked Tower (*Eğri Kulle*, i.e. Tancred's Tower) which is the second corner of the fortress.

From here one heads north (!). Going east of this Crooked Tower in the moat, one walks down the slope through gardens and orchards, till one comes in 900 paces to the Gate of the Iron War-mace (Damascus Gate) which looks towards the north and consists of two strong iron gates. It has been given this name because a mighty mace is suspended above the gate. Outside this gate one follows the moat in an eastern direction and comes after 100 paces to the rock-cut Cave of the Demons, referring to the demons that were here imprisoned by the prophet Solomon. It is a cave protected by a talisman and worth seeing. Continuing eastward, in the moat, in front of the Cave Tower, for another 300 paces, one comes to the Flower Gate, a small iron gate facing east (!). Thence, walking along the edge of the moat toward the east, it is 500 paces to the next corner, the Gate of Rüstem Pasha.

From here one now turns to the south, walking in the moat down the slope, it is 500 paces to the of the Tribes; it is also called the Gate of Mary, since she lies buried there (Gate of St Stephen). It is a double iron gate on the eastern side facing the Mount of Olives. From here along the moatless walls of the Aqsa Mosque it is 600 paces to the Tower of the Shrine of Mary (the Cradle of Jesus) which is the fourth corner of the fortress. This completes the square circuit of the castle of Jerusalem.

From this tower one proceeds westward, with no moat, passing through chasms and frightful places in front of the Aqsa Mosque prayer-niche, and after 800 paces arrives again at the Gate of the Maghrebis.

According to this calculation the circumference of the fortress is 7,050 paces. It has fifty-seven well-fortified towers; seventy-eight bends, i.e. corners looking at the other walls; and 4,040 embrasures between the battlements of the wall. Only there is no moat for a stretch of 1,700 paces over very stony ground from the Gate of Mary to the Gate of the Maghrebis and thence past the Gate of David as far as the northern (!) corner. The moat is not necessary along this stretch, nor is there space for it. And the moats on the other sides are not very deep, only the height of two or three men.

The citadel, just inside the Gate of Khalil al-Rahman, is small – 400 paces in circumference – and connected on one side with the main fortress. It has three layers of iron gates giving into the inside of the large fortress. From the first gate one crosses a wooden bridge to the inside of the citadel. The area between the gates is an audience hall embellished with a great many war implements. In the citadel live the castle warden and the governor's deputy; an imam, preacher and muezzins; and the garrison soldiers. There are seventy houses covered with lime, very small chambers. The castle warden has a stuccoed garden in the moat of the citadel.

The corner tower at the right-hand side of the citadel gate is the Tower of David and his noble dwelling, built by David himself. For the sake of a blessing, it is not inhabited, but is used as an ammunition depot and treasury. It has an iron door. The tower is built with ashlars measuring five to six cubits. There is no doubt that it was constructed by demons.

The moat of this citadel outside the Gate of the Friend is about 40 cubits deep and 50 Meccan cubits broad. The citadel has three storeys strongly built. Every stone is the size of an elephant. Inside is the Mosque of David with its qibla originally facing north to the Aqsa Mosque. Then, when the verse *Turn your face towards the Holy Mosque* (2:144) was revealed to Muhammad, the direction during prayers was instituted towards Mecca. Sultan Isa of the Ayyubids had this small mosque of David transformed into a Friday mosque, as attested by this chronogram inscribed on a white marble slab left of the prayer-niche:

In the name of God the Merciful the Compassionate. There is no god but God. Muhammad is the messenger of God. 'Whether he is better who founds his house on the fear of God and His good pleasure' (9:109). *'Help from God and a speedy victory'* (61:13). *This blessed tower was built by order of our lord, the glory of the world and of religion, al-Malik al-Muʿazzam ibn al-Malik al-Adil ibn Sayf al-Din ibn Abi Bakr ibn Muhammad ibn Ayyubiyan ibn Shadi, may God perpetuate his kingdom. The construction was directed by Izz al-Din, in the land of Palestine, in the year 610 (1213–4). Praise be to God, Lord of the universe.*

There are no buildings outside the fortress of Jerusalem except for the Suburb of David, which consists of 40 houses. There are only gardens and vineyards, all the buildings being inside the fortress. There are (—) Muslim quarters and 1,000 castle-like lofty palaces and other houses. All the buildings are of masonry; there is no wooden construction except for the doors. And all the houses are completely covered with lime.

There are (—) prayer-niches, two of them Friday mosques, the one within the citadel, and the other being that one designated by the decisive Koranic text: *Glory be to Him who made His servant go by night from the Sacred Temple (of Mecca) to the farther Temple* (17:1). God mentioned it in the noble Koran. Besides these there are no Friday mosques, all others being ordinary ones.

Description of the ancient *mescid*, the Mosque (*cami*) of Aqsa[66]

The building was begun by David. During his caliphate a plague broke out among the Children of Israel. When it subsided, due to the prayer of the prophet David, the *mescid* of Aqsa was built on the site of his prayer. Before its completion, however, David passed away and the prophet Solomon carried on the construction. David went to God's mercy after the *gaza* against Goliath, the foundation of this mosque having been raised to the height of a man.

The caliphate passed to Solomon who, being sultan over all creatures, ordered the demons to complete the construction, which they did after a long period. But on that very day, as Solomon was leaning on his royal staff while watching the finishing of the mosque, the divine command came forth: *Return to your Lord* (89:28), and his noble spirit ascended to heaven while his body was still leaning on his staff. No one was aware of this event.

As the *mescid* of Aqsa was being purified, Solomon's wise men, including the vizier Asaf Barkhaya, realised that the work was complete. They dismissed the jinns and fairies before the sunset prayer and confined the demons in the ancient prison, situated in the moat outside the Gate of the Pillar (Damascus Gate), and bound them with a talisman. In the course of time they all perished. Even nowadays one may witness their skeletons in that cave. But it is a gloomy place and one shudders on looking into it.

Later on a worm gnawed into Solomon's staff, who thus fell to the ground. The learned men buried him next to his father David. These events are told at length in many estimable books.

Then a divine command made the Aqsa Mosque into a qibla. Many kings followed. Each built an annex to the mosque so that it became as beautiful as paradise. When the Prophet had spent ten years in Medina after the Hijra, the verse *Turn your face towards the Holy Mosque* (2:144) was revealed, whereupon the qibla was changed from Jerusalem to Mecca. But it was about Jerusalem that the verse *Let them circle the Ancient House* (22:29) was revealed. At present it is the Ka'ba of the poor (or of the dervishes).

It is a large light-filled mosque, 300 feet in length from the qibla gate to

---

66 Evliya usually carefully distinguishes between *mescid*, a small neighbourhood mosque, and *cami*, a large mosque used for the Friday congregational worship. The Aqsa Mosque clearly falls in the second category; but Evliya also refers to it as *mescid* because it is identified with the mosque called *al-masjid al-aqsa* in Koran 17:1 (translated as 'the farther Temple' in the citation just above).

Jerusalem

the prayer-niche. Its width from the prayer-niche of Umar on the eastern side to that of the Malikis is 400 feet. Inside are seventy large and small columns of porphyry, etc., both artificial and natural.[67] Each column is a jewel in itself, worth an Egyptian treasure.

Both aisles of the mosque are later additions, with arches and domes raised above artificial columns. But the original building in the centre is in tiers, one above the other, with arches above natural columns, topped by a ridged wooden ceiling, painted in various colours, resting on twenty beams of cypress wood – a marvellous sight. The central dome rises 40 cubits from the floor, while the annexes on either side are twenty cubits high.

The interior of the mosque has a total of 120 arches, large and small.

The light-filled dome over the prayer-niche is the highest part of the building and unrivalled on the face of the earth. It is 50 cubits high and supported by the other domes as though it were their crown. It is elliptical, while the other domes are round. Inside it is embellished with gilded glass-mosaic designs in iridescent colours representing the Tuba tree of paradise and multicoloured flowers. It is a dome of *light upon light* around which is the verse *God is the light of the heavens and the earth* (24:35).

The restoration of the mosque by Sultan Süleyman and the prayer-niche and pulpit are beyond description. True, the pulpit is of wood; yet, in order to show his skill, the accomplished master designed such a finely-wrought pulpit that it is like witchcraft. As to the prayer-niche, it is profusely gilded, as if it were a lapis-lazuli enamel work studded with jewels. Whatever of precious metals or stones is known on earth has been carved like bird's eyes and inserted by the accomplished master into that jewel-like prayer-niche of indescribably beauty.

Above the prayer-niche – and in accordance with the artistry of the prayer-niche, pulpit and dome – the master glass artisan Serhoş İbro ('Drunkard Abe'), who was one of Sultan Süleyman's teachers, made twelve magical mosaic panels of multicoloured iridescent bits of glass. As they reflect the rays of the sun, the mosque, which was light, becomes *light upon light* and the congregants' eyes shine with reverence and humility as they pray. Aside from these panels there are 105 panes of rock-crystal and cut glass.

---

67 Here 'artificial' or 'man-made' (*ameli*) probably means joined out of several pieces, while 'natural' or 'God-made' (*sunʿ-ı huda*) means carved out of a single piece. 'Natural' in the next paragraph translates *yed-i kudret*, lit. 'Hand of Power', also implying God-made not man-made.

The wall on the prayer-niche side is covered with coloured and veined marble slabs the height of three men. If you examine them closely you can observe God's handiwork, so shiny and polished are they. In this wall also, to the left and right of the prayer-niche, are seven windows that look onto the Rock outside. Facing the pulpit is the muezzins' gallery set like a pavilion on twelve well-proportioned slender columns. There is also a preacher's seat, like the throne of Solomon, with cunningly carved Indian woodwork like Fahri cutouts.

The silk prayer-carpets in this mosque are marvellous, each one a masterpiece of Turkish or Arab or Persian weaving, unmatched in other mosques. And there are thousands of costly and highly-wrought chandeliers and 7,000 lamps. 1,000 of these latter are lit every night, and the rest on holidays and festivals, so that the interior of the mosque, already luminous, becomes *light upon light*.

The mosque has ten gates, seven of which open to the south. The central gate rises to a height of fifteen cubits. It is of ancient make and of enamelled brass. The three gates flanking it on either side are shorter but also masterworks and worth seeing. To the left is the Gate of Hızır; to the right, the Gate of the Malikis; at the foot of the minber, the Gate of the Medrese. Outside the south gates are vaults over six piers, forming a kind of vestibule.

When one visits the Aqsa Mosque, one comes first to the prayer-niche of Umar, in the east corner, where he performed his prayers during a whole week after the conquest. Next is the prayer-niche of David, where prayers used to be offered while the foundations were dug. To the left of it, on a stand, is the ancient Koran in the handwriting of Uthman, in Kufic characters, as though written by the Hand of Power. One visits next the Station of Jesus, to the right of the pulpit; it is a praying-place behind a well-wrought iron grill and has a separate entrance. Finally one comes to the Station of Hızır at the gate on the left side of the mosque. God be praised, I visited all of them and offered at each two prostrations beseeching their intercession.

There are 800 salaried servants employed at this Aqsa Mosque. It has imams for the four Sunni rites and as many preachers. On Fridays the preacher ascends the pulpit with sword in hand – it is the sharp sword that belonged to Umar himself. Each preacher is on duty for a week. There are fifty muezzins, reciters of litanies, masters of ceremonies, chanters of hymns in praise of the Prophet, chanters of *devir*, reciters of one of the thirty parts of the Koran, and caretakers. All these offices are paid from

Jerusalem

the private purse of the Sultan. The agent in charge of the annual sultanic gifts comes every year and distributes the emoluments.

The domes of the Aqsa Mosque are completely covered with lead. All the domes are topped by golden finials, to the height of a man, dazzling to behold.

Description of the Dome of the Rock

From the Aqsa Mosque one proceeds north through a meadow and then 200 paces over flagstones of white unhewn marble laid out by order of Sultan Süleyman. There is a large round basin made of one huge block of marble; Sultan Süleyman saw it in his dream and it was constructed to his specification when he woke up in the morning. It is unmatched on the face of the earth, a remarkable radiant basin made by God's handwork that occupies the centre of this great courtyard.

Passing this, one continues northward another twelve paces and comes to a flight of twenty-two white marble steps leading to the Dome of the Rock. Their width is twenty cubits, so that 1,000 pilgrims could ascend them without crowding. At the top of these steps one beholds the Holy Rock, or rather the structure that encloses it, in the very centre of the courtyard. When one sees it, gleeming like a plastered pavilion, one recites this prayer: *O God, put a light in my heart and a light in my ear and a light in my eye. Make me a light by Your mercy, O most merciful of the merciful.*

Coming from the direction of the Aqsa Mosque, there is a tiny pulpit at the foot of the courtyard gate. Here pilgrims take their shoes in their hands and walk barefoot 100 paces over the white marble flagstones until they arrive at the gate of the Dome of the Rock where they leave their shoes in the custody of the doorkeepers and start their visit.

It was Abd al-Malik ibn Marwan who first started the construction of this Holy Rock in the year 85 (704). Subsequently, since it is the former qibla, many kings and sultans built annexes to it.

In the year (—) Sultan Süleyman, having conquered Belgrade at the beginning of his reign and having taken Rhodes from the (Knights of) Malta and got the wealth of Korah, and having become an independent sultan, one blessed night saw the Prophet in his dream.

'O Süleyman,' he said, 'you will live forty-eight years and make many *gazas*. Your descendants will not be cut off till the end of time. My intercession will be always extended to you. However, you should spend these spoils on Mecca and Medina, and for the fortification of Jerusalem, lest the infidels invade it during the reigns of your followers. You should also install a water-basin in its courtyard and embellish the Dome of the Rock and offer annual gifts to the dervishes there and rebuild Jerusalem.'

Such being the order of the Prophet, Sultan Süleyman at once rose from his sleep and sent from his spoils of *gaza* 1,000 purses each to Mecca and Medina and Jerusalem. He dispatched the Grand Architect (Sinan) to Jerusalem with the required material. And he transferred Lala Mustafa Pasha from the governorship of Egypt to that of Syria, charging him with carrying out the restoration of Jerusalem. The pasha gathered all the master measurers and marble-carvers and painters available in Cairo, Damascus and Aleppo and sent them to Jerusalem.

They embellished the noble city and the elegant Rock to such an extent that the verse *These are the gardens of Eden, enter and dwell there forever* (cf. 39:73) was justly written over the Gate of Paradise of the noble Rock. Verily, it is a replica of a pavilion in paradise. This humble one has travelled for thirty-eight years through seventeen empires and has viewed countless buildings, but I have never seen one that so resembled paradise.

When a person enters, he stands dumbfounded and amazed, with finger to mouth. It is a light-filled mosque (*cami*!) like a Palace of Khawarnaq in the middle of a plain paved with white marble. From the outside the courtyard is 300 paces in circumference. The building is octagonal. The outside is covered with veined marble and porphyry casements, to the height of three men, each slab manifesting God's handiwork.

Between these casements and the eaves of the dome is a layer of finely-wrought and delightfully painted tiles inscribed in blue with the *Ya Sin*, the calligraphy being in the style of Ahmed Karahisari. At each corner (of the octagon) such verses as *'Peace!' shall be the word spoken by a merciful God* (36:58) and *Nor can I succeed without God's help* (11:88) are written in large letters.

Above these inscribed tiles are spouts for the rain-water made of tinned copper. Further up are the eaves of the dome, covered all around by lead sheets. And above the eaves, the drum is enclosed with painted tiles, ten cubits high and of excellent execution.

Then the blue and light-filled dome rises into the sky. It is not round like other domes, but elliptical like the dome over the shrine of Jalaladdin Rumi in Konya. The finial is twelve cubits high, so they say, and so richly gilt that its glittering can be seen at a distance of a day's journey. The Rock is under this lofty dome.

This shrine has four doors: the (—) Gate looking south, the (—) Gate

Jerusalem

looking east, the Gate of Paradise looking north, and the (—) Gate looking west. These double doors are of yellow brass, like gold – no master could nowadays execute such work – and are ten cubits high. Each one has double curtains of embroidered broadcloth, for the rainy season in Jerusalem is severe.

Inside these doors there are four zones (concentric circles) until one reaches the Rock. In the first zone, the inner wall, like the outer wall just described, is covered with varicoloured and veined marble and porphyry slabs. They are so cut as to form pairs: placed side by side, they produce many curious inscriptions and designs. This is so on the outside as well. Thus, as one enters the (—) Gate in the direction of the Rock, on the encasing marble to the right of the door is the picture of two cocks, beak against beak, with outspread wings. By God's command, there are many such animal and floral designs in this veined marble that are visible when one looks close.

In the wall of this first zone are (—) windows overlooking the courtyard. Above them are panels of stained glass with marvellous colours and such inscriptions as *There is no god but God, Muhammad is the messenger of God* and *God is the light of the heavens and the earth* (24:35), or the names of the first four caliphs. It is licit magic.

The inner part of the first zone is not a wall but a circle of twenty-four lofty columns connected by arches which support the high dome. Sixteen of the twenty-four are monoliths, wrought by the Hand of Power, veined porphyry columns of indescribable beauty. The other eight are artificial square piers. The master builder lavishly adorned them with richly gilt ornamentations, like the enamel on a timepiece or the paintings of Mani. When the sun's rays fall through the stained window glass on these piers, the effect is dazzling to one unaccustomed to the sight.

The ceiling between these twenty-four columns and the wall is tooled camel leather, with designs that Bihzad, Mani, Shah Quli, Vali Jan or Agha Riza could not achieve with a paintbrush. This ceiling is divided into eight compartments, each with designs in a different pattern.

Under the arches supported by this colonnade are balconies for people to walk around and light the oil lamps. In front of this row of columns, in the first wall, is the Hanafi prayer-niche where a large congregation offers the five daily prayers. It has an imam and muezzins attached to it, and there is a muezzins' gallery over the door leading to the cave of the Rock, but there is no pulpit. Costly silken carpets are spread out on the floor.

The inner part of the second zone has another row of variegated porphyry columns, numbering twelve in all, like rubies, each worth the annual *harac* of Turkey. The dome above, full of divine lights, rests on this circle of columns. The ceiling between the second row of columns and this third row is also tooled camel leather. It is divided into sixteen compartments, each displaying the magical skill of a past master.

Between these columns of the third row, all around, an iron grill has been placed. It is almost miraculous, like the work of David the ironmonger. There are doors in four places through this iron grill to enter the Holy Rock. They are highly-wrought doors that open to the four cardinal points.

Inward from this grill is another layer, a railing of cypress-wood inlaid with mother-of-pearl, that surrounds the Holy Rock. It has no door or chute, and no one is allowed to go beyond it. Only the very noble *(—) -zade* enters the enclosure once a year to sweep the dust. All pilgrims circumambulate the Rock outside the railing.

Description of the Holy Rock

It should not be concealed from my brethren pilgrims and travellers that the so-called Holy Rock is a white rock enclosed by this railing and, following its edge, 100 paces in circumference. Through the railing one perceives a flat rock, called the Holy Rock (*Sakhrat Allah*, lit. Rock of God). Some commentators are of the opinion that the verse *His are the keys of the heavens and the earth* (42:12) means to say, 'My beloved Muhammad! I created the face of the earth, then I locked it with keys, i.e., I secured it with mountains.' Others interpret 'keys' as first of all Mt Arafat and second the Holy Rock; and upon this second key the divine glance was fastened, so that Jerusalem was the place of prayer of the tribes of jinn.

Even in that remote time the Holy Rock was a place of pilgrimage and the qibla of mankind, as mentioned above. Then the Prophet received the gift of prophecy at the age of forty in Mecca where he lived for another thirteen years. When he was fifty-one years and nine months old, Gabriel the Trustworthy came from God and said, 'O Muhammad! God greets you and wishes that you visit His Jerusalem by means of the rolling up of space.'[68]

So the Beloved of God performed the rolling up of space together with

---

68 *Tayy-i mekan*, defined by Redhouse as a going from one place to another in a miraculous way regardless of distance.

Gabriel the Trustworthy. Some intoxicated (?) persons say no, he went from Mecca to Jerusalem together with Buraq. While there is controversy on this point, all agree that he came to Jerusalem (on the Night Journey) where all the spirits of the prophets welcomed him. He performed his prayers in the grotto under the Holy Rock. No sooner did he pass his hands over his face than Gabriel again came from God and said, 'O Muhammad! God greets you and has sent Buraq, who is a spark from the paradise of Firdaws, bidding you mount and see His Throne and Seat, His Tablet and Pen, and His eight paradises, and to behold His beauty without intermediary.'

The Prophet obeyed the divine order, left the Grotto of the Rock and made two prostrations on the Holy Rock. Even now the marks of his noble head while prostrating and the impressions made by his blessed knees on the Rock are still visible – so they say, but no one is allowed to visit them.

After that the Prophet mounted Buraq with a *besmele* and, reciting the verse *Embark, in the name of God it shall set sail and cast anchor* (11:41) and striking Buraq with the whip of monotheism he easily rose to the highest heaven. Hearing a loud noise behind him he turned his blessed head and saw that the Holy Rock had left its mooring and was crying, 'O Muhammad! Take me along into God's presence.' Immediately the Prophet addressed the Rock thus, '*O Holy Rock! Remain suspended, by God's permission.*' Thereupon the Rock remained suspended in the air, by God's permission, at the point it had reached, not touching the ground anywhere. And because it is suspended between heaven and earth it is called the Hanging Rock. But it is the Holy Rock and, according to the chroniclers, the second of the two 'keys' that were created on the face of the earth. *Knowledge is with God.*

According to the *Tevarih-i Tuhfe* there are two rocks which came from the heavenly paradise. One is the Black Stone (in the Ka'ba) which was originally ruby-red. During Noah's flood it remained in the water of the abyss, and sinners wiped their faces against it. Thus it changed its colour and became the Black Stone. And the other is this Holy Rock. *Knowledge is with God.*

The late Sultan Ahmed (I, reg. 1603–17) had a richly gilt canopy made, the cover of which was a curtain studded with gold and jewels, and fastened it to the surrounding columns to make a baldachin over the Rock. From this baldachin to the highest point of the dome is a height of 40 to 50 cubits. The interior of this indigo-coloured dome is covered over its whole surface with gold, studded with precious stones set in enamel. The one who painted all four sides is the painter known as Shah Quli.

When the Holy Rock flew after the Prophet and remained suspended in midair by his command, a large cavern remained underneath, which is a shrine that can hold 200 men. It is entered through a door of grilled iron that is reached after descending (—) stone steps under the muezzins' gallery behind the Hanafi prayer-niche. Below it there is a spacious room and a prayer place for pious pilgrims.

One of the Caliphs of bygone days had a thin partition wall erected underneath the Holy Rock so that pilgrims would not be overawed at seeing it suspended, but could offer their prayers with presence of mind and absence of fear. For many a pregnant woman who had entered the cavern and seen the Rock suspended had miscarried at the very sight. Yet there is still a space between the wall and the rock, enough to put a finger or, in some places, an entire hand!

[...]

God be praised, I visited all the sites (in the Haram area) in ten days and ten nights during Ramadan of 1082 (January 1672). And I completed a Koran recitation on the Night of Power (27 Ramadan) in the temple of the Aqsa Mosque and bestowed the religious merit accrued therefrom upon the spirits of those departed believers buried in Jerusalem.

[...]

Description of the interior of the settlement of Jerusalem

It should be known to the world-viewing lovers that this city of Jerusalem, although it appears small, yet contains 240 prayer-niches. Aside from the Aqsa Mosque and the congregational mosque in the citadel they are all medreses and dervish convents and small neighbourhood mosques.

There are seven Hadith schools, ten schools of Koran recitation, and forty primary schools.

Each of the seventy dervish orders has a convent, including the Qadiri, the Badawi, the Sa'di and the Rufa'i. The most frequented is the Mevlevi convent just inside the Gate of the Pillar; it is also a place of promenade. All of these have a contingent of dervishes who perform a Muhammadan ceremony (i.e., *zikr*) every blessed night, and all have sound endowments.

There are six great *hans*, including those of Ghawriya, Khasakiya, the Soup Kitchen, and the Marketplace.

There are six public baths: the Mother Mary Bath, with fine air and water; the Sultan Bath; the Shifa Bath, whose water has curative properties; the Bath of the Spring; the Bath of the Rock; and the Bath of the Patriarch, called so because it is mainly frequented by Christians and is near their quarter.

There are three soup kitchens that distribute food to sojourners. The Khasakiya soup kitchen has sound endowments.

There are eighteen fountains, including that of Sultan Süleyman. They all have chronograms indicating the year 947 (1540–1). Aside from these there are seventy places in the city with flowing water in pools and jets. The water was brought from a stony and forested area near Khalil al-Rahman (Hebron), four hours away, by Sultan Süleyman. He spent an Egyptian treasure and made Jerusalem run with water – a remarkable public works.

Previously the only water in the city was what accumulated in cisterns. Thus, between the Gate of Mary and the Hıtta Gate there is a large cistern, now empty, known as the Lake of the Children of Israel; it is 50 cubits deep, 100 paces long and 80 paces wide. Other cisterns are found in the moat outside the Gate of the Pillar. There are also lakes, now dried up, in the moat outside the Gate of Mary. And there used to be cisterns in the Harams of the Aqsa Mosque and the Rock. The city depended on them; but Sultan Süleyman obviated the need for them by channeling a great river, so now all who satisfy their thirst utter a Fatiha on behalf of his noble spirit – *may God have mercy on him*.

The royal marketplace of this city contains 2,045 shops, according to the market inspector's register. But the roads are narrow. Most of the market consists of vaulted stone buildings, like those in Aleppo. All around the Han of the Marketplace is the bazaar of the mounted troops where precious items of every sort can be found. The Long Market and the markets of the goldsmiths, wool carders and silk merchants are vaulted stone buildings, never marred with mud. The shoe market, just inside the (—) Gate near the Rock, is also a stone building.

All the streets in this city are paved with pure white polished stone. The major thoroughfare – extending from the grain market to the door of Umar's mosque, attached to the wall of the Church of the Holy Sepulchre – has paving-stones the size of kilims. They say it was constructed by Solomon's demons.

There are water dispensaries in forty places.

While there is no separate bedestan with iron gates, precious stuffs from all over the world are found here, because it is a prosperous city and crowded entrepôt.

There are seven churches in this city, two Jewish (!), two Armenian, and three Greek. Among them is the **Church of the Holy Sepulchre**, belonging to the Greeks. It was built by Yanko ibn Madyan (who is?) Alexander of the Greeks. Above the door is an inscription in Greek language giving the date of construction. It was – *saving the comparison!* – the Ka'ba of the Christians during the lifetime of Jesus.

Even now 5,000 or 10,000 hell-destined infidels gather here every year on their infamous Festival of the Red Egg (Easter). Greeks and Armenians come from the seven climes, and fractious Franks from eighteen kingdoms. On the days of their assembly here, the Pasha and the Molla and *şeyhülislam* and the notables of the province, as well as all the Ottoman military personnel, fully armed, stand ready in front of the Church to prevent 10,000 infidels from swarming into it to perform their pilgrimage. The trustee of the Church utters a benediction upon the Sultan of Islam and a malediction upon the infidels. The Pasha and the Molla break the seal of the Church's door and open it, because for the rest of the year it is sealed shut.

Notwithstanding, there are 200 or 300 permanent residents – more like prisoners, actually – priests, monks, patriarchs and other kinds of ecclesiastics belonging to the Franks, Greeks, Armenians, Copts, and other Christian communities. Their food and drink comes from their soup kitchens attached to the churches in the surrounding districts. It is brought by servants and handed to the priests inside through a hole in the door.

Thus the churchmen on the inside practise their austerities for an entire year, shut off from the world. On the day when the door is opened, in the presence of the Pasha and the Molla, there is an exchange of personnel, some going in and some coming out. At this juncture, those infidels who wish to perform their pilgrimage are charged ten gold pieces each for the privilege of entering, and this sum is divided between the Pasha and the Molla.

On that day and until the evening there is pandemonium, as the infidels celebrate their infelicitous festival. After the evening prayer the Pasha shuts the door and everyone leaves the Church. But armed guards remain stationed in the rest of the city and at the fortifications, because sometimes 20,000 infelicitous infidels are gathered here.

The same procedure occurs for three consecutive days, with the Church

Jerusalem 333

door opened in the morning and closed at night. The funds accrued thereby are distributed among the *ulema* and sheikhs and other pious men of the Muslims; for the income of the Church of the Holy Sepulchre is a kind of *zeamet* belonging to the populace of Jerusalem. At the end of three days, when their infamous festival is finished, criers go through the town announcing the fact, and all the infidel pilgrims scatter to perform their other visits.

In sum, there is no great cathedral on the face of the earth so worthy of notice, unless it be the Stephan Monastery in Vienna. But this one is even more finely built and embellished. The walls are covered with variegated designs, the work of masters who practise their art even today. The intricate carving in the marble revetments at the windows and arches is beyond compare, like Fahri paper cutouts. On either side of the door are three slender marble columns. Left of the door is a highly-wrought cupola-topped pavilion of Constantine, reached by seventeen stone steps – a marvellous vault like the pavilion of Chosroes. In front of the door the courtyard is paved with white marble.

This humble one visited Jerusalem several times. But in the year 1058 (1648) – the year of the enthronement of Sultan Mehmed (IV) – when Zileli Çavuşzade Mehmed Pasha was governor of Jerusalem province, I received permission to break the seal and tour the inside of the Church of the Holy Sepulchre.

The door opens to the Muhammadan qibla (i.e., south). I entered, saying '*I take refuge in God.*' Upon entering, seven domes, great and small, come into view. The central dome is that of the ridged roof, a large inverted (?) dome constructed on artificial piers. The interior is gilded glass enamel, at the level of magical Rumi painting.

Another well-proportioned dome is constructed on four red porphyry columns, each one worth the annual revenue of Turkey. These columns are so highly polished that one can see one's features reflected in them.

The 'qibla' of this church – *saving the comparison!* – is a gilt semi-dome on the eastern side.

Another lofty dome, attached to the western side of the central dome, resembles that of Aya Sofya in Salonica, except that this one is open in the middle. According to the chronicle of Ibn Abbas, there were 882 years between the death of Alexander the Great and the birth of the Beloved of God (the Prophet); and according to the Greek histories there were 600 years from the time of Jesus to that of the Seal of the Prophets. When he was born on the night of Monday, the 12th of the month of Rabiʿ al-awwal, the Vault of Chosroes and the Pavilion of Khawarnaq and the dome of Aya Sofya (in Istanbul) and this dome of the Church of the Holy Sepulchre all collapsed. Repairs were attempted several times with the aid of the kings, but failed each time. Now the cover is open and birds are kept out with wire mesh. Later, with funds provided by one of the kings, a smaller dome was constructed underneath this open dome; it too is a remarkably fine object.

The Christian Greeks reside to the south of this dome. The Franks reside toward the large door. The Armenians are to the north. Every corner has a different nation and language. But the Greeks are in charge. The reason is that when Umar conquered Jerusalem from the Byzantine emperor, he renewed the pact that had been drawn up between the monks and the Prophet and gave this Church of the Holy Sepulchre into the hands of the Greeks, exempting all the monks from the poll tax. Later, when Sultan Selim I conquered Jerusalem, the monks produced the pacts of the Prophet and Umar and the other kings of Egypt. Selim confirmed them, and they are reconfirmed whenever an Ottoman sultan assumes the throne. That is why the Greeks are in charge.

The cellars of this church, which run underneath it from end to end, are full of the votive offerings that have arrived here from the various Christian kingdoms of the seven climes for thousands of years – only God could reckon them. The highly-wrought and jewel-encrusted chandeliers and oil-lamps are not to be found in any other church. And I can't tell you how many idols and icons and statues there are, each one like Wadd and Suwaʿ and Yaghuth and Yaʿuq (pre-Islamic idols mentioned in 71:23). There are also the portraits of the kings who endowed repairs and sent votives, like the work of Azar (father of Abraham), which astound the observer.

On the side of the prayer-niches (i.e. altar), over a gallery, is a statue of Jesus – *saving the comparison!* – with his hands raised in prayer as though in supplication. I enquired about it and they told me it was the Spirit of God (i.e. Jesus). Indeed, the statue seemed alive (lit. having a spirit – *ẕi-ruḥ*). Whatever direction you look, it too looks in that direction. If you move right or left, it seems to follow you. If you smile it smiles back, and if you cry it starts to weep. God knows, even Mani or Bihzad, Arzhang or Vali Jan would be incapable of drawing such a figure. This ancient church contains many such magical depictions, recalling the verse:

> You can depict the fuzz on his cheek
> And the beauty-mark on his arm;
> But, O Bihzad, how can you draw
> His coquetries and charm?

In front of this statue of Jesus is a large crystal lamp, suspended in the middle of the dome. There is a superstitious belief that this lamp burns by a divine miracle. But this humble one examined it very closely and discovered the secret. The lamp is made of precious rock-crystal or cut glass or plain crystal, and is highly-wrought and studded with gems. The chain by which it is suspended in the middle of the dome is curiously wrought and jewelled as well.

The reason it burns on their notorious Festival of the Red Egg (Easter) is this: There is a zinc jar concealed in lead at the apogee of the dome. It contains olive oil mixed with a small amount of naphtha. During the days of the festival, because of the heat, the oil in the jar drips down through that highly-wrought chain and fills the lamp, with none of the infidels aware of it. The wall on the eastern side of the Church, above the prayer-niche which is their 'qibla' (i.e., altar), has been embellished by the clever master builder with panes of crystal and/or glass. At noon on the Red Egg days, the glass panes get very hot from the beating of the sun. This heat in turn affects the large lamp, which bursts into flame.

If the weather happens to be cloudy on those days, and the sun is not strong enough to produce this effect, one of the clever monks secretly climbs on top of the dome and kindles the oil mixed with naphtha at the tip of the chain. The fire runs down the chain, in plain view of the infidels standing below, who think that it is fire from heaven. Awestruck, they remove their hats and cry *Kiryeleys, Kiryeleys!*

In this manner the fire of Nimrod descends into that lamp and lights up the interior of the Church. The monks use the fire in that lamp to kindle the thousands of candles that the infidels have in their hands, and the infidels in turn take those nefarious camphor candles and distribute the fire throughout the Christian world. Vast sums are earned from this trade as well. It is indeed a strange art of the lamp. Even the monks who expend their lives in this church are not aware of it. Only the one who attends this lamp knows about it, and he keeps it to himself, only passing on the secret to another one before he dies.

In the middle of this dome there is a canopy attached to the piers on all four sides by tent ropes. It is precious stuff of thin material, embroidered with gold. The floor of the church has no carpets, but rather is paved with tiny precious stones, 'bird's-eye' work, like Indian marquetry.

All around this church are hundreds of expensive chairs, each one the memento of a king or other sort of infidel nobility. On the eastern side, under an arch, is a statue of Mother Mary holding, as it were, the baby Jesus in her embrace. This statue too seems alive (lit. having a spirit – *zi-ruh*), the mother of the Spirit of God (*Ruhullah*, i.e. Jesus). Her necklace of pearls and rubies and diamonds is worth five Egyptian treasures. There are various other statues as well, each the relic of one infidel or another.

This Church also houses Jesus's clogs, his black cloak, his waistband made of date-palm fronds, and his black turban. On one jewelled casket is one of his genuine Gospels; in another, the pact of the Prophet, sealed with his seal reading *There is no god but God*. All the pacts acceded to by his successors are also preserved in this Church.

The austerities practised by the monks here are certainly admirable, though we do not look favourably on them; for, according to our religion, *There is no monkery in Islam*.

The wonder of this place is that, with so much beautiful adornment, it lacks spirituality; it is more like a tourist attraction.

After touring the Church and performing two prostrations in a corner, I prayed that it one day become a Muslim place of worship, and came outside. The monk who showed me around had the appearance of being a heretic of the infidels. I put this question to him, 'You devils! Why do you worship these idols you have made? Why do you greet them and revere them and take them as your gods?'

'By God,' he replied, 'we do not worship them, nor do we bow down before them. Only our Greeks are a bunch of stupid and credulous people. Our priests cannot get them to understand religious doctrines through preaching, so they point to those images. Also, anyone who sends a votive offering to our monastery, or who sponsors some repair, we make a statue of him and inscribe his name on it as so-and-so the donor of such-and-such. Or we bury him in the monastery, having got thousands of ducats from him, and people who see his grave or his statue pay him reverence. This constitutes our *zeamet*. This is how we earn money for ourselves and for the pashas and for you. As for bowing down and worshipping, that we do to God alone.'

Thus he put a good construction on their idol-worship.

Jerusalem

Seven steps southward from this Church along the main road is a bell-tower connected to the church wall. It rises twenty storeys into the sky. But the bell does not function, since Umar tore down the summit of the tower. But there is an organ-loft here, again attached to the church. On their unholidays they play the Psalms of David on the organ in the *rehavi* musical mode, which stuns the listener.

Here we went up some stairs and through a door inside. It turned out to be the Church's soup kitchen, with some 200 dirty and ignorant cooks. The food prepared here suits the austere diet of the monks – we were told it is completely vegetarian.

All the buildings of this Church are covered with thick lead, each tile being four spans square, not three cubits as in Istanbul. The lead is mixed with quite a bit of gold, as we were told by some goldsmiths, and wherever there is gold there is also lead.

Emerging from the kitchen door back out to the main road (one comes to the Mosque of Umar).

{**Concerning the founder of the Church of the Holy Sepulchre.** According to the Greek chronicles, Constantine founded Istanbul 328 years after the birth of Jesus. His mother, Lady (*Mayfirav*) Helena, was the daughter of a king of the city of Ruha (Urfa, Edessa). She came to Jerusalem with 40 million of Constantine's money and found some relics of Jesus. While constructing buildings she had endowed, she found in Jerusalem an ancient patriarch of the Magi named Makarios. It seems that the Jews had crucified Jesus at this priest's instigation and he knew the tree (or piece of wood) on which the crucifixion happened. Eventually he showed Helena the place. She excavated and found a grave and three trees (or pieces of wood) in the shape of crosses.

The Christians claim that they lay those trees (or pieces of wood) one by one over the corpse inside that grave and it suddenly came to life and stood up. That day – which is the 14th of September – is still observed by Christians who throw crosses into water (? – lacuna in the text). The infidels' reverence for the cross stems from this event. The resurrection of that corpse when the crosses were laid on it is recorded in the Coptic and Greek chronicles.

After discovering these crosses Helena had them preserved in a jewelled gold casket. She built this Church of the Holy Sepulchre in seven years. The Christians believe (? – lacuna in the text) that it was built over that resurrected corpse, and that that was actually the corpse of Jesus – God forbid! – and that he subsequently rose into heaven. Others say no, after being resurrected he summoned his people (to faith) and then died. Still others are the messianics who say he is the Spirit of God, and that the prophet Idris and the prophet Jesus are alive in heaven (? – lacuna in the text). Such are the wayward Christians among whom doubt and dissention have arisen.

The aforementioned Helena repaired (!) the Church of the Holy Sepulchre and the Aqsa Mosque, embellished the Dome of the Rock, and renovated Bethlehem, making each of them like paradise and endowing soup kitchens. On her way back to Turkey, she slaughtered myriads of Jews. She entered Constantinople in grand procession and presented Constantine with the golden casket containing the crosses from Jesus's grave, saying they were relics of Jesus and the name of God. He rubbed his face on the crosses and preserved them. This is how the Church of the Holy Sepulchre was founded.}

5. Sheikh Bekkar the Naked in Damascus

One day, while I was paying court to Kara Murtaza Pasha in Damascus, ten stalwart youths in his retinue came to me and said: 'Evliya Çelebi, please get a leave for us from the treasurer. We're going to visit our relatives in the Turkman district.'

I didn't like the idea. 'Perhaps the Pasha will want to go out riding when you are gone,' I said. 'If he asks where you are, and is told that you went out, what will become of you?' I did not ask leave from the treasurer, but they got it anyway, using the key-boy as intermediary. Then they came to my room and said, 'Without you we have no life. Don't be a spoil-sport. You have to come with us.' So I went along, willy-nilly.

As the eleven of us fine gentlemen were sauntering through the crowd in the Sinaniye Market, we saw coming toward us the above-mentioned Sheikh Bekkar, stark naked, with his hands on his shoulders and his genitals swaying to and fro. Suddenly he came up to me and slapped my face with the slap of a holy idiot. I reeled, and blood gushed from my nose onto my green cloak. When I looked up, I saw that all my companions had fled. Sheikh Bekkar seized me by the hand and began to parade me around the marketplace as though he were a slave broker, shouting, '*One sinner for sale! One new one! For sale! One new one!*' He was actually auctioning me off! I was so humiliated that my entire body broke into goose bumps. The crowd looked on amazed, and some boys even asked the sheikh how much he was selling me for. I was bathed in sweat from the shame of it.

He kept parading me about until we came to the convent of his holiness Sheikh Arslan. There he allowed me to renew my ablutions, after which we entered the shrine and he said: '*Recite the Sura of the Emissaries.*' I recited it in a loud voice. '*Recite the Sura of the Soul-Snatchers.*' I recited that as well.[69] When I finished, he opened his hands and babbled a kind of nonsensical prayer. '*This prayer nice, nice,*' he said, addressing me. He finished with: '*Say, I ask forgiveness of God,*' and I replied: '*Turn to God in repentance.*' Then he stood up and kissed my forehead, saying, '*This tomb my master, you my child.*' Seizing me by the hand once again, he ushered me out of the convent. As we stepped outside, he kissed my shoes and placed them in front of me. I kissed his hand and put on my shoes, thinking, 'What can I do? He is naked and crazy, and he has me in his clutches.'

We returned to the central marketplace. Dragging me along by the hand, he kept shouting, '*O lookers, O nobles, this my son, despised, forgiven, for sale, a thousand thousand purses!*' He made a public scandal out of me; but I was not upset about it as I had been before. In this manner he brought me to the palace square and ushered me into the council hall, shouting the while. Then he delivered me to Murtaza Pasha, hand to hand, saying, '*This my spiritual son.*' Once again he kissed me on the forehead, then departed.

As I was recounting the entire misadventure to Murtaza Pasha, seventy or eighty Damascus janissaries, accompanied by the municipal police chief, brought three dead men loaded on horses and seven or eight wounded men through the palace gate. 'My lord,' they said, 'we raided a party of fornicators in a house in the Turkman district, not realising that they were your officers. They killed three of our men and wounded these others. Now they have walled themselves up inside that house and are fighting it out.' They deposited the corpses in front of the Pasha and kissed the ground.

The Pasha leapt up like an eagle. 'Call the treasurer!' he cried. When the treasurer arrived he pummelled him mercilessly, wounding him with his dagger in several places. Then he mounted with his retinue and bodyguard and galloped off to the den of vice. A terrific battle ensued, in which three

---

69 i.e., Suras 77 and 79, both containing vivid depictions of punishments on judgement day.

of the officers were killed; the other seven were brought back after the evening prayer, strangled, and buried along with the first three in the vicinity of Sheikh Reyhan.

The moral of the story is: I was on my way with these men to that den of vice. But because I am one of those who bear God's holy word, having memorised the Koran, his holiness Sheikh Bekkar received a divine inspiration and seized me from the midst of those doomed men. He paraded me round about, crying, '*One sinner!*' and so rescued me – may his secret be sanctified. Owing to that saintly man I was saved from that abyss.

6. The Hajj caravan; Muzayrib, the Hajj bazaar

First of all, the vizier Hüseyn Pasha, younger brother of the late Siyavuş Pasha, being governor of Damascus, was charged with conducting the Damascus pilgrims to and from the noble Ka'ba. For it had been reported to the Porte that every year Arab brigands plundered the pilgrims and caused them great harm and loss. So Hüseyn Pasha was grand commander, and under him the *sancak(-beys)* and *timar* and *zeamet* holders of Damascus province, along with 500 Damascus janissaries and their officers.

Hoca Bekir Agha brought forty purses each from Kara Mehmed Pasha in Syrian Tripoli and Hacı İshak Pasha, governor of Sidon. When Hüseyn Pasha received these sums he disbursed them among his retinue. First he gave each of his twenty chief doorkeepers 300 *guruş*, five camels, one muleteer, one water carrier, and one torchbearer. The 100 individuals deserving of esteem, each 50 *guruş*; 100 *müteferrikas*, each 40 *guruş* 100 *delis*, 100 *gönüllüs*, 20 regiments of Segban and Sarıca troops, a total of 2,000 *levend* horsemen, each 100 *guruş*; those mounted on camel-litters, each 50 *guruş*; two regiments of Tatars, including 200 fully armed warriors, each 100 *guruş*; 50 each of saddlers, cooks, tasters, panters and tent-pitchers, each 50 *guruş*; 30 players of the military band, five purses; 1,000 water carriers, 300 torchbearers, 300 muleteers, 1,000 camel-drivers, each 10 Venetian *guruş*; and 100 of his personal retinue, each 100 *guruş*. In short, a total of 5,120 men were given 270 purses. And 300 more purses were spent on provisions and other expenses.

On the (—) day of the month of Shawwal, he paraded the sacred litter of the Prophet around the city of Damascus, while all the pilgrims went about readying their provisions for the journey.

By God's wisdom, on that day 2,000 Persian pilgrims arrived from the direction of Erzurum and Diyarbekir, with much wealth. They showered our lord Hüseyn Pasha with presents. He in turn appointed one of his officers over them. According to imperial *kanun* he got twenty gold pieces for each stop (? – *durma*) and fifteen for each man – a very helpful sum.

That same day he gave this humble one 200 fine coins (i.e. gold pieces); five camels, one riding-camel, one grey mare, four camel litters, one tent; one tent-pitcher, one water carrier, one baggage attendant, one torchbearer; ten *guruş* for each of my slaveboys. He appointed us a daily ration of two complete meals; four measures of fodder for my three horses; for breakfast every morning, five China bowls of whatever food is available; one candle; and other food and drink and other necessities. And he ordered that we pitch our tents in the shadow of his pavilion.

On the 20th of Shawwal in the year 1081 (sic. error for 1082 = 19 February 1672), with a *besmele*, we departed Damascus in grand procession with so many troops pertaining to that province; and the troops of the Emir of the Hajj, Harmuş Pasha; and the well-armed and well-ordered soldiery of the Pasha (i.e. Hüseyn Pasha) consisting of 5,120 men.

[...]

The grain pertaining to the imperial purse and belonging to the pashas, the Emir of the Hajj, the agent of the imperial pantry, and the other officials going on the Hajj, as well as the foodstuffs of the merchants, had been piling up here in storage for the past five or six months. All the Muslim pilgrims crossed the bridge over the Hurrayan River that flows here at the foot of the castle. This river originates in the east, in the mountains of Bosra, flows west and empties into the Lake of Minya.

After crossing, Hüseyn Pasha pitched his tent-pavilion along the river bank and the rest of the pilgrimage caravan settled down in their rows of tents. Criers went through the camp announcing a ten-day halt, until the beginning of the month of Dhu'l-qaʿda, and warning us to see to our provisions. We all busied ourselves making preparations for the journey. Day by day pilgrims kept coming from all directions, until the reckoning of tents and marquees stood at 6,300. For this was the Greatest Hajj and only God knows how many pilgrims there were.

In addition, outside the camp, there were 5,000 tents and huts belonging to tradesmen. This bazaar increased day and night. There were 300 bread shops, also cook shops and textile shops, so you can extrapolate from these. This humble one strolled from one end of the camp (i.e., the bazaar) to the other and it came to 8,000 paces. It was a sea of men, all jostling shoulders. Everything was for sale except the elixir of life, including silks and brocades and satins and other precious stuffs. In this bazaar, 40,000 or 50,000 Damascus pilgrims spend five or six Egyptian treasures and then get 40,000 or 50,000 camels from the Arab tribes. The Arab tribesmen get rich as well and come here once a year with their wives and children to buy precious stuffs. So it is a sea of men.

First of all, according to the *kanun* of Sultan Süleyman, the sheikhs of the following tribes bring camels to this plain of Muzayrib to assist the Muslim pilgrims: Bani (—), Al Umur, Al Rashd, Al Ribah, Al Ma'an, Al Shahab, Al Turabi, Ibn Harfush, Ibn Hanah, Ibn Sa'id, Bani Ibrahim, Bani Salim, Bani Ata, Bani Atiya, Bani Safar, Bani Zuhd, Bani Wahidat. Also the sheikhs of Nablus, Ajlun, Bani Zayt, Safed, Acre, Ramla, Gazza, Jerusalem and Khalil al-Rahman (Hebron).

In short, it is a *kanun* of Sultan Süleyman that the sheikhs of seventy-seven tribes come annually to this plain of Muzayrib with their followers to serve the pilgrims with 40,000 or 50,000 camels, for which service they receive sultanic gifts from the Damascus treasury. The plain becomes crowded with people, so everyone has to keep an eye on his own suite, because they will steal the collyrium from your eyes!

The pashas get 3,000 free-ranging camels from these sheikhs, 2,000 of which are for carrying water – four goatskins of water per camel – and 1,000 for barley and beans. In addition, the Pasha has 200 camel-trains for his other supplies and fifty mule-trains loaded with his own provisions. Mules actually bear up quite well between Damascus and Mecca. His personal retinue and some of his troops use thoroughbred mares as their mounts. But stallions do not bear up very well.

By God's wisdom, while we were buying and selling and securing provisions for the journey in this plain of Muzayrib, on the 25th of Shawwal (24 February) at noon the air became thick and a storm arose that sent everyone scurrying for their lives. The rain fell as though the clouds had let down their hair and were weeping, and anyone with a tent or marquee or baggage was left moaning and sighing. That day and night it rained so much that no one could visit anyone else and all the tents were engulfed in the flood. When the Arabs saw the situation they gave up haggling and took shelter with their camels in some valleys outside the camp. Only a few stuck it out and stayed behind.

That night there was a wintry blizzard, with snowflakes the size of sparrows' heads. Two hundred camels and seventy or eighty naked Arabs gave up the ghost. That night several thousand horses and mules, dragging their tethers and hobbles, turned their rumps to the desert wind and took refuge in the hamlets. In the morning we saw that some horses, mules and donkeys had disappeared. Praise God, none was permanently lost, but all the animals were returned to their owners for fear of Hüseyn Pasha.

That day the rain continued as though flowing out of a water-carrier's skin. Horses and mules and camels were up to their knees in water and shivering like autumn leaves. The people were alarmed, crying 'My lord, what is going on?' Everyone was worried what would happen to them, since one in a thousand provisions for the journey was not yet ready, and only three days remained until the first of the month of Dhu'l-qa'da.

Finally everyone piled up their clothing inside their tents and sat on them. I wrapped my three horses in kilims and felts, raced them over the ground (?) and turned their rumps to the wind. Nor did I deprive their heads of provender-bags filled with barley and straw. But the rain gave us no respite.

Now, by God's wisdom, the mice that normally make their home underground had nowhere to find shelter except amidst the clothing piled up inside the tents, which they gnawed to shreds. Some of the horses that were lying on the ground had their manes and tails eaten up by mice, so those mature thoroughbreds were turned into immature foals. God knows, some of them that dozed off got their noses and ears bitten. This too was a calamity.

A contingent of pilgrim latecomers that had been left behind in Damascus, including the janissary colonel Ahmed Agha and the grand vizier's son-in-law and superintendent of the doorkeepers Siyavuş Agha, got caught in the storm in the place called Sanamayn. They were separated from their goods and provisions, and some died of the cold. After suffering a myriad pains and troubles, and just escaping with their lives, they entered the camp here at Muzayrib, but there was no place for them to rest. Finally the Pasha took them into his tent-pavilion.

By God's wisdom, that day a terrible wind blew apart all the tents. A man was assigned to hold down each tent-rope, but it was no use: the ropes were left in their hands and the tents, that had been pitched on the ground, were now flapping in the air.

So everyone was moaning and groaning. With bare feet, in concord complete, they came to consult Hüseyn Pasha in his tent-pavilion.

'The rest of the pilgrims,' they said, 'have been unable to get here from Damascus. And the sheikhs of the Arabs have been unable to bring camels because of the winter weather. The Muslim pilgrims have been battered by all sorts of troubles and travails. Now the month of Dhu'l-qa'da is upon us. Ahead of us are various stages of the journey. If we get behind schedule for a single day, the noble *mahmil* (the sacred litter of the Prophet) will not reach Arafat on time, and your noble reputation will suffer a breach. My lord, we must do something about this. The pilgrims from Damascus are drowning, they have suffered loss of life and property, and have been subject to pillage.'

'*Judgement belongs to God*,' replied the Pasha. 'If the pilgrims are unable to go this year, well, the Hajj is not obligatory as long as the road is not safe. And my charge is not to convey the pilgrims, but rather to convey the noble *mahmil* and the two Egyptian treasures of the holy endowment (i.e., the *surre*, the Sultan's annual gifts) to Mecca. If the *mahmil* of Egypt reaches there but the *mahmil* of Damascus fails to, that would be a stain on the honour of the Ottoman dynasty. How could my own honour otherwise be diminished? I will dismantle the noble *mahmil*, wrap it carefully, and load it on my mules, which are serviceable. By God's command, I will roll three stages into one and reach the Ka'ba on time. So whoever is able, let him join me in such a forced march; and whoever is not, let him go back. For concerning the Hajj, God has commanded in the glorious Koran, in the Sura of al-Imran: *Pilgrimage to the House is a duty to God for all who can make the journey* (3:97).'

Everyone young and old applauded this sentiment, saying it was the reasonable course, and a Fatiha was recited. Criers went through the camp announcing the plan. Seven grandees who were being conveyed in palanquins got off in Muzayrib and mounted horses. Four or five hundred pilgrims (with mounts) and quite a few merchants, also 600 miserable men on foot, went back to Muzayrib castle.

That day and night there was no let-up of snow and rain. It was a period of days that betokened Noah's flood. This night as well the animals broke loose and took refuge in the hamlets, and again the villagers returned them – some naked, some wounded – to their owners.

That day the Pasha ordered his personal retinue to recite 1,000 Sura of al-An'am (6) to ward off calamity. And to all the Muslim pilgrims he dealt out the assignment of reciting 200,000 blessings on the Prophet and 100,000 Sura of al-Ikhlas (112). By God's command, as soon as the recitations began, the rain of torment stopped and the sun showed its head from the tower of the firmament. The men and the animals revived somewhat. But men and horses were mired in mud – judge what condition the camels were in! That night, the (—) of the month of Dhu'l-qaʿda, (? – lacuna in the text), the cannon was fired and the caravan set out – but how was this possible, seeing that all the baggage was waterlogged?

7. Medina

Description of the stage of Old Wadi al-Kura

It is also known as Old Medina. In a desert area, there are wells with fine drinking water, sufficient for all the pilgrims. The people who live in the flourishing villages that are in these wadis came to this place to offer their wares to the pilgrims for sale at a cheap price. In the afternoon the horns again were sounded and we continued on our way, passing over stony tracts and areas with thorn bushes and pebble stones and through narrow passes. After sunset, according to *kanun* – because of harassment from the infidels (i.e., rebellious Bedouin?) of the Khaybar region – the pilgrimage caravan was lighted with thousands of torches, resembling the stars in the night sky; it was as though the crescent moon had become full and it was as bright as day. Again according to *kanun*, the pilgrims were surrounded by Muslim soldiers and could proceed in complete security. The next day we continued from the time of the morning prayer until the mid-afternoon prayer, uninterruptedly like a flowing river. After walking about seventeen hours, without untying our loads, we came to:

Stage of Wadi al-Istiqbal and Dar Wadaʿ

It is also known as Dar Jurf. This place is surrounded by bare mountains. If one reaches this place from Damascus, the mountains seem to be as naked as poor Arabs. No trees grow here, only in the wadis there are numerous thorn bushes, date palms, acacias and toothpick trees. In Dar Wadaʿ all the animals are fed on barley and beans. Since the entire population of Medina comes out to greet the pilgrims here after the muezzin has called them to prayer, it is known as Wadi al-Istiqbal ('Wadi of Welcome'). The notables of Medina and the pilgrim guides, dressed entirely in white, men with beaming faces, wide-eyed, with sweet words on their lips, with glowing cheeks, courteous, gentle and good-tempered, came out with their gifts and went from tent to tent looking for their friends.

Even those whose friends had died attached themselves to one or another of the notables and were honoured. They all said to Hüseyn Pasha 'My lord, this year you have come seven days later than in previous years; but God willing you will reach Mecca safe and sound and be able to stay there an extra day.' The pilgrims were cheered at this good news.

After a stay of two hours the drums sounded for departure. Time was short, since there was only one more day until Dhu'l-hijja (the month of pilgrimage). There are ten stages from Medina to Mecca, and with a stay of one day in Medina and one day in Mecca you need twelve days for this journey. The halt on Mt Arafat takes place on the 10th of Dhu'l-hijja. From fear of not arriving there on time, no rest was permitted from Muzayrib until this point except in Ula and Ma'an and we marched for periods of twenty-five to thirty hours. Everyone kept on walking while munching on biscuit from his own scrip. Even the camels were fed their balls of dough while walking. We kept flowing like a human stream. This was the reason why so many horses, camels, mules and donkeys were left behind.

Also we did not stop at the usual pilgrim stations, but only when necessary. Under normal circumstances there are twenty-four stages between Damascus and Medina. This is about 350 hours riding on a camel. It is possible to cover this stretch on a horse or mule in 100 hours if the roads are well kept and supplies assured. But the roads are in poor condition and supplies have to be carried by camels, which also are fed from their loads. A person can satisfy hunger with a piece of bread; but it is not worth the trouble incurred because of the animals. If the authorities made an effort and kept good care of the road from Damascus to Medina, one could manage without camels and cover the stretch on horseback in comfort. *May God grant ease!*

Thanks to God's providential care, camels are endowed with such strength that they can walk and sleep at the same time. And, as God is my witness, some of the torchbearers are as tough as Nakhchivan steel and they too can walk and sleep at the same time, while bearing torches on their shoulders. This is simply one of God's amazing mysteries.

In short, we set off from Wadi'l-istikbal immediately. It is from this point that the guides begin to take their task seriously, pointing out the landmark mountains and valleys.

After one hour of travelling we arrived at the top of a hill. When one reaches this point and turns south one sees the orchards and gardens of Medina and the dome of the Mosque of the Prophet reaching to the sky.

From the gleam of the gilded pinnacle on the dome, the plain of Medina becomes *light upon light* and one's eyes are dazzled.

Here the sincere lover gets off his horse or camel or mule and says the following prayer: *Peace and blessing be upon you, O Messenger of God; peace and blessing be upon you, O Beloved of God; peace and blessing be upon you, O lord of the first ones and the last ones; and peace be upon the apostles of God.* This is a matter of love (i.e., not obligatory). If the pilgrim feels strong enough, he proceeds from here as far as Medina by foot, a five-hour downhill stroll. If he is handicapped or old, he remounts his horse or camel or mule or donkey and continues the journey, repeating again and again the noble blessings on the Prophet. There are many varieties of this prayer, but the following is short and practical: *O God, bless Muhammad and his people!* As soon as Medina comes into view and one sees the dome of the Mosque of the Prophet, one should not neglect this prayer: *Intercession, O Messenger of God!*

It is quite a marvel that when this hill is reached and the dome of the Prophet comes into view, and when the company of believers begins to cry out, a change comes over the animals as well. The camels that were exhausted suddenly regain their strength and grumble like thunder, the horses whinny and the mules and donkeys cry out in the *segah* musical mode: *The harshest of voices is the braying of the ass* (31:19). It is then impossible to hold the animals back, but they head toward Medina at great speed.

When the pilgrims have reached this hill and viewed Medina, some of the lovers put on the pilgrim's robe and proceed barefoot escorted by some of the inhabitants of Medina. At Ali's Well one does not have to wear the pilgrim's robe nor say these prayers but only repeats the noble blessings on the Prophet. There is no obstacle according to the Sharia, however. If, out of love, one puts on the pilgrim's robe here and does not have one's head shaved, that is even more fitting. Would that poor, needy man always wore the pilgrim's garb and turned to God; how much more fitting that would be, and how heavy his goods will weigh on God's scales. For this reason many lovers of God will recite the following verse:

> *Let us abandon the crown of transience,*
> *Let us be naked for a while.*

To put on the pilgrim's robe means to separate oneself from all things but God. Verse: *The unmarried state is truly the greatest sultanate.* For this reason the Prophet ordered putting on the pilgrim's robe as a sign of separation from all that is worldly and as a form of turning to God. That is why many pilgrims come to visit the Prophet's tomb dressed in the pilgrim's robe beginning at this point.

Concerning the inhabitants of Medina
As soon as the city of Medina becomes visible, that plain is transformed into a sea of people and everyone, young and old and schoolchildren come to greet the pilgrims. Some children bind little baskets on palm branches to beg the pilgrims for alms. The pilgrims come on litters mounted high on the humps of the camels. The naked Arab boys reach out these baskets and say: *Praise be to God, o pilgrims, go unhurt and in peace! May God accept your visit to Him!* And the pilgrims say: *Praise be to God, we have arrived at the shrine of our Prophet who came as a mercy for both worlds.* They do not allow a single one to go empty-handed, as they believe them to be the neighbours of the Prophet.

The children accompany the pilgrims on their way to Medina, which takes five hours, and as they go they sing eloquent *kasides* (odes) and *na't* (poetry describing the Prophet). Some children, those with tuneful and melancholic voices, sing *kasides* in such a way that one's flesh tingles with elation. And most of the womenfolk recite the noble *mevlud* (poetry on the birth of the Prophet). This crowd accompanies the pilgrims to Medina, and some of the pilgrims are carried on sedans and some on litters.

Praise for the soldiers of Sarı Hüseyn Pasha
From this point Hüseyn Pasha drowned his sea-like soldiery in blue iron (i.e., had them put on coats of mail). The Emir of the Hajj and the vanguard, then the Damascus army and the Pasha's troops put on their golden uniforms and marched in procession. The entry of the great Sarı Arslan Hüseyn Pasha into the city was beyond description. Such a well-ordered and decorated and well-armed troop had not entered since the conqueror of Yemen, Sinan Pasha, Rıdvan Pasha and Tavaşi Süleyman Pasha. The prominent citizens of Medina gathered to receive these soldiers. The learned, the religious, the imams and preachers, sheikhs and descendants of the Prophet, young and old, rich and poor came out to greet them. The tradesmen set out their goods for sale, and hundreds of sheep and rams were slaughtered. There were crowds on both sides of the highway. Women, dressed in gauze and cloth-of-gold, ululated from the windows and roofs of all the houses, their voices reaching up to heaven.

The Pasha marched in with his horse-tail and banner and his spare horses, dressed in a sable-fur cloak and girded with a quiver. He had a turban on his head wrapped after the fashion of Sultan Selim. His runners were dressed in cloth-of-gold, wearing vests with pearl buttons, and on their heads were gold plates set with plumes. The canteen-bearers and musketeers wore red broadcloth and gold-embroidered felt cloaks, with jewelled muskets in their hands and gem-inlaid swords at their waists. The chief canteen-bearer held a canteen decorated with precious stones, the likes of which I had never seen even belonging to a vizier. One hundred of the Pasha's personal retinue sat on full-blooded Arabian horses, each worth 1,000 *guruş*, and was adorned with gilded saddle bags and a tall headdress. Each Aga was drenched in sky-blue armour wearing a turban made in Baghdad. The swordbearer and footman, with their quivers of gold-embroidered silk and their breeches and gold-stitched felt hats on their heads, accompanied the Pasha as he paraded past. After them came the banner and flag, then the military band in rows of eight. They beat the Muhammadan drum and stopped at the vizierial tent. The people of Medina were utterly astounded at this, as they had never seen such a magnificent vizier.

After the Pasha had taken his seat in his tent-pavilion, seventy to eighty cannon shots were fired from the towers and ramparts of Medina castle. The surrounding plain reverberated at the sound. From the place where Hüseyn Pasha drew up this procession, one could see Medina to the south and Mt Uhud to the north. This lofty red-coloured mountain will be described in due course. It was from here that the Pasha entered Medina in formation. As for this humble one, deeming it more fitting to visit the pilgrimage sites than to participate in the procession, I took a slaveboy and a guide and mounted my horse.

[...]

While in the suburb I went straight to the (—) Bath where I bathed using a clean bath-glove and soap. Then I came to my tent, took off all my travel garments, uttered a *besmele*, and put on the pilgrim's garment. Barefoot and bare headed, free from all worldly attachments, I became a roselike dervish.

I immediately left my tent and entered the walled city of Medina through the Egyptian gate. At this point one must recite the following verse: *Lord, grant me a goodly entrance and a goodly exit, and sustain me with Your power* (17:80). I went straight to the shrine of the Prophet, that *mercy for the worlds* (21:107), and entered through the Gate of Peace (*Bab-ı Selam*). I did not go on foot like the other lovers, but lay my sinful face on his precious ground and crawled in, fishlike, without using hands or feet. Thanks be to God, there is mercy among men, as is expressed in the proverb: 'No one treads on the face of one who lies on the floor.' In the crowd of forty to fifty thousand pilgrims I made my way through to the railed precinct *müvacehe* of the Messenger of God. There I kissed the threshold, prayed beseeching, and knelt down. As I bowed humbly I spoke the following words: *Peace be upon you, O messenger of God.* I prayed for his intercession and I nearly fainted. When I came to myself, I completed a Koran-recital that I had left off at the Sura of al-Ikhlas (112) then retired backwards according to etiquette. God willing, the form and manner of the visit will be explained in detail in the proper place.

From there I returned to my tent and took something to eat. The sergeants at arms announced a halt of two days and two nights. Then the noble vizier held a *divan*. The eight-layered military band played. When that was finished, all the notables of the province had an audience with the Pasha. After coffee, sherbet and rose water, and after fumigation with incense, the Arab highwaymen who had been captured on the way were brought to the place of execution in chains.

'Let no one be put to death in the shrine of the messenger of God,' said the Pasha. 'Give them over to the warden of the castle.' The warden was immediately summoned. Then all the notables of the province came forward – the religious scholars, pious individuals, and foreign residents – and asked for the release of the condemned men.

'I know how they should be forgiven!' said the Pasha. 'Who went to summon the warden?'

Now among these men was one in janissary dress with a magnificent sable fur. 'My lord,' he said, 'I am the warden.'

'So it's you, is it?' As the Pasha rose to greet him I saw that his cheeks were flushed and the hair of his beard and moustache were standing on end. 'Hey, warden, who are you in fact?'

'I'm a janissary.'

'So you are a servitor of the Sultan?'

'Yes,' the fellow replied.

'Damn you!' said the Pasha. 'Don't I have a chief doorkeeper and a captain of the janissaries? You could have spoken with them and they could have reported to me. You are a servitor of the Sultan, yet you come hobnobbing with these foreign residents and sit here without a qualm. I call for the warden and you just stand there! Where did you let your beard grow grey? Remove this infidel! Shut him up in the tower with these Arab infidels!'

The warden was handed over to the chief canteen-bearer who confined him in the tower and made his deputy warden in his place. After watching all this, I got my weapon from my tent and put it in my belt, then began to visit the Pilgrimage sites and tour the city and the castle.

[...]

In 959 (1552) it was under the rule of (—) Sherif and governed on his behalf by another sherif at the rank of *sancak-bey*. The decree was issued by Mehmed IV that whoever was the Sheikh of the Haram should be the ruler of Medina. The subordinate governor was dismissed. It was further decreed that the Sherif would come once a year, lodge outside Medina, and visit the grave of the Prophet; and would not interfere in any way in the affairs of the city.

The Molla in Medina by ancient statute received a salary of 500 *akçe* per diem. Nevertheless, because it was such an unprofitable place and so far away (from Istanbul), it was not considered a prestigious mollaship. However, Sultan Mehmed issued a law according to which no one could become a molla in Istanbul if he had not already been a molla in Mecca and Medina.

The reason was that this Medina is a very unprofitable place and a haunt of dervishes. There are no arguments, disagreements or differences of opinion. The inhabitants are all good-tempered, honest people. If there is a legal claim required to be registered by the *kadi* it is resolved quickly and easily, then everyone says a Fatiha and the parties go their separate ways.

At present, 1,000 gold pieces from the imperial *surre* and 200 bushels of wheat from Egypt are set aside for the Molla and the same for the Sheikh of the Haram. The Sheikh of the Haram runs the government with about 500 soldiers and the Molla decides cases with forty or fifty men saying 'This is the judgement of the messenger of God.'

[...]

Inside the walls are 2,000 four- or five-storey tall houses, some small, some larger, well-constructed and decorated, the roofs completely covered with lime. Most of the public buildings are *hans*, mosques, medreses, water dispensaries, soup kitchens, dervish convents, primary schools, Hadith and Koran schools. There are no other prayer houses or mosques inside the walled city, they are all outside. There are many markets and also some public baths.

Among the houses there are no orchards and gardens or public squares. Only seven houses have courtyards; the rest are packed layer on layer. Within the city walls there are a total of five quarters and (—) prayer-niches. There is another small mosque in the citadel where the soldiers perform their ritual prayers. For from fear of bandits the fortress is continuously garrisoned and never left empty. This citadel is the soul of Medina. The entire contents of the treasury and all its wealth are secreted inside it.

In the city there is an iron gate which faces eastward and in front of which is a large assembly hall where the watchmen are stationed. Moreover there are weapons decorating all the walls of the fortress. In the assembly hall a lofty dome covers a vast arena paved with marble. In the centre of this arena is an elegant pool and water jet, whose water is drawn by means of a water wheel. All the watchmen, young and old, perform their ritual ablutions from this pool and station themselves around it. This hall is used regularly by the castle warden and the other notables for meetings and council assemblies.

No one from outside is allowed into the fortress, only they do let in Muslim pilgrims. But Arab tribesmen are strictly prohibited from entering.

In the citadel there are no markets, *hans* or baths, only a few grain bins, an ammunition store and seventy to eighty small houses. It is a very strong and resistant citadel. Its mosque is very well built, the construction dating from the time of Sultan Süleyman. The other small mosques in the outer fortress are not very spacious or imposing. It is only in the Great Mosque where sermons are preached.

Description of the Mosque of the Sacred Garden

The noble grave of the Prophet, that light-filled garden which is the aim and goal of all the community of Muhammad, may be found in this mosque. Since Friday prayers are not performed in any other mosque within the Medina fortress, this mosque (The Mosque of the Prophet) attracts a large congregation. Especially during the Pilgrimage, it is hard to find a place to kneel. It is a grand mosque and it would be hard to find such a spiritual house of prayer in all the seven climes of the Islamic lands. The former rulers, for the sake of the Prophet, made it so well-constructed and adorned and jewel-like as though it were Paradise itself.

It is indeed a paradise, for concerning this mosque there is a sound Hadith: *The area between my pulpit and my grave is one of the gardens of paradise.*
[...]
The mosque together with the courtyard measures 800 paces in circumference from the outside. But the area in front of the wall on the prayer-niche side has a garden and one of the city quarters, so one enters through the Gate of Peace from where, as one respectfully passes by the Prophet's grave, it is 200 paces as far as the Umar Corner of the mosque. By this reckoning, the circumference of the mosque measures 1,000 paces.

From there one continues to pace off the mosque from the inside, past the foot of the Prophet's grave, Gabriel's Gate, the forecourt of the Sheikh of the Haram and the Gate of Healing. It is 170 paces from the interior of the courtyard to the area in front of the oil magazines. From the corner of the oil magazine through the courtyard as far as the corner where the barrels for the soup kitchen stand, it is 150 paces. From there one again crosses the courtyard, passes the Gate of Mercy and returns to the Gate of Peace with 170. By this reckoning, the interior of the mosque measures 690 paces, the outside 1,000 paces.

The courtyard is completely covered with pebbles. It measures 600 paces in circumference. There is a lofty cupola in the centre where the olive oil is stored that is used for the many lamps in the mosque; the oil comes from Sousse in the Maghreb to Egypt and then via Yanbu to Medina.

In front of this oil-cupola there is a small square terrace surrounded by a railing. Here there is a date palm reaching to the sky. The Prophet planted it with his own hands. Next to it, by God's will, a sapling date palm is sprouting. Precisely this spot was the courtyard of the house of Abu Ayyub Ansari. It is now the courtyard of the mosque.

There are terraces on all four sides of this courtyard and, in due order, fifty-two varicoloured precious lofty pillars, of white marble and porphyry and 'honeycombed' marble, such as are found in the Dome of the Rock. Around the courtyard are fifty-two finely-constructed arches, and between every two arches the names of God are written in Karahisari style calligraphy.

Around the courtyard are three minarets stretching up to the sky. Each is finely constructed and well-proportioned and has three balconies. One of these minarets, at the Umar Corner, points upward like a stylus, architecturally very impressive. Another, outside the Gate of Mercy, rises over the gate of the Sultan Qaytbay Medrese; this too is a noteworthy minaret and station of Bilal for giving the prayer-call in the *uzzal* musical mode. The third, in the corner on the northern side of the courtyard, is a large minaret built in the old manner, not as finely constructed as the others.

This noble mosque is completely covered in (—). In the compass of the mosque there are a total of 300 columns, large and small. Above the columns are 300 arches with twenty (—) each, like so many rainbows. And above these vaults are the coloured ceilings, so masterly executed that even Mani and Bihzad and Arzhang could not paint this ornamentation with their brushes of hair. It is so magical and wonderful, that even after so many centuries it still shines with the glimmer of gold and azure.

Above the precinct of the Prophet's grave are six small stone cupolas, each decorated on the inside like a Chinese picture gallery. When the sun shines through the windows all around these cupolas, the inside of the Prophet's tomb becomes *light upon light.*

The pillars of the mosque, which the Prophet built first and which Uthman extended, as far as the Gate of Peace, are a man's height and covered in green tiles. But the columns of the gallery around the courtyard are bare. Between the buildings added on by Uthman and the old Prophet's mosque, as far as the Gate of Peace, and between the columns, are varicoloured lattices, some of cypress, some of walnut or acacia wood. In the wall built by Uthman is an ornate prayer-niche. No one is permitted to pray here since the old mosque of the Prophet lies beyond it and the pulpit is also there. The building by Uthman has simply become the courtyard of the Prophet's mosque. Some people perform two prostrations here as they believe their prayer will be answered.

The courtyard is not covered with straw mats since it serves as a public thoroughfare from the Gate of Peace. However, the master builder paved this courtyard with small precious stones as though it were Indian inlay-work. It is so overlaid with raw marble and jasper, porphyry, etc., that one is dazzled by it.

The floor of the Prophet's mosque is completely covered with rich gold-embroidered carpets bestowed by many different rulers and viziers. It is a mosque of divine light. By God, if I were not so besmirched with worldly affairs and not so inclined to travel, I would not budge from this mosque. Thousands of people, indeed, have withdrawn from the world and become foreign residents in this mosque, worshipping before the grave of the Prophet.

The muezzins' gallery is made of pure white marble and stands on eight slender columns. All around it is an enclosure decorated with ornamental marble work.

Close by the grave of the Prophet is the lowly prayer-niche of Imam Hanafi. This is also decorated with tiny stones shining like birds' eyes and is one of the most beautiful prayer-niches that I have ever seen. It is flanked by golden candlesticks as tall as a man, and on these are eight white wax and camphor candles, each eight cubits high, stretching upwards like a pillar and so thick that a man can just put his arms around it. They come from Egypt and shine like the light of God.

To the right of this prayer-niche Sultan Murad III had a lofty pulpit built of finely-wrought marble, the like of which I have never seen in any house of prayer in all the Islamic lands. It embodies the spirit of this mosque of the Sacred Garden. These verses are written on the elegant door of the pulpit:

> *It was the will of Sultan Murad, son of Selim, to set up this pulpit.*
> *He prays that his reward may be multiplied in Heaven.*
> *Sa'd says: As for its chronogram and date:*
> *A pulpit built by Sultan Murad.*
> Year 1002 (1593–4)

Also to the right of this prayer-niche are the niches of Imam Shafi'i, Imam Malik and Imam Hanbali. They are also elaborate prayer-niches. The five daily prayers are performed first of all by the Shafi'i school, then the Hanafis, then the Malikis, and finally the Hanbalis. The muezzins, however, do not leave the gallery but wait until the Shafi'is are finished and then call the members of the other three schools to prayer.

The chronogram under the arch on the inside of the Gate of Peace: *Sultan Sultan Qaytbay ordered this sacred building to be constructed. May God multiply his success, in the year (—)*. It is a richly ornate door, made of shining brass, the work of a goldsmith. People who see the door believe it to be made of gold.

The four gates leading into the mosque – the Gate of Mercy, the Gate of Peace, Gate of Healing and Gabriel's Gate – consist of finely-worked brass and are polished the colour of amber. When one enters through the Gate of Peace, on the left hand side in the corner is a calligraphic inscription at the height of a man on a blue paper plaque in large letters, as follows:

> *The custom of the Arabs: if someone is a great prince*
> *It is usual to let slaves go free at his graveside.*
> *You who are the pride of the world and prince of this world and the next:*
> *God forbid that he who rubs his face on your grave should not go free.*

This is very suitable, demonstrating poetic skill like that of Hassan (ibn Thabit); may God bless you a hundredfold.

And when you come through the Gate of Peace, you see on the right-hand corner at the height of a man, the following verses from the Koran: *I take refuge in God from Satan the cursed. In the name of God, the Compassionate, the Merciful. He who founds his house on the fear of God and His good pleasure* (9:109); *Their Lord has promised them joy and mercy from Himself* (9:21); and from the same Sura: *None should visit the mosques of God except those who believe in God and the Last Day* (9:18). And the verses continue in clearly legible gold writing as one moves towards Uthman's prayer-niche. From these texts to the paved work below, the wall built by Uthman is covered with a varicoloured mosaic of porphyry and jasper green marble. Over these decorated stones *Victory/al-Fath* (Sura 48) is inscribed in another layer of clearly legible gold writing, all the way from the Gate of Peace to Gabriel's Gate. It must be the calligraphy of Yaqut Musta'simi – but God knows for sure —as it is an ancient inscription and the style is close to his.

With regard to the repair and maintenance of Uthman's wall, in the Shafi'i corner on a square piece of white marble is the following chronogram:

> *He is the intercessor at the place of resurrection and the place*
> *where the Archangel Gabriel was sent down;*
> *Leader in prayer of all the prophets and crown of the heads of the*
> *mystics.*
> *By God's grace this chronogram has been made with a benediction:*
> *God grant that he flourish in both worlds.*
>
> Year 1043 (1633–34)

On this wall built by Uthman there are no windows except for one window with brass bars, at half the height of a man, in the precinct before the Prophet's grave. Outside it is a rose garden of Iram with roses, hyacinths and sweet basil. And there is another window in front of the railings at the foot of the prophet's grave that looks out onto the main street. Apart from these there are no other windows in the mosque, so it is like a castle guarded on four sides. It really is a castle within a fortress, like a jewel in its setting.

Inside the mosque, in front of the Sheikh of the Haram pavilion is the bench of the People of the Bench (*Arbab-ı Suffa* – a group of pietists during the lifetime of the Prophet). This is another place of worship, a terrace facing the grave of Fatima within the railings of the grave of the Prophet.

Above the iron railings on this side there are calligraphic plaques by thousands of scholars. Thanks be to God, I too, lowly Evliya, have written in clearly legible writing a plaque saying, *Seyyah-ı alem Evliya ruhiyçün el-fatiha* (For the spirit of the world-traveller Evliya, a Fatiha). There is some more calligraphy of mine, on the wall in front of the aforementioned railings of the Prophet's grave, in large letters reading: 'Intercession, O Muhammad, for Evliya (or, for the saints). Year 1082 (1671–2).' Moreover I set up a crystal oil lamp as big as a turban beside the others.

These oil lamps were made in Egypt. There are 7,000 all together. They are lit every night by the mosque servants and by their light all the residents and visitors can read the Koran and engage in religious discussions until the morning prayer.

If I were to write everything I know about this mosque it would fill a very thick volume. The reason why I did not describe the fortress first of all was to inform you that the mosque of the Prophet is right in the middle of the fortress, and where the Prophet's resting place is in this mosque.

[...]

Description of the interior of the Sacred Garden and account of how we entered the tomb of the Prophet with our patron, Vizier Hüseyn Pasha

First you must put on clean and ritually pure clothes and constantly recite the noble greetings upon the Prophet. The Sheikh of the Haram and twelve of his black eunuchs are girded in white cotton loincloths. These aghas of the Haram are saintly men at the level of the Pole of Poles. They have dedicated their lives on behalf of the Prophet – black eunuchs who have given forty or fifty years of their lives to this service. They each carry jewelled censers and rose-water sprayers with which they approach the gate of the railing of the grave of the Prophet. First the Sheikh of the Haram girds the Pasha with a white loincloth and gives him a besom, i.e. a broom.

In sum, there were seven of us altogether, including this humble one, who entered the sanctuary. With us were the viziers, deputies, ulema and other religious dignitaries, town notables and sweepers. Their representatives reside here in Medina. The sweepers' deputy of the Ottoman Sultan is the Sheikh of the Haram himself. He also takes a broom in his hand and praying and praising, opens the noble gate of the Prophet's railing from the direction of the grave of Fatima. The twelve eunuchs and the deputy sweepers enter and close the gate of felicity, after which no one is allowed inside the Sacred Garden.

All the sweepers are trustworthy people. They too are allowed into the Sacred Garden once a year by the black eunuchs. For the rest of the time they sweep the outer mosque and kiss the Ka'ba cover. Entreating Fatima's intercession, they recite a Fatiha for her spirit and enter crying, 'O daughter of the messenger of God!' For one reaches the grave of the Prophet by going past the grave of Fatima. They burn incense of aloes, ambergris, camphor, hyacinth and dressed aloes. Crying 'Allah!' with tearful eyes, they proceed until they are at a level with her felicitous head and burn pastilles of raw ambergris.

The marriage of Ali to Fatima took place in the second year after the Hijra. Fatima was eighteen years old and Ali was twenty. He was a courageous youth. After the wedding night he killed Abu Jahl and seventy of his followers in heroic battle and took captive the Prophet's uncle Abbas and the Prophet's cousin Uqayl ibn Abi Talib along with seventy other deniers. Later many of them converted to Islam and so became Companions of the Prophet. After the death of Fatima, mother of Hasan and Husayn, her grave was made within this railing at the feet of the Prophet.

All visitors to this place outside the Sacred Garden perfume their brains with the incense and cry out: *Intercession, O Messenger of God!* The Pasha and this humble one kissed the ground and prayed for the intercession of the Prophet. We then began to sweep the noble pavement. The black eunuchs assisted with their seven lamps. The deputy sweepers swept once or twice each and removed the sweepings. We and fifteen others were left there; but I was drained of energy, intoxicated and bewildered from love. I asked for help from his noble spirit and my senses revived enough to light three more lamps.

A large netting is suspended beneath this lofty dome. It is a pavilion of cloth-of-gold and set with jewels, worth several Egyptian treasures. No emperor has possessed its like. No one may enter within this netting, for the Beloved of God himself lies here in a sarcophagus covered with a green embroidered Ka'ba cloth. This pavilion of the messenger of God contains numerous precious and bejewelled items – candlesticks, oil lamps, censers, rose-water sprayers, and the like – sent as votive offerings by sultans, viziers, deputies and great notables. These have accumulated from the death of the Prophet up to this date of 1082 (1671–2) and are heaped up inside the pavilion, not suspended. Only God knows how many items there are. It is for this reason that no one is allowed within the curtain; it is reserved for the Prophet. But once a year some of the more pious servants are permitted to enter and clean the dust off.

8. The People of Mecca

It is not concealed to men of discernment that, as recorded in the *Kıyafetname* of Akşemseddinzade Hamdi Çelebi (d. 1503), the people of Mecca are dark skinned, some of them reddish or brownish, with eyes like gazelles, sweet speech, rounded faces, keeping their own counsel, gentlemen of pure Hashimite lineage. But because of the hot climate they are very skinny. They are not much versed in the crafts, and do not have the ability to work with heavy loads; rather, most of them are merchants, while another class get by on the charity of the Sultan.

The majority of Meccans, being of a melancholic humour, are not very sociable. They are rough spoken in their trade dealings and in conventional discourse. If you wish to buy some merchandise from them it is customary to ask the price. They will say, for example, 'Ten *guruş*.' You may think it appropriate to bargain and counter with eight, but if you do, they will flare up and demand fifteen. If you say nine they will say twenty, and stubbornly stick to that price. That is how contentious they are. Among themselves, on the other hand, they join hands under their sleeves and engage in dumb barter over prices by squeezing with conventional signs, like the Pythagoreans. So it is better to just give the first price they ask, since they won't engage in bargaining and they eschew ill-gotten gains.

Indeed they are very fine gentlemen, all of them pure in lineage and descendants of the Prophet. However, because of their rebelliousness during the reign of the Egyptian Sultan Qaytbay (reg. 1468–96), the Sultan made a surprise attack on Mecca with 12,000 piebald horsemen and put all the sherifs in chains. He exiled most of them, retaining only seven noble *seyyids* inside Mecca. The sherifs agreed that henceforth they would not wear green turbans but only white. They also agreed not to mount horses with docked tails, to put on their saddle cloths front to back, and to mount barefoot. This agreement is still in force, although in the course of time the sherifs returned and Mecca is now full of them. But they never wear green turbans.

As for the rest of their attire, they use splendid Indian silks, plain white shirts with embroidery, *zaği* and *mollayi* stuffs, weaves and *germsud* and *hümaşahi* and mohair cloaks of various colours, which they proudly prance about in. From their white turbans in front and back they let down Muhammadan turban-ends, each a Meccan cubit long.

Some wear varicoloured precious Kashmir and Lahore cottons. The reason is that the sherifs receive such items as gifts from the emperors and notables of India. From the Ottomans, on the other hand, they mostly get grain.

The Meccans never wear trousers but rather baggy pants and *beddavi* shirts. On their feet they wear Circassian and *cimcime* shoes and slippers. A scarf of Kashmir cotton around their neck is *de rigeur*. They put kohl on their eyes, following the Sunna of the Prophet, and put henna on their hands and feet and beards.

They never eat greasy foods, only coffee and hard bread, beans, olives, dates, sweetmeats, sherbets, pilavs and soups. They are very abstemious. If they eat too much they cannot digest it, because the heat anyway roasts a man. Living so abstemiously they are very healthy, so healthy that there are no physicians in Mecca; if one does come he cannot make a living and moves elsewhere. The people of Mecca also abstain from sex six months of the year because of the heat. One day they go to the summer pasture known as Wadi Abbas . . . . (?— lacuna in the text). They do not light fires, except for the merchants and the sherifs.

They are 100 per cent Shafi'i. Some . . . (?— lacuna in the text) are called Zaydi. (They are thought to practice) *mut'a* marriage. This is an arrangement whereby a man on a campaign or journey can contract to have sexual relations with a woman for up to one month for one *guruş*. At the end of the month he pays the fee and goes elsewhere. If he has to stay more than a month he contracts with the same woman for one *guruş* or five *guruş*, or else with a different woman, and they can do what they will. This is called *mut'a* marriage. It is said to have been the practice in Mecca in olden times, and the Meccans are reproached for it, but in our day I have not been aware that it is practised. It is a vicious slander. They are gentlemen of pure religion. And they have little boys who are charming and clever; as in the verse:

When he walks he is spirit in form in motion;
When he talks he breathes life like the words of Jesus.

The people are well-born, high and mighty individuals. They don't like the Turks who sojourn in Mecca. The Turks (on the other hand) are quite comfortable in Medina, where indeed most of them live and where the sherifs hardly have any influence.

The clay of Mecca is so fine and delicate that they fashion from it all sorts of jugs and pitchers which they use for the water of Zamzam.

The women here are known for their beauty and grace; with fairy faces and angel looks, like the moon at mid-month or like garden peacocks; and with gaits like skipping partridges; pure virgins and mature matrons who are clearly the object of the Koranic verse: *You may marry other women who seem good to you: two, three, or four of them* (4:3). They are the source and origin of mankind. They too wear fine fabrics and put on jewellery from head to toe. On their heads they wear caps of gold and silver or else cloth threaded with gold, wrapping a black silk cover over that, and they cover their radiant faces with veils of multicoloured silk so that one sees only their gazelle-like eyes daubed with kohl. They are very covered-up women.

But there are also Ethiopian slavegirls, actually singing-girls, tawny as raw ambergris, who set hearts aflutter. Some dance in public in the coffee houses. They are the pride of Arabia and no cause for shame. They all wear light-blue stockings and blue slippers. If a woman passes by a man of God, his brain is suffused with the perfumes of musk and ambergris and civet. One day as I was going to visit the shrine of Sufyan al-Thawri (scholar of early Islam, d. 778) I ran into a flock of women. It turned out to be a wedding procession. One of the maiden girls was drowned in gold bangles. Even from a distance of ten paces my brain was suffused with fragrances. More than 500 schoolboys followed the procession crying *Amin amin!* as they made their way to their destination.

[...]

But the Meccans, being of a melancholic and saturnine disposition, are not much engaged in learning. They are all merchants. The study of Hadith and the memorisation of the Koran are rather Egyptian specialities. In Mecca it is only some of the Turkish sojourners who engage in the religious sciences; other than that, Mecca has no reputation for it. Also one does not find saintly individuals engaged in mystical exercises and performing miracles as one finds in other countries. The reason is that, being of melancholic humour, they are more given to frivolity and also to building activities. The multi-storeyed buildings here are not to be found in Aleppo or Damascus or in Iraq, though one does find them in Cairo.

Another quality of the Meccans is uxoriousness. They are in thrall to their wives: whatever their wives tell them to do, they do. In this respect, the men are the wings of the women. You never find a Meccan who is prominent for courage. They only put on fine clothes, apply henna to their feet and beards, go from coffee house to coffee house, then go home with a coffee mug in one hand and a biscuit in the other and fall asleep on their pillow sipping coffee and munching on biscuit.

For food and drink they completely rely on the marketplace. Since they are in thrall to their wives, nothing gets cooked in their houses. The women themselves are slow and heavy. They never do any work, never wash laundry or spin yarn or sweep the house. All their needs are supplied from the marketplace.

These are very extravagant people; but since they possess the wealth of Korah, they spend freely and indulge in magnificent clothes and furnishings. That is how it has been over the generations. My aim (in reporting this) is not to reproach them in any way – *God forbid!* I have only recorded the facts.

9. Uyun al-qasab

Stage of Uyun al-qasab: In Arabic it means Sugar Cane River, or else Sugar Well, there being wells of fresh water. It is under the rulership of the sheikhs of the tribe of Awlad Salih Nabi. If something gets lost, one has recourse to them. We stayed here for one hour and gave the camels fodder, then the trumpets were sounded and we set out again at noon.

By God's wisdom, it was my fate on this noble Hajj to travel hurriedly toward Mecca with the Syrian caravan, and then, on my return, to again travel hurriedly with the Egypt caravan. In fact, while the Syrian caravan is always in a hurry going to Mecca, its return journey is leisurely. The Syrians enjoy a stay of twenty days in Mecca and twelve in Medina, and they have long stops at the stages on their return journey, not entering Damascus until the month of the Prophet's birthday (i.e., Rabi' al-awwal, three months after the Hajj). The Egyptians, on the other hand, take their time going to the Ka'ba, walking leisurely between stages for eight or ten or (at the most) fifteen hours, then enjoying a stay of twenty-five days in Mecca. But on their return journey they walk fifteen or seventeen hours between stages, have only two days in Medina, and sometimes in their haste join two stages into one to get back to Cairo as soon as possible. For this reason it is well-known among the pilgrims that you should go with Egypt and return with Syria. In my case, I had to go in haste from Syria and return in haste to Egypt. Nevertheless, God be praised, I went with pleasure and returned with pleasure.

The Egyptian pilgrims do have one good practice. For the five daily prayers, the guides have watches and whenever it is prayer time – whether on hill or dale or wherever they may be – the caravan stops for what is termed *rada*. They make the camels kneel, everyone dismounts and performs the prayer. They give fodder to the camels and horses, and they themselves have a meal and rest for one hour, with an elaborate coffee-service.

But every night (!) until the *rada* halt for the evening prayer they make the camels kneel with their loads and they sleep like the Seven Sleepers of Ephesus and enter the Valley of the Silent as though following the dictum *Die by God's command!* Even the camels and the other beasts lie sprawling and snoring in the sand, because the road to Egypt is very secure.

Then the guides in the front raise their banner, beat their kettle-drums and set off. It takes an hour for the news to reach the rear guard and for them to set out as well. For the roads to Egypt go through narrow ravines. This year, with the two caravan trains travelling side by side, the length from one end to the other was 87 steps (or degrees? – *derece*). Because it was a year of the Great Hajj, the caravan was very large.

These halts, which are called *rada*, are not made by the Syria caravan going to Mecca because that road is not secure, there are many Arab brigands. The Syria road is, however, a broad plain and summer pasture. Four trains of palanquins can go side by side, flanked by three trains of free-ranging camels, and guarded on the extreme right flank by the Emir of the Hajj's Jerusalem and Nablus soldiery and on the extreme left flank by the Damascus troops. And they travel night and day, because the stages are very far from one another. So they only halt long enough to perform the ritual prayer and then go on. But the streams of water are sweet, and the roads are open plains. And on the return trip they do proceed by leisurely *rada* halts.

The Egypt roads, in contrast, are rocky, with hills and valleys, and the streams of water are bitter. There is security, however. The caravan is surrounded by seven regiments of troops: the Emir of the Hajj's deputy with the Circassian soldiery on the right flank; the Emir of the Hajj's troops in the rear; the *sipahis* and *gönüllüs* on the left flank; and the guards, *azeb* troops and gunners with the treasure and the cannons, all fully-armed and mounted on imperial dromedaries and camel mares. The Bey of Azlam with six cannons guards the rear. The Egyptian caravan has no rear guard until the Azlam troops arrive; but the Syrian caravan has an obligatory rear guard.

There is another good custom that is due to the cheapness and abundance of foodstuffs among the Egyptian soldiery. When they make the *rada* halts for the five daily prayers, they light the torches and, in the middle of the night, offer coffee to any and all comers. They hand out sweetmeats and sugar, stuffed pastries, hazelnuts and peanuts and walnuts, dates and roasted chickpeas, pastries and candies, so freely that God knows, everyone's pockets are filled with enough candy and nuts to munch on while walking the next day.

There is a contingent of bedouin Arabs, known as Ibn Halwan – forty men with red shawls. One hour before the caravan reaches a stage, this group of men go to a nearby high point and cry: '*O pilgrims! God be praised, the blessed stage is near!*' When the pilgrims hear this they become cheerful. Even the camels, that had been exhausted by the trek, become like seven-headed dragons when they hear this cry, and go so fast that those on foot cannot keep up with them.

In fact, before this cry, some of the camels trek on with their heavy loads while they are sleeping. I have often witnessed this, and God knows I am telling the truth. Even some of the men – the torch-bearers in particular, with wood on their backs weighing 15 or 20 *okkas*, and bearing a lighted torch on their shoulder – walk in their sleep or sleep while walking, a very strange sight. But camel-drivers observe that camels are often asleep while walking, and when they come to a rocky or difficult spot they cry out *Idak, idak!* to the camels who suddenly wake up and get past that difficult spot. At such rough places the tent-pitchers and water-carriers and torch-bearers beat their drums and tambourines crying '*God save the Sultan!*' and clap their hands and make jokes as they proceed on the way.

They travel until morning, avoiding settling into a stage in the dark of the night. For when that happens, a hue and cry rises among the troops,

Uyun al-qasab

everyone has trouble finding his regiment and finding his train with all the backing and forthing. So they wait until morning to call a halt and make the camels kneel.

There is another fear that keeps them from reaching a stage at night. There are, to be sure, no rebels or bandits on the Egyptian roads that would carry out a night raid. But the pilgrims are afraid of thieves among the camel-drivers and tent-pitchers and guards and water-carriers and military musicians and torch-bearers; and especially the pickpockets and sharpers and spoilers who come along with the Azlam soldiery. These people will separate an entire camel from its train, with its load and a sleeping man on top, then waken the man and strip him and sneak away with the camel and the load. Many such losses have been incurred in the dark of night, and Egyptian pilgrims have to be on their guard against these house-thieves. That is why the caravan does not stop at night.

10. St Catherine's Monastery on Mt Sinai

Description of the stage of Mt Sinai

In the (—) language they call all mountains *tur*. Examples are (Tur Hiraven) near Ayn Tujjar, the Mount of Olives (*Tur Zayta*) in Jerusalem, and this Mt Sinai (*Tur Sina*). It is a lofty mountain, from the summit of which one can see the minarets of the ruined city of Madyan of the prophet Shu'ayb. Mt Aqaba is visible below, and one can also make out the waves of the Red Sea, although Mt Sinai lies amidst mountains a distance of three hours north of the sea.

Because Moses and Jesus both spoke to God without intermediary on this mountain, Ptolemy Alexander built a great monastery at its very summit, unmatched in its beauty. Indeed, compared to the embellishment here, the ornamentation in the Church of the Holy Sepulchre in Jerusalem and in the church in Bethlehem is a mote in the sun.

It has over 1,000 monks and patriarchs and priests and liars from twenty-six nations of the Christians. They practice such austerities and false fasts that they turn into Ahlat skeletons, and for their unholy breakfasts consume a date or olive or almond and a cup of milk. Votive offerings come here from throughout the Christian world. There are immature Magian boys and lovely *kaladite* (?) youths who service any and all comers day and night.

The kitchen of Kay Kavus in this monastery has over 100 cooks who will prepare whatever food you desire. Even bird's-milk and soul-water can be found in their pantry. There are numerous monks, but ever since the reign of Selim I, the Greek infidels have been in charge.

There is a nine-arched dome illuminated day and night by an oil-lamp. We asked the nasty priests for permission to tour it. They would not let us in. We cited the verse:

> Yesterday I went to see you in church
> But the monks would not let me in.
> I swear that on Judgement Day
> I will complain about you to Jesus.

Out of fear of Jesus they opened the door of the sky-coloured dome and we went inside.

Stations of Moses, Jesus, and Mother Mary. And, east of these, **Station of the Apostles**: twelve stations. All these shrines are so embellished that one cannot express it with tongues or record it with pens.

Their water is mainly from cisterns. They also haul up water from below with donkeys.

When God revealed Himself to Moses on this mountain the voice of the Lord of Power broke it asunder and all the trees and vegetation were burned. The following Koranic verses were revealed about this: *And when his Lord revealed Himself to the Mountain, He levelled it into dust. Moses fell down senseless* (7:143). *The tree which on Mount Sinai grows gives oil and a condiment for men* (23:20). And when He revealed Himself, the *gamam* – i.e., cloud – descended upon this mountain. Even now, traces of those events are sometimes visible. In short, it is a wondrous shrine.

However, it has remained in the hands of the Christians. But were it in the possession of Islam, it would be in ruins. The infidels have made it prosperous, and strive to maintain its endowments. They keep on good terms with the authorities by giving presents to the governor of Egypt, the notables of the seven regiments, the Agha of Suez and the Arab sheikhs. They even gave this humble one a leathern tobacco-pouch that smelled like musk and ambergris. And the Frankish patriarch gave me a watch.

I also received patents (*papintalar*, safe-conducts) from the seven patriarchs, to the effect that: 'He is a world traveller, he has visited Mt Sinai, no one should hinder him in his travels to the country of the Seven Kings.'

St Catherine's Monastery on Mt Sinai

I wanted to go to the castle of Tur and from there to Suez, but they dissuaded me, saying the roads were too hard and I would not be able to catch up with the Hajj caravan. Seeing that it was a small castle on the seacoast, I thought I could at least tour it. So I walked down from Mt Sinai in the company of a few of the monks. We went through a broad valley with rose gardens and orchards ... apples, pears, pomegranates, quinces, and grapes ... that are shipped to Suez and from there to Cairo, providing that city with cheap fruit.

There are streams flowing in these orchards that empty into the Red Sea at the foot of Tur Castle. All the Suez ships stop here to take on water, and also to transport water to Suez where a single waterskin sells for ten *para*. They gave me a lot of fruit and I hurried back. It turned out that the pilgrimage caravan had left the castle of Nahil and we met in mid-journey in the moonlight at midnight. Toward morning a *rada* halt was announced. I distributed the Tur fruit among the brethren of purity, and pleased all my friends.

VOLUME TEN

Egypt and Sudan

EVLIYA'S FINAL VOLUME, covering the last ten years of his life, is devoted to Cairo and journeys along the Nile. His description of Cairo, the second great city of the Ottoman Empire, provides a survey, full of anecdotes and asides, on a par with his account of Istanbul in Volume 1. And again we find chapter divisions – a feature found only in this and in the first volume.

Evliya dwells on the unusual customs of various groups whom he meets in Egypt – snake charmers, beggars, the Hadari fellahin with their elaborate wedding ceremonies and an Arab tribe that claims to have sex with crocodiles. He explores the inside of one of the great pyramids. He attends the colourful *mevlud* of Seyyid Ahmad al-Badawi in Tanta. (With regard to the acrobatic performances, cf. Volume 4, selection 2 for similar entertainments in Anatolia. The festive atmosphere of these *mevluds* has its counterpart in the fairs of the Balkans; cf. Volume 8, selection 10).) Even more than elsewhere, Evliya gives very rich descriptions of the animal world in relation to the people: snakes and crocodiles, domestic fowl and migratory birds (cf. Volume 8, selection 1), elephants and monkeys.

Evliya had a special interest in the Nile, as attested by the surviving map of the Nile in the Vatican Library that can be attributed to him. His journeys along the Nile take him as far as Alexandria to the north and the land of the Funj in Sudan to the south; and there is an excursion to Ethiopia and the Red Sea coast. As is the case with the Kalmyks earlier, Evliya's description of the Funj is rich in fantasy – if thus we should interpret his encounter with two Bektashi dervishes and their unusual mounts.

Evliya relates events in Cairo up until 1683 and concludes by claiming that he has retired into obscurity after fifty-one years of travel.

1. Adam's prayer for Egypt in 'Hebrew'

Adam's first earthly home was Sarandil (or Sarandib, Ceylon, Sri Lanka). The second was Mt Arafat. The third, by God's leave, was Mecca. After dwelling there for some time he had, according to the chroniclers, 40,000 sons. Every year he and his descendants used to circumambulate the Holy House and perform the Hajj. But since there was no sown land in Mecca, they had difficulty feeding themselves. So, by God's command, they migrated to Egypt and settled on the bank of the Nile. This was their fourth home.

In Egypt sowing was so easy and crops were so plentiful that one grain of wheat produced 100 ears and every ear 100 grains, as attested by the Koranic verse *each bearing a hundred grains* (2:261).

At first Adam and his descendants all lived together in Egypt, and this is the prayer he recited. It is in the Hebrew language, because when Adam fell from paradise, in his rebellion he forgot the language of paradise, which is Arabic, and instructed by Gabriel he began to speak Hebrew instead. I record here his prayer for Egypt (or Cairo – *Mısr*) which I got from the Coptic chronicles:

Hidam	My God
tıt jedilem	My faith
huji çiji riba	Preserve from the devil
felaj riba felaj riba	Save me, save me
şujüm jaken	All your angels
tarj dilem şerij tena	May they serve me
sıja riyeji zehriba	Give wheat I'll make bread
jedilem jiraj jiraj	In the end death occurs, death
Hidam kidam	My God
hirj bijti jar binti	For my sons this my city
jari mjni jar mjni	Make prosper, make prosper.

Such is Adam's prayer for Egypt in the Hebrew language in the meter *müfte'ilün*. That is why first of all lands Cairo is so prosperous, a city that is half the world.

2. Relation among Nile overflow, plenty and poverty, crowdedness of Cairo, people and donkeys

Because God blessed Egypt with the Nile, there is great abundance and an accumulation of imperial wealth (or tax money). This wealth is assured as long as the Nile overflow reaches 18 cubits. If it reaches 20 cubits, then the Pasha, agents, tax farmers, provincial governors and peasants all become rich. If it does not reach 18 cubits, then – *God save us!* – the land is not watered and dearth and famine ensue, the agents and tax farmers are cut off, imperial wealth is not produced, the Pasha is forced to make up the loss to the treasury out of his own pocket, and he in turn wrings it out of his subordinates.

There are 300,000 holders of religious offices – imams, preachers, ulema, sheikhs, descendants of the Prophet – who demand their salaries, amounting to two Egyptian treasures, from the supervisors of endowments. If they don't get their salaries, there is a public uprising. But if there is abundance in the land, then their salaries are forthcoming and they shower benedictions on the Sultan and the benefactors.

{But if the Nile rises above the point indicated in the geomancy of Muhyiddin-i Arabi[70] by the phrases *The water was equal to the wood* and *From the mountain to the mountain*, if the overflow is three cubits too high, then Cairo becomes flooded. This actually occurred during the governorship of Kethüda Ibrahim Pasha (1669–73), when one could see the Nile flood from the threshold of Demirkapu and from in front of the Ibrahim Gülşeni convent, and the Cairo populace was alarmed.}

In short, there is no city in the entire world, let alone in the Ottoman Empire, that is such a sea of men and with such productive land as this. Cairo is called Mother of the World, because if the whole world is suffering dearth and famine, Egypt can feed it; but if, God forbid, Cairo suffers famine for a single day, not all the world's crops could sustain it. For Cairo is a sea of men.

In particular, when this humble one in the course of my travels arrived in Cairo in 1082 (1671–2), 800,000 men had died of plague that year, according to the court records of the four Sunni rites. In fact, there was one village whose tax farm was taken over by the state and in the course of

---

70 Evliya frequently cites geomantic and onomantic prognostications wrongly attributed to Ibn Arabi (d. 1240); see Dankoff 2004, 103.

two months Ibrahim Pasha sold it to nine different men for twenty purses each. Despite this loss of life, the markets were so crowded that one could not walk through without jostling shoulders.

In Cairo, flocks of animals – horses and mules, camels, cows, water-buffaloes, sheep and goats – roam about in the marketplace. And donkeys are so numerous that they have taken over the city. One can hardly pass through the streets because the donkey drivers are constantly shouting '*Behind you! On your side! In front of you! On your right! On your left!*' Sometimes they pick out naive Turks for abuse, crying '*Give way, Efendi!*' and trample them with their donkeys.

The first *temcid* one hears in Cairo is the braying of donkeys, in the *segah* musical mode. If one donkey in its stable starts to bray in the middle of the night, then – in accordance with the Koranic verse *The harshest of voices is the braying of the ass* (31:19) – there is braying in Cairo for the next two hours, making one think that doomsday has come and the antichrist has emerged.

All the notables of Cairo, and even the womenfolk, ride donkeys. You see women on donkey-back – with silver harness and velvet saddle-cloth and the donkeys dyed with henna – riding as far as Özbekiye (Azbakiya) and Salibiya and Old Cairo (Fustat) and Bulaq and Qaytbay, crying '*Behind you! On your side!*' and shooting jereed (!). And this is not considered shameful, because the donkey is Egypt's caique and ferryboat.

There was a certain Ali Bey from Girga who had 40,000 donkeys, each of which earned him 10 *para* a day for carrying grain. He is famous throughout Egypt. And it is certain that the Emir of the Hajj, Rıdvan Bey, had 40,000 camels. Even now it is impossible to pass through the streets of Cairo because of the water-carrying camels and donkeys.

There are twelve festivals a year in Cairo, which will be described in due course; on those days especially it is impossible to move in the marketplace because of the crowds of people and the crowds of donkey drivers and camel drivers. It is a sight worth seeing, part of the glory of the city!

3. Snake medicine and snake charming

Description of the preparation of the greatest electuary, the theriac of Faruq

Let it be known to intelligent travellers that in every country throughout the world there are physicians who make the theriac of Faruq, but they cannot make it like the Egyptian kind. The tablet of Faruq is peculiar to

Egypt. One should understand that the term 'tablet' in the first place refers to something that is extracted from the body of a snake.

There are forty persons receiving salaries from the endowments of this hospital of Sultan Qala'un who are charged with providing this service once a year. They are a guild and reside in the villages of the Habiroğlu in the district of Giza. Once a year in the month of July, they hunt the snakes from which the theriac of Faruq is made.

When it is the proper time to hunt snakes, they gather together and put on clothing of thick felt from head to foot. They even cover their faces; only their eyes are visible. They attach pieces of white felt to long sticks and head for Bahnasa, the Fayyum and Jabal Akhdar. They reach the place where the Faruq snakes are found in the cool of the morning when the snakes are indolent before being warmed by the heat of the day. Even in that condition it is a great struggle to catch them.

Having caught several thousand, they put them in baskets that are smeared with Faruq, and the snakes become intoxicated and bewildered. While the snakes are in this state, they sew up the openings of the baskets.

It sometimes happens that while struggling to catch the snakes, one of them will spring at the face of a hunter. If it strikes him in the eye he cannot be saved and falls a martyr to this profession. For they are deadly poisonous snakes. If they bite a camel on the ear or a mule on the hoof, they kill it instantly.

Hunting these snakes is reserved for the above-mentioned individuals. No one else is able to carry out the task. By God's command, the members of their guild belong to the Sa'diye brotherhood; but they are very upright individuals.

This group caught a great many snakes, loaded them in baskets on donkeys, and took them to Cairo. On the way, near a garden of Iram called Basatin, one of the snakes escaped and bit the donkey carrying its basket. The poor donkey collapsed head first, and in the twinkling of an eye its body swelled up to the size of an elephant. When it died, each leg had turned into a huge pillar. Some of the hunters drove away the people dwelling nearby, saying that the carcass of the donkey would split open and they would be ill affected by the stench. They removed the baskets of snakes that had been loaded on that donkey and placed them on another one. As this was going on, the carcass of the poisoned donkey split open and everything, even the bones, dissolved and flowed away. Thank God no one was harmed. The people who were there immediately piled dirt

Snake medicine and snake charming 375

over the carcass of the donkey and buried it. They brought the cargo of snakes on the other donkeys to the hospital of Qala'un and turned it over to the chief physician and superintendent.

This humble one had previously asked the chief physician if I could watch the process; so now they sent me word. I immediately mounted my horse and went to the hospital of Qala'un. They opened the door of the Faruq chamber and let me in, then barred the door. They do not normally let in outsiders because it is a dangerous place, full of thousands of pitiless snakes, and also because they want to keep their knowledge secret, on the grounds that *The Evil Eye is a reality*.

This Faruq chamber is a large medrese. Walls and floor are covered with varicoloured raw marble. It is a medrese devoted to the science of medicine. All around the courtyard are terraces which on that day were covered with carpets.

We were some thirty people all told, including the chief physician, the superintendent, the secretary of the endowment, the administrator of the endowment, ten assistants of the chief physician, the reciter of prayers, and twelve snake-hunters, cooks and butchers. There was no reason for anyone to knock on the door and want to come in. Still, they barred the door firmly and told me not to fear. I got up on a low stool which they used to light lamps and got ready to watch. All thirty people arose, performed an ablution and two prostrations, then brought out their tools and equipment.

First, there were 100 blocks of wood, each three spans long. In the middle of each was a *gevele* nail, one span in height. There were 100 sharp meat-cleavers, like so many swords of Zahhak, the backs of which were made of thick Frankish iron. There were 100 large glazed earthenware crocks, large enough for a man to fit inside. Some were full of water, others empty. There were several tinned trays from the time of Qala'un (Mamluk sultan, reg. 1279–90); one *ardeb* of finely sifted salt; and some fifty large vessels, like earthenware water jars, glazed inside and out, but with wide bases and mouths big enough for a man to put his head in.

Everyone readied these copper and earthenware vessels. When the reciter of prayers stood up, all those present also rose to their feet. After the *besmele* and praises of God and blessings on the Prophet, he mentioned in order the Ottoman dynasty, the benefactor Sultan Qala'un, the Physician Loqman, Pythagoras the Monotheist, the Sultan of Physicians Abu Ali Sina (Ibn Sina, Avicenna), and the spirits of the other physicians. He then prayed for the safety of those present, mentioning the chief physician, the superintendent, the secretary, the chief cook and all the assistants and servants. After the prayer he said '*God is great*' and recited a Fatiha, and we touched our faces with our hands.

Now the old chief hunter and three snake-butchers cut open the top of one of the twelve baskets that were standing in the middle of the courtyard. Great God! Some thousands of merciless snakes with poisonous fangs slithered out. I was stupefied with fear, although I was watching from a high perch. Some of them jumped as high as a man to the left and right. Hissing and whistling, they threw themselves at the wall.

While the terrified snakes were leaping about, the chief physician's servants joined with the snake-hunters and prodded them inside yellow cloaks that were smeared with Faruq, and they all quieted down. The chief hunter and three butchers sat themselves next to the post-blocks mentioned above with cleavers in their hands and took the snakes out of the cloaks one by one.

One type of snake to emerge was small and white, with an intoxicating musky smell. These the hunters put in their bosoms. I asked the chief physician about them, and he said, 'That is the musk snake. It is not used for making Faruq, but for other medicaments. You'll see shortly.'

As I observed, they collected together all these little white snakes and arranged them on a long red silken cord, hanging by their throats. The cord was tied to a shaded place in a corner of the medrese and stretched from wall to wall. Using cotton, they dripped some Sousse olive oil into the mouths of the snakes, at which they died and began to swell up. The snakes would remain hanging this way for forty days and nights, the snake skins granulating into musk like cardamom seeds, with an odour so sharp that it makes one's nose bleed.

Another type of small snake was short and mottled, with rounded heads like half of a walnut shell. The men set these to one side as well. When I inquired about them, the chief physician said, 'They are called snake of Adam the Pure and are descended from the snakes that were banished from paradise along with Adam. These too are not used for making Faruq, but for other medicaments.'

He searched through ten baskets of snakes and set aside the musk snakes and the round-headed snakes of Adam the Pure. The latter, like the Faruq snake, does not hatch eggs but gives birth like other animals, by God's wisdom and contrary to the nature of snakes.

Then they counted the Faruq snakes that were left. There were 8,300, large and small. There were handed over to the administrator of the endowment, and the secretaries and instructors recorded in ledgers that there were 800 *guruş* worth of snakes.

The chief snake-hunter and three snake-butchers were seated at the post-blocks. Uttering a *besmele* and the intention of healing, he took out a large snake from the cloak, put the middle of the snake on the nail of one of the blocks, and holding the head and tail together with his left hand, struck once with the cleaver in his right hand. The body of the snake, minus head and tail, began to squirm about the marble floor, while head and tail remained in the chief hunter's hand. He used the back of the cleaver to crush the snake's head and left it on the floor, saying *'Declare God's unity.'* All those present shouted, *'There is no god but God!'*

When he cuts a snake, he does so holding it stretched out and leaving behind four inches (lit. three fingers) of the head and tail. Another butcher takes the body of the snake and slices open its abdomen with a golden knife, extracts the intestines and eggs, and throws it to a third butcher who, pulling on the snakeskin with his fingernails, flays it from end to end. Apparently the skin was makeshift to begin with, so now the white flesh easily slips out. But the snake is still writhing!

With this the job of the butchers is done and the snake falls into the hands of the physicians. The chief physician's assistants take the peeled snake, wash it thoroughly in the aforementioned crocks, and put it into one of the glazed jars, adding salt. When these jars are full they place them on the fire. The chief physician holds a watch. They burn acacia wood under the jars, and the fire becomes extremely hot.

Meanwhile everyone is in a state of fear and reciting litanies. Sometimes when they remove a snake from the cloak they spit into its mouth, so the snake is intoxicated and bewildered, then they put it on the log and chop it. In this manner the twelve hunters and butchers kill ten baskets of snakes.

As for the heads and tails, they fill large apothecary bottles with them and save them to make other medicaments. I persisted in questioning them about this, but they refused to answer. From what I understand, however – and God knows best – they extract the poison from the heads and send them to Frengistan. Because one time a gift of 1,000 snake heads strung on a cord was brought to the king of Dunkerque. He was pleased with the gift, took the snake heads off the cord, and gave them over to the Graf.

If the butchers do not strike accurately while killing these snakes and one tiny part of the head or tail is still slightly attached to the body, the chief physician immediately leaps from his place and cries out, '*irmi, irmi al-ḥayya*' meaning 'Throw it away! Throw away the snake!' (Once) they did not throw the body of the snake with its head in with the intestines and eggs of the other snakes, but they put it in a place apart. That snake immediately swelled up as big as one's arm, although it was originally only as thick as one's thumb. The improperly severed head had affected the body and it swelled up. So (whenever the head was improperly severed) the chief physician immediately cried out and had them throw it away. They also discarded the log and cleaver that were used and brought out different ones. By God's wisdom, on that day seventy-five snakes from ten baskets were not properly killed and the men threw them all away along with the implements. The discarded snakes are not charged on the account of the endowment; rather, they are charged against the account of the snake-hunters and butchers and the cost deducted from their fees. It is an amazing spectacle.

Another noteworthy event occurred that day. When the skins and intestines and eggs of the butchered snakes had piled up like mountains, the snake-butchers regrouped and sprinkled some of the aforementioned sifted salt on this snake-rubbish. As this was going on, one of the butchers withdrew his hand and gave a heart-rending sigh. The chief hunter immediately spat onto the fellow's injured finger, brought three of the snakes that had been washed in the crocks, and wrapped his finger with them. The three snakes immediately swelled to the size of a man's arm. He removed them and wrapped the finger with three more; they did not swell up, but they did change colour, and were also removed. Now the chief hunter took the fellow's finger into his mouth, sucked at the wound and spat a yellow substance on the ground. They rubbed a bit of Greatest Faruq on the fellow's finger. The pain subsided; the man was saved from being poisoned.

Apparently the head and tail of one of the snakes being killed had not been properly severed in a single blow and were accidentally left amidst the snakes' eggs and rubbish. Then, while the butchers were sprinkling salt on the snakes' eggs and innards, some poison from that improperly severed snake got on that fellow's finger. They treated him as I described and saved his life.

In sum, I never saw such hard-hearted and cold-blooded men as these snake-hunters and snake-butchers – I wonder if they should even be considered human beings. To be sure, I witnessed a remarkable scene; but at every moment I nearly took leave of my senses, and I began to regret having come to watch. Now I asked the chief physician, 'You have salted the skins and innards and eggs of these snakes and pickled them in jars to preserve them. What will you do with them?'

'What are you after? Don't ask!' he said. I persisted and questioned him again. Finally he answered, 'There are Frankish bailos (i.e., ambassadors from Venice and other European states) here. They purchase these jars from us and take them to the physicians of Frengistan, who use this substance to treat various ailments. They treat every limb of the body in a different manner, and this substance is very effective.'

They put the cleaned and salted snakes into twelve glazed earthenware jars, placed the jars on the kitchen hearths in one corner of the courtyard, and burned acacia wood under them to make the fire extremely hot. The chief physician had his staff in one hand and a watch in the other. The cooks were again his students, having mastered the sciences under his tutorship; the chief physician was only present to watch the time. The snakes boiled for three hours. An amber-like yellow oil appeared at the top of the jars. The chief physician took up a ladle, spooned out yellow snake oil and filled the large apothecary bottles that were there. Once again they made the fire very hot under the jars – please note that the vessels used to cook the snakes are not copper saucepans or kettles but, as I mentioned, earthenware jars glazed inside and out.

Next the chief physician weighed the snake oil, that he had spooned out with the ladle, against olive oil that comes from Sousse in the Maghreb – it is the finest olive oil, like Water of Life. He filled the bottles with five *okkas* of snake oil and five of pure olive oil, then put them over a low heat which they later increased. After three hours the oil took on the consistency of clarified butter and the fragrance of musk and raw ambergris, perfuming the brains of those present. I was impatient to learn what it was for, and again questioned the chief physician.

'To tell you the truth,' he said, 'there are an enormous number of people in India with leprous conditions, and this oil is very beneficial for that climate. If it is rubbed just once on the bodies of those afflicted with such diseases, by God's command the malady disappears and they become as clear-skinned as pearls or eggs. But it has no benefit here in Egypt, even if it is rubbed on a thousand times. On the other hand, in Egypt, if you make those suffering from mange or palpitations swallow one dram of it for forty days, by God's command they are cured.'

They cooked the snakes in the jars for three more hours and boiled off one span of water, then removed the jars from the fire and put the shredded snake meat on large copper trays to cool. The snake broth left in the jars was for local consumption. For the past month, bowls and ewers and copper buckets had been arriving from the Egyptian notables along with prescriptions, and these were now taken out of the cupboards. The name and illness of each patient were written on a piece of cloth wrapped in paper and attached to each vessel. They filled the bowls and buckets with that snake broth, sometimes adding other medicaments according to the illness, and returned them to their owners. Thus, the snake soup went to hundreds of places.

Their work complete, all the assistants filled dishes with snake soup, crumbled some bread on top, and sat down to eat. I nearly took leave of my senses. The chief physician, superintendent, secretary and other servants also began to drink the snake broth by the cup. They brought me a cup too. I refused it, but the chief physician and superintendent were insistent, 'Truly, my lord, it is very invigorating. It increases the faculty of vision and eliminates the odour of haemorrhoids.'

'It is God's to command,' I said, mustering my courage. 'A trouble shared is a trouble halved.[71] They drank it, so I'll drink it too.' I closed my eyes and gritted my teeth, uttered a *besmele* with the intention of healing, and drank off a cup. It smelled like musk. They brought another cup, in which, with the tip of a knife, they put a small amount of the snake oil mixed with the aforementioned olive oil. I drank that too. God knows, that musky smell did not leave my brain for an entire week.

On the benefits of snake broth. I described above how we were attacked by Arabs on the night we were approaching Badr-i Hunayn after departing from Mecca.[72] During that period I was quite anxious and my body became feverish. Praise be to God, I drank two cups of this snake broth and within a week not a hint or trace of the malady remained, my body turned to pure silver, and I was well again. I experienced other benefits as well.

My adventure. One such benefit relates to something that occurred to me in the year 1056 (1646). I was with Tekeli Mustafa Pasha at the siege of

---

71 This English expression is offered by Redhouse as the equivalent of *El ile gelen düğün bayramdır*, 'What is suffered with other people is a wedding party and holiday.'
72 The reference is to Vol. 9, fol. 367b.

Şebenik (Sebenico) castle, one of the Venetian strongholds on the Bosnian frontier. After pounding the fortress with cannons for forty days and forty nights we were unable to conquer it and retreated, making camp in the place called Danilova. There we were surrounded by 200,000 Uskok (Christian Bosnian) and Carinthian and Frankish and Croatian infidels and had a great battle that lasted seven hours. The Ottoman troops were routed and the infidels began to massacre the Muslims on one flank.

At that period this humble one was travelling with the janissary regiment as commissary, and before my very eyes the infidels put my seven slaveboys and 380 companions to the sword. I abandoned all my money and goods and galloped off on an Arab steed that the grand vizier Kara Mustafa Pasha had given me. The infidels pursued me round about that endless plain, but were unable to catch me and eventually lost track – God the Preserver hid it from them.

When night fell I was in a desperate state. Abandoning my horse, I entered a forest with my sword and quiver and bow case and spent seven days and six nights in the mountains, with no companions but birds and wild beasts, and subsisting on roots and berries. But going on foot with quiver and bow case and sword, and 80 Venetian *guruş* and 150 ducats in my waistband, exhausted me. Finally I removed the arrows from the quiver, took the bow by the handle, put the quiver and two hand-guns and the waistband with the *guruş* into the bow-case and buried it under a rock, leaving sword, guns and waistband in trust to God. Lightened of my load, I came to a stream, performed an ablution and two prostrations of prayer in need, and sought spiritual aid from all the prophets and saints.

While in this bewildered state, I overheard a conversation in Bosnian:
'*Bre Meho!*' (Hey, Meho!)
'*İşo veliş?*' – i.e., What do you have to say?
'*Hodamu sinko, hodamu*' – i.e., Come here, dear son, come!

When I heard these voices speaking Bosnian, my spirits revived. Still, I had anxious thoughts. Weren't all the people in these mountains Croatian Uskoks? They had submitted to the infidels and put the Ottomans to the sword. Might not these voices belong to them?

It turned out that they were father and son who had come to the mountain to cut wood, and when it was the time of the noon prayer they recited the call to prayer, so I knew they were Muslims. I came forward and greeted them, and we became acquainted.

'Welcome,' said the old fellow in (Turkish in) Bosnian dialect. 'Are you all right? What are you doing in these mountains?'

'I'm with a few friends,' I replied. 'We know these mountains. We came up here to hunt. We're janissaries from Livno castle.'

'Do you have any news about the routed army?'

'They were routed a week ago and fled to Kinin and Livno castles.'

'It's fate,' he said. 'And how did the infidels take Kilis castle?'

As for this humble one, I was at death's door and charged with guarding the castle of my body. To make a long story short, we became friends and I accompanied them at a leisurely pace toward Glamoch castle. As we approached we ran into the castle warden. I related the entire sad story to him. He immediately had one of his servants dismount and bid me mount instead. I wept with joy, giving God a thousand praises. Two hours later we entered Glamoch Castle in procession and I stayed that night as guest in the warden's house.

The wonder is that there was a Muslim castle one hour from where I was, but in my fear I spent seven days with foxes and jackals and rabbits and deer as my companions and bedfellows.

In the morning I requested the warden to lend me ten horsemen, saying that I had left some friends in the mountain among the rocks and wished to search for them. We went back into the mountains by the same roads we had come out, straight to the place where I had left my quiver and guns and waistband. Saying that I had to pee, I gave my horse to the guides and went ahead. I turned over some rocks and took my weapons. The strap of my quiver had been eaten by a fox or a jackal, but I somehow attached the quiver to my waist along with my waistband, into which I stuck my handguns. Praising God, I rejoined my guides, mounted my horse, and returned to Glamoch Castle in an hour.

I stayed there as guest for seven nights. By God's wisdom, one night, in my sleep, I had something like a nocturnal emission and awoke with lumbago. Gobs of blood mixed with pus and seminal fluid oozed onto the bedclothes for an hour. I was ill for another seven days.

When I recovered, the castle warden, Mehmed Agha, gave me a horse and a suit of clothes, and I got presents from the other officials as well. Out of consideration, they gave me a servant and several men to accompany me. We reached Tekeli Pasha in the Livno plain, and my spirits revived. But I found not one of my friends; all had been martyred at the hands of the infidels, who had taken Kilis Castle and massacred the soldiers garrisoned there. But Tekeli Pasha had raised a general levy and begun to protect the province and its populace. When we met, he gave me a horse and a suit of clothes. Our acquaintance was ancient, he having known (?) Melek Ahmed Pasha's father-in-law and Kaya Sultan's mother.

To come to the point – *One subject leads to another* – after the ejaculation that occurred on that night in Glamoch castle, this humble one lost sexual potency; I did not even have any nocturnal emission. And I was despondent, thinking that my progeny had been cut off. Now, twenty-seven years later, I came to Egypt and drank two cups of snake broth with oil on the day of Faruq in the Qala'un hospital. That night I had two nocturnal emissions in succession. In the morning I went to the hospital and told the whole story to the chief physician. He gave me ten *okkas* of snake broth and one canister of snake oil and olive oil mixed. I used the snake broth for five or six days and became so healthy that I could break hazelnut shells on my flesh, so hard had my body become. I experienced other benefits as well.

In short, the chief physician distributed this snake broth to all the people (who had left their vessels and prescriptions), and the snake stew that they had cooked was cooling on the trays. The chief physician sat down at the trays with his students and attendants. They all washed their hands thoroughly, rolled up their sleeves, and one by one took some snake stew in their hands. From the back of each snake, from both sides of the spine, which they call the backbone, they extracted long cordlike strings as thick as the handle of a pen-sharpener. The length differed according to the size of the snake that was cut.

This is what is termed the 'tablet' of the theriac of Faruq, which is the Great Theriac and is drawn out from the snake-meat like a string. Each snake produces just one tablet weighing one *miskal*. All this toil and trouble, all this fear and anxiety, is for the sake of tablets weighing one *miskal* each. None of the other parts of the snake that are cooked are used for Faruq; they are thrown away, or given to the poor to eat, or else are buried in some out-of-the-way place.

An enjoyable anecdote for sex addicts. Some of it was once given to a man who was no longer able to have sexual intercourse. He ate snake stew and then had sex five or ten times with his wife. She became annoyed because he could not get enough. The next morning she presented a cohabitation suit in court. As plaintiff, her complaint was: 'God forbid it, I cannot endure this affliction!' As defendant, he admitted: 'I ate snake meat and had sex ten times.' The *kadi* reconciled them to having sex twenty times (a day?). Those who heard of this suit wanted to drink snake soup as well, and prayed: '*O God, make it possible!*'

In short, they pounded the meat extracted from the back of those snakes with wooden mortars and pestles, pulverised it into a paste, and weighed it on a scale. At this juncture it becomes a white 'greatest electuary' and is called 'viper's tablet'. Now all the medicaments are passed through a fine sieve and weighed out in precise amounts, then mixed with the viper's tablet together with pure Anatolian honey that has been repeatedly boiled.

Every year they cook three cauldrons of theriac of Faruq. First they send two jars of it to the felicitous sultan and one jar each to the grand vizier, *şeyhülislam* and chief physician in Istanbul and the molla of Cairo as gifts. The rest they save for the superintendent of Qala'un's endowment; it is dispensed to the bed-ridden patients in the hospital according to their illnesses.

The theriac of Faruq is exported from Egypt to Turkey and Arabia and Persia and Frengistan – in short, to the seven climes. It is produced in the manner described. They usually cook it once a year, but while this humble one was in Egypt, the chief physician, being the perfect master, cooked it three times a year.

As for the white snakes of Adam the Pure, mentioned above, their number exceeded 1,000. The medrese where the theriac of Faruq is made has a small room fitted with glass panes and a cord stretched from one corner to the other. The chief physician hung those white snakes in a row along this cord, attaching them one by one by the tail with red silk thread. Struggling for their lives, the snakes bit one another and, formerly thin and white, they all swelled up as thick as one's arm. Now they closed all the windows of the room and went out, shutting the door behind them. When they opened it forty days later, the snakes of Adam the Pure had shrunk and become like thin strings. Even the bones were now black as cardamom seeds, having turned into a narcotic – the odour deprives a man of his senses, making him intoxicated and dizzy.

As for the snakes with the round head like half a walnut shell that we described above, the snake-butchers cut them in two and pickle them with their speckled skins. The halves with heads are strung on strings, the tails are buried in the ground. After 40 days they dry out and turn red. Then they are taken (off the strings and out of the ground) and kept in lead

Snake medicine and snake charming 385

canisters. Otherwise they would be eaten by ants, since snake meat and human flesh are very tasty.

A wonderful anecdote. The fact that human flesh is tasty is something I witnessed among the Kalmyk cannibals in the Kipchak Steppe. They eat the corpses of their dead, and they also strangle and eat some of their poor Nogay captives – they do not cut their throats, so as not to lose their blood, but just strangle them, cook them and eat them. The Kalmyks claim that there is nothing tastier than human flesh, snake meat, and pork; and the tastiest part is the pig's tail and the 'tail' or coccyx of humans. There are in fact many men of the Kalmyk persuasion in Turkey who know of this taste. But I myself can testify that human flesh is tasty, for if a man kisses his beloved just once, he finds eternal life and is overjoyed. That is how I know that human flesh is tasty.

To sum up, anyone who goes to Egypt and does not see how this Greatest Faruq is made has seen nothing remarkable on the face of the earth. That is all on this subject.

In Egypt, if a snake invades your house or pigeon coop and the tranquillity of the home is disturbed, you find one of these snake-hunters and, of course, pay him a few *para*. He enters the house and shouts once at the top of his voice, then blows a whistle that he carries at his waist and makes a hissing sound with his mouth. The snakes immediately begin to appear from various places. They raise their heads and dart threateningly at the hunter, but as they approach he captures them and fills his bag with them. So the house is rid of snakes. These house snakes, however, are not used for Faruq; that is only made from other snakes that live in the desert.

My tale has been long, like the tail of a snake, and you may think it is a tall tale; but as God is my witness, this is the way it was.[73]

In the year 1085 (1674–5) snakes had infested the quarters of Ahmed Efendi – he was the imam of our lord Canpoladzade Hüseyn Pasha – and forced him to flee. One day, while the imam's purebred Arabian horse was eating fodder, a snake bit it on the nose and it died. The carcass swelled to the size of an elephant, and it was impossible to move it. Finally they dug a hole right there and buried it. Anyway, the imam was still unable to go home.

---

73 Note play on words: *yılan* 'snake'; *yılan hikayeti* 'snake story' – i.e. a long drawn-out story, a shaggy-dog story; *yalan* 'lie' – a tall tale.

One day I happened to meet one of the snake-hunters and took him to the imam's quarters. He shouted once at the top of his voice and began to blow on the whistle. Five or ten snakes, each as thick as one's arm and over a fathom in length, raised their heads and gathered around him. Everyone else fled, including this humble one – I ran to the house of the governor's secretary and watched from the window. The snakes did battle with the hunter for perhaps an hour. He eventually put eleven of them in his sack and left, uttering the benediction, 'May God bless you!' With his house rid of snakes, the imam returned to his quarters and stayed there.

The strangest story of all. A few days later I went to Rumeli Square. It turned out that the snake-hunter had sold the eleven snakes to snake-charmers there for eleven *guruş*. God knows, each one was as dreadful and frightful as a dragon. But within a few days the snake-charmers had taught them tricks, and they danced like monkeys on Rumeli Square. What strange and marvellous spells and magical charms these snake-hunters have – God knows, they have been vouchsafed the miraculous graces of the saints! The strange thing is that they are terribly funny and entertaining.

While the charmers were making the imam's snakes dance and perform on Rumeli Square, one of them darted from its place and bit a small boy on the foot. By God's wisdom, a dervish of the Sa'diye brotherhood was there. He sucked the venom from the boy's foot and spat it out on the ground. The boy's foot was rid of the venom and returned to normal. But the Sa'di dervish did not stop there. Crying '*O Living and Eternal One! Peace be upon Noah in the two worlds!*' he seized the snake that had bitten the boy and started to gobble it up.

'O woe!' cried the snake-charmer. 'This was the Pasha's imam's snake that I bought for eleven *guruş*.'

Finally an officer of the agent in charge of public spectacles,[74] who had authority over the snake-charmers, came and took the Sa'di dervish to the Pasha. He continued eating the snake, even in the Pasha's presence, and was foaming at the mouth.

'My snake that was as big as a dragon is gone!' shouted the snake-charmer. He was furious. All present testified that the sheikh (i.e., the Sa'di dervish) had saved the boy from being poisoned. The Pasha was pleased with the sheikh and had him eat two more snakes in his presence. He

---

74 *Hurde emini yasakcısı* – see Shaw 1966, p. 137.

bestowed fifty gold pieces on the sheikh, ten on the snake-charmer, and five on the boy who was saved from the poison. Then he dismissed everyone. It was a strange spectacle.

4. Rain, snow and hail in Egypt in 1083 (1672)

In Cairo when it rains, there is a shortage of water. Unlike other places, where rain brings rejoicing and the people bask in the water of mercy, in Cairo the people devour one another from a dearth of water. The reason is that the soil is oily (and so turns to slick mud). If it rains just a little, neither horse nor man nor donkey nor camel – *God save them* – can go outdoors and fetch water, which is why there is a water shortage. Then the price of one goatskin of water brought on the back of a water-carrier goes up to five *para*. The water dispensaries open to dispense drinking-water, and water for any other purpose becomes very scarce.

So the governor of the province, or rather the constable, brings 40,000 or 50,000 (!) donkey-driving rubbish sweepers with dry earth which they pour over the public thoroughfares so that people can walk about a bit. Because none of the roads in Cairo is paved, therefore there is so much mud – *God save us* – it rivals Silistria. Since it is a coastal climate, however, it only rains once or twice a year. If it were like Turkey, then every time it rained, Egypt would be ruined.

In fact, in the year (10)83 (1672–3), there was rain mixed with snow that lasted for seven days and seven nights. People could not go outdoors to visit each other, or go to the public prayer-grounds and offer a prayer for rain (!). Twenty-two houses of Hadari Fellahin were destroyed, and the water shortage was so severe that people still talk about it. When it snowed and the roofs and the people were covered with white snow, the Arabs said, *Ash hadha nazala mina's-sama al-qutni*, meaning, 'What is this? It's raining down cotton from the sky!' The Turks said, 'God be praised, look at God's mercy!' and they ate the snow. The Arabs gathered here and there and when they tasted the snow said, *Lahha'ad barda'n-nar*, meaning, 'My goodness, cold fire!' In Cairo the snowfall was light and soon disappeared, but in Buhayra it stayed on the ground for five hours. And that year in Cairo there was a hailstorm in which every hailstone weighed five or six drams.

Fortunately the plants and crops of Egypt have no need of rain, because the Nile overflows and for three months the country turns into a red sea; then the water recedes, crops are planted, and in sixty days they reach maturity, are harvested and stored. That is why there is no need for rain. 'God's custom' operates in this fashion, a marvellous example of divine wisdom.

5. Crocodiles

On the animals that occur in the Nile and their properties
First, there are thousands of fishes in the Nile. But the one they call crocodile is a frightful and harmful beast, similar to the animals known in Turkey as lizard, monitor lizard, and gecko lizard. It has four legs and a tail. In Arabic it is called *timsah*, in Persian *nahang*, in Turkish *luy*, in Mongolian *selkun*, in the province of Nubia *wuli*, in the province of Ulwi *shunshar*. It is an accursed creature, up to fifteen cubits in length. Its back is covered with scales, such that even a musket shot cannot penetrate. Only under the armpit is a soft spot, tender like an earlobe, where it can be shot; or else it can be killed with the shot of a one dram musket striking the head.

Medicinal property. Hunters take its fat, which relieves pain when rubbed on the body in the heat of summer.

In most animals, the lower jaw moves, but in the crocodile the upper jaw opens and shuts while the lower jaw is immobile. There are sixty teeth in the upper jaw and forty in the lower. It also has two long fangs in the lower jaw, while in the upper jaw it has two holes through which the points of its fangs emerge just next to the nostrils. On close inspection I observed that those two fangs are not found in the young of the crocodile, but in adults they emerge like Zahhak's sword at the ends of the lower jaw.

When a sheep or lamb, or a man, a horse, a cow or a camel, is drinking at the edge of the Nile, the crocodile approaches very stealthily and first strikes with its tail, then drags the animal into the water. If the victim is a man or a sheep, it gives no quarter but swallows the victim in an instant.

By God's wisdom, it has no hind quarters for the excretion of waste. Instead, when nature calls, it emerges from the Nile onto one of the islands and strolls about. By God's command, there is a kind of pied bird, like the duck in Turkey, with short legs and a beak and claws. While flying phoenix-like along the river's edge, it spies the crocodile on the island and approaches it, just as a lynx approaches a lion, and flutters once or twice. The crocodile becomes happy when it sees this bird. It may not even have come out on the island to relieve nature, but simply for a pleasure stroll with its mate. And if the bird is hungry, it will nudge the crocodile on the nose to make it open its mouth. Or the crocodile will open its mouth of its own accord.

The bird then goes into the crocodile's mouth all the way to its stomach. It kicks and scratches at the filth and takes some into its mouth. The crocodile then opens its mouth like a cave and lets the bird take out all its filth. This makes the crocodile happy, while satisfying the bird's hunger with the worms it finds amidst the filth. So the bird gets the benefit, and the crocodile gets relief, a marvellous example of divine wisdom.

There is a proverb that 'The magpie does not groom the calf out of love.' It picks out lice and worms from the calf's back in order to get something to eat. This bird performs a similar service for the crocodile.

It sometimes happens that the bird finds nothing good to eat the first time and enters the crocodile's stomach again to get more filth, but the crocodile, while swallowing, swallows the bird as well. The bird then makes its way back to the crocodile's mouth and, in its frustration, strikes a few times at a sharp bone that the crocodile has in its upper palate. Because of the pain, the crocodile will then open its mouth like a dragon and let the bird go out.

It is a wonder and a marvel that, while having no hind quarters, every crocodile has a bird appointed to service it. *God does what He wills by His power.*

A wonder. This crocodile is the dragon of the Nile. All creatures fear it, and it eats any and all. There is no animal in the Nile more swift or more terrible. But on land it is very slow-moving, because its legs and arms are short and it must drag its belly on the ground. So it cannot move fast or go far, and if it is out of water for more than three days it will die.

The crocodile's mortal enemy. But God has created one creature that is deadly to such a dragon. It is a four-legged furry animal (the ichneumen), quite similar to the one in Turkey known as the weasel which is an enemy of mice. It lives in the Nile and, like the crocodile, also lives on land. It comes out on one of the islands and crawls around the fine sand, seeking crocodiles, for which it nurses undying hostility. It is a small weasel-like creature that also hunts the birds that remove the crocodile's waste.

As soon as the crocodile comes ashore to relieve itself, this weasel approaches it walking over the sand. It is invisible to the crocodile, whose eyes are at the top of its head and, since it has no neck, cannot look down or left or right. When the aforementioned bird comes to service the crocodile and satisfy its own hunger, the crocodile opens its mouth and the bird goes inside. Then this weasel leaps up and also goes inside the crocodile's mouth. Now this crocodile, free of guile and full of bile, starts to thrash about and hurls itself into the Nile in a life-or-death struggle.

Once indeed, as I was returning to Cairo from Aswan by boat, a large crocodile caused a surge of waves, swimming right and left like an arrow let loose from a taut bow. I asked our captain, 'O Hacı Reşid! Why is this crocodile acting like this?'

'My lord,' he said, 'a larger crocodile must be chasing it.'

'But I don't see any.'

'Well, it must be seeking its mate.'

Now the crocodile came very close to our boat, and I told my slaveboys to shoot it. They let loose one or two bullets, but to no effect. Finally it came out onto the western shore, struggling and flaying about, climbed up the slope and stayed there. We followed it onto the shore and, as we were observing, a weasel came out of its mouth and ran into the Nile. The crocodile died then and there. It was 30 feet long.

There are crocodiles that reach a length of 40 or 50 feet. Indeed, there is no region of the Nile with more gigantic crocodiles than these provinces of Isna and Aswan. In Hafir-i Kabir – that is the fortress of Kör Hüseyn Bey, who acts as vizier to the king of Funjistan – the fortress gate is not made of iron but rather is the skin of a huge crocodile, nailed to the wall with nails weighing three *okkas* apiece. It is just the torso, minus the head and tail. I made a point of measuring it with a cubit-measure: it came to fourteen cubits high and seven cubits wide. I was amazed. Some of the Funj elders told me that they had seen even larger ones.

{The crocodile actually has another enemy, which is the hippopotamus. In Nubia, and also near the city of Dongola in the province of Barbaristan, crocodiles are few because there are so many hippopotami. But in Nubia the crocodile is called *wuli*, in the province of Ulwi it is called *shushar*.}

A wonder. The crocodile, when it wishes to have sex, emerges onto one of the islands with its mate, and the male lays the female on her back. Some Arab tribesmen, in order to rid themselves of gonorrhoea, or else prompted by lust, hide in the sand and scrub and, while the female is lying on her back and before the male has done the deed, rushes out of his ambush with a shout. The male runs off into the Nile, but the female is left

Crocodiles

paralysed, like a tortoise, unable to move. This is because her forelegs are short, her locomotion in the water being through her tail and mouth; and unless the male, after sex, turns her right side up, she is stuck there with her vagina sticking out beneath her hind legs. So the lustful pervert covers her hind legs with sand and piles sand over her tail as well, then fearlessly performs the ugly deed – *God be our refuge!*

But the rakish devil swears that the pleasure derived from a crocodile is greater than that from a virgin maid, indeed that the female crocodile is exceedingly hot and that each time she has sex she is a virgin and gushes with blood. Also, the pudendum of a man who has sex with a crocodile exudes a musk-like perfume for an entire week. As for the crocodile's vagina, it is reportedly white and 'Chinese' like that of an Ethiopian slavegirl. And that is a fact, as I can testify, since they once brought a female crocodile to Özbek Bey, the governor of Girga, and it had a rounded vagina exactly as I have described.

As for this crocodile (i.e., the 30-foot one observed near Aswan?), its back was as pied and mottled as a chameleon's.

{Another marvellous creature of the Nile is the Old Man of the Sea, called (? — lacuna in text), the upper part (?) man and the lower part fish (? — lacuna in text).}

A marvellous story concerning the Nile crocodile. Indeed, while I was travelling in the region of Shallal (the First Cataract) the conversation turned to crocodiles. Our host was a certain Abu Jaddullah, a venerable sheikh, one who had experienced the vicissitudes of fortune, one who belonged to the class of lovers (i.e., those mystically inclined), an upright individual. He related as follows, 'When I was young I had a crocodile in the Nile. It was a female. At that time I was making a living by fishing with nets. Sometimes I netted a big fish and set it aside. One day this crocodile swam by. It was a very beautiful specimen. I snipped off some fish heads and threw them to her. She ate them and went on. This continued for several days: I gave her fish like this every day. One day she just strode out of the water, raised her tail and lay on her back. I recalled that our Arabs have sex with crocodiles. So I too girded my loins and went to it. The pleasure drove me out of my mind. Afterward I took a club and propped it between the sand and the crocodile's back, then stood to one side. She wriggled onto her feet, gave me a glance, then went back into the river and cavorted like mad.

'I cohabited with her for three years. All my clansmen in Shallal knew about it. If one day I failed to show up she would look for me. Eventually I stopped going to the edge of the Nile out of fear of the other crocodiles. Whenever my crocodile came to the shore she left a kind of fragrant oil like civet. I used to fill jars with it and sell them for ten *guruş* a piece. I earned my living that way for three years.

'Then one day I happened to go over to one of the islands in the Nile, and my crocodile followed me onto the shore. She walked around a bit, then rolled over and expired. Suddenly it grew dark, and when the darkness lifted what should I see: the crocodile's head and torso had transformed into that of a beautiful girl. But her legs and her vulva were still those of a crocodile. It turned out that she was the daughter of the sheikh of the Kunuz Arabs and had been bewitched. By God's command, at the moment she died the spell became ineffective and she resumed her original form. The people of that island and I buried her.'

This was the story the sheikh related, and some local residents who were present approved it and bore witness that it was true. For in that country, having sex with crocodiles, and killing crocodiles and nailing their skins to the gates, are nothing to be ashamed of but are rather considered heroic deeds. And anyone who does not do battle with a crocodile is not considered a man. There is a distinct rivalry among them, and they only give their daughters in marriage to one who has killed a crocodile or has killed an elephant. For in that country, the crocodile is a dragon, very harmful and accursed, since it snatches men and animals as they are drinking and children as they are swimming near the shore.

The basic reason why men of this region have sex with crocodiles is that they suffer from incontinence and gonorrhoea, and they engage in intercourse with crocodiles in order to rid themselves of these afflictions. Some, who will not commit that act, have sex instead with Ethiopian slavegirls who, being very hot and attractive, drain men of sperm and other things.

{**The Nilometre talisman for crocodiles.** There are several stories among the people giving the reason why the nilometre is called Umm al-qiyas ('Mother of Measure'). In one version, a sultan had a beautiful daughter named Miqyas ('Measure'). One day, while she was swimming near the shore of the Nile, a crocodile snatched her and took her away. When the Sultan heard of this, he moaned and groaned. One of the great saints, Sheikh Abu Bakr al-Batrini, who happened to be present, uttered a

Crocodiles 393

prayer of supplication that the girl be saved. By God's command, the crocodile left her where it had found her, safe and sound. The sultan, in his joy, built a pavilion on that spot and named it Umm al-qiyas after his daughter. Later Sheikh Batrini had a marble figure of a crocodile made and buried it under the Nilometre pool. It is a Greatest Talisman. From that day to this, if a crocodile passes below the Nilometre, it immediately flips over and withdraws to the shore, where it is killed. That is why there are no crocodiles below Cairo.}

Peculiarity of the crocodile. After the crocodile and its mate have sex on the shore, the female lays eggs, the size of ostrich eggs, only they are not round but oval and mottled. She buries them in the sand and returns to the water, but every day she comes out to check them. It sometimes happens that an egg is exposed to the heat and the white of the egg gets cooked. In that case, on the fortieth day a skink emerges, having formed from the yellow of the egg. But those eggs that remain in the sand (protected from the heat) become crocodiles, by God's command.

The crocodile has a membrane on its brain that makes it suitable for living in the Nile; but the skink does not develop that membrane and so remains on land. The female crocodile lays ten or twelve eggs, of which some become crocodiles and some skinks. The skink does go into the water, but must come out again; it cannot make its home in the Nile. The physicians call it the water skink. Its progeny however, which they call the land skink, never goes into the Nile and never drinks water, but is bound to the sand and the desert. The physicians have noted its extremely beneficial medicinal qualities.

6. The Cairo underworld and unusual trades

On the vices of Egypt and the police guilds

The accursed and irreligious tribe is this group.

Guild of prostitutes of Babulluq. 800 harlots of the class of rebellious ladies. Their huts are amongst the rubbish-heaps and at the foot of the Babulluq Gate.

Guild of home-bound prostitutes. These are the she-devils of the covered and honourable women. They ply their trade in their homes, but they have pimps. They are 2,000 in number who are listed in the police chief's register and pay a tax. And there is an incalculable number under the control of the military groups, whom the police chief cannot touch.

Babulluq boys. In the coffee houses, *boza* shops and taverns, and in Rumeli Square, are to be found all the catamites. They too pay a tax.

Sheikh of the Arasat. Three men, one in Bulaq, one in Old Cairo (Fustat), one in New Cairo. All the male and female prostitutes are noted in their registers, and they exact taxes from them.

Sergeants of Babulluq. Forty individuals. They know each prostitute's house and whether a women slept at home or not.

Guild of pimps of Babulluq. They go from house to house in the whorehouse district with *akçe* counting-boards in hand and wheel and deal as though trading in horses and mules.

Guild of female panders. These are old hags who get a wage from would-be fornicators for finding the finest of fornicatresses. 300 ancient crones.

Guild of bazaar jobbers. They bring items from the *boza* shops and taverns and kebab-houses and other places of entertainment in Babulluq and sell them to make a living. Sometimes a silly and inexperienced youth gets leave from his master to go to the bath house and instead comes to Babulluq where he makes out with a sweetheart in one of the huts. At some point he wants wine and kebab, so he gives three *akçe* to the bazaar jobber who obtains whatever the youth desires. But into the wine or the *boza*, the bazaar jobber puts white clove or datura or earwax or rush ashes, and when that youth drinks a cup, he topples over like a sack of henna. At once he is relieved of his clothes and his knife or dagger and his purse. Some low-life gallows-birds use him as they wish, then dump him in a corner or a remote spot. When the refined youth recovers he sees that he is naked, but what can he do? He cannot even tell anyone what happened. And whatever is lost is gone. If he has a lot of money on him, they kill him right away and bury him.

God knows that many such incidents occurred during the governorship of Canpoladzade Hüseyn Pasha. When he was told about them, he realised that they constituted a loss of revenue, and that he would be liable, so he ordered his chief doorkeeper to tear down the houses of prostitution. That agha assembled a few thousand Barbaris and fellahin who tore down all the whorehouses and *boza* shops and taverns and banished all the prostitutes from the city. So Cairo was cleansed.

My aim in recording these scurrilous matters is to warn the heedless. There are sections of Cairo that one should avoid. Those who know the city are aware that there are dangers lurking in every corner.

Sheikh of the beggars. One man. Their convent is in Rumeli Square. All the beggars forgather there. They have twelve sergeants who attend at the Pasha's and the chief *kadi*'s gates. Whatever direction the Pasha goes, he informs the beggars and they stand there in rows along the highway.

All the beggars of Cairo, numbering 9,000, are listed in the sheikh's register. They offer prayers for the Pasha and the notables, to the degree of the alms received from them. But if a beggar curses anyone, the sheikh is informed and punishes him.

On the day that the noble Ka'ba cover leaves the city, the sheikh of the beggars is mounted on a donkey, with his *örf-i izafet* (a type of large ceremonial turban) on his head, accompanied by his one-eyed and one-armed and scald-headed servants carrying bastinados, and thousands of beggars pass in procession. This custom is only found in Cairo.

Guild of oil-lamp lighters. Forty shops, 200 individuals. On nights of saint's birthdays (*mevlud*) and nights when the town is decked out, also in the months of Rajab, Sha'ban and Ramadan, when the shops are open every night until the dawn prayer, these people provide illumination with oil-lamps. They are sure to light one in front of every great merchant's shop that is not open. However many thousands of oil-lamps you may wish to be lit, they will haggle with you and then provide illumination for houses and highways. This also is a custom peculiar to Cairo.

Guild of slave merchants. 2,000 individuals, in the *hans* of Cairo. They go once a year to the provinces of Funjistan, Afnu, Qirmanqa and Baghanisqa and bring back black slaves. They themselves are dark-skinned men from the provinces of the Oases, Aswan and Ibrim.

Guild of eunuch surgeons. Ten individuals, in their homes. Their trade – *God preserve us!* – is to make eunuchs out of black-skinned young boys from May Burnu and Jaju, Qirmanqa and Baghanisqa, Ethiopia and Funj and Afnu. They feed the boys and give them saffron sherbet, then line up 100 or 200 in a row and cut off their penis and testicles with a razor. They stick a reed where the penis was and sprinkle a kind of dust made from vegetation in order to staunch the bleeding. Over that they put dust made from acacia leaves, then pieces of oiled black leather, and wrap everything in rags. In this way they cut off these boys' progeny. They are ruthless Sudanese merchants, ten in number, hideous black-skinned men of ill-omen, with dark faces and lustreless eyes.

Kethüda Ibrahim Pasha once had 100 or 200 little black Arab boys eunuched to give them as gifts. I went on purpose to watch the operation. *God preserve us!* Some of the boys in their anguish thrashed about like chickens with their heads cut off and had to be tied down; some were so weakened, they took to their beds; some died within a few days.

Such are these merciless executioners and ruthless Sudanese merchants. This too is something peculiar to Cairo.

Guild of carpet makers. Twenty workshops, 300 individuals. They weave silk carpets and prayer-rugs, in praise of which the tongue falls short. True, carpets are also woven in (the Anatolian towns of) Uşak, Kula and Alaşehir. But nowhere will you find the quality of these Egyptian carpets, except perhaps in Isfahan.

Guild of donkey drivers. As many as 3,000 individuals; because Cairo's ferryboat and caique are the donkey. They amble so nimbly, even an ambling horse cannot keep up with them. It is said that there are 40,000 donkeys in Cairo. All the notables ride them, with no stigma attached. It is, after all, a Sunna of the Prophet, since the noble Prophet had a donkey named Yağfur and always used to ride it. I have even heard it quoted as a Hadith, that anyone who makes fun of someone riding a donkey is an infidel.

Guild of donkey shearers. They have no shop, but there are certain places where they are usually to be found. Once a month they shear all of Cairo's donkeys and camels. 200 individuals. They shear so closely that not a sign of fur is left, as though they used a razor instead of shears.

Guild of pickpockets. They are under the authority of the chief of police. They will steal a man's purse, or his knife or dagger, out of his pocket or out of his bosom, without hesitation or regret. 300 individuals. One must be very wary of these people in crowded places. They are such masters of their trade, they will steal an eye and leave the eye-salve in its place. They have a sheikh of their own. If the chief of police wants to, he can find the stolen item that very hour; because all the thieves and pickpockets are in his register.

Guild of cot makers. They make sugar cages (!?) and cots out of date-palm wood. (—) individuals. This trade is also not found elsewhere.

Guild of rubbish sweepers. (—) individuals. They sweep up the rubbish in all the highways and bring it to the stokeholes of baths, glass works, bakeries, gypsum works, lime kilns, and pottery kilns to be burnt.

There is no group of people in Cairo more misshapen and fantastical than these. They are like creatures that have been metamorphosed. Nevertheless – in accordance with the verse,

> Ecstatics know what ecstasy is.
> What need is there to talk about it?

– I have seen some pious men in Cairo who, when they catch sight of these detestable individuals, do not pass them by without kissing their hands. Many people believe that in Egypt, the saints of God are to be found among these rubbish sweepers, eccentric dervishes, junk dealers and street barbers. *No one has knowledge of what is hidden except God* (27:65). And note the Hadith Qudsi (Hadith in which the speaker is God): *My saints are under my collar; no one knows them but I.*

Guild of camel meat and camel liver cooks. Ten shops and individuals, on Rumeli Square. It is food for the poverty-stricken, but very tasty; I have eaten it often.

Guild of earth rat hunters. They have no shop but operate out of huts and tents in Rumeli Square. Twenty individuals. The season for these rats is the breaching of the Nile (flooding of the Nile canal). At that time these hunters catch them and bring them to Rumeli Square to be sold.

They are a small animal, more like a rabbit than a rat, and emerge out of the soil, by God's command; they are half soil and half dust. I have seen them bleeding on the ground when a farmer driving his team turned over their den with his ploughshare. So eating them is permitted according to the four Sunni rites.

When these rats mature they make mounds like moles. When the hunters see that, they know that there are mature earth-rats and dig them out. They are a small, nicely-formed animal with fur like a squirrel. A live one weighs 50 or 60 drams. They are very plump, and their flesh is light, invigorating and easy to digest. I often ate them when I was going to the

Oases. Their diet is completely vegetarian, consisting of underground roots and grasses.

Guild of sherbet makers from henbane. Two shops in Rumeli Square. They soak the henbane overnight, then strain the liquid, add a bit of purified honey, and sell it by the bowlful. The dervishes who drink it are stunned when they look into the faces of their beloveds and can recite 1,001 verses of poetry while standing on one leg. It is said to be a narcotic.

Guild of *subya* makers. It is *boza* made from rice, as described above. Peculiar to Egypt.

Guild of sherbet makers from licorice. It is described above. Peculiar to Egypt.

Guild of sherbet makers from tamarind. Has a laxative effect. Also peculiar to Egypt.

Guild of *akve* makers. Arab daggers as large as swords. Not found in Turkey.

Guild of rush mat makers. They make fine patterned rush mats that sell for 40 or 50 *guruş* apiece.

Guild of cooks. They make the Egyptian specialties, which are cous-cous pilav, Jews' mallow, okra, taro and cauliflower.

Guild of *miray* halva. No shop, forty individuals. They put a mirror on the end of a mottled stick. When the sugar has reached the proper consistency and been made into halva, they stick it underneath the mirror (? – text confused) and draw out the halva. They go from shop to shop reciting poems and at each couplet give out some halva, for which they receive one *para*. They utter a benediction and go on to the next. It is a type of dervish-style halva.

Guild of Bahari dervishes. For the most part they are Yemenite dervishes. They put various flowers – sweet basil, hyacinth, rose, jasmine – inside a bath towel and to any of the notables whom they meet on the main roads they give a syringa or anemone and get something in return. Seventy or eighty individuals. These too are peculiar to Egypt.

7. Trades and products lacking in Egypt

Trades and products lacking in Egypt

It is well-known among the cognoscenti, and it has become proverbial, that in Egypt there are many horses but no master farriers – there are only makers of shoes for donkeys; there are many sick people but no physicians (*hekim*) or magistrates (*hakım*); many blind people but no eye-doctors.

There is a great deal of truth to this. One man out of two, by God's command, is blind or rheumy-eyed. If someone has trouble seeing, they say – and this too has become a proverb – 'Your eyes are like those of the son of an Egyptian janissary;' and that is because a child born to a Turk in Egypt is bound to have watery eyes and poor vision.

When they say there are no magistrates, what they mean is that no magistrate – whether religious or secular – carries out his duties, but everything is 'under protection'[75] and the governor is only a tax farmer trying to maximise his income.

There are no water mills or springs, but there are many wells.

There are no public weighing machines specifically for flour or oil or honey. To be sure, there are scales for silks; and customs dues are exacted on candles, household slaves, gold and silver thread, captive slaves, and merchandise in the bedestans. But none of these has a specific place or office for collecting the tax. Regarding bedestans, there is really no room for them; only the Khan-i Khalil might be considered one.

There are no shops selling flour or sheep's-heads. No makers of mariner's compasses or bowstrings. No one selling mustard or salad or grape syrup. No one manufacturing mail armour, shields, shagreen, gun barrels or triggers. Mail armour comes from Dagestan and Circassia, shields from Aleppo, shagreen from all over, gun barrels from Algeria.

There is no one making shoe nails, scales for iron, scales for rice, augers, adzes, or saws. No one making thimbles, needles, wire thread, or arrowheads. No one making trumpets, shawms, cylindrical drums, reed flutes, panpipes, or small kettledrums – but they do make marvellous large kettledrums for the district governors. No one making glass bowls or casting bronze plates; no knife-grinders; no diamond cutters; not even

---

75 *Cümle şey himayededir* – probably a reference to *mal-i himaye* 'protection taxes' – see Shaw 1962, 138; Shaw 1966, 157–8.

anyone drawing wire from iron – wire is imported ready-made from Europe. No one making tin buttons, lead whetstones for barbers, or lead slabs. Concerning the latter, however, a certain mature individual named Hacı Nasır, at my instruction, produced the workbench and mold, and cast around 1,000 lead slabs; they were worked into water containers and sent to the Haseki Sultan imaret and hospital in Mecca.

There are no shops for thumbstalls, toothpicks, drill masters, glue, cudgels, turban crests, deerskin, muslin caps, janissary felt caps, or whips. But all these items are imported to Cairo and can be found in the marketplace at a cheap price.

There is no one making Kashan tiles; no one extracting silver with aquafortis;[76] no one making barrels, lime mortar, or putty; no one cleaning water conduits, laying roof tiles, or repairing pavements. None of these trades is found here, nor indeed does Cairo have any need for them. As for precious fabrics, they are imported from India and Yemen, and are plentiful.

8. Chicken incubation; Sabil Allam stones

Another marvel is that they bury 10,000 eggs in horse manure and in twenty days 10,000 chicks going cheep-cheep begin to walk about. It is an amazing sight. But not everyone can do this. In the *kadi*-district of Abyar, in a village called Barma which belongs to Serdar Süleyman, one of the Egyptian *beys*, there is a noble lineage. Incubating chickens in manure belongs to that family. Anyone who wishes to raise chickens in this fashion must get a man from this lineage. He will go to whatever *kadi*-district you want to take him.

First he builds a special oven for incubating chickens. It is a large oven, like a bread oven, with a dome on top and empty below. He divides the inside with brick into compartments. In each compartment he lays down manure, two fingers thick – the manure is unburnt and soft, fluffed like wool – and fifty eggs. But he checks each egg, holding it up to the sun: if it is fresh, he puts it in; if it is addled, he doesn't. An addled egg will split from the heat of the manure and infect the other eggs, so the chicks won't come out. Therefore he only uses fresh eggs. One can also tell by looking at the egg whether the chick that emerges will be a rooster or a hen.

Over the eggs he puts another layer of manure, two fingers thick. Once

---

76 See Vol. 1, fol. 187a for the process referred to.

the oven is filled up, he lights the fire underneath, again using manure as the fuel rather than wood. The fire is kept going for three days. On the fourth day, the chicken-father strips and goes inside the oven, clucking like a hen, and turns over all the eggs. For this operation he uses a special glove made of chicken feathers. He turns over each of the fifty eggs in each compartment, one by one, and puts a few feathers in between them. Then he fumigates the oven with a kind of incense, closes the mouth and leaves.

The master incubator never shows this operation to anyone. But this humble one went to that village for the express purpose of seeing it with my own eyes. During the twenty days I stayed there, the chicken-mother (!) entered the oven and turned over the eggs three times.

Before twenty days are up, the chicks start to hatch like an army of jinn and they begin to scratch at the manure. They are immediately removed from the oven, so as not to harm the eggs that have not yet cooked and are still covered with manure. Outside the oven are some broody hens, and the chicks going cheep-cheep begin to march behind them.

One drawback is that the chickens incubated in horse manure do not have the same flavour as those hatched beneath a hen, and the meat is a bit tough. Also the kite, otherwise Pharaoh's falcon, is very hostile to these chicks. There are little boys who keep guard over them; otherwise in one day they would all be snatched away by kites. There is no bird in Egypt more harmful than the kite.

Ten days after hatching, these chicks are stuffed into bushel baskets.[77] They give five or ten bushels each to the peasants (i.e., to sell in the cities?). Praise be to God that I have seen chickens bought and sold by the bushel in Egypt.

These chickens sold by the bushel are, for the most part, a government monopoly. There is a special officer, charged by the Pasha's chief panter, who has thousands of chickens produced in this way. 500 chickens are slaughtered for the Pasha's kitchen every day and given to his retinue as part of their ration.

Unless you have seen how these chickens are produced, you can have no idea what devils these Egyptian fellahin are. Indeed, it is a marvel and a mystery, hard for the mind to conceive. But *God creates what He pleases by His power and decides what He wills by His might* (24:45).

---

77 Instead of simply *kile* 'bushel', Evliya uses the phrase *dipsiz kile* 'bottomless bushel', an idiom for a spendthrift.

A noteworthy work of God (i.e. natural phenomenon). In the place called Sabil Allam, described above, are some small stones of various colours. The Sabil Allam stones are famous in Egypt. They are of various colours and shinier than diamonds or rubies. They are found in that plain and sell for 100 or 500 *guruş*. And there are numerous stones of the cat's-eye and fish's-eye variety that sell for five or ten *guruş*. Sometimes a windstorm blows away the sand and reveals countless such stones. Cheap to begin with, they sell at a great price after an engraver polishes them and carves them into various shapes. Some of them are more lustrous than Badakhshan rubies and more radiant than diamonds.

The Egyptian chroniclers and ulema agree that it was in Sabil Allam that Shaddad ibn Ad built *the many-columned city of Iram* (89:7). Indeed, the foundations of great buildings are evident here and there in this valley of Sabil Allam. Also, when Kethüda Ibrahim Pasha was removed from office he stayed for seventy-seven days in this plain of Sabil Allam, during which time his servants, at loose ends, gathered these Sabil Allam stones and used them to play board games. Later they gave some to an engraver who used them as ring stones, so all the servants came into possession of a seal ring. One finds stones of that value – it is a wonderful phenomenon.

Another stone found in the Sabil Allam plain, hard and bright yellow, is the object of Frankish physicians who come and look for it in the heat of summer. Its medicinal property is that if a man holds it in both hands, he immediately becomes nauseous and starts vomiting, and the nausea does not let up until he lets go of the stone. It effectively purges the stomach of all yellow and black bile.

Finally, there is a pied stone like a bead. A woman who binds it to her waist during intercourse will definitely not conceive. In fact, this stone is very common among the prostitutes of Babulluq in Cairo. When my mother gave birth to this humble one, my head passed through her womb only with great difficulty, and as a result her vagina was disfigured. To avoid getting pregnant thereafter she always used to carry some of these Sabil Allam stones, and would bind them to her waist whenever she had intercourse with my father.

9. Exploring a pyramid

One hour from the town of Giza on the west bank of the Nile are the three 'mountains' known as the pyramids. They are the tallest and most ancient buildings on the face of the earth. They are huge man-made mountains, each one a veritable Mt Qaf, and each one pertaining to an idol. Thus they call the large pyramid Mt Balbahith (Belhib), the middle one Mt Malhawiya (Belhube), and the lowest one Mt Abu'l-hawl (the Sphinx).

There are thousands of stories about these artificial mountains. Some chroniclers say they were built before the Flood by Ad ibn Shaddad. Others maintain that before the Flood, King Surid, at the urging of his soothsayers, built them as a tomb for himself. When they were finished he filled the three pyramids with treasure, put in weapons, and also placed therein the books of all the sciences written by the prophet Idris. He set up talismans and guardians (?) and covered the pyramids with brocade, making them a hidden treasure. He also built a great city on the shore of the Nile where the guards of the pyramids resided. Every year, in spring, all the people of the world came and circumambulated the pyramids, as they do the Ka'ba. (Marginal notes with additional information)

Even now, in the northern pyramid, there is a south-facing gate, inside of which, on the right side, is a Hebrew inscription carved on the rocks. It reads, 'I who built the pyramids completed them in six years. May those who come after me be able to tear them down from their foundation in 600 years. Indeed, it is easier to tear down than to build up. And I covered them with brocade. May the kings who come after me be able to cover them with reed mats.'

In fact, the Caliph Ma'mun (Abbasid caliph, reg. 813-33) came from Baghdad to Cairo and girt his loins to conquer Pharaoh's treasure buried in the pyramids. He made great efforts, piling wood and lighting fires, pouring vinegar, hurling large stones with mangonels. In seven months he was able to tear down an area of 20 cubits. He found a large chrysolite jar encrusted with gems and containing 1,000 gold pieces weighing one *okka* apiece. On a rock the following was inscribed, 'O you who wish to conquer this tomb for its treasure! However much effort and expense you put into it, so much will you take out. If you covet too much, you will depart this perishing world.'

When Ma'mun and his soldiers saw this, they were amazed. Those 1,000 gold pieces exactly corresponded to the troubles they had undergone and the expenses they had incurred over the past seven months.

They also realised that the phrase on the rock inside the gate on the northern side – 'May the kings who come after me cover them with reed mats' – was pregnant with meaning. So Ma'mun ordered that the pyramids be covered with Egyptian reed mats. When they were half covered, a strong wind arose and swept the mats and the workers up into the air like a falconer's lure, breaking the mats asunder and rendering the workers lifeless.

Finally, heeding the advice of Caliph Ma'mun's vizier Husayn ibn Sahl, they gave up and returned to Baghdad. The places on the pyramids that were destroyed during the reign of Caliph Ma'mun are still visible.

When Yusuf Salah al-Din (Saladin, Ayyubid sultan, reg. 1169–93) was renovating the fortifications of Cairo, he removed stones from the pyramids and used them for the citadel and the lower castle. Sultan Mu'ayyad (Mu'ayyad Shaykh, Mamluk sultan, reg. 1412–21) also used stones from the pyramids to construct the eleven dikes nearby. Those places too (where stones were removed) are still visible.

As for the saying of Surid – 'I built the pyramids in six years. May the kings who come after me be able to tear them down in 600 years' – the interpretation of this humble one is: If I were to mine the pyramids with 100 quintals of black powder and one 'six-treasure' mine that was used in the siege of Candia castle, the mountains of *Ahram* (the pyramids) would be blown sky-high like an *ihram* (pilgrim's garment) and no trace would be left of the building, not even the foundation, but all would crumble to the ground and melt into the Nile.

But, to tell the truth, I have never seen such a huge building on the face of the earth. God be praised that, during the governorship of Ibrahim Pasha, I spent five or ten days partying next to the pyramids, while our horses were grazing in the nearby meadow, and I had occasion to tour them several times and marvel at them.

On one occasion there were forty-five of us, including some in the retinue of the Master of the Horse and Behlul Agha and other officers. We brought torches, oilcloth lanterns and wind-tapers. After clearing away the sand and rubbish from the door on the northern side of the large pyramid, we took refuge in God and entered with a *besmele*. This humble one kept an eye on the compass and the watch.

The first 700 paces in a southern direction was a broad highway, fifteen cubits wide and surmounted by vaults 20 cubits high. There were numerous caves on either side, also man-made halls with domes carved from the soft rock stratum and gilded and decorated as though just emerged from the hand of Bihzad. Every cell was full of human bones, and every skull could hold 100 bushels of wheat. Only God knows how many skulls there were, both large and small. In our path lay a shinbone, still covered with its skin, that was 71 spans as measured by this humble one's hand. There were an abundance of such bones.

One large cave was full of human corpses that lay shrouded in date-palm fibres. And there were several hundred skeletons (or mummies), each 70 or 80 paces tall. But we nearly suffocated from the smell of bat droppings, the bats being as large as crows and hanging from the rocks by their claws. Some hurled themselves at the lanterns and torches and scorched their wings. Some struck us in the face.

At this juncture, a few of our companions got frightened and went back with one or two lanterns. The thirty-five of us who were left summoned our courage and went on for another hour, along a gently descending slope, our compass pointing south. We saw vaulted halls like the Vault of Chosroes, each containing mummified human corpses, and near them, trampled in the dust, rotted reed mats and pieces of cloth woven of date-palm fibre.

Fifty paces further on, continuing on a downward slope, we came upon a large pool of clear water. But all around the edge sat frightful birds, as large as eagles or geese. As soon as they saw us, they flapped their wings and produced a thunderous noise that made our brains ooze from our ears. And the bats besmirched us and our clothes with their droppings. Meanwhile the torchbearers informed us they were running out of kindling. The noise produced by those eagles' wings was particularly dreadful.

We had no heart to advance a single step beyond that pool, and had just decided to turn around, when a freezing-cold wind from the direction of the birds made us shudder with apprehension. What would we do if our torches and lanterns went out? The bats meanwhile, that were the size of pigeons, kept fluttering at the flames like moths and brushing against our faces with their wings. It nearly drove us crazy.

To make a long story short, guided by the piles of stones we had set up along the way, we somehow managed to make our way back and emerged safe and sound. Our companions who had fled earlier teased us, saying, 'Where did you get these filthy faces and strange looks?' God knows, though we emerged safely, we were completely exhausted. But it was a tremendous experience! Only God knows what lies beyond that pool.

Thus this humble one saw the inside of one of the pyramids. There was no buried treasure, only buried men. But there is no doubt that it is under a talismanic power. For when we came to that pool, all of us were confounded, and we remained in this stunned condition until we came out into the air, when we recovered our souls. *God save us!* May I never be vouchsafed to enter it again.

After returning to our tents for breakfast and coffee, we surveyed the pyramids from all sides. Two of them have a square base with each side 200 paces long, making the circumference 800 paces. Each of the stones is 20 or 30 cubits long and broad. And the height from the ground to the top is 200 cubits. The large pyramid has a door on the northern side through which we entered, but the other two have no visible entrance. The Abu'l-hawl pyramid (the Sphinx) is quite small, but both are mountains with square base and pointed tip reaching to the sky.

I climbed up the pyramid that we had entered. At the top there is a square or arena large enough to pitch a pup-tent with ten flaps. In some of the crevices I found jesses and hoods and pigeon rings and anklets. All Cairo was spread out beneath my feet – so lofty are these mountains. There are also structures built of black stone and guarded by talismans all around the pyramids. I would need an entire volume to describe them all.

10. Weddings, circumcision, etc.

Wedding ceremony of the Egyptian fellahin

Mentioned here is the rule of the Hadari fellahin as passed down from their ancestors.

When they want to marry an Arab girl to a Muslim man, the religious ceremony takes place according to the rule, then on the night of the wedding procession 1,000 or 2,000 relatives and associates and hangers-on assemble in a broad plain. They eat Jews' mallow, okra, taro and cheeses.

When this feast is over, and after the evening prayer, a lovely young janissary appears from one side of this plain. With shawl and turban and a motley waistband, a silver-handled knife in one hand and a club in the other, shouting raucously and striking anyone in his path, he makes his way through the crowd, chases away some people and breaks some objects, thrashes with his knife and walks and talks like a drunkard. As this sweetheart approaches, some men get up and stop him, kiss his face and seat him in a corner.

Now it turns out that this bandit boy is actually the bride! She stands up again and cries, '*Where is our master?*' She is supposed to find her husband and try to kill him. Some men plead for him. She says, '*I don't care, my dear.*' She greets those present with hugs and kisses, girds up the skirts of her dolman, puts down the two knives and departs.

As soon as the bride is gone, they find the groom and bring him. He settles in a corner, dressed in finery. Some of his friends go and tell him, 'Thank God, your beloved came and was very angry but she couldn't find you. There must be some mistake.' He gets up and says, 'Fie! My beloved apparently wants to kill me. What is my crime? I've spent ten purses for her sake, etc. etc.' – and item by item, like a talking ledger, he recounts all his expenses for the past month or two. The audience actually takes great pride, boasting that so-and-so's daughter got married and got so much money.

Now the groom gets angry and starts brandishing his knife, saying 'I spent so much money' and 'If I find my beloved I'll kill her.' As he is stalking about, the bride reappears on one side of the plain and the groom runs away and hides in a corner.

This time the bride is out-fitted as a lovely scholar from a good family, with a red mohair cloak over her shoulders, a scarf round her throat and an ulema's turban on her head. As she approaches, some relatives go to greet her and some scholarly types stand up and invite her to sit with them.

'No,' she says, 'I have a legal dispute with so-and-so' – meaning her husband. 'He apparently wants to kill me. My parents married me to him and gave so many purses and jewels and gold and silver vessels as a dowry.' She too lists her dowry items one by one, so everyone knows that the virgin so-and-so was married with so much wealth and so many purses. If the girl is not a good speaker she gets prompted by some relatives nearby.

Then the girl takes out her knife again and pretends to be searching for the groom. He takes flight. When the bride has left, the groom comes back in another outfit and once again repeats the precise amount he has paid, how much went to the bride's mother, how much to her father, her mother's sister and her father's sister, and lists all the presents he has given.

Then it is the bride's turn again. This time she is dressed as a cavalry-man, with red trousers and a dagger in her belt. She searches for the groom, brandishing the dagger, and again lists all the valuable items in her dowry. The next time she comes dressed as a sheikh and imparts all sorts of sheikhly counsel. When it is the groom's turn he shows up as a dervish, with a staff in one hand and prayer-beads in the other, shaking his head and reciting litanies.

In short, during that long night until the glimmer of dawn, bride and groom appear ten times each in various costumes and have all sorts of disputes. And the bride sits on the knee of any man she likes and they talk and kiss.

Meanwhile the plain is adorned with hundreds of torches and thousands of oil-lamps; kettledrums and five-layered military bands are played; poems are recited in loud voices, both in classical Arabic and in colloquial; and everyone has a wonderful time.

A torch procession comes in from one side, with numerous people on foot accompanying the bride who is mounted on a horse with bejewelled saddle. She is smothered in sable furs and wearing all her gold and finery, a Pharaonic crown with three forked crests on her head, and her face still unveiled. She greets the crowd on either side. All the fellahin rise to their feet and return the greeting. Hundreds of boys and girls holding candles and crying '*God save the Sultan!*' accompany the bride to the middle of the plain. She rubs her handkerchief on the crown and waves it over the crowd. All the fellahin click their heels.

Description of the Pharaonic crown. It is a wadded turban of camel's leather, the size of a frying-pan, with eight corners. Every corner is woven with gold thread, and there is evidence that the spaces between the corners were originally studded with pearls. The inside is cotton lined with velvet and embroidery. At the very top is a garnet the size of an apple. The edges are adorned with turquoises and carnelians, and the edging is crenellated. It is a strange and wonderful crown.

Now the bride dismounts and looks for the groom, saying: 'Where is he who will marry me, this humble one with the noble heart?'

The groom emerges from his tent with a swagger, but the bride grabs him by the beard and holds up her unsheathed dagger as though she is about to cut his throat. Some peacemakers intervene and reconcile the bride to the proceeding by making the groom promise to give her a house or an orchard or a few slavegirls or a few purses – in short, whatever he can afford. All present serve as witnesses and recite a Fatiha.

Weddings, circumcision, etc. 409

The groom immediately snatches the bride from amidst the crowd and takes her into a nuptial chamber or a tent or into a corner, where he lays her down, Pharaonic crown and all, and removes her maidenhead. The girl emerges, bleeding and panting as though escaped from a cudgel. She shows her blood to her father and mother and everyone else, and utters some plaintive words. They again boast to one another, saying 'Our daughter proved a virgin.' For among these Arabs, and particularly this tribe of Hadari fellahin, finding a virgin is not easy.

Then the girl is consoled by her parents and relatives. They finally remove the Pharaonic crown. As she sighs and groans, the father and mother wipe off the blood and toss the bloody rags over the congregation. Summoning the groom, they ask him why he has bloodied their daughter in this fashion. He denies it, but she says, 'Look at his clothes. They are still covered with my maidenhead blood.'

Everyone examines his clothes and sees that they are covered with blood. The girl grabs him by the penis, the father and mother hold him by the waist crying '*Sharia justice for the wedding!*' and demand the blood-price from the groom. Again some peacemakers intervene and extract more presents for the father and mother as blood-price for their daughter. As they demand more and more, the groom's parents and relations come forward and a huge battle ensues.

'You have stripped our boy naked and extorted money from him,' they claim. And those present bear witness that it is so.

Again men from both sides act as mediators. The girl's parents give substantial presents to the boy's parents and relatives as hush-money.

Now that the two sides are reconciled, they sit down together and proceed to celebrate. From then until the morning prayer there is such rejoicing and shooting of muskets and rockets and raucousness of singing-girls and dancing-boys and musicians that Pharaoh's drooping spirit perks up.

Such is the wedding ceremony of the Hadari fellahin. But they never allow strangers to participate. And they are very careful to preserve that Pharaonic crown. This is the permanent custom of the fellahin.

Description of the ceremony of female circumcision. A similar great celebration and wedding occurs when the girls are circumcised. Thousands of women go in grand procession, mounted on donkeys, accompanied by a musical band. They first bring the girl to the public bath, then to her house where that night female surgeons perform the operation. The girl has a reddish tongue that does not speak in the crevice of her chestnut grove. They cut out that tongue in order that desire be more eloquent.

{In fact, this female circumcision among the Hadari has come down from the time of Abraham. When the prophet Abraham was in Mecca, King Tawtis of Egypt sent him a slavegirl named Hagar as a present. Mother Sarah was jealous and one night she cut out the extraneous flesh in Mother Hagar's vagina. It turned out, however, that the operation actually increased sexual pleasure. From that time on, the bedouin Arabs circumcise their daughters, a practice that has come down from Hagar the mother of Ishmael.}

Description of the ceremony of circumcision of boys. This is the most refined of the Egyptian ceremonies. In observance of the Sunna (or circumcision – *sünnet*) of the Prophet, when they are about to circumcise their sons – whether high or low, rich or poor – they help one another out.

Accompanied by an eightfold musical band are ten or fifteen or twenty little boys, bathed and smothered in gold and trinkets, with magnificent crests on their turbans, and mounted on Arab thoroughbreds. Before them in the procession go riderless horses with jewel-encrusted saddles and golden shields. At the head of the parade are old men of the quarter and surrounding neighbourhoods, bearing arms and smothered in cloth-of-gold, who pass by row on row cracking all sorts of jokes. In the midst of the troop are various highly-wrought palm tree festoons, oil-lamps, flags and banners.

Then comes the learned surgeon mounted on an Arab horse and preceded by a man bearing on his head a chest adorned with the circumcision instruments. Walking alongside the surgeon are his journeymen girded with silken waist cloths.

Just in front of the boys to be circumcised are a group of clowns and mimes, mounted on oxen and donkeys and emaciated horses – with henna on their hides, straw on their flanks and fox-tail crests on their manes – who pass with a thousand jests and pranks.

In this fashion, with band playing, they parade the boys about to be circumcised all around the marketplaces of Cairo. Rich or poor, this is what they do.

There are other festivities as well that go on for three days and three nights, with a hue and cry and feasts and pandemonium. Practically every night you can find such celebrations going on in a hundred places in Cairo. On those nights, all the streets of those quarters of the city are illuminated

Weddings, circumcision, etc.

with thousands of oil-lamps, and food is liberally dispensed. For three months criers sent by the governor make the announcement, so the coffee shops and the eating and drinking establishments of the district remain open and there is buying and selling until the morning.

But the wedding parties are the most raucous and splendid, because they observe the Hadith: *Proclaim weddings, even with tambourines.* In short, they are Egypt's pomp and circumstance, not found in other countries.

Good customs of the populace of Cairo

If a man falls ill, all the people of the quarter inquire after his health and bring presents and make sure that he has made his last will and testament. As soon as he dies, they inform the treasury agent and prepare his shroud. All the neighbours gather in front of his door. Reciting *tevhid* and *tezkir*, they wash his body and place it in a coffin according to *kanun*, either one so many fingers' length all around (? – *parmakh*) or else one on the Turkish model. They adorn the coffin with roses and rose-water and sweet basil.

All the sheikhs and ulema attend the funeral procession with flags and banners, *tevhid* and *tezkir*. They first put the coffin inside the Azhar Mosque where they perform the funeral prayer, then take it to the Qarafa (burial grounds). Or else they bring it to Rumeli Square, perform the funeral prayer in the place known as Zawiyat al-Janaza or Sabil al-Mu'minin, then take it to Imam Shafi'i or one of the twelve other cemeteries. But the most prestigious is the main Qarafa at the foot of Mt Jushi (Mt Muqattam) where one can be buried next to Benjamin the brother of Joseph or Sheikh Uqba.

The fellahin, however, bury their dead near Old Cairo (Fustat), because that is the ancient burial grounds. When the Pharaoh was in charge, he drew a wall all around that cemetery and charged a toll for every corpse that entered. The fellahin bring their coffins there accompanied by banners and followed by the womenfolk mounted on donkeys. The women pass by waving their handkerchiefs, baring their faces and tearing their hair. The coffins of the fellahin are borne on step-ladders like the hatched roofs of the infidels in Turkey. But they pay great respect to the dead, adorn the coffins, and observe the Sharia with regard to shrouding and burial and the *iskat* prayer.[78]

---

78 *Iskat*, defined in Redhouse as alms given on behalf of the dead as compensation for their neglected religious duties.

Another good custom is that every Friday eve (Thursday night) myriads of men and women mount their donkeys and go to visit the twelve Cairo burial grounds. They complete Koran recitals, recite *Ya Sin* (Sura 36), give alms to the poor and visit the dead.

The tombs are masonry-built underground vaults known as *fisqiya*, each one a hut of sorrows. The doors of these structures are sealed with earth and reopened whenever there is a burial. One *fisqiya* may contain 100 or 200 corpses. They do not cover the bodies with earth but simply place them inside, in their shrouds, so the flesh rots away and they are left as skeletons. After the burial they seal up the entrance with mortar and gypsum; because in Egypt there are very many shroud-robbers. Indeed, during the governorship of Canpoladzade Hüseyn Pasha, a number of them were apprehended and, for the sake of *purging the world of evil* (cf. 7:56), they were put on stakes with the shrouds they had stolen around their necks.

Every grave has a headstone engraved with the date of the deceased's death. They also erect a variety of domes, open at the top. They pour out water and grains of wheat for the birds. They put roses and myrtles and sprigs of sweet basil on the gravestones.

On these days, a woman needs no permission from her husband in order to visit the graveyards. Nor can her husband question her about where she has been, because a stipulation to this effect was included in the marriage contract. In other matters as well, Egyptian men cannot question their wives about their whereabouts; for just as Potiphar was defeated by his wife, so nowadays the husbands of Cairo are defeated by their wives.

Such is the *kanun* of Egypt. In no other country is there such affection for the people of the graves.

{Another strange custom relates to the *mevlud* of Imam Husayn in the month of Muharram. On the night of the festival, thousands of Cairene Jews go around in groups of three, carrying large baskets with various kinds of incense. Crying their wares with fine voices, the Jews light incense and sell it. This is a custom that has come down from the time of Sitt Nafisa, ever since the head of Imam Husayn came to Egypt. At least, this is what I was told.}

How the poor of Cairo earn a living

Whatever manufactured items there are in the world, the poor of Cairo get hold of them, set them out and trade in them. They get by in this fashion.

But there are many beggars with no trade at all. On Friday and Monday eves (Thursday and Sunday nights) there are so many of these importuners in the graveyards that one can hardly walk through. If there is a well-outfitted man, one of these beggars is sure to approach and greet him and engage him in conversation. Suddenly and fearlessly he will say, '*A'ti ya sultanım masrufa ehli beyti*' – thus demanding that the man provide his expenses for his wife and family!

As for the poor, they do not let a man walk about the marketplace.

My adventure. One day I went into the latrines at the Mosque of Sultan Hasan in order to answer the call of nature. I shut the door and was going about my business when some fellow opened the door, stuck in his hand and asked me for alms. Since I was just wiping myself, I spared nothing but gave him whatever was in my hand.

'*May God increase your excrement,*' he said and went away.

I finished wiping myself, went out into the courtyard to renew my ablutions, then re-entered the mosque. After performing the prayer, I happened to see a friend and told him what had happened.

'Are you crazy?' he said. 'May God reform you! Does one put excrement in the hand of a man like that?'

'Well,' said I, 'does a man like that open the door of the latrine, while the person inside has his privates exposed, and demand money, saying *Something for God?*'[79]

'Was he a man of blessed aspect,' he asked, 'with a yellow beard, of medium height, a flat forehead and a round face like a Tatar?'

'Yes,' I replied, 'one with a Tatar face and a yellow beard.'

'O cruel one!' he said. 'That man is the Pole (i.e., chief of the saints) of Cairo. He was testing you by showing up that way in the latrine. Why did you look at him scornfully and put excrement in his hand? And he uttered a benediction, saying, '*May God increase your excrement.*' Be very wary of him.'

I was stunned. And indeed, I had diarrhoea for the next two months. His prayer that God increase my excrement came to pass! God be praised, through giving alms I eventually recovered my health.

---

79 *Shay'an li'llah*, a common demand of beggars.

11. *Mevlud* of Seyyid Ahmad al-Badawi in Tanta

Chapter 65: Stages and shrines of our journey to visit Seyyid Ahmad al-Badawi in the year 1083 (1672) and our journey to the entrepôts of Damietta, Rosetta, Alexandria, and other villages and towns and cities

I had completed, as far as possible, my tours of Cairo and my visitations of its shrines, and I wished to visit also the shrine of the world-famous Pole and Father of Orphans, Seyyid Ahmad al-Badawi. 'How will I manage,' said I to myself, 'to rub my face on that threshold and to seek succour from his noble spirit?'

As I was pondering this dilemma, by God's wisdom, in the year 1083, on the 12th day of the month of Rabi' al-akhir (7 August 1672), a hubbub arose in the city, and the sounds of drums and tambourines and kettledrums, *zikrs* and litanies, rose to the skies. I questioned one of my friends in our house of sorrows, and he said, 'Today is the day on which all the sheikhs and dervishes of Seyyid Ahmad al-Badawi gather together to perform *zikr* and go up to the viceroy (i.e., go up to the Cairo citadel to the palace of the Ottoman governor Kethüda Ibrahim Pasha) in order to obtain the warrant authorising the *mevlud* for the year (—). It is a great and boisterous procession of dervishes.'

I immediately betook myself to the court of the Pasha's palace and, secluding myself in a corner, busied myself with watching events.

Glory to God! More than 10,000 Badawi dervishes filled up the palace square and the royal markets, playing on their drums and tambourines and displaying their pennants and banners. Some were drenched in instruments of war, with staffs or cudgels in their hands, *palheng*-stones and skirts at their waists,[80] and *zikr* on their tongues.

A myriad of motley flags and banners turned the city of Cairo into a tulip garden.

In the palace square, in the Pasha's presence, the sheikhs' chief deputy said *'Mention the name of God!'* and thousands of dervishes uttered their *zikr* with a single voice. Golden banners fluttered, drums and tambourines and small kettledrums were sounded, trumpets were blown like the trumpet of

---

80 For pictures of these items see Atasoy 2000, fig. 122, 123 (banners), 336 (skirt, *tennure*) 353, 356 (*palheng*), 362, 363 (staff, *zerdeste*).

Israfil (announcing the resurrection). 3,700 sheikhs and 10,000 barefoot and bareheaded dervishes engaged in *zikr*. Ecstatics cried out on every side. The royal *tevhid* in the palace square was such that, by the Lord of the Ka'ba, the cry of *Allah Allah!* reached up to the sky and the angels in heaven cried *Sübhanallah* ('Praise God') in astonished rivalry.

When this was over, and the leader of the dervishes had uttered formulas of praise to God and blessing upon the Prophet, they cried benedictions upon Sultan Mehmed IV, conqueror of Candia and Kaminiec, and lauds upon Kethüda Ibrahim Pasha, and group by group and in good order took their places before the Pasha.

Now Ibrahim Pasha issued the warrant of Sultan Qaytbay, ordering the provincial governors of Gharbiya and Manufiya, Hasan Agha and Ali Agha, along with the seven guard regiments and other janissary aghas, to attend the noble *mevlud* with all their soldiery fully armed; to protect the Malaqa square; to prevent the brigands of the Arab tribes from coming to the arena and bearing cudgels and *akve* daggers; and to close the wine and *boza* taverns and the houses of prostitution.

The Pasha also presented the sheikhs with gifts, more than those of previous viziers, including two green turbans for the noble tomb of Seyyid Ahmad al-Badawi; two *batmans* of aloes and 50 *miskals* of raw ambergris; one silken carpet and one silken prayer-rug; two beeswax candles, each the height of a man and weighing 100 *batmans*. To the dervishes he gave 100 gold pieces as sacrifice money, which he handed over to the chief deputy Sheikh Mustafa Rumi. The sheikhs uttered a benediction and kissed the Pasha's hand.

The royal *tevhid* recommenced, so loud as to stun any deniers. When it was over, and after further benedictions and lauds, the Pasha's servants took up his gifts – the carpet and prayer-rug, aloes and ambergris and turbans – and the chief executioner, in a loud voice, read out the warrant in the palace square and announced that the Badawi *mevlud* would take place in the middle of the month of Jumadi al-akhir.

Thus all the sheikhs and dervishes marched off in procession, row on row and wave on wave, and everyone returned to his abode.

At this juncture I was overcome with the urge to travel. 'How,' said I to myself, 'can I perform this very important visitation?' While I was pondering this, after the evening prayer a chamberlain came and informed me that the governor wished to see me. Immediately I went into Ibrahim Pasha's presence, where the subject of conversation was the festival of

Seyyid Ahmad al-Badawi. Seizing the opportunity, I said, 'My lord, if you grant me leave, this humble one and full of fault will be present at that harvest-home of prayer, where I will recall my lord with benedictions and at the same time I will have visited that shrine.'

He accepted my supplication. Summoning Nişli Ali Kethüda, he ordered that I be given 100 gold pieces as travel expenses and made me an official attendant at the Badawi *mevlud*. He entrusted me with the orders for the *kashifs* of Gharbiya and Manufiya. And it being the end of the year and the month of *Tut* (i.e., the first month of the Coptic calendar, corresponding to September), when the *kashifs'* authority lapses, he also gave me the orders for them to come to the *divan* in Cairo and settle their accounts. And he entrusted me with letters of good news to Hasan Agha, the *kashif* of Gharbiya, appointing him deputy of the sergeants for the *divan* of Cairo. He also bestowed on me one well-furnished tent; ten quintals of biscuit and other supplies of food and drink, including 100 *okkas* of coffee and three quintals of sugar; and 100 candles.

We bid each other farewell and I proceeded to the house of Nişli Ali Kethüda. He too gave me letters addressing the *kadis* and *kashifs* and *multazims*[81] en route, to the following effect:

> The bearer of this document, Evliya Efendi, is the boon-companion and ancient friend of our viceroy, and is our own dear father. To whomever of you this love-styled letter arrives, it will please us very much if you treat Evliya Çelebi with due consideration and convey him safely and soundly from one of you to the next.

He too offered me 5,000 *para* as travel expenses.

I took leave of all my friends and that night was guest in the house of the delivery agent[82] Ibrahim Agha in Bulaq. For three days and three nights the city of Bulaq was illuminated with myriads of oil-lamps and there were continual celebrations. On the second night, all the sheikhs attended in front of the janissaries' lodge and the delivery agent's palace, decorating the bank of the Nile with lamps and torches, and carrying out the imperial *tevhid* and noble *mevlud* until the morning.

The next morning, the *nakibüleşraf* hosted a banquet in the convent of Ibrahim Gülşeni in Bulaq, according to *kanun*. The great notables and

---

81 Tax farmers, at this period equivalent to the *kashifs* – see Shaw 1962, 60.
82 *Risale ağası* – see Shaw 1962, 81.

ulema and sheikhs of Cairo came, in particular the *kadi* of the military and the *şeyhülislams* of the four Sunni rites, and a Muhammadan feast was consumed. That night the Gülşeni convent became the light-filled rose-garden (*gülşen*) of Iram, and there was a noble *mevlud* in the style of the above *mevluds*, which it would be monotonous to repeat.

The next morning, the Badawi dervishes, the ecstatic dervishes of the other Sufi brotherhoods, and the wealthy sea-going merchants, all boarded twelve *aqaba* ships. Each one of these holds 2,000 men – thus a sea of men rode on the river that was like a sea. These ships are similar to caravels, with stern-castles four stories high. The lowest storey is for the storage of food and drink and other provisions; the second is filled with womenfolk; the third has the dervishes and sheikhs; the fourth is filled to the brim with fellahin and sailors and servants and ship's-captains and other pilgrims. Raised platforms and pavilions are constructed on the decks where everyone carouses and jests with his lovers and friends.

These twelve *aqaba* ships belong to the *waqf*-endowments of Seyyid Ahmad al-Badawi. All expenses are covered by the endowment. The masts and yard-arms are all out-fitted with pennants and banners, and on all sides are thousands of oil-lamps and banners of the sheikhs.

There were several thousand additional pilgrims and sheikhs who did not board these *aqaba* ships but rather hired boats of their own – *qayasa* fishing-boats and caiques – which they boarded with their friends. These numbered 200. So the face of the Nile was adorned with boats proceeding caravan-style, the twelve *aqaba* ships along with 600 or 700 (!) caiques and *qayasas*, holding 40,000 or 50,000 men.

We set off from the city of Bulaq in mid-morning, putting our trust in God. The military personnel in all the ships fired a salute, one volley with their muskets and one volley of cannon shot. As the report died away, the Badawi chief deputy struck up the drums and kettledrums and bells and began the performance of the royal *tevhid*. We were carried along by the Nile current, to the sound of kettledrums and trumpets.

When the flotilla came opposite the city of Inbaba, the dervishes together sang out a Muhammadan call-to-prayer on behalf of the saint İnbaba, then each one recited a Fatiha and declared his intention of performing the Badawi visitation.

At that juncture, this humble one transferred to a smaller boat with seven or eight servants and faithful lovers. Now communing with Sheikh Mustafa Rumi, now with Sheikh Uthman Kannasi, now with Sheikh Inbabi, now with Sheikh Ahmad Qalyubi, we toured the paradise-like and prosperous villages and towns on either side of the Nile, and recorded their descriptions.

[...]

Shrine of Seyyid Ahmad al-Badawi. Attached to the door on the right side is the wall of Seyyid Ahmad al-Badawi. Among the domes of the side terrace on the right side of this mosque is the lofty dome of the shrine of the Lordly Pole (chief of the saints). It is round and uninterrupted like a white pearl, covered in white plaster and with a green bronze finial.

The saint himself (d. 1276) lies inside the square catafalque, made of cypress wood and covered with a Ka'ba covering of cloth-of-gold studded with jewels. It is in the centre of that light-filled dome and surrounded by a cypress-wood railing. Each of the four corners of the catafalque is adorned with a ball of fine polished silver, the size of a man's head.

The green turban in the middle of this square catafalque, marking the place of his blessed head, was sent by the governor of Egypt, Ebü'l-hayr Kethüda Ibrahim Pasha. 4,000 Badawi sheikhs and 20,000 Alawi dervishes[83] brought the noble turban in grand procession, playing their drums and tambourines, trumpets and small kettle-drums, and performing their *zikr*. With a *tekbir* the chief deputy wrapped the turban around the station (*makam* – meaning the headstone?) of his blessed head. Underneath the turban they wrapped the gold-weave napkins that were on all sides. These multicoloured napkins, enough for a sultana's dowry, had been left rotting one upon the other. Only God knows how many there were. No one but the shrine servants is allowed to touch them or remove them; the hand withered up of many a man who tried to do so.

They also lay down the carpet and prayer-rug which the Pasha had sent, and they lit the aloes and ambergris, perfuming the brains of those in the noble dome.

Above the railings that surround the catafalque are expensive chandeliers, each one worth the *harac* of Turkey. Among the votive gifts are silver candlesticks the height of a man, gilded and tinned copper candlesticks, gold and silver censers and rose-water sprinklers and silver scissors.

---

83 Alawi signifies a connection with Ali, but here seems to serve mainly as a rhyme for Badawi.

On the reading-stands inlaid with mother-of-pearl are hundreds of ancient Korans, calligraphed by Yaqut Musta'simi and the Sheikh (Hamdullah) and Karahisari.

Suspended around the lofty dome are several hundred candles the height of a man, each one weighing three or four quintals. These candles come as gifts from the kings of the infidels. For the infidels also believe in this saint, because it often happened that thousands of captives were delivered from these kings' prisons when their iron shackles were broken into bits, thanks to the miraculous graces of Badawi. So the iron fetters and chains, weighing 40 or 50 *okkas*, which these Muslim captives bore for forty or fifty years, are now suspended next to these candles, which are never lit but serve only as ornament.

The Muslim emperors of the seven climes have also sent precious gifts for the sake of a blessing, such as jewel-encrusted oil-lamps and lamp-stands, porcelain cups, ostrich eggs of various sizes, gold and silver balls and decanters. They are suspended here too, in countless numbers.

The world-travelling lovers have also left behind mementoes, such as a dervish staff, *palheng*-stone, drum and tambourine, trumpet and bell, sling of David, banner and lamp, braids and feathers and bells, a hatchet of Abu Muslim, headgear of various sorts, a begging-bowl, fire-stick, water-pot and ribbons, leathern apron, dervish woolen cloaks, wooden swords, curiously shaped fish-bones, leathern knapsacks, and things of this sort that are the equipment of dervishes. Each of these items was hanging in a corner, and 1,001 items besides.

Every master calligrapher has left a handwriting sample here adorning the walls. This humble one also, with my usual impertinence, wrote the Koranic verse, *Nor can I succeed without God's help* (11:88), in large letters on a plaque and deposited it by the side of the prayer-niche.

Within this lofty dome, in the corner containing Badawi's blessed head, is the imprint of the Prophet's foot on black granite. It is visible in that corner; it is not inside the catafalque. All the pilgrims rub their faces on it and say *Intercession, O Messenger of God!*

All around the dome are windows with bronze gratings that look out onto the public thoroughfare.

The prayer-niche is small but highly-wrought with tiny stones like mother-of-pearl inlay.

Around the dome are varicoloured glass panes.

The cupboards of this shrine contain so many precious jewelled vessels and ancient Korans and *waqf*-endowment documents that only God knows their number.

The door of this light-filled dome opens eastward to the courtyard of the mosque. The door leaves are covered with silver roses and sequins and rings and varicoloured silver bosses attached with nails. Every generous patron has adorned this sublime door with some work of art. The frame is painted porcelain and the surrounding wall is covered with varicoloured tiles. Over the lintel the following chronogram is written in large letters on a round plaque of gilded marble: *Our lord Sultan Qaytbay, may his victory be perfect, ordered the construction of this holy place in the year (—).*

He who performs two prostrations of prayer in the prayer-niche of this light-filled dome will be protected from all vicissitudes of fate; no foe will stand up against him; and he will never see the face of poverty.

And if a murderer or thief or debtor takes refuge in this shrine from fear of the magistrate, he cannot be touched or apprehended. If he has in fact committed a crime and deserves punishment, he will not last there forty days but will waste away and die of hunger. But if he is innocent, he has nothing to fear and will go free.

Indeed, during the governorship of Ibrahim Pasha, a *kashif* who had a debt outstanding to the state treasury ran away and took refuge in the shrine of Badawi. Ibrahim Pasha twice sent officers to apprehend him, but they did not dare to and left.

One day, a brute of an officer from the *müteferrika* corps named Ali Agha came and berated the sheikhs in charge – Sheikh Salama and Sheikh Ahmad – waving the warrant in their face and demanding they turn over the *kashif*.

'Bring him forth from the shrine immediately,' he said. 'Otherwise, by the head of my efendi, I will clap you in irons and take you to the presence of the vizier.'

He went on in this Pharaoh-like fashion. But the sheikhs responded, 'God forbid, we cannot remove him. Here are the keys, go and open the door, if you dare, and arrest the *kashif* according to the vizier's order.'

'What have I to do with keys?' he said. 'You must open the door and hand the fellow over to me. Otherwise I will break the door down and take him out and put him in chains.'

This humble one happened to be present. 'Come now, Ali Agha,' I said. 'Don't act like that. Take the keys.'

After much counsel of this sort, he eventually took the keys, but after expending much effort for a full hour he was unable to open the door. Roused to anger, he and his henchmen wrenched the blessed door out of its socket, removed the *kashif* by force, and dragged him kicking and screaming to the sheikhs' assembly. All present were in a state of shock, murmuring *God is sufficient for me!* I too was dumbfounded. Sheikh Salama counselled patience and gentleness and went home.

The aforementioned officer and his henchmen mounted and left. But as soon as they set foot outside Tanta, on the road to the village of Tuh Nasara, Ali Agha was overcome with colic and, moaning and groaning, gave up the ghost then and there.

The next thing we saw was the *kashif* and the agha's henchmen bringing the corpse back to Tanta. They buried him in the cemetery. The *kashif* returned to the shrine and stayed there. One of Ali Agha's henchmen abandoned the world and remained in a corner of solitude as a Badawi dervish.

When I reported this event to the Pasha, he sent an order freeing the *kashif* and also gave the dervishes in the shrine 10,000 *para* as alms. In short, he is a mighty saint, one of those who dispose as they will, *may his noble secret be sanctified.*

[...]

The *mevlud* of Seyyid Ahmad al-Badawi in the city of Tanta

It is held in a valley between the town of Tanta and the town of Mahallat al-Marhum, 3,000 paces distant from each. Beginning twenty days before the breaching of the Nile in Cairo, all the shopkeepers and merchants make their way to Tanta, group by group. On either side of the main road going out of the city, and half way to Mahallat al-Marhum, they start to set up thousands of shops and coffee-houses, using tents, reed-mats and reeds, carpets and embroidered kilims.

Next come the Badawi sheikhs. In that arena of delight north of the city, next to these miniature markets, first the twelve vicars of Seyyid Ahmad al-Badawi take up quarters in their jerry-built pasha-pavilions, laid out tent rope to tent rope along with the tents of their dervishes, according to the *kanun* of the Abu'l-Al Ahmadi (the clan of Seyyid Ahmad al-Badawi).

First, according to sheikhly protocol, they set up the tents of Sheikh Mustafa Rumi – he is sheikh of the Marzuq Kifafi brotherhood, which however derives from the Badawi. Then come those of Sheikh Inbabi, Sheikh Kannasi, Sheikh Shinnawi with his 10,000 dervishes, Sheikh Ahmad

Qalyubi, Sheikh Uthman, and Sheikh Ghamrawi. In sum, first the vicars take up quarters in their proper places, then whatever other sheikhs arrive find a place as well.

Following the sheikhs, the *kashif* of Manufiya sets up his tent-pavilion with his 1,000 chosen troops, armed and mustered. Their sheikhs (!) undertake to guard the camp bazaars, which they patrol every night with so many soldiers and, if they find a rogue or bandit, put him to death in summary fashion.

Day after day a sea of men throng to this happy valley – from India and Yemen, Ethiopia, Persia, and Aden – settling with bag and baggage in tents and pavilions, joined tent rope to tent rope, so the plain becomes a tulip-garden of tents and banners.

On day six, according to the decree of the vizier of Egypt, the *kashif* of Gharbiya arrives with his 2,000 troops, 1,000 Arab horsemen, and 500 boys on foot, with cudgels in their hands, serving as military guards. They march in beating their drums, raising up their dragon-imaged banners, and shaking their horse-tail standards like the locks of a lovely lad. The *kashif* of Manufiya comes out to greet him with his soldiery fully armed and striking his kettledrums.

The *kashif* of Manufiya, however, does not have a five-layered military band like the *kashif* of Gharbiya. The latter is at the rank of *beylerbey*, occupying the throne of Tahir Baybars (i.e., the Mamluk sultan al-Malik al-Zahir Baybars, reg. 1260-77), so he takes precedence; although he does not take precedence over the governor of Girga, whose rank is higher than Upper Egypt (!).

Then the *kashif* of Manufiya stood up to greet the *kashif* of Gharbiya and their two troops paraded in grand procession from the Malaqa square, through a sea of men. When the two *kashifs* had taken up quarters in their tent pavilions, this humble one mounted with my retinue and presented the gifts sent by Ibrahim Pasha.

Also the orders he sent were read out, one of which was: 'You who are the *kashif* of Gharbiya, Hasan Agha: after the Badawi *mevlud* you will proceed to the Threshold of Egypt (i.e. the *divan* in Cairo) to settle your account and carry out my noble command.'

Another was: 'You who are the magistrate of Gharbiya: you will supervise the noble *mevlud* of Seyyid Ahmad al-Badawi, which takes place in your province, until its dispersal, giving protection to all the pilgrims and merchants. You will prevent the brigands of the Arab tribes from riding about on horseback in the Mal'aba ('Playground') arena with their javelins and swords and *akve* daggers, and will punish such malefactors.'

When these orders were read out, they cried: '*To hear is to obey!*'

I also gave him the letter of the Pasha's deputy, which was to the following effect, 'The viceroy has appointed you deputy of the sergeants for the *divan* of Cairo. Give Evliya Çelebi one horse with saddle and one Egyptian purse. It will please us if you treat him with due consideration and convey him back to us in happy condition.'

When this letter was read out publicly, he presented me one Arab horse with silver trappings and gilded stirrups and blanket; one other horse with its horse cloth; one purse as reward for bringing good news; 5,000 *para* as a gratuity for bringing the order; and one additional horse as a tip. He furnished me a tent next to his tent-pavilion where I stayed as his guest three days and three nights, partying and carousing. After that I was guest in the house of the sheikhs' chief deputy for ten more days.

Once these two *kashifs* had taken up quarters in the arena of the *mevlud*, there was a great sense of safety and security. All the merchants and pilgrims brought out their goods and displayed them openly. The amount of buying and selling that went on was phenomenal. And everyone decorated the front of his tent or pavilion with lamps and pennants and flags and standards.

In fact, there is a terrace in the arena of the *mevlud* where Seyyid Ahmad al-Badawi used to pray whenever he sought solitude outside of the city – it is called the Station of Badawi and is still a place of worship. Here, for the sake of a blessing, a certain benefactor planted a ship's mast, 80 cubits high, with thousands of ship's ropes stretched all around it. Every night of the celebration they string 40,000 oil-lamps on these ropes, illuminating the surroundings in grand fashion. It is something like a vizier's tent-pavilion with a central pillar. At the very top of the mast is a Catherine wheel that turns like the revolving sphere of heaven. It uses as many as 1,000 oil-lamps. When viewed from some distance away, it appears that a light emerges from the pavilion and settles on the arena. In the Arab regions this kind of lamp display is termed *eşare*. It requires forty attendants to operate it and burns 10 quintals of sesame oil every night. The benefactor has endowed 20,000 *para* for the fifteen nights of this display. It is a 'bride' that has to be seen, as though it were the royal pavilion of Pythagoras the Monotheist.

They have similar *eşares*, large and small, in thousands of places – with oil-lamps figured in the pattern of a tent-pavilion or prayer-niche or pulpit or Seal of Solomon or sun disc or cup or squash – that illuminate this arena of delight.

But especially in the year that we witnessed this event, when the sheikhs went to the presence of Ibrahim Pasha in order to get permission for the noble *mevlud*, the Pasha warned them, 'O sheikhs and efendis! I have high expectations of you. This year watch out that you perform the *mevlud* of the Prophet with even greater celebrations than last year. For those celebrations are the emblems of Islam!'

'Upon our heads, we will do it, O vizier!' they replied.

News of this warning spread among the Egyptians, who spared no effort or expense to carry out the Pasha's wishes. They are in any case given to pleasure and enjoyment, and celebrating is second nature with them.

So this year the notables of the entire province of Egypt, as well as those of Damascus and Aleppo, and the Arabs and Persians more generally, assembled for the Badawi *mevlud* in such numbers that, aside from Bedouin tents and kilim-shelters and huts, there were counted 1,700 tents and pup-tents and royal tent-pavilions. Only God knows the number of huts-of-sorrows of the poorer sort (or dervishes).

And many benefactors set up water-dispensaries, consisting of large earthenware jars, at crossroads. For water is scarce in this arena. There are some wells, to be sure, but not enough for so many myriads of people in mid-summer. As for the Nile, it is an hour's distance from this arena, in the direction of Mahallat al-Marhum.

The two *kashifs* with their soldiery keep guard day and night over all the pilgrims. And in every quarter guards are furnished by the Egyptian notables and their retinues. For in such a huge gathering, vermin of every stripe, members of the Harami and Juzami (rival clans) and other tribal riffraff are always present. Every day in this Mal'aba arena 10,000 or 15,000 naked Arabs stand ready with their spears bristling like a forest. Sometimes the Harami and Juzami clansmen seize the opportunity to kidnap one another in this open field, or do battle with one another, and hundreds of brigands get killed on each side. But the quarrels quickly subside due to the spirituality of Badawi.

So the pilgrims set up camp here, tent rope to tent rope, making a fortress of tents. That is why the *kashifs'* soldiery stand ready. For in these days in this arena there are hundreds of Egyptian treasures worth of property. That is how great a gathering it is.

In fact, Kashif Hasan Agha's chief equerry and chief camel-driver, outfitting the spare horses with weapons and the camels with flags and banners and fine garments of many colours, go around from shop to shop and extract a one *para* toll from each one. They told me they had taken patrol-money from 5,060 shops, and if they could go into the town they would have got 5,000 *akçe* more. That is how prosperous a gathering it is.

These shops all consist of tents and reed mats and reeds. No shops are more popular than the ones selling dried chickpeas. For Badawi chickpeas are taken as presents to all the regions of Islam. Thousands of camel loads of raw chickpeas come here and are dried to make this product.

There are 600 coffee houses, 300 cookshops, 200 butchers, 50 herbalists, 100 fritter shops, 100 bread shops, 200 *boza* shops, 500 sherbet shops, and hundreds of other types of shops adorning this arena of affection. While only God the Concealer of faults knows the number of shopless men peddling their wares.

Larger marketplaces are found in seventy places. For example, there is a bazaar for baked bread, one for (dried?) fruit, another with thousands of camel loads of melons and watermelons and *abdüllavi* melons; and bazaars for horses, sheep, cattle, camels, mules, and donkeys. The trumpeting noise of braying animals in the donkey bazaar is enough to drive one crazy.

There is also a bazaar for bedouin cloaks, one for Maghrebi stuffs, and one for white and coloured cloth and thread – this last is frequented by men and women both.

Speaking of women, there is a special bazaar for them – over 1,000 tents and huts of fornication, where women's skirts are lifted and men's breeches are untied, and the women are auctioned off to the highest bidder.

And there is a bazaar for boys in every coffee house, where pretty boys are on display, with earrings on their ears and their doe-like eyes smeared with collyrium. This is a special bazaar of filth, especially frequented by the Hadari fellahin. One or two thousand such men forgather in every coffee house and raise a ruckus beyond description. Day and night a thousand boy dancers prance about with coquettish gestures, catching the hearts of lovers in the traps of their flowing locks. Other groups of entertainers – singers, instrumentalists, ghazal-reciters, itinerant musicians, mimics, eulogists, comedians, mimes and buffoons – are everywhere, conducting as it were sessions of Husayn Bayqara.

Also in this town of Tanta is a playground for jereed shooting. It is kept completely clear: there are no tents and pavilions, no animals grazing, not even a stone the size of a bean that might strike a horse's hoof. Before dawn, in the cool of the morning, all the cavalrymen gather there with their thoroughbreds to perform their equestrian exercises and play their games with seventy-seven kinds of weapons. On one side they hurl spears, on the other side clash with cudgels or swords. They fire their muskets or practice archery on horseback; gallop their horses while standing up on the horses' backs or crouching down with their hands on the stirrups and legs in the air; and display their skills in Egyptian-style jereed and other games. For all of which they are rewarded by the *kashifs*. And all of this takes place to the beating of Ottoman drums on one side and kettledrums on the other.

Until the heat of the day, this arena is the site of many a spectacle that can only be appreciated by someone who himself rides horses and girds on swords. In fact, the Lord of Power has created the horse out of wind, and to perform such feats while mounted on wind is truly a heroic deed. These equestrian arts are peculiar to the Egyptian cavaliers; no kings on earth can rival them.

This humble one takes great pleasure at watching such exercises on wind-swift steeds. For I saw five or ten turns each of cudgel-play and swordplay and archery during the time when Murtaza Pasha was ensconced in Revan.[84] For this reason I greatly enjoy watching equestrian exercises, and so I have recorded them here.

Once this Mal'aba arena is free of the cavaliers, it is the turn of whatever entertainers and acrobats there are on the face of the earth to display their skills.

First come several hundred lovers of the Sa'di and Badawi brotherhoods who, to still their own ardour, lick red-hot irons with their tongues and break and knead them with their hands. Some even take the pieces of iron that are glowing like carnelians and, crying *Ya Hay!* swallow them. Then come the fire-eaters, tumblers, jugglers, rope-dancers, shadow-puppeteers; players with bottles or bowls or jars or jugs or goblets; beads players and gamblers; tricksters with straps; trainers of donkeys, roosters and monkeys; strong-men, cudgel-wielders, mace-wielders, sword-swallowers; mirror-conjurors; alchemists; trainers of dogs, goats, bears, human beings, and cows; snake-charmers – in short, seventy-seven guilds of prestidigitators

---

84 Translation of this sentence is conjectural; the meaning of *baba harbi zandısından* is unclear, also what *hane* means in this context. The incident referred to, following Murad IV's conquest of Erevan in 1635, is described in Vol. 2, fol. 309b.

whose feats, were I to record them as I witnessed them, would require an entire volume.

The huge gaping crowd in this arena provides a ripe opportunity for pickpockets. So one has to be cautious, since they have picked the pocket of many a heedless innocent and bankrupted many a foolish man. People speak of stealing the eye-salve from an eye, but the thieves of Egypt aren't like that, rather they steal an eye and leave the eye-salve in its place. Such masters are they of the pickpocket trade. For there are many wondrous sights in this arena, and if you get caught up in the spectacle and pay no heed to who is around you, you can end up naked. *God preserve us from the evil of mankind.*

A marvellous feat. This humble one applauded all the entertainers whom I watched in this Mal'aba arena. But the ones I admired the most were the snake-charmers, who made the snakes dance like monkeys. They were huge and fearful creatures, dragon-like, as thick as one's arm, and Faruq vipers.

The strange thing is that each snake has a name. If a snake-charmer calls to one and say 'Come,' it comes and hurls itself onto him, slithers up his shoulder and into and out of his bosom. If he says '*Go,*' it goes away. If a snake makes a mistake and comes when he has called a different one, he takes the snake that doesn't know its name and hurls it at a giant yellow snake nearby, which wraps it in a deadly embrace.

The snake-charmer beats a rhythm with his tambourine, in the *segah* musical mode, and amazingly, the snakes dance precisely to that rhythm, not departing from it one jot. Certain snakes, while they are dancing, raise up their heads to a man's height, flatten out their necks, stick out their tongues and make their eyes red.

On that day, I noticed that snakes never shut their eyes, because they have no eyelids. Grasshoppers also lack eyelids and so their eyes are always open. And some snakes wrestle with each other, intertwining and embracing.

This snake-charmer has a kind of Faruq drug that renders the snake unconscious as soon as he touches it to the snake's nose. Anyone who gets hold of some of this Faruq can set himself up as a snake-charmer and make a living. In short, snake-charming is something at the level of a saintly miracle.

A marvel. One day while a snake-charmer was making some snakes dance in this arena, a Badawi dervish who happened to be present went crazy and screamed 'Allah!' The snakes became agitated and started fleeing into their bags. But before they could get away, the dervish grabbed hold of one and began to eat it. The poor snake twisted and turned, and wrapped itself round his arm; but the dervish gave no quarter and continued to eat it. All the spectators were aghast. The snake-charmer cried, 'O people of Muhammad! O you Muslims! He has eaten my prize dancing snake, the one I trained for twelve years. He has eaten my snake that provides me a living for my family.'

He collared the Badawi dervish and a struggle ensued. The dervish's eyes turned to bowls of blood (signifying rage). Without a qualm, he ate up the snake, quite raw. Finally the snake-charmer hauled the Badawi before the Sharia court.

'My lord,' he said to the *kadi*, 'he ate my prize snake. My livelihood was bound up with that snake. I earned a living and paid what I owed to the tax agent. I demand justice!' Such was his plea.

'Why did you eat the snake?' the *kadi* asked the Badawi.

'Truly, my lord,' he replied, 'a fat snake and delicious, but one accursed and vicious, my lord.'

The *kadi* asked the snake-charmer how much the snake was worth, and the charmer told him ten *guruş*. The *kadi* reconciled him to one gold piece. The Badawi gave him one gold piece, wiped his mouth, and left.

That is the kind of snake-charming that goes on in this arena of affection.

Another marvel. A Badawi dervish wearing a woolen cloak had a rooster that he made dance in this arena. The rooster had a horn on its head in front of its comb. It always sat on the Badawi's head. Whenever someone gave the rooster a *para*, it swallowed it, then beat its wings and gave a cock's crow, but a cock's crow the likes of which I have never heard. Then the Badawi said, '*Say, O rooster, that God is one!*'

The rooster immediately beat its wings three times and said in a loud voice, '*There is no god but God and Muhammad is the messenger of God.*' And as God is my witness, it enunciated every letter perfectly. Then it danced in a circle three times on the ground and once again took up its position on the Badawi's head.

It was a marvellous spectacle. But they told me that the Badawi was an individual suspected of miraculous powers. Also that the rooster swallowed up to 1,000 *para* a day in this gathering; in the evening it defecated the coins, and the rooster-father took them and spent them.

Another marvel was a show of white magic that we witnessed in this arena of contention. A certain Nasr al-din Tanjawi from (Tangiers in) the Maghreb, a master magician, invited all the great notables who were in their tents, each with a green leaf (for cleaning teeth?) and a toothpick, to come to the arena, which became packed with people. Together with his attendants, he struck a flourish on the tambourine and drove a stake into the ground.

Now from his knapsack of love, he took out several red cannonballs, the size of an orange, and began to juggle with them. Then he took out three larger balls from the Sea of Grace (i.e., the knapsack) and showed his skill with them. He rolled one of them in front of the spectators and let them examine it and kick it. It made the rounds of the arena as though it were being played in a game of polo. The magician then took it and, as he tossed it in the air, a rope seemed to unravel from it. He gave the end of the rope to one of the spectators, who pulled it and pulled it, then tied it to the stake in the ground. The strange thing was that the ball was the size of a man's head, but the rope that unravelled from it was enough for a porter's load.

Once the rope was tied to the stake, the magician threw the ball high in the air, where it stayed suspended with the rope in between, one end at the stake and the other end at the ball. Now he grasped the rope with his hand and shook it, crying, '*Come down, O red ball, come down!*' He addressed the ball in this fashion several times, but it stayed in the air and would not descend. Some stalwart youths among the spectators joined his own attendants and kept pulling on the rope, until there were three skeins of rope piled up at their feet, but still the ball would not descend. As they kept pulling, the rope kept getting thicker, so what started as thin as a cord became as thick as a hawser. The entire audience was amazed.

The magician once again addressed the ball, telling it to come down. After some conversation with the ball, he addressed the audience and said, 'O people of Muhammad! The ball says, 'I have put on such a fine show, now let all the notables, my aghas, give my master one Egyptian *para* each; then I will come down and do some more tricks.' So, you lovers, we desire one speck of silver from each of you.'

He collected 10,000 *para* from the great notables. Then he grasped the rope again and shook it. 'O ball!' he said, 'Your wish is fulfilled – may God grant it as a blessing. We have come up with a purse of *para*. So now it's time to come down.' Still the ball would not descend.

'O Muslims!' he said. 'Let all of you request the ball to come down.' Everyone great and small clapped their hands and shouted, *'Come down! come down!'*

At once the ball started swaying back and forth, and descended to the ground. The magician picked it up and put it in his knapsack. The ropes piled on the ground turned out to be thin thread. He put it all in his sack and proceeded to perform some other tricks.

I found each one of them astounding. With my faulty intellect, however, I speculated that the above mentioned ball was full of dew, which has the property of turning into air when it is exposed to heat; and when he threw the ball into the air, the heat of the day was extreme. By the time he had finished his patter and collected his coins, the dew had all dissipated, and the ball fell to the ground. Otherwise, my trifling intellect could not comprehend it, but I gathered it by means of *knowledge of certainty* (102:5 – i.e., by deduction, not ocular evidence). Making the ropes appear thick as hawsers, however, is a trick of alchemy.

In (10)74 (1663) after the conquest of Uyvar, I saw a magician in the city of (—) in Austria who also kept a ball suspended in mid-air in this fashion. He was a great magician, and his tricks have been described in detail. But this magician in the Badawi arena also performed noteworthy feats. If I recorded everything that I witnessed, it would require a large volume.

In various corners of this Tanta arena are set up swings, merry-go-rounds, cradles, litters, Catherine wheels and carousels. Great and small, lovers and beloveds, mount the swings and swing back and forth to the sound of drums and shawms. The days of the Badawi *mevlud* are like festival days, the blessed nights like the Night of Power. There are also gatherings in tents where the faithful lovers celebrate with drum and tambourine and small kettledrum, *tevhid* and *tezkir*. And on every side are thousands of cauldrons in which delicious foods are cooked, and people eating and drinking. But, by God's wisdom, if any wine should enter this arena, it turns to vinegar by the secret of Badawi. There are *boza* houses, however, and apricot sherbets. But the sherbets of licorice, barberry, tamarind and treacle are especially fine. It is a divine wisdom that wine in this arena turns to vinegar.

Amidst all the hubbub and commotion, the sheikhs and dervishes of the Sufi brotherhoods go off troop by troop – beating their drums and tambourines, jangling their bells, raising up their standards, shouting aloud and performing *zikr*, the dervishes dancing – to visit the tomb of Seyyid

Ahmad al-Badawi. Then the thoroughfares are so crowded that sometimes a woman or child has been trampled to death in sight of the holy shrine. Even the pilgrimage visitations of Mecca and Medina do not get this crowded, except when the Noble House (i.e., the Ka'ba) is opened, but then after an hour things settle down. This Badawi visitation, however, goes on for ten days and nights, and it is like the gathering of the Last Judgement. Shoulder rubs shoulder, with everyone crying *Hu!* and *Hayy al-Qayyum!* and performing *zikr*.

In this arena, certain wealthy individuals among the great notables outfit their tents and pavilions with silk carpets and brocades, satins and velvets, Indian cushions with embroidered needlework and mottled velvet pillows and curtains, also various kinds of weapons and expensive chandeliers. The front of each tent is decorated with 100 or 150 poles topped with flags. Oil-lamps and torches provide illumination. The tents are decked out with pennants and standards, like so many idol-temples of China. Night and day there are private parties and intimate conversations, where benedictions are uttered for the continuance of the Ottoman state.

The sheikhs as well decorate their tents with myriads of oil-lamps and flags, as they engage in their worship. In short, whatever sort of pleasure you may desire can be found in this Badawi *mevlud*. But – in accordance with the verse:

> In the world of multiplicity take pleasure in unity
> And look to the Beloved.
> Make your heart pure like a mirror
> And gaze at the Beloved's face.

– the knower of God is he who looks closely at the world's adornment and is not deceived thereby, who in the midst of multiplicity takes pleasure in unity, and amidst transience polishes the mirror of his heart so that it will reflect eternity. For the trinkets and ornaments of this world are of a day, and the sound and fury are gone tomorrow; as in the Koranic verse: *Your worldly riches are transitory, but God's reward is everlasting* (16:96). So while those concerned with appearances go in one direction and sleep the sleep of heedlessness, those concerned with inner truths, who are the knowers of God, are awake at midnight performing royal *tevhid* and remembering the Eternal One.

In numerous places noble *mevlud*-poems and odes in praise of the Prophet are recited by cantors and eulogists, with fine voices that delight the cherubs in heaven and the children of fairies and of men on earth. And because this plain is embellished with countless lamps and torches, every night is like the fourteenth of the month (when the moon is full) or is bright as day. So there is something to occupy everyone during all these nights; as in the verse:

> When the Eternal revealed Himself
> And did the world create
> He gave each creature consolation
> In one or another state.

There is another group of men in this arena of delight whose job it is to set off muskets and rockets and various types of fireworks. Over the ten nights there are elaborate displays – with firecrackers, basilisks, kingfishers, butterflies, rams, falcons, chestnuts, peacocks, roosters, horses, castles, priests, Jews, demons, fairies, beauties, jets, mortars, waterspouts, bats, moths, rocket-donkeys, dogs and water buffaloes – imaged forth from rockets, lanterns filled with gunpowder and naphtha, Catherine wheels, tents of fire. The crowds get frightened at these animals. There is a hue and cry like the clamour of India. Dark night is bright as day, and the city of Tanta remains like a salamander (i.e., unburnt) in the midst of the flames.

The first three days of these fireworks displays are at the charge of the *kashifs* of Gharbiya and Manufiya, who out-rival one another, spending each night 2,000 *guruş* on rockets that sometimes set tents ablaze. This is an ancient *kanun* going back to the time of Sultan Qaytbay who used to attend the Badawi *mevlud* in person and spend great sums on its celebrations.

In sum, this humble one, the globetrotter Evliya, has spend forty-one years journeying throughout the eighteen empires, but I have never seen anything like the Sultanate of Egypt.

I have been fortunate to witness the breaching of the blessed Nile in Cairo; imperial wedding and circumcision festivities in Istanbul; the decking out of the admiral's fleet on the sea at Sarayburnu (the Topkapı Palace promontory); celebrations for the conquest of castles and the birth of Ottoman princes; festivities when the Sultan returned from performing *gaza*; the hoopla in Kağıthane in Istanbul in the months of Rajab and Sha'ban; parties on the Bosphorus for the Judas tree flowering in Göksu, the cherry season in Rumeli Hisar, and the season (of white cherries and chestnuts) in Akbaba Sultan (in Beykoz); The gunpowder festival in Pécs in the province of Buda (in Hungary); the garden seasons of Meram in Konya and Azpuzu in Malatya; the summer-pasture paradise of Istanaz in the Antalya region; the promenade of Büzürg Seng in the city of Elbasan in Albania; the fairs of Doyran, Maskoluri, Alasonya and Ösek; the *ful* (?) of Lonçat (Rotterdam?) in Germany; the orchard of Sudak in Kaffa; Pençi Hasan near Irak-ı Dadyan in Dagestan; in Persia, the bazaar of Gilan, the shrine of Imam Riza in Mashhad (!) and the Ashura ceremonies for the martyrdom of Husayn in Tabriz; and in Baghdad, the annual ceremonies at the shrines of Salman Pak, Imam Husayn and Imam Ali.

Yes, I have been vouchsafed in the course of my travels to see all of these pilgrimage sites and visitations, tourist attractions and promenades, grand gatherings and celebrations that are the envy of kings and the adornment of the world. But if all of these that I have listed were gathered into one, they would only make up one particle of the festivities at the Badawi *mevlud* and would perhaps answer to one day or one night of that festival.

The reason for its magnificence is that the majestic Badawi is a mighty saint, one of those who dispose as they will, even now as in his lifetime. Indeed he has not died; for this noble Hadith pertains to the great saints and believers: *Those who believe do not die but are transported from the abode of transience to the abode of eternity.* We believe in this noble Hadith – *The messenger of God has spoken true* – and are certain that he is alive and that this grand assembly takes place at his behest.

The rulers of this world have myriads of servitors in their employ. When they wish to assemble an army, they can do so by force, pressing men into service and massacring those who resist. But such huge numbers of God's creatures from Hind and Sind, Arabia and Persia and Turkey, come at great expense to themselves, abandoning their possessions and their families and undertaking the journey, in order to rub their faces at the threshold of Badawi and celebrate his *mevlud* crying *Ya Badawi!* And, by God above, anyone who does rub his face just once at that lofty threshold is cured of various illnesses, is protected from guile and bewitchment, and is free of all pain and fear and danger. This is tried and tested.

There is one other grand gathering that is comparable to this one, and that is the Mina bazaar in Mecca when the pilgrims return from Mt Arafat. 70,000 pilgrims gather there for three days and three nights. Indeed, as regards religious merit, as well as the sheer number of men and animals, the Mina bazaar festival is even greater than the Badawi *mevlud*. In that arena of delight, the soul experiences a different kind of expansiveness and inward joy, since all except God is far from one's consciousness and only the veil of modesty remains between everyone and his Lord. For there, everyone is as innocent as when he emerged from his mother's womb; as is signified by the noble Hadith: *He who repents of his sin is as though he has never sinned.* He finds his Lord, and he experiences the unity in multiplicity that is the goal at Mecca and Medina as it is at Badawi.

But the Pole of Poles (i.e. Seyyid Ahmad al-Badawi) is himself present every year at the Badawi *mevlud*, as has been witnessed many times. You may object that after so many people have gathered in one place, there is all sorts of rubbish and filth. That is true, but it is the way of the world. And he is a deep ocean and the Greatest Help (*gavs-ı a'zam*, a title of the greatest saint) – rubbish does not cause any harm to the ocean. And anyone tainted by corrupt and scandalous deeds, in that great place is certain to be reformed. Such a master of the grand gathering is he, the Father of Orphans – may his spiritual effort by ever present.

On the eighth day of this Badawi *mevlud*, criers circulate among the pilgrims to announce that on Friday in the city of Nahariya will be the noble *mevlud* of Sheikh Muhammad ibn Zayn. As soon as they hear this, some pilgrims and merchants strike their tents and shops on Thursday and move to Nahariya.

During the days of the festival, 1,000 camel loads of dried chickpeas and several thousand quintals of halva are sold in the bazaar of the Badawi *mevlud*. This is no exaggeration; for all the visitors that come from the various regions of Islam must take home chickpeas, as a blessing, when they return to their countries. They are indeed quite delicious. They sprinkle sesame oil on the raw chickpeas and bake them in red-hot sand. It is a process found nowhere else, which gives the chickpeas a distinctive flavour and makes them world-famous. They also make a kind of *lokum* (Turkish delight) with (sesame) oil, cut up in small pieces like 'pilgrims' *lokum*', that is also considered a blessing and is taken as gifts to all the countries.

The following day, Friday, all the *kashifs* and the soldiery, fully armed, assemble at the tent-pavilion of the *kashif* of Gharbiya and consume a huge Muhammadan spread. Each of the colonels of the Gharbiya guards gets a gratuity consisting of one horse and one camel. The Gharbiya troops take their leave, amidst prayers and blessings, and everyone makes his way to his home town or village, having served for six months.

Towards noon, the Muhammadan spread is the turn of the *kashif* of Manufiya. He too has a great feast, and his colonels too get one horse and one camel apiece as gratuity. Having received Sharia vouchers that they have performed their service, they take their leave and go off to their homes.

Now the *kashif* of Gharbiya and Manufiya proceed with their own soldiery to the shrine of Badawi. They open the cloak room and have one of the sheikhs put on a Badawi cloak and turban, then they parade him through the city in grand procession. They perform the Friday worship at the mosque of Sheikh Ibrahim Matbuli. As they conduct him back to the shrine, everyone comes out on the street to watch the parade and greet the sheikh. Back at the shrine he removes the cloak and turban and secludes himself once again in his cell. The *kashifs* receive Sharia vouchers that they have performed their service, make a farewell visit, and head off for Cairo.

The reason for all this is that when the Badawi *mevlud* breaks up, Tanta is left as a frontier zone. The Nile submerges the countryside; the *kashifs* are left without authority; deputies and representatives seize control; and the naked Bedouin brigands begin their banditries.

Now the tents and pavilions in this Badawi arena start to be dismantled. This too is a noteworthy scene, full of commotion. Myriads of horses and mules, camels and donkeys move off with their loads, and after a great deal of shouting and toing and froing, not a single pilgrim is left in this plain. For once the *kashifs* in charge have taken their leave and are gone, the pilgrims and merchants are fearful of the bedouin vermin. This too is a day of terror. The world becomes a kind of shadow-puppet theatre. One moment there is pandemonium, the next moment not a fly remains in this valley. Where is that grand gathering, that hue and cry? It is scattered in a trice, and in its place only ants and snakes. Truly, the pomp of this world is no more substantial than a dream. One should take a lesson from this as well.

The (leading sheikhs or) vicars decamp from this plain and remove to the city of Tanta. For on Saturday they purify the shrine of Badawi and that night assemble in that gate of felicity and perform a noble *mevlud* that is attended, so they say, by the spirits of all the saints. And that night the sheikhs and dervishes complete more than 1,000 Koran recitals.

The next day, the sheikhs and dervishes too make their farewell visit and everyone sets out for his own dwelling. Those sheikhs and dervishes who attend the shrine now clean it with rose-water, wash every stone of the noble courtyard, cover the floor with silk carpets, and resume their life of quiet.

On the following day, the citizens open a channel of the Qarnayn Canal in the territory of Manuf and – glory to God! – the blessed Nile comes billowing and submerges the entire plain where the Badawi *mevlud* took place. All the rubbish that was left behind is swept away, and that plain becomes a sea. It is as though no one ever set foot in this open field. This too is a noteworthy event.

This humble one took careful note of thousands of sights in this city of Tanta. When my tour was complete, I bid farewell to all my friends, Sheikh Salama and Sheikh Ahmad the vicar and Sheikh Çelebi, and all the imams and preachers. I completed one last Koran recital in the shrine of Badawi, seeking succour from his noble spirit, and performed the farewell visit. Then I kissed the threshold, according to protocol, and set out for the city of Nahariya.

12. Mountain of the Birds

Description of the Mountain of the Birds

{It is also called Mt Taylimun.} It is a wondrous spectacle. The tongue falls short at describing this great mountain. Every year in the spring several hundred thousand birds of various kinds – but mainly storks and goldfinches – come from the direction of Turkey and settle on this mountain. The mountain plains swarm with them, so that one can hardly find a place to set one's foot, and their cries are loud enough to make one's gall-bladder burst. The people of the region are aware of the spectacle and come to view it from a distance; but no one can seize any of the birds or throw stones at them.

On top of the mountain, on a sandy plain, is a cemetery. Each sarcophagus contains thousands of birds of various sorts – but mainly storks – buried in their shrouds (i.e. mummified). The (living) birds all come to visit this cemetery, circling above it and squawking and lamenting. Then they land in the mountain plains. Most of the buried birds are visible outside the graveyard. Their bodies and feathers are fresh and undecayed inside their shrouds, which are made of date-palm fibres.

No one knows the reason why these birds are buried here in their shrouds. Nor have I seen it mentioned in any of the histories. This humble one actually brought two of these mummified birds to Kethüda Ibrahim Pasha so he could see them.

After resting for one night, the birds arise at the crack of dawn and raise such a hue and cry that – glory to God! – one might think all hell broke loose. There is a huge cave on this mountain. As soon as the sun rises, all the birds take wing and, with a great clamour, circle about this cave – or rather, circumambulate it – seven times. Then they settle on the ground again, landing wave after wave, and seem to consult on the next step.

Now one bird from each species goes inside the cave and does not come back out. Until those birds expire inside the dark cavern, none of the others will fly away. Sometimes a bird that has entered the cave rushes back out in fear of its life. When that happens, the other birds strike it and drive it back inside. If it comes out again, they kill it with their beaks and make another one go in.

As the day declines, first the cranes take off, then the vultures, the eagles, the kites, and finally the storks. Eventually all the birds take wing and for an entire hour – with sad voices and lamenting cries that would comfort the soul of any mournful listener – they once again fly seven times around this mountain. As night falls, all God's birds draw up in their formations and, flock by flock, fly away heading south. After crossing over the country of Funjistan and the headwaters of the Nile, they continue beyond the confines of this Egyptian peninsula (i.e., the African continent). Portuguese and Indian mariners have observed them flying southward over the ocean; but where they go after that, nobody knows.

Actually, it is only the storks that cross the ocean. The other birds do not go beyond Africa, which is their winter home. For the migrating birds of every country have a summer pasture (in the north) as well as winter quarters where the climate is tropical. But they cannot breed in the tropics, because the intense heat cooks their eggs. This humble one, when I was going to Mecca, once found two ostrich eggs. I bored holes in them, thinking that I would empty them and take them back to Turkey; but I found that they were hard-boiled from the heat of the sun.

When those birds had flown away, I climbed with a few other individuals to the top of the mountain to see the bird mummies in their cemetery. When we got to the cave, we went inside. It is not too dark, and is a huge cavern; but the stench of countless avian corpses soon drove us back out. We did notice, however, that the representatives of the various bird species that had come into the cave had latched onto holes in the domes of the cavern with their beaks and claws and were now hanging there, dead. And the bird corpses underfoot were the remains of previous ones that had hung by their claws and then fallen.

The various bird species come every year and visit this mountain in the manner I have described. Then, after sacrificing one of their number in this cave, they cross the lands of Aswan and Sudan and fly out over the ocean. In spring, when they return from their winter home in the tropics, they once again visit this marvellous mountain. They circumnavigate it seven times as previously, but do not sacrifice any of their number in the cave and do not rest there overnight, but continue on.

Only God knows the number of dead birds piled up inside this cave. It is an annual spectacle.

The people of the province know about the annual sacrifice, and it has come down from their ancestors that if no bird remains suspended by its claws but they all fall to the bottom of the cave, it is a sign of impending drought. So when that happens, they put all their grain in storage bins and guard it carefully until the drought is over. If a single dead bird remains suspended, the harvest will be slight. If there are two, the peasants will get just enough crops for subsistence. If three, there will be plenty, the blessed Nile will rise to 16 cubits, and the Sultan will be paid his tax. If there are four hanging birds, the Nile will overflow to 20 cubits and all the government agents and tax farmers will get rich. If there are five, the Nile flood will be 22 cubits and all the peasants of Egypt will get rich. If there are six, it will be 26 cubits and the crops will be so abundant – *each bearing a hundred grains* (2:261) – that peasants and *emirs* and governors and tax farmers together will be unable to remove them all from the threshing floors. This is tested wisdom and a firm belief of the fellahin of Upper Egypt, and it occurs by God's command.

It is a strange quirk of nature that wild creatures and denizens of the air should come of their own volition, latch on to the holes in the rock at the top of this cave, and hang there by their beaks and claws until they die. It is a wondrous act of divination, an ancient talisman that is effective until today – truly white magic! God be praised that in the course of my travels I have been vouchsafed to witness this tremendous spectacle.

13. Map of the Nile

The sages of old spent the length of their lives travelling in these countries, measuring altitudes with their astrolabes and learning about God's bounties, making maps and writing the books of *Geography* and *Pa[d]riye* and *Koloniye* (i.e. Ptolemy on the Old World and Christopher Columbus on the New). This humble one, full of fault, also has taken great pains to record the villages, towns, cities, mountains, rivers, and stages north and south that I have traversed in the course of my travels, in order to expound upon the countries where I have sojourned and to set down their contours in writing. I have also recorded many castles and countries, rivers, mountains and lakes, as in the *Mappa Mundi*, in the fashion that I have seen done by my master Nakkaş Hükmizade Ali Bey. If God permits me to complete this journey of the Nile and Funjistan, I plan to record their features (in such a map).

14. Meeting with Kör Husayn Qan

The great plain of Hankoc

It is governed by the *dabir* (chief accountant) of the king of Funjistan. All our soldiery encamped here, tent rope to tent rope. In the morning, a cry of *Allah Allah!* arose at the eastern end of the plain. It seems that Kör Husayn Qan's army was waiting there, and when they heard that our troops had arrived with grain, in their joy they let out the cry of *God is Great!* The Funj castle magistrates who had accompanied us left their baggage and prepared to race forward on their riding-camels unburdened.

This humble one also took my letters and joined the forced march. After traversing this wilderness for three hours we reached a sea of men and squabbling camels. The plain was covered with black tents and *ihram derim* (a kind of tent), and there were countless soldiers with javelins, bows and arrows, crossbows, slings and spears.

When we had made our way through them, we came upon another troop from whose heads in the heat of the sun there wafted a sweet fragrance that perfumed our brains. They had anointed themselves with civet. A swarthy people with handsome faces, they were the forces of the king of Qirmanqa, myriads of men who had come to join forces with the Funj king and whose black tents covered the ground.

After passing through them we entered upon another troop that resembled Egyptian soldiers and even had Ottoman tents here and there. We rejoiced to see these familiar tents and baggage, and the *derim* tents that looked like those of bedouin Arabs.

Continuing forward, we saw about 2,000 varicoloured tents and pup-tents and tent-pavilions, and a royal pavilions with golden balls and precious gauze. The shiny balls glittered in the bright sun and dazzled our eyes. This, as it turned out, belonged to Husayn Qan.

The castle *qans* (magistrates) approached the pavilion, with this humble one in front, walking fearlessly but properly. Husayn Qan came as far as the pavilion door to greet us. After shaking hands, I showered him with some flattering phrases, then he took me by the hand and sat me down opposite him knee to knee.

'Welcome!' he said in Turkish. '*Safa geldin, hoş geldin!*' It turned out that he spoke excellent Turkish, since he was from the Kalafish Bedouins near Aswan. We exchanged pleasantries, and I wished him well on his campaign, which pleased him mightily. He served tea and fennel. After drinking a cup of each, I begged leave to let the castle *qans* come forward one by one and kiss his hand.

The king of Barbari came first. He honoured him mightily and took him on his right side. Then the *dabir* of the Funj emperor kissed his hand. He greeted him according to their protocol and said, 'Have your baggage brought immediately, so we can give grain to the troops. In the morning, God willing, we'll advance against the enemy.'

He also addressed this humble one, saying, 'We'll take you on the *gaza* as well. You are most welcome here.'

I handed over the letter of the vizier (i.e., Ottoman governor) of Egypt and the letters of the Girga, Der, Ibrim and Say notables. The *dabir* of the Funj read out the Arabic letters with excellent articulation. When Husayn Qan understood their contents, he rose to his feet and tried to kiss my hand, but I would not let him. That very hour he ordered his deputy to felicitate me with a tent and to supply all our needs. So we camped in his circle.

He had a pastille of ambergris in his hand and gave it to me. In return, I gave him a lime-coloured gold-embroidered Kaya Sultan handkerchief that I had in my bosom. He immediately used it to tie together the locks of his hair, letting it hang down like a Muhammadan turban-end.

'This will bring us luck, God willing,' he said. 'We have got a gift from the Turks, so we will get much booty and will be victorious.'

I arose and went to his tents where I rested for an hour while his soldiers and our servants came and set up our tents. At the time of the mid-afternoon prayer, Hüseyn Bey (i.e., Husayn Qan) came to our tent and raised us from the ground (i.e., treated us with great honour). I brought out some tidbits and candies that I happened to have. He drank a cup of sherbet flavoured with musk and took great pleasure. When he was about to leave, I presented him with a skein of mohair, two pieces of Damietta striped stuff and two jars of sorrel sherbet flavoured with musk, which pleased him exceedingly. He returned to his pavilion and distributed the newly-arrived grain supplies to his troops.

At the time of the sunset prayer, an enormous clamour arose from among the countless soldiery, causing my heart to leap. It turned out to be the call to prayer! At midnight they sounded the kettledrums, took down the tents, and got ready to march. At the time of the morning prayer, the trumpets and drums and kettledrums sounded and the march began.

Now Husayn Qan summoned this humble one and offered to take me up on his Mahmudi elephant, where he was already mounted.

'By God,' said I, 'this is the first time I have ridden an elephant.' He let down a ladder woven of elephant skin. Reciting the *Mu'avvizeteyn* I clambered up to the kiosk on the back of the elephant, settled in knee to knee with Husayn Qan, and we set out. The king of Barbari was also with us, as was the *dabir* of Funjistan – indeed, he had invited thirteen men to join him on the elephant's back, and we sat there clustered together, eating our breakfast and cutting stages (i.e., travelling fast). But this elephant moved in such stately fashion that the tea and fennel in our cups did not spill one drop, although a thousand elephants and even horses could not keep up with him.

After breakfast, other elephants came abreast with ours. They had mounted on them the *firdilans* – i.e., the singers and musicians. They played a kind of square *rebab* (rebec), and another instrument consisting of 200 iron rings attached to a hoop and making the sound *kıvış kıvış*, also reed instruments (?) accompanying the songs sung in a fine and melancholy voice by the Funji singer. So we rolled up stations (i.e., travelled apace) enjoying these 'Bayqara' musical sessions.

15. Meeting with Qan Girgis; encounter with two Bektashi dervishes

Description of the great and ancient fortress of Arbaji

It is a lovely city on the east bank of the Nile, built in the middle of a vast and fruitful plain. The fortification is made of lofty trees trunks, joined together with wooden planks and mud bricks morticed with millet stalks and sedge. In this country there are trees used in building construction that are 2,000 or 3,000 years old and have never decayed – trees such as the wild date-palm, acacia, tamarisk, teak, oleander, and ilex.

The fortress is rectangular in shape, 1,000 paces in circumference. Inside are 700 houses made of reeds and mud bricks – there is no sign of stone in this. The door leaves are made of wild date-palm wood. Outside the fortress are 3,000 reed and mud brick houses, seven Friday mosques, and eleven *boza* shops. There are no other amenities – no minaret, *han*, public bath, water dispensary, or medrese – and no orchards or flower gardens, though there are many vegetable gardens.

This city was originally the residence of the Funj king's vizier, Qan Pir, and is now the residence of the king's brother, Qan Girgis. He is in command of 40,000 troops and 600,000 Barbari peasants.

Qan Girgis is a good-natured individual, and I was honoured with the pleasure of his company. I handed over some of the booty that Kör Hüseyn Bey had got from the Firdaniya *gaza*, plus the gifts of the *kadi* of the Barbari king, saying, 'Husayn Qan sends his greetings.'

He inquired about the *gaza*, and when they related how it came out, he performed a prostration of thanksgiving. He was also very pleased with the gifts of the Barbari king. At this juncture, I presented him with one jar of sorrel sherbet flavoured with musk, one handkerchief, and one shirt with a pair of breeches, which pleased him exceedingly.

This Qan Girgis was, however, a rather simple-minded person. When he first caught sight of me and my retinue he got up and hid in a corner, shouting to his interpreter, 'Who are these raw men?'

'They are from the vizier of Egypt and are going to your brother, the Sultan of Funj,' he replied.

'Why then are they so white and raw?' he asked. 'Why aren't they *qaqan* (i.e., cooked?) like us?'

The interpreter turned to me and said, 'Qan Girgis wishes to know why these men are so white? Have they come to complain about someone having flayed the skin off their faces? If they are seeking justice against someone who has made them so white and raw, he will certainly give them justice and punish the offender.'

I was somewhat taken aback at this absurd speech, and I began to bemoan my state, thinking that I had travelled through eighteen empires and kingdoms only to end up in this country and to hear such foolishness. But then I considered that I had come here of my own free will, so I praised God and began to answer the interpreter thus, 'We are servants of the Sultan of Mecca and Medina, king of the Arabs and Persians and Turks, and Caesar of Constantinople, Sultan Mehmed Khan. We reside on the soil of his jurisdiction. By command of God most High, and in accordance with divine custom (i.e., natural law), all the people of that region are white like us. In your country of Funjistan, in Barbari and Sudan and Baghanisqa – in short, everywhere in the Egyptian peninsula (i.e., the African continent) – the people are descended from Ham son of Noah, and like you their faces are black and their eyes are black and even there words are black. God, Lord of the Worlds, created you black and created us white. Otherwise, no one flayed the skin of our faces; had they done so, our faces would be bleeding. And we have not come to complain and seek justice. The one who makes our faces white (i.e., proves our innocence) in this world and the next is God – and who can demand justice of God?'

In this preacher-like fashion I made my reply, and the interpreter conveyed it point by point to Qan Girgis the Silly. In his amazement he kept crying *İlalla illalla!* and, addressing his crow-like cronies, said, 'Have you ever seen uncooked men like these?'

Among those present was a Barbari man who had travelled as far as Cairo and Gaza. He replied, '*May God increase your life*, O Qan Girgis! I have seen such uncooked men in Egypt. In that country the sun does not blaze so hot as it does here, and that is why the people there stay so raw.'

At this I nearly went out of my mind, thinking that now this madman was going to strip us naked and grill us in the sun for a few days so that we get cooked. 'My lord, I take refuge in You,' I muttered, and continually recited the *Mu'avvizeteyn* and repeatedly called on God the Preserver.

God be praised, he did not do anything of that sort. But he did get up from his place and come toward me. I just stood there, without flinching, though my eye was on my servants and theirs was on their weapons. He approached with his cronies and said, 'Let's see what sort of clothing they wear. Let's see if the rest of their bodies are a raw as their faces.'

He tried to get me to loosen my waistband, and was very insistent about it. All sorts of fearful fancies started going through my mind. I pulled up the sleeves of my robe as far as the elbows and showed him my arms, but he was not satisfied.

'You must loosen your waistband,' he said. 'Let us see your clothes and your body.'

I began to get angry at such an unreasonable proposal. But I was also still afraid that he was going to strip us and cook us in the sun, and I began to cry for help. With us were some Ethiopian Jabarti men (Ethiopian Muslims) from Dongola, who now intervened.

'O Qan Girgis,' they said. 'These are Turks. They have never seen such behaviour or heard such proposals. They think you will loosen their waistbands, take their clothing, leave them naked, and steal their money and goods. You see that their servants are fully armed, with three or four muskets apiece. It looks as though there will be a tussle and we'll end up like the sword bazaar in Arbaji. Then how will you answer your brother Malik Qaqan?'

He returned to his seat and, with a smile, called me over. I tried to beg off, but he begged and wheedled, so I went and settled next to him knee to knee. He said lots of things, and also apologised.

'In my entire life,' he said, 'I have never seen such raw men in this country as you are. That is why I requested to see your skin. Otherwise, God forbid, we had no designs on your person.'

He stood up and once again tried to kiss my hand.

'At least undo your turban so we can see your head,' he said.

I realised that this man had a screw loose, and it is crazy to consort with someone who is crazy. So I said, 'The reason we have such long turbans is that we are those who struggle in God's path (or, those who engage in jihad). When we are martyred, we will be wrapped and buried in our turbans. It is a token of the Prophet and signifies Muhammadan honour and dignity. To undo a man's turban from his head is to undo his honour. It is now such a sign on our heads.'

This was how I answered him, and I did not undo my turban.

He took out six pastilles of white ambergris from behind his leathern cushion and gave them to me. He also gave me a bag of aloes wood, two bags of carnelians, and large seeds of coral the size of nutmegs. And he gave me two black virgin maidens and eight swarthy boys. In return, and to lighten my load, I gave him an elephant. He was delighted with this exchange, but I was even more delighted, since these elephants consumed 100 camel loads of grass per day and drank half the Nile.

On the third day we bade each other farewell and our party, along with his donation of soldiery, headed toward Funjistan along the shore of the Nile. That day we went for twelve hours.

Description of the fortress of Itshan

A round fortress of mud brick on the west bank of the Nile, with one Friday mosque and 600 houses of mud brick and thatch.

By God's wisdom, its governor was Rumlu Kara Ali Çelebi, an elegant and eloquent gentleman (*çelebi*) who had been born of an Ethiopian slavegirl in Tophane (in Istanbul). In his youth, while journeying from Ethiopia to Zayla (in Yemen), he had fallen captive to these Funj and for these fifty years was unable to free himself. He had wife and children, and was a good-natured and sweet-spoken 'mad lover' (i.e., one inclined to poetry and mysticism).

We toured the mosque and the weekly market places of the town, enjoyed the singers and musicians in the *boza* shops, then proceeded to the gardens outside the town where we indulged in melons and watermelons.

A melancholy incident

This humble one, the world traveller and boon-companion of mankind, Evliya-i Gülşeni, having traversed the globe and viewed its cities and countries, had now set foot in Itshan, one of the cities of Sudan in the country of the blacks; and after diligently touring the town, and studiously visiting its streets and markets, I was now enjoying the melon season in its gardens, while my slaveboys Kazım and Sührab stood nearby surveying all four directions – for I never went a single moment without a guard and a sentry, since that is what they advised me in Ibrim and Say.

'Agha,' they said, 'two men have appeared. They are approaching, mounted on I don't know what.'

'Keep your weapons at hand,' I told them, and busied myself eating watermelon.

They arrived. Both were white men, but I had never seen the likes of their mounts. As I pondered what animals they could be, I heard the resounding noise of a Bektashi trumpet.

I stood up to observe these individuals. Two lovers of God appeared, graceful and lively, Bektashi dervishes in their Kalender outfits. As they came near, they sounded some reverberating salutes with their trumpets, in the muʻaṣṣer (?) musical mode. After greetings, they dismounted and we kissed and embraced. Then they sat down, holding the reins of their beasts in their hands.

'Boys,' I said to my servants, 'take these lovers' animals from their hands and let them graze.'

'No,' said the Bektashis, 'these animals will not go near any man who eats meat, nor can such men go near them.'

I was dumbfounded. Taking a closer look at these beasts, I saw that one was a rhinoceros. [...] (described at length). The other was an oryx (*kazık boynuz*, lit. stake horn), known in Arabic as *baghal barri* (a wild mule). It is indeed very much like a mule, except that it has two thin black nodose horns just below its ears, the tips of which are like lancets, and cloven hoofs. Its flesh can be eaten, according to the four Sunni rites. It is very swift, like a gazelle, and the female gives birth once every two years – a marvellous creature indeed! These lovers had tamed these beasts, attached reins and put saddles on their backs, and rode them.

Having examined these creatures, I sat with the Bektashis in the garden and had much lively discourse with them. At dinner time, we offered what we had – since *The best food is what is readily at hand* – consisting of camel meat and chicken. But they refused, saying they had not tasted meat for seven years, and began to weep.

When we inquired the reason, they related as follows, 'We were three brothers travelling with India-merchant ships from India to Ethiopia. Portuguese infidels seized our ships and took all three of us captive. They imprisoned us in their hold. By God's wisdom, one of our brothers died, and they roasted his body and forced us to eat it. We fed on our brother's flesh for an entire month. At the end of a month, by God's wisdom, as we were sailing in the Indian Ocean, a storm hurled us ashore and our ship broke apart. We fled to a mountain top where we bathed in a stream and performed two prostrations of thanksgiving. And we swore never to eat the flesh of any living thing. That is the reason.'

They wept as they told us this, then continued, 'The next day, these two animals came and associated with us. Though dumb creatures, they conveyed a thousand sentiments. It is now seven years that we have been wandering with these animals, and we have not yet reached a place of safety. We are left amidst negro blacks who treat us with contempt, saying that we are raw men.'

They complained bitterly, but gave thanks to God and ate a little barley bread and millet bread and some melons and watermelons. It turned out that they had been grazing with their animals for the past seven months, subsisting on grass. Sometimes when they went into cities, people were abusive and refused to give them food.

'Of what garden are you the roses?' I boldly inquired. 'Of what country's pure earth do you derive, and of what river's water have you drunk? What is your birthplace?'

'We are from Larende near Konya in the land of Turkey,' they replied.

'I have seen your home town,' I said. 'I have visited the tomb of the mother of Mawlana (Jalaladdin Rumi) in her mosque, and have toured the noteworthy medreses of Karamanoğlu Ya'kub and Ibrahim Bey.' They were pleased at this response.

'O faithful brethren,' I continued, 'if you wish to reach a place of safety, do not depart a single step from this humble one, but accept our fellowship and, by God's command, I will bring you to the country of Egypt in honour and security.'

We joined hands, made vows, and exchanged pieces of bread. The three of us became brothers in this world and the next, and we had many fine conversations together. It warmed my heart to see Turkish dervishes in such inhospitable coasts as these.

Leaving the garden, we made our way back to our quarters in Itshan castle where I indicated a place for these Bektashis among our companions. In the course of our conversations I learned that their names were Seyyid Ni'metullah and Seyyid Carullah. I also offered them each a suit of clothing that I had on hand, but they refused, saying they would not depart from their dervish habit, nor would they sully themselves with this world's refuse. I saw that they were pure souls who nested like the phoenix on the Qaf of contentment. And I gave thanks to God, mindful of the proverb, *First the companion, then the road.*

16. Elephants and monkeys

From there (Wadi Qoz) the next day, as we were travelling in the desert heading north, a black dust-cloud appeared in the sky ahead of us. Wondering what it could be, we continued forward. It turned out that an eagle had seized a baby elephant and, while starting to eat it, the mother elephant had come and was battling with the eagle. That was the reason for the cloud of dust hanging in the air. We observed from a distance, without making a sound. The big elephant tried to protect the little one with her trunk, but it was no use; she was overcome by the terrible eagle and seriously wounded.

Now our companions took pity. Crying *Allah Allah!* with a single voice, and shooting their muskets, they spurred on their horses and made the eagle take flight. It was like a black cloud, its wing-spread casting a shadow on the ground that blocked the sun light. The mother elephant seized the opportunity and ran away. We approached the baby elephant. The terrible eagle had gouged out its eyes and gnawed at several parts of its body. It staggered about in that plain, fearing for its life.

We resumed our journey. When we had moved off some distance, the eagle swooped down from the sky, took the baby elephant in its beak, flew up into the air and dropped it on the ground, where it broke into pieces. The eagle settled over it and began to feed. We passed by that place,

[...]

Departing from Poragha the following morning, we proceeded through an uninhabited valley. Eleven huge Mahmudi elephants accompanied us, five of them milk-white, six of them black. They paid us little heed, sometimes walking in front of us, sometimes to our right or left, chasing one another, or playing, or fighting. This went on for seven hours. Though we were armed, we agreed not to shoot at them, but simply to watch.

One of them was a very large old elephant. He did not prance around like the others, but several times came close to the soldiers in order, as it seemed, to exhibit his beauty. He was a very clever animal. His legs were like minarets, tusks like ship-masts, trunk like a chimney, belly like an Isfahan kettledrum, hide like a worn carpet, mouth like the mouth of a stokehold, eyes like gazelle eyes, tail like the staff of a dervish sheikh, anus like the Cave of Orphans.

These eleven elephants accompanied us all the way to the next stage, and no one laid a hand on them.

[...]

Elephants and monkeys

Departing from there (Nazdi) in the morning, we again headed north, encountering herds of elephant and rhinoceros, deer, gazelle, wild mule and oryx – so many animals that only God knows their number. And – glory to God! – this was a plain completely covered with trees and other vegetation. Birds in every corner cheered our spirits with their plaintive song. Actually, this bird jungle is quite well-known in the province of Dombiya, under the name of Wadisha. Once a year the king of Dombiya comes here to hunt – here and there one can see benches for his tents and cooking places. We stayed in this jungle plain for three days, camping and hiking, and saw many wonderful things.

There are monkeys here as big as Merzifon donkeys. They use one another as mounts, and sometimes use goats. They are different colours – white, pied, red, black, gray, and blue – and only the Creator knows their number. Some carry clubs on their shoulders, as though they were doorkeepers or going somewhere urgently on official business. Some are huge lumbering creatures that make the earth tremble when they run. In short, there are many kinds of monkey, one more comical than the next. This humble one found three infant monkeys on the road, which we put on the pack-horses and fed.

In this plain we reached the border of the Sultan of Dombiya and crossed into Ethiopia in the first clime. We made a thanksgiving sacrifice for getting this far in safety. The next day, however, the effect of the first clime began to make itself felt, and our heads were cooked from the heat of the sun; but by God's command, it did us no harm.

We always had ten men go in front as a vanguard, and at this stage, while we watched, the man at the front slid off his horse and the horse ran back toward us. The other nine men fell on their horses' necks and came to us panting heavily.

'What's going on?' we asked.

'By God, there's a scoop-tail (*kepçe kuyruk* – i.e., horned viper?). It sprinkled its urine on that unfortunate fellow, who was riding in front of us. He fell off his horse and the horse ran to you.'

As they reported this, the horse also fell to the ground and gave up the ghost. It immediately swelled up, like a mountain. Everyone fled from its side, and the horse burst like a cannon.

'What should we do now? Can we take a different road?'

With such a hue and cry, and shooting our muskets, we plucked up our courage and went forward. That damned creature known as scoop-tail –

it is somewhat like a gazelle in size and appearance, but its tail hangs down raggedly – scurried away into the mountains. We approached the poor fellow who suffered the attack. His body had turned into a coagulated mass.

'Don't go near him,' they cried. 'Don't even look at him. The stench of the poison will affect you badly.'

We left him there and resumed our journey. Some of his companions sighed in regret, since the dead man had 700 gold pieces in his belt. But what could they do? The fellow's corpse had turned to pudding

[...]

The next day we continued north. The Sea of Suez (Red Sea) appeared before us. From now on we went east along the shore, skirting black mountains (on our right), and cut stages for six days, until we entered the land of monkeys (*Vilayet-i Maymunistan*). Everywhere, both mountain and plain, was taken over by monkeys, baboons, chimpanzees, etc. They all engaged in some comical behaviour, viewing us from the trees, chattering *ah ah* or *kah kah* or *vah vah*, doing somersaults and tumbling and performing all sorts of acrobatics. Watching them made us forget the hardship of the journey. In short, the Creator of the world has not created any creature as funny and clever as the monkey. But they are ill-omened (although *maymun* means well-omened!). Watching them dispels grief, to be sure; but feeding them betokens that one will inherit poverty. It is great fun to watch them, however. The elephant is also a clever animal.

17. Envoi

Final Word and Farewell to the Reader

As they say in the Hindi language, *Izid Alla kipanah chalti hun* ('I desire the refuge of God'). Praises without end to the Lord Creator, by whose assistance these scattered folios of ours, having turned many colours like dervish robes, are now completed in Cairo, the rare one of the age. The writing of it, the beginning and end of it, was in the year (—) when the governor of Egypt was (—) Pasha, *may God vouchsafe him what he desires*. But in the eyes of the intelligent it is not complete. I only hope that they will attribute its shortcomings to the length of my travels, and will disregard the lack of fancy phrases and fine expressions; that they will cover its faults with the skirt of forgiveness, and will scratch out its errors with the pen-sharpener of improvement.

For it is fifty-one years now that this humble one, full of fault, having

Envoi

sojourned in the seven climes, has brought these rough copies to completion. After so many travels I have now withdrawn into obscurity. It is not vouchsafed to me to study chronicles and histories, nor have I recorded in this my *Book of Travels* any other traveller's adventures or any other writer's compositions. Only I have, where appropriate, added Koran commentaries and prophetic Hadiths that I learned from my master Sheikh Ali al-Shumurlisi, with his permission.

Aside from that, these rough copies are all the record of my own adventures and of my travels which I have taken pains to record in such shameless detail. *Apologies are acceptable among the noble* – may my apology be acceptable, may I be remembered with a benediction.

APPENDIX

Outline of Journeys and Events in the Ten Volumes of the *Book of Travels*

Selections in the present anthology are highlighted in **bold**, with indication of folios translated from the original manuscripts (see Bibliography).

VOLUME 1

1. Introduction; The dream (Vol. 1, fol. 6b–8a)

[Chapter 1]	Hadiths on Istanbul
Chapter 2	Founding of Istanbul
Chapter 3	Black Sea
Chapter 4	Walls of Istanbul (built by Constantine)
Chapter 5	Circumference of Istanbul
Chapter 6	Talismans
Chapter 7	Mines; resumption of historical narrative: the rise of Islam
Chapter 8	Sieges
Chapter 9	Seljuk and Ottoman conquests of Rum
Chapter 10	Siege and conquest
Chapter 11	Capture of Frankish ships; fulfilment of Akşemseddin's prophecy; kin relationship of the Ottomans and French royalty
Chapter 12	New palace
Chapter 13	Old palace
Chapter 14	Public officers
Chapter 15	Imperial mosques: Aya Sofya
[Chapter 16]	Layout of Aya Sofya
Chapter 17	Shrines at Aya Sofya
[Chs. 18/19]	Küçük Aya Sofya/Zirekbaşı
[Chapter 20]	Mosque of Fatih Mehmed II
Chapter 21	Mosque of Bayezid
Chapter 24	Mosque of Selim I
[Chapter ?]	

2. The Süleymaniye Mosque (Vol. 1, fol. 43a–45b)

Chapter 2[?]	Şehzade mosque
Chapter 31	Grand viziers
Chapter 32	Viziers of the cupola
Chapter 3[?]	Admirals
[Chapter ?]	The organisation and divisions of the empire according to the *Kanun-name* of Süleyman
[Chapter ?]	Reign of Selim II
Chapter 41	Viziers
Chapter 42	*Beylerbeys*
Chapter 43	Defterdars
Chapter 44	Ulema
Chapter 45	Physicians
Chapter 46	Sheikhs
Chapter 47	Conquests
Chapter 48	Death
Chapter 49	Reign of Murad III
Chapter [5]2	Reign of Mehmed III
Chapter [5]3	Conquests
[Chapter ?]	Reign of Ahmed
Chapter [5]6	Princes
Chapter [5]7	Grand viziers
Chapter 58	Viziers
Chapter 59	Ulema
Chapter 60	Sheikhs
Chapter 61	Conquests
[Chapter ?]	Mosque
Chapter 64	Reign of Mustafa
Chapter 65	Reign of Osman II
Chapter 66	Chotin campaign
Chapter 67	(Second) reign of Mustafa
Chapter 68	Reign of Murad IV
[Chapter ?]	Revolt of Abaza Mehmed Pasha
Chapter 70	Revan campaign
[Chapter ?]	Baghdad campaign
Chapter 75	Events in his reign
Chapter 81	Husrev Pasha

Appendix

Chapter 82	Hafız Pasha
Chapter 83	Receb Pasha
Chapter 84	
Chapter 85	
Chapter 86	
Chapter 88	Character of Murad IV
Chapter 89	Habits of Murad IV
Chapter 90	Admirals
[Chapter ?]	Chief muftis
Chapter 93	Ulema and mollas (chief *kadis*)
Chapter 94	Janissary aghas
Chapter 95	Malta campaign
Chapter 96	Death
Chapter 97	Reign of Ibrahim
Chapter 98	Viziers
Chs. 99–109	
Chapter 110	Conquests
Chapter 11[?]	Killing of Sultan Ibrahim
Chapter 11[?]	Reign of Mehmed IV
Chapter 119	[Childhood]
Chapter 120	Viziers
Chapter 12[1]	Provincial governors
Chs. [12]2–130	Princes, etc.
Chs. 131–7	Buildings, etc.
Chapter 138	*Gazas* and conquests
Chs. 139–94	
Chapter 195	Valide Sultan mosque
Chs. 196–200	Other mosques
Chapter 205	Mosques of viziers, etc.
Chapter 206	*Mescids* (neighbourhood mosques)
Chapter 207	Medreses
Chapter 208	Koran schools
Chapter 209	Primary schools
Chapter 210	Hadith schools
Chapter 211	*Tekkes* (dervish convents)
Chapter 212	Imarets (public soup-kitchens)
Chapter 213	Hospitals

Chapter 214	Palaces
Chapter 215	*Hans* (inns)
Chapter 216	Caravanserais
Chapter 217	*Bekar-odaları* (bachelor barracks)
Chapter 218	Fountains
Chapter 219	*Sebilhane* (water dispensaries)
Chapter 220	Baths
Chapter 221	Imperial Tombs: Fatih Mehmed II
Chapter 222	Bayezid II
Chapter 223	Selim I
Chapter 224	Süleyman
Chapter 225	Selim II
Chapter 226	Murad III
Chapter 227	Mehmed III
Chapter 228	Ahmed I; Osman II; Murad IV
Chapter 229	Mustafa; Ibrahim (same tomb as Mustafa)

3. The antiquity of smoking (Vol. 1, fol. 105a)

Chapter 230	Tombs of the viziers
Chapter 231	Tombs of the saints and ulema
Chapter 232	Saint-fools, etc.
[Chapter ?]	Kadizade; ulema who died in reign of Murad IV; sheikhs of the Sufi orders
Chapter 235	Description of the three molla-districts outside Istanbul: Yedikule
Chapter 236	Yenikapu
Chapter 237	Topçular
Chapter 238	Otakçılar
Chapter 239	Nişancıpaşa
Chapter 240	Çömlekçiyan
Chapter 241	Eyub
Chapter 242	Südlice
Chapter 243	Karapiripaşa
Chapter 244	Hasköy
Chapter 245	Kasımpaşa
Chapter 246	Galata

Appendix 457

4. Galata (Vol. 1, fol. 128a–130a)

Chapter 247	Tophane; the gun foundry
Chapter 248	Beşiktaş
Chapter 249	Ortaköy
Chapter 250	Kuruçeşme
Chapter 251	Arnavudköy
Chapter 252	Rumelihisarı
Chapter 253	Istinye
Chapter 254	Yeniköy
Chapter 255	Trabya
Chapter 256	Büyükdere
Chapter 257	Sarıyar (Sarıyer)
Chapter 258	Boğazhisarı (Rumeli Kavağı)
Chapter 259	Anadolu Kilidü'l-bahir kal'esi (Anadolu Kavağı); village of Kavak; Yoroz castle
Chapter 260	Beykoz; hunting parks; Incirli; Çubuklı
Chapter 261	Kanlıca
Chapter 262	Anadoluhisarı; Göksu; Kandilli
Chapter 263	Çengelliköyi = Çengalköyi
Chapter 264	Istavriz = Istavroz; Kuzkuncık
Chapter 265	Üsküdar
Chapter 266	Kadiköy
Chapter 267	Imperial gardens
Chapter 268	Pleasure-outings

5. Kağıthane (Vol. 1, fol. 145a–146a)

Chapter 268 (!)	Merchants and craftsmen, their shops, their patron saints, etc.
Chapter 269	Description of Istanbul made in 1048/1638
Chapter 270	Guilds, shops, patron saints, etc.; 1100 guilds listed in 57 (!) Chapters

1 parade sergeants, etc.
2 guards, police, etc.
3 military judges, etc.
4 physicians
5 farmers and peasants
6 bakers
7 Black Sea captains
8 Mediterranean captains
9 Egyptian grain-merchants
10 butchers, etc.
11 sheep-drovers, etc.
12 cooks
13 confectioners
14 fishermen
15 the imperial inspectors

16 grocers, etc.	27 tent-makers	38 The New Bedestan
17 fresh fruiters	28 fur-dealers	39 joiners
18 sword-cutlers	29 tanners	40 military-band
19 musket-makers	30 saddlers	41 acrobats
20 blacksmiths	31 shoemakers	42 architects
21 hinge-makers, etc..	32 shoe-sellers	43 singers
22 kettle-makers	33 druggists	44 musicians
23 goldsmiths, etc.	34 barbers	45 jesters, dancers, etc.
24 bronze-founders	35 bath-keepers	46 mimics
25 bow-makers, etc.	36 painters, etc.	47 *boza*-sellers
26 tailors	37 The Old Bedestan	

6. Guilds parade (Vol. 1, fol. 165a–b, 193a–b, 198a, 204a)

Chapter 271 Population of Istanbul
Chapter 272 Poets and *littérateurs* in the reign of Murad IV
Chapter 273 Hezarfens (masters of all trades)

7. Lağari Hasan Çelebi (Vol. 1, fol. 216b)

VOLUME 2

1. Setting out (Vol. 2, fol. 220b)

Description of Bursa

2. Hot Springs of Bursa (Vol. 2, fol. 227a–228a)

3. Return to Istanbul (Vol. 2, fol. 241a–242a)

Izmit. The Princes' Islands. Return to Istanbul. Departure for Trabzon (19 August 1640) with Ketenci Ömer Pasha. Sinop. Samsun. Trabzon.

4. Hamsi in Trabzon (Vol. 2, fol. 252b–253a)

Travels in the Caucasus with Ketenci Ömer Pasha's deputy, Hüseyn Agha. Abkhazia; specimens of Abaza and Ubykh. The Azov campaign. Crimea: Bagchesaray. Balıklava.

5. Black Sea adventure (264b–266a, 267a–268b)

Canea campaign. Evliya is appointed customs clerk and chief caller-to-prayer and boon companion to Defterdarzade Mehmed Pasha, commander-in-chief and governor of Erzurum. Departure for Erzurum in 1646. Bolu. Amasya. Erzurum. Shushik campaign.

Evliya is appointed envoy to the Safavid governor of Tabriz requesting him to send caravans to Erzurum. Journey to Armenia and Azerbaijan. Nakhchivan; specimen of Persian. Qarabagh. Marand.

6. Tabriz (Vol. 2, fol. 297a–298a, 300b–303a)

Maragha. Ardabil.

7. Cat-brokers of Ardabil (Vol. 2, fol. 306b)

Khuy. Erevan. Ganja. Shamakhi. Baku.

8. Oil wells of Baku (Vol. 2, fol. 314b–315a)

Journey to Georgia and Armenia. Darband. Tiflis; specimen of Georgian. Akhiska. Kars. Ani. Üç Kilise ("Three Churches," i.e. Echmiadzin).

9. Cathedral of Echmiadzin (Vol. 2, fol. 325a–325b)

Return to Erzurum. Gümüşhane. Bayburd. Tortum. Joins Seydi Ahmed Pasha for a raid on the Cossacks at Günye. Mingrelia; specimen of Mingrelian. Return to Erzurum.

Defterdarzade Mehmed Pasha, dismissed in mid-winter as governor of Erzurum and ordered to go to Kars, instead turns rebel ('Celali') and marches toward Istanbul in alliance with Varvar Ali Pasha, the dismissed governor of Sivas.

Kemah. Erzincan. Şebinkarahisar. Ladik. Merzifon. Departure from Merzifon on 27 Muharrem 1058 (22 February 1648) with irregular battalions (Segban and Sarıca troops).

10. Ankara (Vol. 2, fol. 355b–360a)

Beypazarı; Evliya gets news of his father's death and quickly returns to Istanbul to settle family affairs.

VOLUME 3

Departure for Syria with Murtaza Pasha (September 1648). Iznik. Akşehir.

1. Nasreddin Hoca in Akşehir (Vol. 3, fol. 9a)

Konya. Eregli. Payas. Iskenderun. Antakya. Hama. Hims. Damascus; specimen of Arabic. Round-trip to Istanbul to witness grand vizier Kara Murad Pasha's routing of Celali Gürci Nebi in Üsküdar. Expedition against Ma'noğlu in Mt Lebanon. Baalbek. Tyre. Specimen of Taymani. Acre.

2. Safed (Vol. 3, fol. 44a–45a)

Dead Sea. Ramla. Return to Damascus.

3. Sheikh Bekkar the Naked on the road outside Damascus (Vol. 3, fol. 50a–50b)

Ma'arrat al-Nu'man. Aleppo. Birecik. Raqqa. Urfa, Harran, Maraş. Kayseri. Bor. Aksaray. Elbistan. Sivas.

4. The girl who gave birth to an elephant (Vol. 3, fol. 79a–79b)

5. Armenian (Vol. 3, fol. 79b)

Divriği

6. The cats of Divriği (Vol. 3, fol. 81a–81b)

Egin. Arabgir. Harput. Pertek. Palu. Genc. Muş. Bin Göl. Zile. Iskilib. Çankırı. Mudurnu. Return to Istanbul (14 July 1650). Melek Ahmed Pasha grand vizier (30 July 1650–21 August 1651). Departure for Özü with Melek Pasha. Silivri. Çorlu. Burgaz. Aydos. Pravadi. Shumnu. Hezargrad. Ruschuk. Nikebolu. The Danube. Round-trip to Istanbul. Silistre. Balçık. Mankalya. Köstence. Babadağı. Karasu.

7. Witchcraft in a Bulgarian village (Vol. 3, fol. 130a–130b)

Zagra Yenicesi. Eski Zagra. Filibe. Tatar Bazarcığı. Sofia.

8. Sofia (Vol. 3, fol. 139b–140b, 142a–143b)

Melek Pasha, recovered, is dismissed from office. Departure for Istanbul (27 June 1653). Köstence. Edirne. Havsa. Baba Eski. Çatalca. Return to Istanbul. Melek deputy vizier. Round-trip to Konya to meet with Ipir Pasha. Ipir becomes grand vizier, 'exiles' Melek to Van.

VOLUME 4

Departure for Van (9 March 1655). Melek Pasha gathers regiments of Segban and Sarıca troops. Malatya. Evliya is sent to Diyarbekir to collect Melek's debt from Firari Mustafa Pasha.

1. Diyarbekir (Vol. 4, fol. 202b–203a, 207b–208a)

Mardin. Sincar. Miyafarkin; specimen of Kurdish. Çemender Bayırı, south of Bitlis.

2. Bitlis (Vol. 4, fol. 221a–222b, 229a–236b)

Ahlat.

3. The ruined city of Ahlat (Vol. 4, fol. 239b–240a)

Adilcevaz. Mt Subhan. Erciş. Amik. Van. Expedition against Abdal Khan in Bitlis. Return to Van (8 August 1655). Evliya is sent on a mission to Azerbaijan. Hoşab. Pinyanişi. Kotur. Berdük. Gazikıran. Urmia.

4. On 'extinguishing the candle' (Vol. 4, fol. 296b–297a)

Dumbuli. Return to Urmia. Salmas. Tabriz. Ardabil. Sahand. Nihavand. Hamadan. Darguzin. Qasr-ı Shirin. Qazvin. Daylam. Mihriban. Qum. Qashan. Qaan. Sava. Rayy. Damavand. Darna. Baghdad (9 January 1656). Karbala. Hilla. Najaf. Kufa. Qurna. Basra. Abadan. Wasit. Return to Baghdad. Havar. Erbil. Shahrazul. Aqra. Imadiya. Jizra. Hisn-kayfa. Nisibin. Mosul. Tikrit. Return to Baghdad. Evliya takes leave of Murtaza Pasha.

VOLUME 5

Mosul. Siirt. Return to Van after eight months' absence. Melek Pasha sends Evliya to Istanbul as courier. Departs Istanbul (5 April 1656).

1. Highwaymen in the Bolu pass; return to Van (Vol. 5, fol. 8a)

2. Escape from Bitlis (Vol. 5, fol. 9a–14a)

Melazgird. Erzurum. Ilıca. Tokat. Return to Istanbul (23 June 1656). Melek Pasha is appointed governor of Özü. Depart Istanbul (8 August 1656). Kırkkilise. Varna. Polish campaign against George II Rákóczi prince of Transylvania. Akkirman. Bender. Chotin. Kamaniçse. Podhaniçse. İşçerez. Lvov. Kiev (?). Çehril. Uman; specimen of Ukrainian. Özü. Akkirman. Kili. Babadağı. Hırsova. Return to Istanbul (7 January 1658). Melek is appointed governor of Bosnia. Depart Istanbul 15 March 1659. Evliya refuses an administrative post, enters the service of grand vizier Köprülü Mehmed Pasha. Expedition against the Celali rebels. Gemlik. Ilıbat. Erdik. Aydıncık. Karabıga. Gallipoli. Bolayır. Ipsala. Malkara. Edirne (25 October 1659).

Moldavia and Wallachia campaigns. Jassi. Return to Edirne (16 February 1660).

Transylvania campaign. Nish. Belgrade; specimen of Serbian. Temesvar. Lipova. Yanova. Siege of Varat (Oradea).

Evliya is sent with a victory announcement (*fethname*) to Bosnia. Sarajevo; specimen of Bosnian. Travnik. Akhisar. Livno (Hilevne); reunion with

Melek. Departure for Dalmatia to conduct raids against the Venetians. Klisz. Kinin. Zadra. Shibenik. Ribniçse. Dirnish; specimen of Croatian. Evliya is sent as envoy to Split.

3. Diplomacy in Split (Spalato) (Vol. 5, fol. 149a–150b)

Yayiçse. Banaluka (Banya Luca). Yenihisar. Zagreb. Çakaturna. Lıgradıck. Evliya returns to Istanbul; Melek Pasha is dismissed from Bosnia, appointed to Rumeli province (Sofia).

Evliya sets out for Rumeli (15 November 1660). Vishigrad. Yenibazar (Novi Pazar). Kosovo. Vuçitrin. Üsküp (Skopje). Kıratova. Köstendil. Arrival in Sofia (2 January 1661).

Melek is ordered to join the Transylvania campaign; Evliya is sent to collect grain requisitions. Manastır. Göl-i Kesri.

4. The bandit Yano (Vol. 5, fol. 179b–180a)

Serfice. Semendire. Evliya reports to Melek Pasha in Temesvar. Execution of Seydi Ahmed Pasha (17 June 1661).

VOLUME 6

Transylvania campaign. Erdel Belgradı (Alba Julia). Kolojvar (Cluj). Nagy Banya; specimen of Hungarian. Kaschau. Bistiriçse. Saray. Kokol. Mkisvar. Conquest of Seykel Tabur under the commander Ismail Pasha, governor of Buda (23 October 1661).

1. An incident on the battlefield (Vol. 6, fol. 21a–21b)

Ferdenvar. Kıhalom (Cohalm). Fogaras. Pıraşov (Kronstadt). Sibin (Hermannstadt). Turvin plain. Sebes (Mühlbach). Melek Pasha is recalled from Belgrade to become the deputy grand vizier and to marry Fatma Sultan; Evliya is sent to Albania to collect the Pasha's debts.

2. Shkodër (Scutari) (Vol. 6, fol. 33a–35a)

Podgoriç. Iştip. Samakov.

3. The Samakov iron works (Vol. 6, fol. 40a)

Reunion with Melek Pasha in Sofia. Pınarhisar. Return to Istanbul (1 April 1662). Death of Melek. Evliya sets out on the German campaign (11 March 1663).

Lofça. Plevna. Vireca. Vidin. Slankamen. Mitrovica. Vukovar. Eszék. Mohacs. Pécs. Földvár. Cankurtaran. Buda. Pest. Evliya sets out on the

Appendix

Uyvar campaign (21 July 1663). Esztergom. Cigerdelen (Párkány). Siege of Uyvar. Nyitra campaign.

4. An adventure near Komorn; Tatar raid into Western Europe (Vol. 6, fol. 123b–130a)

Uyvar. Léva campaign. Nögrád campgain. Rudnik. Return to Belgrade. Evliya departs on a mission to Herzegovina and Dubrovnik (19 April 1664). Uzice. Prijopolje. Pljevlja. Çayniçse. Foça. Nevesinje. Ljubinje.

5. Dubrovnik (Ragusa) (Vol. 6, fol. 150b–153a)

Nova. Kotor. Risna. Kaçka plain; Evliya is assigned to join the relief party against the Uskok raiders for those conducting the Dubrovnik treasure to the Porte. Blagaj. Kabele. Mostar.

6. The great bridge at Mostar (Vol. 6, fol. 164b–165a)

Return to Sarajevo; Evliya sets out on the Kanizsa and Yenikale campaign. Izvornik. Raça. Valpova. Siklös. Szigetvar. Babócsa. Berzencze. Kanizsa. Siege of Yenikale.

VOLUME 7

1. Raiding expeditions in 'Germany'; a fabulous tree in Krokondar (Vol. 7, fol. 4a–5a)

Return to Kanizsa and departure on the Raab expedition (July 1664). Lake Balaton. Stolnibelgrad (Székesfehérvár, Stuhlweissenburg).

2. The battle on the Raab River (Battle of Saint Gotthard) (Vol. 7, fol. 18a–22a)

Treaty negotiations in Visegrád (1 October 1664). Belgrade: the grand vizier appoints Evliya to join Kara Mehmed Pasha on an embassy to the Austrian emperor. Departure (20 April 1665). Petrovardin. Ilok. Hatvan. Egri (Eger, Erlau). Fülek. Kermat. Tata. Papa. Komorn. Senmartin (Sz. Márton). Ovar: the beginning of 'Germany'.

3. Comparison of Austrians and Hungarians (Vol. 7, fol. 49b)

4. A pleasure resort near Vienna; the free conduct of women (Vol. 7, fol. 51a)

5. Vienna (Vol. 7, fol. 57b–72b)

29 June 1665: sets off to Western Europe. (Text breaks off.) Returns to Austria after two and a half years. Pojon. Szolnok. Sombor. Bács. Szegedin. Czanad. Gyula, Varat. Sekelhit (Székelyhid). Erdelbelgrad (Alba Julia). Severin. Bucharest; specimen of Rumanian. Sets out for Crimea. Ferahkirman (Perekop). A raid into Muscovy. Return to Perekop (November 1665).

6. Crimea (Vol. 7, fol. 117b, 121b, 125a, 134a, 141b)

Perekop. Gözlev. Inkirman. Balıklava. Menkup. Baghche-saray. Akmescid; specimen of Tatar. Karasu (Cherson). Sudak. Eski Kırım. Kefe (Kaffa). Kerch. Taman. Temrük. Çoban; specimen of Nogay. Circassia.

7. A meal of strange honey in Circassia (Vol. 7, fol. 155a)

Kabartay; specimen of Kabardian. Iraq-ı Dadyan. Dagestan (5 May 1666). Tarkhu. The Caspian. Endiri. Terek. Astrakhan. Saray (Saratov). Kazan. Alatır. Balukhan. Türkorı. Kalmyks.

8. Kalmyks and cannabilism (Vol. 7, fol. 176b)

Specimen of Kalmyk – the most difficult of the 147 languages he encountered in 51 years of travel. The Don. Azov.

VOLUME 8

Evliya departs Azov for Istanbul to join the Crete campaign.

1. Return to Crimea (Vol. 8, fol. 188b–194a)

Taman. Kerch. Kefe (Kaffa). Baghche-saray. Perekop. Yeni Bazar. Yanboli. 2. Report to the vizier's deputy in Edirne and return home to Istanbul.

2. Report to the Sultan in Edirne (Vol. 8, fol. 204b)

Gümülcine (Komotini)

3. The Gypsies of Gümülcine (Komotini) (Vol. 8, fol. 208a – 210b)

Sidrekapsi. Aynaroz (Mt Athos). Toyran. Kavala. Drama. Serres. Salonika. Vardar Yenicesi. Vodina. Karaferye. Alasonya. Yenişehir. Tirhala. Fener. Izdin. Modonice. Livadya. Istifa. Agriboz. Kızılhisar.

4. Athens (Vol. 8, fol. 250b–257a)

Evliya departs on a mission to the Dodecanese to collect war materials for the Crete campaign. Corinth. Vostitsa. Balibadra.

5. Balibadra: A great cypress tree and the five ethnic groups of the Morea (Vol. 8, fol. 261b)

Glarentsa. Holomiç. Kefalonya. Arkadiya. Navarino. Koron. Kalematya. Mistra. Tsakonya; specimen of Tsakonian Greek. Monemvasia. Tirabolice. Argos. Anaboli. Thermisi. Return to Corinth.

Passage to Crete (4 October 1667). Canea. Retima. Siege of Candia.

6. Siege of Candia: Ministrations to the wounded and Saint Green-Arm (Vol. 8, fol. 292b–293a)

Surrender; Evliya recites the victory *ezan* (2 September 1669). Candia. Tour of Crete. Sets out on Maina campaign (30 May 1670). Specimen of Maina Greek.

7. A captive woman in Kolorya (Vol. 8, fol. 337a)

Zarnata; Evliya departs on a mission to Albania and the Porte. Lepanto. Angeli Kasri. Ayamavra. Preveze. Narda. Ioanina. Aydonat (Paramithia). Delvine. Ergiri Kasri. Albanian Belgrade. Mikat. Kanye. Avlonya. Pekin. Elbasan. Struga. Ohrid. Vlandiva. Strumica.

8. Fair at Doyran (Vol. 8, fol. 375b–376a)

Return to Edirne. Hayreboli. Tekirdağ. Return to Istanbul (28 December 1670).

VOLUME 9

Evliya has been searching for a spiritual guide (*mürşid-i kamil*) in his travels.

1. Setting out on the Hajj (Vol. 9, fol. 2a–3a)

Inegöl. Kütahya. Afyon-karahisar. Uşak. Simav. Demirci. Alaşehir. Gördes. Akhisar. Marmara. Durkutlı. Manisa. Bergama. Menemen. Halkalıpınar. Izmir. Urla. Karaburun. Çeşme. Sakız (Chios). Sivrihisar.

2. Brigands at the Alman Pass; Ephesus (Vol. 9, fol. 66a–68a)

Kuşadası. Balat. Güzelhisar (Aydın). Tire. Birgi. Nazilli. Denizli. Muğla. Milas. Bodrum. Istanköy (Cos). Marmaris. Sönbeki. Rhodes. Elmalı. Antalya. Alanya. Ermenak. Larende (Karaman). Takyanos. Silifke. Akliman. Görgös (Korykos). Tarsus. Adana. Maraş. Ayntab. Kilis. Aleppo. Ceble. Betis. Hüsnabad. Tripoli. Cübeyle. Beirut. Sidon. Tyre.

3. Safed and the land of Canaan (Vol. 9, fol. 198b –201b)

4. Jerusalem (Vol. 9, fol. 208a–214a)

Bethlehem. Khalil al-Rahman ('Friend of the Merciful' = Hebron). Evliya returns to Jerusalem; performs the festival prayer of Ramadan (= 1 Shawwal 1082 / 31 January 1672) in the Aqsa Mosque; decides to alter his itinerary and take advantage of the pilgrimage caravan from Damascus rather than going directly to Egypt; accompanies the governor of Jerusalem, Harmuş Pasha, who received an imperial order to join the pilgrimage caravan.

5. Sheikh Bekkar the Naked in Damascus (Vol. 9, fol. 249b–250b)

6. The Hajj caravan; Muzayrib, the Hajj bazaar (Vol. 9, fol. 257b–258a; 260a–261b)

Salih. Fahlatayn.

7. Medina (Vol. 9, fol. 275b–283a, 290b–291b)

Mecca; Hajj ceremonies.

8. The People of Mecca (Vol. 9, fol. 358a–359a)

Jidda. Evliya returns to Mecca, gets permission to join the Egyptian pilgrims. Departs Mecca 27 Dhu'l-hijja 1082 (25 April 1672). Medina. Yanbu' al-barr. Yanbu' al-bahr. Muwaylah.

9. Uyun al-qasab (Vol. 9, fol. 375b–377a)

Aqaba.

10. St. Catherine's Monastery on Mt Sinai (Vol. 9, fol. 380b–381a)

Wilderness of Tih (Sinai Desert). Suez. Evliya arrives in Cairo, 6 Safar 1083 (3 June 1672).

VOLUME 10

1. Adam's prayer for Egypt in 'Hebrew' (Vol. 10, fol. 2a–2b)

Evliya enters Cairo, 7 Safar 1083/4 June 1672

Chapter 1   Fustat: kings before the flood
Chapter 2   Kings after the flood
Chapter 3   Amalekites
Chapter 4   Joseph and the Fayyum
Chapter 5   Dynasty of the Pharaoh Reyyan
Chapter 6   Prophets who entered Egypt
Chapter 7   Amr ibn al-As and the dragon, etc.

Appendix

Chapter 8   Koranic verses and Hadiths concerning Egypt
Chapter 9   The Arab conquest
Chapter 10   The Islamic dynasties
Chapter 11   The forty-eight sultans and kings of Africa
Chapter 12   The non-Islamic dynasties
Chapter 14   Selim I in Damietta, Alexandria, etc.
Chapter 15   *Kanuns* of Egypt in the reign of Sultan Selim (I)
Chapter 16   Government officials
Chapter 17   Regulations of the *divan*

2. Relation among Nile overflow, plenty and poverty, crowdedness of Cairo, people and donkeys (Vol. 10, fol. 63b–64a)

Chapter 18   Garrisons; the military establishment
Chapter 19   [1st] grand procession: Pasha's entrance
Chapter 20   Ulema; the religious establishment
Chapter 21   Cairo: first builders
Chapter 22   Vizier's palace
Chapter 23   City walls
Chapter 24   Quarters, palaces
Chapter 25   Friday mosques
Chapter 26   *Mescids*
Chapter 27   Medreses
Chapter 28   Hadith schools
Chapter 29   Koran schools
Chapter 30   Primary schools
Chapter 31   Dervish convents
Chapter 32   Soup kitchens
Chapter 33   Public baths
Chapter 34   Commercial buildings
Chapter 35   Hospitals

3. Snake medicine and snake charming (Vol. 10, fol. 120b–126b)

Chapter 36   Water dispensaries

4. Rain, snow and hail in Egypt in 1083 (1672) (Vol. 10, fol. 128a)

Chapter 37   Fountains
Chapter 38   Wells, water-wheels, basins, etc.
Chapter 38 (!) Canals and waterways
Chapter 39   Dikes

Chapter 40   Ponds
Chapter 41   Bulaq
Chapter 42   Qaytbay Yaylası
Chapter 43   Fustat = Eski Mısır (Old Cairo)
Chapter 44   Nile flood; the Nilometer; Roda Island
Chapter 45   [2nd] grand procession: breaching the Nile
Chapter 46   The Nile

5. Crocodiles (Vol. 10, fol. 160b–163a)

Chapter 48   3rd procession: first night of Ramadan
Chapter 49   Merchants and craftsmen, their shops, etc.

1 police	12 sword-cutlers	22 shoe makers, etc.
2 farmers, etc.	13 blacksmiths	23 saddlers, etc.
3 beverages	14 kettle-makers	24 druggists, etc.
4 linseed-oil	15 goldsmiths, etc.	25 barbers
5 architects	16 tailors	26 painters, etc.
6 ship's carpenters	17 tent makers	27 Khan-ı Khalil
7 bakers	18 bow and arrow makers	28 acrobats
8 butchers		29 musicians
9 cooks, greengrocers	19 furriers, etc.	30 Egyptian soldiery
10 dry-goods grocers	20 Ka'ba covering	
11 surgeons	21 tanners, etc.	

Chapter 49(!) Industries and products special to Egypt

6. The Cairo underworld and unusual trades (Vol. 10, fol. 177a–178a)

7. Trades and products lacking in Egypt (Vol. 10, fol. 179b–180a)

Chapter 51   4th procession: festival of Ramadan
    5th procession: festival of sacrifice
Chapter 52   6th procession: pasha's entrance
    7th procession: pasha's departure
    8th procession: pasha's confirmation
    9th procession: forwarding the Egyptian Treasure to the Porte
    10th procession: janissaries' conveying of the Treasure
    11th procession: forwarding of the Pasha's 'pocket-money' to the Sultan and high Ottoman officials
    12th procession: arrival of sword and caftan (royal insignia)

Appendix

13th procession: forwarding the *surre-i Muhammedi* (annual gift from the Sultan to the holy cities) to Damascus

14th procession: Ka'ba cover

15th procession: pilgrimage convoy procession: the noble *mahmil* (the sacred litter of the Prophet)

16th procession: torchbearers' forwarding the noble *mahmil* to Bilbays

16th (!) procession: forwarding gifts for the Arab tribal sheikhs along the pilgrimage route

17th procession: expenses for repairs and gifts for the holy cities

18th procession: daily expenses for the pilgrimage convoy

19th procession: surrender of *waqf* funds to the Emir of the Hajj

19th (!) procession: military entourage

20th procession: Azlam soldiery and supplies

21st procession: Aqaba soldiery and supplies

22nd procession: Burka fireworks (Cf. IX 386b.mid)

22nd (!) procession: return of pilgrimage convoy to Cairo

23rd procession: falconer's treasure

24th procession: falconer's trousers, sword, and robe

25th procession: entrance of the molla of Cairo

26th procession: Girga Beyi

27th procession: Sur-ı Hümayun Donanması (celebration of an imperial victory; royal birth, circumcision, marriage; enthronement of new Sultan)

28th procession: candles, incense, etc. for the holy cities

22nd (!)[1] treasure: foodstuffs for the imperial kitchens and pantries in Istanbul

23rd treasure: gunpowder

24th treasure: wages for the religious personnel

25th treasure: inspection of the *waqf* funds

29th treasure: funds accruing to the Pasha

33th treasure: funds accruing to the Pasha's 23 grandees

36th treasure: funds accruing to the emirs, Circassian begs, and other notables

44th treasure: funds to inspectors, administrators, etc.

---

1 Here *alay* ('procession, festivity, celebration') shades off into *hazine* ('treasure, funds, expenses') and the numeration becomes erratic.

48th treasure: peasants' tithe
55th treasure: taxes on merchants in the seven ports
60th treasure: (ditto)
65th treasure: earnings of the 170 guilds; expenditures of pilgrims
73rd treasure: grain magazines
Total of 35 Grand Processions and 81 Treasures

Chapter 52(!) Protocol of revenues
Chapter 53   Mevluds
Chapter 54   Pleasure-outings
Chapter 55   Wonders and marvels; characteristics of the populace; trades and occupations; Pyramids and Sphinx

8. Chicken incubation; Sebil-i Allam stones (Vol. 10, fol. 229a–230a)

9. Exploring a pyramid (Vol. 10, fol. 232a–233b)

Chapter 56   Trees, etc. found in Egypt but not in Turkey
Chapter 57   Native plants, etc.
Chapter 58   Things not found in Egypt
Chapter 59   Climate; customs and characteristics of the populace

10. Weddings, circumcisions, etc. (Vol. 10, fol. 243b–246b)

Chapter 60   Ulema
Chapter 61   Notables (Ottoman beys, efendis, aghas, etc.)
Chapter 62   Climes, etc.
Chapter 63   Tombs and shrines
Chapter 64   Main roads and quarters
Chapter 65   Journey down the Nile from Cairo to Rosetta

11. *Mevlud* of Seyyid Ahmad al-Badawi in Tanta (Vol. 10, fol. 277b–279a, 285a–286b, 289a–295a)

Chapter 66   Return up the Nile from Rosetta to Cairo
Chapter 67   Inspection tour to Damietta
Chapter 68   Return up the Nile from Damietta to Cairo
Chapter 69   Journey up the Nile south of Cairo

12. Mountain of the Birds (Vol. 10, fol. 369b–370b)

[Chapter 70?] Ibrim

13. Map of the Nile (Vol. 10, fol. 392b)

Chapter 71   Journey in the Sudan

Appendix

14. Meeting with Kör Hüseyn Qan (Vol. 10, fol. 398b – 399b)

Kör Hüseyn Kan defeats the heathen tribes; Evliya recites the *Victory* Sura (48). Rajab 1083/October-November 1672: Hüseyn Kan loads Evliya with gifts and sends him off in the company of the king of Berberi.

15. Meeting with Qan Girgis; encounter with two Bektashi dervishes (Vol. 10, fol. 409a–412a)

Chapter 72   Sources of the Nile
Chapter 73   Journey to Ethiopia

16. Elephants and monkeys (Vol. 10, fol. 432b– 435a)

Chapter 74   Return journey from Ethiopia to Egypt
Chapter 7[5]   Events in [10]94 (1683)

17. Envoi (Vol. 10, fol. 450b)

BIBLIOGRAPHY

An on-line bibliography, updated periodically, has been posted on the Bilkent University website: http://www.bilkent.edu.tr/~tebsite/kaynaklar/kaynakcalar.htm.

Manuscripts

References to Volumes 1–8 of the *Seyahatname* are to the autograph ms. as follows:
    Bağdat 304   Volumes 1 and 2
    Bağdat 305   Volumes 3 and 4
    Bağdat 307   Volume 5
    Revan 1457   Volume 6
    Bağdat 308   Volumes 7 and 8
References to Volumes 9–10 are to:
    Bağdat 306   Volume 9
    İÜTY 5973   Volume 10
Some references to Volume 10 are instead to ms. Beşir Ağa 452, cited as Q. These references can be traced in the YKY edition, ed. Yücel Dağlı et. al. For the precise folios translated in this anthology, see Appendix.

Editions

Evliya Çelebi Seyahatnamesi, vols. 1–6 ed. Ahmed Cevdet (Istanbul, 1314–1318 H. = 1896–1901; vols. 7–8 ed. Kilisli Rif'at (Istanbul, 1928); vols. 9–10 ed. Ahmed Refik Altnay [unnamed in the edition] (Istanbul, 1935, 1938).

Evliya Çelebi Seyahatnamesi (Istanbul: Yapı Kredi Yayınları), 10 vols., under the editorship of Yücel Dağlı, Robert Dankoff, Seyit Ali Kahraman, Zekeriya Kurşun and İbrahim Sezgin, as follows:

Volume 1: 2006, ed. Dankoff, Kahraman, Dağlı [This edition is intended to replace the inadequate edition of Orhan Şaik Gökyay, 1996]

Volume 2: 1999, ed. Kurşun, Kahraman, Dağlı [New edition in press]

Volume 3: 1999, ed. Kahraman, Dağlı [New edition in press]

Volume 4: 2001, ed. Dağlı, Kahraman [New edition in press]
Volume 5: 2001, ed. Dağlı, Kahraman, Sezgin
Volume 6: 2002, ed. Kahraman, Dağlı
Volume 7: 2003, ed. Dağlı, Kahraman, Dankoff
Volume 8: 2003, ed. Kahraman, Dağlı, Dankoff
Volume 9: 2005, ed. Dağlı, Kahraman, Dankoff
Volume 10: 2007, ed. Kahraman, Dağlı, Dankoff.

Translations

Faruk Bilici, *La Guerre des Turcs: Récits de batailles* (extraits du 'Livre de voyages') (Paris [?], 2000).

Martin van Bruinessen and Hendrik Boeschoten, *Evliya Çelebi in Diyarbekir* (Leiden, 1988).

Korkut Buğday, *Evliya Çelebis Anatolienreise* (Leiden, 1996).

Robert Dankoff, *The Intimate Life of an Ottoman Statesman: Melek Ahmed Pasha (1588–1662), as portrayed in Evliya Çelebi's Book of Travels (Seyahatname)* (Binghamton, 1991).

—— *Evliya Çelebi in Bitlis* (Leiden, 1990).

Robert Dankoff and Robert Elsie, *Evliya Çelebi in Albania and Adjacent Regions* (Kosovo, Montenegro, Ohrid (Leiden, 2000).

Joseph van Hammer [-Purgstall], *Narrative of Travels in Europe, Asia, and Africa in the Seventeenth Century by Evliya Efendi*, I (i, ii), II. London, 1834, 1846, 1850) [Reprint: New York, 1968].

Ulrich Haarmann, 'Evliya Čelebis Bericht über die Altertümer von Gize', *Turcica* 8.1 (1976), 157–230.

Hasan Javadi and Willem Floor, *Evliya Chelebi: Travels in Iran and the Caucasus in 1647 and 1654* (Washington, 2010).

Richard Kreutel, *Im Reiche des goldenen Apfels. Des türkischen Weltenbummlers Evliyâ Çelebi denkwürdige Reise in das Giaurenland und in die Stadt und Festung Wien anno 1665* (Graz, 1957) [2nd ed. 1987: stark vermehrte Ausgabe besorgt von Erich Prokosch und Karl Teply].

J. W. Livingston, 'Evliya Çelebi on Surgical Operations in Vienna', *Al-Abhath* 23 (1970), 223–45.

Pierre MacKay, 'A Turkish Description of the Tower of the Winds', *American Journal of Archaeology* 73 (1969), 468–69.

Erich Prokosch, *Ins Land der geheimnisvollen Func: Des türkischen Weltenbummlers Evliya Çelebi Reise durch Oberägypten und den Sudan nebst der osmanischen Provinz Habe in den Jahren 1672/73* (Graz, 1994).

—— *Kairo in der zweiten Hälfte des 17. Jahrhunderts beschreiben von Evliya Çelebi* (Istanbul, 2000).

Luciano Rocchi, *Tra guerra e diplomazia. Un viaggiatore turco nella Dalmazia del Seicento – Passi scelti dal Seyahatname di Evliya Çelebi* (Trieste, 2008).

St. H. Stephan, 'Evliya Tshelebi's Travels in Palestine', *Quarterly of Dept. of Antiquities in Palestine* 4 (1935), 103–08, 154–64; 5 (1936), 69–73; 6 (1938), 84–97; 8 (1939), 137–56; 9 (1942), 81–104 [Reprint: Jerusalem: Ariel, 1980].

Nuran Tezcan, *Manisa nach Evliya Çelebi* (Leiden, 1999).

H. Turková, *Die Reisen und Streifzüge Evliya a Čelebis in Dalmatien und Bosnien in den Jahren 1659/61* (Prague, 1965).

Studies

C. F. Beckingham, 'The *rihla*: Fact or Fiction?' In I. R. Netton (ed.), *Golden Roads: Migration, Pilgrimage and Travel in Mediaeval and Modern Islam* (Richmond, 1993), 86–94.

Robert Dankoff, *An Evliya Çelebi Glossary: Unusual, Dialectal and Foreign Words in the Seyahat-name* (Cambridge, Mass., 1991) [In: *Sources of Oriental Languages and Literatures*, ed. Şinasi Tekin & Gönül Alpay Tekin]; expanded Turkish version, with Semih Tezcan: *Evliya Çelebi Seyahatnamesi Okuma Sözlüğü* (Istanbul, 2004; 2nd edition, 2008).

—— *An Ottoman Mentality: The World of Evliya Çelebi* [with an Afterword by Gottfried Hagen] (Leiden, 2004; 2nd edition, 2006).

Robert Dankoff and Semih Tezcan, 'Seyahat-name'den Bir Atasözü', *Türk Dilleri Araştrmalar* 8 (1998), 15–28.

Henry George Farmer, 'Turkish Instruments of Music in the Seventeenth Century', *Journal of the Royal Asiatic Society* (1936), 1–43.

Markus Köhbach, 'Die Beschreibung der Kathedralen von Iaşi, Kaschau und Wien bei Evliyā Čelebi: Klischee und Wirklichkeit', *Südost-Forschungen* 38 (1979), 213–22.

F. R. Kreutel, 'Neues zur Evliya-Çelebi-Forschung', *Der Islam* 48 (1972), 269–79.

Albert Howe Lybyer, 'The Travels of Evliya Efendi', *Journal of the American Oriental Society* 37 (1917), 224–39 [repr. *Journal of Turkish Literature* 2 (2005), 127–43].

Pierre MacKay, 'The Manuscripts of the *Seyahatname* of Evliya Çelebi, Part I: the Archetype', *Der Islam* 52 (1975), 278–98

—— 'An Introduction for the World Traveler', 2007 http://angiolello.net/EvliyaLetter-2.pdf.

—— 'Real and Fictitious Journeys in Evliya Çelebi's Scyahatname: Some examples from Book VIII', *Journal of Turkish Literature* 6 (2009), 110–29.

Alexandros A. Pallis (1941), In the Days of the Janissaries: Old Turkish Life as Depicted in the *Travel-Book* of Evliyá Chelebí (London, 1951).

—— 'A Seventeenth-Century Turkish Baedeker: *The Travel-Book* of Evliya Cheleby'. In Greek Miscellany: A Collection of Essays on Mediaeval Greece (Athens, 1964), 84–101.

Erich Prokosch, 'Die Gedenkinschriften des Evliya Çelebi', *Jahrbuch des Österreichischen St. Georgskollgs Istanbul* (1988–89), 320–36.

Ettore Rossi, 'A Turkish Map of the Nile River, about 1685', Imago Mundi 6 (1949), 73–75.

Pinelopi Stathi, 'A Greek Patriarchal Letter for Evliya Çelebi', Archivum Ottomanicum 23, 263–68.

Karl Teply, 'Evliya Çelebi in Wien', *Der Islam* 52 (1975), 125–31.

Nicolas Vatin, 'Pourquoi un Turc ottoman racontait-il son voyage? Note sur les relations de voyage chez les Ottomans des *Vak'at-ı Sultan Cem* au *Seyahatname* d'Evliya Çelebi', *Études Turques et Ottomanes: Documents de travail* 4 (1995), 5–15.

Other works cited

Muzaffar Alam and Sanjay Subrahmanyam, *Indo-Persian Travels in the Age of Discoveries, 1400–1800* (Cambridge, 2007).

Nurhan Atasoy, *Derviş Çeyizi* (Istanbul, 2000).

—— *A Garden for the Sultan* (Istanbul, 2002).

Ross E. Dunn, *The Adventures of Ibn Battuta: A Muslim Traveler of the 14th Century* (Berkeley, 1989).

EI2 = *Encyclopedia of Islam*, 2nd edition.

Jane Hathaway, *Beshir Agha: Chief Eunuch of the Ottoman Imperial Harem* (Oxford, 2006).

Cemal Kafadar, 'Self and Others: The Diary of a Dervish in Seventeenth Century Istanbul and First-Person Narratives in Ottoman Literature', *Studia Islamica* 69 (1989), 121–50.

Meninski = François de Mesgnien (Meninski), *Thesaurus linguarum orientalium* . . . , 6 vols. (Vienna, 1680) [Reprint: Istanbul, 2000].

Naima = *Tarih-i Naima*, 6 vols. (Istanbul 1281–83/1864–66); ed. Mehmet İpşirli, 4 vols. (Ankara, 2007).

Pakalın = Mehmet Zeki Pakalın. *Osmanlı Tarih Deyimleri ve Terimleri Sözlüğü*, I–III. İstanbul, 1946–56. [Reprint: Istanbul, 1971–72].

Rd1 = James W. Redhouse, *A Turkish and English Lexicon* (Istanbul, 1890).

Rd2 = *New Redhouse Turkish–English Dictionary* (Istanbul, 1968).

Joan-Pau Rubiés, *Travel and Ethnology in the Renaissance: South India through European Eyes* (Cambridge, 2000).

Stanford J. Shaw, *The Financial and Administrative Organization and Development of Ottoman Egypt, 1517–1798* (Princeton, 1962).

—— *Ottoman Egypt in the Age of the French Revolution* (Cambridge, MA, 1966).

Richard E. Strassberg, *Inscribed Landscapes: Travel Writing from Imperial China* (Berkeley, 1994).

Zdzislaw Zygulski Jr., *Ottoman Art in the Service of the Empire* (New York, 1992).

ACKNOWLEDGEMENTS

The publishers would like to thank the following for sharing their enthusiasm for Evliya Çelebi with us over the years: Patricia Daunt, Jason Goodwin, Robert Irwin, Donna Landry, Gerald MacLean, Philip Mansel, John Scott and Ali Tuysuz. We are particularly grateful to Caroline Finkel, who introduced us to the work of Professor Robert Dankoff.

We would also like to thank the following for granting permission to use material in their copyright:

The Gypsy Lore Society for permission to quote from 'The Earliest Text in Balkan (Rumelian) Romani: A Passage from Evliya Çelebi's *Seyahatname*', published in the *Journal of Gypsy Lore* (1991) and Koninklijke Brill NV for permission to quote from *Evliya Çelebi in Diyarbekir* edited by Martin van Bruinessen and Hendrik Boeschoten, *Evliya Çelebi in Bitlis* edited by Robert Dankoff, *Evliya Çelebi in Albania and Adjacent Regions* edited by Robert Dankoff and Robert Elise and *An Ottoman Mentality: The World of Evliya Çelebi* by Robert Dankoff.

INDEX

Abaza Pasha: and Dubrovnik, 211
Abdal Khan of Bitlis, 112; family of, 124, 145, 147, 156
Ahlat: Emir Kay Mosque, 134–5; castle of, 144, 163; population of, 135
Ahmed, Sultan: and Dome of the Rock, 329–30
Ahmed Giray, Sultan: family of, 189; troops of, 189
Ak Mehmed Pasha, 261, 270, 272; retinue of, 266–7, 269–70, 273–4
al-Badawi, Seyyid Ahmad: tomb of, 430–1
Albania, 258; language of, 179–80; population of, 226
Alexander the Great, xxxi, 17, 45; death of, 333
Alman Pass; bandits of, 306–8
Altı Kulaç,: murderer of Mehmed, Molla, 153–4
Ankara, 81, 83, 87; architecture of, 73–4; governor of, 85; history of, 71–2; Jewish population of, 78; mohair cloth, 78; population of, 72–6
Armenia, xii, 113, 134, 332; and Christianity, 99; Echmiadzin, 34; ethnicity of, xvii, 18–9, 69, 87, 103, 113, 207–8, 252, 332–4; Jacobites, 99; language of, xxvi, 90, 99–100
Athens, 278, 286, 292; Acropolis, 280; origins of, 278–9; Parthenon, 281; population of, 280, 287–8
Austria, 218; and Catholicism, 230; Ottoman embassy, 218; population of, 231; Vienna, 218, 221, 232–4, 237, 240–1, 246, 275, 333
Azerbaijan, xvi, xxvii 112; borders of, 142; population of, 60; traditions of, 66; Van, 71, 142
Azov, 266; military of, 259, 266; sea of, 259–61, 263; wildlife of, 268

Bayezid the Thunderbolt, Sultan: death of, 82, 91; military campaigns of, 309; mosque of, 250; reign of, 82
Bayram Veli, Haci, 76–8; background of, 82; tomb of, 71, 78, 81, 84
Bekkar, Sheikh, 95–6, 338–9; and Kara Murtaza Pasha, 339; background of, 96
Nureddehir, son of Khan of Bitlis, 124, 145, 147, 156: murderer of his brother Ziyaeddin, 160–1

Catholicism: and Austria, 230
Çelebi, Evliya, 79, 90, 118; and Efendi, Evliya Mehmed, xi–xii; and Sultan Murad IV, xii; *Book of Travels*, xi, xvii–xviii, xxi–xxiii, xxvi, 2, 44, 93, 451; family of, xi; military career of, xii–xiii; writing style of, xxvii–xxviii, xxxi
Christianity, 37, 64, 69–70, 94, 189, 192, 195, 212, 235, 246–7, 366, 381; and Armenia, 99; and Germany, 200, 239; Easter, 317, 332; Gospel, 236, 248; language of, 205; Old Testament, xxxii

Index

Crete, 276; conquest of (1669), 258
Crimea, 249, 259, 275; Akmescid (Simferopol), 251–2; khanate of, 251–2; population of, 250

Damascus, 90, 94–6, 311, 317, 338, 340–4, 346, 362, 424; and Persia, 138; artisans of, 326; Manjik Garden, 114; Jacobite population of, 99; military of, 348, 363; produce of, 124; Sazenekler, 138
Defterdarzade Mehmed Pasha, xxiv
Dubrovnik: castle of, 206–7; celebrations of, 208–9; palace of, 211; population of, 205, 207

Efendi, Evliya Mehmed: and Çelebi, Evliya, xi–xii; imam of Murad IV, Sultan, xi
Egypt, xvii, xix, 30, 94, 146, 277, 298, 310–11, 353, 379, 399–400, 411, 424, 427; Afnu, 395; Aswan, 264, 390, 438, 440; Baghanisqa, 395; Cairo, xxi, xxiv–xxv, 4, 300, 311, 326, 362, 370–1, 373–4, 387, 393–7, 402, 404, 410, 414, 416–17, 435, 443, 450; Funjistan, 395, 437, 439, 441, 443; Fustat, 411; Ibrim, 395; Isna, 264; Jewish population of, 406, 412; Mosque of Sultan Hasan, 413; oases, 395, 397–8; population of, 380; pyramids of, 403–4; Qala'un hospital, 383–4; Qirmanqa, 395; River Nile, 300, 370–2, 387–92, 397, 402, 404, 416–18, 421, 424, 436–9, 442, 445; Tanta, 425, 430; treasure of, 232, 235–6, 358, 424; wildlife of, 193

France, 220; and Galata, 19; military of, 224; royalty of, 166; territory of, 198

Franks, 12, 78, 106, 164, 193–4, 197–8, 200, 288, 317, 334, 381, 402; and Venice, 179, 280, 292, 379; artisans of, 16, 85, 149, 170, 221, 231, 241, 279; ethnicity of, 18–19; 207, 214, 235, 294; language of, 166–7; navy of, 295; Patriarch of, 286; produce of, 78, 85, 166, 375; territory of, xxviii, 195, 286, 312, 332

Galata: and France 19; harbour of, 21; population of, 18–20; Tower, 18, 30
Germany, 275; and Christianity, 200, 239; borders of, 200; language of, 218, 221, 248–9; military of, 247; mountains of, 220; population of, 200–1; Raytinad Fortress, 219–20; River Danube, 221, 231; territory of, 224
Greece, 332; language of, 292–4; population of, 366
Gürci Mehmed Pasha, 222, 226; troops of, 181–2, 185, 189
Gypsies: Anatolian, 276–8; language of 277–8; Rumelian, 276, 278

Habsburg Empire, xvi; court of, xviii; Peace of Vasvár, 218; territory of, 218
Holland, 275; military campaign against, 190; territory of, 190, 194
Hungary: and Protestantism, 230; Buda, 432; Derinma'den, 202; Holçar Castle, 201–2; military of, 201; Pécs, 432; population of, xvii, 231
Hüsameddin, Sheikh: tomb of, 82–3
Hüseyn Pasha, 341, 343, 346, 348–9; governor of Damascus, 340, 412

Ibrahim, Sultan: retinue of, 37
Iraq, 112, 298, 362; and
  Muhammad, Prophet, xxxii, 283;
  and Ottoman Empire, 69;
  Baghdad, xii, xviii, xxv, xxxi, 3,
  35, 64, 95–6, 112, 137, 213, 221,
  264–5, 290, 349, 403–4, 433;
  Jacobite population of, 99;
  Karbala, xxxiii; Najaf, xxxii
Islam, 366, 425; Hadith, 361, 397,
  411; Hajj, xvi, xx, xxiv, 34–5, 93,
  168, 225, 302, 340, 344, 362, 367,
  371; Koran, xi–xii, xviii, xxxi–
  xxxii, 3, 10, 15, 25–6, 30, 35–6,
  49–50, 53, 59, 67, 71, 76, 79–80,
  93, 98, 144, 186, 227–8, 236–7,
  273, 297, 303, 305, 308, 311, 321,
  324, 330, 340, 350, 361, 373, 412,
  419–20, 435–6; Rajab, 395;
  Ramadan, 55, 146, 276, 303, 330,
  395; saints of, xxxii–xxxiii;
  Sha'ban, 395; Shi'i, xii, 56; Sufism,
  xiii, xx, 417, 430; Sunni, 56, 58,
  397
Ismail Pasha, 173–4, 222, 226
Istanbul, xiii, xvii–xviii, 3, 42, 55,
  90, 259, 305, 443; Aya Sofia, xii,
  9, 17, 220, 284, 310, 333–4:
  fortress of, 17; Jewish population
  of, 13; Kağithane, 432; origins of,
  337; Ottoman conquest of (1453),
  xii; Tophane, 445
Istanoz: population of, 84; valley of,
  85

Jerusalem, xvii, 302, 311, 329; and
  Khan, Sultan Süleyman, 326;
  Aqsa Mosque, 321–2, 324, 330,
  338; Church of the Holy
  Sepulchre, 316, 331–4, 337–8,
  365; Dome of the Rock, 302, 319,
  324–5, 328, 331 Fortress of, 319–
  21, 325; history of, 315–17;
  military presence in, 318, 363
Judaism, 64, 102–3, 230, 250, 322,
  331; and Ankara, 78; and
  Constantinople, 13; and Egypt,
  406, 412; and Safed, 92; Book of
  Psalms, 93–4, 236, 239, 250;
  Hebrew, 93–4, 371, 403;
  Passover, 276; Rabbinic, 103;
  Torah, 93–4, 236, 239, 250

Kağithane: bridge of, 24; pleasure
  gardens of, 21–3; population of,
  23–4
Kalmyks, 260–1, 267–8, 270–1,
  273–4, 370, 385; language of, 271
Kara Murtaza Pasha: and Bekkar,
  Sheikh, 339; governor of
  Damascus, 154–5, 338
Kara Mustafa Pasha: grand vizier,
  381
Karınca Kapudan: and Khan,
  Süleyman, 9
Katib Salahaddin: tomb of, 83
Kelp Ali Khan, 61–2; beating of
  Naghdi Hoca, 62
Kethüda Ibrahim Pasha, 372, 396,
  415–16, 421, 424, 436; dismissal
  of, 402; governor of Egypt, xvii,
  372, 414, 418, 420; palace of, 414
Kipchak Steppe, 275, 385; River
  Kuban, 266–7, 270, 272;
  landscape of, 264, 266; wildlife of,
  264–5, 268
Komorn, 187; castle of, 181–3
Köprülü Mehmed Pasha, 140
Kör Hüseyn Bey: fortress of, 390
Kör Husayn Qan, 440–2; military
  forces of, 439
Korol: history of, 190; territory of,
  191
Kurdistan, xvi; bridges of, 214;

و بر قپوسو دخمه ایچ قلعه قیو سیدر بو قلعه کرجی مستکل مثلثه
و حصنه ندعا مک توپله مولمه حصار در هر بولمه الک کبیر
قلعه در اماعا متیندم والمحصار دیب اسمیتایا لمعنو سنده
مده سا ایله یا ملبس علی یر وجود لها در دم اعرسعا معلو علی
اما سو لیا ر جه ملسو بلر ع لها ده مرسو کو یر فرد کنز رنده یطر لیا
مر منده ملعبه عدد سوار لری الجاه امد لکن انلید دار اخرکر حو در
و غیری عباد تگاه مؤمنا حمله سدر عدد جوا معلم دم
ییکار تعدیم مسجد کا معظمه در اند دو درام ندسرای قرب ندن
ندن کوچک قپوسو جا مع آندن بیسغا دبه جا مع آندن نور ته
بینه جنبه خانیه متصل یاز بیعه ی جا مع آندن بیوک قپودن طنزه تعر قبیله
در قاتها مکتب صبیا غیبا
مسلم لو ایی جا مع عظیم اولو پر سمه یاسد و صا باره حلعه
فقر ادر حمله جا مع صاحبی محمد افندی عکه که محمود زرتندی
حلوه سدر و بو لمه حصار ده عزیر محمد احمد علم سومی دکر
معار وصا بلنا موسدط شیخ عمر افندی تکیه بر والشیخ
اولو عدد علا مسر لید ر حملدا مکلف جا مع اولما عه متعهد